D0721900

The Greek Achievement

CHARLES FREEMAN

The Greek Achievement

The Foundation of the Western World

ALLEN LANE
THE PENGUIN PRESS

ALLEN LANE
THE PENGUIN PRESS

Published by the Penguin Group
Penguin Books Ltd, 27 Wrights Lane, London W8 5TZ, England
Penguin Putnam Inc., 375 Hudson Street, New York, New York 10014, USA
Penguin Books Australia Ltd, Ringwood, Victoria, Australia
Penguin Books Canada Ltd, 10 Alcorn Avenue, Toronto, Ontario, Canada M4V 3B2
Penguin Books (NZ) Ltd, Private Bag 102902, NSMC, Auckland, New Zealand

Penguin Books Ltd, Registered Offices: Harmondsworth, Middlesex, England

First published in the USA by Viking Penguin, a member of Penguin Putnam Inc. 1999
First published in Great Britain by Allen Lane The Penguin Press 1999
1 3 5 7 9 10 8 6 4 2

Grateful acknowledgement is made for permission to use the following copyrighted works:
Maps and plans of the temple of Artemis at Ephesus, the Parthenon and the Acropolis at Pergamum from Egypt, Greece and Rome by Charles Freeman, Oxford University Press (1998), themselves adapted from The Oxford History of the Classical World, edited by Oswyn Murray, et al., Oxford University Press (1986). By permission of Oxford University Press.
Excerpts from poetry by Tyrtaios and Solon, translated by Oswyn Murray from his work Early Greece, Fontana Books (1993). By permission of HarperCollins Publishers Ltd (London).
Poem by Sappho and poem by Archilochus, translated by Anne Pippin Burnett from her work Three Archaic Poets: Archilochus, Alcaeus, Sappho. Copyright © Anne Pippin Burnett, 1983. Reprinted by permission of Harvard University Press and Gerald Duckworth and Company Ltd.
'Peer of Immortal Gods' by Sappho, translated by Peter Green from his work Shadow of the Parthenon: Studies in Ancient History and Literature. Copyright © Peter Green, 1973. by permission of University of California Press.
Excerpts from The Iliad by Homer, translated by Robert Fagles. Copyright © Robert Fagles, 1990. Used by permission of Viking Penguin, a division of Penguin Putnam Inc.
Excerpts from The Odyssey by Homer, translated by Robert Fagles. Copyright © Robert Fagles, 1996. Used by permission of Viking Penguin, a division of Penguin Putnam Inc.

Printed and bound in Great Britain by The Bath Press, Bath

A CIP catalogue record for this book is available from the British Library

ISBN 0-713-99224-7

To the Freemans, Hilary, Barney, Issie, Tom, and Cordelia, in the hope that this book and the memories of a Greek experience on the island of Symi in August 1998 will bring them new Greek adventures in the years to come.

Whither, O city, are your profits and your gilded shrines,
And your barbecues of great oxen,
And the tall women walking your streets, in gilt clothes,
With their perfumes in little alabaster boxes?
Where is the work of your home-born sculptors?

Time's tooth is into the lot, and war's and fate's too.
Envy has taken your all,
*Save your douth** *and your story.*

—Translation by Ezra Pound (1916) from the Greek poet Agathias who lived in Constantinople in the sixth century A.D.

**Douth* means worth, nobility.

Preface

This book is an exploration of the culture and history of ancient Greece. It is written for the general reader in the strong belief that some appreciation of the achievements of ancient Greece is essential for any full understanding of the western tradition.

The central focus of this book is, inevitably, on the classical period (480–330 B.C.) but historians are now stressing the achievements of the earlier "Archaic" and the later "Hellenistic" ages. This book aims to provide an overview of the period from 1500 B.C. right through to the conquest of Greece by Rome (finally in the first century B.C.) and beyond. Greek city culture continued to flourish and even expand under the Roman empire, and the coming of Christianity in the fourth and fifth centuries has been chosen as the closing point.

I have not pretended the Greeks were "like us." Important elements of the western political tradition such as human rights were lacking and there was very little practical (as against theoretical) understanding of science or technology. Fundamental to Greek society was a rich spiritual tradition, supported by a complex and fertile mythology, but this was eclipsed or absorbed by Christianity. Yet the range of the Greek cultural experience and its impact on the western tradition remains. It is this range that most impresses and *The Greek Achievement* attempts to cover it. There are individual chapters on drama, philosophy, science, and mathematics. Plato and Aristotle are given full treatment, not relegated to a "culture" chapter tagged on at the end as in some recent surveys. Homer, whose influence pervades Greek history, has also been given his own chapter. The Greek historians are woven into the political narrative as they provide the best surviving accounts of it and it is here too, alongside the chapters on philosophy, that the Greek contribution to political thought is covered. Despite their diversity the many aspects of Greek culture were interlinked and so much of Greek art appears also in the narrative chapters, although separate sections are provided for key achievements, the sculptures of the temple of Zeus at Olympia or the Parthenon, for instance. By covering "the Greek Achievement" through time and through its own breadth I have hoped to provide a comprehensive introduction to the subject that reveals the full fascination of ancient Greece and its remarkable culture.

My interest in Greek history came when I first discovered the Minoans and Mycenaeans at the age of thirteen. It was followed by extensive travels in Greece in my twenties and a period working on the site of Hellenistic Cnidus in southwestern Turkey. (The remains of the famous shrine to Aphrodite were discovered the year *after* I worked there!) I returned to the study of the ancient world when working on a major world history project in the early 1990s and have stayed with it since. In 1998, I was able to revisit many of the Greek cities of Turkey, including some, such as Aphrodisias, I had not seen before.

The idea for this book came from my agent, Bill Hamilton, and like all good agents he used telepathy, in this case with the effect of landing the proposal with Penguin the day after they had decided to update their ancient world list. I am grateful to Simon Winder, the history editor, for taking it on and providing such consistent and congenial support while it was being written, and for Cecilia Mackay, Penguin's picture researcher, for taking such enormous care in searching out illustrations. Academic support was given by Nigel Spivey of Emmanuel College, Cambridge. Nigel can take responsibility for many of the ideas but need take no responsibility at all for the way I have chosen to present them! Staff at the Cambridge University Library and London Library have always been helpful and I have happy memories of the camaraderie and encouragement I encountered on the Historical Association's Study Tour of Classical Turkey in September 1998.

A hectic publishing schedule meant that this book was actually produced in the United States. Michael Millman at Penguin Putnam in

New York generously took the project in hand and I am indebted to William Troffer for meticulous copyediting and to S. W. Cohen and Associates for compiling the index.

One July night in 1968, I was making my way in a small boat along the Turkish coast to the ancient site of Cnidus. We sprang a leak and were forced to take refuge on Symi, a small island in the Dodecanese. I shall never forget the moment as we slipped into Symi's magnificent harbor at sunrise. Thirty years on, in 1998, we holidayed as a family on Symi. Still relatively untouched by tourism (thanks to its lack of water) the island provided us with a memorable Greek experience. It is in the hope that this book and memories of Symi will encourage my family to enjoy further Greek experiences in the years to come that I dedicate it to them.

Buxhall Vale,
Suffolk
April 1999

Contents

List of Maps and Illustrations

The Greeks and Phoenicians in the Mediterranean	66–67
The City of Megara Hyblaia	69
The Doric and Ionic Orders	77
The Greek World from the Seventh and Fourth Centuries B.C.	196–197
The Athenian Empire at Its Height	203
Parthenon/Temple of Artemis	236
The Campaigns of Alexander the Great	328–329
The Hellenistic Kingdoms	344–345
The Acropolis at Pergamum	355
The Roman Empire in the East	412–413

Plate Section 1

Page

1 The Apollo Belvedere, marble, Roman copy after original Greek sculpture of c. 330 B.C. (Museo Pio-Clementino, Vatican/Scala)

2 The Lion Gate, 1350–1330 B.C., Mycenae (F. Birch/Sonia Halliday Photographs)

The Royal Grave Circle, 1650–1500 b.c., Mycenae (F. Birch/Sonia Halliday Photographs)

3 View of the remains of the Southeast Gate, Troy, drawing by Heinrich Schliemann from his book *Troy: Results of the Latest Researches*, London, 1884 (AKG London)

Bronze statue of warrior, attributed to Pheidias, from Riace, c. 450 B.C. (Museo Nazionale Reggio Calabria/Scala)

4 The Acropolis, Athens (G. Garvey/Ancient Art & Architecture)

Model of Olympia (R. Sheridan/Ancient Art & Architecture)

Model of the Acropolis of Pergamum from the southwest (Antikensammlung, Berlin/BPK)

5 The stadium, Aphrodisias, 1st/2nd century A.D. (R. Sheridan/Ancient Art & Architecture)

Plate Section 3

Page

1

Recreating the World of Ancient Greece

If there is one icon (Greek *eikon,* an image or likeness) that stands for ancient Greece and its leading city-state of the fifth century B.C., Athens, it is the Parthenon, the temple dedicated to Athena, as maiden, *parthenos,* which rises in splendor on the Acropolis of Athens. Millions of visitors to Greece each year toil upwards through the summer heat of Athens to offer it the appropriate homage. It is seen as standing for purity, beauty, and even a form of moral and intellectual integrity. It is proclaimed as the crowning achievement of the society which founded Western civilization.

The period of Greek history, the classical period, in which the Parthenon was built has also been given iconic status. Athens was basking in the glory of having defeated two invasions by the largest empire, the Persian, the world had yet seen. It was exulted as the defender of freedom against the forces of tyranny. "If to die well be the chief part of virtue, fortune granted this to us above all others; for striving to endure Greece with freedom we lie here possessed of praise that grows not old," wrote the poet Simonides. "Our city is an education to Greece . . . Future ages will wonder at us, as the present age wonders at us now," enthused her statesman Pericles, the man responsible for building the Parthenon, in 431 B.C. The city was run democratically with every citizen having the right to speak in its Assembly.

This too was a city where there was fine pottery and stunning sculpture, stimulating theater and great philosophers. A popular image of Athens has survived in which the marble is always shining, the streets are clean, and there is a lot of time for passionate philosophical discussions about art, theater, or the meaning of life.

There is, however, another picture of ancient Athens. The historian Thucydides prided himself on his careful reconstruction of the events of the Peloponnesian War, the great struggle between Athens and Sparta in the late fifth century B.C. The year is 430 B.C., only two years after the completion of the Parthenon. The farmers of Attica have crowded into the city to escape from Spartan raids but plague has broken out in the city. Thucydides goes on:

> There were no houses for the newcomers, and living as they did during the hot season in badly ventilated huts, they died like flies. The bodies of the dying were heaped one on top of the other, and half-dead creatures could be seen staggering about in the streets or flocking around the fountains in their desire for water. The temples in which they took up their quarters were full of dead bodies of people who had died inside them. For the catastrophe was so overwhelming that men, not knowing what would happen next to them, became indifferent to every rule of religion or of law . . . As for the gods, it seemed the same thing whether one worshipped them or not, when one saw the good and the bad dying indiscriminately. As for offences against human law, no one expected to be brought to trial or punished . . . All the funeral ceremonies which used to be observed were now disorganised, and they buried the dead as best they could.
>
> (Translation: Rex Warner)

So Athens was not always a resplendent city. Thucydides was describing, of course, a natural disaster, unavoidable in an age where understanding of disease was limited but there are many, more ominous passages in his work. He continues with the war and for the year 416 B.C. he tells the story of the Aegean island of Melos, one of the Cyclades. Melos was one of Sparta's colonies but had remained neutral in the war at least until, according to Thucydides, "the Athenians laid waste to the Melians' land and made them their enemies." Now Athenian representatives were sent to the island to encourage surrender and subservience to Athens. The Athenians were met by representatives of the Melians and a debate took place. When the Melians pleaded the right to neutrality and warned the Athenians of the effect on Athens' image if the Athenians subdued them, they were met with an unyielding and brutal response. " 'If we were on friendly terms with you, our subjects [of the Athenian empire] would regard that as a sign of weakness in us, whereas your hatred is evidence of our power.' " The plucky Melians argued on and concluded in words that the Athenians themselves would surely have used if they had been confronted by Persian envoys, " 'Our decision, Athenians, is just the same as it was at first. We are not prepared to give up in a short moment the liberty which our city has enjoyed from its foundation for 700 years.' " "Siege operations were now carried on vigorously," records Thucydides, "and the Melians surrendered unconditionally to the Athenians who put to death all the men of military age whom they took, and sold the women and children as slaves."

Thucydides destroys any illusions one might have that nobility was inherent in the Greek character. Whatever the achievements of the Greeks might have been, and as will be seen in this book they were considerable, they developed against the backdrop of a real world, one in which human beings were degraded by disease and where brutality was an everyday part of life. It certainly can be argued that the Melian atrocity was an inevitable result of the strain of war, but war was endemic in Greek society and there was hardly a year in the fifth century that Athens was not fighting someone somewhere. Other cities were subdued as Athens constructed an empire in the century. One of them, Mytilene, reduced after a revolt, was subject to a decree by Athens' democratic Assembly that it, too, should have all its male citizens killed and its women and children enslaved, though this was rescinded at the last moment and only those specifically guilty of revolt were actually executed. Even so these numbered one thousand. Athens was a city too that depended on the labor of possibly as many as one hundred thousand slaves, many of them uprooted from their native cultures in the lands neighboring Greece. Yet, it is remarkable that there are still books available on Greece where slavery is hardly mentioned. J. B. Bury's *History of Greece*, first published in 1900 but now in a fourth edition, which has been reprinted several times in the 1980s and 1990s, has only six references to slavery in the index to its five hundred pages.

Why has this sanitized picture of ancient Greece survived? The answer lies partly in the superb public relations image Pericles created for Athens in the speech he made in honor of the city's war dead in 431–430 B.C., but there had to be other forces that sustained the Periclean image of Athens and they are rooted in the late eighteenth and early nineteenth centuries A.D. Of course the Greeks had not been totally forgotten before then. Certainly the actual land of Greece had been cut off from western Europe after the fifth century A.D. as a result of the fall of the Roman empire in the west, the emergence of the Byzantine empire, and then the absorption of Greece into the Ottoman empire in the fifteenth century, but the philosopher Aristotle had enjoyed canonical status right through the Middle Ages and beyond (although, in an age which had forgotten Greek, through Latin translations of Arabic versions). A professorship in Greek had been founded in Florence in 1360 and the first printed copies of Homer's epics appeared in 1488, also in Florence. The works of the Greek historian Plutarch, which contrasted the achievements of selected Greek and Roman heroes, were highly influential in the sixteenth century. The mathematical breakthroughs of Archimedes had been essential inspirations for the mathematicians of the seventeenth century.

However, it needed something more to restore Greece to the European consciousness. By the end of the eighteenth century, travelers were returning to mainland Greece, then still ruled by the Ottomans. In 1762, a Scotsman, James Stuart, and an Englishman, Nicholas Revett, who had traveled to Greece together in the 1750s, published a scholarly and illustrated account of their travels (with other volumes to come in later years). It caused a sensation. For the first time, Greek temples portrayed in their original settings could be enjoyed by the armchair traveler. The influence of Stuart and Revett was particularly strong in classical architecture where Greek columns and pediments came to replace the heavier Roman style (as in several public buildings in Edinburgh, now dubbed "the Athens of the north"), but other enthusiasms were aroused. Greece became a place for the more adventuresome to explore (just as in the twentieth century exotic and remote locations suddenly become fashionable). One scholar, Robert Wood, wandered around Greece with his copy of Homer searching, as others have done ever since, for the original sites of the places described in the epics. His essay on Homer raced through several editions and was a major influence on German scholars.

Paradoxically, however, the most powerful influence was a man who never visited Greece, never saw original Greek art, and yet who revolutionized the history of taste by elevating Greek art to the height of perfection. Johann Winckelmann, born in Germany, was a poor, self-educated student of Greek literature who, after a conversion to Catholicism, found himself Librarian and Keeper of Antiquities in the Vatican. Rome was his base and it was here that he came across copies of Greek art which he used as sources for his *History of Ancient Art* published in 1764. For Winckelmann there were peak moments in history, the highest points of cycles that saw the birth, flowering, and then the inevitable decay of civilizations. For Greece the high point was the fifth century, the classical period. (The word *classical* originates with the Latin "belonging to the highest class of citizens" but was used by some Roman writers to describe those earlier writers and sculptors whose work was considered especially authoritative. It was adopted by later Europeans to describe periods of history that appeared to have achieved cultural excellence and, in general terms, for Roman and Greek architecture and the study of their literature and civilization.) Here the combination of a perfect climate and an enthusiasm for freedom provided "the peak." It was not just Winckelmann's elevation of the classical period that was important, it was his idealization of Greek art. His particular enthusiasm was for the apparent purity of classical Greek sculpture, what he described as "its noble simplicity and calm grandeur."

Winckelmann was not the first to enjoy Greek sculpture, but he could write effectively and his enthusiasm proved infectious. This is how he describes the Apollo Belvedere (actually a Roman copy of a late fourth-century Greek bronze original, then as now in the Vatican Museum). It is a description affected perhaps by Winckelmann's homosexuality:

> This statue surpasses all other representations of the god, just as Homer's description surpasses those attempted by all other poets . . . An eternal spring time, like that which reigns in the happy fields of Elysium, clothes his body with the charms of youth and softly shines on the proud structure of his limbs . . .

> This body, marked by no vein, moved by no nerve, is animated by a celestial spirit which courses like a sweet vapour through every part . . . Like the soft tendrils of the vine his beautiful hair flows round his head, as if gently brushed by the breath of the zephyr. It seems to be perfumed by the essence of the gods . . . In the presence of this miracle of art I forget the whole universe and my soul acquires a loftiness appropriate to its dignity. From admiration I pass to ecstasy, I feel my breasts dilate and rise as if I were filled with the spirit of prophecy . . . I am transported to Delos and the sacred groves of Lycia—places Apollo honoured with his presence . . .

Winckelmann's enthusiasm caught the mood of Romanticism then sweeping Europe. The German poet Goethe was right when he said "we learn nothing by reading Winckelmann, but we become something." Winckelmann affected a whole generation of Romantics, particularly in his own country, who adopted Greece as their own inspiration. As the Romantic philosopher Johann Herder put it, "In the history of mankind Greece will eternally remain the place where mankind experienced its fairest youth and bridal beauty . . . noble youth with fair anointed limbs, favourite of all the graces, beloved of all the Muses, victor in Olympia and all the other games, spirit and body together, one single flower in bloom."

This was certainly a sanitized version of the original Greece and one could be forgiven for believing that ordinary human beings did not exist in ancient Greece at all. Nevertheless, the Greeks were appropriated as the forerunners of European civilization, especially in Prussia, the leading German state, where some inspiration was needed to revive the state after its humiliation at the hands of Napoleon (at the battles of Jena and Auerstadt, 1806). "In the Greeks alone we find the ideal of that which we should like to be and produce," remarked the scholar Wilhelm von Humboldt, who became Education Minister in Prussia after Prussia's defeat. It was Humboldt more than anyone who was responsible for installing the study of Greece as the core of the curriculum in the *Gymnasien,* the only schools which prepared students for entrance to universities and the professions.

The content of Greek studies was not so much its history or art as its surviving texts. There was already a revered tradition dating back to the fourteenth-century Italian scholar Petrarch of collecting ancient texts, collating different versions of them, and analyzing their structure and language. Petrarch was convinced that his age was a dark one in comparison to that of Rome and he elevated Roman literature over that of his own day. (There were some Greek texts among his collection but Petrarch could not read them.) In the centuries that followed, the surviving manuscripts (many of them eighth- or ninth-century copies of original versions) were minutely analyzed and an introduction to Latin authors, Livy and Virgil, in particular, became the core of the European school curriculum. However, philology, the interpretation and analysis of ancient texts, was as much concerned with the biblical as with the Latin or Greek survivals. It was the German scholar Friedrich August Wolf (1759–1824) who insisted on making a distinction between the Bible and other ancient sources. His enthusiasm was for the latter and he went further to argue that among the ancient cultures, the Greeks reigned supreme; only the Greeks, he argued, showed the qualities "of true humanness." Studying the Greeks was seen to be a serious business. Students had to immerse themselves not only in the texts but in every other aspect of Greek society so that they could understand the content and detail of what they had read. There was a moral purpose involved. Through mastering the ancient authors, Wolf argued, one could not only penetrate the secret of the greatness of the Greeks but absorb self-discipline, idealism, even nobility of character. It was Wolf who persuaded Humboldt that text analysis should be at the center of Greek studies and this became the core of the *Gymnasium* curriculum. The Germans were to remain at the forefront of Greek scholarship during the nineteenth century although much of their work was pedantic and obscure. The spirit of Romanticism died in the dusty classrooms of the *Gymnasien* and studies of university professors. However, their influence on the rest of Europe, and, in particular, the development of classical studies in the United States was profound.

Meanwhile there was a somewhat unseemly scramble to acquire Greek antiquities for the national museums of Europe. Each nation wanted to show its own commitment to Greece and its status as an heir to the Greeks by having original works under its own control. A shipment of statues from the temple of Aphaea on the island of Aigina was pursued around the Mediterranean by French, English, and Bavarian agents in 1812. (The Bavarians won and the sculptures are still in Munich.) The British Museum acquired one of the greatest of prizes, the sculptures of the Parthenon, by purchasing them from Lord Elgin who had appropriated them on the Acropolis and shipped them to England. The French acquired the celebrated Venus of Milo (a statue of the Greek goddess Aphrodite from the island of Melos) in 1820 and carried off further sculptures from Olympia in 1829.

Now, however, the real world intruded. In 1821 the Greeks launched their War of Independence against the Ottoman empire. Some three hundred Germans went to fight alongside other Romantics such as the English Lord Byron who actually died (of a fever) in Greece in 1824. (Byron remains venerated in Greece with streets, and even babies, still named after him.) The war, although ultimately successful, was a messy affair and many of the more idealistic volunteers were deeply disillusioned by its brutality. It also presented the European nations with the tricky problem of how to treat the supposed heirs of the founding civilization of Europe now that they were once again an independent nation. In the end they were largely airbrushed out of the European consciousness. A Bavarian king and German administrators were foisted on them and there was even a theory that the inhabitants of Greece were no more than descendants of Slavs who had migrated there in the seventh and eighth centuries A.D. This was deeply humiliating. It is little wonder that when a Greek shepherd, Spiro Louis, untrained as an athlete, won the first Marathon of the revived Olympic Games in Athens in 1896, he became an enduring national hero. He had shown the gathered potentates of Europe that in the one race that really mattered the Greeks were still the best.

The forces of philhellenism (love of ancient Greece) also influenced the way that the Acropolis was recreated when it came under the control of the new, largely German, administrators of Greece. On the rocky but leveled hilltop the surviving fifth-century buildings of Pericles nestled within a mass of medieval Byzantine structures, a Frankish tower, later Ottoman defenses, and a mosque. These the new administrators, many of whom were imbued with the enthusiasms of Winckelmann, decided to remove. They were supported by the Greeks who wished to forget the long years of servitude to the Ottomans and who even saw the Christian Byzantine period as inferior to the original glories of Greece. In the 1830s and 1840s all the later buildings of the Acropolis were demolished, often without any proper records being kept of how they had looked. In their place the four major buildings of the fifth-century Acropolis, the Parthenon, the Erechtheum, the Propylaea, and the temple to Athena Nike were highlighted, the last having to be reconstructed from surviving fragments on its original site. But was this anything like the ancient Acropolis? Certainly not. The site was originally crammed with statues of gods and goddesses, votive offerings and portraits. The white marble and the emptiness between the surviving buildings that characterize the site today were never there in the fifth century. The sculptures, including those of the Parthenon frieze, had originally been painted, as purists are often horrified to learn. The "new" Acropolis, and the one, though further restored, which is seen today, reflect as much the ideals of the nineteenth century as those of the fifth century B.C.

This passion for whiteness in Greek sculpture was responsible for one of the most bizarre stories in museum history. In 1928 a millionaire picture dealer, Sir Joseph, later Lord, Duveen, had agreed to finance a new gallery for the Elgin marbles, the sculptures of the Parthenon frieze that had been bought from Lord Elgin by the British Museum in 1816. His influence became so great that he and workmen under his control were allowed direct access to the sculptures as they were stored waiting for their new home. In September 1938 the director of the museum discovered on a bench three of the Parthenon sculptures, whose surfaces appeared to have been scraped down. Although the work was stopped immediately the damage had been done to these and others of the marbles. As one of the masons later confirmed he had been asked by Lord Duveen to make the sculptures as white as possible, removing the surface of the marble when necessary. (A full account of this extraordinary story is to be found in the third edition of William St. Clair, *Lord Elgin and the Marbles* [Oxford, 1998].)

Germany was not the only country to enshrine the study of ancient Greece within its school curriculum. It was part of a general European movement, which spread also to the United States. There were good reasons for this. The nineteenth century saw the old landed hierarchies threatened by new economic forces (arising from industrialization and international trade) and social and political change. The study of Greek was difficult and required dedication and so it was an ideal subject for those who wished to preserve high standards in education. It had the advantage of having no useful function (in contrast to, say, science, mathematics, or modern languages) so it served the purposes of continuing the isolation of an upper class, whose members did not have to earn a living, from the rest of the community who did. It is impossible to disentangle the institution of Greek studies in the English public schools from the determination to maintain the British class system. The Greeks provided, through Plato's *Republic*, for instance, a model for a leisured ruling class whose right to rule depended on a specialized education denied to the majority who were not considered worthy of it. Of course, not all of those who turned up at an English public school were able to master Greek but for these the Greek ideal of achieving glory through competition in games was adapted for the soggy school playing fields of Britain. If the competitive but essentially amateur enthusiasm for sports was believed to have ennobled the Greeks, so might it ennoble young British gentlemen.

The main Greek texts adopted for study, Homer, Thucydides, Plato's *Republic*, and Aristotle's *Ethics*, were used to reinforce the ideals of nobility, self-sacrifice, and dedication to others which the public schools claimed was their purpose. Selections had to be made to meet this purpose. While Athens could be seen as the parent of democracy, and hence unsettling for those who feared its emergence in nineteenth-century Europe, there had always been Greeks who ridiculed democracy, in particular Plato in his *Republic*. This was one text, therefore, which was singled out for study. The eighth book of the *Republic*, which contained Plato's bitterest attack on democracy, was said by the historian Macaulay to be unsurpassed in Greek philosophy for its profundity, ingenuity, and eloquence. (It is interesting to note, however, the most popular history of ancient Greece, that by George Grote, published between 1846 and 1856, championed Athenian democracy, although Grote presented the Athenian Assembly as if it were like the Victorian House of Commons and ignored slavery.) Even the Spartans, whose system was essentially totalitarian, had their advocates. Their harsh social system was often seen as a forerunner of the rigor of an English public-school education, with its emphasis on training in hardiness. The awkward features of Greek society were distorted or ignored (as Grote ignored Athenian slavery). How could Greek homosexuality be dealt with? The widow of the poet Shelley was advised that his translations of Plato's *Symposium*, which deals with homosexual experience, could only be published if references to homosexuality were erased. Thus *lover* should be translated as "friend," *men* as "human beings," *youths* as "young people."

Lesbian relationships caused the same problems. The poems of Sappho, with their frank assertions of physical attractions between Sappho and the maidens surrounding her, proved particularly difficult to handle. One German scholar did his best to resolve the issue when he suggested that "no educated Greek would have thought these were beautiful love poems if something monstrous and disgusting had been going on in them." An English classicist assured his readers that "she (Sappho) preferred conscious rectitude to every other source of human enjoyment." The fact that Greeks enjoyed a range of bisexual attachments without guilt was incompatible with their adoption as exemplars for schoolboys and so the truth was doctored. The same was done with the examination system to ensure that the high status of Greek was recognized. While candidates for the British civil service, including the Foreign Office, could be awarded a maximum of 350 points for each of the German and French papers, there were no fewer than a total of 700 for the Greek papers.

In so far as the Greeks were presented as an isolated race of genius who laid the foundations of European civilization, they could be used to support the idea of superior cultures based on racial purity. While the Romans would provide the model for the practical administration of an empire, the Greeks helped provide the *ideology* for imperialism. In the first volume of his *Black Athena* Martin Bernal has argued that the image of the Greeks was deliberately shaped to provide a rationale for European racism. This may be an overstatement of the case but there is no doubt that scholars such as the influential German Karl Muller (*A Handbook of the Archaeology of Art*, 1830) did stress, as Winckelmann had done, that Greek art had reached a pinnacle because of the superior qualities of the Greeks as a people. In this case, argued Muller, the secret lay in "their spiritual harmony." Such views did not actually create racism but they became part of the milieu in which it was ideologically possible to sustain it.

If mastery of the texts remained the core of Greek studies a potentially new and threatening Greek world was provided by archaeology. In the 1870s it was seen just how powerful a force the discipline might prove when a complete amateur, the German businessman Heinrich Schliemann, dug up the citadels of Troy and Mycenae. At Troy he claimed to have found the evidence of the Trojan War, at Mycenae the remains of King Agamemnon who had led the Greek invading forces. (The story of Schliemann is told in Chapter Two.) Archaeology could possibly confirm, but, equally, destroy the traditional picture of Greece, here by adding the hitherto unknown Mycenaean civilization to Greek history. Were the Mycenaeans really Greek and if so where did they fit in the cycles of history? Worst of all, archaeology threatened to bring out into the open a society of ordinary human beings (although Schliemann himself was obsessed with the discovery of "heroic" Greece). As Ian Morris has shown in an important essay "Archaeologies of Greece," the archaeology of Greece was clearly a discipline which had to be controlled by the scholars. As a subject in its own right classical archeology was given an inferior status as against textual analysis and it was not until 1890 that one could study it at Oxford University and then only as an option. The content of classical archaeology seemed designed to keep the human side of Greek life well concealed. It focused on the excavations of great buildings, predominantly temples and sanctuaries. In the later nineteenth century there were major excavations of Olympia, Delphi, and when it became harder to export finds from Greece itself, the Hellenistic city of Pergamum in Asia Minor. One hundred thirty slabs of sculpture from the famous Pergamum frieze and 462 crates of other material, a total of 350 tons in all, were shipped to Berlin in 1880 alone. The finds from these sites were described by scholars in meticulous detail but as aesthetic objects rather than human creations. Also within this tradition was the work of Sir John Beazley (1885–1970, professor of classical archaeology and art at Oxford between 1925 and 1956). Beazley examined a vast number of Greek pots, analyzed their styles and produced groups and schools by painters and dates. It was a towering achievement but one that completely isolated the pots from the society which made them.

It would be wrong to see Greek studies in the nineteenth and twentieth century as ossified. The sheer weight of intellectual pressure placed on the Greeks, and the continual interaction between different approaches as a variety of political and cultural movements drew inspiration from Greece saw to that. There were important new interpretations. The Swiss historian Jacob Burckhardt, lecturing in 1872, placed his emphasis on the political achievements of the Greeks and also on the degree to which Greek society was competitive, not as serene and harmonious as many depicted it. In his *Birth of Tragedy* (1872) the German philosopher Friedrich Nietzsche shocked his contemporaries by insisting on the importance of the forces of unreason, typified by Dionysus and early tragedy, in Greek society. The rationalist approach of such philosophers as Socrates and his followers, argued Nietzsche, marked not the pinnacle of the Greek achievement but the moment when it lost its true essence. An interest in anthropology rather than archaeology drew scholars such as the English Jane Harrison toward similar themes. By exploring the mythology of Greece she uncovered a very different spiritual world from that of the Olympian gods which had dominated studies in Greek religion. If one looked at the cult worship of Greece, she argued in 1890, "one would find a classical world peopled, not by the stately and plastic forms of Zeus, Hera, Artemis, Apollo, Athena, and Hephaestus, but by a motley gathering of demigods and deified saints, household gods and tribal gods." This was a world where powerful forces, both benevolent and malevolent, contended with each other, a far cry from the ordered society of Greeks so beloved by other scholars. Even so, the fascination with myth still left Greek myth as privileged among other mythologies, those of the ancient Near East or Egypt, for instance. In the 1890s Sigmund Freud was even to argue that one myth, that of Oedipus who unwittingly kills his father and marries his mother, represented unconscious impulses to be found in *every* society.

A watershed in Greek studies came with the First World War. Many young men brought up on the classics went off into battle as if they were Homeric heroes sure of finding glory. Their own disillusionment, in the British case in the mud of Flanders or in the Gallipoli campaign near the ancient site of Troy itself, merged with a disillusionment with authority in general. It was not so much Greece itself that was rejected immediately after the war as the ideologies, class-ridden education, imperialism, canons of perfect art, which had helped sustain a distorted image of Greece. There was a major reaction. In his influential *The Decline of the West*, published (in German) in July 1918 just before the war ended, the historian Oswald Spengler challenged the whole idea that world history should be centered on the achievements of the civilization of Greece. He questioned the greatness of Socrates, Thucydides, and even Plato. ("In Plato we fail to observe any conscious evolution of doctrine; his separate works are merely treatises written from very different standpoints which he took up from time to time, and it gave him no concern whether and how they hung together.") The Greeks were even criticized for "losing" most of the plays of Aeschylus and the works of the pre-Socratic philosophers in the Hellenistic period. In his work, on the other hand, Spengler would give no privileged place "to the classical or Western culture as against the cultures of India, Babylon, China, Egypt, the Arabs, Mexico—separate worlds of dynamic being which in point of mass count for just as much in the general picture of history as the Classical, while frequently surpassing it in point of spiritual greatness and power." In Germany as a whole philhellenism had become so closely associated with the monarchy and German nationalism that it never recovered from the overthrow of the kaiser and German militarism at the end of the war.

By the 1930s, the influential art critic Roger Fry had set in motion "a frank attempt to dethrone Greek art altogether." The cynicism of the 1930s, an age that had more than traditional images of ancient Greece to be cynical about, was also expressed by the poet Louis MacNeice, himself a classicist. While Athens had been presented in the nineteenth century as the paternalistic ruler of an empire, much as England was believed to be, the image was now reversed in line with the times. England, said MacNeice, was like fifth-century Athens, but only in so far as it was "able to maintain free speech and a comparatively high standard of living . . . on the basis of gagged and impoverished subject peoples."

In one of his poems, *Autumn Journal*, MacNeice expressed his disillusion more harshly:

When I should remember the paragons of Hellas
I think instead
Of the crooks, the adventurers, the opportunists,
The careless athletes and the fancy boys,
The hairsplitters, the pedants, the hard-boiled sceptics
And the Agora and the noise
Of the demagogues and the quacks; and the women pouring
Libations over graves
And the trimmers at Delphi and the dummies at Sparta and lastly
I think of the slaves.

For MacNeice his own frustrations with hierarchies were projected onto an ancient society which had become inextricably tied up with the class system of the Britain of his day.

There were other forces which undermined the supremacy of

Greece. In Germany, so long at the forefront of Greek scholarship, further assaults on the study of Greek were launched from two sides when the Nazis came to power in 1933. The new regime demanded a more technical school and college curriculum to meet its demands for modernization and rearmament. At the same time within the field of ancient history there was a shift toward the study of the German race and its creation, an obsession for many Nazis. (Hitler, it is interesting to note, stood against this trend; he showed some understandable enthusiasm for the Spartans.) There was a temporary revival of the traditional *Gymnasium* education after the war. A reaction to the excesses of Nazism and the coming of the Cold War led some German scholars to applaud the Greeks as the founders of Western democracy, but in Germany as elsewhere in Europe, traditional Greek classical education was in decline.

In the United States a classical education had never been so important as in Europe. Moreover, the rejection of traditional authority was not so profound as it was in Europe after the First World War. Perhaps for these reasons the status of the classics persisted longer. The coming of the Cold War even sponsored a revival of interest in the classics. As the scholar W. R. Connor put it (speaking of the 1950s), a study of Greece and Rome seemed well able to "create a citizen elite suited for an activist world power." The disillusionment came with the 1960s when canons of all kinds were questioned in the intellectual turmoil brought about by the Vietnam experience. The collapse of a traditional, text-based classical education in the Western world has been complete. It is astonishing to find that among one million students admitted to British universities over three years in the 1990s, only twelve of these chose a single degree course in classical Greek.

This did not mean than an interest in ancient Greece in itself disappeared—in fact the opposite. Knowing something about the Greek achievement is still seen as an essential part of education (enshrined for instance in the history syllabus of the British National Curriculum). What has disappeared are two things: first, the treatment of Greek texts as if they presented an intellectual obstacle race in which a search to grasp the meaning and etymology of every word and an analysis of grammatical rarities was an end in itself, and, secondly, the ideologies which sustained a distorted and sanitized image of ancient Greece. This does not mean that Greece, any more than society, can be studied today without ideological preconceptions. The modern student is naturally drawn to Athenian democracy and repelled by Spartan totalitarianism. For many students in the nineteenth century the opposite was the case. However, there is not the same need to justify the Greeks as there was when a ruling class's survival, including its education system, even its imperialist adventures, seemed to depend on the Greeks for their legitimacy. This enables the student to stand back and assess who the Greeks actually were in a more detached way.

The many texts which survive, histories, poems, speeches, if only a tiny proportion of the total that were written, still provide essential material for the study of Greece, as, it is hoped, the breadth and range of those quoted in this book will show. However, these texts are no longer accorded the authority they once held when they were embedded in an elitist education system which they were used to uphold. Nor are they regarded as necessarily accurate descriptions of ancient Greece and its history. The histories of Herodotus and Thucydides, for instance, can now be seen as products of their own time, with their writers having agendas of their own. The struggle of modern scholarship is to understand these agendas and to use the texts more creatively and flexibly to penetrate the assumptions within which the Greeks viewed their world.

There has been a similar revolution in classical archaeology. Archaeology continues to provide a mass of objects to study but the collection of objects as an end in itself, in particular to provide models for admiration, has long since gone. Sir John Beazley's work on Greek vases was in itself impressive and it was certainly important in helping classify the style and schools of vase painting but the fundamental question of where all this meticulous analysis of vase paintings led was left unanswered. Modern scholarship stresses that Greek art was created not for connoisseurs to linger over (at least not until Greek sculptors began providing for the Roman market in the first century B.C.) but to be used for a purpose. A temple is not just a building to be admired for its aesthetic beauty; it is also a symbol of city power, and a mediating force between man and gods. Much of Greek pottery was provided for the *symposia,* the drinking parties of the Greek elites. The subjects of the vase paintings reflect the drinkers' own concerns, sometimes to portray their own activities, sometimes to highlight a favorite myth. Unraveling what these concerns might be is a major area of scholarship. Although it is impossible to recreate with much confidence exactly how the Greek used images and what they saw in particular myths, the approach itself is an exciting one and has done much to create a more penetrating and less idealistic assessment of ancient Greece. The artificial gulf between archaeologists and texts (artificial in so far as both are, or should be, concerned with the study of Greek society as a whole) has largely been bridged.

New movements in classical archaeology have also been responsible for a shift from a study of buildings to a study of the environment which sustained them. Ninety percent of Greeks made their living on the land and it was their surpluses which underpinned city life. Yet until recently virtually nothing was known about the Greeks as farmers. The rise of the field survey in which sites are discovered through the patient accumulation of pottery and other evidence as a result of systematic walking over a region has allowed maps of the different patterns of settlement to be drawn. Land use can be shown to have shifted against the background of a harsh and relatively unchanging environment. It is certainly instructive to walk over a depopulated area of modern Greece, as this author did recently on the island of Symi (one of the islands of the Dodecanese), and see the extent to which walls and enclosures, many dating from classical times, have been used and reused to sustain the same mix of crops and animals. This is the underlying pattern of Greek life and was always sustained or returned to during times of crisis.

How far scholarship has moved can be seen in two recent books, one on Greek art and one on Athenian society. Andrew Stewart is an authority on Greek sculpture and his book of that title is a highly respected survey of the whole field. In his *Art, Desire and the Body in Ancient Greece* (1997) he stands aside from pure aesthetic responses to sculpture to show how the Greeks used their portrayals of the human body to reflect political and social ideals. From public statues of city heroes or individuals such as Alexander to the scenes of love-making on fifth-century B.C. pottery, the body carries its own messages, messages designed to show the ideal citizen, the warrior-hero, or the dominance of men sexually over women. Nakedness, such a pervasive element in Greek sculpture, can be seen as a "costume" in its own right, one to be "worn" during heroic activities such as the games, the most competitive of Greek activities (outside war, where nakedness was scarcely feasible). Stewart contrasts the naked man with the clothed woman, suggesting that here the placing of clothes on representations of women symbolized male control over them. While the connotations of the presentation of a particular style of body are impossible to explore in full, Stewart challenges more traditional approaches to Greek art, those, for instance, which saw it designed by its creators to be an aesthetic experience. This is not to say that, technically and aesthetically, Greek art has nothing to say (Stewart's approach to sculpture in his major work on the subject suggests the very opposite) but here he shows how a range of other meanings can be teased out from the way it presents its subjects.

In his *Courtesans and Fishcakes: The Consuming Passions of Classical Athens* (1997) James Davidson examines a very different world, that of the elite of Athens and its pleasures. Although the traditional picture of Athens is of an austere citizenry, torn between contemplating beauty and obsessively running their state, Davidson digs through the surviving texts to recreate a world of sensual pleasures. Fish occupied a special place as a food which had no connection with the sacred rituals surrounding sacrifice. Normally sacrificial foods had to be divided equally among participants so there was little chance to gorge on them. Fish were free of such restrictions and so might be enjoyed hedonistically. Davidson goes on to explore the wide range of sexual pleasures available to the Athenian elite but he shows how the search for pleasure had to be tempered by the political and social demands of a society that was a radical democracy. The "good" citizen had to appear restrained and therefore live within conventions that defined how, when, and to what degree pleasures could be enjoyed. The wine had to be mixed with water according to understood proportions and, in a well-run *symposium,* the number of mixing bowls to be consumed by the participants limited. In short, Davidson draws on literary sources to describe and define the parameters within which Greek behavior was conducted. It is an excellent example of how texts can still widen our perspectives of the Athenian past.

As the ideological cladding surrounding Greek studies fragmented, the Greeks could no longer be portrayed as a pure race who had a natural supremacy over those around them. There was no ethnic Greek race, however much the Greeks, in particular the Athenians, liked to think there was. The original population of Greece was itself a mix of natives and newcomers. Greece was accessible to the cultures of the East and drew on them for population and ideas. Its own settlers intermarried with local populations throughout the Mediterranean. A relatively coherent Greek culture based on a common language, shared religious beliefs, and experiences certainly emerged but this is not the same as a distinct racial identity. While the classical period (traditionally dated between 480 B.C., the year of the second Persian invasion, and 323 B.C., if the death of Alexander is taken as a conclusion) did see major achievements, it is hard to see it as a peak. It was dominated by war and instability. Many of the fundamental transformations of Greek culture took place in the so-called Archaic age (720 to 480 B.C.), *before* the Persian invasion which has been traditionally seen as the cultural watershed in Greek history. The Hellenistic age, which succeeded the classical, was not so much a period of decline, as Winckelmann and his followers would have argued, as one in which Greeks made important and often successful adaptations to new challenges. Nor, as used to be assumed by scholars, was Greek culture automatically accepted as superior and hence worthy of imitation by surrounding peoples. Research on, say, the Etruscans in the eighth to sixth centuries B.C., when they were in close contact with Greek cities and traders, and the Babylonians and Egyptians, peoples with a far longer history than the Greeks, show they were resilient to Greek contact and bypassed, used, even transformed, Greek culture for their own ends. These trends in recent scholarship are reflected in this book.

A survey of ancient Greek history has to have a starting point and an end. The starting point is relatively easy to choose. The Mycenaeans of the Bronze Age were not only the first civilization on the Greek mainland but spoke an early form of Greek. They provide a natural place to begin. The end is harder to pinpoint. Traditionally, Greek history ended with the conquests of Alexander. This reflected the old obsession with the classical period, and it led to such absurdities as the elimination of most Greek mathematics and science, astronomy, and medicine. (It is still possible to find books on ancient Greece which do not even mention Archimedes.) More recently, histories of Greece have added the Hellenistic period, from the death of Alexander to the final submission of the last Greek kingdom, that of the Ptolemies in Egypt, to the Romans in 30 B.C. It is arguable, however, that one should go further still. The Romans did shatter parts of the Greek world (one has only to think of the complete destruction of

Corinth in 146 B.C. or the Roman general Sulla's plunder of Athens in 86 B.C.) but they did not destroy Greek civilization and in fact, after some hesitations, absorbed many aspects of it. This deserves to be part of the story of Greek civilization. Under Roman rule Greece itself may have been a relative backwater, but many of the Greek cities of Asia Minor enjoyed enormous prosperity and there were important new "Greek" foundations such as Constantinople. The Romans could not afford to destroy the Greek elites; they needed their support if the empire was to remain at peace. By 100 A.D. shrewd Greeks realized that their own survival depended on acquiescing in Roman rule. Open praise could lead to massive Roman patronage, and one is conscious, surveying the remains of wealthier cities in the eastern empire, of the enormous energy which was still available in the Greek world. Nor were the Greeks intellectually dead in the Roman period. One only has to look at the sophisticated work of Ptolemy in astronomy, Plotinus in philosophy, and Galen in medicine.

A more sustainable cutoff point can be seen in the coming of Christianity to the Greek world. Christianity was first given tolerance and imperial support in the early fourth century. Although the traditional culture of Greece did survive, in some areas as late as the sixth century—and in many spheres of life Christianity and "paganism," as the rich Greek spiritual heritage was now dubbed, coexisted and even worked on each other—Christianity did eventually supplant the spiritual world of the Greeks. The Christian world, which merged into that of the Byzantine empire, though still predominantly Greek speaking, had very different concerns and loyalties to the one it had succeeded. This seems an appropriate moment to end.

But first the beginning . . .

2

The Formation of the Greek World

In the earliest times, it was said, the god Zeus had released two eagles, one in the west and one in the east. They had met over Greece at the mountain sanctuary of Delphi, later the shrine and oracle to the god Apollo. This then was for the Greeks the center of the world. Not only this. Greek historians and philosophers claimed with some arrogance that Greece was favored by the gods in being blessed with exactly the right balance between heat and cold and between aridity and abundant fertility for breeding men of spirit and hardiness. For the historian Herodotus it was the rugged terrain of Greece which nourished the soldiers who were able to fight off the great Persian invasions of the fifth century. For the philosopher Aristotle the Greek climate stimulated not only intelligence but free political institutions, in contrast to the oppressive climates of the east where the people lacked spirit and easily submitted to tyrants.

Greece is certainly rugged: It is part of the crumpled strip of the earth's surface which stretches across the eastern Mediterranean through Turkey as far east as the Himalayas. Mountains make up three quarters of its land surface and the mountain ranges, which typically sweep from northwest to southeast, are carried on in the islands of the Aegean. There are only a few areas of fertile lowland, the largest centering on the plains of Thessaly, one of the few landscapes in Greece where pasture is rich enough to sustain horses. (The ownership of horses was always an extravagance in Greece and in Homer's *Odyssey,* Telemachus, the son of Odysseus, has to refuse the gift of three stallions from King Menelaus of Sparta because his home, Ithaca, has not enough pasture or "running-room" for them.) In the Peloponnese, the peninsula at the southern end of Greece, there are fertile lowlands along the coast, such as Messenia in the southwest notoriously held by the Spartans for centuries through the brutal subjection of its native inhabitants (the helots), and the valley of the river Alpheus, which runs past the ancient site of the Olympic Games. But these are exceptions. Mountains predominate in the Peloponnese as everywhere else in Greece and as late as the 1930s only one sixth of the land in the peninsula was actually being cultivated. Those who want to make a living from the land have little alternative but to exploit the niches left between mountains: hilly slopes, narrow valleys, the occasional larger plain or lowland.

There are many other challenges for the Greek farmer. Rainfall is unpredictable with dramatic variations from one year to the next. Droughts of several weeks are common but when they are broken it is often by sudden storms that sweep away fertile soil. (Longer droughts, one of seven years on the island of Thera in the sixth century B.C., have been recorded.) Even in normal times rain tends to cascade down the slopes, making it difficult to gather for irrigation, and the ground has to be pulverized regularly to ensure it absorbs and holds moisture more easily. This is a tough environment and it made for a tough, hardy people. When the Greeks began to travel and settle in other parts of the Mediterranean they found almost everywhere outside Greece more fertile and easier to work.

Anyone visiting Greece is struck with the contrast between the white limestone of the mountains and the deep-blue, "wine dark" sea of Homer. Familiarity with the sea dates from the dawn of Greek history. As early as 12,000 B.C. obsidian deposits on the island of Melos were being exploited by seafarers from the Peloponnese. Sea travel was fostered not only by impenetrable mountain ranges but the scatter of Aegean islands which makes the eastern Mediterranean relatively easy to cross. It is possible to sail from mainland Greece across to the southern coast of Asia Minor (modern Turkey) and from there along the coast to the Near East almost always in sight of land.

Eastern Greece is full of sheltered bays and the normal practice of the early seafarers was to beach ships, although they could be also anchored off shore, the early anchors being heavy stones. In Homer's *Iliad,* the massed rows of the beached ships (here on the coast of Asia Minor), protected from the Trojans by a ditch, provide the natural gathering place for the Greeks as they plan their conquest of Troy. When Chryseis, a beautiful girl taken as a prize by the Greeks, is returned to her father on an island neighboring the mainland, a landing must be made. The sail was replaced by oars as the beach came closer:

And once they had entered the harbour deep in bays
they furled and stowed the sail in the black ship.
They lowered the mast by the forestays, smoothly,
quickly let it down on the forked mast-crutch
and rowed her into a mooring under oars.
Out went the bow-stones—cables far astern—
and the crews themselves swung out in the breaking surf . . .

(All translations from the *Iliad* and the *Odyssey* are by Robert Fagles)

and later, on their return, they enjoy the exhilaration of a following wind in a manageable sea:

they stepped the mast, spread white sails wide,
the wind hit full and the canvas bellied out
and a dark blue wave, foaming at the bow,
sang out loud and strong as the ship made way,
skimming the whitecaps, cutting towards her goal . . .

So there was intimacy with the sea by the eighth century B.C. and travelers could range widely. Even in the relatively safe environment of the Aegean, however, the sea was respected and feared, normally avoided during the winter months. "Go to sea if you must, but only from mid-June to September, and even then you will be a fool," was the poet Hesiod's advice. Homer's *Odyssey* is the archetypal epic of the sea, its natural hazards and unexpected challenges thwarting the traveler as he tries to reach home.

It was within this setting of mountain and sea with all the challenges they brought both to seafarers and to farmers that a Greek identity was cradled. It is impossible to pinpoint the origins of Greekness. The Athenians, in a typical display of arrogance after their defeat of the Persians, were to argue that they were the only people in Greece to be racially pure and of unbroken descent. However, despite evidence of occupation of the Acropolis for over five thousand years, this was a mythical distortion. There was certainly never a separate ethnic group which could be called Greek. The archaeological evidence suggests that even the early inhabitants of Greece, like those of most parts of the Mediterranean, were a mixture of native and immigrant stock. Homer, writing about 700 B.C., used several names for them, Achaeans, Danaans, and Argives, and "the Greeks" he describes fighting before Troy maintained a loose unity among themselves which was easily fragmented by personal rivalries. He was echoed by the historian Thucydides, writing in the fifth century B.C. "In his [Homer's] time the Hellenes [Greeks] were not yet known by one name and so marked off as something separate from the outside world." Some "Greek" peoples themselves even preserved memories of themselves as outsiders to the peninsula. The city of Thebes in Boeotia, for instance, attributed its foundation to one Cadmus, a Phoenician. The earliest evidence that the Greeks recognized themselves as a distinctive culture comes from an inscription at Olympia dating from 600 B.C. which talks of the judges of the games as *hellanodikai* ("Greek judges"). Previously, the word *Hellene* had been used (in Homer) only for one group of Greeks living near Thermopylae. Now it seems to have acquired a more general use and as only Greeks had the right to participate in the Olympic Games implies that more general criteria for "Greekness" had been recognized. In the fifth century B.C. the Greeks, in particular the Athenians, defined themselves rigidly as Greeks as a contrast to "the barbarians" outside whom they had defeated in the Persian Wars (see Chapter Nine) but this was an artificial definition. Who was actually Greek and how Greekness could be defined were always fluid concepts. The historian Sir John Myres put it nicely in his *Who were the Greeks?* (London, 1930) when he ended, "The general conclusion is that the Greeks never wholly were 'one people' but were ever in the process of becoming."

Despite the difficulties in pinning down Greek origins it seems fair to begin a history of Greece with the first peoples of the Greek mainland who can be linked, however tenuously, to the Greeks of the classical age, the fifth and fourth centuries B.C. One hundred fifty years ago, with only literary rather than archaeological evidence available, it was difficult to take the story back beyond the eighth century B.C. One

Hippias of Elis, the city which presided over the Olympic Games, argued that Greek history began with the first Olympics, an event which can be traced back, from his calculations, to "our" date of 776 B.C. The eighth century B.C. did mark a fresh beginning to Greek history. It was a period when essential traits of Greek culture, the *polis,* the shared sanctuaries such as Delphi and Olympia, the adoption of literacy, became rooted in the Greek world and to this extent Hippias' view makes sense. However, the fifth-century-B.C. historians Herodotus and Thucydides both recorded legends of Greek peoples which suggested an earlier history, largely of migration, of "Greek" peoples, Ionians, and Dorians, to and from mainland Greece.

The question was whether these legends could be trusted as historical sources. George Grote, the shrewd author of one of the great nineteenth-century histories of Greece, published in England between 1846 and 1856, was a doubter. He summed up the legends as belonging to "a past that was never present—a region essentially mythical, neither approachable by the critic nor measurable by the chronographer"—and refused to push his history back beyond the eighth century. As historians grew to understand that oral myths are shaped and developed to suit present concerns (just as the memories of individual human beings have been shown to be) and that the stories of Ionian and Dorian migrations reflected the later rivalries of the two peoples, then the literary sources came to be treated with greater scepticism.

It was archaeology that allowed the history of the early Greeks to be given some coherence. The story starts with the excavations of the flamboyant German financier Heinrich Schliemann (1822–90). Schliemann was a versatile and energetic businessman and an accomplished linguist who had acquired a passion for the works of Homer. Having made his fortune he was determined to spend it on the rediscovery of the world of the Trojan War, the great expedition of the Greeks to take and sack the city of Troy, after Helen, the wife of Menelaus, the king of Sparta, had been abducted there by Paris. The story was embedded in the Homeric epics and other legends. Exploring the area immediately south of the Hellespont with the works of Homer in his hand, Schliemann focussed on a hill, Hisserlik, as the true site of the ancient city of Troy. (It seems clear, however, that Schliemann's choice was heavily influenced by a contemporary expert, Frank Calvert, who showed the area to him.) Schliemann began digging there in 1871. It proved indeed to be a complex ancient city site and most scholars accept that it is the "real" Troy. However, in his enthusiasm to discover what he was looking for, an early pre-classical city that showed signs of being destroyed, Schliemann tore his way through the overlying jumble of buried ruins. His massive trench still scars the site. The eventual discovery of a double gateway reminiscent of the Scaean Gate described by Homer and a cache of precious objects nearby, which Schliemann called Priam's Treasure after the king of Troy at the time of the Greek siege, convinced Schliemann that the war had really taken place and he had found the evidence for it. (The "treasure of Priam" has had an interesting history. At one point Schliemann decked out his wife in it. It was then taken back to Berlin, looted from there by the Russians in 1945, and has only just reappeared on display in Russia.) In later excavations at Troy, however, Schliemann became aware of just how complex the site was and he had to continually rethink, as archaeologists have had to ever since, what each layer of the city represented. The "treasure of Priam" has been dated in fact to 2500–2200 B.C., at least a thousand years before any destruction of the city which might tie in with Homer, and it is the latest, uppermost, layers, not those at the bottom, which date to 3000 B.C., which would provide evidence, if any exists, of a Greek sacking of the city. (The relationship of Homer's epics to actual historical events will be discussed in the next chapter.)

Meanwhile, following a dispute with the Ottoman authorities over the treasure that he had smuggled out of the country, Schliemann returned to the Greek mainland to the Peloponnesian site of Mycenae whose stone walls and great "Lion Gate" had always stood above ground. Another lucky hunch (based on a reading of the *Description of Greece* of the second century A.D. Greek Pausanias) led him in 1876 to the celebrated shaft graves. These had been dug within a ceremonial circle (now known to archaeologists as Circle A), originally outside the city but incorporated into it when its walls were extended at a later date. The graves were those of an elite group, women and children among them, who had been buried in deep shafts along with weapons, spears and daggers, gold and silver ornaments, including gold face masks, and exotic trinkets from Crete, Africa, and the Near East. The Homeric figure associated with Mycenae was Agamemnon, who had led the Greek expedition to Troy, but had been murdered on his return by his wife's lover, Aegisthus. Here, proclaimed Schliemann, were the graves of Agamemnon and his men and he even pinpointed one of the bodies, and its gold mask, as that of the murdered hero himself. Again Schliemann had overreached himself. Like the treasure of Priam the graves were dated to much earlier than any conceivable Trojan War (to c. 1550 B.C.). The importance of the finds remains and they are, unlike many other treasures of Greece, still in the country, displayed in the National Archaeological Museum in Athens.

Schliemann's flamboyance, gift for publicity (he reported his finds well both in newspapers and in detailed reports), and ruthlessness in the pursuit of his ends had succeeded in bringing to life a forgotten civilization, the Mycenaeans (as they came to be called after the stronghold at Mycenae) of the Aegean Bronze Age. (The Bronze Age, called after its most widespread metal, is normally defined as running between 3000 and 1200 B.C. though in the Aegean, unlike in the Near East, there are only civilizations in the later part of the period.) Schliemann's methods could be deplored and his attributions scorned but his achievement still leaves him as a dominating figure in the history of archaeology.

At about the time of Schliemann's death in 1890 the first reliable dates were being given for the Mycenaeans. Mycenaean pottery had been found on the Nile at El-Amarna, the site of the capital of the heretic Egyptian Pharaoh Akhenaten, and was securely datable from a chronology established there to the mid-fourteenth century B.C. Eventually, Mycenaean civilization was defined as stretching from about 1600 B.C. to its collapse in the twelfth century. Mycenae continues to be regarded as the center of the civilization, but a number of other important Mycenaean sites—Tiryns, Pylos, and outside the Peloponnese, Gla, Thebes, and Athens—have also been rediscovered.

Schliemann had assumed that the Mycenaeans, as Homer's heroes, were Greeks who were linked through Homer to the classical world. He could claim therefore that there was an underlying continuity between the Bronze Age and later Greek history and this view was shared by many of the scholars of his time. By the early twentieth century a reaction had taken place. Many scholars felt that the so-called Dark Ages, the period between the collapse of Mycenaean civilization and the revival of prosperity on the Greek mainland in the eighth century, presented a gulf which was too deep to cross. Perhaps there was some intellectual snobbery involved in that scholars of the classically "pure" fifth-century Greece did not want their civilization associated with the more barbaric Bronze Age! The argument could only be settled if something specifically "Greek" could be pinned to the Mycenaeans.

The link came in a somewhat prosaic way, in a series of clay tablets. In the early 1900s another major Bronze Age civilization had been discovered, by the English archaeologist Sir Arthur Evans, on the island of Crete. It took its name, Minoan, from a king Minos of Crete, who, legends suggested, lived some three generations before the Trojan war. Excavations showed that Minoan civilization, at its peak between 1600 and 1450 B.C., centered on expansive palaces, the largest of which was at Knossos in the center of the north of the island. These were sophisticated buildings, adorned with large courtyards and colourful frescoes, even designed so as to absorb the impact of earthquakes. They acted as centers for the gathering and recording of local agricultural produce that was then traded overseas for stone and metals. Minoan traders were found throughout the southern Aegean (the most spectacular trading center yet discovered is Akrotiri, a thriving town on the Aegean island of Thera, still partially preserved under the lava of a volcanic eruption which destroyed it in 1626 B.C.) and evidence of communities of Minoan craftsmen has been found in northern Egypt (Avaris in the Nile Delta) and modern Israel.

To help record quantities of goods, the Minoans had evolved their own system of writing, known as Linear A. It is a syllabic script (each sign represents a syllable) though some signs are ideograms (pictorial symbols) of particular commodities. The surviving examples are inscribed on clay tablets which had been hardened and preserved by the very fires which had destroyed the palaces. Alongside the Linear A tablets, were others inscribed with a similar though distinct script. These were termed Linear B. Thousands of Linear B tablets were found at Knossos and Arthur Evans assumed that the two scripts had co-existed. Neither could be deciphered but in 1939 the story took a new twist when an American archaeologist Carl Blegen digging at the Mycenaean site of Pylos on the Greek mainland found a large cache of Linear B tablets, preserved here too when the palace was destroyed by fire about 1200 B.C. At first they were taken as evidence of Minoan expansion overseas but then a more radical theory suggested itself. There was increasing evidence that the Mycenaeans had settled in Crete in the mid-fifteenth century. Was it possible that they had adopted the use of writing from Linear A in order to write their own language? The work of an American scholar, Alice Kober, in the 1940s established that the languages of Linear A and Linear B were probably different and gradually the theory of Mycenaean expansion became the preferred explanation.

This still left the language in which the Linear B tablets were written, whatever it was, undeciphered. There had been a suggestion from Arthur Evans that it might be Greek. He got tantalizingly close to proving the point when he was shown that a later, deciphered Greek syllabary from Cyprus had some similarities with Linear B and two syllables reading "*po-lo*" in the Greek Cypriot were next to an ideogram of a horse on a Linear B tablet. (*Polos* is the Greek for foal.) However, he dismissed the similarity as a coincidence. Even so he inadvertently opened the way to the decipherment. Among the audience of a lecture on the Minoan world Evans gave in 1936 was a fourteen-year-old schoolboy, Michael Ventris. Ventris became inspired by the challenge of decipherment. He had enormous linguistic ability and a passion for cryptography. Although he later became an architect, in his spare time he stuck to the analysis of the tablets. He did not expect, at first, to find that Linear B was Greek; some relationship to Etruscan was his first guess, but then he, too, noted the similarities with the Cypriot syllabary (which is now known to be derived from Linear B). The real step forward came when he tried to fit the names of Cretan cities—Knossos; its harbor, Amnissos; and another local town, Tylissos—which he assumed might have remained unchanged over the centuries, with syllables from Linear B. He began to get some matches (again using links with the Cypriot syllabary) and thus some syllabic sounds which he could use in other contexts. An exciting moment came when the sounds *ko-wo* and *ko-we*, the *kouros* (boy) and *kore* (girl) of Homer's Greek (the earliest Greek texts to have survived) emerged. The Homeric words for *shepherd, bronzesmith,* and *goldsmith* were similarly deciphered. In June 1952 Ventris went public. "During the last few weeks," he announced triumphantly in a BBC radio broadcast, "I have come to the conclusion that the Knossos and Pylos tablets must after all have been written in Greek—a difficult and archaic Greek, seeing that it is five hundred years earlier than Homer, and written in a rather abbreviated form, but Greek nevertheless." A newly discovered batch of tablets from Pylos clinched his claim. A picture of a vessel with three supports was accompanied by a text reading "*ti-ri-po*" and one of two similar vessels with the text "*ti-ri-po-de.*" This corresponded to the Homeric Greek for one and two *tripods.* As remaining texts were unraveled (some of the words are still indecipherable as they had disappeared by Homer's time) names of Greek gods emerged, among them Poseidon, Zeus, and Athena. It was not just Greek language but other elements of Greek culture which had been born in the Bronze Age. Moreover, the discovery established for Greek the longest continuous history of any European language which survives today and a language which has fed into others. (Colin Renfrew, an authority on the early Aegean, has suggested that the Greek language may have evolved from early Indo-European roots in Thessaly and further south between 5000 and 2000 B.C.). The word *tripod* remains with us.

Now that the position of Mycenaeans as forerunners of the later Greeks seemed secure, their own origins needed to be explored. There have been suggestions that they originated outside Greece. One theory is that they were charioteers from the east—the remains of chariots, unknown before this in Greece, have been found in their graves. Another, put forward by Martin Bernal in his book *Black Athena*, is that the Egyptians (or an Egyptianized people, the Hyksos) colonized Greece. The sheer difficulty of conquering a fragmented, mountainous landscape such as the Peloponnese and the failure to find any archaeological evidence for outsiders has discredited this approach. (The chariots, not of particular use for fighting or transport in a rocky landscape, were probably imported as status symbols.) Archaeology, in fact, pointed in a different direction. In 1952 further excavations at Mycenae had uncovered another grave circle. It was earlier than Grave Circle A (though given the name Grave Circle B) and its graves dated between 1650 and 1550 B.C. (Grave Circle A's graves overlapped those of Circle B in time—the earliest dated to about 1600, the latest to 1450.) The graves in Circle B varied in opulence but the earlier ones, simple, individual tombs, lined with stones, resembled those known in the region earlier. This suggests that Mycenaean civilization was an indigenous development. The *tholos* tomb, a circular chamber with a corbelled roof, buried under a mound, known first in Messenia, but with later examples found in the other Mycenaean centers, is further evidence for local development. (It is typical of Mycenaean burials that the body is buried intact [inhumation] and not burnt before burial [cremation].) The evidence that the Mycenaeans originated within Greece seems convincing.

There is no obvious explanation as to how and why a group of chieftains in mainland Greece should have elevated themselves above their fellows and gained access to goods from across the eastern Mediterranean. Mycenae, for instance, is no richer in resources than the rest of Greece and has no immediate access to the sea. However, Greece was on the edge of the thriving Minoan trading empire and it can only be assumed that determined individuals were able to exploit the opportunity to trade any surplus produce they could squeeze from their locality, grain, hides, wool woven into textiles, timber, oil, even slaves, for the riches and other resources of the east. It has been argued that the real driving force of Aegean trade was the search for the constituents of bronze, copper, and tin. Copper was relatively plentiful, in Crete and Cyprus, for instance. Tin, essential for hardening copper into an effective metal compound, was more elusive. The main source was probably Anatolia but the Mycenaeans may have been involved in passing copper and tin into the Aegean from Europe.

By 1500 there is growing evidence that the local elites of the Greek mainland were forging closer links with each other and producing a more coherent culture. There was now a typical Mycenaean stronghold, a ruler's citadel on a low hill in an area where the land was reasonably fertile and the water supply good. The *tholos* tomb was adopted throughout the Peloponnese and constructed with increasing expertise as stone-working skills improved. Large chamber tombs, cut into soft rock, were used by elite families over several generations, a sign of political stability. The tastes of these families were increasingly sophisticated as shown by the finely worked ivory and gold they had left. (Perhaps the finest of the gold work was imported. Two gold cups found in a Mycenaean tomb at Vapheio [in the southern Peloponnese] portray the capture of bulls, one by force, one by the lure of a female. They are brilliantly observed and executed and probably the work of Minoan craftsmen.) Overseas travel was conducted with increasing confidence. While the Mycenaeans may not yet have been able to challenge the Minoan monopoly of trade in the Aegean, their pottery is now found spreading to the central Mediterranean (in the Lipari islands, north of Sicily, for instance). They had mastered the crossing (tricky because it takes place over open water often against the prevailing wind) between Italy and Greece.

Around 1450 the palaces of Crete, with the exception of Knossos, were destroyed. Shortly afterwards there are signs of Mycenaean influence at Knossos. The famous throne room in the palace seems to have been modeled on the typical *megaron,* or hall, of a Mycenaean stronghold, and chamber tombs in Mycenaean style appear in the area. What actually happened to the Minoans in the mid-fifteenth century is uncertain. Their civilization may have been destroyed by earthquakes or invaders but there is some evidence that tensions between the various palaces of the island erupted into local conflicts which weakened the civilization so severely that Mycenaeans, already in close contact with Crete, were able to expand onto the island.

The Mycenaeans appear to have retained some awe for the Minoan achievement and were ready to adopt much of Minoan culture rather than destroy it. A system of writing was essential for any efficient recording and distribution of goods and the Minoan Linear A provided the inspiration (see above). Linear B was the result. The Mycenaeans built their own palaces on the Minoan model and these were adorned with frescos and Cretan motifs. However, they are never so large nor so well built as the Cretan examples—the central block of the palace of Nestor at Pylos, the best preserved of the mainland palaces, is only slightly bigger than the central courtyard of Knossos. Moreover there is little evidence of "civilization" affecting the mass of inhabitants of Mycenaean settlements. These are little more than a scatter of buildings, not consolidated along streets with drainage systems as towns such as Gournia in Crete or Akrotiri on Thera are. The elaborate cult activities of the Minoans appear much more sophisticated than those of the Mycenaeans.

Mycenaean rulers have left the impression that they dominated their peoples through showy displays of their power, partly perhaps through the ownership of exotic goods but even more so through the effective use of stone for imposing fortifications and tombs. The great *tholos* tombs carry a message with them. The so-called "Treasury of Atreus" (Atreus was in legend the father of Agamemnon) at Mycenae, the best preserved, is a massive domed construction in stone, thirty-two feet high inside, with a *dromos,* a ceremonial entranceway leading to its great doorway (itself over 16 feet high) nearly 120 feet long. It has to be seen as a statement of strength. The fortifications around Mycenae and the neighboring citadel of Tiryns have some defensive purpose but well beyond what would be needed to fight off intruders armed only with bronze weapons.

The best "documented" of the Mycenaean communities is that of Pylos although the preserved tablets which provide the evidence of its day-to-day existence date only from the final days of the palace, about 1200 B.C. Interpretations of the surviving texts are difficult but they suggest a hierarchical society under a presiding ruler, the *wanax,* who was supported by local landowners and who may also have been responsible for cult activity. There is evidence of an effective administration able to coordinate the raising of extra supplies and organize defense at times of crisis, such as the community experienced at its destruction, the moment when the surviving tablets were written. It appears that the palace had direct control of some land, specialized in the gathering of flax for making linen, and supported its own craftsmen. For daily food supplies it may have raised a levy of wheat from the surrounding landowners and peasantry but these maintained their independence. Traces of unprotected outlying settlements found by archaeological field surveys supplement the evidence of the texts and are a testimony to the overall security of a Mycenaean "state" in its heyday. Evidence from other sites show that the staples of each palace's economy varied—Mycenae and Knossos specialized in wool, Thebes in wool and livestock. The landscape was manipulated to improve yields. At Gla in Boeotia a lake was drained in order to increase the supply of arable land while the citadel of the city was enlarged, presumably so that the palace's flock of sheep could be guarded safely. At Tiryns a river was diverted to lessen the risk of flooding in the settlement. Overall, Mycenaean societies appear to have enjoyed a modest prosperity, even if most of their surpluses were channeled toward the ruler and his palace.

The most impressive feature of the Mycenaean economy was its trading networks. In the eastern Mediterranean of the fourteenth and thirteenth centuries there were no clearly defined borders between peoples, no obstacles to unlimited travel other than those raised by language difficulties or local violence. The stable Egyptian and the Hittite empires each respected the other's sphere of influence in the Near East and so conditions were settled. Free enterprise could now flourish and its nature can be guessed from the finds made in the famous Ulu Burun (or Kas) ship, wrecked off the coast of southern Turkey in about 1350. The hopes and livelihood of an ambitious trader who was making his way round the eastern Mediterranean, collecting and offloading cargo as he went, had been drowned in the wreck. Metals, predominantly copper (six tons of it) and tin, were the main cargo but there were raw materials and artifacts from at least seven different cultures, resin in Canaanite amphoras, pottery from Cyprus, ebony from Africa, a gold scarab from Egypt, and cylinder seals from the Near East. The finds even included a frame for a writing tablet arousing speculation that writing might have spread to the Aegean long before the normally accepted date of the eighth century.

The Mycenaeans flourished in this world. The major export which survives in archaeological evidence was in the shape of small vases, jars, and jugs that probably contained perfumed oil but which were valued in their own right (as can be seen from the many attempts to copy them). The pottery is found throughout the Mediterranean along the coast of Asia Minor; in Syria and Palestine; in Egypt, far up the Nile; and as far west as Sardinia (an important source of copper), Sicily, and Malta. It is assumed that it was traded primarily for copper and tin—another wrecked ship of about 1200, found also in southern Turkey off Cape Gelidonya, was loaded with copper and tin from the Levantine coast and Cyprus on its way to Greece.

It is hard to know where the legendary image of the Mycenaeans as warriors fit into this picture. The overall stability of the Aegean and of the Mycenaean settlements themselves has cast some doubt on major military expeditions painted by Homer, but the Mycenaeans were certainly used to conflict. As material evidence of warfare, there is the famous suit of bronze armour of about 1400 B.C. found at Dendra and a mass of bronze weaponry—swords, both for slashing and stabbing, daggers, and javelin heads. A fresco on the palace walls at Pylos depicts warriors (on another, from Mycenae, ox-hide shields are shown hanging on the palace walls) and a papyrus from El-Amarna appears to show Mycenaean mercenaries in the service of the Egyptian kings. There are depictions of sieges on silver and stone. Again if the "Ahhiyawa" mentioned in Hittite sources are, as many believe, Mycenaeans, then there is evidence for warlike raids on the coast of Asia Minor, possibly, recent redating of the Hittite sources suggest, about 1400 B.C. Was there, among all this activity, really a Mycenaean raid on Troy, a city whose position overlooking the entrance to the Hellespont would have made it a coveted prize? The question will be explored further in the next chapter.

The sheer range of the Mycenaean presence and the stability of their internal economies over many decades is impressive evidence of their success. Yet the Mycenaean rulers remained vulnerable. To survive they had to maintain a delicate balance, holding the allegiance of their subjects, living at peace with neighboring communities, as well as keeping their trading links intact. Any weakness in the chain of control could bring collapse, and disintegration did come in the century after 1200 B.C. The evidence is of destruction of individual sites followed by short-term revivals throughout the twelfth century B.C., with some Mycenaean communities, that of Athens, for instance, surviving largely unscathed. It is consistent with gradual dislocation rather than sudden collapse.

What upset the balance is unclear but it was probably a combination of misfortunes. Earthquakes, severe drought, and rulers greedy for more resources than their economies would provide, are all possibilities. Initially, a collapse may have been precipitated by the disruption of trade routes. In Egyptian records there are accounts of raids by the mysterious Sea Peoples around 1200 B.C. It would be easy for these disruptions to become magnified in the telling, deterring traders from venturing across the Mediterranean at all. If resources failed to arrive, the rulers would have lost both credibility and the means (weapons, for example) to keep control. There would have been temptation to grab new sources of raw materials by attacking neighbors and then there would have been further disruptions as these fled as refugees. Tangled into the accounts are legends of invaders, the Dorians, entering Greece from the north but the archaeological evidence is inconclusive. The most important of the later Dorian cities, Sparta, was only founded as late as 900 B.C.

Overall, the archaeological evidence is suggestive of a movement from the Mycenaean centers eastward during the twelfth century B.C. as the old world fragmented. New settlements are found at Perati on the eastern coast of Attica and Lefkandi on the island of Euboea, but there is even evidence of Mycenaean refugees as far east as Cyprus and Rhodes and at Emborio on the island of Chios in the Aegean. Later (c. 1050) there may have been another migration from Athens, a refounding of the ancient city of Miletus on the coast of Asia Minor, for instance, and possibly other settlements along the same coast.

The trend of the next decades, into the eleventh century, was toward isolation. There was a narrowing of horizons as communities lost a sense of being in contact with the world overseas and became preoccupied with their own survival. Population levels fell drastically and many settlements were abandoned. Traditions of craftsmanship were sustained only for a few years before faltering through lack of patronage and raw materials. The collapse of the Mycenaean states meant, in short, the end of all their rulers fostered and sustained, impressive halls, imposing stonework, frescos, fine craftsmanship, and the knowledge of writing. In art the figure, human and animal, disappears.

What could be carried and sustained more easily was an oral tradition of the past, repeated and enriched by wandering singers. This helped preserve a common Greek language, though one with several different dialects—Arcadian (the survivor of Mycenaean Greek) in Arcadia, in the central Peloponnese, and Cyprus; Doric in the Peloponnese; Aeolic in Thessaly and Boeotia; and Ionic in Athens, Euboea and, later, on the coast of Asia Minor. Many but not all the Mycenaean gods named in Linear B texts lived on and in some places, at Calapodi in central Greece and Cato Syme in Crete, for example, cult activity continued throughout the centuries, although its form changed with time.

What followed in the three centuries 1100–800 B.C. has traditionally been known as the Dark Ages but archaeology is lifting some of the darkness. A significant development was the coming of iron to Greece. Iron is very much harder than bronze but there was a major technological problem concerned with its production. The ore requires a temperature of above 2,732 degrees Fahrenheit (1,500 degrees centigrade) if it is to be reduced to pure iron (copper ores require only 1,981 degrees Fahrenheit [1,083 degrees centigrade]). The higher temperature could only be achieved through charcoal-burning furnaces and sustained by continual bellowing. Even then the so-called bloom, a spongy ball of iron, was all that would emerge and this was still solid enough to require beating into shape (by a blacksmith, a profession which has maintained itself over three thousand years). Tradition and archaeology combine to suggest that it was in Cyprus and Crete, areas rich in ore, that Mediterranean iron working began, though gradually other sources of ore, including the island of Euboea, became known. Iron is first used for weapons, daggers, and then from about 1050 larger objects such as swords. From about 1000 B.C. it is used for agricultural implements. All this encouraged the search for the sources of iron ore. Soon travelers are heading back west to Sardinia and the Italian peninsula in search of it.

Some enterprising communities did manage to survive and even prosper in the Dark Ages. The best known is Lefkandi on the island of Euboea, settled by Mycenaean refugees in the eleventh century. At first it kept up some contact with the East but then in the late eleventh century it appears to have lost touch with the outside world. It remained prosperous, however, and in about 1000 B.C., one of its rulers was buried alongside his wife in a building larger (150 by 30 feet) and more sophisticated (it was surrounded by a colonnade of timbers) than any other known in Greece. It remains unique for its time, a chieftain's hall which appears to have been converted into his final resting place. Among the grave finds is good evidence of the spread of iron by this time, a spear, a sword, iron pins for holding clothing, and iron bits in the mouths of four horses buried near the bodies. Later, the settlement shows signs of its own metalworking and a renewed contact with the East.

Lefkandi also had contacts with the city of Athens, particularly after 900 B.C. The community here, like so many others in the period, appears to have contracted during the eleventh century before enjoying a slow revival. Most of the evidence of its size, social structure, and relationships with the outside world come from cemeteries. The pottery from graves has proved particularly interesting. About 1050 a distinct form, owing nothing to outside influences, emerges. Known as protogeometric, it consists of neat, squat vases with concentric and regular semicircles, drawn with a compass, above circular bands on their necks. It is an ordered if simple style and endures over 150 years, suggestive of social stability in the community. In one sense protogeometric pottery can be seen as the first Greek art but it is lacking the most characteristic feature of later periods, the human figure (though the odd vase sports a daubed horse). This lack of figures is typical of all Greek art of the period though characteristically Lefkandi bucks the trend with a pottery centaur (a man with the body of a horse) from about 900 B.C. This figure, writes Andrew Stewart in his *Greek Sculpture*, "inaugurates the use of myth in Greek sculpture—a truly momentous occasion."

By 900 B.C. Athenian pottery develops further as geometric motifs, rectangles, swastikas, meanders, become more prevalent and spread outwards from the middle and neck of a pot to fill it completely. By 800 the typical Athenian pot is a tightly packed mass of geometrical forms (the style, not surprisingly, is known as geometric). There is very occasionally a human figure but there were clearly inhibitions about representing any, and in this sense true Greek art, which reveled in the human form, can hardly be said to have begun. These pots have been interpreted as status symbols for the elite and their increasing elaboration in design is associated with other signs of wealth in Athenian graves, gold worked finely into wire and beads, ivory and bronze work from the east. It fits with evidence of a few families able to maintain some dominance in the small community which made up the settlement.

However, it would be wrong to see the elite of the period, such as it was in those impoverished times, as urban dwellers. It is possible to reconstruct from the poems of Homer, which contain some material from these centuries, a world where a local nobility, the *basilees* (singular *basileus*), form an elite based in the countryside. The *basilees* are a hereditary class, passing their wealth and homesteads on from generation to generation, though land is split between their sons. They see themselves as set apart, flaunting their individuality through military achievement and their duty is not to any local community but to themselves, their family, and their class. Women of the class have a status of their own, as acceptable marriage partners (witness the frenzied wooing of Odysseus' wife Penelope by rival *basilees* when he fails to return from Troy), and also as overseers of the domestic arrangements of the household, the *oikos,* but often there is found something more, the adulation of a woman for herself. Arete, the wife of Alcinous, ruler of Phaeacia, is described as honored by her husband as no other wife in the world is honored. "Such is her pride of place, and always will be so: dear to her loving children, to Alcinous himself and all our people. They gaze on her as a god, saluting her warmly on her walks through town." (Translation: Walter Shewring.) Women of lower status enjoyed no such respect and are there to be freely exploited as menial workers or sexual playthings.

The household itself centers on a hall with benches around the walls, a courtyard, stables, and private quarters. The whole is supported by a pastoral economy. Odysseus' riches in Ithaca, enough, according to Homer, to place him among the twenty richest men in the world, are described as "a dozen herds of cattle . . . just as many herds of sheep, as many droves of pig and goat flocks ranging free." This is not opulence on the scale that could be found in the Near East (that was hardly to be expected in Greece), but it shows that ownership of cattle is a status symbol and helps explain why Homeric sacrifices and feasts centered so exclusively on meat. They provided the opportunity for orgies of conspicuous consumption that only the *basilees* could afford.

An attractive feature is the mutual cooperation between members of this class which helps sustain an Aegean-wide system of supportive relationships. In the *Odyssey*, Odysseus, washed up naked in the land of the Phaeacians, manages to persuade Nausicaa, the daughter of their king, that he is worthy of her father's hospitality. After delicate negotiations, she promises him help, "the right of worn-out suppliants come our way." Once his credentials have been accepted there are honored conventions of welcome, bathing, clothing, and the respectful listening to his story by the king and his entourage before the visitor is bedded down and then, refreshed and restored, helped on his way. Gifts, horses, cattle, or *objets d'art* are provided to cement the relationship on the understanding that the traveler would return the help in similar circumstances.

In the eighth century, however, the world of this noble class came under threat from new social and economic forces. Population growth in Greece was demanding a more intensive exploitation of the land (see further Chapter Three). Cattle may have provided status but they were a hopelessly inefficient way of using all but marginal land. It made more sense to grow crops for immediate consumption or sale and gradually there emerged small holdings based on the staple crops of Mediterranean agriculture, olives, vines, and cereals. It is a highly pragmatic way of farming. Only in the most disastrous of years will all three fail.

The olive is native to Greece and well adapted to the climate. It can endure drought and the comparatively warm winters of Greece guard it from frost which will otherwise kill it. This does not make it an easy crop to grow. The trees take some years to mature (for the ancient historian the cultivation of new olive trees suggests political stability or the rise of lucrative new markets, usually in neighboring cities) and normally crop only every other year. The fruit is difficult to pick, especially from larger trees. Yet in a marginal environment such as Greece, olives have proved their worth. The trees cling to life with tenacity. (The legend that when the Persians sacked the Athenian Acropolis in 480, Athena's sacred olive tree was burned to the ground but resprouted within a day may be rooted in reality.) Olives are high in calories, so are a food in themselves, and the extracted oil can be used in lighting and cooking, for treating wool, and even for perfume. As the fruits mature and stay on the tree for some weeks, the crop can be harvested between autumn and winter, giving the farmer some welcome flexibility in the way he focuses his labor.

The vine appears to have been introduced in Greece about 5000 B.C., while the dates for domestication of vines, as opposed to the exploitation of wild varieties, have been placed well before 2000 B.C. Drinking cups for wine were certainly known this early and by the time of Homer (c.700 B.C. but the poems often refer to conditions in earlier centuries) wines are being classified by quality. Nestor, king of Pylos, has, for instance, a coveted vintage which has been sealed and left to mature for eleven years. The skill of successful viticulture comes from knowing when to pick. Hang on too long and run the risk of losing everything through rain; pick too early and the immature grapes can only be left in the sun to dry into raisins.

Barley was the most common cereal crop in ancient Greece as it needed only two thirds of the rainfall of wheat, but it had little prestige and was mixed into a kind of cake only acceptable to slaves or the poor. Wheat was always the aristocratic choice, even if, as in Athens, much of it had to be imported from abroad. (Barley was the most common crop in Athens' territory Attica until as late as the fourth century B.C.) The problem with cereal crops lay in finding enough labor to plough, sow, and then harvest a crop. The harvesting of crops took place in a concentrated period in late May or early June and would need several fit people working together to secure the crop before the grain overripened and was lost. Oxen could be used for ploughing but, as they were heavy consumers of grain themselves, only a larger farm would benefit from them. Farms with older dependents or young children to feed would have been at a real disadvantage in finding enough labor and there was an incentive to provide slave labor to fill the shortfall. (It is probable that household slaves were diverted from domestic work at harvest time.) There was not quite so much of a rush to thresh and winnow the grain as to harvest it and these tasks could be fitted in before the vines and olives needed to be harvested in the autumn or winter. Greek agricultural life mixed periods of intensive labor with more relaxed ones.

The luckier farmer would be able to supplement his diet with fruit and pulses. As Odysseus, returned to his native Ithaca after twenty years, tries to prove to his father, the aged Laertes, that he is really his son, he remembers himself:

> *. . . a little boy*
> *trailing you through the orchard, picking our way*
> *among the trees, and you named them one by one.*
> *You gave me thirteen pear, ten apple trees*
> *and forty figs . . .*

Laertes is also shown to have vegetables, probably beans. Flax was grown to provide linen and rope.

Animals, predominantly sheep and goats, played an important part on the Greek small holding. They could survive on fallow land and were used to provide manure as well as wool and cheese. The smaller farmers preferred a mix of arable with pasture and it was the larger herds which were farmed separately on pastureland higher on the mountain slopes and moved between summer and winter grazing. There were upland settlements that specialized in processing wool and leather, and also in the production of charcoal for heating and cooking.

There is a fine early account of the tribulations of the Greek farmer in the *Works and Days* of Hesiod, written around 700 B.C. Its central passage is a manual of practical advice, possibly based on Hesiod's own experience of farming in Boeotia, an area he rates as "bad in winter, troublesome in summer, good at no time." The description sets the tone of his work. Hesiod has no illusions about life. He is bitter over a brother who has taken more than his fair share of the family inheritance, leaving him with no other option but backbreaking labor on the land. The moral imperatives of hard work, frugality, the steady accumulation of surpluses, pervade his writings. "If there is a desire for wealth in your heart, then do the following, work with work on top of work." In short, peasant farming was a constant battle against unpredictable forces. There was a stress on endurance, hard work, and sheer ingenuity—in preserving water for regular irrigation, for instance. The increase in yield from land which was well turned, and thus able to retain more moisture, seems to have been considerable but tools remained primitive. The earth had first to be cut through by an *ard*, a rudimentary wooden plough sometimes tipped with iron, then broken up with a mattock. Furthermore, the farmer required an intimate knowledge of the triad of crops, and the soils on which each best flourished, and some shrewd judgment of the ways the limited reserves of human strength could be distributed to maximize a return.

Hesiod's is the world which pervades Greek history, as well of that of preindustrial Europe, that of the hardy and self-reliant peasant, suspicious of luxury and cautious of change. It was the underlying pattern of all Greek life—even the wealthier Greek cities could not survive without their farmers. With experience and good judgment a small surplus could be expected in an average year. Hesiod assumes that a modest prosperity is there to be won by the hardworking farmer and it was this that was to sustain the Greek city-state and hence the possibilities of civilization itself.

3

Homer's World: Heroes and the Coming of the City-State

The eighth century is the age of Homer. The two great epics, the *Iliad* and the *Odyssey,* attributed to a poet of whom almost nothing is known, can be said to mark the beginning of the European cultural heritage. As they exist now the *Iliad* and *Odyssey* are two episodes from a much larger cycle of epic poems covering a war between bands of, possibly Mycenaean, Greeks and the city of Troy, after Paris, the son of Priam, king of the city, has abducted Helen, the wife of Menelaus, the king of Sparta. The war will end eventually in a Greek victory (after the celebrated ruse of introducing a wooden horse crammed with Greeks into the city) but only after ten years of siege and bloodshed. There were probably five poems dealing with the siege and capture of the city, with the *Iliad* the second of the five. The *Odyssey* seems to have been the second of three epics dealing with the aftermath of the siege as the heroes returned home.

The episode covered in the *Iliad* centers on the Greek camp at Troy. Here there is acute rivalry between Agamemnon of Mycenae, who claims overall leadership of the Greek forces, and Achilles, the proud, touchy hero, son of the goddess Thetis and hero Peleus and leader of the Myrmidons, one of the groups making up the Greek army. A row between them over a girl, Briseis, captured as booty, leads to Achilles' threatening to withdraw all his men from the siege. However, he eventually relents to the extent of allowing his beloved companion,

Patroclus, to borrow his armor and enter battle. Patroclus is killed by the Trojan hero Hector but Achilles has his own revenge by killing Hector. Hector's body is reclaimed from the Greek camp by his aged father Priam, and in a moving scene, Achilles and Priam break down in mutual grief as they understand the futility of war.

In the *Odyssey* Odysseus, one of the Greek leaders, is coming home, a journey which will take ten years and involve him in countless adventures. As the poem opens, Odysseus' wife, Penelope, besieged by suitors, waits for him in Ithaca, unaware of whether he has survived the siege of Troy or not. In fact Odysseus is alive and the *Odyssey* recounts his adventures as he makes his way home. They include the sexy nymph Calypso who lures him to her mountain retreat, tempting Sirens, monsters, and whirlpools. He experiences the extremes of society, from the uncivilized Cyclops, "lawless brutes with no meeting place for council, no laws either," from whom he escapes only with the greatest cunning, to the well-tended city-state of the Phaeacians where all is good order. It is the Phaeacians who eventually land him on the shores of Ithaca. After being recognized first by his dog and then his old retainers he deals brutally with Penelope's suitors and he is then reunited with her.

In the past fifty years it has come to be appreciated how these epic poems were transmitted orally over centuries. They may have been recited first as the songs of warriors, to the lyre, in the Mycenaean chieftain halls of 1500 B.C., with the siege of Troy as a later event being woven in over time. Some scholars have gone back further, claiming that the *Odyssey* may come from the same Indo-European root as the Indian epic *Mahabharata,* itself over eight times as long as the *Odyssey* and *Iliad* combined. It was the American scholar Milman Parry who, drawing on parallels in Bosnian oral poetry, showed how the poet had a creative role, drawing on legends and preexisting patterns of verse but always developing them, adapting his lines, or composing new ones as he went along. For Greek epic a satisfying meter, technically known as the dactylic hexameter, was evolved. The meter combines order with diversity (each line has six metrical units which may consist of either two long syllables [a spondee] or one long syllable followed by two short ones [a dactyl]; every line ends in a spondee but within the line spondees may be mixed with dactyls) and this is part of its emotional appeal to audiences who get used to a rhythm whose internal variations preserve it from monotony. Inevitably, as Parry showed, some lines become so satisfying that they become embedded in the poems. There are formulaic phrases or lines "swift-footed Achilles"; "crafty Odysseus"; or "when early born rosy-fingered Dawn appeared"; and stock ways of describing feasts, sacrifices, or the arming for battle. Yet there was always room for improvisation. The Bosnian poets would never repeat a poem in the same form; they were adept at molding it to their audiences, and the same can be assumed for the singers of the Greek epics.

The Homeric epics, therefore, contain a pastiche of events and scenes which reflect the long history of the poems. Most weapons are bronze as they would have been in Mycenaean times, yet then an iron arrowhead is mentioned quite casually in a line which must have been added later. Similarly, at funeral games for Patroclus one of the prizes is a lump of iron, reflecting a moment when it was seen as a precious metal, before smelting and trade in ore became commonplace. Boar tusk helmets, known from pictures to have been among Mycenaean armor, survive in some scenes as does inhumation, the normal burial practice in Mycenaean times. Cremation, only introduced later, exists alongside it. Marriage customs in which a bride is expected to bring a dowry exist alongside ones in which she is lured by the wealth of her suitor. The nobles of the epics live sometimes on country estates, sometimes in walled cities. The farm of Laertes, father of Odysseus, is the farm of a prosperous eighth-century peasant while the nearby court of Ithaca comes from an earlier age.

In short, this is a composite world with no historical coherence to it. As the poet developed the story any new background details would reflect the experiences of his audiences of the day and he would not bother to remove lines which described an earlier, vanished world. Studies of other epics have shown how easily they become distorted by time and the imagination of the singers. The French epic, the *Song of Roland,* first written down about 1150 A.D., has been shown to bear little resemblance to what is known historically of the eighth century battle it describes. In his book *Roumeli* the travel writer Patrick Leigh Fermor describes listening to the epics of the nomadic Sarakatsan people of northern Greece. They originate in the struggles against the Ottoman Turkish overlords but the word *makaronades,* a derogatory term for Italians, was simply substituted for "Turks" after the Italian invasion of 1940. So easily can the context of a poem be changed. The final form of the epic normally reflects something of the world in which it is sung. Many of the features of the eighth-century Greek world which will be described below, the *polis*, the oracle at Delphi, athletic games, overseas colonization, appear in the Homeric epics and this has enabled them to be given an approximate date, 750 B.C. for the *Iliad,* possibly 725 B.C. or later for the *Odyssey.*

One hesitates to question the reality of the Trojan War. It is such a powerful and pervasive event in Greek epic, it is hard to accept that there is no truth at all in stories of an attack on the city. It is clear from Mycenaean sources that sieges were common in the period and would be an appropriate setting for a war. Moreover, Troy itself, with its commanding position at the entrance to the Hellespont and hence to the Black Sea, and its control of the land route between Europe and Asia, would have been a much coveted prize. It is impossible to stand on the ruined walls of the city today looking out over the surrounding plain and not to feel some resonances of the epic. (The less scrupulous tour guides on the site work with enthusiasm to make the link, confidently tying specific events described by Homer to exact locations along the walls. An imposing wooden horse stands by the entrance to the site.)

Excavators have shown that the city which stood at the time of the Mycenaeans (labeled Troy VI) enjoyed sophisticated fortified walls, some 1800 feet in total length, 21 feet high, and between 12 and 15 feet thick. Outside these impressive fortifications a large city built mostly in wood has been recently discovered and a total population for Troy VI is now estimated as seven thousand. It was certainly one of the biggest trading cities of Asia Minor and the Near East. There is evidence of widespread trade with the Aegean and a quantity of Mycenaean pottery has been found. Tantalizingly, the city was destroyed in around 1250, a traditional date for the Trojan War. However, the cause seems to have been an earthquake and meticulous excavation of the site has failed to find any definitive evidence of a Greek conquest. Troy VI's successor, Troy VIIa, was destroyed by fire and some archaeologists have linked this destruction to a Mycenaean conquest but again no conclusive evidence has been found to back this claim. The whole story may have a kernel of truth but equally, in the present state of archaeological knowledge, could be an invention, the creation of a story around a city which would be familiar to the whole Greek world, a fantasy tale of what the Mycenaeans would have liked to have achieved if they *had* been superhuman.

The final form of the poems cannot be separated from the famous and enduring "Homeric questions" that have worried scholars over the centuries. Did one person, "Homer," bring coherence to each poem and if so how much did he have to do, simply order the episodes into a story or work on them over decades perhaps, to improve overall consistency both of character and narrative? Was the final composer the same person for both poems? The structure of the *Iliad* in particular does suggest a poet who made the poem his own and worked on it until it reached its present coherence. The *Odyssey* is a more fragmented poem, with more diversions from the central narrative, though it, too, has a final coherence. Some scholars feel, however, that its approach to the art of poetry, about which it is extremely self-conscious, its notion of a hero, its acquaintance with a wider Mediterranean world, and its mood of individual adventure make it the work of a different poet altogether. Where did the composition take place? Tradition places the composition within the Ionian communities of the Asia Minor coast although it has more recently been argued that the Greek mainland or the offshore island of Euboea is as likely an origin. There are in fact traces of several dialects as one would expect of a poem worked on over centuries.

There has to be some incentive to preserve epics of this length and detail and a means of doing so. A means became available in Greece in the mid-eighth century when an alphabet from the Near East was adopted by the Greeks. The source was the Phoenicians, a collective word used for the peoples of the independent cities of the Levantine coast, which included Tyre, Sidon, Byblos, and Beirut. (The name *Phoenician* probably comes from the purple dye which was one of their products—the Phoenicians called themselves Canaanites.) The Phoenicians had intruded into the Greek world in search of metal ores (probably to satisfy the needs of the Assyrian empire) and seem to have stimulated a revival of Greek trade as a result of which the Greeks began to use Phoenician trading routes with increasing confidence.

The Phoenicians already had an alphabet, with some twenty-odd consonants, though like the other alphabets of the Near East, which first appeared about 1500 B.C., it lacked vowels. The consonant *t* could, theoretically, stand for the sound *ta, te, ti, to,* or *tu.* Somewhere, about 750 B.C., perhaps in Crete, perhaps in Cyprus, perhaps even in the western Mediterranean, Greek traders started using the Phoenician alphabetic script themselves. However, almost immediately they took the alphabet a step forward. They introduced vowels, adapting Phoenician letter forms for the purpose. Vowels are crucial to Greek grammar and it is probable that it would have been impossible to have written Greek satisfactorily without them; nevertheless, it proved an inspired development and made the Greek alphabet (actually alphabet*s* as different Greek communities used slightly different letter shapes) the direct ancestor of the Western alphabet, much more accessible and useful than the consonantal alphabets of the ancient Near East. It also showed that the Greeks were not mere imitators of the Phoenicians but able to transform what they had learned for their own ends; in other words, they were, in the eighth century, developing a distinct cultural identity. (Despite the variations in script *all* the Greek alphabets adopted vowels and this can only suggest some cultural coherence within the Greek world.)

Fairly soon writing was being used in various contexts, to record names and goods, of course, but also to make dedications to the gods and to jot down lines of verse. As they mastered the new technique the Greeks were able to record their thoughts in a much more sophisticated way than ever before. It would therefore have been possible to record the *Iliad* and the *Odyssey* in the eighth century though the process would have been a laborious one. (The earliest reference to a written version is, in fact, not before the sixth century in Athens, but there has been a suggestion [by Barry Powell] that the alphabet was actually adapted from the Phoenician model for the express purpose of recording the poems.)

The question that remains is why poems of this particular type with their emphasis on the hero had become so popular. An answer can only be suggested by exploring the world of the eighth century.

While trade was reviving in the eighth century, and presumably bringing some modest prosperity, Greece itself was undergoing a significant growth in population. The evidence is drawn from an increase in the number of graves and new settlements and has been calculated by some scholars to have been as high as 4 percent a year on a scale equal to the most fertile of third-world countries today. Presumably greater stability, slow improvements in agricultural productivity, or modest prosperity from trade were enough to lift populations above the levels of mere subsistence and thus increase the chances of survival. It is likely, however, that a change from a pastoral economy to one based on arable farming with a more consistent production of surplus crops was the most important single factor. As field surveys collect further evidence, a slower growth rate stretching further back in time may be revealed, with population growth encouraging the shift to arable farming and the shift itself then enabling a larger population to be supported.

One result was the growth of larger communities. There are not only many more of them but those close together tend to coalesce into larger units, incipient towns (some of them around defensible high ground, the Acropolis at Athens or Acrocorinth in Corinth, for instance). Most significant of all, these communities begin, in the eighth century, to make a distinction between a "city" area and the surrounding countryside. It can be seen most clearly in the exclusion of activities such as burials from a defined central space. In Corinth, cemeteries were moved outside city limits in about 750 B.C. and the same happened in Athens and the Peloponnesian city of Argos about 700 B.C. This suggests that the community is exerting control over its citizens' activities. A further step is for the city to be defined by walls—an early and perhaps not typical example is the Greek settlement at Old Smyrna on the coast of Asia Minor enclosed possibly as early as the middle of the ninth century and then rebuilt in the late eighth—but there are other examples in Greece, including Athens, before 700 B.C. It may have been the Phoenician cities of the Levantine coast which provided the model, though these were much more crowded than the typical Greek city which from early times marked out space for different city functions.

It was typical for a new city to find a protecting god, Athena, at Athens, Apollo in Corinth, for instance, and sacred areas, both inside and outside of the city were set aside for temples, the first in Greece, in which to worship them. An example from Argos, the temple to Hera (the wife of Zeus), and a terra-cotta model from the shrine at Perachora north of Corinth suggests that the earliest form was like a nobleman's house with a porch and a steep concave roof. However, during the eighth century there is the emergence of the recognizable Greek temple with columns placed around a central hall, which now houses a cult statue to the god or goddess. (The predominant use of a temple was not to provide a meeting place for worshippers but to house and honor this statue.) Examples are the temple to Hera on the island of Samos (where the base of the cult statue has been found), and that to Artemis at Ephesus which had eight columns along each side and four on the facades. Columns may have been used to support an extended roof so that mudbrick walls could be given some protection from the elements or simply added to create impact. The temple is set within an enclosed precinct, the *temenos,* which holds an altar where sacrifices to the presiding god or goddess take place. (There is so much blood, smoke, and general mess in a Greek sacrifice that it has to be an outdoors activity.)

The temple to Hera at Samos has a further importance. It is several miles (kilometers) from the city of Samos although its size and sophistication make clear that it can only have been constructed by the city itself. The evidence suggests that here, and in other cases such as the shrine of Perachora, the sanctuary was deliberately placed to mark the city's control of marginal land or a disputed border. Here is the city defining its own wider territory, essential if it is to have the means to defend and to support itself. This relationship between town and a defined territory which produces food is, physically, what makes the *polis,* the city-state. Another way in which this marking of territory took place around the cities of the Argolid (the eastern spur of the Peloponnese) was for Mycenaean tombs in the surrounding area to be reopened and presented with offerings as if a link with ancestors was being reclaimed and control of the territory sanctioned as a result.

The *polis* is, however, a human organization. The ancient Greeks could never conceive of a *polis* independently of its citizens (it has been suggested that the word be translated "citizen-state" rather than "city-state") and the emergence of this comparatively sophisticated political structure deserves an explanation which goes further than population growth. It probably lies in the emergence of a peasant class of farmers as arable farming takes root. What do such farmers require? Security is one need and this presupposes some form of community organization so that all can join in the protection of their land, and the stores of surplus food they accumulate, against rival communities. Yet with each individual attuned to self-reliance, any form of surrender to an outside ruler will be anathema. Here is the potential for political structures based on the involvement of citizens in their own government, at least through participation in an assembly in a local center. (Assemblies and debates were already known in the Homeric world. Success in debate was valued as highly by the *basilees* as success in war and warriors were expected to give approval to the decisions of their leaders.) In other words, the urban center is the deliberate creation of the rural community and moreover it reflects its values. It is a male community, suspicious of the old nobility, and sensitive to its own identity. The rise of the middling peasant farmer is accompanied with an increase in the use of slaves. This may have been because such labor was essential to provide the manpower to run an effective farm but the presence of slaves also enhanced the status of the owner. To work for others was for a Greek a humiliation, the lowest form of life, and the institution of slavery reinforced the concept of the free individual, an essential one in Greek culture. Hand in hand with the rise of slavery, comes the marginalization of women. The Dark Ages village was open, allowing easy access between members of the community, but after about 700 the typical Greek house is enclosed, centered on a secluded courtyard with women segregated from the wider community. The community also expects to do its own fighting and so evolves citizen armies, the hoplites, a heavy infantry drawn from those peasants rich enough to buy their own armor. (The earliest known example of hoplite armor, a helmet, comes from the city of Argos and is dated to c. 725 B.C. though hoplite warfare is essentially a feature of the seventh century onward.) Fifth-century Athenian democracy, in which a male citizen body, its freedom supported by slavery, ruled the city and defended it on land and sea, was the eventual heir of this revolution (see Chapter Eleven).

Evidence that serious thought about the nature of government is emerging at this time can be seen in Hesiod's the *Theogony* (c. 700 B.C.). The theme of the poem, which draws heavily on Eastern myth, is the origins and genealogies of the god but Zeus is portrayed as the protector of mankind through a daughter Dike, justice. In Hesiod's second poem, *Works and Days,* Dike is offended and complains to Zeus when justice is betrayed. The emergence of an abstract, if personified, concept such as justice is an indication that such concepts have entered Greek thinking this early and represent "higher" values that can be appealed to in debate. In a nutshell, an agricultural revolution has fostered a political revolution. By 730 the concept of a *polis* is so well developed that new settlements founded overseas by Greeks in the second half of the eighth century are planned from the start as *poleis,* with marked-out areas, temples, and accompanying land.

The story is not finished here. Revolutions presuppose the overthrow of dominant classes. So did the *basilees,* the aristocratic class, simply disappear? Certainly their way of farming was comparatively inefficient and appears to have been eclipsed in many, but not all, parts of Greece. (The Athenian aristocracy maintained territorial power bases in Attica well into the sixth century.) However, noble birth and status were not easily eliminated. The aristocracy seem to have created new roles for themselves which allowed them to maintain status in different forms. The evidence is inevitably fragmentary and it is easy to base too much on it but it is possible to piece it together to produce the story of a class which sustained itself in a new and potentially threatening world.

An early indicator of aristocratic self-definition can be seen in pottery from Athens. In 800 B.C. the human figure on pottery was still virtually unknown (although there are some decorative friezes of animals and birds). Then in a cemetery at the Dipylon gate in Athens an astonishing development takes place about 770 B.C. Large pots, over five feet tall appear, probably placed as markers alongside graves. A number appear to be by one painter (the so-called Dipylon master) and his associates and they contain pictures of human figures placed within rectangles inserted in their geometric patterning. The human bodies are abstract in form (with triangular torsos) and they are engaged in activities surrounding death, at funerals as mourners with horses, and occasionally in battles, both on land or sea. The scenes are set out carefully but there is no emotional input or hint of individuality. The figures do not overlap. The artist concentrates on providing a clear picture of what is going on.

The Dipylon master deserves the credit for the way he created his images. Although crude in comparison to later Greek art they, and the context in which they were presented, were totally original. However, the "master" can hardly have constructed and painted such large vases as he did without some prompting from his patrons. Some kind of statement is being made in these pots and it is all the more significant when the accompanying graves are examined. The bodies they contained were no longer cremated, as was the Athenian tradition, but buried untouched as was typical in the rest of Greece. It is possible that noble families were trying to maintain their identity against popular pressures within the city by insisting on their membership of a wider Greek world. It is also possible that they were defining themselves as a class by emphasizing their past glories and achievements. This suggestion is supported by a scene on a pot of about 750 B.C. where one of the human figures has four legs. There was a myth in which King Nestor of Pylos defeated two warriors whose bodies were joined together. The picture acquires real fascination when it is known that one of the aristocratic families of Athens, the Neleids, claimed descent from Nestor. Within the next few years the "Siamese Twins" reappear in other Athenian pots. Is there evidence here therefore that an aristocratic family, under threat from the new order, was preserving its identity, its treasured and ancient family history, through an artistic statement? If so, and the suggestion can only be pure speculation, the depiction of the human figure, the narrative of events, the portrayal of myth, all crucial ingredients of later Greek art, may have been born from the stresses of the eighth-century social revolution.

If social forces in the city-state are focusing new pressures on the aristocrats they can look for self-advertisement outside the city. The appearance of the temple, complete with cult statue, within a sanctuary in the eighth century has already been mentioned. Again it has been noted how many of these sanctuaries were on marginal land, between the territories of states. Some were on important trade routes. Olympia, in the western Peloponnese is at the junction of two rivers, the Alpheus and Cladeus. Another is at Isthmia, on the narrowest point of the isthmus between the Peloponnese and mainland Greece, the natural crossing point for traders who wish to avoid the tricky voyage around the south of the Peloponnese. Yet another is Delphi, the oracle sacred to Apollo, on the slopes of Mount Parnassus. Its earliest dedication dates from 800 B.C. These sanctuaries receive an enormous increase in dedicated goods in the eighth century. Particularly notable are bronze tripods. These are known to have been used as competition prizes but seem also to have been status symbols in themselves. A dedication was a way in which a member of the nobility could advertise his status to the wider world. At Olympia, there is evidence of resident craftsmen from whom tripods could even be ordered on the spot. Often dedications of arms accompany the tripods. The argument that the sanctuaries are being used for self-display by marginalized groups is strengthened by the rise of another sanctuary to Hera, at Perachora, north of Corinth. Here the dedicators are overwhelmingly women. Their dedications are exotic ornaments, such as Phoenician scarabs, evidence that the women, too, come from the richer classes. Are they too fighting against the eclipse of their traditional roles?

There is another way in which the nobility could express their prowess to a wider Greek world and that is through competition in games. Games are a noble concern. Again Homer puts it well. When Odysseus is hosted by the Phaeacians and games are thrown in his honor, he hesitates to take part. One of the Phaeacians taunts him—perhaps he is not truly of the noble class but only a mere trader, a calling always despised by aristocratic Greeks:

> *I never took you for someone skilled in games,*
> *the kind that* real *men play throughout the world.*
> *Not a chance. You are some skipper of profiteers,*
> *roving the high sea in his scudding craft,*
> *reckoning up his freight with a keen eye out*
> *for home-cargo, grabbing the gold he can!*
> *You are no athlete. I can see that.*

Odysseus cannot, of course, resist the challenge and seizing a discus throws it farther than any other competitor. He has thereby confirmed his noble status.

Games had traditionally been thrown to mark specific but irregular events such as deaths (the games held at the funeral of Achilles' companion Patroclus in the *Iliad,* for instance). The Olympic Games (held for the first time it was said in 776 B.C. but dates either side of this have been proposed by scholars), in contrast, appear to have been formally set up as a regular opportunity every four years for young nobles to show themselves off. Significantly, the competition was not for any worldly goods, as this would be below the dignity of the competitors, but for honor. The victor won only a wreath of wild olive. Thus the noble preserved himself "above" those who had to earn a living. Moreover his victory was not just for himself—it also brought him status within his home city. Later sources suggest that the victors in games were welcomed home through city walls which had been broken down for the purpose. It is as if their heroic status as victors gave them talismanic powers that transcended the need for physical defences. It is not certain how early this enhancement of the victor took place but it suggests a way in which the nobility survived not only with some of their class values intact but with a role in the emerging city-state. In short, they had found a way of negotiating their survival into the city age.

The eighth century also saw an intense interest in "the hero." The hero as an individual is difficult to define but typically he lies somewhere between an ordinary mortal and the gods and is often the son of a god himself. Most heroes were placed in a mythical past but they retained their power through being linked by descent to an existing group, maybe a clan or a particular city. It was accepted that they needed some kind of cult worship, perhaps through a festival in their memory. As Carla Antonaccio has argued, it seems that the consolidation of a link between a city or a family and a founding hero was an important development of the eighth century. She goes on to suggest that epic poetry is used in the same way, to preserve memories of a heroic past in such a way that existing social groups can use the exploits of heroes to legitimize their own status as descendants. However, there is an alternative view, suggested by Gregory Nagy and based on comparison with epic performances from India, that by invoking legends of heroic ancestors in a public performance, the community *as a whole,* evokes their support. Oliver Taplin, in his *Homeric Soundings,* has argued that the poems were presented in a Panhellenic setting, during the feastings and festivals that surrounded the games which were now becoming a feature of Greek life. He argues that each epic could have been recited at all-night sittings, the *Iliad* over three nights, the *Odyssey* over two. If so, they could have become part of a communal ritual, their value resting in their unchanging nature. This might explain why they were consolidated into a more formal, finished text by the late eighth century. They could have been written down then or preserved in the memory of poets, the unchanging nature of the texts reinforced by competitive declamations in which an accurate rendering of an agreed text was important. (There is evidence of a guild of public reciters, the rhapsodes or "song-stitchers," who specialized in Homer and these played a major role in Athens in the sixth and fifth centuries.)

If a prime concern of Homeric epics is the exploits of heroes, how does Homer portray such men? During his mortal life, the hero has superhuman strength and endurance even if, unlike in other folk traditions, he is not given any magical powers. (He cannot transform himself into an animal at a moment of crisis, for instance.) His exploits are always recognizably human ones, though carried out at a higher level of achievement. Here is the Trojan hero Hector approaching the gates which guarded the Greek ships. He grasps a boulder which would normally have taken two men to lift:

Planting his body right in front, legs spread wide,
his weight in the blow to give it total impact,
Hector hurled at the gates, full centre, smashing
the hinges left and right and the boulder tore through,
dropped with a crash and both gates groaned and thundered
. . . and Hector burst through in glory, his face dark
as the sudden rushing night but he blazed on in bronze
and terrible fire broke from the gear that wrapped his body,
two spears in his fist. No one could fight him, stop him,
none but the gods as Hector hurtled through the gates
and his eyes flashed fire.

The hero can change the course of battles as Achilles, roused to implacable anger by the death of his beloved companion Patroclus, does in the *Iliad.* The hero can show heroic attributes in other settings; Odysseus in the *Odyssey,* for instance, is a different kind of hero from the warrior-superman, one who relies on cunning and resourcefulness for his survival. There is an element of the trickster, known from other folk-tale traditions, in his behavior and Homer allows him other virtues, endurance, statesmanship (he is presented as having been the ideal king of Ithaca before his departure for Troy), and athletic prowess, though in the final scenes of the epic, he does emerge as a powerful warrior able to wreak destruction on his enemies. It is in the heat of battle, in fact, that the ideal of heroism can most easily be achieved. In war the hero raises himself high above ordinary mortals—partly because the risks of death are so high and the intensity of the moment so strong—but partly because it is through the act of killing that fame can be won. Yet the hero is mortal. Although he can be given help by the gods, so, too, the gods can will or allow his death. In a final scene of the *Iliad* between Achilles and Priam Homer shows that even the greatest hero is not immune to the horrors of war and human fate. When death comes, there is no special reward for the hero. In the *Odyssey* Achilles meets Odysseus in the underworld and tells him that even life on earth laboring for others would be preferable to death. The only appropriate response for the hero is nobility in the face of suffering that cannot be avoided.

The Greek concept of the hero is important, above all because the human attributes of the hero are never lost. This fostered the idea that every Greek, though most usually those from the noble class, could become heroic, achieve *arete,* excellence, in his own life. Glory could be achieved through *agones,* competitive participation in battle or in games. Victory raises the victor to near godlike status. Death is something worth risking for the sake of everlasting fame and those who appeared to have avoided it could be reviled as were those who competed but lost in the games. (One of the Spartan survivors from the battle of Thermopylae was so effectively ostracized by his home community that he committed suicide.) Alongside heroic behavior comes the idealization of the heroic male body. The search for perfection in the human form was to prove one of the driving forces of Greek art. In short, the heroic ethos, and the competitive instincts it released were essential elements in the Greek achievement.

However, the Homeric epics are not concerned simply with the glorification of the hero. This would make the epics little more than propaganda hymns concerned with the ease with which a hero conquers and achieves glory for his community. The greatness of the *Iliad* and *Odyssey* as literature arguably lies in the way they illustrate the *difficulties* inherent in the heroic role. The greatest glory for the hero comes from activities which court death and yet death brings nothing but a shadowy existence in the underworld. Here is the ultimate and inexplicable human tragedy. The Homeric heroes are actively fearful of death, yet they cannot risk the taunt of cowardice. How then can the heroic role be maintained in a way that is psychologically bearable?

The dilemma is explored in its most intense form in a moving scene between Hector and his wife Andromache, before Hector goes out to battle. Andromache knows that if Hector is killed, her life will be shattered, her status as a noble woman destroyed. She will probably be sexually abused, then dragged off to Greece and forced to serve as a menial servant in the halls of her captors. Hector, aware that Troy will indeed fall, knows this to be the truth and he imagines her in captivity:

> *And a man may say, who sees you streaming tears,*
> *"There is the wife of Hector, the bravest fighter*
> *they could field, those stallion-breaking Trojans,*
> *long ago when the men fought for Troy." So he will say*
> *and the fresh grief will swell your heart once more,*
> *widowed, robbed of the one man strong enough*
> *to fight off your day of slavery.*

The scene is given added poignancy by the presence of Hector's small son who recoils in fear as his father dons his armor. Yet Hector has to fight—"I would die of shame to face the men of Troy and the Trojan women trailing their long robes, if I would shrink from battle now, a coward"—and he has to go into battle bearing the dreadful weight of responsibility for Andromache and his son, if, as does happen, he is to die. In short, Homer has highlighted the terrible dilemmas involved in war, notably the demands of the community for service on its behalf that conflict with personal relationships.

There are other dilemmas for the hero presented in the poems. The clash between Agamemnon and Achilles reflects what must have been very real problems in defining the authority of leaders. On what grounds can one man be expected to accept the supremacy of another's demands at a moment of crisis; how can individual honor be preserved in the face of such demands? In the *Odyssey,* there is much talk of good government, of hospitality within the noble class, of laws and assemblies, yet the only way open to Odysseus to deal with the suitors who have been importuning his wife is to kill them without mercy. There is no legal structure in Ithaca by which they can be judged and dealt with within the community. A major function of epic poetry is to address these concerns. "Epic," writes Oliver Taplin in his *Homeric Soundings*, "was a way of exploring political development by setting up difficult questions, questions which in real life might be intolerably confused and explosive." This public airing—and potential diffusion of emotive issues as a result—was to reappear in Greek tragedy two centuries later.

The key moment in Homer's exploration of the tragedy of war comes at the end of the *Iliad*. Priam has come to seek the body of his son, Hector, from Achilles. This was in itself a remarkable gesture, a humiliating experience for one of Priam's status (normally a herald would have been sent), and the Greek audience would have been acutely sensitive to this self-abasement:

But Priam prayed his heart out to Achilles:
"Remember your own father, great godlike Achilles—
as old as I am, past the threshold of deadly old age!
No doubt the countrymen round him plague him now,
with no one there to defend him, beat away disaster.
No one—but at least he hears you are still alive

and his old heart rejoices, hopes rising day by day
to see his beloved son come sailing home from Troy.
But I—dear god, my life so cursed by fate . . .
I fathered hero sons in the wide realms of Troy . . .
. . . one, one was left me, to guard my walls, my people—
the one you killed the other day, defending his fatherland,
my Hector! It's all for him I've come to the ships now
to win him back from you—I bring a priceless ransom.
Revere the gods, Achilles! Pity me in my own right,
remember your own father! I deserve more pity . . .
I have endured what no man on earth has ever done before—
I put to my lips the hand of the man who killed my son."
Those words stirred within Achilles a deep desire
to grieve for his own father. Taking the old man's hand
he gently moved him back. And overpowered by memory
both men gave way to grief. Priam wept freely
for man-killing Hector, throbbing, crouching
before Achilles' feet, as Achilles wept himself,
now for his father, now for Patroclus once again,
And their sobbing rose and fell throughout the house . . .

Homer makes no secret of the brutality of war. Men die horribly, if quickly, their guts or their brains spilling out as they fall slashed by swords or pierced by arrows. The horror of war is made more explicit through placing it in contrast with a world at peace. Civilization for Homer is based on good order in the state, the hospitality of rulers, love between men and women, and appropriate relationships between mortal men and the gods. Often the contrast between peace and war is conveyed almost in passing. Hector pursued by Achilles runs alongside the edge of the city, past:

washing pools
scooped out in the hollow rocks and broad and smooth
where the wives of Troy and all their lovely daughters
would wash their glistening robes in the old days,
the days of peace before the sons of Achaea came . . .

The poet has paused just to remind the listener of the realities of war and how the spot where washing, among the most domestic of activities, should be taking place has been transformed into a backdrop for death.

Domestic life is held together by the marriage bond. Odysseus offers his hopes to Nausicaa, the girl who has offered him her family's hospitality:

And may the good gods give you all your heart desires:
husband and house, and lasting harmony too.
No finer, greater gift in the world than that . . .
when man and woman possess their home, two minds,
two hearts that work as one. Despair to their enemies,
joy to all their friends. Their own best claim to glory.

The sense of emotional involvement in a happy marriage is well conveyed and again shows that Homer is concerned with more than the macho achievements of warriors. When Odysseus is finally reunited with Penelope, Penelope, distraught that she has not recognized her husband, implores forgiveness:

The more she spoke, the more a deep desire for tears
welled up inside his breast—he wept as he held the wife
he loved, the soul of loyalty, in his arms at last.
Joy, warm as the joy that shipwrecked sailors feel
when they catch sight of land . . . So joyous now to her
the sight of her husband, vivid in her gaze,
that her white arms embracing his neck would never for a moment let him go . . .

Dawn with her rose-red fingers might have shone
upon their tears, if with her glinting eyes
Athena had not thought of one more thing.
She held back the night, and night lingered long
at the western edge of the earth, while in the east
she reined in Dawn of the golden throne at ocean's banks,
commanding her not to yoke the wind swift team that brings men light,
Blaze and Aurora, the young colts that race the Morning on

. . . Rejoicing in each other, they returned to their bed,
the old familiar place they knew so well.

These are intensely moving movements in themselves but all the more so in the hand of a poet who can deal so explicitly with the horrors of war.

It was the historian Herodotus who wrote that "Homer and Hesiod first fixed for the Greeks the genealogy of the gods, gave the gods their titles, divided among them their honors and functions, and defined their images." Even so, the Homeric epics do not provide a coherent role for the gods. They can protect human beings but they can also destroy them. In the *Iliad* and the *Odyssey* the gods often seem to act unfairly. They let their personal grudges predominate, they act with total lack of concern for the fate of humans. This often leaves the heroes exasperated or frustrated, unable to combat the fate that the gods define for them. Yet they also show tremendous spirit: They are not crushed by destiny. Homer accepts that there is a place for free will, that human beings can and often have to fashion the world for themselves. Human endeavour is not threatened by the gods, as it seems to have been in some of the more autocratic societies of the East, and Greek life was to prove all the richer for it.

Yet there is also a sense in Homer that impious behavior will receive the wrath of the gods. The suitors in Ithaca have offered the conventions of hospitality and they are killed by Odysseus, rightly it seems and with the support of Athena. Despite the fickleness of the gods it is hoped that they will respond to appropriate honoring and this can be achieved by the holding of the correct rituals. There is something more. The gods are associated with the underlying order of the natural world. Homer describes how the Greeks' base is destroyed by Poseidon, the earthshaker and the god of the sea, and things return to an original pattern:

> *The earth-shaker himself, trident locked in his grip,*
> *led the way, rocking loose, sweeping up in his breakers*
> *all the bastions strong supports of logs and stones . . .*
> *He made all smooth along the rip of the Hellespont*
> *and piled the endless beaches deep in sand again*
> *and once he had levelled the Argives' mighty wall*
> *he turned the rivers flowing back in their beds again*
> *where their fresh clear tides had run since time began.*

> *So in the years to come Poseidon and the god Apollo*
> *would set all things to rights once more.*

For later generations Homer remained a great moral teacher. In fifth-century Athens boys would learn the poems by heart and not only absorb a heritage but understand the appropriate behavior for people in different stations in life, men and women, slave and free, ruler and ruled. There was virtually no situation, either in the ways humans relate to each other or to the way the gods relate to men and the natural world, that is not covered somewhere in the epics. Furthermore, the epics had enormous emotional power. In Plato's *Ion* Socrates is used by Plato to question one of the rhapsodes. He freely admits that his role is to arouse emotion. "I look down at my audience from the platform . . . they are crying, and they turn awestruck eyes upon me, and they yield themselves to the amazement of what I relate." The impact continued past the classical age. Alexander the Great was steeped in Homer and when he crossed over into Asia Minor he appropriated the Homeric heritage in support of his adventure by sacrificing at the supposed tombs of the heroes Ajax and Achilles. In the great cache of papyri found in the Greek city of Oxyrhynchus in Egypt, much of which dated from Roman and Byzantine times, Homer was still the single most popular author. There was a sense in which the Greeks never ceased emotionally to live within the age of heroes.

4

An Expanding World: 800–550 B.C.

About the year 650 a band of adventurers from the Cycladic island of Paros arrived on Thasos, an island in the northern Aegean. There was much to attract them and other seafaring Greeks to the site. The island was fertile, particularly rich in timber and minerals including gold but, despite the rich pickings to be had, it was also threatening territory. There were earlier non-Greek settlements on the island and the Thracians on the mainland were hostile to the intruders from the south. It must have been a tough undertaking for the settlers to establish a toehold on the island, tougher still to exploit its resources. Yet the newcomers succeeded. By 600, as archaeologists have established, the first primitive settlement had been transformed into a well-planned Greek city complete with sanctuaries and an agora, a meeting place for its citizens.

Among the band of early settlers, the son of its leader, in fact, was a poet, Archilochus, and fragments of his experiences have survived. Archilochus may have been of noble birth but he has little time for gentility. His writing is vivid, his attitudes abrasive. Thasos is a dump. "All the dregs of Greece are drawn to Thasos." There is no room for showing off by "gentlemen" officers in the everyday crises the settlers faced:

Not for me the six-foot general, strutting round on lanky legs,
Fondling his fancy hair-do, stroking his close shaven chin—

Let me have a short-arsed leader, one with bandy legs astride,
One with both feet firmly anchored, full of guts and full of fight.
(Translation: Alan Griffiths)

This is an uncertain and ephemeral world. In one of his poems Archilochus portrays a father with an ugly and apparently unmarriageable daughter who nevertheless had found herself a suitor. The outcome is a total surprise and Archilochus/the father compares it to an eclipse of the sun he has just seen:

Nothing is too odd or wonderful.
nothing is beyond belief since Father Zeus
made night from noon, hid away the sun
and laid a shrinking fear on men.
From that time all things were possible
and so no man should marvel if
the forest beasts remove to dolphins'
salty fields, finding roaring waves
a sweeter home than land, while fishes plunge
high up on wooded mountain slopes.
(Translation: Anne Pippin Burnett)

The overpowering experience of an eclipse (it can be dated to 648 B.C.), together with the day-to-day struggles for survival in the frontier settlements of the north Aegean must have emphasized the precariousness and unexpected nature of human life. While Homer's heroes are presented in a distanced past, this is life very much in the present. Moreover, Archilochus himself makes no pretense to be a hero. There is a famous passage where he relates how, when escaping from a skirmish with a Thracian, he leaves behind his shield. He admits to no dishonor here—he tells the reader that he will simply get hold of a new one. He brags of his sexual appetites and conquests and brutally insults a fellow settler who promised him his daughter in marriage but then went back on his deal. (A legend survives that the unlucky man, his wife, and the daughter all committed suicide as a result of his invective.) Nevertheless, Archilochus has a rough sense of values. He warms to those of his fellows who will fight alongside him, and although in his longest surviving poem he persuades a girl he fancies to submit to his sexual advances, at the moment of climax he holds back from taking her virginity. Memories of him as a courageous patriot lingered on in his native Paros and a shrine to him was built there in the third century B.C. (Archilochus was also honored as the first of the so-called lyric poets.)

There were overseas Greek settlements before the Parians reached Thasos. By 750 a number of Greek cities on the western coast of Asia Minor (prominent among them, Smyrna, Ephesus, and Miletus) and the neighboring islands (Lesbos, Samos, Chios) were already flourishing, exploiting inland resources and trading in the eastern Mediterranean. They forged a common Ionian heritage which was rooted in legends that they had been founded by migrants from Athens, the Ionian mother city. However, between 750 and 550 there was a Greek expansion overseas on a much larger scale. Some hundreds of settlements were founded throughout the Aegean and then the Mediterranean, from the eastern coast of Spain to the shores of the Black Sea in the northeast and to the north coast of Africa.

The Greek migrations of these centuries were not a single mass movement with a well-defined cause but rather a series of distinct initiatives whose roots lay within the internal conflicts and and economic difficulties of individual cities as much as with the attraction of trading and farming opportunities overseas. Moreover, there were different phases of expansion each with a different pattern of underlying causes. The movement begins in earnest in the eighth century and the initiative was taken by the Euboeans, in particular the traders of two Euboean cities, Chalcis and Eretria. The Euboeans may have been stimulated to overseas activity by Phoenicians visiting their island in search of copper and iron but they were particularly well placed for trading themselves. The channel which runs between the island and the mainland is well sheltered and once open sea is reached in the south it is only seven and a half miles (twelve kilometers) to the island of Andros. From there it is possible to cross from island to island through the Cyclades to the coast of Asia. By the early eighth century networks of Euboean trade had already been established in the east, and reached to Cyprus, where Greek was still spoken as a result of the Mycenaean migrations of the eleventh century, and the Middle East through a mixed trading community at Al-Mina on the Orontes River where Euboeans seem to have traded alongside Phoenicians and Cypriots from 825 B.C. It is probable too that Euboeans had penetrated the northern Aegean and some of their earliest overseas settlements,

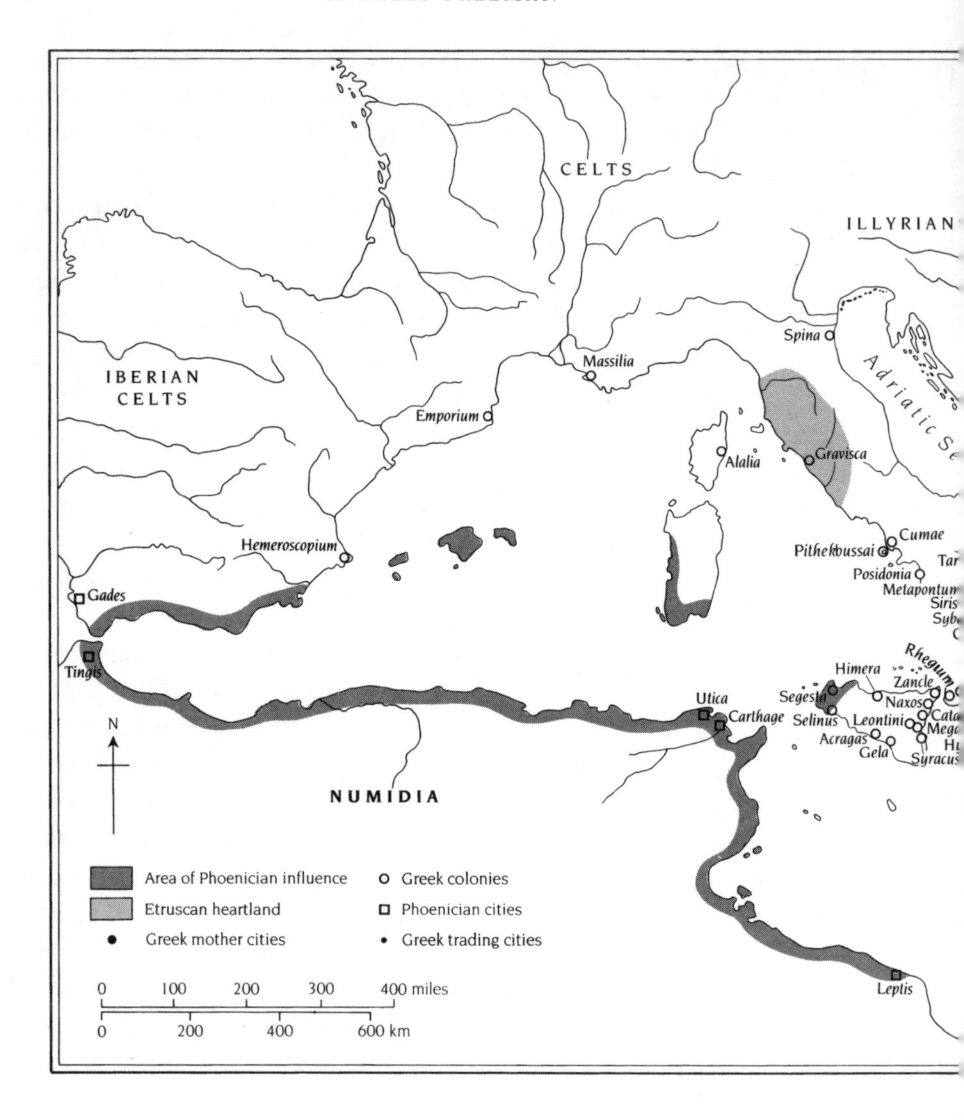

(*apoikiai* as the Greeks called them, as distinct from centers devoted to trading, *emporia*) may have been there.

By the early eighth century the Euboeans had learned that the richest pickings of all in the lucrative metals markets were to be found in the western Mediterranean. Sardinia, Spain, and central Italy all had large reserves of ores. Voyaging to find these resources was, however, a much more hazardous affair than island-hopping in the Aegean, and it is assumed that the Greeks only followed across the open sea between Greece and Italy where the Phoenicians had led. While the Phoenicians consolidated their position in Sardinia and farther west (what was to

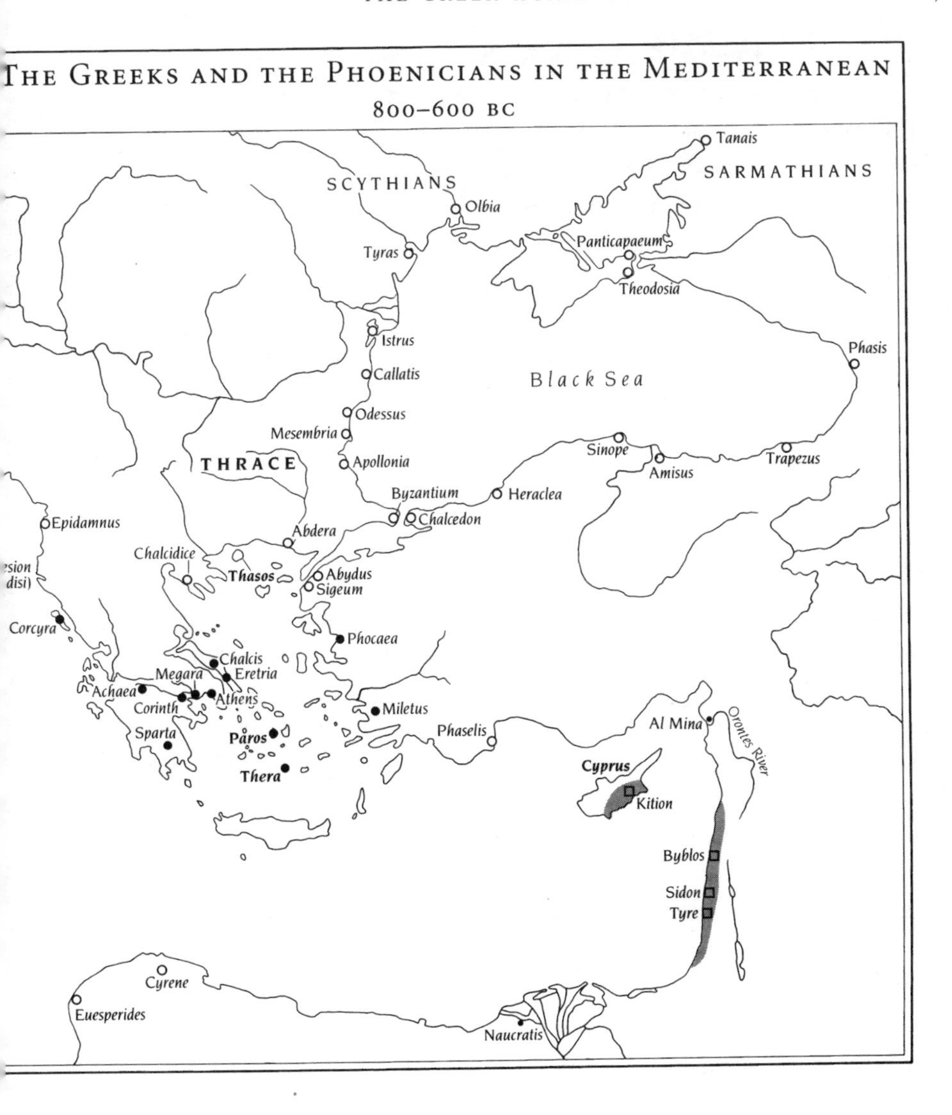

become the greatest overseas Phoenician city of all, Carthage, was founded, according to tradition, in 814), the Euboeans seem to have been given a fairly free hand to settle perhaps as early as 775 B.C. on the island of Ischia and there they built up, at Pithecusae, a thriving commercial and metalworking center, an *emporion,* which was able to draw its raw materials from central Italy.

The Euboeans of Pithecusae traded directly with the Etruscans whose heartland was centered on the area between the rivers Arno and Tiber. The Etruscans had already begun to exploit the Colline Metallifere, metal-bearing hills, which had reserves of iron, copper and silver, for themselves but now their leaders began to appreciate the opportunities offered by trade. There were good profits for both sides. While an Etruscan aristocracy began to enjoy luxuries from Greece and the East, the flourishing settlement at Pithecusae may eventually have been home to as many as ten thousand Greeks, with a smattering of eastern traders and craftsmen among them. (For Greek contact with Italy see the Afterword to this chapter and Chapter Nineteen.)

Soon there were other Greek settlements on the route west. There was an Eretrian settlement on the island of Corfu, the last land before the crossing to Italy, by the 730s, and Chalcis, with help from settlers from the Cycladic island of Naxos, was credited with founding a city (itself called Naxos) on the headland on Sicily which was the first landfall on the island for those rounding the toe of Italy from the east. Ischia had little in the way of fertile land—it grew little more than vines—but mainland sites offered much more. Naxos, for instance, had a fertile valley behind the headland. Once this was recognized, the lure of good agricultural land became a powerful force. In about 730 the community at Pithecusae split and a new settlement was made on the Italian mainland at Cumae. The site was very much more fertile than Ischia and was soon self-supporting. It founded in its turn other settlements, including Neapolis, "the new city," the modern Naples. Other Greek cities were now joining the move west. Corinth, fast becoming a major trading city in its own right, pushed the Eretrians off Corfu (making the island in effect its colony) and Corinthians grabbed one of the finest Sicilian sites of all, Syracuse, with its double harbor and excellent fresh water supply. The native Sicels were driven inland (a layer of destruction found by archaeologists may mark this event) and later ended up as labor for the expanding settlement. The Achaeans from the northeast of the Peloponnese were other major players in this intrusion. They founded Sybaris, Croton, and Metapontum on the instep of Italy, and Posidonia (later the Roman city of Paestum) across the "foot" on the west coast. The Spartan settlement at Tarentum, a fine harbor high on the instep of Italy (late eighth century) shows another motive for settlement. Its founders were the illegitimate children of Spartan women and helots the slave class of the Spartan state. There was no place for them at Sparta; a new start was their only hope.

Excavations at one of these new settlements, Megara Hyblaia founded by the city of Megara in the late eighth century, have shown

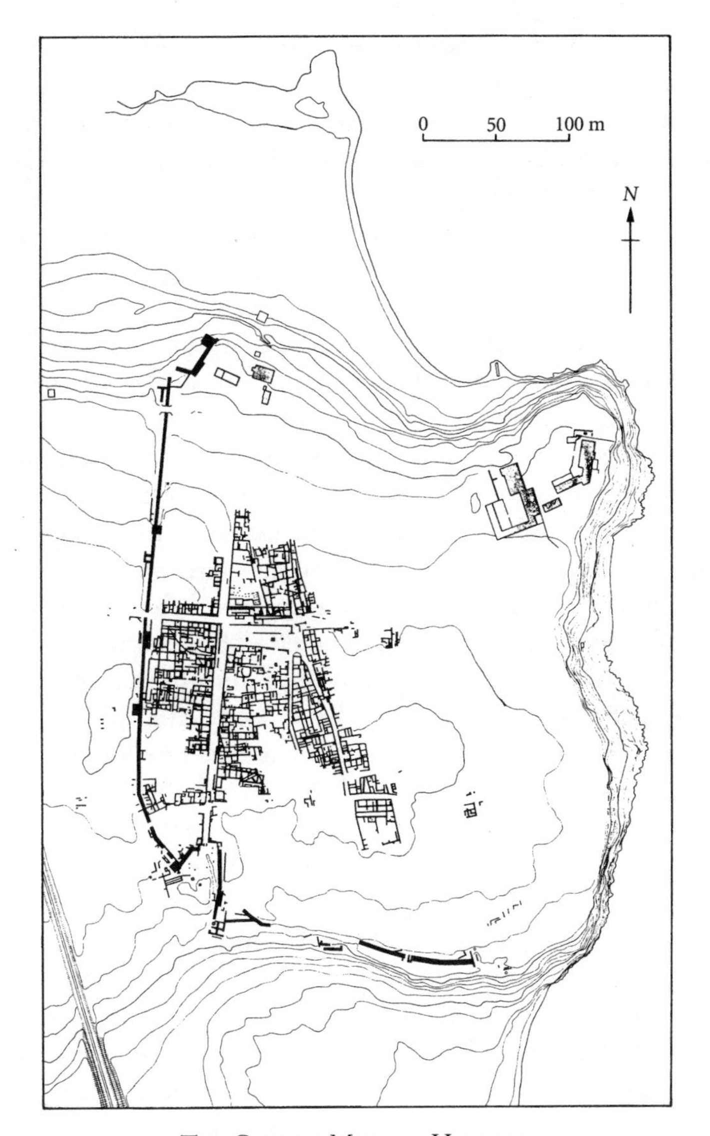

THE CITY OF MEGARA HYBLAIA

how sophisticated a foundation could be. The Megarans chose an uninhabited site on the east coast of Sicily and so were free to plan their new city from the beginning. A city area was distinguished from a cemetery area, streets set out in grids, and space left for public buildings. These were constructed as the city grew in the seventh century and the first known stoa, an open colonnade, has been found in the city. It has been argued in fact that these new cities, designed as they had to be from scratch, stimulated a conception of what a city ought to be and, in effect, provided models for the emerging cities back on the mainland.

Megara Hyblaia appears to have attracted settlers from a wide variety of sources. There is pottery from Athens, Rhodes, Corinth, and Argos but the city soon develops its own distinctive style of pottery making. Like Cumae, Megara Hyblaia, whose territory was hemmed in by neighbors, then began searching out new sites for its population. In about 650 it founded the city of Selinus on the western coast of Sicily. Selinus was another planned city, a central grid of streets was by the sixth century overlooked by temples placed dramatically on the surrounding higher land.

It was by means such as this that the coastline of Sicily and southern Italy became dotted with Greek settlements. The founding expeditions were probably small, perhaps two to three hundred young men in *pentekonters,* fifty-oared warships, who may have already been bound to each other through common kinship groups but whose sense of community would have been strengthened by the challenges of the voyage. The initial contact of determined and isolated men far from home with the natives must often have been brutal (as Archilochus' poems and the destruction layer at Syracuse suggest) though on some sites such as Metapontum there is evidence that Greeks and natives lived alongside each other until a Greek presence came to predominate. Intermarriage with the natives would have been inevitable if the settlement was to endure. The historian Herodotus mentions that the Greeks who settled his homeland Caria (southwest Turkey) murdered the men so as to be able to seize their women as wives, but in eighth-century Italy there is evidence that intermarriage between Greek and Italian took place peaceably, the women, as finds from graves suggest, continuing to wear their native dress. Selinus, on the west coast of Sicily, even made formal arrangements for wives to be supplied from the native town of Segesta with which it had strong commercial links.

Later, often somewhat mythological, accounts of the era gave great prominence to an expedition's leader, the *oikistes.* It was he who would seek guidance from the oracle of Apollo at Delphi before the expedition left as to which route to take and where to land. He would have a specific religious role in allocating the land for temples and sanctuaries on the new site and establishing cults. In his turn he would receive cult status as a hero after his death (in contrast to the normal practice of only giving cult status to long dead and usually mythical heroes).

(There is evidence of a cult building to Megara Hyblaia's founder in the center of the excavated city.) The scholar Carol Dougherty has explored a further link between the *oikistes* and Apollo. Many legends suggest that *oikistai* adopted a new role as founders after they had murdered rivals or been involved in political struggles in their home city. The normal punishment for such activities was exile but the city was also left polluted and it was important to call on the god Apollo for purification. Dougherty suggests that hand in hand with the purification of the guilty one at Delphi was his charging with the foundation of an overseas colony. In his new role as *oikistes* the murderer or dissident was able to transform himself into a potential hero but in a distant setting, and as result the original disorder in the home city could be both purged and its recurrence avoided. "Founding a colony creates a new civic identity out of the troubles and trauma of the mother city," as Dougherty puts it. It is a reminder that internal tensions on the mainland were a major factor in overseas settlement. These tensions will be explored further in the next chapter.

Dougherty and most historians use the word *colony* for these new settlements. In some cases the word is clearly justified. Corinth, for instance, seems to have maintained direct control of her settlements, sending out her own magistrates to them, insisting on a common pattern of coinage (when coinage was invented in the sixth century) and exerting some direction over their affairs. (It led to persistent tensions with Corcyra.) However, while most settlements in the west brought their home city's cults with them and honored the city's gods, their very distance from home and the urgent need to adapt to their new environment seems to have led to almost immediate political independence and a new distinct citizenship. This would certainly have been expected of cities founded by dissidents. The word *colonization* can be more aptly used to describe the process by which these cities extended inland, subduing the native population and building up large territories. Syracuse acquired some 1,500 square miles, and her inland settlements appear to have been garrisoned. Cities such as this reveled in their opulence, building vast temples, often set out in rows (as at Acragas in Sicily), as a demonstration of their wealth and Greek identity. Like many white settlers of the British Empire they appear to have clung to their home culture more tenaciously than those who had been left at home and they were always avid for the latest news from Greece.

These early settlements in the west took place at a time of increasing tension within the Greek world which eventually broke out in open warfare about 700 B.C. It centered on rivalry between Chalcis and Eretria ostensibly over the fertile Lelantine Plain between the the cities on Euboea (and thus is known as the Lelantine War), but with Corinth siding with Chalcis and Megara with Eretria the conflict may also reflect growing rivalry over trade. The war is often seen as the last of the vanishing age of heroic Greece. It seems to have been fought between aristocratic heroes in hand-to-hand combat. Archilochus talked later of such combat's being the style of the "spear-famed lords of Euboea" and burials of warriors with swords and spears from this date have been found in Eretria. The war ended in some exhaustion and both cities are less vital in the centuries that followed, though Eretria, with Megaran support, continued to found settlements in the Chalcidice peninsula (the name itself a reminder of earlier settlements there by Chalcis) in the northern Aegean.

The beneficiary of the war was Corinth and the seventh century is Corinth's century. The city was superbly placed for Mediterranean-wide trade. The crossing to the west along the southern coast of the Peloponnese was a risky one and so there was every incentive to use the Gulf of Corinth instead. This meant that traffic had to cross land at the Isthmus but a special roadway, the *diolkos,* was constructed along which boats or their unloaded cargoes could be dragged. Control of the Isthmus, which may have come after Corinth defeated Megara in the Lelantine War, also gave Corinth access to north-south land routes. The city itself had a good reserve of fertile land and access to fresh water. It was also well known for favoring craftsmen, in contrast to the disdain in which they were held by the ruling classes of most cities. Shipbuilding was a major activity. Herodotus was to credit the Corinthians with the invention of the trireme, the highly effective warship of fifth-century Greece, in about 600 B.C. and Corinthian shippers probably grew rich as carriers of goods from other cities. The city was also open to other Greeks and the pottery from Ionian Greece, Athens, and Sparta has been found there. This was, in short, a thriving commercial community, a haven of free enterprise.

In its early days of commercial supremacy the city was ruled by an aristocratic clan, the Bacchiadae. They were exclusive, marrying only among themselves, and their position in a vibrant and expanding city soon became isolated and precarious. There were stories of their using violence to keep control. About 657 B.C. they were overthrown by one Cypselus, apparently a popular leader, whose mother, according to legend, was a Bacchiad by birth who had married outside the family when rejected by them for her lameness. It may have been Cypselus' grievance over this which gave him the incentive to seize power. This was among the first of the so-called tyrannies which were to prove a common form of government in seventh and sixth-century Greece (see Chapter Five). Cypselus consolidated his position. He spread the fame of Corinth abroad by building a temple at Delphi and donating a gold statue to the temple of Zeus at Olympia. In his search for new sources of timber, for shipping, and flowers, for perfumes, he founded Corinthian colonies along the coast of northwest Greece, and so paved the way for further Greek expansion into the Adriatic just at a time when most of the best southern Italian sites had been filled. Later, about 600 B.C., another important overseas colony, Potidaea, on the Chalcidice peninsula was founded to open the way to further raw materials. Cypselus' tyranny was to be passed on to his son, Periander, and then, in 587, to his great-nephew, Psammatichus. Although by this time the tyranny was deeply unpopular, Corinth had enjoyed many decades of stability.

Wealthy trading cities are often associated with cultural innovation and Corinth was no exception. The inspiration came from the East. Many Greeks had visited the Near East—Corinthian pottery is found in quantities at Al-Mina after 700—while the goods of the East, particularly its metalwork, wooden statues, and textiles were already well known through the Phoenician contacts. As a result of a turbulent expansion of the Assyrian empire in the late eighth and early seventh centuries (which brought the Assyrians right up to the Levantine coastline and as far south as the great Egyptian religious center of Thebes on the Nile) many craftsmen fled to the West, bringing their skills with them. A host of images drawn from Egyptian, Syrian, and Assyrian art engraved on metalwork or woven into textiles had thus become familiar to Greeks. In the seventh century many were adopted by them in what has been called "the Orientalizing revolution."

Orientalizing is first seen in Corinth in the city's pottery. The dominant artistic style of the eighth century developed in Athens had been geometric, but once a pot has been filled up with meanders and rectangles, the style had nowhere else to go. Geometric pottery proved, in short, to be an artistic dead end. Inspiration for something new was luckily at hand. The Corinthians had built up a flourishing trade in perfume. It was probably obtained from the East and exported to the West, particularly to Cumae and Syracuse. It was "packaged" in small flasks known as *aryballoi,* and in about 720 some painter in Corinth had the inspired idea of covering the pots in images from the East. They are beautifully done. Figures of animals, dogs, lions, panthers, sphinxes form the main subjects with floral designs set in friezes above and below the animals. The figures are painted in black but then incised to give more detail of ornament or anatomy in a technique probably copied from Eastern metalworking. The whole process seems to have been a liberation, ushering in an exuberance in the parade of animals, flowers, and rosettes that surround the typical pot. Very soon cups and jugs in the same motifs are appearing. The new style achieved instant and sustained commercial success. Corinthian pottery dominates the trade of the Greek world for the next 150 years.

Yet the Corinthian painters were more than just inspired copy artists. Perhaps the finest surviving example of their mature work, the "Chigi vase" of about 650, shows not only their skills but their intelligent control of foreign images for their own ends. The Chigi vase, so-called from one of its early owners, was found in Italy in 1882, shattered, in a tomb near the major Etruscan town of Veii. Parts of it have never been recovered. Though termed a "vase" it is, in fact, the earliest example of a type of jug known as an *olpe.* An important feature of the jug is the assured use of color, black, buff, and shades of red and brown. The lowest and narrowest of the three friezes around the jug shows boys hunting hares and a fox among thickets, a scene that appears to have been derived from Egyptian or Phoenician models. On the major central frieze are animals: An Assyrian-style lion is being hunted, a double-headed sphinx gazes on while there is also a procession of a chariot and horses. A small scene shows the first known depiction of the judgment of Paris (Paris, the son of Priam, king of Troy, was asked to judge who was the most beautiful among the goddesses, Hera, Athena, and Aphrodite) and the figures are named, another first. However, it is the upper frieze which has excited most attention. Here there is a detailed portrait of the new world of warfare. A boy, standing alone and apart, pipes a hoplite phalanx into battle. Its opponents are just about to make contact with their spears. The composition is masterly, with the figures overlapping yet distinct and they are imbued with a real sense of movement. This is painting of the highest quality with a mature use of perspective far beyond anything in geometric patterning. Not least, the human figure has moved to the forefront of the activity.

At the same time that such skill was being lavished on a small object (the Chigi vase is only twenty-six centimeters high) Corinthians were also involved in developing the most monumental of art works, temples. The original Greek temples had been in wood and mudbrick, though often set on a rough-worked stone base. By 700 local limestone, the softer varieties of which are only slightly more difficult to work than wood, begins to be used in temple building. Then about 675 in the area around Corinth heavy terra-cotta tiles for roofing appear. The tiles had no fastenings, they rested on their own weight, and this meant that the slope of the roof had to be shallow (about fourteen degrees) so that they could be supported without slipping off. It also meant that there were new incentives for strengthening walls and columns, in effect, using stone rather than wood to carry the extra weight.

The problem facing the Greek craftsmen was that they had little experience in working harder stones, such as marble, which were freely available in Greece. They needed a model. Once again the East was to provide it, although this time the source was Egypt.

For centuries Egypt itself had been largely closed off to the outside world and the styles of Egyptian art had only been known at second or third hand—Egyptian motifs and art forms, including that of the sphinx, had entered the Near East when Egypt had controlled the southern part of the area during the New Kingdom (1532–1070 B.C.) and then passed northward into Assyria and westward. In the mid-seventh century, however, a dynamic Pharaoh, Psamtek (known to the Greeks as Psammetichus) revived the country's fortunes. He started to use Greek mercenaries to consolidate his position against the Assyrians and also allowed a Greek trading post to be set up (around 620 B.C.) at Naucratis in the Delta not far from his own capital. The traders were mainly from Ionian cities along the coast of Asia Minor, but the fact that Cypselus' great nephew was named Psammetichus suggests Corinthians must have been involved as well. The Greeks brought oil, wine, and silver, probably in exchange for grain from the wealth of the Nile valley.

The impact of Egypt on these visitors must have been astounding. The pyramids were only 75 miles (120 kilometers) from Naucratis and there was a wealth of other massive stone monuments still intact. Furthermore, Psammetichus followed Egyptian tradition by establishing his authority through mounting his own massive building program. For the first time Greeks could see not only that stone could be used to create large buildings but were able to watch the process of quarrying, transporting, and shaping hard stone for themselves.

The evidence for what impact this had within Corinth itself is fragmentary because the Romans sacked the city with typical thoroughness in 146 B.C. However, in cities under Corinthian influence or control a new style of temple architecture appears, the so-called Doric order. Jeffrey Hurwit sees it in propaganda terms, "a conscious decision to build monumentally and claim Greek architectural superiority for Corinth." The fully developed Doric order consists of fluted columns, their height about six times their diameter. Each column is surmounted by a square block of stone, the *abacus,* and along the top of the row of columns runs the architrave and above this the frieze. The frieze is decorated with the so-called triglyphs, each with three raised grooves, which are spaced regularly. They are a transfer into stone of the original wooden beam ends. In between the triglyphs the rectangular spaces, known as *metopes*, were free to be filled with decoration. One of the earliest examples comes from a temple to Apollo from between 640 to 630 B.C. at Thermon in northwest Greece, an area under Corinthian influence. Here painters from Corinth (judging by the style of what survives) placed painted terra-cotta slabs in the metopes. This temple was in wood (so the triglyphs were actual beam ends) but once stone became regularly used the metopes were covered with carved reliefs. Another early Doric temple, still largely in wood, is that to Hera, the wife of Zeus, at Olympia from about 600 B.C. The first fully Doric temple in stone, to Artemis, comes from Corinth's colony Corfu, also built about 600 or a little later. The Doric order was taken up across the Greek mainland by the cities of Sicily and Italy and by some of the islands of the Cyclades, an indication of just how pervasive was the influence of Corinth. The order was to last almost without further development over the centuries and was revived by the classical architects of later European history.

The pattern of the Greek temple, columns around a central walled building, the *cella,* was a Greek invention. There is a possibility, however, that the Doric order itself was partially inspired by Egyptian examples. The fluted column appears in Egypt as early as 2600 B.C. (the flutes are believed to be the translation into stone of "columns" made up of papyrus stalks) while temple facades such as the shrine to Anubis at the temple to Queen Hatshepsut at Deir el-Bahri near Luxor (c. 1480 B.C.) have columns which are the same proportions as Doric ones, surmounted by similar *abaci*. Other Egyptian influences are seen in eastern Greece, especially in the Ionian cities of Asia Minor that traded heavily through Naucratis. By 600 B.C. the second major Greek architectural order, the Ionic, is being developed here. In the Ionic order each of the columns rests on a plinth and the column is topped by a double volute, a design which is distinctly oriental. The architrave and frieze are left clear (though horizontal lines along the architrave suggest that it was originally made of overlapping boards) but a row

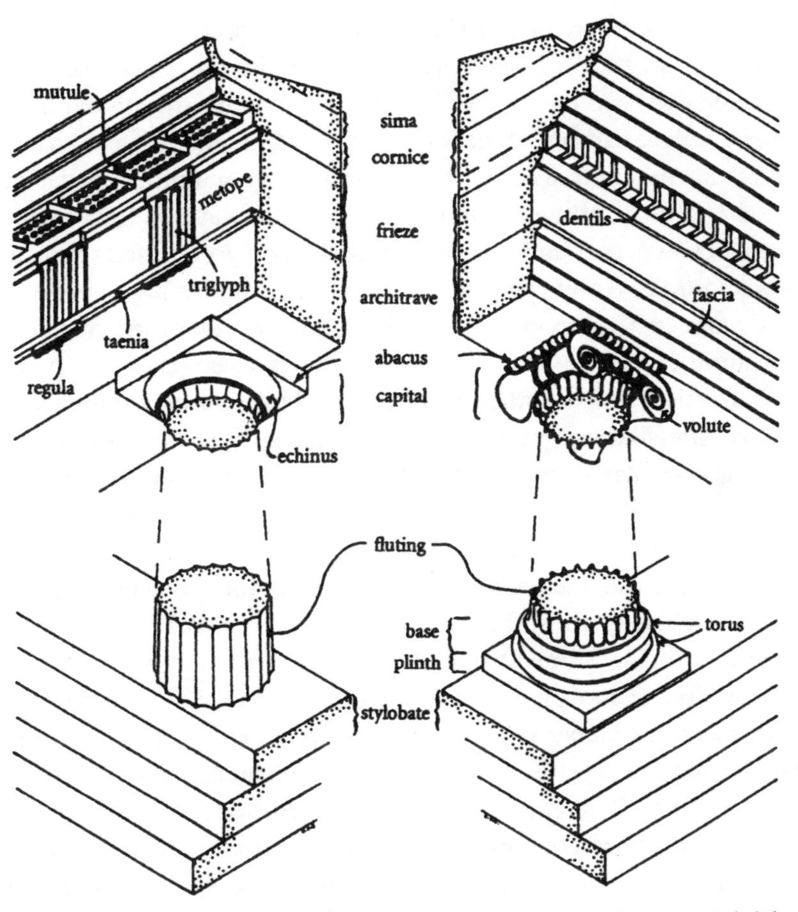

THE DORIC AND IONIC ORDERS. This figure illustrates the essential differences between the two original classical orders.

of dentils, small regularly placed rectangular blocks, runs along the top under the eaves of the roof. The link with Egypt is suggested by double rows of columns, similar to those in large Egyptian temples, found at some of the major Ionian temples such as that to the goddess Artemis at Ephesus. The Ionic order is spread through the cities along the coast of what is now Turkey and was used in some Ionian dedications at Delphi. Later, in the fifth century B.C., Athens, which claimed to be the mother city of the Ionians, used the Ionic order for selected buildings on the Acropolis (the Erectheum is one) and, alongside the Doric order, in the Propylaea, the great gateway to the Acropolis.

Limestone continued to be used as the main building stone for these temples, but from about 650 B.C., just about the time of the first contacts with Egypt, the Greeks were beginning to use marble for figure sculpture. Marble is plentiful in Greece and more tensile than limestone (it is, in fact, a form of recrystallized limestone) but is hard to work and heavy to handle and thus inevitably a prestige material. The pioneers in the carving of marble were the islanders of Naxos where a white marble abounds. Their earliest known sculpture is the celebrated Nikandre *kore* (a *kore* is a young girl) found on the nearby island of Delos, legendary birthplace of the god Apollo, but dedicated by Nikandre to Apollo's sister Artemis. Votive dedications were one of the commonest motives for the creation of works of art and in her dedication Nikandre describes herself through her relationships with men, mentioning her father, brother, and husband by name. Though life-size, the statue is very thin, only nineteen centimeters thick, and this suggests that statues of this type had earlier been worked from planks of wood (none of which have survived). Although the face is very worn, it can be seen to have been triangular in shape, with a pointed chin, and with a wigged hair style divided into blocks, which has parallels with those known in the East. (A much better example survives in a limestone statue of a woman probably made in Crete about 630, the so-called Auxerre goddess.) The style, the triangular head, the front-facing pose with feet tightly held together, is termed Daedalic, after a legendary Greek craftsman, Daedalus (whose name is found as far back as the Linear B tablets). Although the influences on the Nikandre *kore* are both Eastern and Egyptian, the Greeks seemed determined to secure the invention of life-size sculpture as their own. Sarah Morris in her important study *Daedalus and the Origins of Greek Art* suggests that it was the Athenians in the fifth century who successfully expunged memories of the influence of the East by linking a mythical *Greek* craftsman, Daedalus, to this early sculpture.

One of the fascinating things about the Nikandre *kore* is that the proportions of her body exactly match those used by Egyptian sculptors. (These proportions were marked as units by the sculptors on blocks of stone before they began work.) Here is an indisputable instance of direct Egyptian influence on Greek art. Egyptian sculpture was also a major influence on the male equivalent of the *kore,* the *kouros,* a standing nude male, which seems also to have been pioneered in Naxos about 650 B.C. Although the Egyptian figures were clothed there is a marked similarity in the stance; both figures stand with their arms to their sides and the left feet forward. (The story of the *kouroi,* used as grave markers by the Greek aristocracy, will be told in the next chapter.) Units of proportion were not the only Egyptian influence absorbed by the Naxians. Naxians were probably responsible for the avenue of marble lions (c. 600–575 B.C.) on Delos which echoes the great processional routes of the Egyptian temples, and when Naxos made a dedication to the sanctuary to Delphi in about 560 B.C. it was on a large marble sphinx, graciously placed on an Ionic column (though the fine wings of the beast suggest it came to Naxos via the Middle East, rather than directly from Egypt).

The examples of painting and sculpture given above show how the Greeks were adopting Eastern influences for their own needs but Orientalizing was a much more complex and pervasive business than the copying of images to make perfume pots more sellable or providing an inspiration for sculpture. It could be said to include the transmission of the alphabet and also a number of loan words. *Cinnamon, cannabis,* and *crocus* are all Eastern words that passed into Greek (and then into English) and they might be contained in a *sakkos* (the English "sack"). The custom of reclining rather than sitting upright at a meal, which was adopted for the aristocratic *symposia* in the eighth century, originates in Palestine. Many of the Greek gods and goddesses drew some of their attributes and even their origins from Eastern culture. Aphrodite, the goddess of love, seems to originate with the Semitic goddess of love, Ishtar-Astarte. Her cult, with the goddess represented as naked in ornaments and pendants, entered Greece via Cyprus. Adonis (from the Semitic word *Adon*, lord), her youthful lover, comes from the East with her. Apollo, perhaps the most Greek of the gods, acquires his bow and arrow and his power to bring plagues (as in

Book One of the *Iliad*) from another Semitic deity, Resep, a plague god who throws firebrands. Artemis, his sister, the goddess of hunting, is known as Mistress of the Animals in the *Iliad*. There are representations in Eastern art of a goddess standing between animals and her origins may lie here. The cult practices followed in her great temple at Ephesus appear to have been adopted wholesale from farther east (significantly the temple itself faces west in an Eastern tradition rather than east as is normal in the Greek world). Mythological stories of struggles between families of gods (as used by Hesiod) come too from the East and the Greek underworld, Hades, is similar to the realm of mud and darkness found in the celebrated Mesopotamian epic, *Gilgamesh*.

What is clear is there was no inhibition among the Greeks to adopting Eastern images and influences when it suited them, none of the cultural resistance which was to be found in Rome when Greek culture became available to the expanding city in the second and first centuries B.C. (See Chapter Nineteen.) Greek culture, in short, enjoyed in the eighth and seventh centuries a process of enrichment and maturation at a time when it was still malleable and in need of guidance and inspiration. Yet there were also signs of a coming of order, of the establishment of control, particularly in architecture. "An ability to control sources, to translate borrowings into a uniquely Hellenic idiom is," writes Andrew Stewart in his major study *Greek Sculpture*, "one of the salient features of early Greek art which sturdily maintains its independence even as it accepts refreshment from without."

One of the ways in which the Greeks imposed their own style on their art was through the use of mythology as subject matter. As children learn even today, Greek mythology is a treasure-house of stories, most of them dealing with the exploits of gods and heroes. For the Greeks myths were much more than simply stories; they were living parts of their own culture handed on from generation to generation, passed on by word of mouth, whether from parent to child, at the *symposia*, the aristocratic drinking parties, or in formal recitations at the great Panhellenic festivals. The stories were also developed by each generation to meet its own needs as the Homeric epics seem to have been. (For the psychological power of myth in the Greek consciousness see Chapter Seven below.) It is perhaps not surprising therefore that when painters were casting around for subjects with which to decorate their vases they should choose mythological themes. An early theme, known from several seventh-century examples, is the story of the killing of the Cyclops giant Polyphemus by Odysseus. This is a direct translation into art of a story from the *Odyssey* and in the most common version the moment shown is when Odysseus drives a heated stake into Polyphemus' eye. In so far as a point is being made it is that the cunning Greek can triumph over a monstrous brute (it is worth remembering Homer's depiction of the Cyclops as a contrast to the "civilized" Greeks). Another common theme is the killing of the Gorgon Medusa by the hero Perseus. Medusa, whose frightening stare turned onlookers to stone, was another figure borrowed from the East (probably Mesopotamia). In the seventh century her head was used as a symbol of ill omen and her overthrow is another triumph for a quintessentially Greek hero (Perseus kills her by cutting off her head after he has become invisible with the help of the gods). The story itself was linked with Corinth—the city used both Medusa and her child the flying horse Pegasus on its early coinage—and this probably explains its popularity in this century.

The first attempts at portraying these myths are hesitant in their execution, as if the painter is genuinely unsure how to portray a story he has only heard expressed in verse. The most pressing problem was how to use a restricted space to tell a full-length story. If more than one moment was to be captured scenes had either to be shown alongside each other or on different friezes, with the onlooker having to fill in the gaps. There were ingenious attempts to get round this, notably in a famous *pithos,* storage jar, from Mykonos, of about 650 B.C., where the fall of Troy is spelled out in a number of boxes below a large representation of the Trojan horse (complete with Greek warriors who are made to peer through "windows" in its body so that the onlooker can see they are there). It is a brilliant but unique experiment. It is not until eighty years later that the challenge of creating narrative is taken up by painters from Athens as that city embarked on its successful bid to become the leading Greek producer of pottery. In the François (the name of the finder) vase of about 570 B.C., which like the Chigi vase was found in Etruria, an astonishing array of myths surrounding the life of Achilles are produced in five layered friezes. Both the potter's name, Ergotimos, and that of the painter, Kleitias, are signed on what is, in fact, a large *krater* (used for mixing wine with water). The central theme is the marriage of Achilles' parents, Peleus and the nymph Thetis, and it has been guessed that the *krater* may have been a marriage gift. Achilles himself appears, first as a competitor in the games he threw for his dead companion Patroclus and then being carried dead from the battlefield. Altogether some two hundred human figures are shown but this is perhaps not so much a consecutive narrative as an anthology of associations. The vase is also remarkable for its mass of inscriptions.

Most vases were produced for private purposes, primarily for use in the *symposia,* the drinking parties of the wealthier classes, but temples could be used as public show places for mythology. The shallow roof, which was the result of the use of heavy roof tiles, left a triangular space at the front of a temple, the pediment. It was a difficult shape to fill and it also demanded relief sculpture rather than, as in a normal stone figure, sculpture in the round. Many temple builders in Sicily and southern Italy did not even attempt to fill it but the challenge of providing an imposing display of myth for those approaching the temple was taken up by the sculptors of the Greek mainland. In the earliest surviving example, the western pediment at the temple to Artemis on Corfu, of about 600 B.C., the center is filled by none other than Medusa, front on, with her head intact. Medusa, as has been suggested, was associated with Corinth and Corcyra was Corinth's often rebellious colony. It has been argued that the figure was placed so prominently to remind the Corcyrans of Corinth's supremacy. There is more of interest to this sculptured pediment. Medusa is shown with head on but also with her two offspring, the winged horse Pegasus, and her son Chrysoar. In the myth these two were only born at the moment she was decapitated by Perseus (who is not on the pediment). In other words, a story incompatible with the original myth has to be created in order to preserve Medusa in her full power alongside her children. Again the problems of narrative have defeated the artist. In these early pots and sculptures, in short, there is a real sense of artistic struggle, a feeling that the artist knows what he wants to do but is restricted by inexperience and the shapes of his settings, whether vase or pediment, in achieving it. The harsh lesson that a story-telling people had to learn was that their favorite stories could not be translated easily into art.

The metopes of a temple were to offer the sculptor a better chance. In fragments from the temple to Artemis in Corcyra, Achilles may be shown on one metope and an opponent on the neighboring one. The sculptor appears to have grasped that a story could be spelled out along an architrave. By 550 B.C. in a temple to Hera at Foce del Sele, near Paestum in southern Italy, all the metopes of a facade are devoted to one myth, Heracles destroying some goblinlike figures. Ionic friezes were even easier to use for a continuous narrative as there were no triglyphs to break up the story. An example from 530, a treasury building dedicated by the islanders of Siphnos to the shrine at Delphi and built in the Ionic style in the island's own marble, shows what could be achieved. The Siphnians employed two sculptors and one of these, "Master B," produced a continuous frieze of gods battling with giants along the north side of the building, "an intricate weaving of duel upon duel" in the words of Jeffrey Hurwit. This frieze is also remarkable for the quality of the reliefs. "Master B" has used layers of planes so that there is depth and perspective to the action. The Greeks were learning fast. The greatest and most detailed of these sculptured stories was to be the celebrated frieze on the Parthenon in Athens of the 430s.

Expeditions from cities of the Greek mainland continued through the seventh century. A well-documented case (from about 630) is that of the islanders of Thera whose story is told in Herodotus' *History* but which has independent corroboration from a fourth-century inscription that includes the original foundation oath. Thera had known seven years of drought (another source suggests this was accompanied by political unrest) and it was agreed that part of the population had to be shipped off elsewhere. The oracle at Delphi designated a specific site, Libya, which the Therans had never heard of, and even appointed an *oikistes*, from the visiting Therans, one Battus. (It is interesting that Battus is portrayed as an aristocrat but an outsider, illegitimate and only half-Theran, a person therefore who might be better out of the way at a time of political tension.) The expedition was planned in an ordered way. Each family had to provide one young man chosen by lot (if land was split between sons as was the normal Greek practice of inheritance then it was an excellent way of settling the matter fairly) but volunteers could also join. The first expedition set off but returned without having made a settlement. The prospective settlers were forcibly sent off again, landing this time on an island off the Libyan coast from where they eventually made their way inland to the site of Cyrene. The initial contacts with the natives appear to have been friendly and there is evidence of intermarriage with them. Battus founded a monarchy which survived over several generations and it has been suggested he may even have copied Libyan models of leadership. Later Delphi "authorized" other Greek settlements on the coast and there were major conflicts between the original settlers and the newcomers, as well as with the native population itself. Nevertheless, Cyrene survived and prospered, trading in a local plant, silphium, which was used in the ancient world as a cure-all, as well as in ox hides, wool, and grain. Its reputation as a major city lasted into Roman times when it became one of the provincial capitals of the Empire.

The communication of information across the Mediterranean world was inevitably inefficient but the Panhellenic shrines must have acted as clearing houses for it. It is not surprising that the oracle at Delphi should become the hub of the movement to the west. Information could be gathered and given divine sanction by Apollo through the oracle. How much accurate information the priests actually knew is a matter for speculation. The surviving pieces of advice seem hopelessly vague. "Here is Taphiasos, the unploughed, on your path, and there is Chalcis: then the sacred lands of the Kouretes and the Echinades. Great is the ocean on the left. But even so I would not expect you to miss the Lakinian cape, nor sacred Krimissa, nor the river Aisaros," runs one oracle. In many cases, a site would have been found and then the oracle adapted to fit it. When a settlement failed it was said that the correct consultation of the oracle had not been carried out and cities that had never received an oracle tended to forge one. Delphi itself became immensely rich in these centuries and cities could advertise their prosperity and military successes to others through the presentation of temples, sculptures, or the spoils of war. The Siphnian Treasury, mentioned above, was one of these dedications.

There are few better examples of the pressures behind expansion overseas than the story of the prosperous Ionian city of Miletus. Gradually deserted by the sea as the gulf which the city overlooked silted up, its surviving ruins can only provide a haunting reminder of its ancient opulence. Its wealth depended partly on trading and partly on the natural fertility of its surrounding territory. If Gocha Tsetskhladze's interpretation of events is correct, by the seventh century Miletus' territory was coming under severe pressure as a result of the expansion of the kingdom of Lydia under the dynamic Mermnad dynasty. Some new outlets for her population needed to be secured and the Black Sea seemed the only possibility. The Greeks had long been wary of this "inhospitable" sea. The entrance through the Hellespont (past the ancient city of Troy) is a tricky one with strong winds and currents, and the sea itself is deep, cold, and susceptible to storms. The native peoples, the Scythians, were portrayed, perhaps with some exaggeration, as wild, unable even to settle into cities. The Megarans, however, had taken two key sites at the entrance to the Bosporus which marked the final passage into the sea, Chalcedon and Byzantium (later the site of the great city of Constantinople) in the early seventh century, and shortly after this, about 650 B.C., there is the first evidence of a Milesian presence along the coastline, though very little of actual settlement. Tstetskhladze suggests it was a humiliating treaty with the Lydians in about 600 B.C. that impelled the Milesians to make permanent settlements around the Black Sea coast, trading with the Scythians or exploiting the land. Later in the sixth century the conquest of Ionia by the Persians sent a fresh wave of Milesians northward and eventually there were Milesian settlements all around the sea.

The Milesian experience confirms that the best sites for settlement in the Mediterranean were occupied. In the west the Phoenicians had been consolidating what had now become an empire focused on the city of Carthage on the North African coast. Phoenician influence extended not only along the African coast but into southern Spain, western Sicily, and Sardinia and it became more exclusive and defensive. A Greek presence at Tartessus, the "far" side of the Straits of Gibraltar in southern Spain, disappears while an attempted settlement by a band of Greeks from Rhodes on western Sicily was fought off in 580. The only area free of settlement in the western Mediterranean was now southern France and when a new wave of settlers from the Ionian trading city of Phocaea arrived in about 600 B.C. they headed here, picking out a site, Massilia, the modern Marseilles, within easy reach of the mouth of the River Rhone. It was a shrewd choice for a people used to trade. (The Phocaeans' own homeland was barren and they had always relied on trade.) The river led northward into the Celtic heartlands and soon the Phocaeans were sending prestige goods north to consolidate relationships with the local chieftains. In 1953, in an aristocratic tomb at Vix near the important Celtic trading base at Mount Lassois, a massive bronze *krater* was found. It is the largest known, five feet (1.64 meters) high, complete with its lid and decorated with reliefs of warriors and chariots. It was probably made in Sparta and can only have been a gift in the tradition of aristocratic hospitality known from earlier times. The success of the Phocaeans in Massilia and other settlements was a direct affront to the Etruscans who had also traded along this coast. In 540 Etruscans and Phoenicians combined to drive the Phocaeans out of a settlement, Alalia, they had made on the eastern coast of Corsica. From now on the era of easy settlement abroad was at an end.

Afterword: Greeks and Etruscans

The relationship between the Greeks and the Etruscans is a complex one. Traditionally historians have explained it in terms of a superior culture, that of the Greeks, imposing itself on an inferior and unformed peoples who were only too receptive to what the Greeks had to offer. A mass of new archaeological evidence together with a more sophisticated (and less culturally biased) understanding of the relationship between the two cultures has led to a more nuanced explanation. While it may be true, in the words of Tim Cornell, that Hellenism was to be "the single most important factor of change in Roman (and Italian) history," the Italians were still able to preserve important elements of their native culture and even to use Greek influences to enrich and enhance it. The resulting mix, which was to pass into Rome (Chapter Nineteen) was of fundamental importance for the later cultural history of Europe.

There is no evidence from the eighth century of any Greek presence in the Etruscan heartland itself, but there seems to have been some intermarriage between Greek and Etruscans and the exchange of prestige goods. Some Etruscan goods, mostly in metalwork that has not survived, reached Greece. However, increasing contact with Greek and other eastern traders brought an influx of new wealth to Italy (both to Etruscans and to other peoples such as the Latins on the plains of Latium to the south of Etruria) and with it the consolidation of a rich aristocratic class. The evidence is found in their tombs, which are modeled on Greek warrior tombs of the period and are filled with luxury goods. The workmanship of gold and silver shows the influence of Greece and the Near East but there are also Greek drinking cups and mixing bowls imported directly from Greece. One of these, a *krater,* mixing bowl, found in a tomb at Cerveteri, is signed by one

Aristhonos in the Greek alphabet used by the Euboeans and it was through the Euboean Greeks that the concept of the alphabet was now passed on sometime in the eighth century to the Etruscans. The Etruscans adapted Greek letters to write their own language; 120 Etruscan inscriptions have been found from the seventh century. The peoples of Latium (of which the Romans were the most prominent) adopted their own alphabet from southern Etruria and this formed the basis of the modern western alphabet (as one can see from looking at any Latin inscription).

By the early seventh century the influence of Corinth was being felt in Italy, as elsewhere in the Mediterranean. A mass of Corinthian pottery was imported and with it a tradition that the Corinthians (in the shape of one Demaratus, an aristocratic exile from the tyranny of Cypselus) brought to Italy the art of making terra-cotta figures and plaques. Certainly terra-cotta objects now become a major feature of Etruscan art and their subject matter (in a fine figure of Apollo from the city of Veii, for example) is Greek in inspiration. As the Greek presence became more pervasive in southern Italy and the tastes of the Italians more sophisticated and demanding, Greek trading posts were established on the Etruscan coast line itself with their wares targeted at specific Etruscan cities. The best known are Gravisca (founded about 600 B.C.), which traded with the inland city of Tarquinia, and Pyrgi, which traded with Cerveteri. By this time fine Greek pottery is being imported in quantity, predominantly, after 550 B.C. from Athens. What is particularly interesting is that Athenian potters adapted their wares to Etruscan tastes. They copied the shapes of Etruscan *bucchero* (a fine black ware) in Athens and then exported it to Etruria. Naked figures were covered with loin clothes in order not to offend Etruscan sensitivities.

Pottery was primarily used for aristocratic drinking parties, as it was in Athens, but it was also placed in tombs. Funerary pottery was produced illustrating themes that appealed to the Etruscans. Scenes of games were especially popular—it is known that the Etruscans held games at funerals (as the Homeric Greeks did). Another favored myth was the suicide of Ajax. It is a far more common scene on pots found in Etruria than on those of Greece. On the paintings that survive on the walls of tombs, it can be seen how the Etruscans adapted Greek themes to their own ends. Wives were never able to dine with their husbands in Greek society; the women portrayed at banquets were always *hetairai,* courtesans. In Etruscan pictures of banquets the women, as inscriptions attest, are wives. Scenes of the underworld show Hades and Persephone and also the boatman Charon, who took the souls across the Styx. In Greek mythology he is harmless, with the Etruscans he is transformed into a demon figure with a hammer, reflecting a more forbidding view of the after life.

In short, Etruscan culture developed in collaboration with outside influences, of which the Greek was dominant. Public building showed the same trend. Etruscan religion centered heavily on divination, one method of which was to predict future events through the observation of the sky. The Etruscans adopted a Greek-style temple, a *cella,* with a columned facade, but they discarded the surrounding columns (the back was usually a plain wall) and raised the steps at the front so that the front of the temple could be used as a platform for watching the skies. This was the model that passed to the Romans, and hence into Western European architecture. As cities became a more prominent feature in Etruscan society (from 600 onward) the Etruscans borrowed the idea of grid plans from the Greek cities, though again adapting it for their own needs. The town of Marzabotta (its original name is unknown; this is the name of the modern village near the site) near Bologna was laid out on a grid-iron plan about 500 B.C. (at a time when the Etruscans driven from the sea by the Phoenicians were seeking new trading opportunities in northeast Italy). The idea of the plan is borrowed from the Greeks but the Etruscans leave no space for public gatherings. In the late sixth century in a final burst of Etruscan-Greek collaboration, the trading city of Spina was built at the mouth of the Po River at the head of the Adriatic. This was one of the last coast lines of the Mediterranean to be settled by Greeks, who had always been scared of the tricky coast line of the Adriatic Sea, but it offered access across the Alps into northern Europe (as the trading city of Venice was to discover some centuries later). Spina was as much Greek as Etruscan and has yielded more Athenian vases than any other city in Italy.

Seventh- and sixth-century Italy was, therefore, a cultural and social melting pot in which different traditions matured alongside each other, rather than the Greek dominating over others. How the emerging city of Rome was affected by all this will be discussed in Chapter Nineteen.

5

New Identities: The Consolidation of the City-State

The basic need of any Greek *polis* was to exploit its surrounding environment and defend itself from neighboring, often hostile communities. This meant finding a harmonious form of government that could ensure stability. It was in this context that the art of politics, as its name suggests, emerged. Politics were fundamentally a pragmatic activity. A political system actually had to work and the Greeks always gave a hallowed status to the lawgiver, the man who could draw up and enforce a set of laws (*nomoi*) which would ease strife between classes. Yet the very act of being involved in politics also forced men to think about abstract ideals, justice, goodness, the purposes of life, the ultimate nature of things and so hand in hand with political activity came the emergence of political thought. The philosophers Plato and Aristotle both focused on the ideal city-state and their approaches laid the foundations of political theory. Greek words supply modern political terms. Rule *(kratos)* by the people (the *demos*) brings democracy. It is contrasted with rule only by the best (aristocracy, *aristoi,* the best), or of the few (oligarchy). A city was run by magistrates, the *archons*, and this word survives not only in *oligarchy,* but in *monarchy,* rule by one person, and *anarchy,* lawlessness as a result of having no *archon* at all.

By the sixth century the *polis,* the Greek city-state, had already proved itself as a successful institution, flexible enough to be exportable throughout the Mediterranean so that a Greek city in Italy or on the coast of Asia Minor, with its imposing temples and open spaces for its citizens, would have been easily recognizable and distinct from the cultures around it. Not all parts of Greece developed city-states. In the northern Peloponnese and parts of central and northwestern Greece the population was grouped into *ethne,* states with a number of settlements, often no more than fortified villages, spread over its territory. Usually the population of an *ethnos* would meet in an assembly but there would be no civic centre as in a *polis.* (It is worth noting that important shrines such as Olympia and Delphi established themselves in areas where there were few *poleis.*) While those who lived in *ethne* were as Greek as those who lived in *poleis* it was the challenges, possibilities, difficulties of living in a *polis* which dominated the next 350 years of Greek life.

Crucial to the identity and functioning of a Greek *polis* was the concept of citizenship. The citizens of a *polis* took mutual responsibility for the administration of its city's affairs, its defense, and sustaining a correct relationship with its gods, and in return were able to share in its wealth and successes. The word *citizen* itself, *polites,* acquired the connotation of shared ownership of a common concern, and citizenship was often closely linked to ownership of land. Citizenship was not simply a legal status: it implied active involvement in the city's affairs. To Aristotle a human being could only reach his fullest potential as a citizen sharing the government of a *polis.* In this sense citizenship had become a psychological state as much as a legal one, the very essence of being a properly functioning (male) human being. The word *idiotes,* from which the English *idiot* is derived, was used by the Greeks of one who put private pleasures before public affairs and who was hence ignorant of what really mattered in life.

Citizenship transcended, though it did not supplant, membership of traditional kinship or tribal groupings and its definition could be said to mark the moment when a city assumed authority for its own territory over and above other rival allegiances. This marked its foundation as a civic force. For a new settlement, such as Cyrene, whose foundation decree survives in a later inscription, definition of citizenship went hand in hand with foundation. The citizens were the original settlers and their male descendants (while citizens from the "home" city, Thera, also had an automatic right to citizenship if they arrived to settle). Defining citizenship was, however, only one of the elements in setting up a functioning *polis*. Someone had to run the city and so administrative offices, the magistrates, emerge. Some of the earliest *polis* inscriptions (from the late seventh century) deal with the problems of who can be magistrates, how long their period of office should last, and to whom they should be responsible—usually a group of "overseers" but on occasions to the *demos,* "the people," as a whole. The authority of the magistrates had to be backed by a constitution which upheld city authority over all other groupings, the aristocratic clans, for instance.

In most cases the birth of the city-state appears to have been an acutely painful affair with intense infighting between rival clans for control of government and between aristocrats and others, as new social classes, peasant farmers, or traders emerged. Sometimes there was a state of intense conflict, *stasis*. (A later example, in Corcyra in the 420s, ended in a bruising civil war whose terrors were vividly described by the historian Thucydides in Book Three of his *History*.) Often, as suggested in the last chapter, a city disintegrated, with some citizens leaving to find a new home elsewhere. Nevertheless, it was these very challenges, the activity of creating the *polis,* that gave birth to politics.

Resources were always scarce in the Greek world and each state was obsessive about preserving its territories and resources from hungry neighbors. As a result, intercity tension was common. "Peace is merely a name; in truth an undeclared war always exists by nature between every Greek city-state" as a speaker in Plato's *Laws* puts it. Every city needed an effective defense force if it was to hold its boundaries. Few *poleis* could afford to support a full-time force of its own, so the wealthier farmers in each city community, perhaps some 30 to 40 percent of the citizen body, doubled as soldiers. The defense force which evolved gradually over some fifty years (725–675) was the phalanx, a tightly packed body in which lines of men standing shoulder to shoulder, eight or more deep, fought as a single coordinated force.

The secret of the phalanx lay in its armor, in particular, a large shield, the *hoplon,* which gave the name "hoplite" to the new warfare. The *hoplon* was circular, of hardened leather faced with bronze, and often decorated with a suitably terrifying symbol, possibly a Gorgon's head. The left arm of a hoplite passed through a central thong on the inside of the shield and his hand grasped a handle on the rim so that not only the left side of the man holding it was protected but the right side of the next in line. A bronze helmet, leather corslet, and bronze greaves for the legs made up the body armor. The right hand was free to hold weapons, normally a spear used for jabbing and fending off attacks, although a sword was often carried as well. The combined hoplite panoply would not have been prohibitively expensive (and could have been passed from father to son), but as the hoplites were expected to provide their own equipment the adoption of hoplite warfare reflects the success of the new relatively prosperous farming class.

The advantage of the phalanx lay in its weight and mass and the way these could be combined to provide an unstoppable force in advance or an immovable one in defense. It made the old aristocratic hero obsolete—even the most resolute would have been trampled underfoot as a phalanx marched or ran forward. Cavalry were no more effective. Stirrups had not yet been invented and charging horseman would be knocked backward by the array of spears which met them. The phalanx had its vulnerabilities. The armor was heavy so a hoplite army would not have been able to march far and it could only fight effectively on flat ground. However, on the right terrain the only way of breaking a well-organized hoplite force (other than by catching hoplites unawares before they had formed up) was providing another hoplite force of superior weight or morale, and this is why hoplite warfare spread through the Greek world as the essential defense force of any prosperous city-state. Hoplite equipment became standardized across the Greek world and developed little over time. A hoplite shield of 350 B.C. was essentially the same as the one abandoned by Archilochus three hundred years earlier.

There is much to suggest that hoplite warfare was carried out according to well-defined rituals. The Greeks "made public declarations to each other about wars and battles in advance, when they decided to risk them, and even about the places into which they were about to advance and draw up their lines," wrote the historian Polybius in the second century B.C. As the hoplites were full time-farmers there were few times they were free to fight in any case—a short period before the grain was harvested and just after the harvest, in high summer before the olives and grapes were ready.

Once a battle had been arranged, the two armies, in lines perhaps several hundred yards (meters) long and several ranks deep, were drawn up more than 600 feet (some 200 meters) apart. Then after sacrificing, and morale boosting by a general, they would march toward each other, a piper (as on the Chigi vase) or flautist marking the beat. The psychology of presentation was vital. The Spartans had perfected the process. They wore their hair long and were adorned with crimson cloaks for effect, their march forward steady and deliberate and hence frightening in its remorselessness. For a less confident opponent the effect would have been terrifying. "In an instant," writes Plutarch of this moment at the battle of Plataea in 479, "the phalanx took on the look of a wild animal, bristling as it turns at bay." In some battles one side simply turned and fled at this point. As the two sides closed, the spears would be used to jab over and under the enemy's shields, piercing the neck or the groin of those unlucky enough to be caught. The outcome would probably be decided, however, by the coordinated weight of numbers as rear ranks pushed on the front. Eventually, after perhaps an hour, the battle would end with one side losing its nerve or breaking up in exhaustion in the summer heat. This was war won or lost in an afternoon. Pursuit was difficult in hoplite armor and casualties were seldom heavy, perhaps 15 percent in a defeated army it has been calculated. It was the humiliation of defeat that was most wounding.

The advantage of hoplite warfare was that once the equipment had been acquired few extra resources were needed. The actual fighting was short and sharp with some kind of decisive result at the end of it. Usually, it appears from an analysis of known battles, that the defenders were successful. The annual rhythm of farming was unaffected and it has been said, somewhat cynically, that warfare may have been no more than a temporary diversion from the incessant border disputes between farmers which provided the real focus of daily life. Yet this was its importance. To defend their common territory those fighting had to swallow their differences and work together ("to bond" as modern management gurus would put it). They had to create a community spirit and there was no other way than through consolidating their loyalty to a city. Hoplite warfare had the vital effect of helping define city identity and yet, unlike most defense programs, it did not threaten to destroy that identity by its demands on resources.

The poet Tyrtaeus (mid-seventh century) captures the new mood of community action. If a man dies in battle it is not only his family or clan that mourns him but the city community. *Arete,* excellence, comes from dying for one's city:

Young and old alike weep for him,
and the whole city is filled with sad longing,
and a tomb and children and his family survive him.
Never has fame forgotten a brave man or his name,
But though he is under the earth he has become immortal,
whoever excelling, and standing firm, and fighting
for his land and children, is killed by mighty Ares.
(Translation: Oswyn Murray)

The need to unite in defense, therefore, helps to create a sense of community among citizens. It was part of a wider process. In an essay on the development of the archaic *polis,* Pauline Schmitt-Pantel shows how community spirit was fostered as a result of traditional aristocratic values being adopted by the citizens of a *polis* as a whole. The duty of defense passes from the warrior-hero to the hoplite. The aristocratic feast, hitherto reserved for those of wealth and good birth, becomes a city feast in which all citizens participate after a communal sacrifice and are eligible for equal shares. Other traditional associations, memberships of an age group or a hereditary brotherhood, a *phratry,* for instance, do not disappear but are integrated into city life, so there is a linked chain of gatherings, "a ritual of conviviality" in Schmitt-Pantel's phrase, all of which combine to reinforce identity on a social level. Increasingly, the *polis* becomes the focus for religious expression. Within the city new festivals emerge, such as the Panathenaea in Athens (see below), that allow a direct focus on the patron god or goddess. Old ones, such as the Thermospheria, the woman's festival in honor of the goddess Demeter, come to be celebrated in distinct ways in different cities as each places its own imprint on the proceedings. Even the Panhellenic sanctuaries, such as Delphi, were drawn into the world of the *polis,* with *poleis* establishing their own presence at each through the gift of a city treasury.

The authority of the city was imposed in other ways. In the early days the aristocratic clans, with their war bands, land holdings, and prestigious heritage, would have been the main competitors for the allegiance of the local populace. In particular the burial places of their heroic ancestors were a focus for alternative loyalties. Many cities now insist that "heroes" are buried within the city's limits. In Megara the first council chamber had, according to legend, the tombs of the city's heroes constructed into it, a conclusive sign of how citizens rather than aristocratic clans, were appropriating the aura of the dead. (Many centuries later, the triumph of Christianity, too, was symbolized by the digging up of martyrs from outlying Christian burial grounds and the transference of their bones into central city churches.)

It has been suggested, by Richard Seaford in his *Reciprocity and Ritual*, that the emergence of the coinage also aided the strengthening of city authority. Coinage seems to have been devised by the king of Lydia about 600 B.C. as a means of paying his Greek mercenaries. (Hoplites were much sought after outside Greece—a force of thirty thousand was maintained by the Egyptian Pharaoh. Mercenary service may have been as effective a way of dealing with surplus population as an overseas settlement.) A lump of metal (electrum, an alloy of gold and silver, in the case of Lydia where the alloy was found naturally) of standard weight stamped with the mark of the issuing authority, was handed over at the end of a year's service. It could then be passed on by the mercenary in exchange for goods or even melted down for its metal value. The idea spread quickly into the Greek world. A set of early coins, some stamped on one side, some on both, was discovered in the foundation deposit of the temple of Artemis at Ephesus (also c. 600 B.C.). Soon the more prosperous cities of the Isthmus, Corinth, Athens, and the trading island of Aegina were issuing their own. The first issue in Athens, c. 550 B.C. or earlier, seems to have been used by the tyrant Pisistratus to pay his own mercenaries and craftsmen while those in circulation could be returned to the state as a means of paying taxation and fines. Seaford argues that not only was this another way in which the relationship between state and citizen was cemented, but the use of coinage undermined the old gift exchange network of the aristocracy. Soon smaller denominations minted in silver, the most easily accessible metal in the Greek world, began circulating and each city would adopt its own stamping symbol, in Athens an owl, in Aegina a turtle. By the fifth century coinage was to be found throughout the Greek world.

It was vital for the emerging *polis* to create a constitution so that the roles and responsibilities of citizens were clearly understood. The city for which the best evidence remains is Sparta, the home of Tyrtaeus. Like many city-states Sparta grew up from a number of settlements, four distinct villages, in fact, on low hills overlooking the River Eurotas in the southern Peloponnese. It was an easily defensible site and the emerging city also had access to the fertile plain of Laconia which was itself protected from the west by Mount Taygetus. The city prided itself on its Dorian heritage, based on the idea that its citizens were decended from the hero Heracles and hence distinct and superior to those other Greeks living around them. (A sense of being Dorian was enhanced by fifth-century rivalry with "Ionian" Athens.)

Early in its history the city absorbed neighboring villages, allowing their inhabitants, the *perioikoi,* "those living around," freedom without citizenship. In the eighth century there was a major expansion of the city's territory to the west when the fertile plain of Messenia was subdued. Messenia's inhabitants, despite being Greeks living in their own traditional communities, suffered a far worse fate than the *perioikoi.* They were reduced, in effect, to slavery, working the land for their new overlords, though they were allowed to keep a share of the produce for themselves. They never settled to their fate and the Spartans were obsessed with the fear, often realized, of their revenge. Any emerging leaders of the helots were eliminated and one element of the training of adolescent Spartans was to let them loose to cause terror among the helot population.

In the seventh-century Sparta, like most cities, remained under strong aristocratic influence. As the result of some compromise between its ruling families there were two hereditary kings who retained the right to command Sparta's armies and lead the city's religious ceremonial. Its aristocracy maintained their influence through the Greek world, exporting great mixing bowls (the symbol of the aristocratic drinking party) and competing successfully in the Olympic Games. The city imported unworked ivory, an exotic material for Greeks, carved it, and exported it throughout Greece. A council of aristocratic elders, the *gerousia,* advised the kings.

However, the seventh century was also a time of trauma. There was, according to later Messenian legend, a humiliating defeat by the neighboring city of Argos in 669/8 B.C., an uprising of the helots which took twenty years to suppress, and friction between richer and poorer citizens. It seems that a political constitution emerged out of these dramas. The constitution was attributed to one Lycurgus. It was common to associate political change with a named lawgiver, much as the birth of Greek sculpture was associated with a Greek craftsman, Daedalus, and Lycurgus may never have existed. However, evidence from the so-called Great Rhetra (*rhetra* was the Spartan term for a decree) which probably dates from the mid-seventh century, suggests that by 650 the citizen body had been brought into the political system. An assembly of citizens now had the power to pass laws although the kings and *gerousia* retained some power to overrule its decisions. Though they are not mentioned in the Great Rhetra, the assembly also elected five magistrates, the *ephors,* who exercised considerable power during their single year of office, providing "popular" supervision of the activities of the kings and the *gerousia.* There is a record of an ephor telling a king to divorce and remarry so he could get a male heir and another persuading the Spartans to declare war on Athens in 432 B.C. The Spartan constitution was somewhat cumbersome but it succeeded in creating a balance of power between different social groups and Sparta, unlike most cities, never succumbed to tyrannical rule. This was *eunomia,* a "good order," if a despotic one, of which Spartans were inordinately proud.

The rise of the popular assembly in Sparta seems associated with the adoption of hoplite warfare by the city in the mid-seventh century. This was possibly as a direct result of the defeat by Argos in 669. The first dedication of a model of a hoplite soldier in the Orthia sanctuary at Sparta (the first of many) is shortly afterward, c. 650 B.C. Sparta was unique among Greek cities in being able to support a full-time army. It was a condition of citizenship that citizens maintained themselves from private plots in Messenia farmed by the helots. They were thus free for year-round training which was needed to maintain their hold on the very slave class that supported them. Training began at seven and was a brutalizing process with continuous endurance tests as the child grew up, his identity as an individual crushed by the experience. Intensive bonding rituals centered on age groups with each year moving on together. Ceremonies at the city's main sanctuary, Orthia, centered on terra-cotta face masks used in some way to mark the transition from one state of being to another (from youth perhaps to adulthood). While a Spartan citizen seems to have married about the age of twenty-five, he was not free to leave his fellows to live at home with his wife until he was thirty.

Pauline Schmitt-Pantel's claim that aristocratic practices were absorbed by the city-state has support from Sparta. It appears that the transition to hoplite warfare took place under aristocratic supervision. The messes in which the citizens ate and socialized, the *syssitia,* appear to have been a direct descendant of the aristocratic *symposia* with the same number of participants (fifteen). The terms used to describe the hoplite ranks are those used also of the old aristocratic war bands. Yet in the end the Spartan aristocracy became submerged in hoplite life with the result that the citizen body referred to itself as *homoioi*, "the equal ones." Contacts with the outside world withered. There were few Spartan victors in the Olympic Games after 570, trade ceased, and the Spartans clung to iron bars for exchange instead of adopting coins as elsewhere in Greece. There were only a handful of written inscriptions (writing seems only to have been used in treaties with other states). This then was an isolated society obsessed with its own self-preservation. Figures from the past, Lycurgus, even Agamemnon, the legendary leader of the Greeks in the Trojan War, were enshrined as its heroes.

Sparta arrived at its constitution after a period of trauma but few cities resolved the transition to a stable constitution so easily. In many parts of the Greek world from the 650s onward, the conflicts resulted not in an oligarchic constitution as in Sparta but in rule by a single figure, the tyrant. The tyrant normally seized power, usually by force, sometimes with popular support, breaking through any normal rules or conventions to do so. As James McGlew has pointed out in his *Tyranny and Political Culture in Ancient Greece*, later Greeks would see the tyrant as justified in overthrowing an earlier regime, usually on the grounds that it had been abusing "justice." In this sense the tyrant has in the first instance a positive role, not only in removing an unjust ruler but in highlighting "justice" as a concept. However, this role could not be sustained. The tyrant had placed himself above the law and by the very nature of his rule could not be restrained by it. In the ways of things, the later accounts said, he would accumulate great personal wealth, become cruel in the exercise of power, and indulge in unnatural sexual practices (intercourse with a dead wife and a mother are among those recorded). It was now the turn of the citizen body as a whole to take on the role of justice bringers and overthrow the tyrant.

Tyranny is widespread in the Greek world in the seventh to sixth centuries but it cannot be explained as easily as later writers suggested. There was no one route to single rule. There was ample scope within the less stable city for either the leader of one aristocratic clan to seize power, a discontented aristocrat to use hoplite support to overthrow a clique, or even for an individual to use the mass of citizens for his support. Nor did tyrants necessarily deserve all the condemnation they were given. The sources themselves often reflect no more than the prejudices of the writer. The disgruntled aristocratic poet Alcaeus wrote that the Mytileneans "established as tyrant of their cowardly and ill-starred city the lowborn Pittacus, praising him greatly in a single voice." In fact, Pittacus was appointed by the city as a mediator at a time of tension, he proved a moderate reformer who argued that law was the best protector of a city, and he retired quietly at the end of his ten years of office. He was hardly a tyrant in the normal sense of the word.

Nevertheless "tyranny" reflects a lack of maturity in city government. It normally occurred at a time when the old aristocratic order was demoralized or tearing itself apart, but when there was no stable hoplite oligarchy or citizen assembly able to assert its own authority. The mass of citizens could be dominated or manipulated by the charisma of the tyrant, his money, or the hopes of good order that he promised. In many cases it is clear that the tyrant saw himself, whatever his birth, as an antiaristocratic force, using hoplites as his armed supporters and even destroying or redistributing the riches of the wealthy. In Megara the tyrant Theagenes (c. 640) was reputed to have destroyed the flocks of large landowners. The overseas settlement where a founder parceled out land equally among the founding settlers may have provided a model for an alternative distribution of resources.

Tyrants appeared in most Greek cities—Sparta and the trading island of Aegina are the notable exceptions. Typically, tyrants manipulated the prosperity of the era for their own or their city's advantages. Cypselus, tyrant of Corinth, and his successors, his son Periander (ruled c. 627–587) and his great nephew Psammetichus (overthrown c. 582), watched over the economic predominance of their city, deliberately seeking out new sources of trade and flaunting their success through temple building. The Pisistratids at Athens presided over Athens' emergence as a major trading city with a glorification of the Acropolis to match its new status. The building projects attributed to Polycrates of Samos (c. 535–522) by the historian Herodotus illustrate a tyrant's concerns. There was an enormous temple to the city's patron, the goddess Hera; an underground tunnel through which piped water could be brought to the city; and a harbor mole. The protection of the city by divine powers was secured, its citizens able to enjoy fresh water, a precious commodity in the Greek world, and its traders a safer harbor. Polycrates' power was underwritten by a large navy and dominance over the islands surrounding Samos.

The tyrants, therefore, acted within rather than against the spirit of the age. They behaved as if they were members of a Panhellenic elite, often making treaties of mutual support with each other in the tradition of earlier *basilees*. They patronized the great shrines of the Greek world. Corinthian money is to be found at both Olympia and Delphi. Pisistratus instituted a festival for all Ionians on Delos, the island of Apollo. Cleisthenes, tyrant of Sicyon, won the chariot race at the Olympic Games. Some such as Polycrates of Samos were players on an even wider stage. Polycrates had an alliance with the Egyptian Pharaoh Amasis but came to grief when he tried to meddle in Persian politics. (He was apparently lured to the mainland, by then under Persian control, and crucified).

Typically, one generation of tyrants followed another. Corinth was under tyrannical rule for some eighty years under Cypselus and his descendants. In the neighboring city of Sicyon, the Orthagorid family may have held power for about a century from 650 B.C. with Cleisthenes, its most formidable leader, ruling for thirty years from 600 B.C. The Pisistratids in Athens lasted two generations. Long-term dynasties seem, however, to have proved unsustainable. By the nature of things, the heir of a usurping tyrant tended to lack the right mix of opportunism, determination, and personal charisma of his predecessor. The very prosperity which the tyrant could use for his advantage also fostered the consolidation of the new classes who were likely to be resistant to hereditary rule. Concepts such as *isonomia,* equal rights, and *dike,* justice, had become powerful slogans in the cause of oligarchic or democratic government. The second generation of tyrants were more vulnerable than the first and there are stories of petty cruelty as their dominance came under threat. Periander suggested that rivals should be eliminated in the same way as taller stalks of corn could be lopped off and he reputedly ordered the castration of three hundred youths from Corcyra. The last years of Hippias, a son of Pisistratus, were marked by increasingly despotic behavior. There was immense relief when such men were gone and their overthrow was typically followed by oligarchic or democratic governments. Ironically, therefore, tyrants fostered democracy.

The history of Athens shows the challenges involved in the transition from the rule of aristocratic clans to government by the citizen body. The city itself with is impressive stronghold, the Acropolis, was well placed for a prominent role in the Aegean world and had already been an important center in Mycenaean times, acting possibly as a springboard for settlement of the coast of Asia Minor as the Mycenaean world disintegrated. Although a leading player in the Greek world before the eighth century, Athens had been unable to sustain its position. Sparta and Corinth were more successful trading cities and the city was hemmed in by two assertive neighbors. Argos, reputedly the first state to have a hoplite army, and Aegina, whose position made her a natural center for Aegean trade. The response was to colonize inland. The move is well attested from archaeological evidence and gradually a substantial territory just under one thousand square miles (2,500 square kilometers), made up of three plains divided by mountain ranges, Attica, was settled. Such a large area made it easy for individual aristocratic clans to establish their own territories and power bases. (Some sixty are known by name.) By the seventh century aristocratic influence was supreme, at a time when in much of the rest of Greece it was on the defensive. Aristocrats monopolized the magistracies, the archons, and after their term of office became members of the Council of Areopagus (named after the hill in Athens on which it met) that saw itself as the guardian of the state. However, it was an unsettled time. There was intense rivalry among clans as they struggled to control an emerging city government which in turn was attempting to assert its own authority. There were further tensions over land. In some way, much disputed by scholars, poorer landowners had become dependent on the aristocracy. There is some evidence of a sharecropping class which had to provide a sixth of their produce for their aristocratic overlords (though this was not as large a proportion as in most such arrangements and does not appear unduly burdensome). It is also probable that some form of feudal relationship between aristocrat and commoner persisted and it was possible for debts (including those resulting from a failure to pay the sixth) to be attached to an individual so that his creditor could sell him abroad as a slave if he could not pay. Resentment may have been fostered so much by the actual weight of these burdens as by the fact that they existed at all in a society where the emergence of a hoplite force gave new confidence and coherence to the middling peasants. Another ingredient in the crisis was the renewal of Athenian interest in Aegean trade. By the late seventh century craftsmanship was being revived in the city. An overseas colony, Athens' first, Sigeum, was settled on the entrance to the Black Sea (c. 600 B.C.). Two contrasting societies were emerging within the same state, one based on trade and openness to the outside world, the other on a feudal agrarian economy.

Tensions had already shown themselves. In 632 one Cylon, an aristocrat and victor of the Olympic games, tried to seize power in the city, calling in support his father-in-law, Theagenes, tyrant of neighboring Megara. He and his supporters were cornered on the Acropolis and there was an attempt to try them, probably by the Areopagus, the council of former magistrates. However, it was a rival clan, the Alcmaeonids, who set upon Cylon and his supporters as they came down from the Acropolis, killing many of them. The city reasserted its authority by trying the Alcmaeonids and exiling the entire clan. Their family tombs were broken up and the bones of their ancestors thrown over the Athenian border. The episode was followed in 621 by a further attempt to assert city authority through a law code drawn up by one Draco. Its penalties were harsh (the word *Draconian* survives in English as a reminder of this), which may represent a desperation to achieve control, but the main thrust of the code was to outlaw the traditional right of a family to self-help in avenging murder.

None of this brought calm and in 594 a more ambitious attempt was made to create a stable government. One Solon was appointed as a magistrate with supreme power as lawgiver. Little is known of Solon. The main sources of his achievements are Aristotle writing over two hundred years later and Plutarch nearly five hundred years after Aristotle. His reputation as a founding figure of Athenian democracy meant that he was revered as a "sage" and used by later Athenian politicians whenever an authority was required to back a political argument. There were many opportunities to distort his achievements and it is unlikely that more than a few of the many laws attributed to him were really his. By the fourth century, he had become an all-powerful founding father under whose aegis a mass of legislation was protected.

Aristotle described Solon as "among the first in birth and reputation, but among the middle in wealth and property" and he was also associated with a successful war to win the island of Salamis from neighboring Megara. (It was an important acquisition as it allowed the Athenians to develop their port at Piraeus without threat.) One can assume that he had respect due to him from his birth but that he had also consolidated a reputation among nonaristocratic citizens for his military achievements. He saw himself, however, above all factions, an isolated figure with the right to act as he pleased in the service of the city he loved.

The Athens Solon inherited was one in which, in his words, rival aristocrats squabble about everything. His ideal was harmony or good order (*eunomia*). Solon set out his concerns in verse, presumably in the hopes that constant repetition would allow his message to sink in:

> *Eunomia makes all things well ordered and fitted*
> *and often puts chains on the unjust;*
> *she smooths the rough, puts an end to excess, blinds insolence,*
> *withers the flowers of unrighteousness,*
> *straightens crooked judgments and softens deeds of arrogance,*
> *puts an end to works of faction*
> *and to the anger of painful strife; under her*
> *all men's actions are fitting and wise.*
>
> (Translation: Oswyn Murray)

What is remarkable about Solon's thinking is that he sees an abstract entity, *eunomia,* as a living force which is able to calm a city's tensions and influence men's actions for the good. He sees justice, *dike,* in a similar way. If *dike* is offended, another of his poems proclaims, she will unleash tyranny on a city as a punishment. (This idea that the world or society should be in balance and there are forces which redress it if is not is an idea to be found in both Greek religion and philosophy.) However, Solon did not believe that "good order" or "justice" were the gift of the gods. They had to be enshrined in the city's constitution through the actions of human beings and this was the task Solon set himself. He was a pragmatic reformer, prepared to use his power to create a political system that would uphold, not offend, justice. Its essence was stability, with citizens acting with moderation and restraint towards each other under a respected system of law. Solon's reforms had a coherence to this end but as with all moderate reformers at a time of acute social conflict, the problem was how to mobilize opinion behind his curbing of the aristocracy without at the same time releasing unattainable expectations among the poor. Solon was driven to despair by the tensions he released. It was, he said, as if he were a wolf about to be torn to pieces by hounds.

An important task was to curb aristocratic display. It appears that family funerals were being used by aristocrats as a means of flaunting their clan's power and so Solon restricted what could be spent on them and the time they could last. (Other cities are known to have introduced similar laws.) The response of rival clans to these grand funerals was to indulge in abuse of the dead man and this too Solon outlawed. It seems that he introduced a public commemoration of the city's dead to transcend those hosted by their families. Here were the thoughts of Tyrtaeus ("the whole city is filled with sad longing . . .") translated into practice.

If the laws of the *polis* were to be upheld they had to be the concern of everyone and Solon decreed that that anyone could prosecute an injustice even if not a direct victim of it ("those who are not wronged, no less than those who are wronged, [must] exert themselves to punish the wrong doers"). There was to be a right of appeal against the decisions of magistrates (who were invariably aristocrats). This was probably to an assembly of all citizens, the forerunner of the later people's juries of Athens. Solon is also associated with the creation of the Council of Four Hundred (a hundred of its members chosen from each tribe). The functions of this council are not clear but its existence seems to be confirmed independently by public buildings for it to meet in which were erected in the Agora at this date.

The most efficient way of exerting authority through the law was to provide an all-embracing code and this, according to later tradition, Solon did. It may have been the one, inscribed on wooden tables, whose fragments were still to be seen in Athens by Plutarch several centuries later. It was truly comprehensive, dealing not only with the laws of the state, including one on high treason and criminal law, but with relationships within the family and commercial activity (the export of olive oil was specifically encouraged). Good sense prevailed. There was no point, said Solon, in passing laws that no one would respect and it was important that citizens could see the point of each law. "Men preserve agreements that profit no one to violate." In short, laws were to serve a community and this implied they could be changed as a community's needs changed, an important challenge to the concept that laws should be absolute. The code became so hallowed that the Roman statesman Cicero claimed that the Twelve Tables, the early law code of Rome, were based on it.

Solon was no radical. Property rights were important to him and he had no wish to introduce equality in landownership. A major concern was to ensure the freedom of the poor as unburdened landowners. Debt slavery was abolished and Solon searched for those who had been sold abroad so they could return as free men. He declared with some enthusiasm that he had destroyed the boundary markers which were in some way associated with dependent status of the poor (possibly they were reminders of debt or a feudal obligation that went with a specific plot of land). A free self-sufficient peasantry could now emerge, the core of the future Athenian democracy.

The freedom of the small landholder went hand in hand with further measures to dilute aristocratic privilege. Solon divided the citizen body into four classes according to the amount of produce (in grain, wine, or oil) that their land would yield. There were the *pentakosiomedimnoi* (producers of 500 bushels), the *hippeis* (300 bushels), the *zeugitai* (200 bushels, probably the level of wealth at which hoplite service could be expected), and the *thetes,* the remainder. Richard Seaford has suggested that the registration in a particular class may have depended on the size of a landowner's gift of crops at a city festival. Status, in short, was defined by a contribution to the community. Magistrates were drawn only from the wealthiest class but this was an aristocracy of wealth rather than one of birth and the old aristocratic clans now had no privileges other than as result of their wealth. Other offices were open to the second and third classes but not to the *thetes* who had to be content with membership of the assemblies.

Solon attempted to create the city community as a living and healthy organism where there was a respected authority, a curbing of aristocratic privilege, and a class of smaller landowning citizens liberated from aristocratic demands. Unlike Sparta where fear locked the system into an undue reverence for the past, the Athenian state had the potential for future growth and development. Solon did not create Athenian democracy—his ideal was good order essential for the upholding of justice—but through establishing popular assemblies and a comprehensive code of laws, he created the framework in which democracy was a possible outcome. This was the measure of his achievement

It was not an achievement, however, that bore immediate fruit. To his despair Solon's last years were overshadowed by continued conflict between rival clans who still had secure territorial bases on "the

Coast" or on "the Plain." In one year no magistrates could be appointed (the word *anarchy,* from "without archons," survives in English as a result). In the end Athens fell subject to a tyrant, Pisistratus. It was the very outcome that Solon had tried to avoid.

The tyranny of Pisistratus was only firmly established in 546 but Pisistratus himself had been determinedly trying to win and sustain power in the city for some fifteen years before that. He appears to have first come to prominence as a soldier in a war against Megara but he also had a power base as leader of "a Party of the Hills." Whether this meant he controlled an actual region of Attica or drew his support from hill folk (who tended to be poorer than those of "the Coast" and "Plains") is not clear. His struggle was with the other two parties but he was ousted by them after a short period of rule in about 560. He spent his exile in Macedonia where he gathered enough silver from the mines there to be able to return with mercenaries and seize power. One flamboyant gesture to win over the more credulous was to dress up a local girl as Athena and to ride beside her in a chariot claiming that here was the goddess herself come to give him her protection. Once back in power Pisistratus ruled until his death in 527. He was succeeded by his two sons, Hipparchus and Hippies. Hipparchus was assassinated in 514 and Hippies expelled in 510.

Sixth-century Athens was prosperous. The city was well placed for Aegean trade and Solon's economic laws may have encouraged the export of olive oil. By the middle of the century the pottery industry was enjoying a boom. Fine painted wares were being exported throughout the Mediterranean as Corinth's predominance in the trade collapsed. So many Athenian pots have been found in Italy that they were originally believed to be Etruscan not Greek.

Like most tyrants, Pisistratus did nothing to upset this prosperity. He appears to have been a relatively benign ruler and aristocratic families were still able to hold magistracies. He has been linked with the glorification of the Acropolis and the founding of a major city festival, the Greater Panathenaea, though direct evidence to confirm this is lacking. Certainly in the sixth century the Acropolis became the focus of a massive building program (as did the Agora where, recent American excavations suggest, Pisistratus and his family may actually have lived). The site was sacked by the Persians in 480 and so only fragments, some buried in pits, others reused in the city's walls, remain of the temples that stood there. There is much dispute among scholars about what was constructed but there appears to have been an early temple to Athena built about 560 and another dating from about 520. A mass of votive statues surrounded the temples, a sign in itself that aristocratic display was not crushed by the tyranny. The most attractive of these statues that survive is one of the earliest (c. 560), the Calf-Bearer, a figure of a man with a calf nestling around his neck, but there is an important set of *korai,* clothed maidens, many with gentle smiles. They were dedicated by males and may have been considered the most appropriate votive gift to a goddess.

The city's identity was further enhanced by the creation of the Great Panathenaea (sometime in the 560s, possibly in Pisistratus' first, short period of rule). Festivals in honor of Athena were already held annually but the Great Panathenaea was a particularly magnificent celebration held only every four years. A great procession, made up of all the different components of Athenian society, made its way through the Agora and up to the goddess' temple on the Acropolis. There were games and competitions open to all Greeks, in imitation of those held at the Panhellenic shrines. The prizes were amphorae filled with the finest oil. The Panathenaea not only acted to create a focus for Athens within Attica but impressed the prosperity and success of the city on the Greek world as a whole.

The embellishment of Athens continued under the rule of Pisistratus' sons and here the evidence is a little firmer. They embarked on a massive temple to Zeus, the father of Athena, on a ridge to the southeast of the Acropolis although it was not completed until some six hundred years later when the Roman emperor Hadrian, a lover of Greek culture, provided the funds. In the Agora they constructed an "Altar of the Twelve Gods" whose foundations survive. It acted as the point from which all distances from Athens were measured. Fountains were installed so that fresh water could be piped into the city.

Athens was thus well on the way to becoming the showpiece city of the Greek mainland. Those who would have wanted to see the sixth-century Greek city at its most opulent, however, would have traveled either eastward or westward of Greece. Cities here had access to larger and often more fertile territories than mainland Greece and so could consistently squeeze out extra resources. They may also have wished to stress their Greek identity against the neighboring native peoples, some of whom, Phoenicians, Persians, and Lydians, were major threats to them. Their opulence was to be seen in their temples, often several to a city, grouped together as at Posidonia (Roman Paestum) in Italy, or on the heights around the city as at Selinus in Sicily (all in the Doric style). Some of these were massive, especially in the east, here built in the Ionic style. Both the major temples to Hera in Samos built in the sixth century were more than 300 feet long and 150 feet wide (over a hundred meters long and fifty wide). The temple of Artemis in Ephesus was just under 400 feet (115 meters) long (it was the first temple to be built entirely in marble and its massive size earned it a place among the Seven Wonders of the Ancient World); that to Apollo to Didyma, though smaller in area, had columns more than 45 feet (15 meters) high. As has been suggested above it was also a time when streets were becoming paved and lined out in grids while fountains and a few public buildings were appearing. This was the pattern of town life which was to spread outside the Greek world so that eventually planned cities on the Greek model are to be found from northern Britain (via the Romans) to Afghanistan.

This period from 620 to 480 B.C. is commonly known as the Archaic age to distinguish it from the earlier Orientalizing period and the later classical (although often the term is extended backward to include the Oriental period). As has been seen it was one in which there was a gradual coming of order to city life. However, there was no lack of social tensions and these are well recorded by its poets and singers. Elegies and lyrics, rather than epics, now become the normal form of poetic expression. Lyric means no more than a song sung to the lyre but this is hardly an adequate description of the poetry of the period (a flute could be substituted for a lyre or a lyric sung without any accompaniment at all). It is often a short and personal piece in which the poet records his own observations, perhaps about friendship, the uncertainties of the age, the loss of an ideal world. Lyrics could be choral and used to address gods (in particular Apollo and Dionysus), and at betrothals, weddings, and funerals. Elegies were sung to the flute and had a characteristic meter. They were often sung at more private occasions, in particular at the *symposia,* the aristocratic drinking parties, and were often, though not exclusively, laments. Here the concerns of a threatened class are more explicit. They, the *agathoi,* the good ones, noble in birth and heritage, above the concerns of moneymaking, lament the usurpation of power by the *kakoi,* the bad ones, the upstarts who threaten them. Theognis, a disgruntled aristocrat from Megara (? mid-sixth century) sums up the querulous feelings of one whose style of life is threatened by the involvement of those below:

Kyrnos, our city's still the same; its people, though, are different:
the ones who used to have no concept of our laws or rules,
but wrapped their ribs around with goatskin cloaks,
and lived like deers outside the city walls,
it's they who are the masters now, while those who once were fine
are cowards now. Oh, who can bear the sight.

(Translation: Alan Griffiths)

In Mytilene (the city of Lesbos), in the late seventh century, Alcaeus composed for a band of fellow warriors with whom he drank and fought. It is a rough world of sudden quarrels and transient friendships as rival aristocrats strive with each other for advantage but there is a shared concern in their contempt of the tyrants who fight over their city. Semonides, mid-seventh century, from the Aegean island of Amorgos, is remembered for an ill-tempered invective against women. Each type of woman is compared to an animal equivalent—a mare (the aristocratic woman); a sow "whose house is smeared with mud and all within lies in dishevelment"; the donkey, who works only under duress, eats all day, and takes as her lover the first of her husband's friends who comes along. Only "the bee" is worth having. Her love for her husband, her refusal to indulge in tittle-tattle, lead to a flourishing family whose "glorious children rise to fame" as they grow old.

The *symposia* were male gatherings that catered for the sexual and intellectual needs of their members as much as the maintenance of social exclusiveness. Respectable women would not be seen at them but women, too, had groups that shared music and song. Alcman, a seventh-century poet from Sparta, records maiden songs sung in processions and dances in which the participating girls share an easy intimacy with each other. They address each other by name, praising each other for their looks and accomplishments. Their life together appears to be one of short but intense comradeship before marriage takes them to separate homes.

It is probably a similar group of leisured and aristocratic girls who are found on the island of Lesbos in the early sixth century. Their leader or mentor was Sappho whose voice is one of the most personal and beguiling to survive from the ancient world. The group appears to have focused its activity on a cult worship of Aphrodite, the goddess of love. The world Sappho creates for the goddess is one of shimmering sensuality:

Come, ...
for here in this sacred haunt
apple trees crowd in a gracious grove, shrines
are perfumed with smoke.

Here the cool water sings its song
deep in the apple-boughs;
all is rose-shadowed and restless leaves
drop sleep like a spell.

Here is a meadow fit for horses,
thriving with early bloom; sweet
breezes are blowing their honeyed breath. . . .
(Translation: Anne Pippin Burnett)

There is much more in Sappho than a sensuous appreciation of the physical world. She is caught within the powerful emotions that life in her group of young girls arouses in her, "a sweet-bitter resistless creature" as she describes herself. They are particularly intense when men threaten to take off a loved one in marriage:

Peer of immortal gods he seems to me, that
Man who sits beside you, who now can listen
Private and close, so close, to your sweet-sounding
Voice and your lovely

Passionate laughter—ah, how that, as ever,
Sets the heart pounding in my breast; one glance and
I am undone, speech fails me, I can no longer
Utter a word, my

Tongue cleaves to my mouth, while sharp and sudden
Flames lick through me, burning the inward flesh, and

The Apollo Belvedere, a Roman copy of an original Greek statue of *c*. 330 BC. For Johann Winckelmann (in his *History of Ancient Art*, 1764) this statue represented the pinnacle of Greek art.

The age of heroes. The wealthy German businessman Heinrich Schliemann (1822–90) was responsible for rediscovering the earliest Greeks, the Mycenaeans (1600–1200 BC). At Mycenae in the Peloponnese, whose celebrated "Lion Gate" is shown here (*above left*), he excavated in a grave circle (*below left*) and discovered what he claimed was the body of Agamemnon, leader of the Greek expedition to Troy. His earlier excavations had torn through the mound of ancient Troy to reveal its complex building history. The scene reproduced here (*above*) represents the site in 1882.

When the Athenians won the battle of Marathon in 490 BC, they felt they had revived this Homeric age. This powerful bronze figure (known as the Riace warrior) may have come from the Athenian monument at Delphi set up in celebration of the victory. Its imposing presence, its nudity and proportions represent the heroic ideal as seen in the classical period.

The Acropolis, the ceremonial and spiritual centre of Athens, "restored" after being cleared of later buildings in the nineteenth century. (For a description of the site see the Afterword to Chapter Eleven.)

This model of the site of Olympia shows in the foreground the hostel in which distinguished visitors to the Games stayed; beyond is the famous temple to Zeus, and beyond that, in the far center, the stadium for running races.

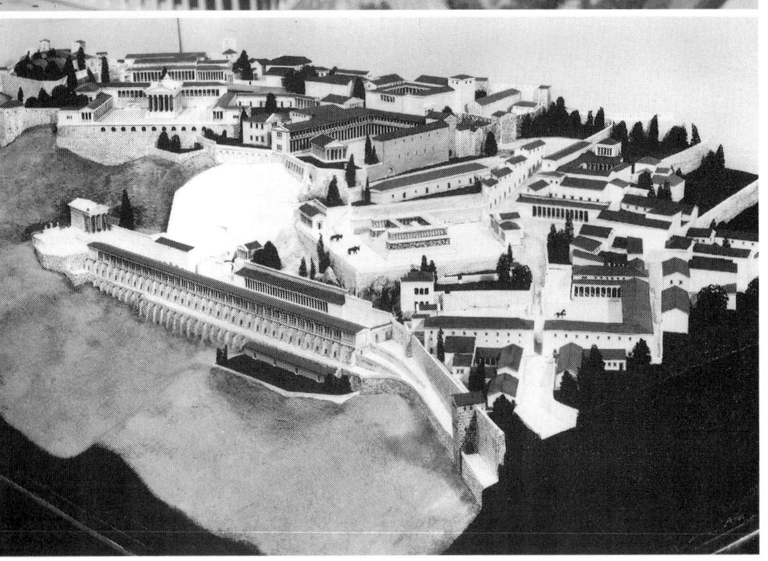

The citadel of Pergamum housed a complete Hellenistic city (of the third century BC) Palaces, barracks for soldiers, a library and theater, temples, *gymnasia*, and other public buildings togethe celebrate the achievements of the Attalid dynasty.

Greek cities flourished in the peaceful conditions of the Roman Empire. At Aphrodisias in Asia Minor the great stadium (first or second century AD, *below*) could seat 30,000 spectators. The theater at Aphrodisias (*right*) overlooked a fourth-century-AD paved area surrounded by *stoas*. The greatest theater of all, at Ephesus (*bottom*), could seat 24,000 spectators. It was here that the preaching of the apostle Paul caused a riot.

Mycenaean pots featured lively designs such as this octopus from an *amphora* of the fifteenth century BC. The style disappeared with the collapse of Mycenaean civilization. By the late eleventh century Athens began developing its own style based on simple geometric designs, as shown in the range of "Protogeometric" pots shown here (*below*). Geometric patterns gradually came to fill the whole surface of the pot. By the eighth century, in the work of the so-called "Dipylon master", stylized "aristocratic" figures appear in a central panel (*above right*).

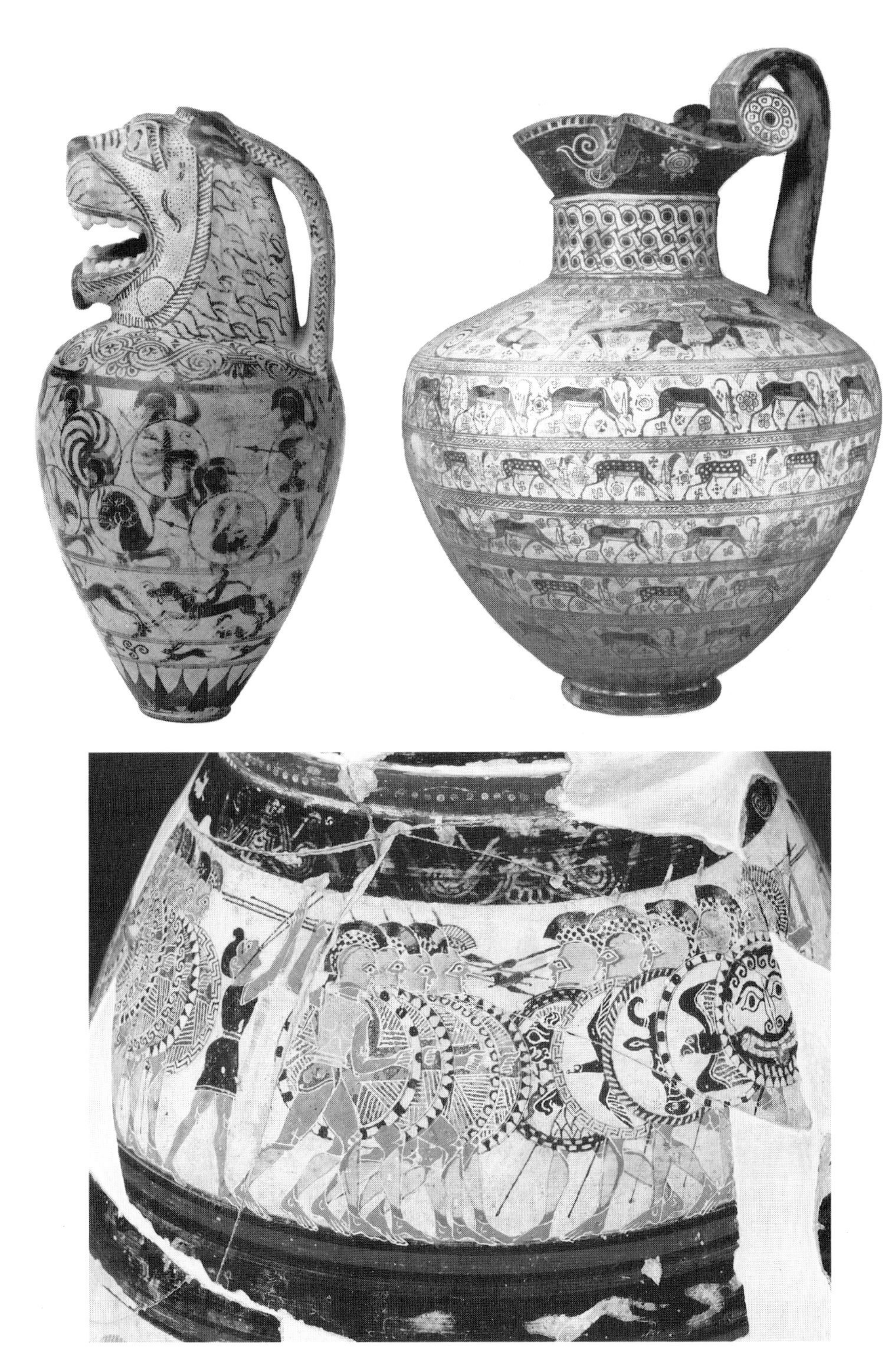

By the mid seventh century Corinthian potters had initiated a luxuriant style which unashamedly drew on images from the east. This tiny jug (*top left*), under three inches high, shows how innovatory the style was. Animals, many fabulous, others recognizable, now run around the surface of pots, as in the wine jar illustrated (*top right*). One of the most famous pots is the Chigi vase (*c.* 650 BC, *above*), which shows hoplite phalanxes advancing toward each other to the sound of the pipes.

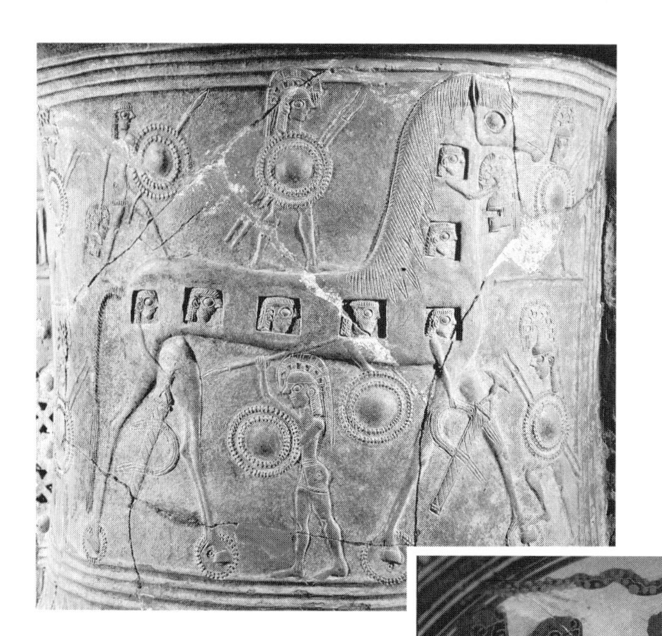

One problem faced by seventh-century potters was how to tell a story in a limited space. The first attempts to do so were ingenious. In a storage jar from Mykonos of about 675 BC (*above*) an attempt is made to convey the story of the fall of Troy by introducing windows into the side of the Trojan horse so that the viewer can see more of the story in one image.

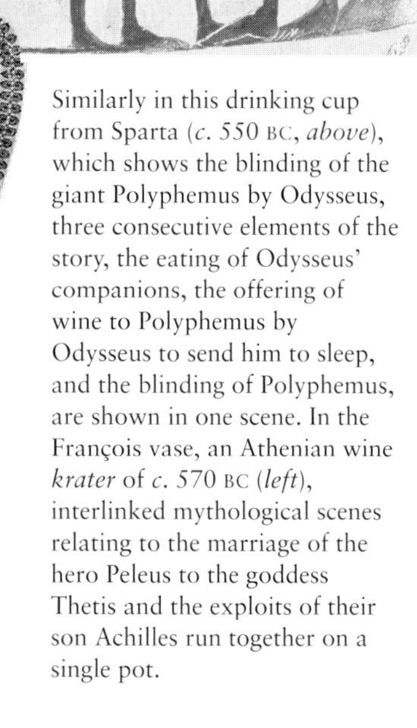

Similarly in this drinking cup from Sparta (*c.* 550 BC, *above*), which shows the blinding of the giant Polyphemus by Odysseus, three consecutive elements of the story, the eating of Odysseus' companions, the offering of wine to Polyphemus by Odysseus to send him to sleep, and the blinding of Polyphemus, are shown in one scene. In the François vase, an Athenian wine *krater* of *c.* 570 BC (*left*), interlinked mythological scenes relating to the marriage of the hero Peleus to the goddess Thetis and the exploits of their son Achilles run together on a single pot.

Sight's eclipsed in my eyes, a clamorous humming
Rings through my eardrums;

Cold sweat drenches down me, shuddering spasms
Rack my whole frame, a greener-than-grassy pallor
Holds me, till I seem a hair's breadth only
This side of dying.

Yet all must be ventured, all endured, since . . .
(Translation: Peter Green)

There is nothing in any of Sappho's poems to suggest that she consummated her love. However, as Kenneth Dover has pointed out, it is just at this time, the late seventh century, that overt homosexuality between men became an accepted part of Greek social life. "A Greek who said 'I'm in love' would not mind being asked 'With a boy, or with a girl?', nor would he mind answering 'With a boy'. . ." There is no reason, despite the lack of evidence, to suppose that women acted differently. With both sexes, homosexuality tended to be confined to the years before marriage, after which heterosexual behavior became the norm.

The openness of Sappho's feelings leads on to another feature of aristocratic Greece, the idealization of the naked male body. The naked body is such a common feature of the artistic world embedded in the Western tradition so successfully that it is made respectable, almost de-eroticized. Yet there are complex cultural inhibitions on the presentation of nakedness in Near Eastern and Egyptian art and these inhibitions are found in Homer. The naked Odysseus covers himself as he encounters Nausicaa after his shipwreck, and in the *Iliad* Odysseus threatens to humiliate the commoner Thersites by stripping off his clothing. However, by the seventh century male nakedness has become acceptable in Greek sculpture. It is found in the *kouros,* the standing naked male in marble, normally presented with its arms stiffly by its side and its left foot forward. (It first appears about 650 B.C.) The proportions and the model are derived from Egypt but the Egyptian statues are clothed. Andrew Stewart in his *Art, Desire and the Body in Ancient Greece* suggests that male nakedness is associated with the portrayal of man in his natural state as the gods created him. Women, however, are presented as clothed as a means of emphasising man's power to control and contain them.

The *kouroi* are found as votive statues, offered normally to the god Apollo—one or two early *kouroi* appear to be representations of the god himself—and found predominantly in his sanctuaries or as grave markers (as was always the case with the Athenian examples). In some areas of Greece, the Peloponnese, for instance, they are hardly found at all. Some were huge, as much as twenty feet (six meters) high, and all must have been expensive commissions. It has become clear that they are associated exclusively with the aristocracy and in cities where the aristocracy is known to have been overthrown they disappear at the same time.

The *kouroi* have to be seen as a statement and it seems to be one concerned with the preservation of aristocratic values at a time when they are threatened. Andrew Stewart sums it up well: "As symbols of a united, ageless, and all enduring aristocracy of individually brilliant men and women, these statues both made concrete and perpetuated its values from generation to generation buttressing it and them against the world at large." The image they present is one of unthreatened and unchanging youthfulness, the moment when the body is at its most perfect. This is a representation of *arete,* excellence, physical beauty allied to nobility of spirit.

The *kouroi* are not simply abstracted shapes. As the sculptor liberates himself from the canonical proportions of Egyptian art, he is free to draw on the actual bodies he sees displayed around him, in the *Gymnasium,* the exercise ground (literally "the place of nakedness"), for instance. Different cities adopted different ideals. In Naxos, the home of marble sculpture, the emphasis was on harmony and grace. The bodies are lean and muscles are not stressed. The Boeotian *kouroi* are much more square set and vigorous. In Athens there is more concern with the structure of the body. However much real bodies are used as models, the archaic *kouroi* still give the impression of being imprisoned in their marble. It was to take the "classical revolution" in art to set them free.

Once the naked male body becomes associated with aristocratic ideals, nakedness becomes, in a word used first by Larissa Bonfante, a "costume" in itself, one which is "worn" in appropriate settings. So in Greek art, heroes, whether they are victors in the games, soldiers who have died defending their city, city founders, or the overthrowers of tyrants, can be displayed naked. In this sense the *kouroi* initiated an important and enduring theme in European art.

Furthermore, it nakedness has become an aristocratic preserve, it is hardly surprising that participants in the games competed naked. After the elimination of "heroic" warfare by the emergence of the hoplite, this was the arena where *arete,* excellence, could best be displayed. In the same way that aristocrats were diverting resources into the production of *kouroi* for their graves and sanctuaries, so too were they focussing on competitive games. By the sixth century the Olympic Games were well established and had taken their final form of nine key events, including running, wrestling, and chariot racing. However, a festival held only once every four years was not enough to satisfy the demand for competitive activity. In the early sixth century more games were founded. The Pythian Games at Delphi were first held in 582, the Isthmian Games the next year, and the Nemean Games at Nemea in the Argolis in 573. The last two were held every two years so in effect there were games somewhere every year. The prizes were, as at Olympia, token ones—a pine crown at the Isthmian games, a crown of wild celery at the Nemean—but the *kudos,* the glory of victory, elevated the victor to heroic status. As Lesley Kurke has suggested, the word *kudos* carried with it connotations of superhuman or talismanic power that stayed with the victor when he returned home. (For more details of the Olympic Games, see Chapter Seven.)

The poet of the games is Pindar (518–438 B.C.), the master of the *epikinia,* the hymns of praise to a victor. *Epikinia* were commissioned by the victors for recital immediately after their victory when still at the games, with another more elaborate version produced for the welcoming ceremony when the victor returned to his home city. The spread of Pindar's patrons are testimony of the success of aristocratic Panhellenism. They came from throughout the Greek world, from Italy and Sicily, Cyrene in Africa, Abdera in Thrace, and the cities of Asia Minor.

There was nothing more magical than a victory at the Olympics. In his first Olympian ode (476 B.C.) Pindar praises Hieron of Syracuse, victor in the horse race:

Water is preeminent and gold, like a fire
burning in the night, outshines
all possessions that magnify men's pride.
But if, my soul, you yearn
to celebrate great games,

look no further
for another star
shining through the deserted ether
brighter than the sun, or for a contest
mightier than Olympia—
where the song
has taken its coronal
design of glory, plaited
in the minds of poets
as they come, calling in Zeus's name,
to the rich radiant hall of Hieron . . .
(Translation: Frank Nisetich)

Pindar's concern is not only to praise the victor. Typically, his victory odes also exalt the victor's family, his household, and this includes any ancestors who have also achieved victory. As Leslie Kurke has shown, Pindar's hymns place the victor within a class, the aristocracy; within a specific family, the *oikos;* but also within the city that gains from his success. In the ode known as *Olympian V* (possibly not by Pindar), a victor, Psaumis, from the city of Kamerina, offers his home city not only the crown he has won in the chariot race and sacrifices of cattle on the city's altars, but the *kudos* itself, with all the talismanic power it brings with it. The city in its turn rewards the victor with a statue, portraying him as he was at the moment of victory, the moment when his *kudos* was at its greatest.

The crucial point made by Lesley Kurke is that by the end of the sixth century B.C. some form of compromise had been made between an aristocracy and city to the mutual benefit of both. The aristocrat is recognized by his city for his victory and given status by it. In return the city benefits from the talismanic power his victory has earned. Aristocratic values are given continued meaning in a changing world. At the same time, the Panhellenic shrines that might offer an alternative focus to the city are transformed into a potential source of glory for the city. They provide the arena in which the city can display its aristocratic citizens in the hope of the rewards brought back by their victory. This successful mediation helps explain why a Panhellenic world could exist alongside a mass of competing city-states and each could take sustenance from the other.

6

Underlying Patterns: Land and Slavery

So when first the time for ploughing appears to mortal men,
then set yourselves hard to it, your slaves and you
yourself, ploughing in wet and dry through the time of the ploughing,
pressing on with the task early in the morning, so your fields may be full.
Plough in the spring; earth turned over also in the summer will not let you down.
Sow the fallow land when the soil is still getting light;
Fallow land is a defense against disaster, and a comfort for the children.
Pray to Zeus of the Earth and to holy Demeter
so that Demeter's holy grain may ripen in good weight,
when first you begin the ploughing, when you take the end of the plough
handle in your hand, and apply the stick to the back of the oxen,
as they pull the yoke-bar by the straps.
Have a slave
keep a little behind with the mattock to make hard work for the birds
by hiding the seed. Good management is best
for mortal men, and bad management is worst . . .

(Translation from *The Cambridge Illustrated History of Greece*, ed. Paul Cartledge)

The poet Hesiod provides a vivid reminder of the demands of agricultural life as they were in the Greek world in 700 B.C. and remained throughout Greek history. As Robin Osborne points out in his *Classical Landscape with Figures* these demands are hardly mentioned in the literary sources and only rarely even on pottery. Yet this was the reality of everyday life for 90 percent of the Greeks. Greek society cannot be understood unless this underlying dependence on the produce of its land is appreciated.

The primary unit for production, the storage of goods and its consumption in the Greek world, was the *oikos,* or household which produced largely for its own needs. (The Greeks used the word *oikonomia* to describe the management of a household and its possessions and this is the source of the English word "economy.") *Oikos* is a difficult word to use as its meaning shifted according to context. The word described not only the house itself but those who lived within, the husband and wife and family and those who sustained their daily life, including their slaves who earned their inclusion not as human members of the *oikos* but as part of the household property. It also included the land on which the household depended for its survival—and could even be used more generally to describe the clan to which the householder belonged (compare Shakespeare's "a plague on both your houses" in *Romeo and Juliet*).

In most parts of Greece the *oikos* was an independent economic unit normally sustained by a landholding. Robin Osborne quotes an extract from a fourth-century-B.C. lawsuit which gives a vivid picture of how the setup worked in the case of a wealthier *oikos:*

> But Theophemos, instead of following on to the money-changer's and collecting the fine, went and took fifty fine soft-woolled sheep of mine and their shepherd and all the hardware involved in shepherding; then he grabbed a young servant boy carrying a bronze water vessel . . . And they weren't satisfied with getting these, they invaded my land—I have a farm near the racecourse and have lived there since I was a young lad—and first they made a surprise assault on the slaves, and when these got away from them and ran off in various directions they went to the house, knocked down the gate that leads to the garden . . . attacked my wife and children and made off with all the goods and chattels that were left to me in the house.
>
> (Quoted in R. Osborne, *Classical Landscape with Figures*)

Here there is a home where the women and children are secluded; a garden, presumably for vegetables, which has to be gated off to protect its crop; a farm worked by slaves and a flock of sheep with its own shepherd and equipment.

The ownership of land brought not only economic self-sufficiency but status and independence (in the sense of lack of dependency on others for work). Evidence from 400 B.C. suggests that only some five thousand out of some twenty-five thousand to thirty thousand Athenian citizens owned no land at all. A typical family unit in Attica seems to have been between ten and fifteen acres (four and six hectares), in Euboea somewhat larger. A study of one Greek colony on the Black Sea showed that its equal plots had an area of some eleven acres (four and a half hectares). As for wealthier individuals, evidence from lists of land confiscated from Athenian aristocrats accused of sacrilege in 415 suggest that they may have held up to seventy-four acres (thirty hectares) of land. Typically this was scattered among several plots (*kleroi,* singular *kleros*). There was a definite advantage in this in that the extreme variability in local climates could be insured against. Some crop somewhere was likely to survive each year. These figures need to be set against modern calculations that a plot of more than seven acres (some three hectares) would have been sufficient in antiquity to support a family of five.

The larger estates were exceptions. The Greek custom of dividing land equally among sons meant that landholdings were easily fragmented and plots of only five acres (two hectares), on or below mere subsistence level, were common. (Fragmentation persists. One study of modern Greek farming found a farmer with seventy-four acres [thirty hectares] divided into twenty different plots, the farthest some five miles [eight kilometers] apart.) The attraction of a new colony in the Black Sea for poorer farmers seems obvious from this, and those who remained with tiny plots would often have been forced into cooperation with each other or to become tenants or sharecroppers to larger landholders. (Many Greek sanctuaries had land of their own which they leased out at what appear to have been reasonable rents, in one case about 4 percent of the estimated annual grain yield of the land.) The very worst fate of all for a free Greek was to become a landless laborer.

In essence, the world of Greek farming was the world of the small to middling peasant with all the attributes of that world, careful husbandry, conservatism, and misogynism ("But then," moans one farmer in Aristophanes, "I married a niece of Megacles . . . a town lady—

proud, luxurious, extravagant . . .") although in comparison to later European examples there were probably less feudal dues or taxation. Karl Marx derided this world, comparing peasants to sacks of potatoes, but what comes through from the growing range of archaeological evidence is the ingenuity and pragmatism of the Greek farmer. He wanted to progress beyond mere survival, to gather resources for sacrifices, dowries, and communal feasting.

How was his surplus to be increased? There is no evidence of any revolution in farming methods in ancient Greece. Agriculture remained, as it had always been, highly labor intensive. Higher productivity, in fifth-century Attica at least, seems to have been achieved through taking in marginal land and using fertilizer, human and animal manure, more intensively. (A study of classical houses in the city of Haleis in the southern Argolid shows that they had stone-lined pits with a capacity of six and a half cubic yards (five cubic meters) in which human and animal excrement was accumulated before dispersal.) However, this does not mean that farmers were inflexible. An important study of a comparatively remote area of the southern Argolid in the Peloponnese, *Beyond the Acropolis, A Rural Greek Past*, by Tjeer van Andel and Curtis Runnels shows how farmers adapted to growing markets. The region is typical of Greece, 80 percent of it mountain, 20 percent plain and valley floors. The soil is of moderate quality and the area has some contact with the wider world through the sea. Like many parts of the Peloponnese the southern Argolid became virtually deserted in the Dark Age and it was not until the eighth century that there was renewed settlement along the valleys. At first only grain was produced but population growth in the following centuries went hand in hand with the exploitation of more marginal land, often steep and stony, and less able to retain moisture. Here olives were grown with possibly some grain among their roots. This was a significant step. Olives take years to mature and require capital, equipment, oil presses and jars, with which to process and store the produce. The greatest period of prosperity for the area was in the fourth century, a time of disruption for much of the rest of Greece. In this period all the region's lowland towns were situated on harbors suggesting that the prosperity was related to growing external markets. Where did the oil go? Athens, relatively accessible by sea, seems to have lost many of her olive trees in the Peloponnesian War and may have been desperate for imports as her population recovered faster than any replanted trees came into crop. Other important fourth-century cities within reach of the Argolid such as Thebes had few olives of their own. So here, it seems, is the population of a comparatively remote area sensing the rise of new markets and exploiting them. It was not to last. The disruptions of the early Hellenistic period and possibly the rise of piracy led to the collapse of the olive industry of the southern Argolid and a retreat by farmers to the more fertile grain-bearing areas.

Within a single estate a Greek farmer might exploit a variety of sources of income, from sheep and goats, woodland (tree cutting was carried out in August when there was free labor after the harvest), and vegetables. The spinning of wool and the weaving of cloth were major contributions of the women who would also bake bread, make cheese, and milk goats. The most common surpluses were in grain, olive oil, and wine. Much of this was traded locally through barter. Grain, in particular, tended to be gathered and stored within the city. It was too precious a resource to trade overseas. In Athens the export of grain was forbidden by law and the Athenian Assembly discussed the state of the grain reserves no less than ten times a year. Although it has been argued that Athens' dependence on grain has been exaggerated, a recent study by Michael Whitby argues that perhaps half her grain needs did come from overseas. It is significant that the trade was in the hands of foreigners. It was apparently too demeaning an occupation for an Athenian citizen whose status depended on producing grain from his own land rather than bringing it from elsewhere.

How much was traded outside the city, with whom and for what in return has proved one of the most difficult and controversial areas of ancient history. Moses Finley in his *The Ancient Economy* (1973) argued that intercity trade was minimal and overwhelmingly based on agricultural products. Local traders took their chances when they saw them on an opportunistic basis. The scale of trade was limited by the difficulty of transporting heavy goods such as grain large distances. There were few trading relationships in which stable markets mutually dependent on each other had grown up and very little in the way of trade in manufactured goods. This view has been challenged but there remains the fundamental problem that there are virtually no data on the perishable goods which made up the bulk of trade, so what can be said with any certainty is limited. Field surveys, such as the one just mentioned in the southern Argolid, do, however, suggest that farmers were prepared to make long-term shifts in their produce in order to supply outside markets. There is also evidence from the pottery trade that Athenian potters, for instance, did create pots for specific communities in Italy. Even if the scale and sophistication of Athenian trade were altogether exceptional it could well be that trade was more developed and more oriented to specific markets than Finley recognized.

Field surveys with their patient accumulation of a mass of pottery have done much to explain the relationships between town and country. There are immense problems in defining what actually constitutes a site or settlement from the scatters of pottery that survive, but the more meticulous surveyors have claimed that they have found up to a hundred times as many sites in a landscape than were previously known. What these surveys have shown is that each city-state evolved its own survival strategies. It had to balance having a population scattered around the city's territory, its *chora,* the land outside the city walls, and so able to exploit its land to the full, with the needs for protection and a social life. The city itself was the core of its identity, a means of expressing its pride through public buildings, the mechanism through which it related to the outside world and mediated its relationship with the gods through community worship. This city would typically be placed near the most fertile land, yet close to a natural feature, such as an acropolis, that could be defended. The advantages of being close to the sea in a mountainous country where the transport of heavy goods by land was all but impossible were obvious.

Surveys show that the relationship between the city itself and settlements outside its walls shifted over time. The island of Melos in the Cyclades has comparatively rich soil and when it was first occupied in the eighth century farmers tended to move out all over the island to exploit its fertility. Over a hundred settlement sites are known over the almost 60 square miles (150 square kilometers) of the island. Over time the number of settlements fall, to eighty by classical times and then down to less than thirty. Meanwhile, the larger settlements on the island such as the city of Melos itself grow. People are moving from the countryside to the city. The city has clearly evolved some functions which it did not have in earlier times. It may have become a center of exchange as farmers became more prosperous. There may have been some prestige or social advantage involved in living in a city rather than in an outlying settlement.

In other situations, in parts of mainland Greece, for instance, the opposite happens. In the classical period, more rather than less outlying settlements appear. Often these settlements begin to achieve some identity of their own with their own temples and theaters, for instance, although they are still subservient to the main city. The demes of Attica are the best example. These were permanent settlements with their own identities and their own legally defined populations—each Athenian citizen was allocated to a particular deme. It is hard to know what were the pressures that led to the greater number of outlying settlements—population increase, perhaps, or the need to forge a social identity in a smaller unit. These settlements may have grown precisely because the authority of the city had become more established so that there was the security in which resources could be transferred to outlying areas and protected there. In other parts of Greece it seems a lack of security remained a problem in more remote areas. Farmers are found building themselves their own towers presumably to shelter inside at time of unrest.

In short, there was no common pattern to the relationship between the main city and its surrounding territory. What is clear is that the relationship between town and country remained very close. Even Athens in its heyday relied heavily on its surrounding natural resources and the vast majority of its citizens were dependent on their own land, rather than an occupation or trade, for income. There is no sense of an urban elite who used the countryside primarily as a leisure resource and looked down on the more ignorant country dweller. Such an idea comes only in Hellenistic times when poems about the countryside are written by urban poets who clearly see the countryside as something to enjoy or use as a backdrop to tales of love and seduction in shady groves.

In his survey of farming, Hesiod mentions in passing the household slave who will help with the harvest. By the fifth and fourth centuries slave owning appears to have spread quite widely among Athenians with a modest household containing two or three (who might be diverted to work in the fields at busy times) and a richer one up to fifteen (Aristotle is credited with thirteen household slaves, one of whom he kept as a sexual partner after the death of his wife, Plato with six). A typical price for a male slave was some 150 drachmas, about what a skilled worker would earn in six months (though in one auction prices for adult slaves ranged from 85 to 240 drachmas). The immediate need of the Athenian citizen would have been to avoid the drudgery of everyday living, a luxury which his status as a beneficiary of a successful *polis* allowed him. Slaves would do all the household work, cooking, baking, and spinning as well as running errands and collecting water. (One disgruntled Athenian complained that slaves were so indistinguishable from everyone else in the streets that people held back from striking slaves for fear of striking a citizen instead.)

The sheer scale and the degree to which Greek society was dependent on slavery has always been difficult for admirers of the ancient Greeks to deal with. However, there is no escaping the reality. There are slaves mentioned in Mycenaean times, in the Pylos tablets, and they are there as a backdrop to everyday aristocratic living in Homer. The problem lies in assessing their status in that period. In the *Odyssey* there are examples of friendship and even emotional intimacy between master (or mistress) and slave. Eumaeus, Odysseus' swineherd, had been carried off by Phoenicians and sold to Odysseus' father. Yet he was trusted and encouraged to tell his story and confides to Odysseus how much slaves enjoy gossip with their mistresses as well as the occasional gift. Odysseus responds by acknowledging the horror of what Eumaeus has been through but suggests that now he is well looked after. It would be naive to think that this was anything like the norm (Eumaeus came originally from a noble family) but it contrasts with a much harsher and more legalistic approach in the coming centuries.

Evidence from both Athens and the island of Chios (from where there is the earliest mention of "barbarians" bought in bulk for money and evidence of slave plantations) links the institutionalization and extension of slavery with the coming of democracy. One of the many ways in which a citizen could define his status as a freeman was by having the absolute power to compel others to labor for him. Not only were the basic chores, whether in the home or on the land, actually completed but the status of the owner was reinforced. In the fourth century Aristotle articulated his theory that some were naturally masters and others necessarily slaves by relating the state of freedom or slavery to the physical environment. As he put it in *The Politics*:

> The nations inhabiting the cold places and those of Europe are full of spirit but somewhat deficient in intelligence and skill, so

> that they continue comparatively free, but lacking in political organisation and capacity to rule their neighbours. The people of Asia on the other hand are intelligent and skillful in temperament, but lack spirit so that they are in continuous subjection and slavery. But the Greek race participates in both characters, just as it occupies the middle position geographically, for it is both spirited and intelligent: hence it continues to be free and to have very good political institutions and to be capable of ruling all mankind.
>
> (Translation: H. Rackham, Loeb Classical Library Edition)

For most Greeks this Aristotelian logic would not have been important—slaves came from the places where there was the opportunity to capture them; the Black Sea area, in particular Thrace, was an early source and then, as the Greek cities of the Asian coastline recovered their independence after the Persian wars and began raiding inland, Caria (the southwest of modern Turkey). Some twenty thousand slaves were taken after the Athenian victory at the Eurymedon River in 468. Typically, a slave was snatched from his or her native culture and sold to a Greek master. There were supposed compensations within the new culture, an ancient ceremony of welcome to the home which had some analogies with those ceremonies of welcome of a new bride, but they can hardly have meant much to those who may have known defeat and the emotional disorientation which came from being uprooted from their homes. It was difficult to make new relationships (Xenophon talks of the women's quarters being closed off from the men's "so that slaves would not breed without permission") and a foreign language can only have deepened the sense of isolation and humiliation. The slave was a possession and his legal identity existed only at this level. He was, according to Aristotle in one of his less happy assertions, not even capable of rational thought. Good treatment tended not to be a reflection of any concern with him as an individual but as a by-product of the Greek concern to behave without excess and to safeguard material possessions. So the slave might have been fed regularly but primarily to keep him in good working order. It was, however, possible for an owner to free slaves and there are several cases known of freedmen in Athens becoming bankers and making their fortunes.

Violence against slaves and their sexual abuse were freely allowed.

In case one retained any illusions about the lot of the domestic slave the potential horror of the relationship could be seen in the Athenian requirement that slaves be tortured before giving evidence in law. The two parties to the case agreed to the degree of torture allowed. As one character in Aristophanes puts it: "Pile bricks on him; stuff his nose with acid; flay, rack him, hoist him; flog him with a scourge of prickly bristles . . . Torture him in any way you please." The master could claim compensation for any long-term disability which resulted from the damage of his "property." In one case where a defendant in a law case refused to hand over his female slaves for torture it was seen as an admission that he knew his case was weak.

It was when they were in a segregated mass that slaves were at their most vulnerable. In the mines they seem to have been particularly expendable. Yvon Garlon in her study of Greek slavery quotes Diodurus Siculus (a Greek historian of the first century B.C.) on mining slaves in Egypt. "No leniency or respite of any kind is given to any man who is sick or maimed, or aged, or in the case of a woman for her weakness, but all without exception are compelled by blows to persevere in their labours, until through ill treatment they die in the midst of their tortures." Very similar conditions were to be found in the Athenian silver mines where slaves were hired out in large teams. (One man, Nicias, alone had a thousand slaves for hire.) This was the world of the forced labor camp and, to the extent that mining underpinned the prosperity of Athens, made it partly a slave economy. During the Peloponnesian War one of the most successful strategies conducted against Athens by the Spartans was to set up a fortified base at Decelea, near Athens, to which slaves could flee. About twenty thousand did so and this was considered by Thucydides to be a major blow to the city's economy.

The helots of Spartan-controlled Messenia were an unusual example of slavery as they were Greeks and they lived in their original homeland, in effect maintaining their sense of identity against their Spartan overlords for centuries. (They set up their own city when freed from Spartan control in the fourth century.) They kept their family units and had some rights to property. They were an essential element of the Spartan economy and also provided a reserve of manpower at times of military crisis. However, it was just their cohesion which made them vulnerable. The possibility of revolt was much greater and so their treatment was correspondingly harsher. Every year there was a formal declaration of war on the helots. Every potential leader was noted and eliminated while part of the training of a Spartan adolescent placed him among the helots and left him free to terrorize them.

Successful farming depended above all on peace, but this seldom obtained in Greece. The period 480 to 431, when the Peloponnesian War broke out, was wholly exceptional in its relative lack of conflict and even then there were wars in Boeotia in the 450s and 440s. After 431 B.C. came a long period of almost continuous warfare and disruption and the scale of warfare became greater as time went on. (See Chapter Fifteen for developments in warfare in the fourth century.) The impact on agriculture must have been severe. Surpluses were never large in any case and two of the three staple crops, the vine and the olive, needed several years (fifteen in the case of olives) to reach maturity. The evidence suggests that in the fourth century hundreds of thousands of Greeks lost their land and were forced into exile. Cities were razed to the ground, their populations transported or sold into slavery. Trade routes were disrupted. (It was the successful closing off of the Hellespont, and hence Athens' grain supplies, which brought the city to its knees in 404 B.C.) These disruptions will be described in later chapters. The Greek economy, near subsistence farming supported by a trading network which allowed some transfer of surpluses, was always vulnerable. It says much for the resilience and ingenuity of the Greek farmer that it worked as well as it did.

7

Underlying Patterns: Spiritual Life

There is one race of men, one race of gods; both have breath of life from a single mother [Gaia, the earth, according to legend]. But sundered power holds us divided, so that the one is nothing, while for the other the brazen sky is established as their sure citadel for ever. Yet we have some likeness, in great intelligence, or strength, to the immortals, though we know not what the day will bring, what course after nightfall destiny has written that we must run to the end.

Pindar, *Nemean* 6. (Translation: Richard Buxton)

While individual city-states were creating their own political and social structures in the Archaic age, Greek culture was developing an underlying cohesion through its shared religious beliefs. While the Egyptians saw gods in the sun, the sky, and in animals and the Jews worshipped a distant, awesome creator God, the Greeks, from earliest times had seen their gods as anthropomorphic, that is, having the attributes of human beings as the result of a common primeval mother (Gaia, the earth). There were no inhibitions in representing the gods, in sculpture and painting, for instance, in human form although there were conventions in the way this was done. Gods were never portrayed as older than middle age and it was not until the fourth century that Praxiteles scandalized the Greek world by presenting a full-size sculpture of Aphrodite naked.

Supreme among the divine powers were the twelve Olympians. The Olympians were not eternal beings; most of them has stories of their births associated with them and they had only achieved their preeminence through overthrowing another group of gods, the Titans. However, they were immortal, nourished by ambrosia, nectar, and the smoke of sacrifices in their home on Mount Olympus. In mythology they were presented as a family. Zeus, the father of the gods, is the brother of Poseidon, god of the sea, and of Demeter, the goddess of corn. Hera, the wife of Zeus, conceived Hephaestus, the smith god, without a male partner, and Ares, the god of war through Zeus, although Zeus hated his son for the destruction he was able to bring to mankind. Zeus fathered through a variety of partners Athena, Apollo, Artemis (a goddess of hunting but also of childbirth), Aphrodite, Hermes, and Dionysus. Hephaestus and Aphrodite are married but Aphrodite frequently cuckolds her husband. The gods are not without feelings; they know grief (Zeus is distraught when he cannot save his son Sarpedon from death in the Trojan War), anger, and sexual desire.

The attributes of the female gods cover the full range of sexuality, from the virginity of Athena and Artemis to the lustful enjoyment of sex by Aphrodite. However, the goddesses can be divided into two groups: the virgins, Athena, Artemis, Hestia (the goddess of the hearth, who is not always classed as an Olympian), and those who do enjoy sexual relationships, Hera (who is ready to wear out Zeus with ardent lovemaking so that she can carry out her own designs while he recovers his strength in sleep), Demeter, and above all Aphrodite, who is the goddess of sexuality itself. The virgin goddesses are usually given specifically protective roles: Athena of cities, Artemis of hunters, and Hestia of the hearth, and hence the home. This may be because their inviolability is seen to give them power (once a real woman submits to marriage and a sexual life she is no longer independent) and so they can be cast in these more powerful roles. It has to be said that the meaning of the myths surrounding goddesses have proved enormously difficult to interpret, particularly when they are given roles that involve masculine traits (Athena as warrior, for example).

Although Greek mythology presented the Olympians as a family, their actual historical origins are very varied. Zeus has an ancient Indo-European ancestry and is present in Greece by Mycenaean times, as are Poseidon and Hera and possibly Athena and Artemis (in the Linear B tablets). Other deities, such as Aphrodite, were later imports from the East while even the "Mycenaean" gods adopted attributes from other cultures or absorbed them from local cults during the following centuries. As a result each god or goddess acquired certain powers, ways of operating and spheres of influence, built up from many different sources over time. There was no sacred book or presiding priesthood that tried to freeze the attributes of any deity, so they developed flexibly to suit local situations. Zeus, for example, is a father figure, the most powerful of the gods, the bringer of military victory, a symbol of sexual potency, the protector of justice, and the upholder of rulers as well as the god of thunder and lightning. Athena was associated with Athens from the earliest times but she is also a more far-reaching protectress of cities and their strongholds (in Argos and Sparta, for instance). She is a goddess of war, urging on the Greeks at Troy, but as so often with Greek deities she is also concerned with the opposites, peaceful interests such as weaving and the protection of olive trees. (Olive oil is the prize in the Panathenaic Games held in her honour.) She is also a goddess of carpenters and credited with the construction of the first ship. She transcends the boundary between masculine and feminine.

The interlocking structure of divine power can be seen by exploring the natures of Apollo and Dionysus, opposites but also complementary to each other. Apollo is not known before the eighth century when he appears in epic poetry and at his main shrines, his birth place on the island of Delos and his remote mountain oracle at Delphi. At Delphi he acts as the communicator between the gods and the human race. He is always portrayed as young, associated with youth and the concerns of youth, athletics and education, poetry and music, and later, philosophy. His origins may, in fact, lie in his role as patron of the initiation ceremonies of youths into adulthood. His instrument is the lyre, a harmonious instrument, and through it he becomes known as the god of order and reason. Yet, like all the Greek gods, he can also be a god of vengeance, the bringer of plague (this is an attribute which seems to have been acquired from the East) but as so often, the power to destroy goes hand in hand with its opposite, the power to heal and purify. He cures those who are polluted and frees them for new roles (murderers are freed to found new colonies, for instance). The healing god Asclepius is his son.

While Apollo stands for order and boundaries, Dionysus is the god who transcends boundaries. He is the god of wine who gave the vine to the human race and thus the possibility of drunkenness and disorder. He is associated with wild places, the rich growth of wild plants, and sexuality. (A model phallus was often carried in his processions.) His routs are ecstatic dances, often performed in the mountains by women worshippers, the Maenads, who work themselves into a frenzy to the sound of flute and drums before collapsing. He is also a god who changes his identity through adopting a mask and hence brings the possibility of personal transformation. The drama festivals are celebrated in his honor (see Chapter Twelve). In legend Dionysus and Apollo are often placed together as if their powers need to feed on each other. Dionysus was given a place at Delphi alongside Apollo. In the passing of time one gives way to the other; Dionysus is associated with winter, Apollo with summer; Apollo with the day, Dionysus with the night. It is a reminder of the completeness of the Greek spiritual experience; reason and unbridled emotions are both given their homes but it is recognized that in a healthy *cosmos* order needs to be balanced by disorder, the measured tones of the lyre by the impassioned fervor of the beating drum. (The idea of Apollo and Dionysus as complementary opposites was stressed by the German philosopher Freidrich Nietzche in his *The Birth of Tragedy* [1872]. He argued that the stress on Apollo and the progressive march of reason, exemplified by Greek culture after Euripides and Socrates [see Chapter Thirteen] had stifled a more primeval, pessimistic aspect of the Greeks represented by Dionysus. The essence of the Greeks, he claimed, is to be found in their early tragic drama.)

In many cases the specific attributes or interests of a god are personified by forces or beings which act as mediators between human beings and the gods. Dike, justice, the special preserve of Zeus, appears in the poems of Hesiod as a woman. Those who feel they have been treated unjustly can appeal to her and she in her turn approaches Zeus on their behalf and he can bring revenge on an impious community. In her turn she has a daughter Eunomia, good order, who works actively to calm unrest in a city. Aphrodite is associated with Eros, love; Athena with victory, Nike, who is personified as a small winged figure held in Athena's hand. Nike is a celebratory figure. Among the glories of the Paris Louvre is the Nike of Samothrace, a Victory with great outstretched wings, which probably commemorated a third-century naval success. Ares, the god of war, on the one hand, is surrounded by more awesome forces, the personifications of Fear and Terror. Asclepius, the god of medicine, on the other hand, has daughters Hygieia and Panacea (both adopted as terms in the later history of medicine). By the fourth century some of these personified forces were being given cult worship in their own right. The most spectacular success was that enjoyed by another daughter of Zeus, Tyche, fortune (normally good fortune), who became a major cult figure in Hellenistic times.

The Olympians stood out from among a mass of lesser gods. Some of these, Hades, for instance, were associated with death and could not even be mentioned by name. Others were local gods whose powers and attributes remained limited even if their cults spread more widely. Pan, the goat god, was centered on Arcadia in the central Peloponnese. A god of shepherds, his cult spread throughout Greece through the fifth and fourth centuries, but he never ranked among the Olympians. He became the god held responsible for spreading panic to armies and also a symbol of sexual obsession. Hestia was universally honored as the goddess of the hearth but was seldom given Olympian status. According to legend her identification with one fixed place, the hearth, prevented her joining the gods on Olympus, while ancient taboos surrounding the hearth seem also to have given her perpetual virginity so that she could never be joined to the Olympian family in marriage.

The minor gods and goddesses merge into the heroes, many of whom are children of the the gods and human partners. Heracles (the Roman Hercules), perhaps the greatest of the heroes, was the son of Zeus and a mortal woman, Alcmene. Hera, Zeus' wife, hated him and attempted to poison him by sending serpents to his cradle. The baby Heracles, already superhuman in strength, killed them with his bare hands. As a response to the hatred of Hera, Heracles acquired the protection of Athena and then embarked on a career in which his enormous strength was used to subdue a variety of awesome animals (the Nemean lion, a Cretan bull, and a boar from Arcadia) and complete seemingly impossible tasks like the cleaning out of the Augean stables. He emerged as a protective figure who was given cult worship by his adherents almost on the same level as that of a god. Rulers of the Peloponnese (where his cult appears to have originated), the Pisistratids of Athens and the royal family of Macedonia all adopted him as their protector. Other heroes enjoyed more local support, as the savior of a particular city. Theseus was the protector of Athens, "appearing" when most needed at the battle of Marathon, and linked to the bringing of democratic government to the city. Heroes may be mythical but some really existed, the founders of new cities, for instance, or overthrowers of tyranny such as Harmodius and Aristogeiton in Athens (page 166).

This profusion of divine figures who ranged from all-powerful but remote Olympian gods to human beings honored after their death (there is no evidence of any Greek general receiving cult worship during his lifetime before the Spartan Lysander in the early fourth century though there were occasions when Olympic victors did so) helped blur the division between the sacred and the profane. There were places and things in the Greek world that had permanent sanctity. They would include temples, for instance, their surrounding sanctuaries, and statues of the gods. For others sanctity was more ephemeral. Places, people, and actions could acquire sacredness when they were endowed with that quality through ritual. An animal brought for sacrifice and the man who carried out the sacrifice had no intrinsic sacred quality until they became involved in the ritual of sacrifice, and even the altar where the sacrifice took place only took on its full readiness for the ceremony when the basket containing the sacrificial knife had been carried around it.

Rituals are ceremonies or a series of activities which accompany any significant moment in a community's life and which are traditionally carried out in the same form from year to year or occasion to occasion. It is the repetition which is important. By placing rituals at fixed times, in designated places, or to mark particular moments, such as the transition of a youth to adulthood, marriage, or death, a human society achieves stability and psychological security. It is probable, in fact, that a society which did not order its existence through rituals would collapse into chaos. (There is a famous anthropological study, *The Mountain People* by Colin Turnbull, which charts the disintegration of the Ik people of central Africa as ancient rituals were abandoned under the stress of economic change.)

In Greek society every kind of relationship could be structured ritualistically, even the way in which a lover was approached or an illness was treated, but normally ritual was concerned with public affairs, the marking of a new season, the welcoming of children as adult citizens, preparation before battle, the opening of a session of the people's Assembly. It was a feature of Greek ritual that it was always carried through under the auspices of the gods. Hence ritual can never be separated from spiritual life. It might be in fact designed as a means of communicating with the gods, as sacrifice was, or as a means of asking the protection of the gods for the event to be celebrated. As in other societies rituals in Greece were reinforced by their repetition over generations so that the abandonment or omission of a ritual (or even its carrying out in the wrong way) brought a sense of foreboding, the fear that the gods would withdraw protection or wreak revenge. When

Thucydides describes the plague of 430 in Athens he seems as much concerned with the abandonment of the rituals of burial, because of the sheer numbers to be buried, as with the loss of life itself.

It was the city that normally mediated between the individual citizen and the gods by providing rituals, festivals, communal feasting, the building of city temples, through which the community as a whole could seek divine protection. In so far as piety can be defined in the Greek world it lay in public participation in the city's rituals. The citizen had to be seen helping his fellow citizens to secure the good will of the gods if he was to be truly a citizen. His participation in the rituals that sustained the support of the gods was as important as any other political activity. Any act of impiety which threatened the relationship had to be condemned. Acts of sacrilege might include the desecration of a sanctuary or the statue of a god (this is why a mutilation of the Herms [figures of Hermes with an erect phallus which served as boundary markers] in Athens in 415 aroused such horror), the introduction of a new god, or the denial of the existence of old gods. Even the incorrect use of words during a ceremony (*blasphemia*) could threaten the relationship. These crimes of sacrilege made their perpetrator polluted and his pollution (*miasma*) could spread the anger of the gods to the whole community in the form, perhaps, of plague, famine, or the infertility of women. The penalty the community had to inflict on the offender was death, or at the very least exile. Similarly the committing of a murder was seen to pollute the whole city. Mythologically it was believed that the murderer would be pursued by the Furies. In real life, a murderer, as a polluted person, could not be approached, talked to, sacrificed with, or welcomed into a home (but he could be purged of his pollution by Apollo and then sent into exile). In Athens it was a responsibility of the murdered man's kinsmen to prosecute the murderer and if they did not act to remove the polluted man they themselves were guilty of impiety. Those who had been associated with the dead, particularly closest relatives, were also assumed to be polluted and could be temporarily excluded from any sanctuary.

While the city community defined and judged the acts of impiety which threatened its own well-being, the wrath of the gods could also fall on any individual. The gods were sensitive to excess of any kind, in particular any act of pride which infringed their own role as controllers of nature. *Hubris,* the humiliation of others simply for one's own pleasure or to show off one's superiority was not only an unpardonable offense against the victim, but offended the gods' sense of moral order. This was Xerxes' offense when he attempted to conquer the Hellespont by building a bridge over it. His humiliation by the Greeks was the gods' revenge.

Even more offensive was any direct attack on objects sacred to the gods. As Sophocles put it in a Chorus from *Oedipus Tyrannus:*

But if any man comes striding, high and mighty
in all he says and does,
no fear of justice, no reverence
for the temples of the gods,
let a rough doom tear him down,
repay his pride, breakneck, ruinous pride!
If he cannot reap his profits fairly,
cannot restrain himself from outrage,
mad, laying hands on holy things untouchable!
Can such a man, so desperate, still boast
he can save his life from the flashing bolts of god?
(Translation: E. F. Watling)

Similarly, when an oath was made the gods were seen as its guarantors and so those breaking an oath could expect divine retribution. Punishment for this and other misdoings could continue down the generations. The curse imposed on the Alcmaeonid clan in seventh-century B.C. Athens was not forgotten and may have affected seven hundred families some two hundred years later. The device of passing the gods' revenge down the generations helped explain, of course, why seemingly pious men might suddenly suffer misfortune. (On the other hand, success in games, in war, or in the overthrowing of tyrants was believed to make the recipients especially honored of the gods, even to the extent of deserving cult worship after death.)

Nor did it matter than an individual knew he had offered the gods. The tragedy of Oedipus lay in his punishment for crimes (killing his father and marrying his mother) which he could not have possibly known he was committing. (He had been separated from his parents at birth and so recognized neither of them.) Retribution could be terrible. In Euripides' *Hippolytus,* Hippolytus is killed after a bull sent by Poseidon drives his chariot onto a great rock. Others die in war as the gods abandon or destroy them. The Greek gods, it has been said, were neither good nor evil, but simply powerful. The protection of humans was not their main concern.

However, human beings were not completely helpless. Although the ways of the gods were unknowable, they honored loyalty to friends, respect given to suppliants (on the grounds that they were without the protection of their city but gained instead the protection of Zeus), and the fulfilling of obligations made to others. The relationship between man and gods rested in fact on this sense of obligation—a sacrifice to the gods was understood to deserve divine favor in return, though this favor could never be guaranteed. In the *Iliad* the priest Chryses, anxious to get the god Apollo to wreak havoc on the Greeks who have humiliated him, reminds the god of the temple he has provided for him and the many sacrifices he has carried out. His hope is that Apollo will reciprocate the favor shown him—as he does—by sending a plague on the Greeks! His prayer takes a typical form in reciting the god's titles, stressing the sacrifices made and then submitting the request:

Hear me,
lord of the silver bow who set your power above Chryse
and Killa, the sacrosanct, who are lord in strength over Tenedos,
Smintheus, if ever it pleased your heart that I built your temple,
if it ever pleased you that I burnt all the rich thigh pieces
of bulls, of goats, then bring to pass this wish I pray for:
let your arrows make the Danaans [Greeks] pay for my tears shed.
(Translation: Richmond Lattimore)

Communication with the gods through sacrifice was believed essential if there was to be any hope of their support. At its most simple, a sacrifice involved a killing of an animal and the division of the body into parts, some of which were offered to the gods and the rest kept for communal consumption. The origins of the ritual lay perhaps in the need to find an appropriate way to kill domesticated animals and consume them and the ritual was designed to make this in some way legitimate through the pretense that the animal died willingly, although there was always the recognition that the transition from life to death was an awesome one.

For a community to survive it is essential that the most nutritious pieces of any killed animal are consumed by the human participants. Otherwise they squander their best resource and starve. As the killing and offering of animals became the way in which the Greeks honored and appeased their gods, this left the problem of how one could justify denying the gods the best of the meat. It was the sort of situation which the Greeks found easiest to resolve through the use of myth, in this case the celebrated story of Prometheus. Prometheus (actually one of the Titans) was present at a feast of men and gods, but hid the best part of the meat after a sacrifice and offered Zeus only the bones concealed in fat. Zeus was furious and removed the use of fire from mankind. From now on there was a chasm between the world of man and the realm of the gods. Prometheus, however, stole fire back and now the gods retaliated by sending mankind women in the shape of Pandora. Pandora brought a storage jar whose cover she removed to release all kinds of evils into the world. Men had to marry women, with all the challenges they brought as partners, to ensure the survival of the human race. Food now was deeply buried underground and had to be worked out from the ground with backbreaking toil. Yet the best meat could be retained on earth and the gods offered the rest.

The rituals of sacrifice were well defined. The animal (a bull was the most prestigious offering, a sheep the most common) was prepared and taken in a joyful procession full of music and song to the place of sacrifice, normally an altar, the only place where blood could be shed, set within a sanctuary. The illusion was always maintained that the animal went to sacrifice willingly as if it wished to offer itself to the human community that would eat it, and it would be sprinkled with water, the shaking of its head which followed being interpreted as its assent to its death. The ceremony would begin with a prayer to the gods followed by each participant's taking a handful of barley from a sacred basket and throwing it at the animal. This was perhaps a means of drawing all the participants into collective responsibility for the death of the animal—the throwing of grains symbolizing an act of violence against it (in some cases stones were thrown instead of barley grains). Then, from the same basket, the sacrificial knife would be drawn and tufts of hair cut from the animal's forehead and thrown into the fire burning by the altar. This act marked a transition, the animal no longer enjoyed any special protection and it was now slaughtered by having its throat cut. The blood was allowed to run over the altar. The moment of death was marked by the impassioned shrieks of women. This sudden outburst of emotion acted as a recognition of the enormity of what had been done in taking the life of a domesticated animal. (There were different rituals involved in the killing of wild animals.)

The animal was then cut up. The *splanchna* (heart, lungs, liver, and kidneys) were roasted and eaten separately by those nearest to the sacrifice. They were seen to contain the emotional essence of the animal. The thigh bones, tail, and other inedible pieces were offered up to the gods by being burnt on the altar. Then there was a transition to a less sacred time as the participants feasted on the rest of the meat. The ceremony was brought to an end by wine being poured over the smoking altar.

Libations, the pouring out of a portion of wine, were an essential part of many rituals. Wine could not be drunk until some had been poured as an offering, and as a ship set sail a *krater* of wine was poured from its stern. Most often the wine was spilled on the ground and libations were above all associated with offerings to the dead and the gods who lived below ground, the chthonic gods. This shadowy world was associated with the dead and the underworld (of which Hades, the brother of Zeus, was overlord.) Some of the darkest forces in Greek mythology, the Furies, for instance, were assumed to live there. This world was approached in a very different way. There were taboos associated with the way the gods could be addressed, sometimes their names could not be used. Sacrifices took place in pits rather than on altars. Lamentations were allowed. It was as if the space was made legitimate for expressions of grief which were taboo as far as worship of the Olympian gods were concerned. Yet the dark earth was also the source of food, the preserve of Persephone, the wife of Hades and daughter of the corn goddess Demeter. Admission to the mysteries of Persephone and Demeter with their life-giving powers helped ward off the terror of death. (See further, page 141.)

Sacrifices could be held in many different contexts and were always the central point of any major festival. At Olympia the morning of the third of the five days of the Games was marked by the sacrifice of a hundred bulls to Zeus which all the judges, competitors, and representatives of cities attended. The great competitive games of the Greek world were irrevocably tied to the worship of the gods. Originally, in Homer, for instance, where Achilles hosts games in memory of his companion Patroclus, games accompany funerals but, as has been suggested earlier, the pressures from aristocrats to have a more formalized setting for a display of their skills led to the emergence of a regular calendar of games. The Olympic Games remained the most prestigious of these.

Olympia set in the valley of the river Alpheus in the northwest of the Peloponnese still holds much of its ancient lushness and there is an atmosphere of peace and gentle fertility there which is different from any other in Greece. For centuries the site of the Games was lost after earthquakes felled the main buildings and silt from the shifting Alpheus covered the site, following the closure of the games by Christians in the 390s A.D. Only in the eighteenth century was it rediscovered and excavations could begin. The core of the ancient site is the Altis, the sacred grove which served as the main sanctuary. Here excavators found the great altar to Zeus placed, according to legend, on the spot where the god had claimed the site as his own by hurling a thunderbolt at it. The ashes from the sacrifices were allowed to accumulate around it from one Games to the next so that the altar became as a great mound. Nearby, the great temple to Zeus, built in the fifth century to house Pheidias' vast statue of the god, one of the Seven Wonders of the Ancient World, lies in ruins after being felled by an earthquake in the sixth century A.D. (although it had been destroyed by fire before this). The massive drums of its columns survive, some still concertinaed where they fell, and most of its fine early classical sculptures have been recovered, preserved in the soil. More intact is the ancient temple to Hera, wife of Zeus, some of whose sixth-century columns still stand. Within this temple was a table of gold and ivory on which the olive crowns of the victors were placed. A sacred olive tree close to the temple of Zeus was used to provide the wreathes of the victors. A mass of statues and altars (reputedly seventy altars in all) dedicated by victors and cities filled the remaining space. Between the north wall of the sanctuary and the overlooking hill of Kronos were treasuries, most of which had been donated by the wealthier Greek cities of southern Italy.

It was around the sanctuary that the Games took place, every four years in the first full moon after the summer solstice. A month beforehand the competitors began to assemble at Elis, the city which supervised the Games. Most were young aristocrats, imbued with the spirit of competitiveness from childhood, though they represented their cities as much as themselves or their class. They had to be Greek by descent. (In one case Alexander king of Macedon, c. 498–452 B.C., managed to convince the scrutineers that he alone of his countrymen was Greek by virtue of direct descent from Heracles.) Two days before the Games were due to start the competitors with the judges and officials would process from Elis to Olympia to arrive for a swearing-in session before a statue of Zeus in the Council Room on the edge of the sanctuary. Then on the second day the sporting events would begin with the chariot races in the hippodrome. Wealthy aristocrats, or occasionally a city, would provide the teams and charioteers for this most dangerous of events but reap the glory of victory for themselves. It was in 416 B.C. that the Athenian Alcibiades entered no less than seven teams and took the first two places, a success which he shamelessly exploited in the Athenian Assembly. That afternoon there was a pentathlon consisting of discus, javelin, jumping, running, and wrestling events. Athletes competed naked. While there were stories to justify this (of one runner who got entangled in his shorts and lost and of another who lost his shorts and then went on to win) nudity went hand in hand with notions of heroism and it was an appropriate "costume" for competitive games. The following morning, the third, saw the great sacrifice to Zeus and it was followed in the afternoon by the most ancient and prestigious of the individual events, the foot races. Originally there was one, of 600 feet (200 meters), the length of the stadium. The winner of this had the Games named after him. Added to this foot race later was one double the length and a much longer one, more than 3 miles, (5,000 meters). The fourth day saw wrestling, boxing, and the *pankration*, a form of wrestling which, unlike the normal wrestling event, allowed the fighting to be taken to the ground. The fifth and final day ended with the crowning of the victors and feasting and celebrations.

The structures which housed these events, the stadium, the palaestra (for wrestling and jumping events), and a *Gymnasium* large enough to accommodate running events and discus and javelin events, survive in ruins though the hippodrome has been lost. It is hard now to recreate the excitement of the games though there are enough existing accounts to give some idea of the noise, tension, and crush of the thousands who massed for the festival. The area around the games would have become a vast tented arena, crammed with food sellers, merchants, prostitutes. For the competitors the glare of publicity and the stress of competing must have been as intense as it is for modern sportsmen. The glory of victory was as exhilarating as the humiliation of defeat was devastating. Some victors, Milo the wrestler who won five times at Olympia and twenty-five times at other games, and Leonidas of Rhodes who won the three foot races at four successive Games, became legendary figures. Leonidas (second century B.C.) became worshipped as a local deity.

A sacrifice, even at so majestic an occasion as the Olympic Games, could only be offered in hope. The favorable response of the gods could never be guaranteed. It is hardly surprising that there was an intense desire to find out the will of the gods, especially when a choice that offended them might have dreadful consequences. This was the function of the oracle, an attempt to find out the will of the gods before a risky action was undertaken. Apollo was the god who was normally used as a source of the Olympians' will but Zeus had an oracle at Dodona (in Epirus, northern Greece), reputedly the oldest of them all, and Asclepius, the god of healing, answered questions on health at his shrine at Epidaurus in the Peloponnese. Normally, a priestess, sometimes in a trance, provided the words of the god. The range of concerns was wide. An individual (and they seem to have formed the majority of the supplicants) approached an oracle to ask, according to Plutarch, "if they shall be victorious, if they shall marry, if it is to their advantage to sail, to farm, to go abroad." Cities sought advice on political matters, how to deal with troublesome neighbors, whether a war would be successful. The oracle of Apollo at Delphi was used to receive advice about the best spots for new colonies. Matters that might offend the sensibilities of the gods always required special guidance. It was wise to approach an oracle before introducing a new cult, for instance, and when founding heroes were needed for the ten new tribes instituted in Athens by Cleisthenes (page 167), a list of a hundred possible figures was drawn up and the oracle at Delphi asked to choose ten.

Oracles appear to have been used as much to provide reassurance and divine sanction for policies already agreed on as to provide a definitive answer. No one ever expected certainty from an oracle. Usually the advice was given in a cryptic or ambiguous message and it was left to the supplicant to decipher what it meant (although some shrines provided interpreters). This gave a supplicant an opportunity to shape an interpretation in his own interests as Themistocles did before the battle of Salamis (page 180). There were famous cases of misinterpretations. King Croesus of Lydia failed to realize that the empire the oracle predicted would be defeated was to be his own, and the Spartans were similarly "wrong-footed" when an attack on the neighboring city of Tegea, undertaken in the belief that the oracle had told them they would win, ended in disaster. If an oracle was unambiguously favorable then it could have real force, in giving title to overseas territory, for instance. An unfavorable oracle, on the other hand, left the responsibility on the shoulders of anyone who persisted in the action warned against.

At least fifteen oracle sites are known from the Greek world but Delphi was by far the most prestigious. Its site on the southern slopes of Mount Parnassus was believed to be the center of the world. Legends told how Apollo took possession of the site after killing a serpent, Python, the guardian of the spot for its original goddess, Gaia, the earth. (This myth may reflect a hope that the Olympian Apollo had triumphed over the Chthonic Gaia.) First and foremost, Delphi was a holy place. A league of neighboring states, the Amphictionic League, oversaw the oracle's activities and could, as they did on four occasions, declare a sacred war on any state which violated the sanctuary or its visitors. It was an accessible place in ancient times: Visitors (who did not have to be Greek although Greeks tended to be placed higher in the queue!) ascended the mountain slope from the sea, and in contrast to Olympia, which seems to have been virtually deserted between games, Delphi was always a hive of activity. So it developed other functions. It was an important center for the exchange of news and it seems, in fact, that the priests could often offer superior advice to supplicants simply from absorbing the mass of gossip that came their way. Cities used the site to show off their wealth or military victories by building treasuries along the Sacred Way which led toward Apollo's temple. There is some evidence that visiting rulers recruited their mercenaries there as well.

In the center of the sanctuary stood a temple to Apollo (the existing ruins date from the fourth century B.C.) and it was here that supplicants came to consult the Pythia, the virgin priestess. Admission was only on the payment of a fee and the carrying out of a sacrifice to see whether the god was willing to be consulted. Then the supplicant would enter the temple and the question to be asked passed on to the priestess. What exactly the Pythia did is unclear (she was invisible to supplicants). She certainly worked herself into some kind of trance but her words were usually intelligible or at least could be made so by interpreters.

While an oracle might give the impression of a real if brief encounter with a god, some individuals felt the need for a more intimate or enduring relationship. The more impassioned rituals of Dionysus, for instance, allowed the participants to feel that they had achieved an ecstatic if temporary unity with the god. Entangled in them are songs and incantations believed to have been passed down by the mythical singer Orpheus (a find of papyri in1962 on a funeral pyre at Derveni in Macedonia has enlarged the body of surviving Orphic texts although these remain notoriously difficult to interpret). A rather different approach, requiring a long period of preparation and more sober series of ceremonies, was that followed by the initiates of the mystery (the Greek *musteria* means "secret things") cult of the goddess of corn, Demeter, and her daughter Persephone at Eleusis. Eleusis was a site which had Mycenaean origins and its central hall, where the climax of the initiation process took place, stood for a thousand years until closed by Christians in the fourth century. The myth of Demeter and Persephone that underlay the rituals dealt with one of the most painful of transitions, that between maidenhood and marriage as a daughter leaves her mother for an unknown man and his home. In the myth, Zeus promises Persephone, his daughter by Demeter, to his brother Hades. To the horror of both, Persephone is abducted by Hades to the underworld and as a result of trauma both she and Demeter give up eating. Then Demeter, disguised as an old woman, visits the world and comes to Eleusis. Here she sees married women going about their daily business and becomes aware that it is only through marriage that the fertility of the human race can be ensured. After Demeter brings a famine to the world, a compromise is made under the auspices of Zeus. Hades accepts that during winter Persephone will stay with him and be given the status of Queen of the Underworld but each spring she will return to the earth, and hence to her mother, bringing the first fruits of spring with her. The human race will enjoy forever the annual rhythm of the seasons.

Those men and women who wished to involve themselves more closely in a celebration of these goddesses could choose to become initiates. The only requirements were that they be Greek speaking (hence slaves might be eligible, and there is the case of one man giving initiation as a gift to his prostitute slave-lover because everything else she earned went to her owner) and were free of impiety. The process stretched over six months, starting appropriately in the spring, and involved a complex of rituals including fasting, retreats, and purifications in water. Finally, each autumn, a great procession of the initiates, followed by a mass of spectators, made its way from Athens (which had taken charge of the rituals) to Eleusis. The initiates were segregated within the great hall and in three days of ever more secret rituals, including the showing of ancient sacred objects and the revelation of texts, they approached the climax of the initiation. What went on at this moment remains secret (no ancient author ever revealed it), but it was clearly a highly emotional experience in which the participants felt they had achieved direct contact with the divine world and would enjoy a blessed afterlife.

This hope of a fulfilled afterlife was a rare thing in the Greek world. The conventional Greek belief was that there was no certainty of happiness in another world. The shades of ordinary mortals would wander without purpose in the darkness under the earth. There are some exceptions to this. In myth gross wrongdoers, such as Sisyphus, who attempted to cheat death, are punished by the gods in the underworld (in Sisyphus' case by perpetually pushing a boulder up a hill). A few, though it was never clearly defined which few, could pass on to Elysium, paradise, where they lived lives like those of the gods. Those outside could only watch. As Pindar put it:

For them the sun shines at full strength . . .
The plains around their city are red with roses
and shaded by incense trees heavy with golden fruit.
And some enjoy horses and wrestling, or table games and the lyre,
and near them blossoms a flower of perfect joy.
Perfumes always hover above the land
from the frankincense strewn in deep-shining fire of the gods' altars.
(Translation: William Barnstone, 1962)

While sacrifices provided an immediate but short-lived means of communication with the gods, centering on the most basic need of the community for food, more permanent offerings to the gods were made as a thanksgiving for favors or as a means of ensuring more in times to come. A votive offering, in effect, involved the permanent renunciation of wealth or resources in favor of the gods. These offerings could take many forms. A temple was the most prestigious and enduring of them, a symbol of a city's pride and its wealth but also the mark of its commitment to the gods. Inside it could be filled with a grandiose cult statue, such as Pheidias' statue of Athena in the Parthenon, precious offerings to the god, or with the city's treasure or trophies from war. The Parthenon also housed a mass of swords and shields.

A temple normally stood in a demarcated sacred area, the sanctuary or *temenos,* a term that went back to Mycenaean times when it described the estate of a ruler. Now that the gods were seen as the supreme forces in the city, this was their estate, an area sacred to them, where processions ended and sacrifices began, at the altar found in every *temenos.* The *temenos* offered a special setting for votive gifts and it was within them at the great Panhellenic shrines that cities would dedicate their treasuries. The sacred way to the the temple of Apollo at Delphi was lined with them. Many sanctuaries also had a mass of statues that had been presented to the gods as offerings. St. Paul visiting Athens in the first century A.D. found the city "a forest of idols" and one excavated sanctuary, Ayia Irini, in Cyprus has yielded some two thousand terra-cotta statues, some greater than life size. It was success in war or in the games that encouraged the giving of votive gifts. The Athenian treasury at Delphi commemorating Marathon, complete with mythical heroes cast in bronze, is a particularly grandiose example of a war offering, and the Athenians followed it with a commemoration of the victory over the Persians at Eurymedon (c. 468, see below), a bronze palm tree with a gilt Athena in its branches. Athletes, or their cities, would celebrate their victories by the dedication of a statue of themselves at their moment of greatest glory.

A specific kind of votive offering was made to Asclepius, the god of healing, at his shrine in Epidaurus in the Peloponnese. Asclepius was originally a hero, the son of Apollo by a mortal woman, Coronis, but he became transformed into a god when legend credited him with the ability to raise men from the dead. His origins were in Thessaly but it seems that the priests at the small shrine at Epidaurus successfully planted a connection there and by the fifth century the shrine had become known to the sick throughout Greece. As Pindar put it:

All who came
Bound fast to sores which their own selves grew,
Or with limbs wounded, by grey bronze

Or a far-flung stone, or wasting in body with summer fire or with winter,
He, loosing them all from their several sorrows,
Delivered them. Some he tended with soft incantations,
Some had juleps to drink,
Or round about their limbs he laid his simples,
And for some the knife; so he set all up straight.
(*Pythian Ode III,* 47–53; translation: C. M. Bowra)

Epidaurus eventually came to host games and theater. (Its theater survives as the best preserved in mainland Greece.) Those seeking cures would have to purify themselves and be free of any pollution before entering the sanctuary and they would then sleep in a special building near the god's temple. It was here that the god would appear to them in a dream and offer them advice. The shrine was littered with offerings of the parts of the body cured (a practice still found in churches in Greece today), but details of cures could also be recorded in writing on pillars inside the sanctuary.

For those who did not survive there would be a commemoration on the site of their burial. In the graves that have been found in Athens, in increasing numbers from the sixth century onward, the dead were commemorated by having oil flasks, *lekythoi,* either placed with the body or brought to the grave. By the beginning of the fifth century these *lekythoi* typically have scenes painted in red against a white background and these show a variety of activities connected with death, a warrior leaving his wife or mother, the family of the deceased around his or her tomb or the journey to the underworld itself. Until the second half of the fifth century there are no more formal grave markers, although there may have been wooden commemorative tablets that have perished. Then after 450 B.C. the stone grave *stele,* a slab with a relief carved on it, appears. These *stelai* are simple and often moving memorials remarkable for the high proportion that contain portrayals of women. It has been suggested that the new status given to women citizens by Pericles' law of 451 B.C. (which stated that only "women of Attica" could bear citizen children to Athenian husbands) accounts for this. Men, who alone would have been able to commission these monuments, must have wanted to honor their wives. Those that do show men are also simple and there is no stress on heroic poses. This is a more sober, community-oriented world than that of the heroes of old.

---

aveling through southern Greece in the sec-
ıd many of the ancient sanctuaries and trea-
ıtion to plunder their riches was irresistible
the revenge of the gods. The Roman con-
first sackings. The destruction of Corinth,
ıs one of the greatest acts of vandalism of
ın general Sulla, determined to finance his
ng of Pontus, in the 80s B.C., plundered
mpia; but there were still five hundred
[illegible] statues remaining at Delphi to be carted off by Nero in the first century A.D. in retaliation for a pronouncement of the oracle's condemning his murder of his mother. In the late fourth century Christian edicts ordered the destruction of pagan temples and as the Roman empire collapsed, successive waves of invaders completed the destruction of the sanctuaries. Those few statues that survive have invariably lost the setting for which they were made. They stand now as isolated works of art divorced from their original role as mediating forces between the Greeks and their gods. Johann Winckelmann must take much of the responsibility for perpetuating this image of sculptures standing in lonely splendor.

The spiritual world of the Greeks was underpinned by myths, *muthoi,* stories of the exploits of gods and heroes. These stories included genealogies of the gods, great epics such as the Trojan War, accounts of the foundation of cities, the adventures of heroes and tense family dramas. Although many myths were tied to a particular locality, Greek mythology gradually came to interlock in a series of connected narratives, often with the major participants related to each other, just as the Olympian gods were. All Greeks were at home with these narratives which were continually being reinforced by being presented in vases, monumental sculpture, and theater.

Where did Greek myths come from? Some, Hesiod's genealogies of the gods, for instance, were imported from abroad, mainly from the East. Some were probably based on real events—there may actually have been some kind of conflict between Mycenaean Greeks and Troy that provided a base for a wide variety of epic narratives. In practice, however, it has proved difficult to tie myth in with historical events. Myths develop their own lives all too easily and are continually being adapted by later generations so that any core of historical reality can easily be lost. (As already mentioned, a study has been made of the French *The Song of Roland,* written down for the first time about A.D. 1150, which shows it to be a massive distortion of the events it claims to record.) As early as the fifth century B.C. educated Greeks recognized that myths may have nothing to do with any real events and distinguished them from *logoi,* stories which did attempt to describe the truth.

So why do myths evolve and hold such psychological prominence? Partly because people love telling and listening to stories but, even more, because myths fulfill deep-rooted needs. "Myths function like shoes: you step into them if they fit. Old shoes, like traditions that are (or seem) ancient, are usually the ones you feel most comfortable with," writes Richard Buxton, in his *Imaginary Greece.* The myths acted to keep alive the idea of a heroic age, the expoits of which provided exemplars for almost any kind of behavior. Myths can be used to give actions legitimacy, to justify, for instance, keeping the best meat for human participants even when the object of a sacrifice is to honor the gods who might thus expect it themselves. In tragic drama they were used as a means of exploring real-life dilemmas in a way that distanced them from any day-to-day context. What were the consequences of women being betrayed by their husbands (Euripides' *Medea*), or defying city laws by honoring obligations to one family (Sophocles' *Antigone*)? These problems could be worked through safely and thus defused as begetters of tension. But myths can also be woven into rituals to give these greater richness and symbolic power. The Greeks, for instance, were profoundly aware of the importance of moments of transition, especially the crucial one for women of the transition from virginity to marriage. The goddess most affected by the transition was Artemis, the virgin goddess of hunting and wild places with whom virgin girls were especially associated. It was recognized that making the transition into marriage meant abandoning the relationship and that recompense had to be made. There were a number of myths which told of how an animal sacred to Artemis, a bear or a deer, for instance, had been killed and the goddess, furious at this intrusion into her domain, had demanded that a girl be sacrificed as compensation. In the rituals which accompanied the transition to womanhood these myths were woven in. The girls would dress up as bears as if they were replacing the life of the dead bear with their own lives and a sacrifice of a goat which had been dressed in girl's clothing would be made. Thus the importance of the transition, the fact that something valuable was owed to the goddess as one moved from one part of life to another, was played out in a way which must have been psychologically satisfying to the participants but without anyone's being hurt.

Myths provided the core of a city's consciousness. A crucial element of Athens' identity and self-confidence rested on the belief that Athenians were the only Greeks of pure blood and there was a myth to support this. It was said that the semen of the god Hephaestus had been placed in the earth of Attica by Athena and that Erechtheus, the first king, had sprung from it. So the Athenians had backing for their claim that they had emerged directly from their native soil, unlike those whose cities had been founded by outsiders. The Spartans, like other Dorians, claimed their ascendancy in the Peloponnese on the grounds that they were banished children of Heracles (who, tradition said, was born in the Peloponnese) simply returning to their heritage, and their earlier presence there had given them the right to rule over other Peloponnesian Greeks such as the Messenians.

As myths were normally passed on orally, only a tiny proportion of the body of original Greek mythology has survived. Some, the Homeric epics, for instance, had such importance that they were written down but most myths were not. On the other hand some of the most popular myths exist in a variety of versions as a result of being developed in different contexts and localities. There is no fixed and hallowed version of a Greek myth as there is, for instance, of the life of Christ as represented in the Christian gospels (and even here the point is made by there being four versions of equal status). So it is impossible to pin down a definitive version of any Greek myth and interpretations of myths are difficult when the context in which any version was developed is missing. The versions of the myths of suppliants or the Eumenides (Furies) in Aeschylus' plays (see pages 223 and 246) are comprehensible largely because the political situation in Athens in which they were set is known as well as are the political biases of their author. Most myths have no such contextual foundation.

Those myths which do survive do tell us something about the concerns of the Greeks but what is not clear. Some scholars believe that every word of any surviving myth, even the color given to an animal, for instance, has its relevance and a complex picture of the Greek worldview can be created through the analysis of myth. This approach tends to assume that the Greeks breathed and lived myths to the exclusion of all else, that details were added for a purpose, rather than simply to make the story more arresting, and that a representative and fairly complete sample of myths has survived. None of these assumptions is likely to be true. Some have gone further. Rather than keep Greek myths within the historical context of ancient Greek society and its specific needs, they have claimed a universal significance for Greek myth. A Greek myth, in short, is assumed to say something fundamental about the human condition. The classic example comes from psychoanalysis where Freud selected one Greek myth, the story of Oedipus, and interpreted it in such a way as to claim that all small sons (in every human society) wish to kill their fathers and marry their mothers. It is beyond the scope of this book to speculate why Freud chose this particular myth and why it was adopted as a universal truth by so many of his followers (Richard Webster's *Why Freud Was Wrong* is a good, if hostile, starting point) but it is an instance of how a myth can be used and developed far beyond its original context and function. This happens, of course, with myths anyway. Freud, however, went further in assuming a myth contained a truth which could be proved scientifically. No educated Greek would have been prepared to do the same.

Whatever the precise part played by myth, it served a major part in defining the spiritual consciousness of the Greeks. There was a sense perhaps to be found also in modern India, that the world of the gods and heroes was never very far away. As one historian Peter Brown has put it, "Greece was a spiritual landscape rustling with invisible presences." Even when a new mood of speculative questioning threatened to undermine traditional religious beliefs, Greek religion retained its power. It was too deeply embedded in Greek culture to be uprooted until the coming of a more powerful and monolithic spiritual force, Christianity (see Chapter Twenty).

8

Revolutions in Wisdom: New Directions in the Archaic Age

While shared religious beliefs and mythology gave a coherence to Greek culture, this culture never fossilized. The inherent tensions within and between city-states brought continual challenges to the conventional ways of seeing things. In the sixth and early fifth century, in particular, a number of developments, predominantly in Ionian and mainland Greece, gave a new impetus and vigor to Greek civilization. Among these was an intellectual revolution which can fairly be said to have planted the seeds of Western science and philosophy.

The revolution had its origins in the Ionian city of Miletus. Miletus was a prosperous trading center enjoying extensive contacts inland and overseas, with the ancient cultures of the Near East, with Egypt, and with its colonies along the coast of the Black Sea, although now that the gulf on which it stood has silted up it is difficult to imagine its past glories. It was a city which had known severe internal tensions, partly as a result of Lydian expansion onto its hinterland. How these may have made it the home of the first philosophers is unclear but a combination of exposure to other cultures with a tradition of intense debate within the city may have shattered conventional ways of thinking.

The arguments of the Milesian thinkers survive only in fragments or in the writings of later philosophers. Since they were feeling their way forward into new territory the concepts they used are not always easy to grasp. However, despite these difficulties, some things are clear. They worked on the assumption that the universe could be seen as a single entity ("*cosmos*" was the word they used) and there were underlying principles in the way it operated. These principles could, they hoped, be identified by the human mind through the use of observation and reason. (They did not go so far as to conduct experiments like "true" scientists.) This was a direct break with the Homeric view where the physical world and its inhabitants were vulnerable to the whims of the gods and where nothing was inherently stable. It was through making this break that the Ionians opened a new era in the history of ideas.

If there is a *cosmos* operating on identifiable principles then cosmic events may be predictable and so it is fitting that the birth of philosophy is traditionally marked by a successful prediction made in 585 B.C. by one Thales of Miletus that there would be an eclipse of the sun. (The eclipse was recorded separately by the historian Herodotus.) No one is clear how this prediction was made or if the story was embellished later, but for Aristotle, writing over two hundred years later, it made Thales the founding figure of Greek philosophy. While in 648 Archilochus saw an eclipse as evidence of the *un*predictability of the world, Thales had suggested the opposite.

Explaining the physical world is not easy. There is such variety and diversity among both animate and inanimate objects. Their interactions are constant and the process of change is continuous. Even so, everyday observations and experience suggest that there is some order in diversity. The stars, sun, and moon operate according to definable patterns. Living things grow from infancy to maturity and then decay. Crops appear each year if planted with care and can be harvested. Yet the Ionian philosophers wanted to go beyond the particular to the universal. Was there some single principle according to which the *cosmos* as a whole operated? Were there primary substances from which all others come? Scientists still ask whether one can penetrate the ultimate meaning of things, find "the theory of everything." Can particle physics reveal the innermost nature of matter? Can one predict the outcome or order of events which appear on the surface to be totally chaotic? The Ionian philosophers were the first to pose the questions and to face the challenge of supplying solutions. In doing so they defined one of the most distinctive features of Western thought.

Thales is history's first absent-minded professor—reputedly so busy looking at the stars one night that he fell headlong into a ditch. His work, according to later sources, covered astronomy, measurement, and engineering. He founded the scientific tradition by arguing that the world may have come from a single substance, water, and that it still rested on water. It is possible that Thales was drawing on Egyptian and Babylonian creation myths which described water as the first substance, but Aristotle suggested that Thales made his choice because water was demonstrably important to life. What Thales was doing, however inadequately, was putting forward an explanation as to why the earth seemed to be stable within the wider universe. His speculations also concerned the very nature (*physis*) of water—what exactly was it made of, what were its properties and functions as a substance (the fact that it could be transformed into both ice and steam made it of special interest). This concentration on the *physis* of a substance was an essential part of the process the Milesians had embarked on. Thales is also recorded as worrying about the property of magnets to attract, suggesting that this is evidence that they may have a soul (*psyche*). He may even have been suggesting that *every* object, however apparently lifeless, had a soul.

Anaximander (mid-sixth century), also of Miletus and an associate or pupil of Thales, took on the task of explaining the origin of the world, its development, and its future, again within the assumption that there was an underlying order to all things. He raised an obvious objection to Thales. If the world rests on water, what does the water rest on? In the first work of prose known in European literature, *On the Nature of Things,* he asserted that the *cosmos* must rest within a larger entity, the Infinite or Boundless, which has existed before all else and from which all things originate and into which all will ultimately dissolve. The creation of the world occurred when opposites, hot and cold, dry and wet, were separated out from the Boundless to form the physical world. Anaximander also suggests, in the only surviving sentence of his work, that material objects are reabsorbed into the Boundless as a result of some form of wrongdoing. This is rather an obscure point (not the most inspiring to choose for the oldest surviving sentence of European prose!) but it has been argued that Anaximander is using the analogy of a city where social order is restored by the punishment of wrongdoers. Meanwhile, the world is stable because the forces surrounding it are equal and there is no reason for it to move from its central position (this is known as the principle of sufficient reason and the first instance of the principle's use).

The third of the founding figures of philosophy, Anaximenes, who worked in Miletus about 550 to 525, and was perhaps a pupil of Anaximander, developed what appears to be a simpler theory. Like Thales, Anaximenes believed there was one fundamental substance in the world, in his case air. The world rested on it and it gave life to living things. (Death was believed to come as the result of air withdrawing itself from the human body.) Anaximenes' particular contribution was to speculate as to how air might change from one substance to another. If steam, surely a form of air, could condense into water and water be cooled into ice, then perhaps every substance, including earth and rocks, was no more than condensed air. The wind was simply air in motion. Here was another attempt to get to the root of the *physis* of a substance, in this case by exploring its properties in different contexts.

These were primitive attempts to make science but they show minds using a combination of observation and reason in an effort to get to the source of identifiable problems. It was the use of abstract reasoning that was important, thinking through a possible explanation for the stability of the world, for instance, that could be defended, however primitively, by reasoned thought. A contrast with the Egyptians can be made. The Egyptians were expert observers. Their medical treatises, for instance, contain meticulous descriptions of every kind of ailment. Yet there is no evidence that the Egyptians reasoned or generalized from their experience so as to create any understanding of how the human body might work. (Illnesses were attributed to the malignant influences of gods and cures were usually little more than spells.) The Greeks were working on a more creative and productive level than this. Geoffrey Lloyd puts the point succinctly, "The extant remains of Egyptian and Babylonian medicine, mathematics and astronomy can be combed in vain for a single example of a text where an individual author explicitly distances himself from, and criticises, the received tradition in order to claim originality for himself, whereas our Greek sources repeatedly do that."

The process can be seen more clearly in two successors of the Milesians, both of whom, in contrasting and totally original ways, tried to explore the nature of reality. Heraclitus, from Ephesus, just north of

Miletus, was working about 500 B.C. He was an unsettled and unsettling figure, one of those somewhat irritating intellectual know-it-alls whose questioning annoys as many as it invigorates. He left about a hundred short statements, many of them baffling. He was the first known relativist, making the point that "truth" in a particular circumstance may be subjective, depending on the observer. A man is seen as giving a blow to another—if he is an official administering a punishment this might be good, if he is someone settling a private feud it might be bad. The act is the same but the context defines goodness or badness. For a fish, sea water is nourishing, for a man it is fatal. If one steps into a river one day and then again on the next day, is it the same river, seeing that its water will have changed completely? Heraclitus is continually questioning the conventions of language and the superficialities of appearance and is suggesting, in fact, that "truth" may never be found.

Heraclitus' views appear to challenge the idea that there can be any coherence to the world. However, he did believe that there was an underlying order to things for which he used the word *logos,* here meaning an account of the world and all that might be revealed in it. (The concept of *logos* is a central one in Greek philosophy—and eventually reappears as "the Word" in Christian theology. It can be seen as a reasoned account of things in contrast, for instance, to *muthos* [myth], a story about the gods that cannot be verified in any way.) This order arises, typically for Heraclitus, *not* because everything is at peace with itself; in fact the very opposite. Harmony is, paradoxically, the result of tension, even strife. Heraclitus takes the analogy (the Greek philosophers enjoyed using analogies) of a lyre or bow. The frame and strings are held in tension with each other but the instrument as a whole exists in harmony. Another analogy Heraclitus uses is of a barley drink whose components are wine, grated cheese, and barley. It only becomes the drink if it is continually stirred (otherwise the wine, cheese, and barley separate). So too the *cosmos.* Its harmony comes because its elements are in a state of constant strife. (Heraclitus argued, somewhat obscurely, that fire was the fundamental substance which underlay the process of change: "All things are an exchange for fire and fire for all things, as goods are for gold and gold for goods.") The city-state, too, suggests Heraclitus, flourishes as a result of the constant interactions of its citizens. Justice is, in fact, strife. This is a world of constant movement and diversity.

There could not have been a greater contrast to Heraclitus' world of constant flux than the account of the physical world given by his contemporary Parmenides. Parmenides came from the other end of the Greek world, Elea in southern Italy. (He and his followers are termed Eleans in contrast to"the Ionians.") Parmenides left the world of observation, even if might be said, of common sense, for the use of pure reasoned argument. In a long poem, much of which survives, he tells how a goddess initiated him into the world of reason. The interpretation of the poem is extraordinarily difficult but the argument seems to begin by saying that one can only talk of that which exists and not of anything which does not exist. (There is an obvious objection here that one surely can talk of, say, an imagined entity such as a unicorn.) He then seems to make a leap by saying that what cannot be talked about, therefore, *cannot* exist. Nothing of what has happened in the past or which will happen in the future can be talked about because it is not existing now, but, it also follows from his earlier point, the past and future *cannot* exist. Similarly, one cannot talk of empty space because one cannot talk of something which does not exist, emptiness (here one has to accept that emptiness is an entity which cannot be talked of). So the only thing which can be talked about and can exist is the material world, without spaces in its makeup, in the present. Reason, on Parmenides' model, does not allow for change or motion (there is no space for objects to move into), or for division of materials. The world is, in short, in Parmenides' words, "like the bulk of a well-rounded ball."

The implications raised by Parmenides' unchanging world were explored by his follower, Zeno. An arrow which has been shot cannot, says Zeno, move. How can this possibly be? Because, answers Zeno, it is always in a place equal to itself and if so it must be at rest in that place. So, as it is *always* at a place equal to itself, it is always at rest. Achilles, the fastest man on foot, will never catch up to a tortoise because when he has reached the place where the tortoise was, it will have moved on, and when he has reached that place, the tortoise will be farther on still. Zeno's purpose in making these paradoxes is unclear. Was he a loyal supporter of Parmenides simply taking his findings further or is he making the point that reason and observation inevitably conflict with each other?

The Eleans thus presented a challenge which every subsequent philosopher had to take up. How could the cold findings of reason be reconciled with the richness and diversity of the observed world? It can be argued, of course, that Parmenides' arguments had too many flaws in them to be called valid reasoning but, as Plato above all was to realize, they deserved some kind of response and a much more sophisticated approach to the underlying nature of the physical world.

One way of dealing with the observable diversity of the world was to suggest that there might be more than one fundamental substance. Empedocles (c. 492–432 B.C.), an aristocrat from the wealthy Sicilian town of Acragas, argued that there were four elements, earth, air, fire, and water (an idea which was to endure for centuries in European culture after the four elements were equated with the four "humors," the balance of which within the human body were said to define health and temperament). A finite amount of these materials had been created (Empedocles agreed with Parmenides on the underlying unchanging nature of the universe) but they could be mixed together in an infinite variety of combinations to produce the material world. Forces of "Strife" and "Love" act to break up and reconcile the elements, hence the observable process of change. A similar approach was taken by Anaxagoras, c. 500–428 B.C., the first philosopher known to have lived in Athens. The amount of material in the world is given. At the beginning it existed as one great mixture but it then separated out and developed into other substances in such a way that everything contains something of everything else. So a lump of iron, though predominantly made of iron, contains every other substance, gold, earth, water, air, even if only in minute quantities. A human sperm contains all the elements which make up a human body (there was a belief that the woman was a passive receptacle for the sperm), its hair, bones, and so on (as well as pieces of everything else besides!). A potentially subversive idea follows from this—if all human beings are made from the same matter what exactly is it that distinguishes a king or hero from any other person?

Suppose one tried to divide up one of Anaxagoras' substances, a lump of iron or a single sperm, for instance. Could one eventually sort out all the components which made it up? Anaxagoras said no, even the smallest particle contained a bit of everything and one could go on subdividing particles forever with the same result. The Atomists, of whom the most prominent were Leucippus and his pupil Democritus, from Abdera in Thrace, disagreed. (Only Democritus's writings survive but many of his ideas are assumed to be derived from Leucippus.)

Every substance, they argued, was made up of *indivisible* particles, which they termed atoms (literally "that which cannot be cut"). All atoms were made up of the same material, a single unchanging substance as Parmenides had argued, but they differed in size and shape. They also moved in a world where, and here the Atomists opposed Parmenides, empty space did exist. Atoms could form themselves in a variety of combinations to make up different physical substances. (Some atoms, Democritus speculated, had hooks on them to make the bonding easier!) In some substances there was more emptiness between atoms than in others (an explanation of why some objects were lighter than others.) This was quite a sophisticated analysis and offers a potentially satisfactory explanation for the diversity of the physical world. The concept of the atom has survived, even if atoms are no longer known to be uncuttable!

The Atomists worried at another problem. The ultimate reality lay in the material which all atoms were made of, but unfortunately one could not see atoms, only speculate on what they might look like. Where did this leave the objects that atoms made up? The Atomists seem to have believed that nothing of certainty could be said about them. Echoing Heraclitus, they observed that some people drinking a mixture might find it sweet, others drinking the same mixture might find it bitter. The mixture cannot be both sweet and bitter and, the Atomists argued, therefore the truth about the mixture could never be told to the satisfaction of all. They concluded that there is no such thing as truth except in relation to the material which makes up the atoms, the ultimate reality. Yet if atoms cannot be seen, what role does this leave for the senses? Democritus imagines a dispute between the senses and the reasoning mind. "Wretched mind," say the senses, "do you take your proofs from us and then overthrow us? Our overthrow is your downfall." If one uses reason to doubt what the senses show, as Parmenides did, then one is doubting the very thing that can provide evidence for reason to work on. One of the most fundamental problems of Western philosophy had been defined.

The Atomists' thoughts on the nature of truth were probably a response to an argument which had been put forward by a fellow Abderan, Protagoras (c. 490–420 B.C.). Protagoras had argued that if a drink is bitter to one person, then it is true to say it *is* bitter; if it sweet to another, then again it *is* sweet. In Protagoras' most famous words

"Man is the measure of all things." All beliefs are true and whatever the senses experience is reality. This was easily challenged by Democritus, and after him, Plato. If all beliefs are true, so too is the belief that no beliefs are true and there is an insoluble contradiction. The search for what could be said to be true remained to be tackled. It was to form the core of the work of Plato.

An alternative approach to the nature of reality had been taken by a refugee from the island of Samos who had made his home in Croton, a Greek city in southern Italy, about 530 B.C., Pythagoras. Pythagoras was such a charismatic character that a host of legends came to surround him, and disentangling the truth is not easy. One early tradition associates him with the theory of migration of souls from one human being to another on death, with a "good" life in one body leading to a better one in the next. Pythagoras founded a sect of fellow believers who through the use of secret ceremonies and special diets worked towards improving their own chances in later incarnations. Pythagoras himself was credited with remembering his previous ones.

Mathematics came to have its own spiritual importance for the sect and here the Pythagoreans made important advances. The Babylonians and Egyptians had always tied numbers to actual physical objects. They could talk of five horses or ten beds, for instance, but not of *five* or *ten* as numbers in themselves. In short, they had no sense of a mathematics that dealt in abstractions. For Pythagoras and his followers numbers had a significance which went far beyond their function as a calculating device. There was, they argued, a mathematical reality underlying the physical world, "numbers in all things," and this could be grasped by reason and observation. To give a single example, take a string stretched across a sounding box and pluck a note from it. Halve the length of the string and try again. The note is one octave higher. There appears to be some kind of relationship between sound and number. This was an important insight and later mathematicians have followed it up with some success. The Italian Leonardo Fibonacci, for instance, discovered around 1200 A.D. that certain numbers, 3, 5, 8, 13, 21, 34, 55, 89, reoccur throughout nature. The petals of almost all flowers occur in one of Fibonacci's numbers. All snowflakes are different but all have a sixfold symmetry. (See Ian Stewart, *Nature's Numbers*, 1995, for a readable overview of the issue.) Even at the highest level of modern mathematics there appears to be underlying order and every mathematician who sees underlying beauty in his abstract work can be said to be working within the mathematical tradition of Pythagoras. As G. H. Hardy put it in his *A Mathematican's Apology* (1940), "The mathematician's patterns like the painter's or poet's must be beautiful. The ideas like the colours or the words must fit together in a harmonious way. Beauty is the first test. There is no permanent place in the world for ugly mathematics."

Pythagoras is known to most for his theorem of the right-angled triangle. A mathematical theorem is a conclusion which follows from taking a series of axioms and working logically forward from them. (The word "theory" comes from the Greek verb *theorein,* to observe something and make a universal judgment as a result of the observation.) The process of working from the axioms to the theorem is the proof. So long as the axioms hold and the logic is correct then the theorem must be true. While traditional mathematicians (in both China and Babylon a thousand years before Pythagoras) had been content to note that in *particular* instances the square of the hypotenuse in a right-angled triangle is equal to the sum of the squares of the other two sides, Pythagoras is credited with the proof that it must be so in *every* instance. It was not simply that he may have discovered this particular proof but the concept itself of mathematical proof, probably the greatest single contribution the Greeks made to mathematics. A way of establishing certainty had been discovered. However, it has to be said that Pythagoras' contribution is shrouded in legend. The first extant writings which show a grasp of mathematical proof are those of the mathematician and astronomer Hippocrates of Chios (not to be confused with the famous physician) a century after Pythagoras.

Where did the gods fit into this early philosophy? The traditional idea that there was a family of gods who intervened in the physical world at random could not co-exist with it. Some philosophers (Parmenides and Empedocles) may have believed in a god who existed *outside* the *cosmos* and this certainly was the belief of another Ionian philosopher Xenophanes (c. 560–480 B.C.). Xenophanes criticizes the unsophisticated approach to the gods taken by ordinary human beings. They imagine them to be in human form. It is the equivalent of horses' seeing their gods as horses and oxen theirs as oxen. Instead, Xenophanes argues there is a supreme divine force above and apart from all other gods and mortals and different in conception to them. The more usual approach of the Ionians, however, was to see a divine force as *part* of the natural order of things. Anaxagoras, for instance, talked of a Mind (*Nous*) which was the underlying force in the *cosmos*, giving it life and direction. Some philosophers saw each object or substance having a purpose intrinsic to its nature—air had the purpose of giving life, for instance. The Atomists, radical thinkers that they were, denied that there were any gods or any purpose to the universe at all. The only reality was the material substance which made up the atoms. (Hellenistic philosophy developed some of these ideas further.)

Intellectually, then, these were exciting times. These early philosophers and the so-called Sophists, who will be discussed later, are normally termed the pre-Socratics, those working before Socrates (who can be seen to introduce a new phase in philosophical thought). They did not form a single school. Some worked on their own, others responded to earlier work. What united them was their readiness to challenge existing conventions, to dig down to bedrock in their attempt to discover what may be called the truth. They raised questions about the underlying purpose and operation of the physical world and the nature of reality. They began to explore the tools with which truth could be found, language, the senses, the use of reason, and see their uses and inadequacies. These remain the central concerns of philosophy to this day. It was a remarkable achievement. And yet the greatest of the Greek philosophers, Socrates, Plato, and Aristotle, were still to come (Chapter Thirteen).

The coming of philosophy has often been linked to the spread of literacy in archaic Greece. The assumption is that literate people are better informed, more able to handle a variety of different viewpoints, and altogether more intellectually aware. In the nineteenth century, when Greece was studied almost exclusively through its texts, scholars tended to associate the literacy of the Greeks with their other intellectual achievements. Recent scholarship reflects a more cautious view and focuses instead on the contexts in which literacy was used on a day-to-day basis.

What seems to be clear is that by 500 a small but significant part of the population in many Greek states could read and write, if only at an elementary level. A good, early example comes from Egypt where in 591 a group of Greek mercenaries carved their names and home cities and, in one or two cases, short texts on a statue of the Pharaoh Rameses II. Nine different hands can be distinguished, most from different cities, suggesting that hoplites from a range of cities (Ionian in this case) could write. The sixth century sees the use of writing in a variety of contexts. The François Vase has no less than 129 inscriptions on it, and one catalogue of known sixth-century texts contains 450 with a geographical range which extends as the century progressed. Thales does not appear to have written anything down but his Milesian successors Anaximander and Anaximenes did and so too Heraclitus and Parmenides. Gravestones and dedications have inscriptions and Solon's laws (590s) were apparently written out in full on wooden tablets. By the sixth century it is known that texts of Homer were circulating—the epics may actually have been written down as early as 750 B.C. So there is no doubt that literacy was widespread and that it had important functions in *recording* material, laws, possessions, and ideas. It had some importance in the city-state for everyday administration, particularly when affairs became more complex, or where it helped for laws to be displayed publicly.

The real question, now asked much more critically than before, is what actual effect did this have on intellectual development. The scholarly reading of texts seems to come much later—in the Hellenistic period when there were the first serious attempts to collect texts in libraries. There is little evidence too to suggest that exposure to what texts there were in archaic Greece would have had any intellectually liberating effect. If, as seems true, the epics of Homer were among the most popular, reading them would only have served to confirm *traditional* ways of thinking. It is quite possible that written texts acted to freeze debate. As Deborah Steiner points out in *The Tyrant's Writ*, in the East the written text was normally used as a means of imposing authority (through the law code of an autocratic ruler, for instance). Socrates hints at the same point in Plato's *Phaedrus*. He compares painting to a written text. You cannot question a painter's work, it maintains "a majestic silence. It is the same with written words; they seem to talk to you as though they were intelligent, but if you ask them anything about what they say, from a wish to know more, they go on telling you the same thing over and over again forever." In an oral encounter, Socrates suggests in contrast, actual intellectual progress can be made through the direct interaction of two or more people. A written text, in short, is not an appropriate way to conduct philosophy and the *Dialogues* of Plato (written accounts of oral interchanges) make the point.

The spread of literacy has also been linked to the coming of democracy on the assumption that only a literate people would be able to cope with affairs of state. There is much truth in this. Fifth-century Athenians, for example, would have benefitted from reading their laws, effecting ostracism, recording decisions, and administering their empire. Even so it has been suggested (by William Harris in his *Ancient Literacy*) that probably only 5 to 10 percent of Athenians were literate. The real business of the democratic state was carried out in the assemblies and the law courts where rhetoric was at a premium. The supremacy of the Athenians, the fourth-century Athenian orator Isocrates proclaimed, lay in the fact that they were better trained *in speech* than other Greeks. Studies of the Greek tragedians show they had a highly sophisticated understanding of the way speech could be used to create meaning and emotion. It was only in the fourth century that literacy in Athens became an essential tool for those involved in administration.

It is precisely within the context of oral, rather than written interchange, that the roots of philosophy may lie. This is the view of Geoffrey Lloyd who has carried out exhaustive studies of the ways in which the Greek philosophers constructed arguments. He stresses that the city-state was an environment in which the pressure of events encouraged innovation. The city could not survive unless it adapted to the stresses of the outside world and this meant not only a process of debate, as alternatives were proposed, but the acceptance of the idea that laws could be changed (implicit, for instance, in Solon's reforms). The cut and thrust of debate whether in the assemblies or in the law courts would in themselves encourage a no-holds-barred approach to political, legal, and moral issues. (As Heraclitus himself said, "Justice is strife.") Although the links between politics and philosophy in the Greek world were bound to be complex, they appear to have operated within the same combative *oral* intellectual climate and one must assume the influence of one on the other.

It is remarkable that while these intellectual revolutions were taking place there were also important developments in painting and sculpture. Those in painting were probably initiated by artists working on wall paintings (one "large-scale" painter, Cimon of Cleonae, has been recorded as being responsible for innovations in foreshortening, for instance) but the surviving examples are on the much more durable material of pottery. Athenian pottery represents one of the paradoxes of the art world. Clay is cheap and easily accessible and pots can be made in large quantities. There is none of the exclusiveness or cost of marble or bronze and it has been estimated that a painted Greek pot might actually have cost the equivalent of only two to three days' wages. Yet in the present day at auction Greek pots can fetch enormous sums.

It is certainly true that the quality of Athenian pottery was high and from the middle of the sixth century Athenian pottery replaced Corinthian as the Mediterranean's finest and most commercially successful. The François Vase of about 570 B.C., mentioned above, could be said to have marked the moment when the Athenians took the lead. It is an enormous *krater,* a mixing bowl, with a mass of figures in black on the red clay background. Perhaps the finest painter of these so-called Black Figure vases is Exekias who worked in the city about 530 B.C. His masterpiece is usually seen to be his portrayal of Achilles and Ajax playing dice, now in the Vatican Museum. The composition of the scene is beautifully judged. Each of the heroes has taken off his armor and placed it behind him so that it frames them as he concentrates on the game. The figures themselves are drawn with great delicacy, details of their hands, faces, and costumes incised on the black paint. Exekias has the gift of being able to isolate his heroes so that they appear as individuals who take absolute responsibility for their own destinies. In another famous vase Ajax is shown intently setting up the sword on which he will soon throw himself when he commits suicide.

In about 530 B.C. there are signs that the Athenian painters have begun to experiment. Individual potters start using a white ground or superimposed colors. The most imaginative change of all, however, was to transpose red-orange and the black so that the figures are left in the original red clay and it is the background which is painted black around them. A number of individual painters are credited with the innovation of Red Figure pottery, most commonly the so-called Andokides painter. (Andokides was a potter who left his name on a selection of pots painted by the same unnamed artist.) This was not merely a change in a coloring scheme. While the details of black figures had to be incised, red figures could have their details painted on them. This allowed a much more natural and free-flowing style. At the same time, a group of painters known as the Pioneers (working about 510 B.C.) revolutionized the use of perspective. Their concern was not to just to tell a story but to portray how figures in a variety of poses, front facing with knees folded, one foot twisted away from another, or in the contortions of a dance, actually looked to an onlooker. This new approach may have originated on wall paintings, as suggested above, but the surface of a pot presented more of a challenge, one which was met with enormous self-confidence, even exuberance. There is a genuine feeling of liberation in the way that figures now suddenly explode across the surface of the pot in poses which would have been unimaginable some years before. "The invention of the technique of representing foreshortened figures was," writes J.J. Pollitt, "both from a technical and conceptual point of view one of the most profound changes ever to have occurred in the history of art. It marks the beginning of a long series of phases [in Western art] in which the artist's role as a recorder of passing sensuous phenomena, and his mastery of the means of making his records exact, comes to rival in importance his role as a narrator of stories and ideas." Much of the pottery was produced for the *symposium* and the painters now have the flexibility to deal with its concerns on the variety of pots, *kraters,* wine coolers, jugs and drinking cups which the rituals demanded. Many of the paintings depict the *symposium* itself, others myths associated with Dionysus, the god of wine.

In the same period, there was also a major shift in the way sculpture was presented. Greater signs of naturalness, copying a real body rather than a pattern set by earlier generations, can be detected in the *kouroi* for some decades before the fifth century but a new technique, the "lost wax" process of casting bronze, now pushed the process beyond the conventions of the archaic age.

Bronze had been used for statues for generations but the size of solid bronze statues had been limited. Not only were large bronze statues prohibitively expensive but the bronze tended to bubble and crack as the metal cooled. A hollow statue avoided these problems. The "lost wax" process worked as follows. A metal stand was set up and then a clay model built up round it. This was then coated with a layer of wax. A further clay covering as put on and the whole heated. The wax melted out and molten bronze was poured in between the two layers of clay. When the bronze had solidified, the clay covering could be broken off. Mishaps were inevitably common, and a large bronze was normally cast as a number of individual pieces which could then be fitted together and the joins smoothed over. The whole was then burnished.

Tradition ascribes the invention of the "lost wax" process to two sculptors from the island of Samos, Rhoikus and Theodorus, who were working there at the time of the tyrant Polycrates in the third quarter of the sixth century. There is archaeological evidence to support the claim. In the sanctuary of the great temple to Hera on the island many statues of hollow bronze from Egypt have been found and it is assumed that they inspired the Samian craftsmen to experiment with their own methods of casting. Once the process was perfected it spread quickly through the Greek world. The evidence is sparse and probably unrepresentative because the temptation to melt down bronze has always been great and few examples survive. The prosperous trading island of Aegina, however, appears to have been making bronze statues early while a cult statue of Apollo, dated, with comparison to marble statues of the period, to c. 510, has been found at Athens' harbor, the Piraeus. A superb example from a slightly later date is the charioteer from Delphi found buried under a landslide. It is the dedication of a Sicilian tyrant after he had achieved a victory in the Pythian games. (The chariot appears to have been salvaged in antiquity and is now lost.) The opportunities allowed by bronze are clearly shown in another sculpture of the period, the large figure of Zeus found in a shipwreck off Cape Artemisium and dating from c. 460. The outstretched arms would not have been possible in a more brittle medium such as marble. Perhaps finest of all among these early bronze figures are the Riace warriors, again a lucky find from an ancient shipwreck off "the toe" of Italy in 1972. They appear to be looted Greek art on its way to Rome.

The experience of working in bronze appears to set an inspiration to those working in marble. The pediments of the temple to Aphaea, carved on the island of Aegina about 500 B.C. in fine Parian marble, are often cited as one example of the direct influence of bronze-working on marble sculpture. The sharp lines of the carving and the addition of, now lost, pieces of bronze to the stone have suggested the link. If, however, there is an icon for the emergence of classical sculpture it is "the Critian boy," a three-quarters-life-size statue of a male nude found on the Acropolis in Athens. It is attributed to Critius, a sculptor who was active in Athens around 490–460 B.C. The statue has been linked to a base found separately on the Acropolis and if the match is correct the Critian boy is in fact one Callias, a victor in the boys' foot race that was part of the celebrations surrounding the Panathenaea. It is dated by most scholars to just before 480 B.C., the year in which the Acropolis was sacked by the Persians.

The Critian boy has had to bear an enormous weight of scholarly enthusiasm—"the first beautiful nude in art" as the art historian Kenneth Clark put it, "a vital novelty in the history of ancient art—life deliberately observed, understood and copied" in the words of John Boardman. It is easy to forget that it is a chance survival and there may have been many other statues of equal quality in marble and bronze in cities others than Athens. Yet it is the Critian boy that has survived and it has become the symbol of the transition from the Archaic to the classical world.

What is the source for this enthusiasm? First the Critian boy deserves to be called beautiful. This sounds an emotive, even sensual, way of approaching him in his nudity and it needs further explanation. The body is finely proportioned, a young man in the bloom of youthful vigor as a successful athlete would be. Yet archaic statues have some sense of proportion too and if proportions can be calculated to some ideal then beauty can be simply replicated from one statue to the next. What seems to give the Critian boy his impact is that the proportions though "right" are not too formal. The head is slightly turned, the right leg is forward of the left which bears the weight of the body so that the right can relax slightly. This allows the right hip to drop slightly lower than the left and there is a corresponding movement in the shoulders. This is no abuse of proportion but a subtle change in the way proportion is managed so that the body becomes natural, relaxed, and, compared to the archaic *kouroi,* approachable as a body. At the same time, and this is perhaps what gives the statue part of its success, there remains an idealization of the human form. The face is serene, not wholly without emotion but somehow removed from the turmoil of real life. If the Critian boy really is an offering of a successful athlete to Athena the patron goddess of Athens, then it is an offering of a boy whose success has placed him emotionally close to the gods, as the poems of Pindar suggest it might.

The Critian boy is often placed within a political context. His air of moderation and self-control is, it is argued, the expression in art of the self-confidence of a city which has not only created a more democratic political system but has successfully led the fight against the Persians (in the invasion of 490 B.C. which led to the Athenian victory at

Marathon). It pays to be careful here. Serene faces, such as that of the Critian boy, lend themselves to all kinds of projections by observers and it cannot be assumed that Critius' main aim was to translate any form of public feeling into his art. He may have had his own preoccupations, and his desire to create an athlete at the moment of his greatest *kudos* may have been stronger than that to create an archetype of an Athenian citizen. What is true, however, is that the Critian boy stood within a city which was brimming with a sense of success. It originated first in its liberation from the Pisistratid tyranny.

The tyranny had first come under direct attack in 514 when two citizens, Harmodius and Aristogeiton, had attempted a coup against Pisistratus' sons, Hippias and Hipparchus. According to the historian Thucydides their initial impulse was personal. Hipparchus had, allegedly, attempted to seduce Harmodius, who was the lover of Aristogeiton, and this was their revenge. However the two conspirators seem to have had wider political ambitions. They chose the Panathenaic festival of 514 for their attack and their supporters, armed, were concealed among the crowds as these gathered for the procession.

The coup began with the successful killing of Hipparchus (Hippias proved too well guarded) but Harmodius died in the ensuing fracas. The supporters melted away and Aristogeiton was later captured and tortured to death by Hippias. So for the time being Hippias survived. He was to cling to power for four more years though his rule was one of increasing brutality.

It was the Spartans who eventually used their army to dislodge him. Sparta had now achieved hegemony in the Peloponnese. It had not been achieved easily. The city had powerful enemies on the peninsula such as Argos, and, potentially, Corinth, and any foreign policy which took Spartan troops too far from home left the city vulnerable to a helot uprising. Under Cleomenes, king between 520 and 490, however, the Spartans embarked on a more adventurous policy. They not only achieved leadership of the Peloponnesian states through a mixture of bullying and compromise (from about 504 the Peloponnesian states, with the exception of Argos, were organized into a league, the Peloponnesian League, under Spartan leadership), they extended their influence northward in what was trumpeted as a crusade to replace tyrannies by oligarchies. As in most such crusades, ideology was used to mask political ambition and there is no doubt that Cleomenes hoped to impose a pro-Spartan government on Athens and reduce the city to the status of a dependent ally.

At first Cleomenes' policy bore success. Hippias was exiled and a pro-Spartan aristocrat, Isagoras, became the leading archon. When Isagoras was challenged by one Cleisthenes, from the Alcmaeonid clan, the Spartans returned to throw out Cleisthenes in his turn together with about seven hundred of his supporters. The victors then attempted to abolish the Council of Four Hundred set up by Solon. A combination of anti-Spartan feeling and popular outrage over the proposed abolition of the council led to what seems to have been a mass uprising of citizenry. Not only were the Spartans expelled for good but Cleisthenes was able to return as undisputed leader of the city.

Cleisthenes proved to be a shrewd politician during his year of office, 508–7. He produced a radical program of political reform that his popular support gave him the chance to implement without fear of opposition from the aristocratic clans. It was a direct attack on the power of the clans (possibly the revenge of an Alcmaeonid for the humiliation imposed on his clan a century earlier). From now on each Athenian citizen was to be linked to a deme, a local community. (The deme was not strictly a territorial unit. Membership of a deme was not lost when a member moved.) Each deme was part of a larger unit, the *trittys,* of which there were thirty in Attica. The *trittys* were grouped into ten freshly created tribes which were given precedence over the four old Ionian tribal groupings, the *phylai.* Each of the new tribes was composed of three *trittys,* but in each case these were selected from different areas, one *trittys* from Athens and its surrounding area, one from the coast, and one from inland. Since each tribe had a mixture of citizens from all parts of Attica, regional loyalties (to aristocratic leaders, for instance) were fragmented and each tribe was allocated an Athenian founding hero in recognition of its new status as an Athenian entity. To replace Solon's Council of Four Hundred there was an enlarged council with five hundred members (the *boule*), fifty chosen from each tribe not by election but by lot. The *boule* prepared business for the citizen assembly. In a later reform, of 501, the city appointed ten generals, who unlike the other magistrates, could hold office from year to year subject to reelection. In 501 the generalships were not important posts. The events of the next few years were to make them the most influential in the city.

This was not true democracy, rather *isonomia,* equality of rights, but it was a further step toward democracy. The demes ran their own affairs and celebrated their own local cults. They gave citizens valuable experience of being involved in local government (and it was in the demes that the citizen lists were maintained). The phratries, the traditional local brotherhoods, were not abolished but seem, in fact, to have been given new vigor and their aristocratic leadership diminished as a result of being integrated into city rituals. Meanwhile, there seems to have been enthusiastic participation in the *boule* and it can be assumed in the assembly (though no firm evidence remains of this). It is probable that the institution of ostracism, the process by which citizens could vote to exile an unpopular political figure, was introduced by Cleisthenes (although there is no record of its use before 487).

What seems to have happened in Athens between 510 and 500 B.C. is a psychological shift in which the citizenry took on responsibility for the government of their own city. The liberation from tyranny became enshrined in popular mythology. It would have been degrading to recognize the role played by Sparta in the liberation so the failed coup of Aristogeiton and Harmodius was highlighted instead. A statue of the two heroes (nude as their heroic status demanded) was erected in the Agora and they became subjects of a cult following. (The original statue itself was carried off by the Persians in 480 B.C. but a copy was made and Roman copies of this survive. It is a unique example from this period of an actual portrait. None other is known until the fourth century.) The hero Theseus becomes a popular subject on pottery in these years. Theseus was the legendary prince of Athens who saved the youth of Athens from being presented as tribute to the Minotaur and he appears to have been adopted as a symbol of the post-tyrannical Athens. His status was elevated further in the years that followed. The hero Heracles, who had been used by the Pisistratids to symbolize their "labors" on behalf of the city, is eclipsed.

Shortly after Cleisthenes' reforms the historian Herodotus records a victory of the Athenians over the neighboring Boeotians. (The cities of Boeotia of which Thebes was the most important were persistent rivals of Athens.) The discredited Pisistratids had fostered links with Boeotia and so the war may have had a retaliatory purpose. One result of the war was the annexation of a border town, Eleutherae, into Athenian territory. To consolidate the new acquisition's incorporation into the city-state its most important festival, that to Dionysus "of the black goatskin," was transferred to Athens where it came to be celebrated every March as the City Dionysia. It has been suggested (by W. R. Connor) that this was the moment that tragic drama was born.

Drama involves the participation in a public display of individuals who portray themselves not as themselves but as characters who engage in a scripted story. According to Aristotle drama began as a development within the dithyramb, a choral ode in celebration of Dionysus. At some point the leader of the dithyramb stood apart from the chorus and engaged in a separate spoken role, relating back to the chorus, perhaps even interpreting its lines for the audience. Dionysiac rituals were originally secret and it has been suggested that the transition of the Eleutherian cult to Athens resulted in the rituals becoming public, performed before audiences, for the first time. The earliest "character" may have, in fact, been a spokesman with the specific role of interpreting the rituals of a rural community to the city audience. Once this role had been performed, further developments were possible. The playwright Aeschylus, whose first production was in 499 B.C., is credited with introducing a second character and allowing interaction between the two, even though the characters still refer back to the chorus. The process would have been helped by the fact that cult worship of Dionysus already included participants changing identity and wearing masks. They also acted out myths associated with the "life" of Dionysus and so the typical tragedy which involved the working through of dilemmas set in the context of myths was born. (The word *tragoidia* means a goat song, or a song performed at the sacrifice of a goat, though the link of this song with drama is not clear.) Dramatic performances were to become one of the key experiences of the Athenian community and will be examined in more detail below (see Chapter Twelve).

This chapter has explored some of the most significant aspects of the Greek achievement. Philosophy and bronze casting are creations of the Ionian world, foreshortening in painting, the reforms of Solon and Cleisthenes, tragic drama, creations of Athens. If there is one link among all these developments it is the particularly competitive and combative arena of the city-state. What came out of the maelstrom of interaction within the city could not have been predicted. There is no inevitability in history. Knowledge of the immense diversity of the physical world can be structured in different ways—the Greeks initiated a particular way of structuring it through the search for assumed fundamental principles. In doing so they set in motion trains of thought which have helped define and elevate the Western scientific approach to life. Again there is no intrinsic reason why the primary function of art should be to copy the physical world as accurately as possible, rather than simply to provide aesthetically pleasing decoration or to set out a story for the illiterate. As it was, the Pioneers of Athens (or their now forgotten inspirers) created an approach to art that proved immensely influential in later European history. Drama is a cultural form which is unique to the West, though copied elsewhere. Human life in no way depends on it but it remains the case that drama fulfills cultural functions that are still found satisfying. Of course this does not mean that twentieth-century drama has a direct relationship with Greek drama; it operates in very different cultural and social contexts, but the idea that human beings can impersonate others and create a story which engages an audience was Greek in origin.

9

Creating the Barbarian: The Persian Wars

There was now to be a very different kind of impact on Greek culture, two major invasions by a foreign empire, the Persian, which helped to define the Greeks', in particular the Athenians', perceptions of themselves in relation to the outside world. This was the moment when the Greeks, again particularly the Athenians, achieved some coherence to their sense of self-identity. Traditionally, the defeat of the Persian invasions has been seen as a turning point in European, even world history, but it pays to be cautious. Accounts of the invasions have come only from Greek sources and the impact was highly dramatized by their writers. There is no record of how the Persians saw the failure of their invasion (although recent discoveries of tablets in the Persian capital Persepolis may change this) or even whether among all the other concerns of a great empire it made much impact at all. The highlighting of the story, as in the traditional account given in this chapter, may be little more than a recognition of the superb public relations skills of the Athenians! It remains a good story.

The Persian or Achaemenid empire appeared suddenly in Asia between 550 and 530. The military genius who created the empire, Cyrus the Great, had inherited the throne of a small kingdom, Persia, in 559 B.C. but within thirty years he had created the largest single political structure the world had yet seen. The Medes were his first conquest and brought with them large resources of horses and manpower (the dominance of Medes in the empire was so marked that the Greeks came to use the word "Mede" for the Persians in general). Then, in 545, came a cunning defeat in a surprise winter campaign of Croesus, king of Lydia, that brought Cyrus the whole of western Anatolia including all the Greek cities of the coast of Asia Minor. Next came the Babylonian empire, the army of its king Nabonidus crushed at the battle of Opis on the river Tigris in 539. The Babylonian empire stretched as far west as the border with Egypt and included Syria, Jerusalem, and the ancient cities of the Phoenicians. All this became part of Cyrus' empire.

Cyrus worked sensitively to consolidate his new conquests. To the Babylonians themselves he presented himself as a traditional king, being crowned in Babylon and showering the city with new buildings. Those who had been the empire's subjects were told they were restored to freedom and the Israelites, for instance who had been conquered by the Babylonians in the early sixth century, acclaimed Cyrus as their liberator. This set a pattern. The empire was given a flexible but effective administrative structure. It was divided into provinces or satrapies, each with a Persian overlord, but at local level native cultures were left intact and even encouraged to flourish. Cyrus finally turned east and, though the details are obscure, added yet more territories and so spread the empire to the borders of modern Afghanistan, where he died in 530. In scope and extent his achievement ranked far above that of the Macedonian king, Alexander ("the Great") who was to demolish the empire in the 320s but fail to provide any stable alternative.

Within five years Cyrus' son, Cambyses, had added Egypt and Cyprus to the empire, and the cities of Libya, including the Greek colony of Cyrene, were forced into surrender. There came a crisis. In 522, in obscure circumstances, Cambyses died and a cousin, Darius, seized the throne, claiming legitimacy as a descendant of Achaemenes, the founder of the Persian dynasty. (The empire now becomes known to historians as the Achaemenid.) Darius consolidated his position with some brutality and then extended the empire even further, both into India and Thrace (c. 513), although a campaign to subdue the Scythian peoples of the Black Sea was unsuccessful. Samos, Lesbos, and Chios were among the Greek islands absorbed. With Persian expansion along the north African coast to a point which was west of mainland Greece, and with the kingdom of Macedon submitting to Persia as a dependent ally, mainland Greece now appeared acutely vulnerable.

Before Darius could move, however, there was trouble among the Greeks whom he had already conquered. The Ionian Greek cities of the coast of Asia Minor had seen their once prosperous trade routes disrupted by the expansion of the empire and they resented it when they were called upon to provide shipping for further Persian conquests. The Persians had appointed local aristocrats as their rulers in what as a form of tyranny. In 499–8 B.C. the tyrant of Miletus, Aristogoras, furious at a betrayal by a local Persian commander, declared *isonomia*, equal rights, for the citizens of Miletus and this inspired other cities along the coast to throw off their Persian-appointed rulers and join in revolt. Athens, which claimed ancient links with the Ionian cities, and Eretria sent help though their forces were soon withdrawn. It was to be four years before the revolt was finally subdued and when it was the Persians allowed more democratic regimes to emerge. However, the prosperity of the cities had gone and in this sense the crushing of the Ionian revolt is one of the markers of the end of the Archaic age.

Darius felt slighted by the intrusion of Athens and Eretria and he decided to punish them. He may also have wished to extend his interest further into the Aegean—he took the island of Thasos in the north Aegean in 492—and the expedition he now planned to Athens involved placing the old tyrant Hippias, now aged eighty, back in charge of the city. In 491 Darius sent envoys to the city-states of the Greek mainland asking for submission. Sparta and Athens killed the envoys. After the insult a Persian attack on mainland Greece was inevitable. Persian forces were gathered in Cilicia with some three hundred triremes assembled to convey them, and were placed under the command of Datis, a Mede, and Artaphrenes, the nephew of Darius. The Greeks expected the invaders to edge their way around the northern Aegean but the Persians grasped the initiative and struck straight across the Aegean, subduing the island of Naxos on the way. Eretria was taken and sacked within a week and a few days later the Persians landed on the mainland on the plain of Marathon, twenty-five miles (forty kilometers) north of Athens (probably on September 10, 490). It was a good site as it had ample water supplies for the troops and the plain was large enough for the Persian cavalry to be deployed. The crushing of the Athenians seemed imminent.

Faced with the sudden arrival of the Persians, the Athenians sent in desperation for help from Sparta but the Spartans were engaged in completing a religious ritual and could only promise to come a week later. The Athenians, with a hoplite force of nine thousand, supported by a contingent of one thousand hoplites from the city of Plataea, had to march north themselves to block the land route to Athens. They were heavily outnumbered, possibly two to one in infantry by the Persians, and were at first content to dig in on the south of the plain. An intense debate then followed among the ten Athenian generals, all of whom had been allocated to the campaign, as to whether to attack. They were evenly divided but under pressure from the most determined of the generals, Miltiades, the War Archon, Callimachus, gave a casting vote to fight.

The Persians, on the other hand, appear to have written off a direct Greek attack. Their strategy, though this is difficult to know for certain, may have been to contain the Athenian army at Marathon while sending a force of men and cavalry southward by sea to the city. They knew there were pro-Persian factions in the city ready to open its gates to them. On 17th September, a week after the landing, it was the turn of Miltiades among the Athenian generals to hold supreme command. He exploited the temporary absence of the Persian cavalry (either they were being loaded for an assault on Athens or were away being watered) to launch the attack. He drew up the hoplites in a narrow line, possibly only three or four ranks deep in the center with each end strengthened to perhaps eight ranks. The men were then ordered to rush headlong toward the Persians in order to engage their infantry before they could be attacked from the side by Persian cavalry or archers. The strategy worked. The hoplites engaged and the heavier wings began to push the Persians backward until they broke and fled toward marshland where many drowned. In the center, where the stronger Persian troops were stationed, the Athenians themselves began to fall back but they were saved when men from the wings, showing remarkable self-control at their own moment of triumph, came back to strengthen the Athenian line and hold the Persian advance. The most bitter of the fighting followed but eventually the Persians were driven back to their ships and made out to sea. It only remained for the exhausted Athenians to march back to their city to reach it before the Persian fleet could disembark. They arrived in time and the Persians had little option now but to sail home. (There is a legend of a courier, Philippides, running from the battlefield to bring news of the victory to Athens. The story was inspiring enough for a race of the same distance, the Marathon, to be created as one of the events of the first Olympic Games of modern times in 1896 when, appropriately, it was won by a Greek, Spiros Louis.)

Tradition relates that the death toll at Marathon was 6,400 Persians and only 192 Athenians, most of them lost in the struggle in the center. It was a stunning achievement, transcending the most epic of heroic legends. No single event was ever to exercise such grip on the imagination of Athens. The Athenian dead were buried in a conical mound which is still to be seen and a marble monument dedicated to Miltiades, the architect of victory, was placed on the battlefield. In Athens itself, a stoa, the *Stoa Poikile*, was built in a corner of the Agora and a paneled painting of the battle was placed next to those of ancient mythical victories of the Athenians, against the Spartans, Amazons, and at Troy. In his epitaph the great Athenian tragedian Aeschylus said he wanted to be remembered primarily for his contribution as a hoplite to the victory. To ensure the wider Greek world appreciated what had happened the Athenians built a treasury at Delphi from the spoils of victory. (It is possible that the treasury was already under construction but was adapted to commemorate the victory). A struggle of Athenians against Amazons was on one of its metopes as was one of Theseus' feats, the humbling of a great bull from the plain of Marathon. It echoed legends that Theseus had been seen in armor rushing ahead of the Athenians into battle. Some years later, perhaps about 450, a bronze group of gods and heroes from Athens' past, including Theseus and Athena, with Miltiades added to them, was placed in front of the treasury. It is possible that the famous Riace warriors, two life-size bronze figures of the highest quality, looted by the Romans and found off the coast of Italy in 1972, were from this monument.

For the Athenians, Marathon may have been a heroic victory, for an empire as large as the Persian, little more than a pinprick, if a humiliating one. There was sure to be a Persian revenge. Athens was lucky in that any complacency about the invincibility of the city was dispelled by an able and articulate aristocrat Themistocles (c. 525–459 B.C.) who realized that the future defense of the city rested not with its land-bound hoplites but with a navy. As archon in 493-2 Themistocles had already persuaded the city to develop a new sheltered harbor at the Piraeus. In the 480s he appears to have gradually strengthened his position as the leader of a dominant anti-Persian faction and when a new strain of silver was found in the Laurion mines in 483 he persuaded the assembly to divert the proceeds to the building of a new fleet of two hundred triremes. (He cunningly seems to have used a state of tension with the island of Aegina to clinch his argument among those who wished to ignore the Persian threat.)

A trireme was, essentially, a long thin rowing boat with a bronze ram which jutted out at the water line. It appears to have been a Phoenician invention, first copied in the Greek world by the Corinthians about 600 B.C. By the fifth century its design had been perfected. Typically it had 170 oarsmen (with 30 other seamen also on board) who sat in three rows, one above the other. Somehow, through piping a beat over the sound of the waves, this large crew was brought into unison. The ship then had to be maneuvered into position at right angles to an enemy ship and the highest possible speed built up before the moment of ramming. (Studies on a modern version, the Olympias, have shown speeds of nine knots are possible.) High morale, meticulous training, and the finest equipment were all essential if the trireme was to be effective.

In the event, the Greeks had a breathing space. Darius had been preoccupied with a revolt in Egypt before his death in 486 and it was not until 484 that his son and successor, Xerxes, began planning another invasion. The historian Herodotus portrayed Xerxes as a man of overweening pride whose behavior was offensive to the gods. Xerxes certainly lacked the sensitivity of his predecessors, preferring to rule in his own right rather than through intermediary titles such as King of Babylon or Pharaoh of Egypt and he may have been impelled not just by revenge but by a desire to equal the three generations of his family who had all conquered new territories for the empire. He was ready to carry out any new conquests in style. He spent four years planning his invasion of Greece and his force, a large army (two hundred thousand men it is estimated) and an accompanying fleet of six hundred triremes, was designed to be so overwhelming that Greek spies were actually encouraged to see it being gathered. To convey it from Asia into Europe he built a bridge of triremes, bound alongside each other with a roadway covering them, across the Hellespont and a canal through the peninsula of Mount Athos.

It was now that any illusions that the Greeks could unite in a common cause were shattered. There were the ancient internal squabbles, those of Athens with Aegina and Sparta with Argos, for instance. Many cities had factions which aimed to use Persian support as a means of coming to power while others felt the realistic course was submission (the sacking of Eretria in 490 had its effect here). Even the oracle at Delphi counseled surrender. Any definition of the coming war as one between Greeks and non-Greeks was, in any case, blurred by the large numbers of Greeks conscripted into Xerxes' forces (mainly oarsmen from the Ionian cities). There was even an exiled king of Sparta, Demaratus, among his advisers while the Hellespont bridge was the creation of a Greek mathematician, Harpalus.

The invading forces would be ready in the summer of 480. The Greek preparations were patchy. Athens decided to resist the invasion at sea and a crash training course for new trireme crews was put in hand through the winter of 481–0. Sparta decided to enlarge her forces by training helots as hoplites but it was not until October 481 that Sparta took the initiative in forming a coordinated response. At a meeting in the city some thirty states united themselves under Spartan leadership and warned that any city which submitted to Persia voluntarily would be stripped of its property. There was a rival bid for leadership from Gelon, the tyrant of Syracuse, who promised an enormous army but his offer was turned down. (Gelon, in fact, played an important role by defeating a Carthaginian attack on Sicily which was launched in 480, possibly in coordination with that of the Persians.) Athens was a potential alternative leader, of the sea forces at least, but the city found little trust among other states and Sparta assumed command on both land and sea.

Then a strategy had to be planned. It could be assumed that the Persian land and sea forces would come down through northern Greece each supporting the other. There needed to be safe anchorages for the Persian ships and access to fresh water for the crews while an army without a protecting fleet would have been vulnerable to a Greek attack in the rear from the sea. The question was where to meet the Persians. The plain of Thessaly was one possibility as it would allow the Greeks the services of the Thessalian cavalry but the Thessalians were lukewarm in their commitment and there was no secure holding place where the Greeks would not be outflanked. In the end the narrow (barely more than two yards [only two meters] wide in places) pass of

Thermopylae which ran between the mountains and the sea near Trachis was chosen as the first holding place on the land. A corresponding station at sea was Cape Artemisium in northern Euboea where the beach was ideal for landing triremes. It was here that the Persian fleet would have to decide where to sail on south, either through the Euripus narrows between Euboea and the mainland, or around the outside of Euboea and then westward around Cape Sounium and up to Athens. Whatever the choice the Greek fleet, two hundred Athenian triremes and seventy more from the Peloponnese, could confront them from Artemisium even though such an encounter in the open sea would have its risks.

The great Persian army and its accompanying shipping did eventually march in the summer of 480. It was an extraordinary and colourful gathering. Persians, Medes, Indians, Arabs, Ethiopians, Libyans, and Lydians were among the assembled troops, each in their native war dress and armed with a bewildering variety of weaponry. The bulk of the shipping was provided by the Phoenicians with some Egyptian support and a contingent from the Ionian cities. Despite the four years of meticulous planning, however, the expedition got off to a bad start. Having delayed in northern Greece to draw on the harvest, it was not until early September that the troops began to move in earnest. The weather was already turning and even before they had encountered any Greeks many Persian ships were lost in storms on the exposed coast of Magnesia.

The fleet that emerged off Cape Artemisium about the 16th September was, however, still larger than the Greek forces. The decision was now made to split it with half stationed off shore to contain the main Greek fleet at Artemisium while the other half was sent along the west coast of Euboea in the hope of sailing around the island, heading back north and catching the Greeks in a pincer movement. The strategy failed miserably. The two hundred triremes of the encircling fleet were lost in a storm which drove them onto a lee shore on the southeastern edge of Euboea and a direct Persian attack on the Greeks at Artemisium ended in stalemate.

The Persian army fared better. Once again the Spartans had been delayed by religious commitments but this time a Spartan force under one of the kings, Leonidas, did manage to leave the city with three hundred hoplites and some trained helots. Gathering other forces along the way to a total of some five thousand men, it eventually moved in to plug the pass at Thermopylae, just before Xerxes' army arrived.

The defense of Thermopylae ranks with the battle of Marathon as one of those great confrontations between Greek and foreigner that became part of the mythology of European heroism against outsiders. Unlike Marathon, however, it was a Greek defeat. Xerxes first attacked the pass on the 17th September and hard fighting continued for two days, the Spartans proving adept at turning the Persian attacks. Xerxes then learned of an inland path which ran across the mountains alongside the pass. It was guarded by a small force from the city of Phocis but a carefully planned night march on the 18th September brought a crack Persian force above the Phocians by dawn and they were easily pushed aside. (Herodotus has an evocative account of how the Phocians heard the Persians rustling through fallen oak leaves.) Once the Greeks knew the pass was surrounded, most retreated but the Spartans remained to the end and were killed almost to the last man. (Two survivors are said to have reached Sparta but at least one of them later died from the humiliation of not having fought to death.)

The Persians were now free to stream down toward Attica. The Greek fleet had little option but to retreat from Artemisium. The Persian warships followed in pursuit through the narrow but sheltered waters between Euboea and the mainland. Athens was their target. Its territory was too large and exposed to be defended and the city itself had been abandoned, except for a few priests and defenders of the Acropolis, well before the Persians arrived on the 27th September. The so-called "Decree of Themistocles," a fourth-century copy of a decree, which may have been passed by the Assembly as early as the autumn of 481, shows where they had gone: the young men to train for the triremes, the old men to the island of Salamis, women and children to Troezen, a city across the Saronic Gulf which had ancient links with Athens. (The inscription including the decree was found at Troezen in 1959.) The deserted city was easily taken and the Acropolis with all its fine temples and sculpture sacked. The Persian fleet arrived in time to watch the flames from the beach at Phaleron. The Greek fleet, meanwhile, had retreated to shelter between the island of Salamis and the mainland.

The next target of the Persians would be the Peloponnese and already, as Athens burned, a protective wall was being constructed along the Isthmus. If the Greeks fell back to here then the whole of

Attica and the surrounding city-states would, in effect, have been surrendered to the Persians and it is hard to see how they could ever have been regained. The Greek hold on the mainland was fast disintegrating in any case. Xerxes began building a mole across from the mainland to Salamis so as to block in the Greek fleet, while on the island itself an estimated eighty thousand men were facing the threat of starvation. The Spartan commander Eurybiades argued that it was vital to get the remaining 380 Greek triremes away quickly to the Peloponnese.

Themistocles, however, knew that an abandonment of his city's territory would be catastrophic. He had two bargaining tools. One was an oracle that Athens had received from Delphi before the invasion which talked of "Divine Salamis" bringing "death to women's sons" and of "a wooden wall which would not fall." He had cleverly presented these at a meeting of the Athenian Assembly in the summer of 481 as evidence from the gods that a naval ("wooden walls") victory at Salamis (which, he said, would hardly have been described as "divine" if a favorable end for Athens was not expected) was predicted. Over a year later he could still cling to the Assembly's endorsement of his interpretation. He also had the remaining Athenian triremes, the bulk of the Greek fleet, as a bargaining tool. He could refuse to withdraw them from Salamis. In an impassioned speech to Eurybiades, the Spartan commander, he argued that in any case the strategy of fortifying the Peloponnese meant nothing if the Persian fleet had control of the sea. Better to face them now at the "divine Salamis" in the hope of defeating them in the narrow waters of the channel.

Themistocles' views prevailed but the situation was so precarious he had to act quickly. The lines of his strategy were clear. The Persian fleet had to be lured up the narrows, the further the better so that their crews would be tired. They could then be ambushed by the Greek fleet, still fresh and probably superior in the ramming skills that effective trireme warfare demanded. The lure was effected by persuading Xerxes, through a slave, Sicinnus, that the Athenians had fallen out with the other Greeks, who were all in a state of demoralization. They would be leaving the next night, the 28th September, rowing in darkness toward the western end of Salamis. The exits from the narrows could easily be blocked in by the Persian fleet.

Xerxes fell for the bait. An easy victory seemed within his grasp. The evidence of Thermopylae, where most of the Greek forces had abandoned Leonidas to his fate, suggested that a lack of a united front among the Greeks was not unusual. A large contingent of Egyptian ships was sent to block the straits of Megara in the west while another squadron of Persian ships patrolled the southern end of the channel. There was a major weakness in this strategy. Once the fleets were at sea communication between them was poor and it was virtually impossible for any change of plan to be effected by Xerxes. As dawn came and a Greek fleet of some seventy ships appeared to be retreating northward, Xerxes, who had placed himself on a "throne" overlooking the narrows, did nothing, and perhaps could have done nothing by this stage, to prevent his fleet rowing after them.

The "retreating" fleet had been placed there by Themistocles, not only to lure the Persians forward but to act as a protective force for the rest of the Greek fleet if the Egyptians had attacked from behind. The main part of the Greek fleet had been concealed behind a promontory on the island so the Persians could not see them as they maneuvered their ships clumsily through the narrowing channel. When the Greeks appeared, fresh and united, the Persian rowers, who by this time had been at sea for twelve hours, had few reserves of strength with which to meet them. A freshening wind brought a swell which made them even more vulnerable as they rolled in the waves.

In Aeschylus' play *The Persians* the battle which ensued is described. There could be no better description of the trireme in action:

> A Greek ship charged first and sheared off the whole high stern of a Phoenician ship and every captain drove his ship against another ship. To begin with the onward flowing Persian fleet held its own; but when the mass of ships was congested in the narrows, and there was no means of helping one another, they were smashed by one another's rams sheathed in bronze. Then they shivered their whole array of oars, and the Greek ships intelligently encircled them and battered them from every angle. Ships turned turtle, piles of wreckage and dead men hid the sea from sight, corpses were awash on shores and reefs, and the entire barbarian fleet rowed away in disorderly flight.
>
> (Translation: N. L. Hammond)

Salamis has gone down in history as one of the great victories of Western history. This is partly due to the skill of the Athenian propagandists who elevated the battle to make it appear the conclusive one of the war. The poet Simonides was paid by the city to write a hymn of praise to those "on their swift-moving ships" who had kept "all Greece from seeing the dawn of slavery." The Athenian playwright Aeschylus elaborated the theme in *The Persians*. The contribution of other contingents from Corinth and Aegina was played down with such lack of scruple that the historian Herodotus had to censure the Athenians for spreading a story that the Corinthians had actually fled during the battle. In fact, the result was not nearly as conclusive as was claimed. Although as many as two hundred Persian ships may have been sunk (for the loss of forty Greek triremes) many escaped and, now that winter was coming, made it back to the coastline of the eastern Aegean to recuperate. The Persian army was still intact and occupying Greece. The war was by no means over and Xerxes, though downcast by his defeat, was determined to continue it. He left an army of one hundred thousand to winter in Greece under a trusted and competent general, Mardonius. Despite the exhilaration after Salamis, the Athenians faced a bleak future. It was hard to see how they could ever regain their territory without making a formal submission to the Persians and many, in fact, argued that this was the only course.

The new election of Athenian generals in March 479, however, brought to power a majority who were determined to fight on (although Themistocles was not among those elected). They turned down an offer from the Persians to surrender back Attica in return for an alliance, but a high-level delegation sent to Sparta pretended that the offer still stood and might well be accepted if the Spartans did not send help. The Spartans were undecided but, according to Herodotus, eventually swayed by independent advice that they would surely lose if the Persians were joined by the Athenians in the battle for the Peloponnese. A force of ten thousand Spartan hoplites under the command of Leonidas' nephew Pausanias, joined by thirty-five thousand helots (an effective way of neutralizing the threat of an uprising while the hoplites were away) slipped secretly over the Isthmus. The Athenians mustered eight thousand hoplites to join them and another eighteen cities sent help. It was a substantial force but always liable to disintegration if internal squabbles broke out between rival commanders.

Mardonius was an experienced general and he had a superiority in numbers, especially in cavalry. After ravaging the crops of Attica during June he moved westward hoping to lure the Greek forces onto the plain of Boeotia and thus expose them to his horsemen. The Greeks were determined to challenge him to battle as it was the only way they could win the war. It was a complicated strategic game which followed with the Greeks following the Persians but sticking to high ground as the Persians tried to draw them off it. Bluff and counter-bluff followed as each side tried to engineer an attack to the best advantage. Accounts and theories of how battle was eventually joined differ. Some suggest that the Greeks, having been cut off from their water supplies on the plain, retreated in disorder; others that their retreat was part of a deliberate strategy. Whatever the truth, Mardonius confidently sent in his troops against the Greeks, who were near the town of Plataea. The Spartans, however, turned in good order to face him and their intensive training proved decisive. Despite a bitter struggle their ranks held and Mardonius, rallying his men on horseback in the center of battle, was killed by a well-aimed boulder. His death led to the disintegration of the Persian forces. Their reserves did not even stay to engage in battle but made straight home for Asia, outstripping the news of the defeat which followed them. The remnants of the defeated Persians followed them.

Plataea, not Salamis, was the decisive battle of the second Persian invasion. It had dislodged the Persian forces from Greece and sent them home in humiliation and so, possibly, had changed the course of European history. However, the Spartans were never as adept propagandists as the Athenians and the importance of their victory is often obscured. There was not much left to do. With Greece free of Persian forces the remainder of the Persian fleet was easily destroyed. Many of its surviving ships were Greek in any case and with the news of the victory of Plataea there was little point in its heading back to Greece. A rising of Ionian Greeks would almost certainly have followed its departure. Most of its vessels was destroyed by the Greek fleet as they lay drawn up on the beach at Mycale (on the mainland opposite Samos). The liberation of Aegean islands, Samos, Chios, and Lesbos, from the Persian yoke followed and it was Athenian ships which then sailed on north to the Hellespont to grab the great ropes which had held the bridge over the Channel as plunder. They were towed back to Athens in triumph.

Only thirty states took part in the defense of Greece against Xerxes' invasion; many more wavered or even gave support to the invasion, but soon even this patchy response was being shaped into something more majestic, a victory of Greeks against barbarians. Herodotus records the moment before Marathon when a casting vote has to be taken by the general Callimachus as to whether the Athenians should attack. " 'It is now in your hands, Callimachus,' says Miltiades, 'either to enslave Athens, or to make her free and to leave behind you for all future generations a memory more glorious than even Harmodius and Aristogeiton left.' " This representation of the wars as a blow for the freedom of the sovereign state is echoed in another verse of Simonides, an epitaph for the dead, already quoted. "If to die well be the chief part of virtue, fortune granted this to us above all others; for striving to endure Hellas with freedom we lie here possessed of praise that grows not old." Freedom here is defined not in terms of rights of the individual, as it would be later in European history, but in the freedom of citizens to share in their own government and make their own decisions about their future. The point was made so successfully that two thousand years later the nineteenth century English liberal John Stuart Mill was to argue that the battle of Marathon was a more important event in English history than the Battle of Hastings, precisely because the saving of Europe from a Persian tyranny allowed peoples such as the Britons and Saxons to forge their own identities.

Hand in hand with freedom went the adulation of supposed Greek virtues, among them moderation and self-restraint. These, it was suggested, not only helped bring victory (in allowing the antagonisms between Greek states to be subsumed in the common cause) but earned the Greeks the support of the gods, in contrast to the pride of Xerxes which forfeited it. The art historian J. J. Pollitt has argued that these virtues can be seen translated into art. He uses the example of the figures from the pediments from the temple to Zeus at Olympia (470–457), one of the great sculptural achievements of the period, to suggest that the victory over the Persians inspired the Greeks to reject "the decorative ornateness of archaic art and of the oriental heritage which was at the root of much of that ornateness." Instead, the expressions of the figures on the pediments comprise resolution, fear, tension, and, in the case of the famous seer, foreboding, but these are never overplayed. Here, perhaps, are a people who quietly delight in their superiority over the less restrained "barbarians" who tried to conquer them.

Just as Greek culture is shaped to a stereotype so too is that of their opponents. The process of defining the barbarian begins in Aeschylus'

The Persians (472 B.C.), which is a dramatic account of Xerxes' invasion set in the royal capital at Susa. Its main moral theme is that the overweening pride of a tyrannical ruler ends with humiliation as the gods retaliate. What defines the barbarian can be summed up under three heads, a love of luxury, a lack of emotional restraint, and a life of subjection to tyrannical rulers. The tyrants that rule barbarians are not chosen by them, exact taxation from them only for their personal benefit and the satisfaction of their greed, and act with brutality when crossed. By humiliating Xerxes, the Greek victory at Salamis struck as great a blow for Persian freedom as for Greek:

> "Not for long now" recites the chorus after Salamis, "will the inhabitants of Asia abide under Persian rule, nor pay further tribute under compulsion to the king, nor fall to the earth in homage, for the kingly power is destroyed. Men will no longer curb their tongues, for the people, unbridled, may chatter freely."
>
> (Translation: Edith Hall)

The barbarian image is elaborated by later writers such as the playwright Euripides. Barbarians do not live under a system of law as Greeks do in their cities. "That is what all barbarians are like. Fathers have intercourse with daughters, sons with mothers, sisters with brothers, close relatives murder each other, and no law forbids such crimes." Greeks, it is implied, live more restrained and regulated lives. These perceptions of the superiority of freedom over dictatorship between Greeks and Eastern peoples helped create a fault line between East and West that survives today.

A sense of a common Greek (rather than simply Athenian) consciousness shaped by the Persian Wars is also to be found in the great account of the wars by the "father of history," Herodotus. *The Histories* date from the 440s or 430s (they were mentioned as complete in an Athenian play of 425) and are remarkable not only for their scope but as the first recognizably "modern" work of history.

Herodotus' own background shows the complexity of the Greek heritage. His home town was Halicarnassus (the modern Bodrum) on the coast of Asia Minor, a Dorian foundation close to the Ionian cities to the north, but one which had a mixed population of Greeks and Carians. (Herodotus himself appears to have had Carian blood though culturally he was Greek and could speak no other language.) Living along this coast he may have been exposed not only to varied cultures but to the Ionian tradition of open enquiry and reasoned observation. (One of his influences appears to have been one Hecataeus, an Ionian, writing about 500 B.C. who adopted a markedly critical approach to tales he heard while compiling a geography of the known world.) By the time of Herodotus' birth (c. 484 B.C.), however, Halicarnassus was under Persian rule and Herodotus himself seems to have been driven out by internal political unrest. He is known to have visited Athens and the Athenian colony of Thurii in southern Italy where he may have died in the late 420s. If his accounts in *The Histories* are to be trusted, however, he also traveled widely through Egypt, around the Black Sea, and deep into the Persian empire as far as Babylon.

The Histories works at two levels. First it is a massive compilation of stories and information, collected from a huge variety of sources but triumphantly welded into a coherent whole. Even when there are digressions, and there are many, they are woven back into the main narrative. The first part of the work explores the causes of the Persian wars by conducting a survey of the Persian empire. It starts with the conquest by Lydia of the Greek cities of the coast of Asia Minor and then the conquest of Lydia itself by Cyrus. In Book Two there is the famous account of Herodotus' visit to Egypt, the fullest ancient description of the country to survive. It acts as a prelude to its conquest by Cambyses. Then comes the reign of Darius, and Herodotus explores his campaigns against the Scythians and along the northern Aegean. Then, starting in Book Five of the nine into which the work was later divided, *The Histories* contains a detailed narrative account of the Persian Wars from the Ionian revolt onward. The Battle of Marathon comes in Book Six; Xerxes' campaign against Greece starts in Book Seven.

Herodotus had an eye for an engaging anecdote. He begins with the tale of Gyges who was encouraged by the king of Lydia to spy on his wife when she was undressing for bed. She spotted him and gave him the challenge of killing himself or killing her husband and becoming king. He chose the latter. It is the first of many such tales occurring in a bewildering variety of contexts and societies. In Egypt, Herodotus was confronted by a culture of great antiquity which was steeped in ritual. He attempted to comprehend it by assuming that everything worked in the opposite way to life in Greece and so created a coherent if not always accurate picture of a highly complex and ordered society. At the other extreme the Scythians, described in relation to Darius' campaign against them, had no coherence to their lives at all, no fixed settlements or agriculture, no temples or altars, as uncivilized as could be, though, Herodotus notes, this nomadic life gave them the advantage of being unconquerable. There is no contempt in Herodotus' description of these people (he was in fact somewhat in awe of the Egyptians) and he proves astonishingly open-minded to the varieties of human experience.

Yet Herodotus was much more than a compiler of travelers' tales. He listened intelligently to what he was told and tried to reason things through for himself. The word he used to describe his work is *historia,* an enquiry, and the word survives in the modern word "history." Herodotus is critical of his sources and often trenchant in his dismissal of what he has been told. "The tale of the Alcmaeonidae treacherously signalling to the Persians with a shield [as the Persian fleet sailed towards Athens after the battle of Marathon] is, to me, quite extraordinary, and I cannot accept it," he writes on one occasion and goes on to sift through the evidence that supports his judgment. When dealing with a matter of geography, why the Nile floods each year, for instance, he works through some hypotheses and comes through to a reasoned, if in this case wrong, explanation for the floods. Herodotus did not discount the actions of the gods entirely in human affairs (he believed that they punish those, like Xerxes, who are guilty of excessive pride, in order, it seems, to restore the *cosmos* to an ordered balance) but, like the Ionian philosophers, he was happy to see the broad sweep of history within the context of the interactions of human rather than divine forces. In his narrative, events follow inexorably from the conquest of the Greek cities of Asia Minor by the Persians. The Ionian revolt is the natural result of the Persian conquest, the Persian counterattack on Greece the consequence of the help given to the revolt by the Athenians. There are also more subtle psychological causes at work. Herodotus is careful to spell out motives and the varying pressures behind decision making—in Xerxes' decision to invade Greece, for instance. In the sense that the discipline of history is the objective assessment of evidence (most of it in Herodotus' case, oral evidence) and the creation of a comprehensive narrative which is held together by cause, effect, and insight, Herodotus, "the father of history," marks the beginning of the Western historical tradition.

No historian can fail to shape his or her material within some form of ideological framework and Herodotus adopts one within lines already laid down by Aeschylus and others earlier in the century. The Persian Wars are defined as a clash between Greek and non-Greek, even though this oversimplifies the actual conflict. The Greeks are given a far greater coherence as a people than they really deserved when they are defined in a famous riposte, supposedly uttered by the Athenian negotiators when they reject a Persian alliance after the sacking of Athens, as having a common culture, religion, language, and customs (and it has been argued that Herodotus was aware that this was only an Athenian view of Greek culture). What really distinguishes them, however, is their love of freedom. Their city-states are their own, their rulers accountable to the citizens. They fight well because they are free and the contrast is made with the Persian troops who, at Thermopylae, have to be whipped into battle.

Herodotus goes further to place the Greek character within an ecological setting. Greece is the center of the world and its rugged terrain is ideal for producing men of hardy spirit. More fertile territories encourage softness and this is, in fact, the final message of *The Histories:* "Soft countries bred soft men . . . It is not the property of any one soil to produce fine fruits and good soldiers too." This is a relatively sophisticated attempt to create an understanding of why some human societies are more effective than others. The danger comes if one people awards itself privileges over those whose climate and ecology is less favorable but this is what happened for the Greeks. A century later Aristotle is writing in his *Politics* that a people's background qualifies them for either life as free citizens or as slaves. The freedom of the Greeks becomes, in short, as Orlando Patterson puts it in *Freedom in the Making of Western Culture*, an invitation to share in the overlordship of all slave peoples, that is all non-Greeks. So one of the most ugly aspects of the Western tradition, the subjugation of others as slaves, is legitimized.

The Athenians took things even further. In a fourth-century text attributed to Plato, Socrates holds forth on the nature of the Athenian identity:

> Such was the natural nobility of this city [says Socrates], so sound and healthy was the spirit of freedom among us, and the instinctive dislike of the barbarian, because we are pure Hel-

> lenes, having no admixture of barbarism in us. For we are not like others, descendants of Pelops or Cadmus or Aegyptus or Danaus, who are by nature barbarians, and by custom Hellenes, but we are pure Hellenes, uncontaminated by any foreign element, and therefore the hatred of the foreign has passed unadulterated into the lifeblood of the city.
>
> Plato, Menexenus (Translation: Jowett. Quoted in Sarah Morris, *Daidalos and the Origins of Greek Art*)

As the next chapters will show, much of Athens' success and failure in the fifth century was to stem from this overbearing confidence.

Afterword: The Temple of Zeus at Olympia

The temple of Zeus at Olympia was commissioned in the 470s by the people of Elis, who were responsible for the Olympic Games, and paid for from the spoils of war with a neighboring city, Pisa. It is a perfect example of a Doric temple although its columns, six along the facade and thirteen along the sides, seem rather thick for its height (much thicker for instance than those of the Parthenon) and may have made it rather forbidding.

Inside was one of the most awe-inspiring creations of the ancient world, Pheidias' vast statue of Zeus, one of the Seven Wonders of the Ancient World. The statue, which was constructed of wood in a large workshop on the site and then had ivory and gold plates added to it (the method is known as chryselephantine), was a little more than 45 feet (some 14 meters) high. It held a statue of Nike in one hand and a scepter topped by an eagle in the other. The whole effect was heightened by the large stone pool of dark limestone filled with olive oil which was placed in front of it to keep the ivory moist.

The statue has long since gone. Having, according to one account, defied an attempt by the Roman emperor Caligula to carry it off to Rome by uttering a spine-chilling laugh, it was finally moved by the emperor Thoedosius II to Constantinople in the fifth century A.D. where it was destroyed in a fire. What have survived from the temple are sculptures from its pediments and the metopes which lined the side walls. (They were preserved under the silt of the shifting river Alpheus.) They make up the finest set of sculptures from the period immediately after the Persian Wars and it is not surprising that scholars have tried to read into them the calm but triumphant atmosphere of the period. They are formal and restrained (in what is often called the "Severe Style") but many of the figures project an intense emotional message.

The subjects of the sculptures, which are carved from imported Parian marble, are all mythological. The east pediment is a serene and balanced scene. A chariot race is about to begin (an event well known to those visiting Olympia) and two chariots are drawn up on either side of a central figure who is probably Zeus. The story is known. King Oinomaos of Elis, attempting to prevent his daughter from marrying as a result of a prediction that her husband would one day kill him, asks any suitor to race against him in a chariot race. As he has magic horses he always wins and the unsuccessful suitors are killed. Finally Pelops defeats him by the ruse of replacing the wooden lynch pins of his chariot with wax ones. They melt, Oinomaos crashes, and as he dies places a curse on Pelops and his family. This does not prevent Pelops marrying Oinomaos' daughter but his descendants, who include Atreus and Agamemnon, are cursed. (They provide rich material for Greek tragedy, see Chapter Twelve.) None of this is known as the chariots prepare but on the right behind a chariot a reclining figure looks on. This is the "seer." He knows before anyone how things will turn out and his pose and gesture are not those of a man of action but of a man of deep reflection and insight. This is something new in Greek sculpture.

The western pediment has at its center a figure of Apollo. The god is shown at his most serene though fully aware of what is a scene of turmoil around him. The story here is of Pirithous, king of the Lapiths, a tribe from Thessaly. He has invited the Centaurs (half men and half horses) to his wedding but they get drunk and cause havoc, even assaulting the bride. An unseemly brawl ensues before the Lapiths throw them out. There are several possible messages here. The Centaurs have certainly abused hospitality and the rules of fair play and deserve defeat. The Lapiths have shown that through determination ordinary mortals can triumph, as the competitors in the games would hope to do. Apollo, the god of reason and order, oversees the victory of the Lapiths over the forces of disorder.

The theme of determination winning through is followed up in the twelve metopes which show the Twelve Labors of Heracles. (It was in fact these metopes which set out the Heracles' Labors in full for the first time.) Heracles was a son of Zeus and as such could be associated with Olympia but his Labors took place in various parts of the Greek world and it could be said that the metopes stress the Panhellenic nature of the Olympic games. Viewers would also have known that it was through his Labors that Heracles became transformed from mere mortal hero into an immortal. So too could victorious athletes reach close to the gods as the odes of Pindar suggested.

10

The Fifth Century: The Politics of Power 479–404 B.C.

Victory in the Persian Wars had made Athens the most influential player in the Greek world. For the next seventy-five years the city was to dominate in the Aegean, successfully using its prestige, wealth, and naval power to prevent a revival of Persian power and while doing so establishing an empire consisting of as many as 150 smaller Greek cities. At home the Athenians were to create a highly sophisticated form of democratic government, one in which ordinary citizens participated directly both as members of the assembly and as its administrators and jurors. The city was also a major cultural center, home to the great building program on the Acropolis, the cradle of western drama, and the breeding ground of the western philosophical tradition.

As the early pages of this book suggested, Athens has been idealized by later generations, and not without reason. The city's achievements were considerable. There were, however, many paradoxes in her "achievement." Athens' democratic system depended on slavery and, to some extent, the income from an empire. Democratic government did not necessarily mean benign or tolerant government. Decrees of the Assembly included those ordering the massacre of the entire male population of another Greek island and the mass enslavement of its women and children. Pericles unscrupulously diverted the tribute raised by the empire (supposedly for common defense) into his building program on the Acropolis. "Greece cannot but consider it as an insufferable affront," said his critics, that treasure provided to defend Greece from the Persians should be "wantonly lavished out by us upon our city, to gild her all over as if it were some vain woman hung round with precious stones." (Quoted in Plutarch's *Life of Pericles.*) The city that had defined and upheld the concept of the sovereignty of the Greek city against the onslaught of the Persians abused and even destroyed the independence of other Greek cities. It is with these paradoxes in mind that the achievements of classical Athens must be explored.

The cultural and political achievements of Athens were linked to each other. The drama festivals were an essential part of the democratic process, and it was the experience of political and social upheaval that sustained developments in philosophy. However, in order to explore each element of the Athenian experience in the fifth and fourth century in detail, the material is here divided, somewhat arbitrarily, among four chapters. In the first, the story is told of how Athens' pride rose during the fifth century but was then humbled by defeat by Sparta in the Peloponnesian War. In the second, Athens' democratic system and the means by which the cohesion of the city was sustained is explored. Chapter Twelve is devoted to drama, Chapter Thirteen to philosophy.

Persia may have been humbled by the defeats of 490 and 480–479 but an empire of its size always had the resources to launch a fresh attack and the city-states of the Aegean, particularly those of the Asian coastline, knew they were very vulnerable. Soon after the war of 480–79 ambassadors from many states approached Athens for protection and the city was happy to respond. Whatever its emotional and cultural links with the Ionian Greeks of Asia Minor, Athens had solid reasons for maintaining an Aegean presence. As the city grew it needed secure trade routes and bases across the sea for grain supplies to come through the Hellespont and for timber (for shipbuilding) and minerals from the northern Aegean coast. There is much debate as to how dependent Athens was on grain supplies from the Black Sea but a recent survey of the evidence by Michael Whitby suggests that in a normal year half Athens' grain came from aboard, above all from the Black Sea. Whitby argues, further, that the Athenians were always ready to import more than they needed, in that a surplus of grain kept prices down in Athens and might even leave some for reexport at a profit. The route through the Hellespont assumed an emotional importance, similar perhaps to the Suez Canal for Britain in the 1950s. If Whitby's analysis is accepted, it is understandable that Athens was bound to welcome any pretext for extending its interests across the Aegean.

The physical expression of Athenian power lay in its triremes. Having gambled successfully on building a great navy and using it with stunning success at Salamis, the city was a major and still-expanding naval power, maintaining 180 triremes in 480, 300 by 431. This was an enormous force at a time when few cities could find the four hundred fit young men needed to man even two of the warships. The vast cost, which included the payment of some sixty thousand men, many of them mercenaries or foreigners living in Athens, was met through the riches of the Laurion silver mines and, from the 440s, tribute from an Aegean empire. Wealthier citizens were also expected to adopt a particular boat and pay for its equipment. The standard of training seems to have been exceptional. Forces of Athenian triremes consistently outmaneuvered their opponents in battle. Leadership was good too, the system of allowing generals (who commanded at sea as well as on land) to stand for election from year to year meant that the most effective could be retained and gain in experience from one campaign to another.

Within the Greek world a challenge to this new force might have come from Sparta, the most powerful Greek *polis* of the sixth century and one whose victory at Plataea confirmed that its hoplite forces remained the best trained and most effective in the Greek world. However, Sparta was always restrained by its position. The city was economically self-sufficient with control of the largest territory of any mainland Greek state, but only so long as it kept the helot population of fertile Messenia under rigid control. In the Peloponnese as a whole, Sparta's influence also remained precarious. There is evidence of renewed conflicts with its oldest enemy Argos and the cities of Arcadia in the years that followed the Persian Wars. Any major Spartan offensive overseas was always a risk (unless, as in the Plataean campaign, a large number of helots were included in it) and Sparta certainly could not have afforded to support a navy as well as an army. By tradition, too, only the hereditary kings could lead expeditions overseas so there was always an element of chance in the quality of leadership. Conservative, inward looking, and, as so often with isolated players, clumsy in its relationships overseas, there was little Sparta could do to to prevent Athens' expansion into the Aegean. Immediately after the victory there *had* been an expeditionary force to the Aegean of twenty triremes led by Pausanias, the Spartan commander at Plataea (himself the son of a king and acting as regent at the time of his command), but it behaved so arrogantly that it threw away any possible hope of winning friends for Sparta. When the Spartans protested at Athens' rebuilding its city walls, Athens simply ignored the protest.

However, the alliance between the two cities, so successful in fighting off the Persians, survived. The dominant figure in Athens after 480 was Cimon whose prestige rested partly on the fact that Miltiades, the victorious general at Marathon, was his father, but whose own vision, energy, and skills as a politician and commander made him a formidable figure in his own right. He respected Sparta for the part she had played in the Persian war and was even prepared, unlike other Athenians, to credit her for her role in throwing out the Pisistratids. He also realized that a quiescent Sparta would allow Athens a free hand in the Aegean and so he kept the alliance in place. The Spartans accepted, if reluctantly, Athens' role as a policeman in the Aegean.

Athens now had to find a vehicle through which her power in the Aegean could be extended. In 477 she masterminded the setting up of a league of states, the so-called Delian League, whose common purpose was stated to be a defensive and offensive alliance against Persia. The number of cities that joined the league from the beginning is not known. (By 450, tribute lists preserved on stone in Athens suggest there were about 150 members.) They were drawn predominantly from the Ionian cities along the coast of Asia Minor but others such as the Dorian city Byzantium and the Aeolian island Lesbos were members as well. A central meeting place had to be found and a traditional cult center for the Ionians, the birthplace of Apollo, the island of Delos (hence the name, Delian), was chosen. Athens provided the treasurers of the league and the bulk of the naval forces and the members agreed to provide either ships or a money payment. Over time most chose to pay money with only Chios and Lesbos till making their commitment in ships by 431. Although the members had an equal voice in the league's council, none could possibly match Athens' power, so in effect the league's expeditions were Athenian-led and this gave Athens the opportunity she may have hoped for from the beginning to shape the activities of the league toward her own self-interest.

THE GREEK WORLD FROM THE SEVENTH AND FOURTH CENTURIES B.C.

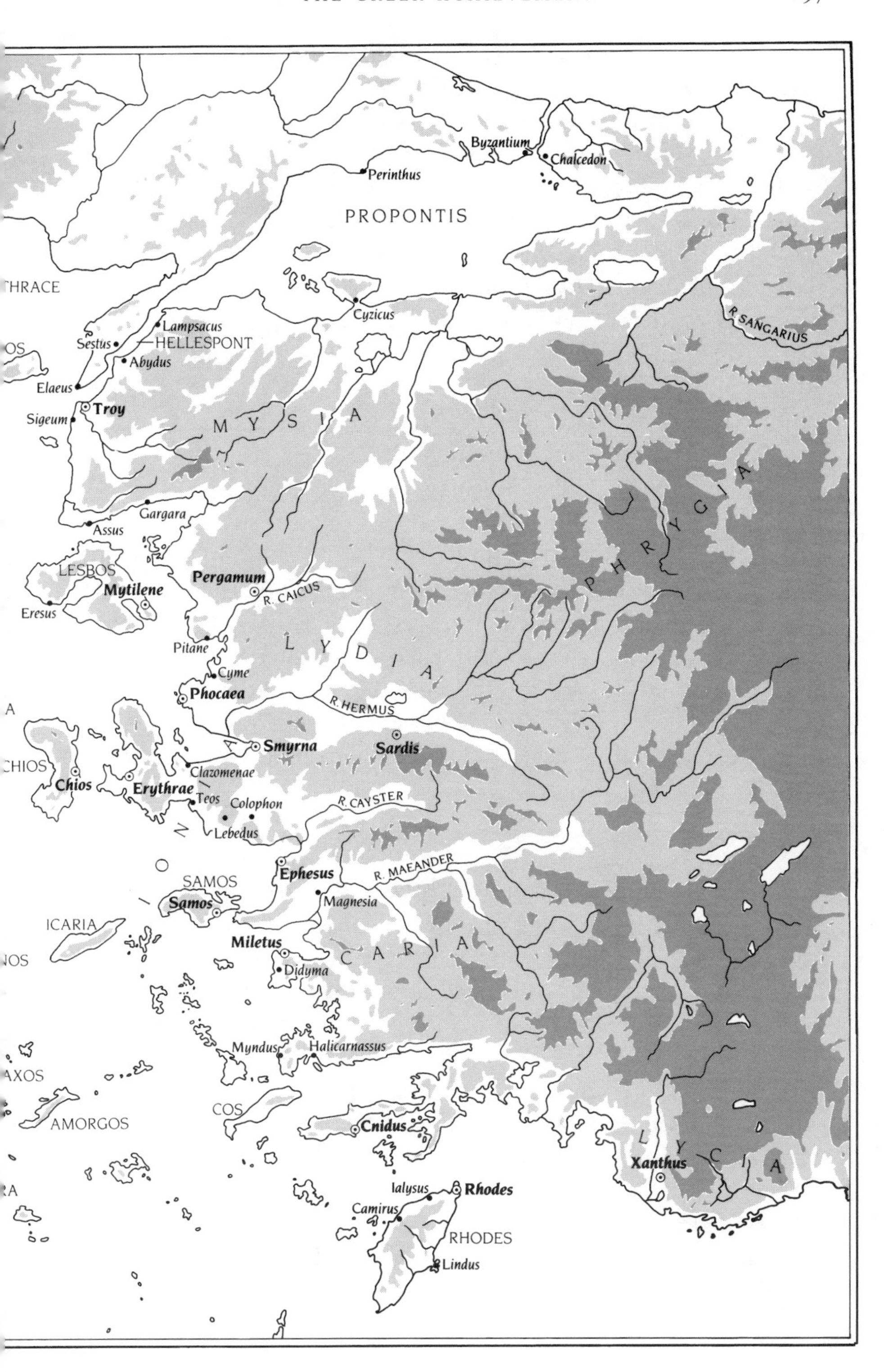
Byzantium
Chalcedon
Perinthus
PROPONTIS
THRACE
Cyzicus
R. SANGARIUS
Lampsacus
Sestus
HELLESPONT
Abydus
Elaeus
Troy
Sigeum
MYSIA
PHRYGIA
Gargara
Assus
LESBOS
Mytilene
Eresus
Pergamum
R. CAICUS
Pitane
LYDIA
Cyme
Phocaea
R. HERMUS
Smyrna
Sardis
CHIOS
Chios
Erythrae
Clazomenae
Teos
Colophon
Lebedus
R. CAYSTER
IONIA
Ephesus
R. MAEANDER
SAMOS
Samos
Magnesia
ICARIA
Miletus
CARIA
Didyma
Myndus
Halicarnassus
AMORGOS
COS
Cnidus
LYCIA
Xanthus
Ialysus
Rhodes
Camirus
RHODES
Lindus

One of the first raids of the league's forces was to oust a Persian garrison from Eion, at the mouth of the River Strymon. This was well-within the original aims of the league but it appears that the Athenian forces then fought their way inland in the hope, which proved unsuccessful, of founding a colony in a region rich in timber. Soon afterward a tidying up operation to clear the island of Scyros of pirates became something more when the Athenians settled the island and enslaved its inhabitants. Its position on the grain route to the Hellespont was doubtless the reason for the takeover. Something even more ruthless in Athenian behaviour was seen in 470 when the island of Naxos attempted to leave the league and was forced back in. Five years later another island city-state, Thasos, attempted to secede in a dispute over its mineral and timber resources but after a siege of two years it also was brought under Athenian influence. The original aims of the league were met more directly when Cimon destroyed a Persian fleet at the Eurymedon River (in Pamphylia) about 468. The plunder was enormous (it included twenty thousand slaves). The overall picture of the Delian League, however, was one of activity in Athenian interests. Trade routes were consolidated, raw materials searched for, and Athenian forces used to crush any states that attempted to keep their independence. Athens' belief in her own superiority as the only truly pure Greek city was being translated into an ideology which justified the right to dominate.

In 465 there came a diversion from Athens' primary aim of hegemony in the Aegean. A devastating earthquake in Sparta (devastating partly because it may have killed many of Sparta's hoplite elite) was followed by a helot revolt. Cimon attempted to use the crisis to cement his alliance with Sparta. He raised a force of four thousand hoplites in Athens and made for the Peloponnese to help. Once the hoplites arrived, however, they appear to have had grave reservations as to their role in suppressing fellow Greeks and the Spartans sent them home. It was a humiliation for Cimon, who was exiled by his city for ten years in the fervor of the so-called "democratic revolution" of 461. This finally shifted power away from aristocratic institutions of the city to the Assembly, which now became the center of Athenian policy making. The mastermind behind the revolution was a young aristocrat,

Pericles, and it is he who becomes the dominant figure in the city in the years to come. (See page 223.)

The democratic revolution meant the rejection of the alliance with Sparta, the known champion of oligarchy, and friend of the disgraced Cimon. Athenian foreign policy was immediately reoriented to box in the new enemy. First an alliance was made with Sparta's old adversary, Argos. Then, when the neighboring city of Megara asked Athens for assistance against the ambitions of Corinth, the Athenians simply brought Megara under control and so gained control of access to the Isthmus over which Spartan land troops would have to cross into central Greece. A counterattack by Corinth was beaten off and so began a tension between Athens and Corinth, still the second largest naval power in Greece, which was to have long-term consequences. In 458 the island of Aegina, a trading rival for centuries, was besieged and bullied into joining the league.

In the same year came a direct clash with the Spartans. The Spartans had sent a force north in support of their mother city Doris (presumably by sea as the Isthmus was blocked off) but there were rumors in Athens that the force was also interested in collaborating with Spartan sympathizers in Athens to overthrow the city's democratic government and regain Athens' friendship. The Athenians were taking no chances and crossed the border of Attica to confront the Spartans at Tanagra. The Spartans seem to have had the upper hand in the fighting but were content to return home after the battle. (They never appear to have had any serious interest in attacking Athens.) It left Athens free to follow the battle up by seizing control of the Boeotian plain, forcing its cities into an alliance with her.

Athens now seemed supreme in central Greece as well as in the Aegean but the city was seriously overstretched. Cimon's forward policy in the Aegean had been successful because all the city's resources could be diverted to it. It could not be maintained now that Sparta was an enemy. This was brought home to Athens in 454 when a large naval force, probably over two hundred triremes, which had been sent to help an Egyptian revolt against Persia in 459, was heavily defeated. Athenian activity against both Persia and the cities of central Greece appears to have been halted in its tracks. Although there was a victory in Cyprus in 451 against Cypriots and Phoenicians, subjects of the Persian empire, Cimon, who had been recalled from exile to command the expedition, died there and his death marked the collapse of the anti-Persian crusade. It must have made sense to make peace with Persia. No details exist but a peace treaty, the so-called Peace of Callias, appears to have been made about 449 and there was no direct fighting with Persia for some time.

The peace did not solve Athens' problems. By 446 the city's control on the mainland was also in jeopardy. A defeat of an Athenian force by a coalition of Boeotian cities at the battle of Coronaea was followed by the restoration of the independence of its cities. The Corinthians helped Megara break free of Athenian control while Athenian forces were busy putting down a revolt on Euboea and a Spartan force, now able to cross the Isthmus, even entered and ravaged Attica. Sparta had regained its freedom to operate on the mainland and Athens was forced to make peace with her in 446/5. Athens appears to have promised not to maintain an alliance with Argos and to surrender two ports of Megara. It was agreed that neither side would directly attack each other without first seeking arbitration. (This period of skirmishing between the two powers and their allies is known as the First Peloponnesian War.)

Although Athens appeared to be the loser in the war, the settlement suggests that Sparta acquiesced in her dominance in the Aegean. At peace both with Persia and Sparta, Athens could now concentrate on her immediate interests in the Aegean and she did so with determination. The shock effect of the defeat in Egypt had led to the withdrawal of the Delian treasury to Athens. Athens was now able to collect the tribute directly and part of the money was transferred without apparent compunction into the city's own great building plans of the 440s. Many of these tribute lists (inscribed on stone) have survived and the number of states paying and their total contributions can be calculated. They show the shift of Athenian energy after the peace with Persia. Tribute was collected in full in 449 and then not at all in 448. In 447 payments resumed but the total was less than in 449. In 446 the full amount was gathered. The numbers can be read to suggest that after the peace with Persia members of the league assumed they could stop paying the league anything (448) but that within two years Athens had forced them back to paying the original levies direct to the city. No mention is now made of the league. Rather, there is a source of the 440s that talks "of the cities the Athenians control." In 446 when the city of Chalcis on Euboea was subdued it promised loyalty to Athens alone with no mention of the league. The council of the league stopped meeting in these years. A league supposedly of equal and independent states (though in practice this had never existed) had been transformed into an Athenian empire.

The purpose of the empire, now that it did not have a defined enemy, was to maintain Athens' economic, cultural, and political supremacy. Athens approached her task with something of the fervor of the American Cold War warriors of the 1950s. Thucydides relates the words of her statesman Pericles. "We inspire wonder now and we shall in the future . . . for we have forced every sea and every land to give access to our daring; and we have in all places established everlasting memorials of evil inflicted on our enemies and of good done to our friends." As in most empires, the methods of control by the imperial power varied from the relatively benign and subtle to the brutal. A sense of common fellowship was maintained through the insistence that all subject cities, not only the Ionian ones, came to celebrate the Great Panathenaea, bringing a cow and a panoply with them and taking part in the procession. One Athenian decree ordered the city of Brea in Thrace (which was actually a settled Athenian colony) to bring a model phallus to carry each year in the procession of the festival to Dionysus.

It is hard to recreate the atmosphere of the Athenian empire and the forces which held it together. There was certainly a coercive element in Athens' control. Underlying Athenian hegemony was the payment of tribute, as the original contributions to the common league's resources had now become. The sums were normally fixed, thirty talents a year for a prosperous city-state such as Thasos, for instance. These were not excessive sums (thirty talents would be enough to keep the men of a fleet of twenty triremes in pay for three months) and exemptions were often granted to buy the loyalty of a city at a time of crisis or in return for an Athenian garrison being allowed to be stationed there, but tribute was still highly resented as a symbol of Athenian power. Inspectors (*episkopoi*) collected the money each year, sealed it with marked identification from the city concerned, and then presented it to the *boule* or Council of Five Hundred in Athens. Confirmation that each subject city had paid, or failed to pay, was made once a year at a meeting of the Athenian Assembly.

In the subject cities themselves, Athenian interests could be represented by a *proxenos*, a leading citizen of that city who agreed to act for the Athenians who visited the city, representing them in court if needs be and so on (here is the origin of the English word *proxy*). Some were prepared to go even further and attempt to influence their city's affairs in Athens' favor. It was a dangerous game. While a *proxenos* might have prestige in the eyes of Athens (and be recognized in his role by a special decree of the Assembly), to his fellow citizens he was often seen as a collaborator. One *proxenos,* Peithias of Corfu, was brought to trial by his people on a charge of having enslaved his people to Athens. He was later lynched.

A much more intrusive form of control was the cleruchy. A cleruch was an Athenian citizen allowed to settle overseas without losing his citizenship at home. Cleruchies were colonies set up on land which was appropriated for the purpose, sometimes from cities which had revolted. One example was the city of Histiaea on Euboea, an important staging post on the way to the Hellespont, which revolted alongside other Euboean cities in 446. The site of the city was completely cleared of its people and then resettled with Athenian colonists. These cleruchies could act as bases for Athenian forces but they were also a way of settling poorer citizens outside Athens—some cleruchies drew settlers only from the lower property groups. Here the social needs of an overcrowded city and the strategic requirement to maintain a presence outside Athens coalesced. J. K. Davies has gone so far as to say that in essence "the Athenian presence in the Aegean amounts to a tremendous land-grab, carried out and protected by Athenian naval power for the benefit of Athenian citizens of all classes."

Although Athens was hardly as exploitative as some later empires (the Romans at their worst were appalling plunderers of their imperial possessions), this was an empire run in Athens' economic self-interest. One decree (possibly of the early 440s) orders all the subject cities of the empire to use Athenian coinage, weights, and measures and not to mint silver coins of their own. The decree can be seen as a symbol of Athenian dominance but it also had the practical effect of making tribute easier to collect. There is even evidence that when the assorted coinage in which tribute had been paid to the Delian treasury was brought to Athens it was melted down and then reminted as Athenian coins. These could then be paid out direct to rowers, officials, and mercenaries.

As the original members of the empire settled, Athens reached out further to strengthen her economic interests. These became more extensive as the needs of the city for raw materials grew. In 437, after two abortive attempts, a settlement, Amphipolis, was finally established up the river Strymon. It was on the coastal route to the Hellespont and thus had strategic value but it also acted as an entre-pôt for goods from farther upstream, for gold and silver from mines of Mount Pangaeus and for timber. Settled with a mixed population (Athenian and others) of some ten thousand it came to have the same kind of emotional and commercial importance to the Athenians as Singapore did for the British. Sometime afterward the reality of Athenian power was impressed on the cities of the Black Sea when Pericles took a fleet along its coastline. A sign of Athens' widening interests came with the settling of an Athenian colony at Thurii, on the instep of Italy, in 443.

Yet there was always a fundamental strategic weakness of the empire in that a concerted revolt would be impossible to suppress, especially if it involved scattered cities. For a start, suppression was

expensive. According to Thucydides the three-year siege of Potidaea and some surrounding cities (432–430) cost 2,000 talents, or 650 talents a year. The annual tribute from the entire empire was only 600 talents (though there was at least as much again from other sources). The failure to respond to the Potidaean revolt, however, would have surely meant outbreaks of rebellion elsewhere and the empire would quickly have unraveled. The larger cities of the empire provided a real challenge if they rebelled. In 440, for instance, Samos, an important city-state with a good-sized navy, revolted. The revolt was suppressed by Athens but only as a result of a number of lucky chances—that the Persians did not see it as a chance to counterattack and that Lesbos and Chios decided to send a handy number of ships to support Athens. In short, Athenian control was relatively precarious and much more vulnerable than it seemed. Pericles, who had no illusions about his city's position, saw the trap in which Athens was caught. "By now the empire you hold is a tyranny," he told the Athenians who had flocked into the city at the start of the Peloponnesian War (431), "it may seem wrong to have taken it, but it is surely dangerous to let it go for you are hated by those you have ruled."

Yet in spite of all these intrusions, the Athenian empire survived until the city's defeat by Sparta in 404. It suggests that there were underlying benefits that balanced the demands. It is probable that the brooding power of Persia and perhaps the threat of attack from other cities may have helped the subject cities acquiesce in Athenian control. Athens seems also to have used her democratic ideology to appeal to the *demoi* of the cities against the oligarchies who ruled most of them. The evidence is very fragmentary but there is some that potential revolts led by oligarchic leaders against Athens were thwarted by the refusal of pro-Athenian democrats to join in. (This may have been one further reason why Samos' oligarchical government was defeated.)

Perhaps the biggest threat to the empire came from the risk of destabilization from outside. The expansion of Athenian interests was bound to incur the suspicion of free states, in particular those of the Peloponnesian League. When Samos revolted, the members of the league actually met to consider whether they should intervene to support the island. The Spartan council voted in favor of war but the league as a whole was restrained by a negative vote from Corinth, which was reluctant to support such a distant revolt. The attitude of Corinth shifted as the Athenians intruded with growing recklessness in the west. In 433 Athenians approached Corinth's colony Corfu, a vital staging post on the way to the west and the state with the third biggest navy in Greece, supporting her in breaking away from Corinth. A small Athenian fleet, of ten triremes, actually clashed with the Corinthian fleet, which withdrew when another Athenian force came up in support. Corfu had been defended but there was now open hostility between Athens and Corinth. Trouble then brewed in the Corinthian colony of Potidaea, which had been a member of the Delian League and thus absorbed into the empire. Athens had been worried about its loyalty and demanded the dismissal of its Corinthian magistrates. The Potidaeans naturally called on Corinth and Sparta for help and then broke into a revolt which was joined by several of their neighbors (432). Altogether seventy Athenian triremes had to be sent to quell the revolt while Corinth retaliated by sending a force of two thousand hoplites. The Athenians were forced to settle down to a three-year siege.

These were symptoms of a deteriorating situation. Corinth was now in total opposition to Athens and was driven towards Sparta, which, Thucydides makes clear, was simmering with resentment at the continued Athenian expansion that, on her own, she could do nothing to prevent. Here at last was a chance for revenge. Athenian forces were in Potidaea, the Corinthian navy was available, and support was offered by the strategically placed Megara, which seems to have been under some trade ban from Athens. Sparta could pose as a liberator of the subject cities of the empire. These were all factors that tipped the balance. A state of war between Sparta and Athens had to be created, however, and this was done by Sparta's encouraging Thebes, one of her allies, to attack Plataea, an ally of Athens since the heady days of Marathon. It was an outrage to the sacred rules of war but it broke the tension. The Peloponnesian War (431–404), actually the second under this name, was under way.

There is a fine contemporary history of the Peloponnesian War, written by Thucydides, an Athenian aristocrat connected to Cimon's family. Thucydides was in the center of things, a survivor of the devastating plague of 430 in Athens and a general in the northern Aegean in 424. When he failed to save the trading center of Amphipolis from the Spartans in that year he was exiled and spent the twenty years to his death outside Athens. He retained contacts there but was now free to travel the Peloponnese to gather the story of the Spartan side of the war. His account had reached the year 411 by the time he died around 400 B.C.

As soon as the war began Thucydides grasped its importance in comparison to earlier wars in Greek history (he was right, the Peloponnesian War was to Greek history what the First World War was to European) and he determined to write a documentary history of events as they unfolded. He took himself and his craft seriously, contrasting himself with Herodotus whom he derided for his loose use of sources and inaccuracies. He, he insisted, was of a different stature, recording what actually happened, not like a poet (and a Herodotus) in an attempt to catch the emotion of the reader, but as someone setting the record straight for all time. His is a much more tightly controlled narrative than Herodotus', altogether more scientific in its approach and one focused with precision on its subject. There are none of Herodotus' colorful digressions here. This does not mean, however, that Thucydides' work lacks emotional impact, as any reader of his vivid description of the horrific end of the Athenian expedition to Sicily discovers. In his penetration to the core of human motivation, his steady gaze on the horrors of war, his superb narrative power, Thucydides ranks as one of Europe's major historians.

Generally, Thucydides has been taken at his own word and the truthfulness and accuracy of what he wrote accepted. This should not mask the fact that what he chose to describe was highly selective (and as other sources for the war, inscriptions among them, are revealed there is increasing questioning of his accuracy). Unlike Herodotus, for instance, Thucydides is not interested in the cultural background to the societies that fought the war, nor, as a modern historian might be, how each side raised the resources to fight it. Rather it is the events of the war themselves that interest him. Although Thucydides could not have known it when he began writing, these events created their own message. The story of the Peloponnesian War is the story of the humbling of Athens, largely as a result of her own blunders. Some scholars have argued that Thucydides deliberately shaped his narrative this way, highlighting the way in which Athenian brutality and arrogance in the massacring of the men of Melos, an island of pro-Spartan sympathies in 416, or the plan to take over all Sicily, for instance, was "revenged" by the city's downfall (in the same way that the playwright Aeschylus argued that the arrogance of the Persian king Xerxes offended the gods and so was punished by them through his humiliating defeat). There may be something in this but essentially Thucydides was the prisoner of unfolding events. His narrative was conditioned by what was actually happening around hm.

What seems to have fascinated Thucydides was not just the events of the war but the way human beings reacted to the pressures these created. Here Thucydides shared one of the preoccupations of his age, intense critical interest in human nature. What conditioned the ways human beings behaved? Were there common human instincts found in every society or did society shape behavior through conventions and custom? Was the way human behaved in particular circumstances predictable, as many other aspects of the physical world were seen to be? The answers could perhaps be found from observation and in this sense Thucydides' detached narrative acts as a laboratory for the dissection of human behavior.

Thucydides' portrayal of human beings is laced with cynicism. As he starts his analysis of the civil war in Corcyra, "And so many terrible things happened to cities through civil conflict, things which happen and will always happen so long as the nature of men is the same." For him, as for many thinkers of the fifth century, human beings stand on their own, independent of any divine or moral forces and they act in self-interest, often with a complete lack of scruple. "The strong do what they have to do, the weak accept what they have to accept," says an Athenian representative as he imposes his city's will on the people of Melos, through the massacring of their menfolk and the enslavement of their women and children. Those who have power structure the world the way they want to. Pragmatism rules over any sense of morality or fair play. When the men of Plataea surrender to the Spartans in 427 they are executed, solely, it seems, to impress Sparta's ally Thebes. Cruelty breeds cruelty, as in the civil war of 427 in Corfu when the warring factions in the city inflict atrocity and counter-atrocity on each other. Thucydides' world is a bleak one, made bleaker by the vicious nature of the fighting he describes. The Peloponnesian War was a war of terror and counterterror, one in which whole cities were destroyed and their inhabitants enslaved or massacred.

When the war began in 431 Pericles had been Athens' leading statesman for over twenty years, a remarkable achievement in a city that was ruled by a volatile assembly of its citizens. He is Thucydides' hero and he is portrayed as having a shrewd and realistic idea of the strengths and weaknesses of his city. What was essential, Pericles argued, was to keep the fleet intact, the trade routes secure, and the empire stable. The Long Walls constructed in 458 that ran around the city and down to enclose the Piraeus had made it impregnable from the land and allowed it to be provisioned by sea. This meant that Attica itself could be abandoned without Athens itself being lost and Pericles ordered those living there to come into the city. There is no better evidence of the strength of community life at the level of the Athenian demes than the bitter complaints of the countrymen that followed. It was not only their homes and fields which were abandoned but the most deeply held convention of Greek warfare—never surrender territory to an invading force without a fight. Further pressures were added when plague swept through Athens in 430, killing perhaps a quarter of the population. Those who had come into the city and settled in closely packed huts were the worst affected. Thucydides describes the plague in one of his great set pieces, analyzing its symptoms with scientific precision but making no attempt to mask the emotional devastation it brought.

The war soon settled into stalemate. There seemed no obvious way that either side could secure a decisive victory. Athens did not have sufficient land forces to defeat Sparta, Sparta the naval forces to destroy Athens. The Spartans ravaged Attica regularly during the 420s but there was no way they could seriously weaken the city by doing so. The Athenians counterattacked along the Peloponnesian coast. A failure by Pericles to take Epidaurus (in the southeastern Peloponnese) in 430 added to the enormous frustrations caused by his defensive policies at home, and led to his being fined and temporarily deposed. Though reinstated as general, he died in 429. Thucydides now records that policy fell into the hands of more unscrupulous leaders from nonaristocratic backgrounds and associates this with a more volatile foreign policy. Cleon, for instance, owner of a tanning shop, persuaded the Assembly to order the execution of all the men of Mytilene and the enslavement of its women and children after the city had revolted in 428. (After reflection, the Assembly reconsidered its decision.) However, in 425 Athens had a stroke of luck when 120 Spartans on the island of Sphacteria off the western Peloponnese were captured and taken back as hostages to Athens. Such a public surrender was deeply humiliating for Sparta and the loss of even such a small force of highly trained men important when Spartan manpower appears to have been in decline. It was followed by the Athenian capture of the island of Cythera, close enough to Sparta for the Spartans to worry that a helot revolt could be sparked off by the Athenian presence. (If Athens had made the instigation of a helot revolt a priority it might have won the war easily.) Some face was saved the following year when a Spartan general Brasidas took an expedition to the northern Aegean and captured the trading city of Amphipolis and several others before being killed in 422. (Cleon who was leading the Athenian expedition against him was killed at the same time.) Both sides were now happy to make peace (the Peace of Nicias, 421 B.C.). Amphipolis was to be returned to Athens and Cythera to Sparta. The Spartan prisoners were also to be sent home. Sparta had failed in its attempt to destabilize the Athenian empire although, to the fury of Athens, Amphipolis chose with Spartan connivance to remain independent of the empire.

The peace, however, did not hold. Thucydides never believed it would; there was simply too much unfinished business. Nothing, for instance, had been done for Megara or for Corinth, which had lost several possessions in the northern Aegean and which now turned against Sparta for failing to protect her interests. By 418 Athens was again meddling in the Peloponnese, exploiting the traditional hostility of Argos for Sparta to create an anti-Spartan coalition. (Argos had made a thirty-year peace with Sparta which had now expired.) Sparta looked to be doomed as the coalition assembled against her. It was now that the Athenians might have finished Sparta once and for all but they missed their chance. Only one thousand hoplites were sent to the Peloponnese, compared to the four thousand Pericles had raised for the Epidaurus expedition of 430. It was not enough. Once again the enormous superiority of Sparta's hoplite training and tactics was shown when at the battle of Mantineia, one of the largest hoplite battles recorded with perhaps twenty thousand men involved, she crushed her enemies. The humiliation of Sphacteria was revenged and Spartan supremacy on land reaffirmed. The survival of Sparta at this moment could, with hindsight, be seen as the turning point of the war (and hence, the failure of Athens to strike at her with every man possible a major misjudgment).

The Athenian intrusion in the Peloponnese had been masterminded by a flamboyant but unscrupulous young aristocrat, Alcibiades. Alcibiades was to prove a competent soldier and a skilled diplomat but these qualities were overlaid by his egotism and personal ambition. He believed that the Assembly would be impressed by his wealth, which he spent with open panache, and the recent success of his chariot teams in the Olympic Games. Some citizens undoubtedly were but others felt that such profligacy was not suited to a democratic city. Their preferred politician was the older and more cautious Nicias who had masterminded the peace of 421 with Sparta. The two men fought openly before the Assembly over what should be the next move in the war.

By chance a city of Sicily, Segesta, had appealed for help to Athens against its neighbor Selinus who was a protégée of Syracuse, the wealthiest city of Sicily (and originally a foundation of Corinth's). Athens had already been probing to the west; an expedition had been sent to support so-called allies of Athens (some of them Ionian foundations) in Sicily in 427, and the fertility of the island and southern Italy was well known. So the possibility of sending an expedition to Sicily to support Athens' allies' there again and to consolidate the economic links was attractive. However, it was difficult to see how such an expedition would help defeat Sparta, except indirectly through cutting off the grain supply of the island to the Peloponnese. A more cautious approach, probably the one Pericles would have adopted, might have been not to risk any further extension of Athenian interests while Athens was still at war. However, a proposal to send an expedition of sixty ships was accepted by the Assembly. A fleet of this size could have been spared, but a few days later in an impassioned debate dominated by Alcibiades who played on the supposed ease with which Sicily could be conquered and the enormous wealth which would accrue to Athens if she was, a plan to send a much larger expedition was adopted by an emotionally charged Assembly. Little thought was given to how Sicily would have been held, and most important of all, what would happen if the expedition failed. Here Thucydides' assertion (reinforced no doubt by his own aristocratic perspective) that democratic assemblies were not always the best decision makers seems justified.

There were three generals appointed to lead the expedition, Alcibiades, the experienced Nicias (who, though he had always opposed the expedition, was not prepared to let his city down by refusing a command), and one Lamarchus, brought in to balance these two political opponents. One hundred thirty-four triremes and five thousand hoplites were ready to sail by the summer of 415 but the expedition's departure was marred when a number of the Herms, marble pillars bearing the head of the god Hermes and an erect phallus which acted as boundary markers in the city, were found with the phalluses (normally a sign of good luck) mutilated. No one can be sure who was behind this vandalism but the city was shaken by the experience and the fleet set off haunted by the episode.

The account of the Sicilian expedition is normally seen as the high point of Thucydides' work. He places it after the episode in which the people of Melos, a neutral Spartan colony in the Cyclades, were massacred by the Athenians, perhaps to make the point that Athens deserved the disaster that followed in Sicily. And it was a disaster. The fleet arrived and found little support from the Sicilians. (Athens' allies in Sicily had exaggerated their resources to attract her support.) It was soon clear that any success would depend on the capture of Syracuse but the three commanders quarreled over how this should be done. Alcibiades' enemies got him recalled on a charge of complicity in the mutilation of the Herms (but he defected to Sparta instead, an indication of the shallowness of his loyalty to his city) and Lamarchus was killed in skirmishing before Syracuse. Nicias, who had opposed the expedition all along, now found himself in charge. He did manage to capture Syracuse's harbor and land the hoplites but before the city itself could be taken its resolve was stiffened by the arrival of a Spartan force. Athens sent reinforcements but the original fleet now found itself blocked into the harbor by Syracuse's own navy. There was a desperate battle to break out, brilliantly told by Thucydides from the perspective of the watching Athenian hoplites:

> As the struggle went on indecisively, the Athenian soldiers revealed the fear in their hearts by the swaying of their bodies; it was a time of agony for them, for escape or destruction seemed every moment just at hand. So long as the issue of the sea-battle was in doubt, you could have heard every kind of sound in one place, the Athenian camp: lamentation, shouting, "We're winning!," "We're losing!," all the cries wrung from a great army in great peril. The feelings of the men on the ships were much the same, until at last, when the battle had gone on for a

> long time, the Syracusans and their allies routed the Athenians and fell upon them, decisive winners, yelling and cheering, and chased them to the land. And then the Athenian sailors, as many of them as had not been captured afloat, beached their ships wherever they could and poured into the camp. The soldiers were not in two minds any more, but all with one impulse, groaning, wailing, lamenting the outcome of the battle, rallied—some of them close to the ships, others to guard the rest of their defensive wall, while the greater part of them began to think now about themselves, about how they were going to survive.
>
> (Translation: Sir Kenneth Dover)

After a final attempt to break out failed, the Athenian army was left with little alternative but to retreat overland. Harassed by Spartans and Syracusans they were finally cowed into surrender and herded back to imprisonment in the stone quarries which surrounded Syracuse. Altogether some forty thousand lives may have been lost as well as half the Athenian fleet.

Athens was weakened in every sense by the Sicilian disaster through the loss of manpower and shipping, through the shattering of her prestige within the empire, through political turmoil at home when her democratic government was overthrown by a pro-Spartan government of Four Hundred. Sparta even set up a base within Athenian territory at Decelea from where she lured some twenty thousand slaves, many of them mine workers, away from Athens. Yet for the time being Athens survived. There were revolts by subject cities in the northern Aegean and along the coast of Asia Minor but most were subdued. Many cities in fact remained loyal largely because Persia was now reemerging as a force in the Aegean and rule by an Athenian democracy was preferable to domination by a barbarian tyranny. Ships were rebuilt and the government of Four Hundred was replaced by a more democratic one (of Five Thousand) when it tried to make peace with Sparta.

It was the reemergence of Persia that was to tip the balance in the war. Persia had the resources to help whichever side was prepared to drop its scruples and accept that something would be demanded in return. Sparta was the one who clinched the deal (411). Abandoning any pretense that it was a liberator of the Greeks, Sparta secured Persian money with which to build a fleet while acquiescing in Persia's reclaiming control of the Greek cities of Asia Minor. Thucydides was right to be cynical about human nature.

As Sparta built ships and recruited mercenaries to man them, the focus of the war now shifted to the northern Aegean. If Sparta's vulnerability lay among the helots of Messenia, Athens' was in the Hellespont, the channel through which the city's essential grain supplies came. The region had now become accessible to Sparta and so the next years of the war were thus dominated by a bitter struggle between the two fleets for control of the Aegean and access to the Black Sea. Byzantium, overlooking the entrance to Bosporus and hence to the Black Sea itself, was captured by the Spartans in 411. The Athenians regained it in 408. Athenian victories in 411 and 410 nearly brought Sparta to sign peace and the city suffered another major defeat at Arginusae (near Lesbos) in 406. As the years passed, however, it was the impact of Persian gold that told as the Spartans were able to continually rebuild and man their fleet. In 405 the Spartan commander, Lysander managed to gain a safe harbor within the Hellespont itself at Lampsachus. The Athenians had no such protection and were forced to use an open beach opposite at Aegospotamae. Every attempt to lure the Spartans out to battle failed and in the end it was a devastating surprise attack on the beached ships by Lysander that decided the issue; 170 out of 180 Athenian triremes were captured and the grain routes of the Hellespont closed.

"As the news of the disaster reached Athens" wrote the historian Xenophon, "one man passed it on to another, and a sound of wailing arose and extended first from the Piraeus, then along the Long Walls until it reached the city. That night no one slept. They mourned for the lost but more still for their own fate. They thought they themselves would now be dealt with as they had dealt with others." (Translation: Rex Warner.) As the food supplies dried up, the city had little option but to surrender (May 404). Even though the city was not razed to the ground, its men killed and its women enslaved (the treatment Athenians had carried out on defeated rivals and what was demanded of the Spartans by Corinth and Thebes), the terms of the peace treaty were harsh: the loss of the empire, much of the remaining fleet, and the destruction of the great walls which had surrounded the city. Lysander then used a perceived delay in pulling down the walls as an excuse for imposing a government of Thirty Men (later dubbed tyrants by the

Athenians) on the city though democratic government reasserted itself in October 403. (See page 303.)

The Peloponnesian War changed the course of Greek history as significantly as the First World War changed Europe's. It is hard to know for how long Athens would have maintained control of her subjects if the war had been won, but there is the possibility that victory in Sicily and the consolidation of the island's resources in the service of Athens could have produced a self-sustaining empire which would eventually have been able to tackle Sparta. With the collapse of the expedition and the defeat of Athens, Greek politics resumed their earlier course, one in which a number of city-states fought among themselves for leadership of their surrounding region without any able to effectively dominate on a wider scale. Athens did regain its democracy and independence, rebuild its fleet and, even for a short time, head a coalition of allied states, but the city's power was broken. It has been estimated that the male population in 395 was perhaps half of what it had been in 431. There were to be no more extravagant building programs on the Acropolis or in the Agora now. In fact there is hardly any evidence for new building of any kind before 350.

As the walls of Athens came down in 404, the historian Xenophon recorded that the demolishers, presumably many of them drafted by the Spartans from former subjects of the empire, danced and rejoiced to the music of flute girls, "thinking that this day was the beginning of freedom for Greece." Of course it was not to be. The power of Persia loomed again on the eastern horizon; Sparta was trying clumsily to build an Aegean empire of her own; and within sixty years a new power, Macedon, was to intrude into Greece from the north. The strain of the Peloponnesian War on the resources of Greece, the disruption of agriculture and the loss of so many men were to leave Greece vulnerable to outsiders. How it succumbed to the most brilliant opportunist among them is the subject of Chapter Fifteen.

11

The Athenian Democracy

Before the debacle of the Peloponnesian War, Athens had been the most prosperous city in the Aegean. One reason was the plunder from war and the tribute from empire (described in the previous chapter) that proved substantial enough not only to sustain a large fleet but to transform the city's Acropolis into an enduring showpiece. However, the city also had its own resources. While Attica, an area of more than 900 square miles (2,500 square kilometers), was not rich land (Plato writing in the fourth century went so far as to describe Attica as a "skeleton of a body wasted by disease; the rich soft soil has all run away leaving the land nothing but skin and bone"), olives grew well in lowland and coastal areas and it produced a healthy surplus of olive oil and wine for export. Crucially, the city also had a major source of mineral wealth in the silver mines of Laurion. Although owned by the state they were leased out to individuals in three- or ten-year concessions with the silver dug out by a harshly treated slave labor force of some thousands. The silver was coined and then, by a means which is not clear, passed back to private individuals. The quality of the silver was such that a trading ship could set off from Athens on its business with nothing but silver coinage aboard and be sure of buying what the trader needed.

Any city on the sea had an enormous advantage over a landlocked one (as could be seen by contrasting Athens with her rival Sparta where almost all economic activity was internal and where even coinage failed to develop). In the early fifth century Athens exploited her central position in the Aegean together with her resources of oil and silver to become the hub of the trading networks of the region. A major step forward came in the 490s with the development of a harbor at the Piraeus. Originally, ships had to anchor off shore and be unloaded by smaller boats; now they could tie up alongside quays and make use of a covered storage area. The way was open to buy staples needed for the survival of a burgeoning city whose population was able to double between 500 and 430 B.C. It is assumed, though some disagree, that wheat from the Black Sea became more essential to the city's survival (barley grew well in Attica but wheat, which requires more rainfall, was preferred for bread) with important implications for Athens' foreign policy. Supplies of timber, most readily available from the northern Aegean, were vital for the maintenance of the fleet. To this has to be added the need for slaves—there were possibly 100,000 of them in Athens brought in from "barbarian" areas or the slave markets. Among these staples were the more exotic imports described in a play by the comedian Hermippus of about 420 B.C.:

> from Cyrene silphium stalks and oxhides, from the Hellespont tunny and saltfish, from Italy salt and ribs of beef . . . Syracuse offers port and cheese . . . from Egypt sailcloth and raw materials for ropes, from Syria frankincense. Fair Crete sends cypress wood for the gods, Libya plentiful ivory to buy, and Rhodes raisins and figs sweet as dreams; from Euboea comes pears and big apples; slaves from Phrygia, mercenaries from Arcadia. Pagasae provides slaves with or without tattoos and the Paphlagonians dates that come from Zeus and shiny almonds . . . Phoenicia supplies the fruit of the date-palm and fine wheat-flour, Carthage rugs and cushions of many colours . . .
>
> (Quoted in M. Ostwald "Athens as a Cultural Centre" in *Cambridge Ancient History*, Vol. V.)

The growing sophistication of the Athenian consumer can also be seen by watching his choice of wines. In a well in Athens close to the Agora a mass of fragments of amphorae (the pottery vessels used for transporting wine) has been found. They came from such diverse areas as Mende (on the Chalcidice peninsula), Corinth and the islands of Thasos, Chios, and Lesbos. Thasos held its prominence into Hellenistic times but by then the wines of the southeastern Aegean, above all those of Rhodes and the city of Cnidus, were the favorites.

(The extent and range of Mediterranean trade routes shown by the origins of all these goods was all the more remarkable because the sailing season was short, from April to mid-September, and ships, still square sailed, were heavily dependent on a following wind. In general, travel from north to south was easiest in the Mediterranean, with a voyage south taking twice the time of one back north against the wind. From Athens it might take three days to get to Rhodes and then another four onto Egypt. Coming back against the wind speed would drop to less than two knots an hour [six knots were possible *with* the wind] with a laborious session of tacking through the Cyclades back to Athens. It took so long to make it up to the Black Sea from Athens that normally only one round-trip a year was possible. The fast currents southward through the Hellespont were another factor which made access there difficult. Another tricky crossing was of the Ionian sea for those heading for the grain-rich cities of Sicily. The winds were particularly unfavorable in midsummer and no more than two round-trips a season were usually possible.)

Trade helped stimulate manufacturing and craftsmanship in the city. Most Greek craftsmanship was small-scale and based on workshops adjoining the homes of the makers. Each industry would have its own area of the city. Pottery, perhaps the finest of the Athenian exports in the fifth century, was concentrated in the Kerameikos (hence *ceramic*) area, alongside the Panathenaic Way, as well in an area alongside the Dipylon Gate in the west of the city. The bronzeworkers clustered around the temple of their patron Hephaestus while sculptors worked in the area to the southwest of the Agora. Even the most successful industries remained small. Despite their domination of a large overseas market, there were probably never more than some 150 potters in Athens at any one time. As the city became more wealthy in the fifth century and was faced with the stimulus of war, more substantial workshops separate from the home emerged. Significantly, the largest workshop recorded in the city employed 120 men making shields.

Economic activity in Athens focused on the Agora, as it did in most cities. The open space was a political and commercial center, a gathering place for almost every communal activity except the specifically religious ones. In such a prosperous city it was a hive of activity. As the orator Lysias put it: "For each of you is in the habit of frequenting some place, a perfumer's shop, a barber's, a cobbler's and so forth and the greatest number visit those who have their establishments nearest the Agora, and the smallest those who are furthest from it." The plays of Aristophanes are full of loud-mouthed dealers competing with others in volume and abuse from stalls alongside the Agora. The city authorities tried to keep some order in this mayhem. To settle the inevitable disputes there was an official set of weights and measures and a tester of money who cut into suspect coins to see if a silver covering hid bronze beneath. (Something like one hundred thousand coins, most of them bronze, have been uncovered in excavations in the Agora.) One inscription found in the Agora laid down the size of container for a measure for nuts, beans, and dates. If anyone attempted to sell anything in a smaller container, then the container had to be destroyed, its contents had to be sold off, and the proceeds given to the state.

Much of the industrial activity of the city was undertaken by the metics (from *metoikoi,* those who came from outside the city). The metics were attracted by the opportunities offered by an expanding city and they must account for a large part of the increase in Athens' population in the fifth century. Eventually they may have made up 40 percent of the population. They were not allowed to own land but the more enterprising could run industrial and commercial concerns. Others are found as laborers, even working alongside slaves on the city's building projects. It was the flexible use of outside talent that helped sustain the economic vibrancy of Athens. While metics could not enjoy the privileges of citizenship and were subject to a special tax, the *metoikion,* they could achieve high social status. Metics appear as participants in Plato's *Dialogues* for instance, and Aristotle himself was a metic (though he was forced to flee the city at a time of anti-Macedonian feeling).

This economic strength and diversity underpinned the cultural, spiritual, and political life of Athens. What was extraordinary about the city community of Athens in the years between 479, the end of the Persian Wars and 322, the year Athenian democracy was eventually extinguished by the Macedonians, was its political and social stability.

There were moments when the political system was overthrown, in 411 and 404, for instance, but it was restored, as a democracy, on both occasions. There were the horrors of the plague of 430 and the humiliating defeat by Sparta in the Peloponnesian War, yet Athens recovered from these. Its traditions and its ways of conducting its political, social and cultural business remained intact, even though economically the city operated at a much reduced level in the first half of the fourth century. The contrast can be made with Germany after the First World War where a similar defeat and humiliation led to the violent political reaction of Nazism. Nothing like this happened in Athens, though the possibility that it might was recognized. Athenian orators frequently stressed how important it was to maintain *homonoia,* consensus, in city life.

This consensus depended on the city's cohesion. Athens' territory, Attica, made the state the largest on the Greek mainland after Sparta. From the sixth century onward Athens exercised increasing influence over the countryside. Country roads were shaped to converge on the city, just as the Aegean sea routes did. Some rural festivals, the festival to Dionysus from Eleutherae, or that to Artemis at Brauron, for instance, were imported into the city while in the countryside itself festivals in honor of Dionysus adopted elements of the great city Dionysia, including drama. The Eleusinian mysteries, which centered on the cult of Demeter and Persephone, became subject to decrees from the Assembly outlining how each deme had to contribute offerings to the ceremonies and came to be directly controlled by the *basileus,* the second most senior of the city's archons. Cleisthenes' reforms themselves linked each deme to the city through the Council of Five Hundred (see farther below). This did not mean that local initiative was stifled. The farther one went from the city the stronger was the identity of the local settlements such as Eleusis or Sounion, with its temple to Poseidon overlooking the sea. Recent archaeological work has shown just how lively many of these communities, or demes, were, especially after the reforms of Cleisthenes. They had their own assemblies, cults, and festivities and some behaved almost as if they were city-states in their own right. In Thorikos, which guarded the maritime approaches to the Laurion silver mines, there is a surviving acropolis, a theater, designed to fit the hillside, a temple, and evidence from inscriptions of a mass of cult activity.

It was the religious festivals of Athens that provided the core of community life and it was appropriate that the Acropolis should finally shed its ancient role as a fortress during the fifth century and become the spiritual center of the city as its ruins were rebuilt from the 440s onward. The most important of the protecting goddesses of the city was Athena, hence the Parthenon on the Acropolis itself, although Athena's father Zeus was also significant and had his own massive temple (begun by the Pisistratids but left unfinished until Roman times) to the east of the Acropolis. The craftworkers sought the protection of Hephaestus, the lame smith god whose temple, one of the best preserved in all Greece, still stands overlooking the Agora in the area originally occupied by blacksmiths. Legend related how Athena had supplanted Poseidon as protector of Athens but Poseidon as god of the sea remained important as the temple built to him on the cliff at Cape Sounion (in 444 B.C.) shows.

The relationship between the city and these and other gods was maintained by an annual round of festivals and rituals that was so deeply embedded in the city's life that no political leader ever dared to disturb it. Many festivals were very ancient, rooted in the agricultural year or marking the changing of the seasons, from the storms of winter to the appearance of the spring blossoms and then to the heat of summer. While the mass processions, the communal feasting that followed sacrifices and the various contests, recitations of Homer, drama, and sport, all helped bring people together, festivals could be used in another sense, to allow a temporary release of energy by groups that could otherwise be seen to be suppressed. At the Kronia festival in the summer, slaves were allowed a day of feasting and free movement throughout the city, while the Thermospheria (a festival known throughout Greece but one which developed its own rituals in different city settings) gave women the chance to have three days running their own affairs free of male interference. Once the festivities were over the normal order of things returned.

Cult activity was deeply conservative in the sense that a festival was seldom dropped from the calendar and the most ancient rituals (in one, men chosen for their ugliness were garlanded with strings of figs and driven from the city, and in another, one among a group of bulls chose itself for sacrifice by being the first to eat an offering of vegetables) continued long after their origins had been forgotten. Each of the twelve months of the calendar (with each year's beginning with the appearance of the first full moon after the summer solstice) was named after a prominent festival which took place in it. (The Athenian year was normally only 354 days with a leap year of 384 days added when necessary.) However, political and religious developments allowed shifts in importance between festivals and the rise of new ones. The two greatest festivals of city life, the Panathenaea and the City Dionysia, originated in the mid- and late-sixth century respectively and both advertised the city's pride not only to its own citizens but to visitors from all over the Greek world. The adding of games and recitals to the Panathenaea (the victors won amphorae of olive oil) appears to have been a deliberate attempt to rival the Panhellenic festivals. The cult of Harmodius and Aristogeiton, the tyrant slayers, was tied in with the liberation from tyranny.

The Persian Wars provided opportunities for new cults and rituals. Theseus had already been adopted by the Athenians as their own "democratic" hero after the expulsion of Hippias and the reforms of Cleisthenes. Following stories that he had been seen rushing ahead of the Athenian hoplites at the Battle of Marathon, his status was now elaborated. He was honored as the king who had consolidated Athens and Attica as a city-state but who had then handed his power on to the people. His cult within the city was boosted after the oracle at Delphi instructed the city to bring his bones back to the city for burial. Legend related that he had died on the island of Scyros and sure enough, when the island was captured by the Athenians in the 470s, some large ancient bones were discovered, announced to be those of Theseus, and transported back in triumph to Athens. A magnificent building in the Agora housed the bones and the Theseia, the festival honoring Theseus, became one of the most important in the calendar.

Some have placed the true beginnings of Athenian democracy with Cleisthenes in 508 B.C. Cleisthenes' reforms had certainly laid the foundations of a democratic state and Cleisthenes was also probably responsible for the institution of ostracism, the process by which the citizen body as a whole could vote to remove an unpopular public figure. The Assembly was asked each year whether it wished to hold an ostracism and if so each voter wrote (or had written for him) on *ostraka,* broken potsherds, the name of the politician he wished removed from the city (for an exile of ten years). The name with the largest number of votes (so long as there were more than six thousand) was thus exiled. The first recorded instance of ostracism was in 487 and the process was used in the 480s to remove politicians suspected of being pro-Persian or sympathetic to a restoration of tyranny.

However, the name most often recorded on those *ostraka* that survive was none other than Themistocles, the architect of victory in 480. Themistocles was in favor of greater democracy in the city and this suggests that in the immediate aftermath of the victory over the Persians conservative influence remained strong. In fact, Themistocles seems to have been the target of a conspiracy. One batch of 170 *ostraka* has been found with his name on each fragment but written in only fourteen different hands. This suggests that votes may have been manufactured in bulk by his opponents and then distributed. Whatever the methods used, the campaign against Themistocles eventually proved successful. He was finally ostracized in 471 and left the city for Argos.

The evidence suggests, in fact, that victory, rather than encouraging a shift toward greater democracy, had given enhanced prestige to *existing* institutions such as the Areopagus, the council of former archons (magistrates), which enjoyed a role as "guardian of the state." The precise powers of the Areopagus are not known but they seem to have included the power to quash decrees of the Assembly, to oversee the behavior of the archons and other officials, and to act as a court for judgment of crimes against the state. As only the higher two property classes could provide archons, the Areopagus was a conservative, even aristocratic body and this seems to have reflected the tenor of Athenian politics as a whole in this period. The leading politician of the city, both at home and abroad, was the aristocratic Cimon. His supremacy in conducting foreign policy, which rested on his election in successive years to one of the generalships, went hand in hand with a dominance within the city where his relationship with the Areopagus seems to have been very close.

By the 460s, however, democratic elements in the city were regaining strength. The archons, originally the most powerful figures in the city, had begun to lose their importance—from 487 they were selected by lot from an elected short list and they could only hold office for one year. The military challenges facing Athens had made the generalships the most prestigious and challenging posts. These were not only elected by the Assembly but the post could be held from year to year. From now on any ambitious politician had to learn to relate to the Assembly (rather than to the Areopagus, for instance) to be sure of sustained political power. As the navy became more important the *thetes*, the poorest class of the citizen body, not only acquired a heightened consciousness of their own importance for their city but also the experience, below decks in the triremes, of working together in a coordinated way. There is no evidence that the *thetes* were powerful or politically conscious enough to initiate a revolution but they would certainly not stand in the way of any move to give increased power or influence to the Assembly of which they were all members by virtue of their citizenship.

That the idea that the Assembly should have the central role in city government was gaining ground in the 460s is supported by the theme of Aeschylus' play *The Suppliants*, performed in Athens c. 463. The suppliants (fifty sisters who have fled from Egypt to escape marriage to their cousins) arrive in Argos asking for refuge. The king of Argos, Pelasgus, afraid that taking them in will lead to war with Egypt, refers the matter to the people's Assembly, which makes the final decision to welcome them on the grounds that it is just to offer refuge and that Zeus will be offended if the Argives do not do so. The risk of war is less serious than the risk of losing the protection of the gods. The crucial point is that it is the Assembly here that overrules the traditional authority of the king and it is a point which must have had its impact on the Athenian audience watching the play.

An opportunity to shift power from the Areopagus to the Athenian Assembly came in 461. Little is known of the "democratic" coup of that year. It seems to have been related to the absence of the powerful Cimon in Sparta, an absence exploited by its leaders, Ephialtes, who died in the ensuing unrest, and a thirty-year-old, up-and-coming statesman, Pericles, himself an aristocrat. It is perhaps naive to see the coup of 461 as a straightforward battle between conservative and progressive forces with the forces of progress winning. There was certainly an element of political infighting involved. Pericles' family had long been involved in a feud with Cimon (see below) and it could be said that Pericles, a highly astute politician who proved able to manipulate democracy in his interests in the decades that followed, used the *demos* to fulfill his own political ambitions.

The political shift achieved by the coup was straightforward. The Assembly was used to strip the Areopagus of most of its powers (on the grounds that these had been wrested illegally from the people) and they were distributed among the Council of Five Hundred, the Assembly, and the people's law courts. The Areopagus was left with a largely ceremonial role.

The democrats consolidated their position with great success. Athenian history was rewritten to suggest that Athens had been a democracy since early times (hence the belief that stripping the Areopagus of its powers was simply returning to what once had been). The key ideological concept of Athenian democracy, the right of every citizen to participate in government and to speak his mind freely both in Assembly debates and in private, became an easily understood and jealously guarded ideal. Democracy came to be as successfully embedded in the Athenian consciousness as the Constitution of the United States is in the American.

The victory of the democrats was, however, never complete. A significant number of aristocratic Athenians continued to believe in an oligarchy based on property qualification and they would use the word *demos* as a term of abuse. ("The ignorant mob" might be an apt translation.) As the aristocratic Alcibiades, who himself was to manipulate the Assembly for his own ends, put it: "As for democracy, we men of sense know what it is . . . but there can be nothing new to say about what is agreed to be absolute insanity." They would, they said, prefer an aristocracy, a government of the best. In the last decades of the century when Athens was at war many were soured by the democratic experience and influential philosophers such as Plato mounted a sophisticated challenge to the whole concept of democracy. Despite this, democracy was to survive in Athens until 322 B.C.

So what did democratic government mean in practice? All male citizens over eighteen (once they had completed two years of military service) could enjoy full and equal involvement in the Assembly's business regardless of how much property or wealth they possessed. This was a very rare privilege in the Greek world. The freedom of anyone to speak was symbolized by the first words of the president of the Assembly at the start of each session: "Who wishes to address the Assembly?" The Assembly itself was free to legislate on any issue, the raising of taxation, conduct of city and foreign affairs, or religious matters. As the wealth of the city and the complexity of its business both at home and abroad increased this gave it enormous power and responsibility. By the end of the fifth century there were some forty meetings of the Assembly each year, four in each of the *prytanies*, the tenths into which the year was divided for administrative purposes. (This was a separate calendar to the religious one mentioned above.) Voting was by a show of hands, in contrast to Sparta where participants shouted out their views.

Altogether some thirty thousand citizens were probably entitled to attend the Assembly although many must have been prevented by demands of work (even with slave labor to cope with the needs of their farms) or the distance which they lived from the city. In any case only some six thousand could be squeezed in on the Pnyx, a hill to the west of the city where the meetings were held. (In about 400 B.C. the space was enlarged to allow as many as eight thousand to fit in.) With so many crammed in to a relatively small space and a mass of business to complete, there had to be efficient organization of debates and it was here that the Council of Five Hundred developed a major role.

The council was not an elected body. Each of the ten tribes put forward volunteers and fifty from each tribe were chosen by lot to serve for one year. It has been argued that the lot was used so that no one's status was threatened by the public humiliation of losing an election (although elections were always used for the generalships where experience and competence were crucial). The short and unrepeatable period of service meant that the council was never able to exercise continuing or powerful influence. It met most days and had a wide variety of responsibilities, including the building and maintenance of the trireme fleet and the supervision of the city's officials. It received the tribute from subject states when it arrived in the city and it watched over the state treasuries. The Assembly therefore depended on it for day-to-day information, particularly about the financial state of the city, and it prepared the agenda for each meeting. (No issue could be raised in the Assembly unless it had been placed on the agenda by the council beforehand, though this seems to have been a straightforward procedure.) Each group of fifty would also take it in turns to be on permanent call for the period of one *prytany,* receiving envoys from other states and conducting day-to-day business. (Before 461 it seems that this role was carried out by the archons.) The group would be based in the Tholos, a circular meeting place in the Agora next to the council chamber, and maintained there at public expense.

Selection by lot was the normal way of appointing not only members of the council but other officials, including the archons (who from 457–456 could be selected from the top three property classes). The only requirement for selection (other than the continuing exclusion of the *thetes* from the post of archon) was to be aged over thirty, a restriction which left a pool of some twenty thousand citizens from which to draw some seven hundred officials each year. The positions to be filled included running the religious affairs of the city and its festivals, presiding over the law courts, administering the treasuries and archives, and at a more prosaic level, responsibility for keeping the streets clean, checking market stalls for moldy food, and running the city prisons. These jobs were demanding ones and expected to be done well. Officials were sworn in at the beginning on their terms of office (the stone on which they stood during the ceremony has been found in the Agora), could be challenged by any citizen at any time during their terms of office, and had to present any financial accounts to a committee of the council at the end of their terms. It was one of many ways in which this was a city run by its citizens for its citizens.

The same pool of 20,000 citizens over the age of 30 was drawn on to decide cases in the law courts (*dikasteria,* from *dikastai,* jurors). A modern legal system operates on the principle that there is a written law against which the guilt of the accused is judged. The police or a prosecutor decides whether there is a case to answer, arrests an accused, and brings him to trial. A judge, aided perhaps by a jury, makes the decision as to guilt. The Athenian courts did not operate in this way. The people not only made the laws, they judged transgressions of the laws. Any citizen could accuse any other citizen of an offense and haul him before the courts. Here there were no independent judges to hear the case but a mass of citizens sitting as a combined judge and jury. They were selected from a list of 6,000 citizens drawn up each year with an agreed number, up to 2,501, sitting for each type of case. (The commitment was a major one; a juror might find himself sitting for 200 days a year, and pay was introduced in the 450s by Pericles so that even the poorest citizen had a chance to serve.) Voting was by secret ballot, through placing a bronze token in a ballot box.

A law case was in essence a battle between the accuser and the accused in front of the jury and was inseparable from political and personal infighting. Athenian society and, it seems, those of other Greek cities were intensely combative. The maintenance of honor (*time*) was crucial. Any slight, in particular an act of *hubris,* an act designed deliberately to humiliate an enemy in public by insulting or hitting him in a way that brought pleasure to the humiliator, had to be avenged, either by the recipient or, in Athens, by another citizen. (An act of *hubris* was considered so potentially disruptive that Solon made it a criminal offense.) In practice it was hard to distinguish between private and public acts of wrongdoing, but in law the distinction became blurred as an extract from a speech by the fourth-century orator Demosthenes neatly shows. "I regarded the man who put me in this predicament," Demosthenes said, "as an enemy with whom no personal reconciliation was possible. But when I discovered that he had defrauded the city as a whole, I proceeded against him . . . thinking it a suitable opportunity to do the city a service and to avenge my wrongs."

In the violent debates that followed such an accusation (and many survive from the mid-fourth century) there was usually little attempt to prove a particular law had been broken. Rather a series of vague assertions, widely drawn and often implying some form of "impiety," were launched by the accuser. The Athenians reveled in a chance to indulge in exuberant rudeness. "Only recently he [one Timarchus] threw off his cloak in the Assembly and his body was in such an appalling and shameful condition thanks to his drunkenness and his vices that decent men had to look away" was a typical taunt. In a celebrated case between Demosthenes and a long term rival of his, Aeschines (who was attempting to deprive Demosthenes of a golden crown awarded him by the council for services to the city), Demosthenes was accused, among other charges, of betrayal of his friends, being the passive partner in a homosexual encounter, behaving as a coward in battle, and failing to respect the gods. Demosthenes retaliated by claiming that Aeschines was a mere upstart, the son, indeed, of a prostitute, who was simply acting out of private enmity. He (Demosthenes), in contrast, was a man of the highest standing, of fine education and social background, who had given everything to the service of the state. He listed the many times his advice had been accepted by the Assembly. (A common defense was to outline the public activities, maintaining a trireme or a drama festival, for instance, which the accused had financed.) It was a compelling speech which won Demosthenes the case. Aeschines was fined for bringing a case which had failed to convince the jury and chose to leave Athens for Rhodes.

Virtually every important politician in fifth- and fourth-century Athens, including Pericles himself, had to face a trial at some time. These were the inevitable bruising political struggles of democratic life. The punishment for one convicted was normally only loss of office or exile, as it was for ostracism, but the death penalty was possible. The best-known example is that of Socrates though he was as much to blame for the penalty as his accusers. Charged in 399 B.C. with impiety and corrupting the young, his defense speeches infuriated the jury so much that the death penalty became the only option. (See page 267.)

Aristocrats, like Homeric heroes, may have expected the ability to speak well to have come with their breeding but the experience of speaking before the Athenian Assembly or the juries must have been daunting. Even Demosthenes, perhaps the most gifted orator in Athenian history, started his life by being humiliated by hecklers and it was some years before he had the experience to make an impact. There may have been some residual deference for the wellborn (which Pericles appears to have exploited and Demosthenes to have used in his speeches against Aeschines) but this could only be taken so far in a city whose ideology stressed the equality of all citizens. The scholar Josiah Ober has shown how the more experienced upper-class speakers negotiated their status with the citizens they were addressing, often proclaiming implausibly that they were simply ordinary citizens like those they were addressing and any wealth they had was in any case used for the benefit of the *demos* and the city. Alternatively, one could elevate the status of the audience by proclaiming that *they* had the virtues of nobility.

By the end of the fifth century, rhetoric was beginning to be recognized as an art in its own right, something that could be acquired by training and experience. The visit of a Sicilian orator, Gorgias in 427 was an important moment. Gorgias, who had gained his experience from fighting property disputes in his native city of Leontini, came to plead with some success his city's case for support against its neighbor Syracuse. It was his style that proved particularly attractive and soon Athenian orators were copying it. Some even began composing speeches for others at a price, although this was never an entirely respectable way of making a living.

One of these speechwriters was Isocrates (436–338 B.C.). Isocrates came from a wealthy background but he was a man without the confidence and strength of voice to be a good speaker himself. As he mastered the techniques of effective rhetoric he turned from speechwriting to teaching. He expected his pupils to master first an understanding of everyday affairs and then learn how to present their ideas within an argument. He had a profound effect on education and by the fourth century Aristotle was able to present rhetoric as a normal part of any education. Students, according to Aristotle, should be able to distinguish between a rhetorical and a philosophical argument, to understand the mind of an audience and the way its opinions might be swayed, and how to construct an argument so that it had maximum impact. Not everyone was impressed. If, Plato was to argue, it was legitimate to construct arguments and play on emotions solely to win over an audience, where did this leave the concept of truth? Supporters of oligarchy reinforced this argument by stressing the ignorance and volatility of the mass of citizens who were vulnerable to the machinations of unscrupulous speakers.

At first sight it *is* hard to see how there could be any stability in the Athenian political system. The Assembly was too large and met too irregularly for coherent policy making to be conducted through it. Like the juries in the law courts it could also be easily swayed by emotional appeals. The council sat regularly but its members, like other officials, served only for a year at a time (and then could not be immediately reselected). The only offices that carried stability with them were the ten generalships whose holders could be elected from year to year. They were crucially important posts. Throughout the fifth (and as it turned out) fourth century warfare was incessant and the efficient organization of the city's defense and its overseas expeditions was essential.

The generals needed to have enough credibility and support with the Assembly to keep their offices (their conduct was scrutinized by the Assembly at regular intervals) and so the ability to present themselves effectively before the Assembly was important. It was common, therefore, for a general to combine his commands overseas with a prominent position within domestic politics. Cimon offers a good example. Although his "rule" took place before the democratic revolution he still had to be elected by the Assembly. He was typical, too, in that he was from the aristocracy, a class whose ability to command men traditionally went hand in hand with the ability to persuade them to fight. What was remarkable is how this class continued to provide the Athenian leaders even after the democratic revolution of 461. The prime example is Pericles whose position in Athenian politics was so assured that the historian Thucydides claimed that the supposedly democratic Athens was in effect ruled by him.

Pericles came from the aristocratic Alcmaeonid clan. (The reformer Cleisthenes, another member of the clan, was his great-uncle.) As a young man he had carried out a traditional aristocratic role by financing the drama festival of 472, which included Aeschylus' play *The Persians*, and may have entered politics to continue a family vendetta against Cimon. (Pericles' father had prosecuted Cimon's father Miltiades in 489). One objective of the coup of 461, it will be remembered, was to oust Cimon. Its success pushed the young Pericles to the center of political life. There is no doubt that he was a politician of genius although it took perhaps ten years after the coup of 461 for this to become fully apparent. In the 450s he seems to have been mainly concerned with domestic matters, masterminding the introduction of pay for juries and in 451 getting a law passed which restricted citizenship to those whose parents were both citizens. (The two measures may be linked in that the greater the rewards of citizenship the greater the political advantage for anyone who limited it.) Despite his political success he maintained the common touch. Plutarch has a good story of how he was abused by "a vile and abandoned fellow" throughout a whole day's business, even being followed home by his tormentor. Unruffled by the experience Pericles arranged for one of his servants to see the man safely home. Gradually he appears to have sensed how he could shape a role for Athens which was so popular with the Assembly that it would sustain him in power as a general year after year. From 443 to 430 he held a generalship every year without a break. The Funeral Oration he made in 431 to commemorate the recent dead of the city is a superb example of how Pericles was able to make his listeners feel good about themselves. This is part of the reconstruction provided by Thucydides:

> In this land of ours there have always been the same stock living from generation to generation till now and they, by their courage and their virtues have handed it on to us, a free country . . . when you realize Athens' greatness, then reflect that what made her great was men with a spirit of adventure, men who knew their duty, men who were ashamed to fall below a certain standard. They gave her their lives, to her and to all of us, and for their own selves they won praises that never grow

> old. Make up your own minds now that happiness depends on being free and freedom depends on being courageous . . . Taking everything together, I declare that our city is an education to Greece, and I declare that in my opinion each single one of our citizens, in all the manifold aspects of life, is able to show himself the rightful lord and owner of his own person, and do this, moreover, with exceptional grace and exceptional versatility . . . this is the kind of city for which these men, who could not bear the thought of losing her, nobly fought and nobly died.
>
> (Translation: Rex Warner)

Central to Pericles' ascendancy lay the drive towards empire. He was probably the driving force behind the transition from the Delian League to empire and the wealth brought in from the tribute was diverted by him to support Athens' democratic system. Alongside his oratory came real personal gain for Athenian citizens and thus he kept his position intact until the outbreak of the Peloponnesian War.

The most visible and enduring of Pericles' achievements was the rebuilding of the Acropolis as the showpiece of democratic and imperial Athens. Here he was following in the tradition of the Pisistratids who had used building programs as a means of glorifying the city and hence their rule. (Such programs also provided work for thousands of craftsmen, from the sculptors and stonecutters to roadcutters and rope makers.) The enormous undertaking which included the massive and opulent statue of Athena by Pheidias, the Parthenon, and two other temples as well as a monumental gateway was of unparalleled extravagance although some of the cost was met by drawing on the tribute from subject cities. At one point the Assembly balked at the expense, at which Pericles announced he would bear it himself and have the temples dedicated in his name. Overcome by this gesture the Assembly said he could have whatever funds he needed and the rebuilding went on.

In 431, as the large stage of building was still under way, the war with Sparta broke out. The frustrations of the long struggle were bound to have their impact on the Athenian political system and even Pericles fell foul of popular feeling before his death in 429. Following his death it is clear that there was now a division of leaders, between those who had to be in command overseas, often for sustained periods, and those who saw their roles at home with the Assembly. The aristocratic Thucydides attributes the greater volatility of the Assembly in these years to nonaristocratic demagogues who swayed the Assembly for their own purposes, but coherent decision making could never be easy under the stresses of war. So there were occasions like the Mytilene debate of 427 when the Assembly, following a violent and uncompromising speech by Cleon, ordered the execution of all the men of the city Mytilene, captured after a revolt against Athenian rule, but then changed its mind the next day (and sent another trireme to rescind the order although this arrived only after the executions had begun). Similarly, the size of the Sicilian expedition of 415 can be seen as the outcome of political infighting in which rival bids for the support of the Assembly led to the serious strategic error of sending a dangerously large force to the west. The best example of a volatile Assembly came with the aftermath of the naval victory at Arginusae (406). The eight generals commanding the Athenian fleet were accused of having failed to pick up a large number of sailors whose ships had sunk. Six of the generals came to Athens to plead their case that a violent storm made any lifesaving impossible. It appears that they were entitled to separate trials before the law courts or the Assembly with time to prepare their defense, but the Assembly was whipped up by speakers so successfully that it forced through a motion that they should be executed en bloc without delay. So they were. As with the Mytileneans' revolt, the Assembly then repented and took action against those speakers who, it said, had "forced" the Assembly to act unconstitutionally.

It was also the Peloponnesian War that provided the backdrop to the two occasions when Athenian democracy was overthrown. The first was in 411 soon after the failure of the Sicilian expedition when a group of upper-class oligarchs with the support of the young bloods of the drinking clubs started a reign of terror, overawed the Assembly, and seized power as a government of Four Hundred. Their motive may have been to produce a government that would impress the Persian king enough for him to offer them financial support, but there was no doubt that this also was a chance to settle old scores with the democratic leaders. After the sailors in the fleet, which was based at Samos, refused to support the coup, the grip of the Four Hundred weakened. In September 411 they were replaced by a more broadly based oligarchy of Five Thousand (the number being an approximation of those wealthy enough to be hoplites, and hence, the oligarchy argued, worthy to take part in government) but even this could not be sustained and democracy was fully restored in 410. In 404, after Athens' defeat the Spartans put in place a Government of Thirty Men (soon dubbed the Thirty Tyrants after they embarked on a reign of terror) backed by a Spartan garrison of seven hundred men. It was soon clear that its position was untenable and the Spartans themselves helped to negotiate a return to democracy. (See further page 303.)

The restoration of democracy in 410 had been accompanied by a decision to draw up a list of all the existing state laws. This took ten years to complete and was the work of one Nichomachus. His achievement in gathering together and codifying fragments of earlier law was a major one. The completed set of laws, which were inscribed on the walls of a stoa, was the fullest law code ever published by a Greek city. Although literacy had been a useful skill and an expected part of education in the fifth century it is now in the early fourth century that literacy became an essential part of professional life. There is the first evidence that pleaders in the law courts would come with extracts from Nichomachus' laws to read out. (It was in the same period that written contracts governing sea voyages became common.)

By this time there had been some reflection on the role of the Assembly as a lawmaker and a new procedure was agreed. The laws gathered by Nichomachus were given a hallowed status, partly by associating most of them with Solon. The Assembly continued to make decrees on immediate issues but these no longer had the full status of law. Any proposed law had to be passed to a council of lawmakers (*nomothetai*) who were selected by lot (in one known case the *nomothetai* were made up of all five hundred councilors plus another thousand citizens). These scrutinized the new law. If it conflicted with an existing law as found on the stoa walls then a debate took place between the supporters of the old and new laws and the *nomothetai* would then make the final decision as to whether the old law should be replaced. Any member of the Assembly who tried to subvert this procedure (by trying to introduce a law directly into the Assembly, for instance) could be prosecuted. It had thus become much more difficult to change laws as a result of impulse. Perhaps most important of all, debates in the law courts now had to refer to written laws and it has been argued (by Kevin Robb), for instance, that this was the moment when literacy became essential for any man of affairs. By the end of the fourth century written documents have replaced oral testimony as the basis for legal business. It was a significant development.

(The historian is the beneficiary of the new passion for recording in stone. Many hundreds of dedications to gods, records of the transactions of officials, lists of officials, laws, reports of decisions by assemblies at deme or city level, inscriptions on gravestones survive, and these now not only allow the religious and political mentality of a city such as Athens to be explored, but comparisons to be made between cities where "archives" of inscriptions survive.)

None of these changes affected the basic principle of Athenian democracy that all should be involved equally in the affairs of state. The Assembly had simply transferred some of its powers as a lawmaker to another democratically selected body. Despite the loss of empire and the economic disruption following the war, democratic principles were in fact enhanced by the decision (sometime between 403 and 399) to pay the members of the Assembly for attending. In the fourth century Athenian democracy settled down to what could be seen as a more mature form and there were no major constitutional changes until a Macedonian takeover of the city in 322 (when a property qualification was introduced). The ideology of democracy was now so deeply rooted that Athenians talked fondly of *patrios democratia,* ancestral democracy. Theseus, who, legend said, had first handed power to the people, and Solon, the father of the most revered set of Athenian laws, received new respect, the latter being honored with a bronze statue in the Agora.

The shortcomings of Athenian democracy have often been stressed. Democratic rights were an elitist male preserve reserved for the minority of Athenians who were citizens. They could not have been sustained without slave labor and, in the fifty century at least, the tribute of Athens' subject cities. It could be argued that democracy for a few in Athens depended on the greater suppression of many, other cities, women, and slaves. Even for those with democratic privileges life was not easy. While all citizens had the right to be involved in politics, political activity carried heavy risks. Officials who failed were severely punished, in the case of unsuccessful generals, with the death penalty. The constant threat of prosecution by political rivals was a major hazard of political life. Public life in fifth-century Athens was not for the faint-hearted. There was no effective protection against the will of the Assembly or a jury, no entrenched human rights. In this sense Athenian democracy cannot be directly compared with modern democracies where the rights of each individual in the community are protected.

However, despite these limitations, Athenian democracy worked surprisingly well and over many decades. A mass of citizens, many with limited administrative experience, did make their own laws, run the daily life of their own city, and oversee and defend an empire. The city was successful in implanting an ideology of democratic government that proved extraordinarily resilient when put to the test. The vast majority of citizens, even the wealthy, got used to paying lip service to the democratic ideal. Equally remarkable were the ways in which the structure of Athenian political life allowed social tensions to be defused. Power struggles between members of the elite could be transferred into the law courts and there were further opportunities for political and social tensions to be defused in the drama festivals (Chapter Twelve, following).

The details of democratic life in Athens have received such scrutiny that it is easy to overlook the power of religion as a force for unity. A Greek city was above all a religious community and Athens was no exception. Pausanias writing in the first century went so far as to say that Athens was the most religious city in Greece. Religious festivals defined the course of the year with every transition of season and political life marked by appropriate commemoration. Of the first eight surviving decrees of the democratic Assembly, six concern religious matters. Sacrilegious behavior, such as the mutilation of the Herms in 415, had an enormous impact on the city's confidence. In short, every activity was shaped in such a way as not to offend the protecting gods of the city. This desire to maintain the balance between humanity and the gods through the mediating presence of the city may in fact provide the key to understanding Athens' comparative social stability in the fifth and fourth centuries.

Afterword: The Acropolis Building Program

When Pericles embarked on his massive building program on the Acropolis the site was bare. Much of the surviving sculpture from archaic times had been incorporated into defensive walls and only the foundations of earlier temples remained. There was thus the opportunity to plan a new complex and to begin with a layered terrace that was created on the summit, which may have been inspired by Persian examples.

The dominant building on the site was, of course, to be the Parthenon. It was built in the first instance to house a massive statue of Athena (in gold and ivory on a wooden frame), the work of the sculptor Pheidias. As with the Olympian Zeus, size was an end in itself. The goddess herself would be impressed with the resources dedicated to her and the statue would also strike awe in viewers with its magnificence. The gold on the statue alone has been calculated as worth $15 million (£9 million). (It was added in plates which could be removed for melting down at times of crisis!) The statue carried a figure of Nike, Victory, in one hand, a spear in another and was helmeted.

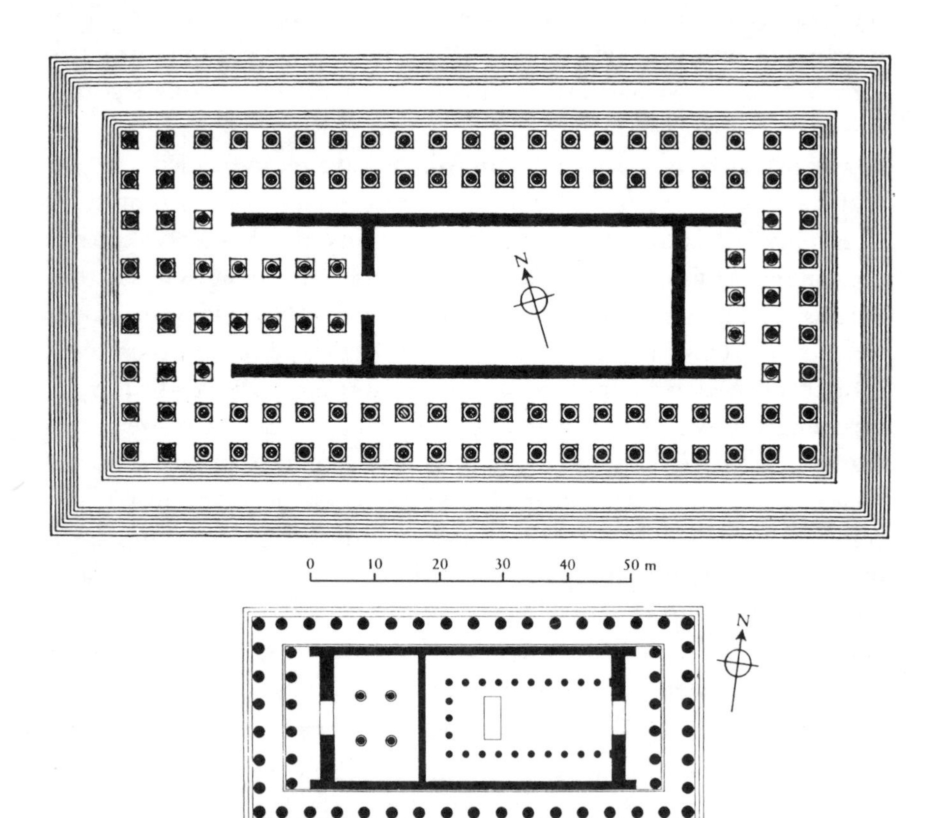

PARTHENON/TEMPLE OF ARTEMIS. Imposing though the Parthenon (bottom) is, and it is the largest of the Doric temples, it was dwarfed by the vast temples of the Ionian Greeks such as the fourth-century Temple of Artemis at Ephesus (top). It is possible that the Ionians were directly influenced by the massive temples of Egypt.

This was a warrior Athena, the protectress of the city, but her simple *peplos,* the dress of the citizen women of Athens, also reminded viewers of her role as chaste maiden.

Pheidias may also have overseen the building of the Parthenon itself though the design is credited to the architect Ictinus. The temple was begun in 447 and the inner colonnade and roof were in place by 438 when Pheidias' statue was formally dedicated. The building was finally completed by 432. It was made of the finest Pentelic marble, 22,000 tons of it dragged to the site by oxcart from mines some ten miles (sixteen kilometers) away. The basic design of the temple was Doric though there were also Ionic elements—in the continuity (without intervening trigylphs) of the famous internal frieze, for instance, and the columns inside the rear chamber. The construction was carried out with great sophistication. It was appreciated that if the lines of stone were left straight, an optical illusion made them appear to be slanted. This was compensated for. The stylobate (the top step) was carved so as to be slightly higher in the center than at the ends and the columns were made marginally wider in the middle. The columns themselves sloped inward, but so slightly that they would only have met in a point almost a mile (1,600 meters) above the temple. (Some idea of how the Parthenon might have been built is provided by the unfinished temple to Apollo at Didyma. Lightly carved out on it walls are lines showing proportioned sketches of column bases. These appear to have provided the blueprint from which the builders worked and they could easily have been erased when the building was completed.)

The glory of the Parthenon lies in its sculptures. The first to be completed, perhaps even being taken from another building, were the metopes around the external colonnade. They showed the Athenians grappling with mythical enemies, Amazons, Centaurs, and Trojans. At each end of the temple was a large carved pediment although the sculptured figures have survived only in fragments. On the west, the side which would have been seen first by those ascending the Acropolis from the Agora, Poseidon and Athena struggled for possession of Athens; on the east, actually the front of the temple, Athena was shown being born from the head of Zeus. Around the internal walls and colonnade of the temple only visible from below at an angle, ran the frieze, most of which is now in the British Museum. It is assumed that its execution was masterminded by Pheidias and is judged by many as the finest achievement in all Greek sculpture in its combination of movement, emotional intensity, and attention to detail.

The frieze would have come into view as the participants in a ceremonial procession approached the western end of the Parthenon. Along this end it showed horsemen being marshaled into position. Participants could then move along either side of the temple and in either case they would follow the flow of a procession shown on the frieze. They would pass horsemen and chariots and then a gathering of men, including elders and musicians, carrying or tending all the offerings needed for a sacrifice, including sheep and cattle. Women carry jugs for libations. As the eastern end, the facade of the temple, is reached, larger figures, which are usually assumed to represent the gods, sit serenely as if unaware of the commotion around them. Finally, between the "gods" there is a scene in which two smaller figures (children?) are carrying bundles while a third is handing over a partially unfolded piece of cloth to an older man.

Most scholars have seen the frieze as a representation of the Panathenaea and it has been suggested (by John Boardman) that it represents the festival of 490, just before the battle of Marathon, with the men on horseback the very young men who were to die as the heroes of the battles. The cloth being handed over is the *peplos* in which an ancient cult statue of Athena housed in the Erechtheum would be clothed at the conclusion of the festivities. Even if the frieze is not a direct representation of the Panathenaea, it might have been designed to show the citizen body of Athens at the height of its democratic and political power and thus was essentially an instrument of propaganda, presumably masterminded by Pericles.

More recently there has been an important reassessment of the Parthenon frieze by Professor Joan Connelly. She makes the point that all known friezes are of mythological rather than contemporary subjects and that on the Parthenon frieze, in particular, there are features that do not fit what is known of the Panathenaea. She suggests instead that the frieze represents an early Athenian myth, details of which only survive in a fragment from a play by Euripides. It tells of an early king of the city, Erechtheus, who sacrificed his three daughters so that the city might be saved from an invading army of Thracians. This would be typical, Connelly argues, of the kind of myth which Pericles, wishing to stress the need of individuals to offer everything for the good of the community, might order for such a prominent temple. The scene

Scenes of Greece. The romantic image of Greece is of white marble set against dark blue seas and distant islands, as at the temple of Poseidon on Cape Sounium shown here (*above*). In reality Greece provides a harsh environment with relatively little fertile land among its rocky hills and mountains. The ruins in this scene (*right*), on the island of Cos, are Byzantine.

In this unusual cup from mid-sixth-century Sparta a ruler (named Arkesilas) oversees the weighing and packing of a white fluffy substance, probably the cure-all herb silphium from Cyrene in Libya.

The height of Athenian black-figure painting was reached in the work of Exekias (*c.* 535 BC). Here (*right*) Achilles and Ajax play dice. The scene is beautifully controlled in itself but there is more to read into it. Achilles was to die on the battlefield, Ajax to carry his body home, but later to commit suicide by falling on his spear. This moment of relaxation and friendship, with their armour laid aside before battle, would have had added poignancy for the knowledgeable Greek viewer.

With the coming of Athenian red-figure pottery about 525 BC, there we new possibilities for treating perspective, possibilities fully exploit by the "Pioneer group" from 510 BC Here (*left*) Heracles wrestles with the giant Antaeus.

Women, sex and music. Respectable women (the wives of Athenian citizens) are portrayed seated, clothed, and with a lyre, the instrument of reason and good order associated with Apollo. The *hetairai*, the women companions of the *symposia*, in contrast, flaunt their sexuality and play on the double pipe, an instrument associated with Dionysus and abandon.

The *symposia* were also the setting for sex between older men and adolescent boys. One is shown here, again naked and with pipes.

The extraordinary quality of fifth-century Greek bronze-working is shown in this head of Zeus, dated stylistically, by the plait in its hair, to *c*. 460 BC.

Two of the great pan-Hellenic sites as they are today: Delphi (*above*) and Olympia (*below*). This view of the fifth-century temple to Athena near the oracle shows Delphi's stunning position on the slopes of Mount Parnassus. The view of Olympia shows the lush lowland setting of the ancient games. The river Alpheus is in the left foreground and the stadium at the top centre. Compare the reconstruction shown earlier.

Mycenaean and Minoan gold-working was of the highest quality, as seen in this cup (*right*) found at Vapheio in the Peloponnese of about 1500 BC.

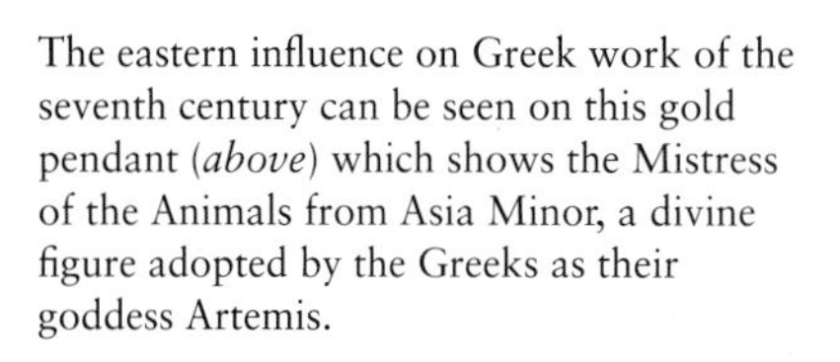

The eastern influence on Greek work of the seventh century can be seen on this gold pendant (*above*) which shows the Mistress of the Animals from Asia Minor, a divine figure adopted by the Greeks as their goddess Artemis.

In the tomb of Philip II of Macedonia at Vergina magnificent gold objects were found, such as this chest (*right*) and gold wreath (*below*). The royal star of Macedonia shown on the top of the chest has been adopted as a national emblem by modern Greece.

The Nile Mosaic from Palestrina (second century BC, *above*) is probably a copy of a commission by the Ptolemies. It shows the fascination of the Greeks with Egypt, its exotic animals (background), its ancient past (centre), and its present (foreground), where Greeks are shown enjoying Egyptian settings.

In this second-century-BC mosaic from Pompeii (*below left*), Alexander is shown at the battle of Issus. At the forefront of the fighting and without even a helmet to protect him, Alexander presents himself as the youthful, unassailable conqueror overthrowing the greatest empire on earth.

In this temple relief from Luxor (*below right*), Alexander is shown being welcomed as Pharaoh of Egypt by the god Amun. The later influence of Christianity can be seen in the hole at the centre of the relief where Amun's phallus has been cut out.

The Erechtheum on the Athenian Acropolis (420s BC) is famous for its Caryatids, women bearing the structur of the building. The Caryatids were one of the examples of classical Greek art copied by Hadrian for his famous villa at Tivoli (begun *c.* AD 118). The villa represents the merging of Greek and Roman artistic taste at its most sophisticated. The Canopus, shown here, used the mode of a Greco-Eygptian temple (of Serapis from Alexandria) se alongside water as a backdrop for the display of Greek sculpture.

on the frieze traditionally seen as the climax of the Panathenaea, where the *peplos,* a garment woven for a statue of Athena on the Acropolis, is shown being handed over, is, suggests Connelly, really a representation of one of the daughters presenting herself for sacrifice. The *peplos* is, in fact, the shroud in which she will be wrapped for the act itself. Other details of the frieze might fit the Erectheus story. The chariots on the frieze, for instance, could represent the army of Erectheus as perceived by later Athenians. The interpretation remains controversial (where, for instance, is the altar and the sacrificial knife?) but seems to have much to commend it.

As the Parthenon neared completion Pericles turned his attention to creating a series of monumental gateways to the Acropolis, the Propylaea (from *propylon,* a gateway). The Propylaea was built between 436 and 432 B.C. It was set on an awkward site at the west end of the rock just where the path upward leveled out. There was a great central opening large enough for processions and animals on their way to sacrifice to pass and then smaller doors on either side. The inner passage through the gateway was flanked by Doric columns. On either side of the gates were public rooms. That to the north appears to have been designed for formal feasts but was then taken over as a picture gallery. The whole provided an appropriate foretaste of what was to come as the visitor or celebrant entered the sacred area itself. As he passed through he would be confronted by a large statue, now lost, of Athena Polias, Athena in her role as the protectress of the city.

By 429 Pericles was dead, the city had been devastated by plague, and was fighting the Peloponnesian War. It says something for the resilience of the city that the construction program went on regardless. An appropriate building was needed for the northern edge of the Acropolis. It was a hallowed site containing a sacred olive tree (allegedly brought forth by Athena in the course of her contest with Poseidon), the ancient cult statue to Athena, an altar to Erectheus, and the grave of Cecrops, a king who was associated with the bringing of civilization in the form of writing and monogamous marriage to the city. The resulting temple, known as the Erechtheum, was not so imposing as the Parthenon but much more complex in design (largely owing to the uneven nature of the site). The eastern facade was that of a normal temple with a *cella* (the main internal room of a temple) behind it and two other *cellas* behind that. The western facade had four Ionic columns set into a wall. On the north and south sides of the western end of the temple were porticoes. The northern is the largest and finest with six elegant Ionic columns. In the southern portico six Caryatids (columns in the shaped of draped women) hold up an ornamental roof on their cushioned heads. The grave of Cecrops and the olive tree were enclosed as part of the complex to the west of the main building. The whole was built between 421 and 405 B.C.

The smallest and for many the most exquisite of the buildings of the Acropolis is the temple to Athena Nike (Athena as victor) which was built on a parapet at the far southwestern tip of the Acropolis in the late 420s. It is the most simple of temples, its facade four Ionic columns in front of an open *cella*. There is an Ionic frieze of Athenians in battle, possibly with Persians, but it is poorly preserved. Sculptures from the surrounding parapet show Athena celebrating victory through the ordering of sacrifices and the piling up of captured armor. One richly draped figure of Victory, who reaches down to adjust her sandal, is one of the most sensual creations in Greek art. The whole is a poignant echo of those glorious days, now some sixty years before, in which the city had triumphed over the most formidable of enemies, the Persians. There was to be no victory to come now. Within a few years Athens would be humbled and it was to be seventy years before the city would be able to embark on another building program.

12

Homage to Dionysus: The Drama Festivals

The previous chapters have shown what a powerful emotional experience living in fifth-century Athens must have been. There were not only the pressures on all citizens to participate in an increasingly complex administrative system but a range of extraordinary and testing political adventures, the creation of empire, a devastating plague, a stressful war, and ultimately, in 404, the humiliation of defeat. This was a city where the impact of events challenged conventional ways of thinking at every level. It was first through drama and then through the more formal approach of the philosophers that the most fundamental concerns of life were explored. The legacy of the exploration has been substantial. Without Greek tragedy and drama and the philosophy of Socrates, Plato, and Aristotle, the European cultural heritage would be very much the poorer.

The city's drama festivals acted as one of the most sophisticated ways through which the city's cohesion was sustained. Their roots, like those of all festivals, were religious, in a celebration of Dionysus, but they were adapted for political and cultural purposes so that they came to perform a crucial psychological function for the community. There were two festivals each year, the most important of which was the City Dionysia, held in the spring; the other, the Lenea, was held in January when the winter seas still isolated the city from the rest of the Aegean. As with so much in Greek life the festivals were competitive occasions. After the opening procession the proceedings began with choruses of fifty men or fifty boys from the ten tribes of Athens competing with each other in singing dithyrambs, choral lyrics. Then came the tragedies with three poets each presenting three plays that could be linked in theme to each other. At the end of his trilogy each dramatist produced a satyr play. The satyrs, often portrayed as uninhibited figures with exaggerated phalluses, were companions of Dionysus and they were shown in a number of stock situations, usually ending in some kind of liberation from captivity. It has been suggested that these plays were used as a sop to Dionysus as the subject matter of the tragedies drifted with time away from themes that were specifically connected with him. On the fourth day of the festival five comic poets each offered a comedy. The winners were chosen by a panel of judges.

The financing of this major occasion (which required at least twelve hundred actors and singers) fell on the wealthier Athenians who would use the occasion to earn the respect of the masses through their contributions. However, the whole community was represented through its participation in the opening processions and as an audience. Drama was a public experience and a highly charged one. Actors would perform in the bright open air on the circular orchestra (which would have space for the chorus) with their audience sitting directly opposite in the semicircular *theatron* (any public space from which an audience watched a spectacle). From the 450s onward a *skene* (the English scene) would provided a backdrop to the orchestra and allow some staging. It is estimated that some fourteen thousand people, many of them from outside the city, attended the plays at the City Dionysia, making it second to the Olympic Games as the largest gathering in the Greek world. (Only half this number would attend a typical Assembly.) The propaganda opportunities were too good to miss. Tribute from the empire was displayed and it was one of the rare occasions when the city's ten generals would appear together and offer libations.

Speaking before a large audience was a well-established part of Greek city life. The recitals of Homer and other poets, the addressing of the Assembly, the use of persuasive rhetoric in the law courts, all had their place in the city-state. In this sense, drama was simply another, if distinct, means of relating to an audience. The chorus, which played a prominent role especially in the earlier tragedies, danced during breaks in the play and music accompanied much of the action as it did in the recital of epic. Masks, which actors used partly to explain their characters but also to help their voices carry up to the higher tiers of the stone seats, had traditionally been used in the Dionysiac rituals. However, once drama became established as a specific form of relationship between speakers and their audience it developed its own conventions and strategies.

The tragedies were invariably based on mythological stories (Aeschylus' *The Persians* is an exception) that would have been well known to the audience but these were manipulated by the poet to illustrate and explore contentious political and social issues. Each of the tragedians had his own approach and favorite themes but they shared a relentless search to find the meaning of life, to understand the factors which cause suffering, to find a way of resolving the inevitable dilemmas of daily existence. How far are human beings at the mercy of a fate which they cannot control or are they doomed by their own emotional flaws or frailties? Often there is no obvious solution to the dilemmas explored but the very fact of exploration within the distanced setting of a myth helps explode their power. At the same time the tragedians do raise the question of how life must be lived if there is no obvious meaning or any moral absolutes, a question seen to be of renewed relevance following the decline of traditional Christian morality in Western society.

There are three major tragedians from fifth-century Athens, Aeschylus, Sophocles, and Euripides. They were seen as outstanding by their contemporaries and by the 330s they enjoyed classic status. A decree of that time ordered the erection of bronze statues of each of the three and the preservation of their plays and stipulated that in performances the original text had to be followed exactly. The earliest of the three and the founder of tragedy was Aeschylus. Aeschylus' life spanned the greatest years of Athens. He possibly came of age around the time of Cleisthenes, fought at Marathon in 490 and maybe at Salamis and Plataea as well, and died in the mid-450s. His epitaph suggests that he regarded the moment of collective glory at Marathon as the crowning achievement of his life rather than his later success in the festivals. His first play was as early as 499 and he was still writing forty years later. He played an important role in using first two and later three actors in addition to the chorus. Six, and possibly seven, of his plays survive from an output which may have totalled ninety in all.

Aeschylus was sensitive to living in an age of rapid change. In his plays he contrasts the world when human beings lived in savagery with a more recent one where the laws of the *polis* have brought civilization and order. In the earliest times, as portrayed in *Agamemnon*, Aeschylus suggests that there is an underlying harmony upheld by the gods but one sustained by brutal punishment. Primitive, revengeful gods such as the Furies harass and destroy those who have offended. The gods punish not only those who infringe their rules but their anger is passed on to their descendants as well. There is a further twist in that the gods often draw men toward their doom. In *The Persians*, the earliest of Aeschylus' plays to survive (472), Xerxes is tempted into the act of extravagant pride, the invasion of Greece, that attracts the revenge of the gods. Aeschylus explains, through the Chorus, how he is trapped as the gods exploit his weaknesses:

Deceitful deception of god—
What mortal man shall avoid it? . . .
Benign and coaxing at first
It leads us astray into nets which
No mortal is able to slip,
Whose doom we can never flee.
(Translation: Seth Bernadete)

In *Seven Against Thebes* (467 B.C.), the gods seem to delight in placing humans in impossible dilemmas. Eteocles, the son of Oedipus, has become king of Thebes but holds on to the throne longer than agreed. He is challenged by an Argive army one of whose leaders is his brother Polyneices. Eteocles is crushed between conflicting demands of defending his city and risking the killing of his brother. The two brothers meet face to face and both die.

In *Seven Against Thebes*, the *polis* is extolled as the nourisher and defender of the human community. Aeschylus argues that it provides a more harmonious and just system on earth than the more brutal rule of the ancient gods. The evolution from a primitive savagery is shown best in the trilogy, the *Oresteia* (the only Greek trilogy to survive in full), which was produced in Athens in 458, shortly after the democratic revolution of 461. The first play, *Agamemnon*, sees the return of Agamemnon from the long but ultimately successful siege of Troy. It should have been a joyful event but Agamemnon has had to make the agonizing decision to sacrifice his daughter so that the fleet could sail for Troy and while he has been away his wife Clytemnestra has taken a lover, Aegisthus. Agamemnon's return is haunted by an atmosphere of foreboding and revenge, powerfully evoked through the poet's most emotive language. It is the creation of atmosphere which is among Aeschylus' greatest gifts. His characters are often undeveloped, defined by their deeds rather than by their personalities. When Agamemnon arrives, Clytemnestra lures him into a palace that she has decked out as if for a celebration. However, once he is inside she murders him in his bath. She exults in the flow of blood:

Words, endless words I've said to serve the moment—
now it makes me proud to tell the truth.
How else to prepare a death for deadly men
who seem to love you? How to rig the nets
of pain so high no man can overleap them?
I brooded on this trial, this ancient blood feud
year by year. At last my hour came,
here I stand and here I struck
and here my work is done.
I did it all. I don't deny it, no.
He had no way to flee or fight his destiny—
Unwinding the robes from Agamemnon's body, spreading them before the altar where the old men cluster round them
our never-ending all embracing net, I cast it
wide for the royal haul, I coil him round and round
in the wealth, the robes of doom, and then I strike him
once, twice, and at each stroke he cries in agony—
he buckles at the knees and crashes here!
And when he's down I add the third, last blow,
to the Zeus who saves the dead beneath the ground
I send that third blow home in homage like a prayer.

So he goes down, and the life is bursting out of him—
great sprays of blood, and the murderous shower
wounds me, dyes me black and I, I revel
like the Earth when the spring rains comes down,
the blessed gifts of god, and the new green spear
splits the sheath and rips to birth in glory!

(Translation: Robert Fagles, 1977)

The murder does not bring an ending but only another transgression for the gods to avenge and this is the theme of the second play in the trilogy, the *Libation Bearers*. Here Orestes, the son of Agamemnon, takes his own revenge on his mother for his father's murder by killing her and Aegisthus. The problem now left for the third play, the *Eumenides*, "the Furies," is how to resolve Orestes' guilt. Orestes is pursued by the Furies (the forces, portrayed in the play as terrible old women, who exact revenge on those who have committed crimes within the family) to Delphi. The matter has to be judged and Apollo is introduced to settle the matter. He is prepared to release Orestes on the ground that the murder of a man is more weighty than the murder of a woman so that Orestes' revenge on his father's murder leaves him with a positive balance but he sends on the matter for final judgment in Athens. Here Athena presides over a court of citizens (in effect this marks the mythical founding of the Areopagus) and when the vote is divided, decides in favor of Orestes. Laws based entirely on fear, she argues, are better replaced by those based on human reason and moderation. He is to be released and the matter brought to a harmonious close. Balance, so beloved by the Greeks, has been restored. Athena then transforms the Furies from evil old hags into protective forces for Athens and the play ends with the goddess presiding over a society where order established through the rule of law is supreme. The city, in this case, Athens, is the finest security. "The stronger your fear, your reverence for the just, the stronger your country's wall and city's safety, stronger by far than all else men possess in Scythia's rugged steppes or Pelops' level plain." The trilogy confronts not only the problem of revenge within the family but shows how the city can provide its own means of upholding justice and peace which transcend the old formal and unyielding rule of the gods. The play thus provides the Athenian audience, and any foreigners who are present, with an endorsement of their new democratic system. As has been described, Aeschylus had already recognized the mood in favor of democracy through his play *The Suppliants* of 463 B.C. (It has also been argued that the trilogy shows the triumph of masculinity, in the shape of city authority, over unrestrained femininity, represented by Clytemnestra.)

The second of the "great" tragedians, Sophocles (c. 496–406 B.C.), first came to prominence as a dramatist in 468 B.C. when he defeated Aeschylus for first prize at the City Dionysia of that year. He is first recorded as the leader of the victory paean (an ode of celebration to

Apollo) after the victory of Salamis, but during his long life he served terms as City Treasurer and as a general and then as one of the investigators appointed by the city after the Sicilian disaster. Only seven of a possible one hundred thirty plays of his have survived, a warning of how tentative any summing up of his life's work must be, but they are enough to confirm him as perhaps the greatest of the dramatists. His own victory record, which included winning the City Dionysia eighteen times, suggests that this was the verdict of his contemporaries as well.

Sophocles develops tragedy by diminishing the role of the chorus and introducing a third character (Aeschylus appears to have adopted this innovation from Sophocles for his later plays). His language is more down to earth than Aeschylus' and his characters more human and well defined as a result. One can know them as rounded individuals in a way which is impossible for those of Aeschylus. Sophocles is more aware of how human beings are trapped by fate though it is often their own personalities that make the ensuing tragedy all the more unavoidable.

The range of Sophoclean drama is extended by his use of women as powerful beings in their own right. In *Antigone*, Antigone, the daughter of Oedipus, has been forbidden to bury her brother Polyneices who has been killed attacking Thebes, by Creon, the ruler who has succeeded Eteocles. She insists on carrying out the ancient rituals. "I do not recognise your decrees, made by mortals, as strong enough to overrule the unwritten and unfailing conventions of the gods, for these are not simply of yesterday and today, but for all time to come." It is not simply that the old laws are there to be obeyed; Antigone's character, which is contrasted with that of her more pliant sister, Ismene, impels her to her action. She burns with her own conviction and scatters dust on her brother's body as the ritual requires. She is now ordered by Creon, who is convinced too that he is upholding the correct moral order, that of the city community, to be buried alive. He relents but she has already committed suicide as has Creon's wife and his son who was in love with Antigone. It is the flaws in Creon's own personality, his own sense of rigidity, which have led him to isolation, although Antigone, too, may be seen as the victim of her own inflexibility. Here is the essence of the tragedy. Individuals are trapped by their personalities and their circumstances.

The theme of the ruler who is flawed but who is also trapped by a situation of his own making reappears in Sophocles' masterpiece *Oedipus Tyrannus*, Oedipus the king (probably written shortly after 430 B.C.). There can be few tragedies in which the dramatic unfolding of a horrific situation is more brilliantly handled. Oedipus is the king of Thebes, married to Jocasta, the widow of the former king Laius who was murdered while on a journey. He is a proud man, perhaps not a great ruler. A plague strikes the city and the oracle of Delphi proclaims it is because the murderer of Laius lives in the city. Oedipus, though he knows that he once killed a man at a crossroads, believes that this can have nothing to do with him. After all, his father, Polybus, and mother rule as king and queen in Corinth. When the news comes that his father has died his first fear is that an ancient prophecy that he will marry his mother might now come true. The truth is gradually revealed that Polybus never was his father. In fact Oedipus was found abandoned at birth. The dreadful story unfolds that he is the son of Laius and Jocasta and so he has indeed killed his father and married his mother. Jocasta kills herself. Oedipus, confronting her body, gouges out his eyes. He is condemned to wander forever deprived of both his sight and a home city. In a sequel, *Oedipus at Colonus*, written many years later, just before his death, Sophocles portrays Oedipus in his last days. He has come to Colonus, a wild place outside Athens where it has been decreed he will die. He is approached by Creon, the brother of Jocasta, who tries to abduct Antigone, her father's companion in exile, and her sister Ismene and to take back Oedipus so that Thebes rather than Athens might have his body. The attempt is foiled as king Theseus of Athens upholds the city's authority over its territory. However, there is no happy ending. Life is one of suffering, often for reasons no man can avoid. The only response can be nobility. Oedipus dies almost alone.

Sophocles' message is one of tragic simplicity but it has haunted through the ages. Even if there is some underlying sense of meaning and justice in the world, human beings often fail to discern it before it is too late. What seems to be right at one moment, the upholding of a city's laws, for instance, turns out in the circumstances to have offended a more deep-rooted law of justice and in retrospect the failure to uphold the older laws over the newer ones can be traced to some flaw within the character concerned. In *Ajax*, the earliest of Sophocles' plays to survive (from before 441 B.C.), the audience learns from a seer that the gods, angered by Ajax's attack on his fellow Greeks, would have forgiven him if he had stayed secluded in his tent. However, before he can be told, he has committed suicide in remorse for what he has done. The possibility that he could be saved existed but was never realized.

In legend, Euripides (480s–406 B.C.) is a more isolated and complex figure then Aeschylus and Sophocles and there is little evidence of his involvement in city affairs. (There is a story that he wrote his plays secluded in a cave on the island of Salamis.) Although he did not have so many victories (only four first prizes in comparison to Sophocles' twenty-four) some nineteen of his plays happen to survive and they suggest a man who was in tune with the most sophisticated thought of his time. Euripides is acutely aware of the fragility of human society. His plays produce characters who wrestle with the complex realities of everyday life where passions, miscalculations, cruelties, and the plottings of revenge override the nobility of character found, for instance, in an Antigone. Sophocles claimed that he, Sophocles, portrayed men as they ought to be while Euripides portrayed them as they really were.

One reason why Euripides is able to focus with such freedom on human relationships is that he is prepared to exclude the overriding power of the gods from human affairs. Like many intellectuals of his time he probed the existence and purpose of the gods. Do they exist at all? If so what is their nature? Are gods inherently good? If so, why do calamities strike men who seem to lead pious lives and why are smaller cities so often overwhelmed by larger ones that just happen to have larger armies and more ruthless leaders? Why is it that the tyrant who commits every kind of crime, including murder and destruction of property, is allowed to become wealthy? If it can be seen that divine figures behave badly what does this imply—that they are not truly gods, or does one have to accept the fact that gods might themselves be bad? Yet without good gods what can be the meaning of life? These are abiding questions, presenting as much difficulty today as they did then.

It is not only that Euripides frees his characters from the brooding intervention of the gods. There is a driving force to his poetry which makes him transform the myths he uses more comprehensively than either Aeschylus or Sophocles. He is never afraid to manipulate or develop a myth when it serves his purpose to do so. As a result he is a highly creative dramatist. Part of his genius lies in the way that he can show human beings as fluctuating between unreasoned passion and calculating revenge. His women are especially strong. Perhaps the most powerful is Medea from the play of that name (431 B.C.). Medea, the daughter of the king of Colchis in the Black Sea, had married Jason after helping him secure the Golden Fleece. Unhappily, she has involved him in murder during the exploit and the couple have fled to Corinth. Now she is being divorced by Jason partly because she is a non-Greek and her two children by Jason cannot be citizens, and partly because he feels polluted by her actions. Jason is marrying the daughter of the Corinthian king in her place. Deprived of the most basic function of a woman, to be a wife, Medea's response is one of uncontrollable fury and yet she retains a clear idea of how most to hurt Jason, through murdering his bride-to-be and her own children. The deed is done and Medea departs in a chariot drawn by dragons after bitter and harrowing exchanges with her former husband as she even refuses him the bodies of his sons for burial. (Jason: "You thought that reason enough to murder them, that I no longer slept with you?" Medea: "And is that injury a slight one, do you imagine, to a woman?") In *Electra* (415 B.C.) a similar passion grips Electra, the daughter of the murdered Agamemnon and sister of Orestes. She has been left in Mycenae after her father's death and Aegisthus, now king, has made her marry a poor farmer, so that she will not maintain her status as daughter of a king. He is a generous man who has vowed not to take her virginity. (The situation allows Euripides to explore the nature of nobility: "There's no clear sign to tell the quality of a man; nature and place turn vice and virtue upside down. I've seen a noble father breed a worthless son, and good sons come of evil parents; a starved soul housed in a rich man's palace, a great heart dressed in rags.") Electra, however, is bitter and when her brother Orestes, who has been in exile from Mycenae, returns they join in killing their mother, Clytemnestra.

As Athens became entangled in the Peloponnesian War, a host of moral dilemmas presented themselves. One might have expected some caution, even self-imposed censorship, in the way that these sensitive issues were dealt with within drama. Euripides shows in his later plays written during the Peloponnesian War that this was not the case. *The Trojan Women*, for instance, written in 415, just after the massacre of the men of Melos and the enslavement of their women and children (pages 2–3), confronts the issue head on. The Trojan women after the fall of Troy are in a similar position to the women of Melos, their men killed and their own future one of captivity. There is nothing they can do to avoid their fate (which is the result of the inhumanity of man rather than the wrath of the gods) and the play ends with their being led off as slaves. In *Helen*, produced in 412, after the disaster in Sicily, Euripides explores the legend that the real Helen was never taken to Troy, only a phantom of her. Thus the entire ten-year siege has been in vain because she was never there to fight over. What then, Euripides suggests to the Athenian audience who were still smarting from the news of the Sicilian debacle which they themselves, as members of the Assembly, had voted to send, is the point of war when "loud and full through Hellas too the same river of weeping runs [as in Athens itself], and hands are clasped over the stricken head, and nerveless fingers clutch and pull the unfeeling flesh till the nails are red"? The impact of the words on his audience, most of whom must have been affected by losses in Sicily, is almost impossible to imagine. (Would such a play have been allowed in London in the aftermath of the battles of attrition of the First World War?) Although Euripides' continual mocking of convention did lead to his being forced to leave Athens (in 408), he had been able to deal freely with the most raw and immediate of public issues over some thirty years.

Euripides' final play, *Bacchae*, brings him back to religious themes. It was written in Macedonia where the poet lived his last years and is outstanding for the lyrical beauty of many of its choruses which exult in the joys of living in the countryside. The god Dionysus appears in Thebes to lead the celebration of his rites. He is opposed by the king Pentheus who is disturbed by the disorder and licentiousness that the unrestrained revelry of the women, of whom his own mother, Agaue, is one, will bring. Pentheus tries to imprison Dionysus but the god escapes to where the women are waiting in the mountains. Pentheus disguises himself to spy on them but Dionysus ensures he is discovered. The women, worked up into a frenzy by the rituals and led by Pentheus' mother, set upon Pentheus, convinced in their ecstasy that he is a mountain lion. His body is ripped apart and Agaue triumphantly returns to Thebes with his head. She boasts of her power to hunt down and destroy even a lion until she examines closely what she is carrying and the terrible truth is revealed. After all his doubts about the gods, Euripides has suggested that to offend them brings retribution. At a deeper level the message of the *Bacchae* may be that it is foolish to stand in the way of a human need to occasionally throw off the conventions and restraints of everyday life. Reason and unreason both have their places in human society.

The philosopher Aristotle examines the nature of tragedy in his (incomplete) *Poetics*. For Aristotle tragedy is one among several poetic arts but it has its own distinct aims or ends. These ends consist of the arousing of pity or fear in such a way that the spectators understand these emotions more profoundly and will be able to see how they operate in day-to-day life. Tragedy, in short, operates as a means of making more complete human beings, who derive a deeper satisfaction, or "pleasure" as Aristotle puts it, from their greater understanding of pity and fear. In tragedy, as in other areas for Aristotle, the end defines the form and Aristotle spells out the essential attributes of a good tragedy. In order to arouse pity and fear a tragedy has to have actors imitating a real-life situation. This must be embedded in a self-contained plot that has its own satisfying and coherent structure. (Aristotle thought that Sophocles' *Oedipus Tyrannus* was outstanding in this respect.) Above all, says Aristotle, it is vital that tragic outcomes are presented as the result of human action (or failure to act). The characters suffer, not because the gods hate them, or they are shipwrecked, or wounded in battle, but because of something they themselves have done as a result of an inadequacy or flaw in their character. Aristotle thus saw tragedy primarily as an emotional experience, with the ability to change human beings for their better. This was in direct contrast to Plato's view that emotion was to be avoided as it clouded the ability to grasp reality through the use of reason. These ideas are explored further in the next chapter.

The tragedians (and the comedians too) heightened the emotional effect of their plays by giving women strong roles in them. Sometimes a myth is developed in tragedy so that a woman moves from the periphery to the center. In the earliest accounts of the murder of Agamemnon it is Clytemnestra's lover Aegisthus who carries out the deed; in Aeschylus' version it is Clytemnestra herself. There have been few subjects that have caused such intense interest or debate as the role of women in Greek tragedy. There is virtually no evidence, in Athens, at least, of women fulfilling in real life the kind of roles they are given in Greek tragedy; so it can be assumed that women are being used (by the male writers) to fulfill some other function. If male characters are presented in tragedy as acting within the constraints that a male-dominated citizen society imposes on them, then, it can be argued, women may be being "used" to act out passionate feelings that have been repressed in the process. In this sense women are not being portrayed as real women but as archetypes for feelings that have been suppressed. It has also been suggested that by allowing women to speak freely about their lot within the "safe" space of the stage, then the anxieties that men have about women can be defused and the conventional treatment of women sustained more easily. (The debate over women in tragedy is covered well in Chapter Fifteen, "Women in Drama," in Sue Blundell's *Women in Ancient Greece* [London, 1995] and in Chapter Five, "Sexuality and Difference," in Simon Goldhill's *Reading Greek Tragedy* [Cambridge, 1986].)

After three days of such searching drama, the day of comedy must have come as a release. The word *komos* itself meant a procession of revelers. A comic play was first performed in Athens in 486 B.C. though the earliest one known dates from 425 B.C. and is one of the eleven extant plays of Aristophanes, the only fifth-century comedian any of whose works survive. Virtually nothing is known of Aristophanes. (He was probably born in the 450s and died in about 386 B.C.) A conventional view has been that he was conservative by nature and inherently suspicious of the new social trends entering Athens in the late fifth century. In the *Frogs* (see below) he favors Aeschylus over Euripides, and in the *Clouds* (also see below) he ridicules new trends in thinking, but the range of his targets is wide and probably no firm conclusions can be drawn from them. He is equally dismissive of the nobility. As a character in the *Frogs* remarks of an aristocratic figure, "How could he not be a nobleman? All he knows is how to drink and screw!" In 411 when Athens fell under oligarchic rule Aristophanes showed no sympathy for the government. It is perhaps easier to see him as a relatively detached figure who penetrated the absurdities of life and the pretensions of individuals wherever he found them.

Aristophanes' plays are set in his own Athens and a wealth of detail about everyday life can be learned from them even though the antics of the characters often transcend any conceivable real life situation. They contain the whole range of comic devices from sophisticated satire through parody (from *parodia,* a burlesque song) to the most unbridled buffoonery and obscenity. Everyone from politicians to philosophers and poets is lampooned. The choruses are dressed up according to the theme of the play. They appear as extravagantly costumed birds, wasps, or frogs. It is the *Birds* (414 B.C.) which is often seen as the finest of Aristophanes' plays. Two Athenians, Peisetairus and Euelpides, wish to escape from the world and eventually team up with the birds to build a walled city in the air (the original "cloud-cuckoo-land"). It will live on the smoke of sacrifices even though this means depriving the gods of them. The Athenians start to grow their own wings and the success of the enterprise encourages all kinds of other human visitors who demand to be made into birds. In the end some accommodation has to be made with the gods and Peisetairus ends up as chief god and married to the daughter of Zeus. This is all pure fantasy brilliantly carried off. In the *Frogs* (405) Aristophanes' theme is tragedy. Euripides has died and there are no good tragedians left. Dionysus has to descend to the underworld to bring one of them back. Aeschylus and Euripides battle it out as to which is best. Aeschylus puts his case:

> Look at the characters I left him. Fine stalwart characters, larger than life, men who didn't shirk their responsibilities. My heroes weren't like these market place loafers, swindlers and rogues they [i.e., Euripides] write about nowadays: they were real heroes, breathing spears and lances, white-plumed helmets, breastplates and greaves, heroes of hearts of good solid leather, seven hides thick.

Euripides won't let him get way with that:

> I wrote about familiar things, things the audience knew about and could take me up on if necessary . . . What I did was to teach the audience to use its brain, introduce a bit of logic into the drama. The public have learnt from me how to think, how to run their households, to ask "Why is this so? What do we mean by that?"

Dionysus then comes in:

> That's right: whenever an Athenian comes home nowadays he shouts at the servants and starts asking, "Why is the flour jar

> not in its proper place? What do you mean by biting the head off this sprat? What's happened to that cup I had last year? Where is yesterday's garlic, who's been nibbling at this olive?" Whereas before Euripides came along they just sat and stared idiotically.
>
> (Translation: David Barrett)

Eventually it is Aeschylus whom Dionysus selects. In other plays Euripides is lampooned as the son of a mere greengrocer.

Despite the hilarity, wit, and sheer buffoonery of the plays of Aristophanes, comedy also had a serious political purpose. It fulfilled a similar function to tragedy in bringing uncomfortable feelings out into the open, although this time through a focus directly on contemporary issues. The use of laughter and ridicule allowed tensions which might otherwise have become destructive to be defused. Aristophanes is completely uninhibited in his criticism of the Athenian leaders, from Pericles to Cleon. Nothing goes unnoticed. Pericles is lampooned for the shape of his head, his relationship with his mistress Aspasia, and his aloof personality, alongside, of course, scrutiny of his policies. Yet these attacks did not discredit the politicians. Aristophanes' most violent attack on the politician Cleon (in the *Knights* in 424) was followed the next year by Cleon's election as a general. An attack on war made in 411 at a crucial moment of the Peloponnesian War in the play *Lysistrata* (women stage a sex strike until their husbands agree to make peace) seems to have done nothing to create a peace party. In short, comedy had an important cathartic effect for the Athenian community, allowing frustrations to be exploded without, apparently, influencing political decisions.

Drama has, therefore, to be seen within the specific context of Athenian political life, but the idea of theater spread to Rome and the Romans borrowed many Greek plays for their own repertoire. The revival of classical learning in the fifteenth and sixteenth centuries saw the plays of the Romans Terence and Plautus being revived rather than the tragedies of ancient Greece. An *Antigone* produced in France in 1580 A.D. was based as much on Roman sources as on Sophocles. There was not even an English translation of *Oedipus Tyrannus* until 1714. Then through the hands of playwrights such as Racine in France whose *Phedre* (1677), an adaptation of Euripides' *Hippolytus*, brought the power of Greek myth back into European theaters, the Greeks were again noticed. They have been exploited ever since, either in original productions or, in the true spirit of Greek drama, through reworkings of the myths. It is largely through tragedy that Greek myth has penetrated so deeply into the European consciousness. While drama serves very different purposes today, it cannot escape its roots in ancient Greece. It is there that the chromosomes of the Western dramatic tradition lie and it is impossible to know what forms of performance might exist today without the Greek initiative.

13

Man Is the Measure: Philosophers and Speculators, 450–330 B.C.

In a famous passage from *Antigone*, Sophocles talks of the nature and achievements of man:

Wonders are many and none more wonderful than man . . .
In the meshes of his woven nets, cunning of mind, ingenious man . . .
He snares the lighthearted birds and the tribes of savage beasts,
and the creatures of the deep seas . . .
He puts the halter round the horse's neck
And rings the nostrils of the angry bull.
He has devised himself a shelter
against the rigors of frost and the pelting rains.
Speech and science he has taught himself,
and artfully formed laws for harmonious civic life . . .
Only against death he fights in vain.
But clear intelligence—a force beyond measure—
moves to work both good and ill . . .
When he obeys the laws and honors justice, the city stands proud . . .
But man swerves from side to side, and when the laws are broken,
and set at naught, he is like a person without a city,
beyond human boundary, a horror, a pollution to be avoided.

(Translation: Amelie Oksenberg Rorty)

Sophocles presents a shrewd assessment of man, his strengths and his vulnerabilities. He has learned how to exert considerable influence on the physical world and he can revel in his powers so long as he does not try to transgress the will of the gods or cheat death.

This confidence in being human is a typical feeling of the fifth century and it is a feeling which is also transmitted through classical sculpture. As seen in the Critian boy, who ushered in this age, the sculptors reveled in the young male nude whose body was taken as representing the peak of human perfection. There was even an attempt, by one Polyceitus of Argos, around 440 B.C., to find mathematical proportions for such perfection. Polycleitus was probably influenced by Pythagoras in believing that number and proportion underlay the structure of the physical world. He appears to have selected an ideal human body, cast it in bronze, and then tried to work out the proportions between different parts of the ensuing structure. His findings were encapsulated in his famous, though lost, *Canon*. The nearest one can get to his ideal is a Roman copy of one of his bronzes, the so-called *The Spear-bearer*, but it is not clear how the "right" proportions should be calculated from it and even whether it is an exact copy of the original. Nevertheless the original caught the imagination and was widely copied in antiquity. It was clearly seen as some kind of ideal by both Greeks and Romans.

Yet what was ideal about it? As any survey of Western art, particularly of female nudes, shows there is no one ideal body. A society accepts different ideals at different times. *The Spear-bearer* is youthful, probably on the brink of manhood, and portrayed as heavily muscled. Andrew Stewart, analyzing the statue in his *Art, Desire and the Body in Ancient Greece*, argues that he stands apart from his viewers as "the perfectly controlled warrior-athlete . . . the quintessence of disinterested male self-discipline." He is unlikely to have been a real spear-bearer as these were associated with tyrants and barbarian kings (the name was given to the statue four hundred years later) but he is almost certainly some kind of warrior and in the fifth century this would have meant a hoplite. Polycleitus has thus chosen man at his most heroic, in war. He is also shown with well-developed muscles. Andrew Stewart teases out some of the messages given out by a muscled body. Muscles suggest masculinity, long hours of disciplined training, and physical power. *The Spear-bearer* may be making a statement about the legitimization of male power and even, in its carefully proportioned state, stand for the city itself in its ideal form, one of equilibrium.

In the fifth century the statues of women always represented them in clothes. So a statue of the fourth century, about 350, of the goddess Aphrodite nude, was bound to cause a sensation. The sculptor was Praxiteles and he produced his statue for the city of Cnidus, on the southwestern tip of Asia Minor where, according to legend, Aphrodite stopped off while traveling from Cyprus to Greece to wash off the sea foam from her body. The model was Praxiteles' own mistress, Phryne. The statue was enshrined in a circular temple open to the winds so that it could be viewed from all sides. (The base of the temple was discovered at Cnidus in 1969.) It became a major tourist attraction and its erotic presence was such that one local youth was overcome by desire and assaulted it, before jumping to his death off the terrace on which the temple was placed. (The semen from his encounter was preserved on the buttock of the statue, doubtless making it even more of a tourist attraction.)

The act of producing such a statue was not only revolutionary in artistic terms but also brave. According to legend, men who saw Aphrodite naked were made impotent. Praxiteles takes these concerns into account. Although the original statue (which like *The Spear-bearer* survives only in copies) was naked except for a hairband and armband, Aphrodite was shown without pubic hair or any hint of her vulva. She could not therefore be violated. Andrew Stewart sees the statue as reversing the normal representation of a woman, as an object capable of being possessed by a dominant and powerful male, into one where the woman herself holds power over those who might try and possess her. "The all-powerful goddess offers the male no closure, no safe haven for his desire . . . the spectator is reduced to the sordid status of a Peeping Tom." The statue had an extraordinary impact. Greeks were still visiting the shrine seven hundred years later and the figure of the statue, small breasts and fairly broad hips, together with the lack of pubic hair, set the model for the classical female nude both in antiquity and in later European art. (One of the most bizarre results of the adoption of this model in European art was that men could be unaware that women had pubic hair. The art critic John Ruskin was so taken aback by this discovery on his wedding night that he was unable to consummate his marriage.)

The place of man in the *cosmos* and the relationship he might have with the gods, his fellow men, his city, and the conventions of society was the subject of ardent debate in the Athens of the fifth century. The wealth and comparative political and social sophistication of the city had made it a magnet for visitors from overseas, in much the same way as Florence in the fifteenth century or New York in the 1970s. Many of the visitors were philosophers. Anaxagoras apparently visited in the 450s, possibly staying twenty years. He caused a stir with his lectures and got on well with Pericles. Parmenides and Democritus also came to Athens although there is no record of any impact they made. More influential was Protagoras of Abdera whose views on the relativity of knowledge have already been described. He arrived in the city in 433. While the earlier natural philosophers had been interested in the exploration of nature for its own sake, Protagoras specifically rejected this concern and in line with the spirit of the age focused his attention on human societies. Notorious for wondering whether the gods existed at all he argued that human beings had to create societies based on those laws, *nomoi* (although the word also means conventions or customs) that suited them best. There were no moral absolutes; rather, appropriate laws could be developed through argument. Man remained the measure of all things and laws therefore the reflection of human society. Pericles was so impressed with Protagoras that he asked him to draw up a constitution for the new Athenian settlement of Thurii in southern Italy.

Protagoras taught his ideas to those who could afford to pay him and he is normally seen as the leading figure of the Sophists (from *sophizesthai,* "making a profession of being inventive and clever"), men who passed on their knowledge either through lectures or personal contact throughout the fifth-century Greek world. Sophistic thought was important not only for the social context within which it was transmitted, but for its nature. Although there was no defined Sophistic school, the Sophists' approach was essentially man-centered, free thinking, and functional. The range of issues and skills explored was wide and many of the Sophists were polymaths. Hippias from Elis, who came to Athens originally as an ambassador from his city, was expert in poetry and music, mathematics, history, and literary criticism. Setting the starting point of the Olympic Games as 776 B.C., and using the records of the Games to list each one in order, he provided a framework for dating which allowed events across the Greek world to be synchronized. (There was no single Greek calender, each city had its own, but they all recorded the Olympic Games so that by securely fixing its dates the calenders of different cities could be correlated.) He also prided himself on his craftsmanship, boasting at one appearance at Olympia that everything he wore including his cloak, his sandals, and his ring had been made by himself. The particular appeal of the Sophists to the young Athenian elite was in their teaching of rhetoric, an essential skill for the aspiring politician, at a time when aristocratic birth no longer brought automatic status or success. For Protagoras rhetoric was important but probably only a minor part of his repertoire of skills. It took the arrival of Gorgias from Leontini in 427 to start the craze for public speaking. Gorgias stressed that effective rhetoric was a means of keeping the ideal of freedom alive as well as providing an avenue through which political power for the individual might be secured. His Sicilian style proved particularly popular and there is a tradition that Alcibiades came under his influence. Another rhetorician, Prodicus, from Ceos in the Cyclades, arrived in Athens as an ambassador and became a friend of Socrates. He became absorbed in the study of the correct use of words and how to distinguish between words that were near synonyms. He has been seen as the founder of linguistics. Prodicus went further than Protagoras in suggesting that religion might actually be a human creation based on an instinct which made gods of those things, the sun and moon, bread and wine, which were seen to be of benefit to humanity. An Athenian Critias (later a leading figure among the "Thirty Tyrants") is recorded in a fragment of a play as going further still. It was rulers who instituted gods as a means of keeping their subjects in check.

The Sophists were fascinated by human nature itself, shown not only in the character of an individual but in the ways human beings in general tended to act, say, in times of stress. They asked what the essence of being human was and then explored what the status of human nature should be. Was human nature stable or did it change under the pressure of events? Was it something inherently good which had to be left to flourish or was it a flawed attribute which had to be constrained by laws? Protagoras argued that human nature by itself was incomplete and had to be tempered by the civilizing influence of laws. These laws, he argued in line with the rest of his beliefs, were not moral absolutes, the product of divine thought, but they had to be created for the particular circumstances by the persuasion "of wise and good political speakers" who "make good things rather than bad to be just to cities." Others, however, doubted that the persuasive skills of the wise or any other force could provide a foundation for laws. They went so far as to argue that there was no foundation at all. Different societies had evolved different customs. (Herodotus had a story of how the Persian king Darius had challenged some Greeks and Indians to adopt each other's burial customs and both had been disgusted by what seemed normal to the other.) It was a small step to seeing laws as the essentially ephemeral results of power struggles between different factions in society. This could lead to cynicism (as found in Thucydides, for instance, who was steeped in the Sophistic thought of his time) or alternatively a more optimistic belief that if human nature was left untrammeled the best society would be the natural outcome. Antiphon, an Athenian of oligarchic sympathies, argued that laws were chains on the natural instincts of man (a forerunner of Rousseau's famous dictum "Man is born free but everywhere he is in chains"). Comparisons were made with the animal kingdom where animals seemed able to work out a system of living with each other without laws.

The influence of the Sophists on intellectual circles within Athens was profound and, as has been suggested, major Athenian thinkers such as Thucydides and Euripides absorbed their ideas. However, for many in the city their ideas were deeply unsettling. Traditionalists placed great emphasis on the transmission of values from old to young through the established education system. There were two underlying objectives of this system. First, the young had to learn self-discipline, through training for physical activity and the mastery of music. "So also the lyre teacher sees to his pupils' restraint and good behaviour. Once they are able to play, he teaches them songs by suitable poets, stringing these into the lesson, and gets the rhythms and tunings into the boys' minds, to make them less wild, and better in tune for effective discourse and action.' (Translation: Peter Levi.) Then moral values had to be absorbed, largely through studying Homer, whose epics were learned by heart (from written texts). Every kind of situation, relationship, and moral dilemma was assumed to be contained in Homer and those who mastered the epics would, it was argued, be well equipped to cope in the real world.

This approach to education was directly threatened by the ethos of Sophistic thinking which encouraged questioning of values rather than the unthinking absorption of them. The Sophists also taught functional skills, something highly attractive to the young Athenian hoping to make his way in politics, but not traditionally part of the education of a "gentleman" whose ability to speak was assumed to come with his breeding. The clash between the Sophists and traditionalists was brilliantly exploited, from the traditionalists' point of view, by Aristophanes in his *Clouds* (423 B.C.). The story tells of a farmer, Strepsiades, whose son Pheidippides has adopted an aristocratic lifestyle and fallen heavily into debt. Not to worry, says his father, he has heard that there is a special school, "the thinking shop of wise fools," where one can learn to win even unjust cases. Both father and son attend in turn. The teachers are absorbed in their own researches, how far a flea can jump relative to its own size and out of which orifice the noise of a gnat comes. Then there is the arrival of none other than Socrates, Athens' most celebrated philosopher, suspended in a basket. He is examining the sun and tells Strepsiades that it is "the clouds" which one must worship not the traditional gods. If there were effective and just gods surely wrongdoers would suffer on earth but there is no evidence that they do more than those who behave well. Pheidippides attends a debate in which traditional thinking is rubbished and emerges to demolish the demands of his creditors. However, he has learned too much. If all authority is discredited so too is the traditional authority of a father over a son. Pheidippides uses an analogy with the animal kingdom, as those who believed in the primacy of human nature did. Young cockerels displace the old when they reach maturity and so, Pheidippides argued, he was entitled to beat up his father.

The *Clouds* is an example of a particularly successful attack on the Sophists and it reflects the views of a city made deeply uneasy by their intellectual probing. In these years Athens was facing a series of profound shocks from plague and military defeat. It was natural for the traditionalists to argue that these were some form of revenge by the gods on those, the Sophists, who ridiculed them. The end result of Sophistic thinking was to spread uncertainty, both about the meaning and purpose of the world and about the nature of moral values. Already around 432 a law had been passed that made it illegal to teach disbelief in things divine. Protagoras was expelled from Athens after a charge of impiety. Then came the mutilation of the Herms in 415, an act of sacrilege which shook the city to its core. Many aristocrats were exiled in the witch hunt that followed.

While the old order could be upheld by new laws and repression, one philosopher wondered whether it might also be possible to find an alternative and more secure foundation for knowledge, in particular for moral values. This was Socrates and his quest was to lead to his death. Socrates was born about 470 B.C. so his early adulthood coincided with the years of Periclean democracy. He played little part in city affairs suggesting that it would compromise his political principles to do so although he does appear to have served on occasions as a hoplite. He was clearly a well-known character in Athens. He would not have "starred" in the *Clouds* otherwise, though the play does not give a fair picture of his role as philosopher. He was not a Sophist, in that he did not charge for his teaching, and he had profound reservations about much of the Sophists' teaching. The fullest account of his philosophy comes in the works of Plato. (There are some memories of him recorded by the historian Xenophon, but Xenophon did not grasp the nature and implications of his philosophy and most scholars prefer Plato's account.) Plato used Socrates as a character in his *Dialogues* in which characters talk through a particular issue. It is assumed that the Socrates of the early *Dialogues* is the "real" Socrates putting forward his own ideas. In the later *Dialogues* Plato may have used the character of Socrates as a front for his own views.

Like most pioneers Socrates was an unconventional and unsettling figure. He was not helped by his appearance, ugly with protruding lips and a flat, turned-up nose, and a paunch, but his personality was magnetic, even disturbing. One account of Socrates' effect on his listeners is given by the aristocratic politician Alcibiades who appears as a character in Plato's *Symposium*:

> When I listen to him, my heart pounds . . . it's a sort of frenzy . . . possessed . . . and the tears stream out of me at what he says. And I can see a lot of other people that he's had just the same effect on. I've heard Pericles, I've heard plenty more good speakers and I thought they did pretty well, but they never had an effect like this on me. My soul wasn't turned upside down by them and it didn't suffer from the feeling that I'm dirt. But that's the feeling I get from him and I know very

> well, at this moment, if I were prepared to lend him my ears, I couldn't hold out, he makes me admit that when there's so much I need, I don't look after myself.
>
> (Translation: Kenneth Dover)

Socrates shifted the concerns of Greek philosophy from a search for understanding of the natural world toward what it meant to live a good life. This was a new beginning in philosophy and all earlier Greek philosophy is conventionally grouped together under the term "pre-Socratic." Socrates started by stressing the inadequacy of conventional thinking, the shortcomings in the kind of everyday opinions most people hold. His method was to go out and question people, often relentlessly, about the everyday words they used and the values they held. When Socrates wanted to explore the nature of bravery, for instance, he sought out an elderly general, Laches. If anyone should know about bravery it was an experienced soldier but as Socrates made clear it was not so easy as that:

> **Socrates** (to Laches): I wanted to get your opinion not only of bravery in the hoplite line, but also in cavalry engagements and in all forms of fighting; and indeed of bravery not only in fighting but also at sea, and in the face of illness and poverty and public affairs. And there is bravery not only in face of pain and fear, but also of desire and pleasure, both fearsome to fight against whether by attack or retreat—for some men are brave in all these encounters, aren't they, Laches?
> **Laches:** Yes, certainly.
> **Socrates:** Then all these are examples of bravery, only some men show it in pleasure, some in pain, some in desire, some in danger. And there are others who show cowardice in the same circumstances.
> **Laches:** Yes.
> **Socrates:** Now what I want to know was just what each of these two qualities is. So try again and tell me first, what is this common characteristic of courage which they all share? Do you understand what I mean?
> **Laches:** I am afraid I don't.
>
> (Translation: Desmond Lee)

Laches has to admit that in effect he had never pondered the full meaning of bravery. Such an approach could leave everyone in a state of frustration but this did not worry Socrates. It was after all, as he said on another occasion, the mark of a wise man that he realized how ignorant he was.

The method of confrontation, *elenchus,* was a pioneering device and one which Plato was to adopt. It enabled a problem to be broken down and examined from every angle. However, it was only a first step in finding knowledge about moral issues. Socrates believed that once one had shown the inadequacies of conventional thinking the way was open to use reason to construct alternative understandings of concepts such as bravery. What, to use the example above, was the common characteristic of the different kinds of bravery? Eventually, through endless questioning and thought about the different situations that bravery might be found, Socrates believed one could construct something called "bravery" that contained all the examples of everyday bravery one could think of. One could carry out a similar exercise for "virtue" or "beauty" or any other kind of quality or even object (the perfect table, for instance). This was the end he aimed for.

It was an essential part of Socrates' philosophy that when one had discovered the meaning of, say, virtue that one would be irresistibly drawn towards it. In effect, the only barrier between man and a good life was ignorance. However, there had to be some element within a human being that provided a home for this impulse and this according to Socrates was the soul, the *psyche.* Here Socrates made a significant development. For the Greeks of the Archaic and classical periods the *psyche* was a sort of double or mirror image of the deceased, the spectral shade that flitted between the worlds of the living and the dead when a corpse had not received the prescribed burial rites. Socrates (and after him Plato) argued that the *psyche* was not only much more substantial than that but distinct from the human body in that it had an existence from before and after that body had died. Moreover, it was a superior part of a human being, endowed with his character and the ability to reason. It stood above and apart from more immediate desires for gratification and sensual pleasure and through its exercise lay the possibility of finding the meaning of moral values. It was within the *psyche* that the impulse to follow the good when it was found lay.

For Socrates, therefore, the search for knowledge was a serious business. One was simply debasing oneself if one just stumbled through life without profound thought on its meaning. Such an approach was no less that a betrayal of the potential of the *psyche*. As Socrates put it in one of his most famous sayings "The unexamined life is not worth living." Once the *psyche* had been used to find knowledge it would come into its own and its owner would be a "good man" without further ado. The man of true virtue would stand apart from the tyrant or even the ancient hero whose prestige depended on his ability to dominate others. He would be driven by his own understanding of virtue (or bravery or beauty) and would not have to depend on the more shallow opinions of others. It goes without saying that a man of virtue would follow his own beliefs and would never try to court popularity for its own sake. Socrates lived up to his principles. In 403, to give an example, during the rule of the Thirty Tyrants Socrates was ordered to seize an opponent of the government for execution but he refused.

For later generations there is something deeply attractive about Socrates, the selfless searcher for truth and virtue whose way and life and beliefs corresponded, but for the Athenians of his own day his presence was unsettling. He had questioned the old ways, upset those whom he questioned, and refused to conform. In 399 B.C., now an old man of seventy, he was arrested. The official charge was "Socrates does wrong by not acknowledging the gods the city acknowledges and introducing other, new powers. He also does wrong by corrupting the young." As suggested earlier, wide-ranging accusations such as these were the normal way of procedure in the law courts and were usually no more than a front for political infighting. Socrates had survived earlier crises such as that of 415 B.C. when there had been a witch hunt against unbelievers after the mutilation of the Herms. One has to dig deeper to discover why Socrates had offended in 399. Athens was in the shadow of a number of collective defeats, of the war, the lost empire, the rule of the Thirty and it is likely that it was the accumulation of these experiences that provided the context for framing scapegoats. Yet what was the essence of Socrates' offense? One suggestion is that he was caught in the backlash against the Thirty Tyrants, some of whom he had taught as boys. Robert Parker in his penetrating study of Athenian religion argues that Socrates' real crime lay in undermining the education system. Since Athenian education had traditionally involved passing on virtuous behavior by personal example and the study of poets such as Homer, Socrates, like the Sophists, was breaking that link by expecting the young to think through what virtue meant for themselves. This, as already suggested above, was what rankled with conservatives.

The normal response to such accusations was to indulge in counter-accusations and hope to sway the jury by sheer force of rhetoric. Even if Socrates had lost, the normal penalty would have been exile. However, Socrates, at least in the account of his trial given by Plato, would not descend to the necessary level of street fighting. He infuriated his listeners by refusing to compromise, even claiming that he should be supported at public expense for his contribution to city life. Such an elevated approach eventually left the jury with little option but to convict him and to pass a death penalty. Plato recorded Socrates' last thoughts (or possibly recreated what he hoped they were) as the hemlock he was given spread through his body. (Death through hemlock was, in fact, a much nastier way of dying than Plato's calm and sanitized account suggests.)

Plato was a young aristocratic Athenian, nearly thirty when Socrates was executed. His own background reflected the turmoil of Athenian politics; his stepfather had been a democrat, a friend of Pericles, while two of his uncles supported the rule of the Thirty Tyrants. He had once considered a political career, and had reached the age at which it would be possible, but now he was disillusioned. He, like Socrates, had been deeply troubled by the threat offered by the Sophists' thinking to the concept of authority. As a result of the new stress on rhetoric, government lay in the hands of those who could speak most persuasively, not necessarily those of the greatest virtue or knowledge. The people could be swayed by passionate argument and do wrong as a result. After all, Socrates, whom Plato considered "the most just man of his time," had been executed by a supposedly democratic process. Plato was also profoundly affected by the collapse of Athens itself and although initially sympathetic to the rule of the Thirty Tyrants (whom he naively hoped would introduce a juster form of government) he soon realized they were even worse than the democrats. "From one point of view," writes G. C. Field in *Plato and his Contemporaries* (London, 1967), "the chief aim of Plato's philosophy may be regarded as the attempt to re-establish standards of thought and conduct for a civilization that seemed on the verge of dissolution."

Plato reputedly left Athens after Socrates' execution and may have visited Egypt and Libya. In 388 B.C. he was in southern Italy trying to find out more about Pythagoras from his followers. He was interested in what Pythagoras had taught about the soul, and his views that the physical world had a mathematical underpinning. He was always to believe, like Pythagoras, that numbers stood apart in some way from the physical world and offered some kind of gateway to a higher understanding. He then went on to Syracuse where he encountered the tyrant Dionysius and his family. The relationship was to be a momentous but ultimately humiliating one. By 386 B.C. Plato was back in Athens and he now set up his Academy—so called from a sanctuary on the outskirts of Athens dedicated to a hero, Academus. It was to last nearly a thousand years before closed down by the Christians in the sixth century A.D. In the Academy scholars could meet in an informal setting and teaching was probably through discussion rather than formal lectures. It seemed possible to come for a short visit or to stay for years. It was a tribute to Plato that he never allowed the Academy to become an institution that simply worked and reworked his own views. Independence of thought was encouraged.

A large body of Plato's work survives and it is impressive, not only for its range and scope but for the lucidity of his writing. As a means of exploring philosophical issues Plato adopts the dialogue in which a number of speakers meet to discuss a problem. Socrates appears throughout the *Dialogues* but other philosophers, among them Protagoras, Zeno, and Parmenides, are represented. Arguments are put forward, often related to the actual views that Plato believed the speaker held, shortcomings dissected, a move made toward further elucidation or the ironing out of contradictions. It was an excellent way of exploring an issue in depth even if a satisfactory conclusion was not always the end result. Plato's ideas were always inventive and searching with vivid analogies to push home his point. It is through Plato that one comes face to face with philosophy as a living subject.

Socrates had attempted to find the true nature of virtue but there is no evidence that he arrived at establishing what virtue was to the satisfaction of anyone but himself. Plato put forward a more radical suggestion. Virtue was not simply a concept which was cobbled together from the common characteristics of many instances of virtue in everyday life; it actually existed as a real entity on a higher level than this material world. This Form of Virtue, as it is normally called, was invisible to the ordinary senses but it could be grasped by the *psyche*'s using its power of reasoning. This is an extraordinary idea but Plato elaborated it with some sophistication. It was not only virtue but almost everything that had a Form, from justice and beauty, to largeness, equality, whiteness, through to a table, that ultimate table which contains all the attributes of everything on earth that can be classified as a table. In other words a whole world exists beyond the one grasped by the senses. While the material world is, as Heraclitus argued, continually in a state of change, the world of the Forms is unchanging (rather in the sense that Parmenides had argued) and each Form represents the most perfect representation of its subject. As Plato says of beauty: "It seems to me that if anything else is beautiful besides the [Form] Beautiful itself it is beautiful for no other reason whatever but that it participates in that Beautiful; and I say the same in all cases." In other words the Form offers perfection of the particular quality because the most beautiful thing on earth can be no more than *part* of the Form of Beauty. As sources of knowledge about reality, the Forms provide something much superior to what can be grasped in the world our senses can see, which is endlessly unstable and unsatisfactory.

Humans could reach the world of the Forms through the reasoning *psyche*. In the most famous of his analogies, Plato (in *The Republic*) presents a group of men chained since childhood in a dark cave and forced by their chains to face only the inner wall of the cave. The sunlight is beyond and between the entrance and the wall is a fire so that their shadows, as well as objects carried in front of the fire, are projected onto the cave. What they saw on the wall they would assume to be reality. They would have no experience of any other reality. However, one of the prisoners might be released and slowly introduced to objects by the light of the fire. It would be painful as his sight adjusted from the darkness but he would have to acknowledge that what he saw was more real than the shadows. Then if he was taken out into the sunlight, he would again be dazzled.

Plato goes on:

> First he would find it easiest to look at shadows, next at the reflections of men and other objects in water, and later on at the objects themselves. After that he would find it easier to observe the heavenly bodies and the sky at night than by day, and to look at the moon and stars, rather than at the sun and its light . . . the thing he would be able to do last would be to look directly at the sun, and observe its nature without using reflec-

> tions in water or any other medium, but just as it is . . . Later on he would come to the conclusion that it is the sun that produces the changing seasons and years and controls everything in the visible world, and is in a sense responsible for everything that he and his fellow prisoners used to see. . . . And when he thought of his first home and what passed for wisdom there, and of his fellow prisoners, don't you think he would congratulate himself on his good fortune and be sorry for them?
>
> (Translation: H.D.P. Lee)

In the analogy of the cave the final goal of the quest is the sun. The sun is not only a force in its own right but it has powers of nurturing other objects in the world. Plato argued that among the Forms there was a supreme Form, the Form of the Good, into which all the attributes of other forms was subsumed. Plato gave this Form the power to sustain and nurture other Forms. It was an original thought which was adopted by Christians to create one of the most powerful and enduring images in theology.

The question remains as to how the Forms can be understood. Plato argued that the Forms were already known to the *psyche* and so it was a question of their being *rediscovered* rather than grasped for the first time. In one Dialogue the *Meno,* Meno, a slave boy, is led through a mathematical proof about the area of a square (the area of a square quadruples when the length of its side is doubled). Plato claims that the slave boy's understanding of the proof in itself proves that his *psyche* knew the argument all along. Plato also used the idea of equality. Nothing on earth is exactly equal to each other, yet one has an idea of equality. Where does it come from if it did not exist already within the *psyche*?

Plato never pretended that finding the Forms would be easy. It would require many years of patient thought. Each step toward understanding involved pain, but once it had been made and consolidated the thinker would immediately recognise how much progress he had made. The real payoff came when one had moved through a hierarchy of Forms and reached that of "the Good." The realization would be obvious: A blinding flash of insight that one had "arrived" is suggested in some of Plato's *Dialogues.* Then there would be a complete understanding of the natural order of things. The traditional order of the Homeric gods in which men and gods were totally separated from each other is replaced by one in which a few individuals can bridge the gap and reach divine knowledge.

Although Plato describes the arrival of an understanding of the Forms as some kind of mystical experience, the knowledge would not lead to a separation from the world as it did among the later Christian mystics. Knowledge for Plato had some practical purpose. By judging the Form of the Good or Justice or Virtue against what is found in the material world, one can set standards for an ideal society. The fully developed philosopher thus has the potential and even the duty to be a ruler. This was the task set for the philosopher in the *The Republic*, the most famous and enduring of Plato's works (completed c. 375).

In *The Republic* Plato took on an unashamedly elitist, and anti-democratic approach to government. The basis of effective and just government is an understanding of the Forms but not everyone has the capacity to understand them. Plato had already argued that the soul, the *psyche,* was divided into three elements, the reasoning part, the "spirited" part, and the part containing everyday human appetites (for sensual pleasure, for instance). So too are the members of human society. There are those best fitted to reason, those best suited to fighting (the "spirited"), and those whose lives would be filled by the search for pleasure. Plato talks condescendingly of the last group as "one lot, the lovers of spectacles and lovers of sounds, who delight in fine voices and colours and shapes and everything that art fashions from that sort of things . . . but their minds are incapable of seeing and delighting in the nature of the beautiful itself." They will never take a part in ruling or defending the state.

Children, Plato argued, should be divided into two groups, those ruled by their appetites, who will be expected to undertake the labor and craft activities of the state, and the rest. These, the rest, will be started on a formal education so that those best suited to reasoning can be distinguished from those who will be the warriors. The former will be trained as potential "guardians" of the state. Both sexes will be considered equally for training as guardians. However, the way ahead is hard. Starting with "easy" subjects such as gymnastics, music, and mathematics, the trainees will be set on a course of disciplined rational thinking. Only then will they be introduced to formal philosophy through the practice of dialogue. By the age of thirty-five the survivors will have understood the whole system of the Forms including the

Form of the Good. Then there is still a fifteen-year period of training in the art of ruling others. During this long apprenticeship the guardians will live together in a shared mess and they will learn that they rule purely out of duty, not because of any love of power or any self-interest. Plato established the ideal of the ruler whose only interest is the public good.

The state which will finally emerge must be a just one so long as it is based on the Forms. However, it is also an authoritarian one because only the guardians understand the Forms and have a right to impose their understanding on others. The guardians are in fact like doctors who know better than their patients what is right for them and have an absolute right to carry out what treatment is necessary for their health. The patients-subjects must not be encouraged to believe they know what is good for themselves or be diverted by emotion. Plato feared the power of the traditional education based on poetry and its accompanying music which aroused emotions at the expense of austere rational thought. He would even ban tragedy in his ideal state. Nor would personal relationships be encouraged—sex, for instance, would be regulated in the interest of breeding more effective citizens. The state would have to be harsh with wrongdoers. "In purging the Polis for the good, they [the guardians] may put some of the citizens to death or banish others, or reduce the population by sending off colonies like bees from the hive . . ."

On his first visit to Sicily, Plato had formed a strong, possibly homosexual, attachment to one Dion, the brother-in-law of the tyrant of Syracuse Dionysius. Dion had absorbed Plato's thought and Plato hoped that on Dionysius' death Dion might become a ruler on the Platonic model. When Dionysius died in 367 he was succeeded by his son Dionysius II. Dion remained an adviser but fell out with the new tyrant. Plato unwisely became involved in the bitter power struggles which followed until Dion was assassinated in 354 B.C. At one point he was even placed under house arrest when visiting Syracuse and had to be rescued by an embassy sent from Athens. Not only had Plato's ideals crumbled in face of an actual political challenge, but Plato himself appeared soured by the experience. In his final years he composed the *Laws*, a massive list of regulations controlling every aspect of life in the state. It was needed, he said, because men were not yet of sufficient birth and education to live in the ideal state of the Republic. The world of the *Laws* was a harsh one. The citizens were to be indoctrinated into goodness and their wrongdoings punished brutally, through flogging, imprisonment, exile, or death.

Plato's thought had continuing power in later European history. It was given a new lease of life in the first centuries A.D. when thinkers such as Plotinus elaborated the idea of a Supreme Good or "the One" who contained the power of love reaching out to those who were searching for it. From here it was a short step to equating the Good with God. St. Augustine came to Christianity through Platonism. As he puts it in his *Confessions*, his fine autobiographical account of his conversion to Christianity (here he is addressing God directly):

> By reading the books of the Platonists I had been prompted to look for truth as something incorporeal, and I caught sight of your invisible nature, as it is known through your creatures. Though I was thwarted of my wish to know more, I was conscious of what it was that my mind was too clouded to see. I was certain both that you are and that you are infinite, though without extent to space either limited or unlimited. I was sure that it is you who truly are, since you are always the same, varying in neither part or motion.

Here God is a supreme Platonic Form, grasped through his creatures, although Augustine is prevented from full understanding by the clouding of the mind. Like the Forms, God is "varying in neither part or motion."

The Platonic legacy has also inspired a number of utopias, states in which rulers claim they have grasped an ideal which they have a right to impose on others. One such was the Republic of Virtue proposed by Maximilien Robespierre to justify the terror in the French Revolution. "What is our ultimate aim?" asked Robespierre, "The peaceful enjoyment of liberty and equality; the reign of eternal justice, whose laws are engraved, not in marble or stone, but in the hearts of all men, even in that of the slave who forgets them [compare *Meno*] and of the tyrant who rejects them." Those who opposed these "eternal" laws (as they were interpreted by Robespierre and his supporters) could be eliminated. The communist leaders were in the same tradition and there is much of the spirit of Plato's *Laws* in the harshness of their unsuccessful attempts to create a communist society.

It should be clear from the above that despite the sparkle, insights, and penetration of the *Dialogues*, there is much to be sceptical about in Plato's thought. Is it true that there are forces outside the real world which can be grasped by the human intellect while remaining inaccessible to the normal senses? How could one actually prove that the Forms exist? Is it enough to say that one has discovered the Form of Good or Virtue? How can one prove that the nature of the Form has been properly grasped? How are varying examples of bravery or virtue related to each other? Can the Form of Good include the Form of Evil? Is the Form of Largeness anything more than something infinitely large (and so comprehensible with very little difficulty)? Plato was sensitive to some of the problems associated with the Forms (there is a section in his Dialogue the *Parmenides* where he explores some of the difficulties) and may have had doubts about them in his later years (possibly as a result of counterarguments put forward by Aristotle), but they are what defines Platonic thought.

By stressing the superiority of the world of the Forms, Plato deflected attention away from the material world we see around us, with all its flux, diversity, and instability. One did not have to find meaning in this world. It was so obviously inferior to the world of the Forms that it was of little interest. As Plato wrote in *The Republic*, "we shall approach astronomy as we do geometry by way of problems, *and ignore what's in the sky* [my italics], if we intend to get a real grasp of astronomy." Important questions about it were left unanswered. Plato never explained, for instance, the relationship between the material world and the world of the Forms, how, say, a Form of Animal related to the actual members of the animal kingdom. His critics have argued that by turning his back on the existing material world and positing the world of the Forms instead, he was opting out of dealing with the really difficult questions, those of how and why a world of change and diversity that is immediately apparent to the senses exists.

It says much for the open nature of the Academy that the challenge to return to a concentration on the material world was taken up by one of Plato's own pupils, Aristotle. Aristotle was not an Athenian by birth, he came from a landed family of the Greek city of Stagira on the Chalcidice peninsula. His father had been physician to King Amyntas of Macedon and Aristotle may have spent some of his childhood at the Macedonian court. If so, the young Aristotle probably knew Amyntas' son, Philip of Macedon, well and this may have been why in the 340s

Philip was to employ Aristotle to be the tutor of his son Alexander ("the Great"). Aristotle was never to shake off the reputation of being pro-Macedonian and his connections were to prove troublesome while he was living in Athens.

Aristotle arrived at the Academy as a student in 367, at the age of seventeen. He apparently retained some of the air of his background in his arrogance and the special care he took to dress well. It is assumed, however, that he had picked up some medical skills, particularly in dissection, before then and his bent was always toward examination of the natural world. At the Academy, of course, he was plunged into the world of Platonic thought. Aristotle always valued Plato highly as a teacher and he may at first have been attracted by the idea of a changeless, imperishable world (as of the Forms) but his real interests lay in the world he could actually experience. It is assumed that by the time of Plato's death in 347 he had rejected Plato's ideas of the Forms and in that year, following an outburst of anti-Macedonian feeling in Athens, he left for the city of Assos in Asia Minor and later moved to the neighboring island of Lesbos. Here he became absorbed in the study of the natural world and compiled detailed accounts of the animals he saw there. Then, in 335, following the humbling of the Greeks by Alexander, he returned to Athens and founded a school for teaching and research known as the Lyceum where he accumulated the first recorded library. He remained in Athens until another burst of anti-Macedonian feeling in 323 drove him to Euboea where he died a year later.

There are major problems involved in exploring Aristotle's ideas. It is assumed that his written works (of which a representative sample of about a fifth of the original remain) were based on lecture notes as his style is comparatively unpolished and discursive. There is a sense of work in progress as befits an endlessly inquiring mind dealing with a diverse world and in these circumstances it would be wrong to expect any final coherence to his ideas. He had no established tradition of scientific experimentation to fall back on and no instruments with which to aid his understanding. The very nature of his undertaking, a relentless probing of almost every sphere of activity, meant that words and concepts of the time were inadequate for what he was trying to say and often he had to invent them. There are further complications in that Aristotle's manuscripts were put together by followers some centuries after his death (the main collection was edited by one Andronicus of Rhodes in Rome about 30 B.C.) and there is no certainty that they were arranged as Aristotle intended.

Aristotle's researches during the twelve years he was in Asia set much of the pattern of his later thought. In his enquiries into the nature of the animal kingdom he examined a vast array of animals and organisms, from the European bison to mites and from octopuses to oysters. Each was described in detail often after dissection. (Aristotle compiled a whole book of his dissections but this is now lost.) The process of growth was observed, in one case by placing a hen over a clutch of eggs and removing and breaking open an egg each day so that the formation of a chick embryo could be charted. These researches which survive make Aristotle the founding father of the discipline of zoology and his work was not to be surpassed for two thousand years.

This was only a start. Aristotle wanted to understand not only the natural world, but the *processes* by which it could be understood. While he was always ready to listen to other opinions (many of his works begin with a survey of earlier thinkers) in the end one had to use one's own senses, what Aristotle called "experience." This is the empirical approach based on collecting facts about the natural world and then making generalizations about that world as a result. Eventually, in studying any particular subject one would be able to come across some basic axioms, such as "all men are mortal." How can one deal with such an axiom? Aristotle broke it up. "All men are mortal" is a proposition, composed of a subject, "men," and a statement about men, the predicate, that they "are mortal." There are other kinds of propositions: "Not all men are fair skinned" or "some men are tall," for instance. A major step taken by Aristotle was to realize that one could make valid arguments from these propositions. For instance, to take a famous example: "All men are mortal, Socrates is a man, therefore Socrates is mortal." In a logical argument the first two statements are known as premises and together, in this example, they lead to a watertight conclusion. This is what Aristotle called a syllogism, "an argument in which certain things being assumed, something different from the things assumed follows from necessity by the fact that they hold." (The key point is "certain things being assumed"—one has to assume that men really are mortal, if they are not then one has no foundation on which to build the process of argument.) One of Aristotle's most brilliant contributions was to substitute letters for actual objects so that one has "All As are B, C is an A, therefore C is B." It seems a simple step but it creates a science of logic which sets out ways in which valid arguments about any subject can be tested. It also provides a means for spotting invalid arguments. "All men are mortal, an elephant is mortal, therefore an elephant is a man" is not a valid argument; neither, it follows, is *any* argument which runs "All A's are B, C is a B, therefore C is B." Aristotle set out a basic means of testing arguments which was not challenged until the nineteenth century.

Logic can only take one so far. A true understanding of the natural world depends on finding deeper underlying reasons for its operation. Aristotle recognized the limitations of earlier materialists such as the Atomists. Surely, he argued, the world is more complex than a set of atoms endlessly rearranging itself. It appeared, for instance, that there was an order which underpinned natural processes. Otherwise why do animals only have sex with their own species so that each species is kept distinct? The attributes of any living organism (the fins of a fish, the legs of a man) seemed designed for a purpose. One does not seem to have attributes one cannot use but why not? Looking at the wider *cosmos,* and drawing on the work of contemporary astronomers (explored in Chapter Eighteen) Aristotle believed the stars enjoyed a similar sort of order, making eternal circlings around an earth which he believed, in line with the conventional thinking of his age, lay at the center of the universe and had no motion of its own. Logically, Aristotle argued, there had to be some Supreme Being which caused the movement of this eternal order and so he talked of "the Unmoved Mover" which existed alongside the material world since the beginning of time. Aristotle shared with Plato and with most other Greek philosophers the belief of an ultimate order, whether visible or invisible.

Within this order one still had to find a way of classifying and explaining the content and activities of the natural world. The problem of finding a meaning to the *cosmos* was discussed in a book which originally had no name but was placed by Aristotle's followers after (*meta*) one on physics. The word *metaphysics* still describes the study of the ultimate nature of things, the purpose of existence, for instance. Although Aristotle certainly believed there was a fundamental unity to knowledge, for practical purposes he divided the sciences into three:

those that are theoretical, mathematics, theology, and the natural sciences; those that are practical, useful for conduct in the real world, such as ethics and politics; and those directly concerned with making things. Each deserved its own approach and methods of working. The study of ethics was different from the study of plants, the study of the arts different from the study of geometry. Aristotle was prepared to consider the fundamental problems of each and this was a measure of his intellectual breadth.

Much of Aristotle's work was taken up with the classification of the natural world, the objects he saw around him. Here he developed the concept of "substance." A substance is any material object with an independent identity, a man, a horse, a table. It might be part of a larger group of similar objects; one man is part of a larger world of men, but the collective group of men does not have any special value over and above the individual men who made up the group. To understand what is meant by a group of men, one had to go back to a single man. In contrast to what Plato had argued there is no transcendent Form of man or horse which exists over and above individual men.

Every substance has certain qualities. A man might be tall, fat, fair-skinned or ugly, a table white or wooden. There were two main points to be made about these qualities as Aristotle conceived them. First, they related only to a particular object. A vase might have the quality of being beautiful, so might a woman. But their beauty attaches only to them. This particular woman or vase is beautiful. Aristotle argued that there is no necessary link between the beauty of a vase and the beauty of a woman, still less a Form called Beauty which can be defined independently. Here again was a rejection of Plato.

Second, qualities can be changed in a substance without affecting its essence. It does not matter whether a man is short and fat or tall and thin, ugly or beautiful, he is still a man. These qualities do not define his "man-ness." There has to be something more profound, some essence of "man-ness" without which he could not be a man. On one level this was the matter that he was made of—his skin, bones, heart, brain—arranged in a particular way so that everyone can see that this is a man and not, say, a donkey. But there is something more than this. No living organism stays static. A baby is born. It is helpless but it can be nurtured and if so it will develop into a child and finally into an adult. This is the only way it can go—it cannot become a donkey at some stage along the way, for instance. Aristotle uses the same word as

Plato, *eidos,* form, to deal with this process of change but Aristotle means something very different. The form is both the force within a substance that drives it to become its most mature state and the organism itself in its most mature state. A man in his prime with a fully developed mind is the form of man but so is the force which drives the body to develop toward this state. The form then decays, "loses hold" as the man gets older. Any living organism goes through the same process. There are immensely complex issues about the relationship between form and matter which still tax philosophers today but Aristotle had provided a means by which change and growth could be explained. In his studies he also coined new words, *dynamis,* the potential within a piece of matter to become its form, and, *energeia,* the actuality of the form.

Another way of approaching an organism or any object was to look at what Aristotle called its causes, or rather the explanations for its being what it was. To take an inanimate object, a bronze bowl, for instance, there are four "causes." The first is its constituent elements, in this case bronze, or rather the metals making up bronze. The second is its actual state, what it actually is—a bowl. Then how did it come into being—in this case through a craftsman. Finally what is its purpose—to hold water. The same questions could be asked of any object, animate or inanimate, but fundamental to Aristotle's thought was the idea of the purpose of an object. "Nature does nothing without a purpose." Every enterprise, every object, every work of craftsmanship, Aristotle argued, had a purpose.

If everything has a purpose there has to be a final end (*telos*) of any organism to which its form is directed. For a fish it might be to swim well. Therefore every move of the form is toward making it swim well. It grows fins, a tail, a means of breathing without air, so that it can fulfill its potential. A bowl is shaped so that it contain liquid. This leads Aristotle on to some of his most important and searching work on the purpose and nature of man. Aristotle argues that the human "substance" is shaped toward the state of *eudaimonia,* well-being, the state of flourishing as a human. What actually did this mean? What really gave a human being satisfaction? Having rejected the mere search for sensual pleasure as an end in itself, Aristotle argued that man was distinct from other living organisms in his ability to reason and it follows that the highest form of pleasure is to be involved in philosophical contemplation. To truly be involved in philosophical activity as an end in itself allowed one to reach a state almost of divinity. This does not mean that one should follow a life of the mystic and do nothing but contemplate. Even philosophers have to live in the real world and Aristotle categorically denied that one should live as an isolated person. Man is by nature a social being. Nor should pleasure be denied completely. One should listen to one's desires (Aristotle believed they were rather like subjects petitioning a king) and then make one's own decision how far to satisfy them. The important thing was the use of rational thought to remain in charge of one's own existence. (Some modern philosophers argue that it is impossible to reconcile Aristotle's view of an ideal life based on contemplation with his assertion that human beings are by nature social animals.)

There still remained the problem posed by Socrates, how did one find virtue? Rather than positing a Platonic Form such as "the Good," Aristotle felt instead that goodness was a quality related to a situation, just as beauty might be (see above). What is right to do might vary from situation to situation. So how could one cope with that? The first need was to develop a desire to do good. Aristotle believed that this could be imbued through education (there was no natural impulse toward good within the *psyche* in the sense Socrates had argued). Aristotle believed it was through a child's upbringing that he or she could be disposed to wanting to find good and thus education and the formation of good character were essential tasks but that in everyday life one still had to use reason and experience to assess what was the correct way to behave. A guiding principle was to avoid extremes although there were occasions when extreme action, anger, for instance, might be necessary. Altogether Aristotle was much more at home with human emotions than Plato ever was and he made a serious attempt to integrate them into his philosophy.

Human beings might be social by nature and friendship was important for Aristotle but was there any higher form of communal activity? The basic human unit, Aristotle observed, was the household (*oikos*). Typically households formed villages and these together made up a *polis*. Each organization represented a more complete community than the one before. Aristotle was fascinated by the *polis* as an organization and he carried out an exhaustive study of different Greek constitutions, 158 in all, although only his account of the Athenian constitution survives. The *polis* is an instance where a group of men living in a particular environment is greater than the individuals who make it up. "Although it is worthwhile to attain the good for one man alone, it is nobler and more divine to do so for nations and cities." The question was how to run the *polis* so that all within would enjoy *eudaimonia*. It depended on how one saw human society and its ends. Aristotle argued that there was a hierarchy in nature, in the way, for instance, human beings controlled animals. Similarly within human society experience suggested there were natural hierarchies. Aristotle noted how men ruled over women, children, and slaves and he suggested that the government of the *polis* should be restricted to free men. Aristotle's attempts to justify this belief were weak. He came up with the argument that only free men enjoyed the attribute of rational thought. As he put it in his *Politics*: "The slave does not possess the faculty of deliberation at all; the female possesses it but in an indecisive form; and the child possesses it but in an imperfect form." The slave is a slave partly because the climate that slaves are brought up in and the types of government they have fit them for the role of slavery.

So if government is confined to the male citizen what form of government is best? It mattered most of all, said Aristotle, that those who ruled cared for the well-being of their subjects. He was prepared to accept that a benevolent monarch or a caring aristocracy might provide just government. The real threat to government was when popular passions ruled as in some forms of democracy, or where an oligarchy or tyrant ruled only in his own interest. Aristotle preferred a state in which most citizens had reasonable resources (rather than one with a small, rich elite and a mass of poor where the temptation for the rich to dominate was too strong) and in which each citizen had the right to rule but could accept being ruled in turn. However, this had to be within the context of reasoned approach to government by those in power. Slavery was essential to ensure that the citizens had the leisure not only to reflect on life but to learn how to defend and rule themselves.

Despite the complexity of his thought, which was inevitable in view of the problems he was dealing with, Aristotle's philosophy remained down-to-earth. He accepted the world as it really was and tried to interpret what he saw within the assumption that there was a wider meaning to the *cosmos*. His greatest weakness lay in allowing the conventions of the day to condition his thinking. For instance, it would have been quite possible for him to argue from what he had already written that all human beings are intrinsically equal, for example, in the way they shared the power of reason. Thus there would be no justification why some should be slaves and others masters. However, Aristotle's aristocratic background proved too confining. He was too firmly embedded in a world where an elite had leisure and could indulge in speculation, academic research, and the art of government and his natural instinct was to find a way to justify preserving it. So, he argued, the slave deserved to be a slave, the woman to stay in the home, and the free Greek citizen to rule over both of them.

This can not detract from the breadth and originality of Aristotle's thinking. His search for a total understanding of the whole range of human experience and the nature of the physical world makes him one of the key figures, perhaps the key figure, in the development of the scientific tradition. In the twelfth century Arab philosophers revived his work and by the thirteenth century it had reentered the Western world. For some centuries Aristotle held his place as *the* great philosopher although at the cost of his works being given canonical status. The inevitable reaction had set in by the seventeenth century but by the twentieth century many of Aristotle's views on ethics and the matter and form of substances were being reassessed and used as the starting point for new debates.

Plato and Aristotle left what Richard Tarnas called in his *The Passion of the Western Mind*, "a dual legacy." On the one hand there is the assumption that there is an underlying, if not immediately visible, order to life which can be grasped by the reasoning mind. Linked to this is the idea that an understanding of the natural order of things will not only bring knowledge as such but a deeper intellectual satisfaction, in religious terms the sense of some kind of relationship or even unity with the divine. Against this stands the empiricist tradition. Here the natural world takes primacy. Everything must be tested against observation and there can be no assumption that there is a higher force watching over the world or giving it an ultimate meaning. Faith has no place here, only observation and reason. In this tradition it is assumed that there is much that can never be known simply because the evidence will always be insufficient. One approach can be attributed to Plato, the other to Aristotle and it is, as Richard Tarnas has argued, the tension between the two approaches which "provided the Western mind with the intellectual basis, at once unstable and highly creative, for what was to become an extremely dynamic evolution lasting over two and a half millennia . . . the secular scepticism of one stream and the metaphysical idealism of the other provided a crucial counter-balance to each other." This is the measure of Plato and Aristotle's achievement.

14

Relationships

Six years before his production of *The Frogs* Aristophanes had already taken on Euripides in his *Thesmophoriazusae* (*The Women Celebrating the Thesmophoria*). Euripides is criticized for exposing the truth about women's lives and arousing the suspicions of their husbands. As one of the female characters puts it:

> I can no longer bear to sit by and see us women besmirched with mud from head to foot by that cabbage woman's son Euripides. The things he says about us, calling us intriguers, strumpets, tipplers, deceivers, gossips, rotten to the core and cursing to mankind. And naturally the men come home from the play and give us that nasty suspicious look and start hunting in all the cupboards for concealed lovers. A woman can't do any of the things she used to do in the old days—why, if you just sit plaiting a wreath your husband thinks you must be in love with someone . . . And then another thing . . . Suppose a woman finds she can't bear her husband a child—she's got to produce one from somewhere, hasn't she? But what chance has she with her husband watching her the whole time? And what's happened to all the rich old men who used to marry young girls? Euripides has put them off completely: "an old man weds a tyrant not a wife," he says. It's all because of him

> that they've started putting bolts and seals on the doors of the women's quarters and keeping those great big Molossian dogs to scare off the boyfriends. . . .
>
> (Translation: David Barrett)

When Aristophanes is not indulging in fantasy he provides some of the best portrayals of life on the streets and in the homes of ordinary Athenians. His women are not silent and submissive. They have feelings and energy, a determination to exploit what limited opportunities there might be for space in their own lives and even hopes for some sexual pleasure. (For this see, in particular, his play *Lysistrata.*)

Yet Aristophanes cannot conceal that in the last resort it is men who control women's space, and often in ways which are highly repressive. All the evidence, from Athens at least, suggests the primacy of the male line and women's subservience to men both socially and sexually. "This is what marriage is" one prosecutor in a law case put it bluntly, "when a man engenders children and presents his sons to the phratries and demesmen and gives his daughters as being his own in marriage to husbands. Mistresses we have for pleasure, concubines for daily service to our body, but wives for the procreation of legitimate children and to be faithful guardians of the household." Here women are adjuncts to men defined not as individuals in their own right but through their sexual or legal relationship to men. This approach pervades Greek life. While both sexes would be welcomed at a ceremony round the family hearth soon after birth, girls were more likely to be exposed to die and their names are usually not mentioned in documents where those of their brothers are. In a law court a man's wife was seldom mentioned by her name. There were even gynecological theories (attested to in Athenian tragedy) which claimed that the male sperm provided the total child with the woman being a passive receptacle in which it grew to maturity. (Aristotle argued that women did provide some of the matter that made up a human being but that all the most vital attributes, intelligence and energy, for instance, came from the male.) In law, children belonged with a father's *oikos* and remained with him if the mother died or was divorced. The feminist scholar Eva Keul's assertion (in the title of her book on women in Athens) that Athenian society was based on "The Reign of the Phallus" has much truth in it. It can certainly be said that sex in the male Greek world was largely defined in terms of phallic pleasure.

The Greek attitude to women was deeply ambivalent. They were both valued and feared. The scholar Charles Segal sums it up well:

> As the one who bears and cares for the children and tends house and hearth, she is at the very centre of what is secure, nurturing, life giving; but in her passionate and emotional nature and the violence of her sexual instincts which she is felt as little able to control, she is regarded as irrational, unstable, dangerous. Hence she is seen as an integral part of the civic structure on the one hand, but also regarded as a threat to that structure on the other . . . She has her place within the sheltered inner domain of the house, but also has affinities with the wild savage world of beasts outside the limits of the city wall.

It was assumed, for instance, that women's sexual feelings were stronger than those of men and they would indulge them if an opportunity was given. (This assumption may have been developed, of course, to justify continuing male control.) In myth, there was the example of the "seer" Tiresias who had experienced life as a member of both sexes and informed Zeus that sex was much more pleasurable for women. In drama, women are freely portrayed as sexual beings and there was the model, too, of the goddess Aphrodite who showed an appetite for sexual pleasure. Phaedra is the extreme, so overcome by sexual passion for her unresponsive stepson Hippolytus that she hangs herself after denouncing him as her seducer. In Aristophanes' comedy *Lysistrata* women refuse to have sex with their menfolk until the war with Sparta is over. They take some persuasion to give up the pleasure. The playwright speculates on life where women control their own sexuality. Not only will men lose the sexual initiative but they will be exhausted by the sexual demands of their womenfolk and the inevitable free love will mean an end of private property because no one will know who is the father of which child.

It was, therefore, the task of men to keep women in order. In Euripides' *Andromache* Menelaus is held responsible for the escape of Helen to Troy because he had not bolted her in and used slaves to watch her. Better still to socialize women from birth so that they would have no notion of independence and little idea of any function other than the support of their husbands. One of the wealthy husbands in Xenophon, for instance, believed that girls should be closely supervised from birth so that "they would see as little as possible, hear as little as possible and learn as little as possible." In Aeschylus' *Agamemnon* Clytemnestra talks of the ideal wife being chaste with regard to sexual matters and as increasing the prosperity of the household so that joy attends the husband when he comes home, and good fortune when he departs. There was no more effective way of enforcing men's control over their wives than by claiming that a man's public reputation rested on a docile wife (as Pericles argued in his Funeral Speech of 431/0).

Marriage marked the major transition in women's lives (as suggested by the myth of Demeter and Persephone described above) and it was often contrasted with a period of relative freedom in the short period of early adulthood before marriage. In myth this is sometimes shown as a time of wildness, with carefree virgins running loose in the countryside from where they are snatched by lustful gods to become the mothers of heroes. (Europa, the daughter of a Phoenician king, is carried off by Zeus, disguised as a bull, and becomes the mother of three of his sons.) Sappho's poems suggest close knit groups of unmarried women in which even sexual intimacy between their members is allowed. The loss which follows on marriage is explored in an extract from an otherwise lost play of Sophocles:

> Unmarried girls, in my own opinion, have the sweetest existence known to mortals in their fathers' homes, for their innocence always keeps such children safe and happy. But when we reach puberty and can understand we are thrust out and sold away from our ancestral gods and from our parents. Some go to strange men's homes, others to foreigners, some to joyless houses, some to hostile. And all this once the first night has yoked us to our husband we are forced to praise and say all is well.
>
> (Translation: Oswyn Murray)

The transition from freedom to subservience in marriage is also explored in the famous speech by Medea in Euripides' play of that name:

> *Of all things that are living and can form a judgment*
> *we women are the most unfortunate creatures.*

First, with an excess of wealth it is required
for us to buy a husband and take for our bodies
a master: for not to take one is even worse.
And now the question is serious whether we take
a good or bad one; for there is no easy escape
for a woman, nor can she say no to her marriage.
She arrives among new modes of behaviour and manners,
and needs prophetic power, unless she has learned at home,
how best to manage him who shares the bed with her.
And if we work this out well and carefully,
and the husband lives with us and lightly bears his yoke,
then life is enviable. If not, I'd rather die.
A man, when he's tired of the company in his home,
goes out of the house and puts an end to his boredom
and turns to a friend and companion of his own age.
But we are forced to keep our eyes on one alone.
What they say of us is that we have a peaceful time
living at home, while they do the fighting in war.
How wrong they are. I would much rather stand
three times in the front of battle than bear one child.
(Translation: Simon Goldhill)

The dominance of the male was reinforced by the differences in the age of couples at marriage. In Athens marriage was structured so that men did not marry until they were thirty, but girls were married at the onset of puberty, perhaps at fourteen. (However, widows of child-bearing age often did remarry and one is recorded whose last children by a second marriage were only slightly older than the grandchildren of her first. Spartan women married later on the assumption that they needed to be adult before bearing children and thus the discrepancy in ages of the partners in Sparta was not nearly so large.) This early age was sustained by arguments that girls' adolescent temperaments needed to be steadied by regular sexual intercourse but this may only have been a rationalization of the need to secure total male dominance. With fifteen years advantage in public life the man would easily have been able to overawe a fourteen-year-old. In Xenophon's *Oeconomicus*, which was essentially a guidebook to household management, it is assumed that a husband may not have have any conversation with his wife, although occasionally there is a mention, on one of Euripides' plays, for instance, of a wife whose large dowry, which would have been withdrawn if she had divorced him, had enabled her to acquire emotional dominance over her husband. It is possible that the late age of marriage for men was related to marriage being seen as a civic duty, taking place at the same age as the mass of city offices were opened to him.

There were three steps in the process of making a marriage in Athens—a process overseen by the state to ensure that any children would be legitimate citizens. First was the formal betrothal of the bride to her future husband. After Pericles' citizenship law of 451, she had to be "a woman of Attica" if the children of the marriage were to be citizens. This was accompanied by a transfer of a dowry. The dowry, and the wife's personal possessions, could only be held by a male protector, the *kyrios*. Before the marriage this would have been the bride's father, if he was alive, or one of her family. During the marriage the husband would hold the dowry but on his death it would either be extracted back to the bride's family or if she had sons they would take it over for her benefit. Next, on the actual day of the marriage, the bride would take a ritual bath of purification and then meet her groom at her father's house where there would be a feast. This was followed by the formal procession by torchlight of the bride from her father's house to that of her husband. She was often welcomed there by the bridegroom's mother (by the time the bridegroom was thirty his father would be unlikely to be alive). After a ceremony of welcome at the hearth of her new home, the third part of the process, the consummation of the marriage, took place. Even at this stage there was some ambivalence about the young wife's role as a married woman. It seems that only when she had actually produced a male heir was her position secure: she could be divorced if she proved barren.

However desperate a man might be for a son there was a large percentage of cases, calculable at around 40 percent, where for natural reasons it did not happen. Alternative means were then used to ensure the continuation of the family line. A father with two sons would allow the second to be adopted by any close male relative who had none. In cases where a daughter had inherited (as a result of her father's dying without having sons), she would be married off to an elderly relative in the hope that she would produce a son who would then be treated as the direct grandson of her father and able to carry on his family line. (It was a condition of these marriages that there should be regular sexual intercourse.) She could even be forced to give up her existing marriage to fulfill her given role.

Within the home women were associated with continuity through the passages of life. They gave birth or helped it to take place, cared for the young (children were introduced to mythology on their mothers' knee), and maintained the home. (The symbol of the "good" wife was as a weaver responsible for creating all the cloth used by the family.) In wealthier homes this was a major responsibility, involving the supervision of slaves and the storage of a variety of goods. "How beautiful it looks," wrote Xenophon, "when shoes are arranged in rows, each kind in its proper place, how beautiful to see all kinds of clothing sorted out, each kind in its proper place: how beautiful bed linen, bronze pots, table ware . . ." There were dry rooms for grains, cool ones for wine. The instruments needed for sacrifices were set in one place, clothes for feasts separated from those for daily use. Stores were sorted according to how long things lasted so that there would no waste. There is evidence that women who had larger households to run were encouraged to be literate. Literacy was here a useful skill rather than a symbol of status. There was some understanding of the importance of exercise for wealthier women. In his *Oikonomikos*, written for this class, Xenophon stressed that stagnating in the home could be avoided by kneading dough, shaking and folding cloaks and bedclothes, and walking around supervising slaves. This, said Xenophon, would improve appetite and general good health, as well as making the wife more sexually attractive to her husband than the slave women!

An average age of death for Greek males has been calculated as forty-six and for women at about thirty-six, one reason for the discrepancy being high rates of death in childbirth. (This is quite a high life expectancy [in India in the early part of this century it was only twenty-four] and doubtless reflects the balanced diet and regular exercise of the average Greek.) Once death had occurred it was women who played the prominent part in the rituals of death, laying out the body and anointing it. The rituals, which included the singing of dirges, served as a social occasion for women who might otherwise not meet together. The burial procession gave an opportunity to go outside the home (in one law case a wife was accused of picking up a lover at her father-in-law's funeral!) though Solon's legislation restricted the number of female relatives who could accompany the procession. After the burial, which took place three days after death, the women would be able to join their menfolk in the funerary banquet. Women were also involved in the subsequent rituals. A *stela,* a grave marker with an inscription or a carved image of the deceased, could mark the grave and reverence to it, including offerings, were expected to last over the years. Women seem to have played some part in presenting these offerings and there are cases of women (for instance a widow Epicteta of Thera in the late third century B.C.) who left money specifically so that their family tombs including that of their husbands be preserved.

As a physical entity the home was considered sacrosanct; any intrusion into it was regarded with horror, and the men's quarters were always placed so that they came between the outside and the women's quarters. Women were not expected to come and answer the door; this would place them within territory in which they might engage with men. In tragedy it was always a charged moment when a woman crossed the threshold into the open air. (The women would have their own rooms, sometimes on a second story, but they would also be able to use the secluded open courtyard at the center of the house.) The orator Demosthenes told how on one occasion his house was invaded by a man who claimed his property. The worst of the matter (though doubtless the incident was played up for rhetorical effect) was that the intruder flung open the doors of the living quarters and used foul language in front of Demosthenes' unmarried sister. A man caught in adultery with a woman in her home was guilty not only of offending the honor of her husband but of transgressing the sacred space of the *oikos*. The householder was justified in killing him on the spot. (The treatment of the woman was more lenient, divorce and, as a polluted person, exclusion from religious activity.)

The contexts in which respectable women could enjoy life outside the home were limited and clearly defined by convention, but in practice, and as Aristophanes suggests, women seem to have used what opportunities there were to the full. One report suggests visiting was common. "My mother and their mother were intimate friends, and were used to visiting one another, as was fitting since they both lived in the country and were neighbours." This was of a wealthier family who would have slaves to carry out the essentials and so were free to enjoy a social life. Women were present alongside men in many festival processions—the best-known representation of this is on the frieze of the Parthenon where girls are shown carrying offerings and even, if the traditional interpretation of the frieze is correct, helping in the sacrifice to Athena. In less wealthy families, the vast majority, women went out to get water and provisions and some, but only the very poor, served at stalls in the Agora, as woolworkers, or as prostitutes (the latter role incompatible with citizen status). Aristophanes' plays are full of such characters. Some aristocratic families enjoyed a traditional right to provide priestesses to serve at the cult of goddesses. (Divinities were always served by members of their own sex.)

In the women's festivals there was an opportunity to engage in much more liberated behavior. At the extreme there were celebrations of Dionysus in which women, known for the festival as Maenads, left the city together, removed their shoes, dressed in fawn skins and engaged in frenzied dancing at the climax of which they would fall exhausted to the ground. In Euripides' *Bacchae* these get completely out of hand. A messenger explains to Pentheus, king of Thebes, what his mother Agaue, who will eventually tear him to pieces, has been up to:

MESSENGER:

About that hour
when the sun lets loose to warm the earth,
our grazing herds of cows had just begun to climb the ridge.
Suddenly I saw three companies of dancing women,
one led by Autonoe, the second captained
by your mother Agaue, while Ion led the third.
There they lay in the deep sleep of exhaustion,
some resting on boughs of fir, others sleeping
where they fell, here and there among the oak leaves—
but all modestly and soberly, not, as you think,
drunk with wine, nor wandering, led astray
by the music of the flute, to hunt their Aphrodite
through the woods.

But your mother heard the lowing
of our horned herds, and springing to her feet,
gave a great cry to waken them from sleep.
And they too, rubbing the bloom of soft sleep
from their eyes, rose up lightly and straight—
a lovely sight to see: all as one,
the old women and the young and the unmarried girls.

First they let their hair fall loose, down
over their shoulders, and those whose straps had slipped
fastened their skins of fawn with writhing snakes
that licked their cheeks. Breasts swollen with milk,
new mothers who had left their babies behind at home
nestled gazelles and young wolves in their arms,
suckling them. Then they crowned their hair with leaves,
ivy and oak and flowering bryony. One woman
struck her thrysus against a rock and a fountain
of cool water came bubbling up. Another drove
her fennel in the ground, and where it struck the earth,
at the touch of a god, a spring of wine poured out.
Those who wanted milk scratched at the soil
with bare fingers and the white milk came welling up.
Pure honey-spurted, streaming from their wands.
if you had been there and seen these wonders for yourself,
you would have gone down on your knees and prayed
to the god you now deny.

(Translation: William Arrowsmith)

Prevalent throughout the Greek world for citizen-wives was the three-day Thesmophoria celebrated in late October. The women organized the event themselves. On the first day women set out from their homes and in Athens encamped on the Pnyx, near where the Assembly met. On the second they fasted and on the third they celebrated. There was an obscure ritual based on the myth that when Pluto came to seize Persephone a chasm had opened up in the earth and a group of pigs had fallen down it. In the Thermospheria rotten meat and clay male genitals were retrieved from the ground each year as symbols of fertility. So this was some kind of fertility rite as well as an opportunity for women to overturn the restrictions of their conventional lives for a short period.

As so often, the Athenian evidence may not be typical of women's lives in Greece as a whole. It is possible that the status of Athenian women was diminished as the citizen elite became more cohesive and determined to maintain its own status as a free, male group against outsiders. A contrast can be made with Sparta, although it is hard to know how far the evidence was distorted by outsiders who were determined to present Sparta as opposite to the rest of Greece. While in

Athens and elsewhere the *oikos* is the core unit of the city economy, in Sparta citizens were supported by plots of land in Messenia which were allocated temporarily to them. They did not descend to their sons on death, for instance, as they would in a private economy such as Athens and elsewhere. While he held a land the citizen was expected to use the produce primarily to support him as a full-time soldier, looked after in a mess. The mess was so much the center of male life that many traditional male roles, head of the household, master of domestic slaves, seem to have been redundant. Nor was the *oikos* a secure home for a family. Whether a child lived or died was left up to the state and instead of being allowed to grow up in the home children were taken into the care of the state when only seven. Even after marriage a man would continue to live in his mess, visiting his wife secretly at night, and it was only when he was older that he would move into the home. One effect of this may have been to free women for a more independent role than they enjoyed in, for instance, Athens. As their husbands were preoccupied with fighting they were given a privileged role as producers of the next generation of hardy children. With the aim of making them fitter for bearing children women were encouraged to live far more in the open air and exercise publicly (naked, to the scandal of outside observers). (It was said that on one occasion when their men were away on campaign the women were allowed to have sex with helots so as not to lose out on the opportunity to conceive fighters, although the offspring of these liaisons were eventually sent off to found a colony in Italy.)

Spartan women were also described as speaking out in ways which an Athenian woman would have found impossible. In some sources (possibly exaggerated by shocked observers) they openly laugh at men, criticizing them for the mistakes, taunting them if they have not married, and taking inordinate pride in the role as producers of children. With the men supported by the city's holdings in Messenia, Aristotle claimed that the majority of private (as distinct from publicly owned land in Messenia) land was actually owned by women and it is true that women from Sparta were the first of their sex to own a chariot which won a victory in the Olympic Games.

In the years before they married, Athenian men were not expected to be celibate. There was a mass of prostitutes, many of them slaves, domestic and otherwise, who were freely used for sexual relief. An extract from a fourth-century dramatist, Xenarchus, shows what was available:

> ... in our city ... there are, after all, very good looking young things in the whore-houses, whom one can readily see basking in the sun, their breasts uncovered, stripped for action and drawn up in battle formation by columns, from among whom one can select whatever sort one likes—thin, fat, squat, tall, shrivelled, young, old, middle-aged, full-ripened—without setting up a ladder and stealthily entering another man's house ... For the girls themselves grab people and drag them in, naming those who are old men "little father," those who are younger "little bro." And each of them can be had without fear, affordable, by day, towards evening, in every way you like.
>
> (Translation: D. M. Halperin)

There could not be much emotional satisfaction from such encounters. There is some evidence, from the coziness of scenes on vases, for instance, that men did look for emotional comfort in their relationships (and they would have the model of Odysseus and Penelope from the *Odyssey* to show it was possible). This may have been provided by marriage but it was also supplied by the *hetairai,* or women companions who were often adopted as live-in lovers by younger men and widowers or as temporary companions at the *symposia,* the drinking parties that women citizens could not attend. No woman citizen would have been able to work as a *hetaira* and hence it was impossible for a *hetaira* to contract a legal marriage with an Athenian citizen. This did not mean that stable relationships between *hetairai* and their lovers did not develop. There are instances where a young man's family are found grumbling that he will not abandon his *hetaira* and settle down properly to family life, with the opportunity of bringing a dowry and legitimate heirs into the family. In New Comedy (fourth-century B.C.) a common story line was for a young man to fall desperately in love with a woman who appeared to be a *heitaira* whom he could not therefore marry. A happy ending was usually achieved by the *hetaira*'s turning out to be a citizen after all.

In practice, only a few very confident and alluring *hetairai* could have expected much independence, as the law case against one Neaera from the 340s in Athens shows. Neaera was born a slave girl and had been successfully trained as a child prostitute. During her career she had been the property of wealthy men in at least three cities, Athens, Corinth, and Megara. Two Corinthian lovers who had shared her but who now wished to marry allowed her to buy her freedom on condition that she leave Corinth. Former clients provided the money and Neaera came to Athens as a free woman with one of these clients, Phrynion. The continuing humiliation of her position was shown when Phrynion had sex with her openly at *symposia* whenever he desired, "making his privilege a display to the onlookers" and she seems to have been freely abused by other guests. Eventually she left Phrynion and found a new lover, Stephanos, with whom she lived together with three daughters from her earlier relationships. Stephanos, an up-and-coming politician, tried to pass her off as his legitimate wife and the daughters as his by a previous marriage (and hence marriageable to Athenian citizens). One of them had even been offered to a credulous archon on the lookout for a wife to help him perform public rituals. Neaera was accused of falsely holding citizen status (although the real motive for the accusation seems to have been to discredit Stephanos).

Despite her change in status from slave to free Neaera appears to have been acutely vulnerable to abuse. There are cases of *hetairai* who seem to have had greater control over their lives and bodies, although a tough personality and alluring sexual appeal must have been essential. A *hetaira* normally kept her body in better trim than a common prostitute and was more sophisticated in her sexual skills. One *hetaira* listed twelve sexual positions in which she was adept—including the intriguing but somewhat daunting "lion on the cheesegrater." The goal was a wealthy lover. As a character in Aristophanes puts it, "They do say those Corinthian *hetairai* pay no attention whatsoever when a man without means tries to seduce them but if a rich man comes along they bend over and present themselves in no time at all." (Vase paintings suggest that penetration from behind was the most common form of sexual intercourse.) In fact, in comparison to the submissive wife and the powerless slave, there was the necessity of some romantic bargaining before the more successful *hetaira* submitted. One writer proclaimed that it was precisely this which gave most pleasure: "You have to struggle a bit, get slapped and punched by gentle hands; a great pleasure, by Zeus, the greatest."

(There was some understanding of the mechanics of conception and attempts were made to avoid it in these varied sexual encounters but these were hampered by the belief that the days immediately before and after menstruation were a woman's most fertile. "Safe sex" would thus have been advised just at the time when a woman was most fertile. Various methods of contraception from *coitus interruptus* to sponges soaked in vinegar, oil, or cedar resin are known to have been used but their reliability is not known. Anal intercourse may also have been used as a form of contraception.)

The most successful of the Athenian *hetairai* was Aspasia, taken as a live-in lover by Pericles after he had divorced his wife. She was clearly an able woman. Even Socrates visited her, accompanied by some of his students, and Socrates jested, according to Plato, that he as well as Pericles had learned the art of rhetoric from her. Inevitably Pericles' enemies accused her of undue influence over him. She came originally from Miletus and one accusation was that she encouraged the Athenian attack on Samos in 440 because Miletus would benefit from it. She was ridiculed in comedies and even prosecuted in the courts (under the usual wide-ranging charge of "impiety"). Pericles himself defended her in court against the charges and won the case.

The *symposia* provided the arena for much of this sexual activity. These were highly ritualized affairs whose origins lay in the banqueting halls of aristocratic warriors. The men were garlanded and reclined one or two to a couch round a central table. (The number of couches was always uneven, usually between seven and fifteen.) Wine was mixed with water by a leader and passed round in drinking bowls according to an order of precedence. A whole set of specialized pottery, mixers, coolers, pourers, and cups was used and provided some of the finest surviving examples of Athenian ware. There were discussions and games, such as *kottabos* which involved flicking the dregs of wine at a target or a favored lover. Many *symposia* were tightly regulated so that good order was always maintained. Often, however, as the evening wore on, the decorum of the proceedings would collapse and eventually sexual desire would then take over. Vase paintings show uninhibited sexual couplings between the participants. Finally the drinkers would take to the streets, celebrating their brotherhood with rowdy behavior.

The *symposia* were perceived by outsiders as threatening to democratic Athens because of the secrecy in which their activities took place and the aristocratic background of many of their participants. There was a degree of license and ostentation that conflicted with the more frugal demands of the committed democrat (this theme is explored in depth by James Davidson in his *Courtesans and Fishcakes*) and participants were assumed to favor oligarchy over democracy. There seems to have been some truth for this in 411 and 404 but there is little evidence that *symposia* were normally used to discuss politics. Rather the opposite; the longest conversation in Plato's *Symposium* is about the nature of homosexual love. When there are competitions for speaking among the participants they were on subjects such as "Who is the best looking" or "Music."

Young boys could attend *symposia* as part of their initiation into society and the *symposium* could act as the setting for pederastic sex. Ancient Greece has often been characterized as if there was a homosexual free-for-all. This is certainly not true. Some cities outlawed homosexual activity altogether while specific homosexual activities were taboo in most of the others. Submission to sexual penetration, for instance, meant placing oneself on the level of a woman and, in Athens at least, led to the loss of citizen rights. One way of humiliating a defeated enemy after battle, some evidence suggests, was to sodomize him. However, many warrior societies also have initiation ceremonies involving sexual contact during which semen is passed from one generation to another, perhaps as a symbol of the strength of the tribe. Such an initiation ceremony is recorded by the geographer Strabo (first century B.C.) in Crete where young boys were kidnapped, taken to a remote part of the country, and then kept there for two months. They were taught hunting, feasting, and military skills within the context of some form of sexual relationship. At the end of the two months the boy was given his warrior costume, his own drinking cup, and treated as an equal. In other words, homosexual initiation was part of the transition from youth to adulthood. In the messes of Sparta, homosexual activity was normal while the warriors of fourth-century Thebes, at one moment the best in Greece, were said to owe their cohesion to paired homosexual bonding. The transition to heterosexual relationships took place naturally. In Sparta it was ritualized by a new wife dressing as a boy for her wedding night and then as a woman thereafter. (In Plato's *Symposium* one of the participants, Aristophanes, does argue that there are men who continue to desire other males as they grow older but they marry women because compelled to by law and custom.)

In general terms the evidence suggests that when men are deprived of women by a late age of marriage, as they were in Athens, they form liaisons with younger boys (a study of Renaissance Florence where a similar age gap existed found that homosexuality was more prevalent there than in Italian city states where the ages of couples on marriage were equal). In this sense young boys may have acted as a substitute for women. In his *Law, Sexuality and Society, The Enforcement of Morals in Classical Athens*, David Cohen argues that a boy on the edge of adolescence could be portrayed as if he was feminine by nature and courted in the same way a girl might be. In Athens the relationship between an older lover (*erastes*) and a young boy (*eromenos*) was dignified as an educational enterprise. A boy would be chosen by his older admirer, perhaps when exercising naked in the *Gymnasium*. There had to be a courtship process in which the dignity and self-respect of the boy and his family was always recognized. The boy had to submit willingly to the attentions of his admirer on the understanding he was gaining by the experience of association. He was not expected to be sexually aroused or have any sexual enjoyment himself and the sexual release of his admirer was by contact against the thighs. There was always the fear that his manhood would be compromised by the encounter and some families employed a tutor to watch over their sons to keep them clear of homosexual activities. As soon as he reached adolescence Cohen suggests the boy was vulnerable to taunts from his age group if he continued to associate with older men.

The insiders of the Greek world were adult male citizens and their predominant stage was the public one. It was public honor, *time,* which was sought after. Before committing suicide, Ajax, in Sophocles' play of that name, meditates on the impossibility of living into old age if one does not enjoy public esteem:

What can I do? Some feat
To make my poor old father understand
He has no soft-bellied coward for a son.
Long life? Who but a coward would ask for it,

Beset by endless evil? Can he enjoy
Counting the days that pass; now a step forward,
Now a step backward on the road to death?
Who'd be that man? To huddle over the coals
Of flickering hope. Not I. Honour in life,
Of honour in death; there is no other thing
A nobleman can ask for. That is all.

As has been seen in this book such public esteem could be earned in war, in the Games, by participation in city rituals, and through rhetoric in the Assembly. Where did this leave private life? It certainly had its duties. As Ajax contemplates suicide, his wife Tecmessa, whom he carried off as a captive from Phrygia, reminds him of his obligations:

On the day you die,
And dying leave me helpless, think of me
That same day roughly carried off by Greeks—
Your son too—to a life of slavery.
Think of the stinging insults aimed at me
By some new owner: "Look! Whom have we here?
Ajax's woman—Ajax, the army's hero—
O what a fall, from such felicity
To such subjection!" Can't you hear them say it?
The blow will fall on me—but on your head,
And on your blood will fall the shame of it.
O Ajax, have you the heart to leave your father
To face old age without you? Have you the heart
To leave your mother a long legacy
Of lonely years? Think how she prays and prays
To have you home alive. Think of your son,
Your son, my lord; must he be left defenceless
So young, without you, under heartless guardians?
(Translations: E. F. Watling)

(The echo here is with Andromache's farewell to Hector, one that an Athenian audience would have recognized.)

Sophocles is perhaps stressing here the concerns of his own age, that the good citizen cares for those in his home and it is one of the attributes of good citizenship that he should do so. In the vicious wrangling between Demosthenes and Aeschines some hundred years after Sophocles the same holds. Aeschines reported that Demosthenes had appeared in public in white only a week after his daughter's death, a sign, Aeschines argued, that he lacked normal familial feelings. This suggests he must be a bad citizen. "The man who hates his child and is a bad father could never become a safe guide to the people . . . the man who is wicked in his private relations would never be found trustworthy in public affairs." This was one of the many ways in which Athenian society reinforced its cohesiveness and married the concept of a stable home to that of a stable city.

15

Transitions: The Greek World in the Fourth Century B.C.

After Athens' defeat in the Peloponnesian War, the Spartans were determined to impose a government on Athens that would prove favorable to themselves. Naturally, it was to be an oligarchy and the Spartans drew on Athenians who were known to be enemies of democracy to set up a council of thirty men. It took office in September 404. In order to demolish the democratic state the new government reversed the law of 461, which had removed the power of the Areopagus and (as archaeological evidence confirms) erased democratic legislation, which had been carved on a wall in the Agora. They envisaged establishing an elite of perhaps 3000 Athenians who alone would enjoy full citizen rights. The Thirty survived their first six months comparatively peacefully. However, for reasons that are not fully clear, the Thirty then began a reign of terror in which some 1500 Athenians, many of them prominent citizens, were killed. The leading figure of this terror was one Critias, a wealthy aristocrat known to have associated with Socrates and Alcibiades. In power he proved particularly violent and unscrupulous but the Thirty shared complicity in agreeing that each should kill at least one metic. One of the Thirty, Theramanes, now broke ranks. He had always been somewhat of an outsider, having markedly more democratic views than his colleagues (he had been one of those responsible for the transition from the Four Hundred to the

5,000 in 411) and he balked at the idea of killing a metic. Such disloyalty could not be tolerated. Theramanes was arrested and put to death (in the early months of 403). By now democratic forces began to regroup both inside the city and in the shape of returning exiles led by Thrasybulus, a successful general who had already played a part in restoring democracy in 411. Thrasybulus managed to enter the city with a thousand of his supporters and defeat the forces of Critias, who was killed (May 403). The Spartans had been called back by the Thirty as their power disintegrated but the Spartan commander Pausanias sensibly supported negotiations with Thrasybulus. The Spartans withdrew and democracy was restored in October 403. Most of the Thirty Tyrants, as they now became known, were killed within a year or two of their overthrow.

Among those associated with the Thirty was Xenophon, an Athenian of the upper classes who had been born about 428. Compromised by his sympathies for the Thirty he decided to leave Athens after their overthrow and enlist as a mercenary commander. The next fifteen years were to see him serving in the Spartan or Persian cause with the inevitable result that he was formally exiled from Athens. The Spartans gave him an estate near Olympia but he was thrown off this after the defeat of the Spartans by the Thebans at the battle of Leuctra in 371 and took refuge in Corinth. In his final years he managed to return to Athens and died there about 354 B.C.

While in Olympia, Xenophon took to writing. His interests were those of an aristocratic Athenian, pious, conventional, and somewhat rigid, but his range was wide. He compiled his reminiscences of the philosopher Socrates, advice on how to run an estate (the *Oeconomicus,* quoted earlier), and treatises on horsemanship and cavalry command. His *Anabasis,* the account of the retreat of a Greek mercenary force, which he helped lead over the snow-covered mountains of Kurdistan and Armenia to the coast after its commander the Persian Cyrus had been killed, is one of the most exciting adventure stories of Greek history. From the historian's point of view he is remembered now for the only full surviving account of these next years, the *Hellenica.* It is not a major work of history, although its pure Attic style was admired in earlier times. Xenophon's model is Thucydides and in fact the *Hellenica* starts where Thucydides left off but Xenophon is much less detailed and less probing than Thucydides and many major events, known from other fragmentary sources, are missing. However, it is an attempt to write a general history of Greece and forms the basis of any later narrative of the tangled events of the next forty years. It is the story of how an overambitious, unscrupulous, and often incoherent foreign policy lost Sparta the advantage of victory.

Sparta was vulnerable even at the moment of her triumph of 404. She had compromised herself in the eyes of other Greeks by accepting Persian money and surrendering the Greek cities of the Asian coast back to Persia. Her determination to let Athens survive had angered Thebes and Corinth both of whom would have benefited from the eclipse of such a major trading and political rival. (It was probably precisely for this reason that Sparta did not destroy Athens.) Nor did Sparta gain many friends in the Aegean. Cities which had not been absorbed by Persia (from Byzantium in the north to Rhodes in the south) found themselves with Spartan governors, garrisons, or pro-Spartan oligarchies imposed on them.

Within Sparta there was a running debate as to where to go next. A conservative faction stressed the city's inherent weaknesses. It was landlocked and always reliant on the successful control of a servile and resentful helot population. For reasons that are not clear, perhaps declining resources in Messenia, the numbers of fighting men was falling. Herodotus had estimated a citizen army of some five thousand men in 480. A century later the total was only fifteen hundred. One result was an increased reliance of freed helots who now made up part of any Spartan army. The conservatives counseled a retreat to Sparta's traditional power base in the Peloponnese and a foreign policy focused on preventing the revival of Athens. However, Lysander, flushed by his victory over Athens in the Aegean, argued for a strong Spartan presence in the Aegean. Lysander was an anomaly in Spartan politics, an outsider who had worked his way up to command at sea through manipulating his position as *erastes,* lover, of Agesilaus, the son of a Spartan king. He had built up a body of supporters among those who saw the chance of booty and prestige in the Aegean and it was probably these supporters who made up the oligarchies which he imposed on various Greek cities at the end of the war. At Samos, and possibly elsewhere, Lysander encouraged cult worship of himself, the first example in Greek history where a living ruler was so honored. He was also involved in activities in the northern Aegean, overthrowing a democratic government in Thasos and intruding into Macedonia and Thrace.

There was much unease in Sparta over the unrestrained behavior of Lysander but now he went further. During the Peloponnesian War he had cultivated a relationship with Cyrus the Persian overlord in western Asia. In 401 Cyrus asked for help from Sparta to overthrow his brother Artaxerxes who had succeeded to the Persian throne. Lysander saw his chance to consolidate his position in the eastern Aegean and he offered Cyrus Spartan support although it was Cyrus himself who was responsible for raising most of a mercenary force of ten thousand Greeks. The strategy misfired. The army marched inland but Cyrus was killed. (The "Ten Thousand" successfully extricated themselves and it was an account of their exploits by Xenophon, their commander, the *Anabasis,* which has lasted as the most vivid of his works.) Sparta was now faced by a hostile Persian king and when the Greek cities of the coast, which had been under Cyrus' control, appealed for help from Sparta, Sparta had little option but to give it. A complete reversal of policy had been forced on her. Agesilaus, who had now become king with Lysander's support, arrived with a Spartan force that campaigned with some success along the Asian coast from 396. (Xenophon served under Agesilaus here and elsewhere and much admired him.)

The danger, of course, was that this forward policy would leave Sparta unprotected at home. In 400 Sparta had further tarnished her image by attacking the city of Elis in the Peloponnese. Elis, which oversaw the Olympic Games, had barred Sparta from them since 420 and some kind of retaliation might have been expected, but the humiliation of Elis (the protective walls of its ports were pulled down and cattle and slaves plundered) scared Thebes and Corinth. The Thebans approached Athens, which was only too willing to join any adventures that might lead to a resurgence of her power. Argos, Sparta's traditional enemy in the Peloponnese, was also prepared to join in any attack. The Persians became aware of these Greek discontents and sent envoys to Greece to exploit them. A war against the Spartans on the Greek mainland was by far the easiest way of getting Agesilaus' army off Persian soil. By 395, only nine years after her victory in the Peloponnesian War, Sparta found a coalition of states arrayed against her.

This was the setting for the Corinthian War (395–386). It is not clear from the (conflicting) sources how the fighting actually started but it centered on land campaigns, largely around Corinth and in Boeotia, which proved inconclusive. The most dramatic events were the death of Lysander in battle in 395 (papers were found in his house suggesting he may have been plotting to overthrow the Spartan monarchy), the withdrawal of Agesilaus from Persia to fight for Sparta at home (as the Persians had hoped), and the complete destruction of the Spartan fleet off Cnidus in the summer of 394 by a Persian fleet under the command of an Athenian admiral, Conon. Conon returned to Athens where he used Persian money to begin rebuilding the city's walls. It was only a partial success for Athens. The Spartans sent a diplomatic mission to Persia (in the winter of 392–391) to remind Persia that a revived Athens would not be in her interest and that Sparta herself would be prepared to acquiesce once again in the surrender of the Greek cities of Asia Minor, something that Athens would never do. The war dragged on until 387 when a Spartan naval force managed to close the Hellespont and force Athens to the negotiating table.

The peace that followed (386) was masterminded by Artaxerxes, the Persian King, and is known as the King's Peace. It was a major diplomatic success for him. His aims were simple, the regaining of the Greek cities of Asia Minor and the prevention of any coalition of Greek states that might seize them from him. No one could prevent him from assuming control of the coast. He then proclaimed the autonomy of all other Greek cities. On the surface this seemed to meet the hopes of the Greek cities that had joined the Persians mainly because of the threat to their autonomy from Sparta but the Spartan initiatives had brought their reward. Artaxerxes made Sparta the guardian of his peace in Greece!

It was an opportunity the city accepted with relish. She could interpret the term *autonomy* as she liked and isolate all her enemies. She dissolved a league of states in Boeotia on the grounds that it was dominated by Thebes, broke up a relationship between Argos and Corinth, and cut the links which Athens was forging with other cities in the Aegean. Mantinaea, a rival city in the Peloponnese, was divided into a cluster of small villages. There was even an expedition to the Chalcidice peninsula, at the request of the king of Macedonia, Amyntas, to warn the city of Olynthos off aggression against its neighbors. The most outrageous intrusion of all occurred in 382. The Spartans accepted an invitation from a pro-Spartan faction to intervene in Thebes' troubled politics and a Spartan force seized the citadel of the city. The leader of the anti-Spartan faction was then executed on the grounds he had conspired with Persia. The whole affair was such a blatant act of aggression (and hypocrisy in view of Sparta's own dealings with the Persians) that Sparta was widely condemned even by sympathizers such as Xenophon. The Spartan garrison was massacred in 379 and anti-Spartan forces regained control.

A predictable result of this high-handed behavior was the revival of an alliance of Athens and Thebes, two states that, sharing a common border, had long-standing suspicions of each other. Athens sent help to Thebes in 379 and had already begun probing for allies among the Aegean cities that had suffered Spartan-imposed governments. It was probably in retaliation that the Spartans unsuccessfully raided the Piraeus but this only stiffened Athens' resolve. By 378 Athens had established a confederacy (the Second Athenian Confederacy) which was eventually to number some seventy states, many of them former members of her empire. She showed considerable diplomatic skill in gaining their allegiance, avoiding charged words such as *tribute* in the agreements for contributions and promising that she would not impose cleruchies or garrisons. Decisions were supposed to be made by a common assembly of all members. With the confederacy in place, a low-level war between Sparta and her enemies persisted through the 370s. The Spartans were defeated twice at sea and in 371 a peace was made in which Sparta acquiesced in Athens' Aegean role, allowing her in fact to uphold autonomy in the area. Athens appears to have become harsher to her confederates as time went on, but despite defections, the confederacy survived until dissolved by the Macedonians in 338.

Thebes had taken part in the same peace talks with Sparta but then refused to sign. Athens' absorption in Aegean affairs had left Thebes free to expand in Boeotia (the one stable aim in her foreign policy was hegemony over the Boeotian plain) and she now claimed that she would sign for all the Boeotian cities unless Sparta agreed to surrender her influence over the neighboring cities of Laconia. This was a deliberate provocation and the Thebans knew it. Thebes had been strengthening its armed forces in the 370s and in 375 a small Theban force had successfully confronted a larger Spartan raiding force of some two thousand men. Sparta failed to take the warning and marched confidently into Boeotia. Her army was made up mainly of allies (there were only some seven hundred trained Spartan soldiers) but at twelve thousand men in total it was twice as large as the Theban army. The Thebans, however, had the advantage of two thousand of their own hoplites and these were brilliantly led by a political leader turned general, Epaminondas. Epaminondas knew that high morale was vital and he had bonded his men into homosexual pairs in the belief that each one of the pair would fight hard to impress his lover. He had studied Spartan tactics and knew he had to smash the right wing of their army, where the elite Spartan troops themselves were positioned, before it enveloped his own. As the armies faced each other near the town of Leuctra he strengthened his left wing and launched an attack of devastating power. The Spartan phalanxes were stunned. Their king Cleombrotas was killed; they fell back and never regained their order. By the end of the day one thousand of the Spartan forces lay dead, among them four hundred of the seven hundred Spartan hoplites. In a humiliating display of victory they were laid out separately for all to gloat over.

This defeat shocked all Greece. Leuctra was a battle which changed the parameters of intercity politics forever. By the next year a Theban army under Epaminondas had entered the Peloponnese. The city of Sparta held out against the onslaught but the helots of Messenia were liberated after 350 years of serfdom. Their own city, Messene, was established on the slopes of Mount Ithome. Protected by strong walls it was impregnable and Sparta would never regain control of her helots. Two further Theban expeditions in 368 and 366 B.C. stripped Sparta of all her allies though the power vacuum allowed the rise of new rivalries among the Peloponnesian city-states. In 364 the cities of Elis and Arcadia actually fought each other within the precincts of the temple of Zeus at Olympia while the Games were in progress. Athens, fearful of this rise in Theban influence, sent forces of her own to the Peloponnese though there was little they could achieve there.

There was now no effective check on Theban power. The city's control of Boeotia was symbolized by the destruction of the rival city of Orchomenus in 364. Its men were killed, its women and children sold into slavery. Thebes even played the old game of Sparta by asking for support from Persia against the power of Athens. The Persians agreed but never offered any effective help. A Boeotian navy was, however, built and attempted without much success to wean Athens' allies from her. The reality was that Thebes had no resources with which to sustain her power other than the brilliance of her commanders, Epaminondas, in particular, and the weaknesses of her enemies.

In 362 Epaminondas marched his men down into the Peloponnese yet again. This time he intervened in support of the cities of Arcadia against Sparta. Men from Messene joined him while Sparta received some help from Athens and Mantinaea. A host of other allies made the ensuing battle of Mantinaea the largest hoplite engagement ever recorded with over fifty thousand men involved. Epaminondas attempted to repeat his tactics of Leuctra but as he charged his left wing toward the Spartans he was fatally wounded. His wing did throw back the Spartans but on the other wing the Athenians held firm so that each side claimed victory. For Xenophon this proved a fitting conclusion to his history. The brief period of Theban dominance was over. Greece, he recorded, was in a state of chaos and confusion, as it had been before. It was time, he concludes, for someone else to recount its history.

The events of these years showed the disastrous instability of intercity politics in mainland Greece. No city had the strength to conduct a coherent foreign policy. There was a continually shifting set of alliances and betrayals as each vulnerable city reacted to the pressure of events. Words such as *liberation* or *autonomy* were bandied about merely for propaganda purposes with Persian money used by whichever state, Sparta, Athens, or Thebes, could gain it. By now the cities themselves were debilitated. The Peloponnesian War had lasted from 431 to 404. Sparta had been at war almost continuously since then, Athens from 396 to 386 and then from 378 onward, Thebes for the same years, with many smaller cities drawn in willingly or unwillingly to the conflicts. The accompanying dislocations to farming and trade had devastated local economies and had placed the governments of these cities under immense strain. There was persistence conflict between rich and poor, and records of the poor calling for the redistribution of land and the cancellation of debts. (Athens, as suggested earlier, was exceptional in preserving cohesion.) This often meant bloodletting within the city. In the Peloponnesian city of Argos in 370 (after the Spartan defeat at Leuctra) supposedly democratic forces clubbed twelve hundred members of the city's elite to death. In Tegea, also in the Peloponnese, in the same year the leaders of the city's oligarchy were hauled out of a temple in which they had sought refuge and slaughtered by a mob.

These were just the conditions in which ambitious men seize power. In several parts of Greece the fourth century saw the rise of tyrants who were to prove more ruthless and innovative than their forerunners of the seventh and sixth centuries and their impact on the Greek world was to be all the greater. They were opportunists who used whatever they could exploit to their advantage, the mass of displaced men who could be recruited as mercenaries, the riches of city treasuries, the fruits of conquered territories, the loyalties inspired by traditional institutions.

The prototype of the new tyrant was Dionysius of Syracuse. The cities of Sicily, of which Syracuse and Acragas were outstanding, were the most prosperous in the Greek world but they faced a major external threat. The Phoenician settlements in the western Mediterranean had transformed themselves into an empire centered on Carthage, the great trading city founded on a peninsula on the North African coast in the ninth century. Defeated in 480 by the Syracusan tyrant Gelon, the Carthaginians had maintained only modest settlements in Sicily but in 410 and 409 they returned to the island in force, apparently in search of revenge for their earlier defeat. In 406 they had a major success when they captured Acragas. In Syracuse the failure to save their sister Greek city brought violent recriminations among the city's generals and it was now that one of them, Dionysius, about twenty-five at the time, forced the others aside. His position was precarious, especially after two more Greek cities fell to the Carthaginians and there was an uprising against him by the Syracusans, but he survived to sign a peace. It was a humiliating one. The Carthaginians were to remain in the west of Sicily and the Greek cities there would not be allowed to fortify themselves. However, in the peace treaty the Carthaginians recognized Dionysius as ruler of Syracuse. Despite another immediate uprising against him he was now to remain as sole ruler in the city for almost forty years.

The sources on Dionysius are limited, especially for the second half of his reign, and it is hard to disentangle the motives and political undercurrents which sustained him in power. It is certainly true that he used the Carthaginian threat as a means of keeping Syracuse mobilized. He instigated no less then three wars, one of which lasted six years (398–392) another eight (382–374), none of which defeated

Carthage but which allowed him to sustain a large mercenary force. To strengthen his position, early in his reign he seized the main cities of the east coast of Sicily, including Naxos, which he razed to the ground and Catane, which he resettled as a base for mercenaries. Messena on the northeastern tip of Sicily fell next and was also resettled and a new city, Tyndaris, was founded along the northern coast. Not surprisingly, Dionysius' expansion aroused hostility, particularly from the city of Rhegium across the straits. Dionysius besieged Rhegium from 391 but before it had fallen other Greek cities of southern Italy, united in a league, attacked him. It took four years of fighting before they had been humbled and Rhegium, finally isolated, fell in 387. Dionysius now had control of the straits and could prevent any attacks on Syracuse from Carthage or Italy through them.

The underlying motive for all this may have been the protection of Syracuse against Carthage but Dionysius seems to have had a love of adventuring for its own sake. The cities of Etruria were in decline and Dionysius was not above raiding them for their wealth. One raid of Pyrgi, an Etruscan port, which probably had a Carthaginian overlord, resulted in a vast haul of gold and silver from its main temple. He made settlements along the Adriatic, had an alliance with the Illyrians, and kept up a lively relationship with the Spartans (whose links with Syracuse had been forged at the time of the Athenian invasion). He would send them resources from Sicily; they would send him commanders and mercenaries. His mercenaries came not only from mainland Greece, but from Italy and even Spain. The famous Celtic "sack" of Rome in 390, made so much of by the Roman historian Livy, may have been no more than an opportunist raid on the city by a band of Celtic mercenaries passing south on the main route to Sicily. Other mercenaries came from the Greek cities Dionysius had sacked. When they were not in action they stationed either in a fortress in Syracuse itself on the island of Ortygia (where Dionysius, his family, and closest advisers also lived) or on settlements in the land that he had conquered.

These sieges and sackings allowed Dionysius to perfect the art of siege warfare. He introduced catapults, battering rams, and siege towers and these innovations, improved further by the Macedonian kings, were to transform the nature of warfare. From now on cities had to have defensive walls and they can be found throughout the Greek world. (See, for instance, the complex of fourth-century walls and fortifications that defend the pass between Attica and Boeotia near the modern Greek village of Fili.) Dionysius' military power may also have allowed him to adopt a more conciliatory line as a ruler. There was never any doubt of his dominance within the city and he could act brutally against immediate rivals. Some sources suggest a touch of paranoia (visitors had to be stripped and reclothed before being allowed in his presence) but he appears to have used his position realistically, avoiding some of the more blatant excesses of personal power. He never seems to have created a title for himself within the city other than "general with full powers" though in agreements with other states he was known as "the governor (archon) of Sicily." He never allowed his head to appear on coins. He kept the traditional institutions of the city intact including its Assembly but manipulated them when he needed. There is a nice story in Aristotle of how he minted some tin coins and then persuaded the Assembly to use them as if they were silver ones. In other ways he acted as a typical Greek tyrant of earlier times, sponsoring public building programs, sending chariot teams to the Olympic Games, and even, in one of the final acts of his life, winning first prize for a tragedy performed in Athens in 367. (The story goes that he drank himself to death at the exciting news of his victory.)

Despite the ambiguities of his political role there is no doubt that Dionysius aimed to found a dynasty. After his first wife died he married two more on the same day, one a Syracusan, one from the allied city of Doris in Italy (both marriages were also consummated on the same night). Altogether there were seven children from the marriages, four of them sons, and they were intermarried with his own relatives to create an integrated but somewhat isolated clan. On his death his son Dionysius II succeeded, with Dion the brother of Dionysius' Syracusan wife as adviser. Dionysius lacked his father's energy while Dion was a serious-minded and rather aloof figure (much approved of by Plato who saw him as an ideal philosopher-king). The two fell out, Dion seized power from Dionysius in 354 and then was himself assassinated the same year. The Syracusan empire collapsed. It took a remarkable Corinthian general, Timoleon, called in by the desperate Syracusans, to restore order to the island.

Dionysius had had role models in earlier Syracusan tyrants such as Gelon but essentially his rule was his own creation. Others were able to manipulate existing institutions to their own ends. This is what happened in Thessaly whose landlocked plains were the most fertile in Greece. There were four main regions of Thessaly and a number of rival cities so there was always the threat of fragmentation, but at times of war the peoples of state united under a military leader, the *tagos,* elected by the Thessalian aristocracy. In the 370s, one Jason, the son of a tyrant of one of the cities, Pherae, became *tagos.* He was a determined and self-disciplined man who had already built up a mercenary force of some six thousand men of his own. (Mercenaries were cheap in the troubled 370s.) He appears to have been elected *tagos* after undertaking military reforms within Thessaly. He then united the country and was able to use his post to recruit Thessalian citizens for his army. (Traditionally the *tagos* commanded a cavalry force of six thousand men and a hoplite one of ten thousand.) Xenophon gives a vivid picture of his dedication to his role and his opportunistic approach (in a speech made by one of his rivals to the Spartans):

> His generalship is of the highest quality—he is one who whether his methods are those of plain force, or working in the dark, or of seizing an unexpected advantage, very seldom fails to achieve his objects. He can use the night-time as well as the day time and when he wants to move fast, he will put breakfast and dinner into one meal so as not to interrupt his work. He will not think it right to rest until he has reached the point for which he set out and done all that had to be done. And he has trained his men to behave in the same way, although he knows how to gratify the feelings of his soldiers when they have won some success as the results of extra hard work. So all who follow him have learned this too—that one can have a good time also, if one works for it. Then, too, he is more self controlled than any man I know with regard to bodily pleasures. These never take up his time and prevent him from doing what has to be done.
>
> (Translation: Rex Warner)

Jason used the traditional powers and aura of the post to the full. Wanting to show off his power to the Greek world he called on the cities of Thessaly to provide offerings for a massive procession and sacrifice at the Pythian games at Delphi. Over eleven thousand animals were eventually assembled for the show. However, it was clear that he saw the *tagos* as merely a stepping stone to greater things. Having seen the Spartans humbled in 371 and the Athenians unable to operate effectively on the mainland, he aimed, according to a speech recorded by Xenophon, to take over Macedonia and use its timber to build a fleet that could challenge Athens. There was even talk of an invasion of Asia Minor—Jason had shrewdly noticed how comparatively easy it had been for the Ten Thousand to make their way inland and for Agesilaus of Sparta to campaign along the coast. All these plans collapsed when Jason was murdered in 370.

It was not surprising that Jason had targeted Macedonia as an area for expansion. The area enjoyed a climate which was much more temperate than in the rest of Greece and was rich in resources, especially timber and minerals (copper, iron, silver, and gold). The challenge for any ruler of the region was its geographical awkwardness. It was divided into two parts, Lower and Upper Macedonia. The settlements of Lower Macedonia, including the ancient capital at Aegae, used as a burial place for the kings, and the more recent one established in the late fifth century at Pella, lay around impenetrable marshland at the head of the Thermaic Gulf. To the west and north of Lower Macedonia was the plateau of Upper Macedonia but this was broken up by impassable mountain chains. Only the strongest Macedonian kings had any effective control over Upper Macedonia although there were boundaries there that could be held against the surrounding peoples of Epirus (the Molossians), Illyria and Thrace. To the south, Macedonia was vulnerable to invasion from Thessaly (as Jason well knew) while the Athenians were continually probing along the coast in search of timber for their navy. Occasionally a larger city in the north Aegean (such as Olynthos in the 380s) took advantage of Macedonian weakness to expand its own territory.

The Macedonians were comparatively isolated from the mainstream of Greek culture and politics although it seems probable that they spoke a dialect of Greek. Attempts to prove that they were or were not Greek at this period are probably fruitless because it is impossible to define what might or might not qualify as "Greekness." To the more sophisticated Greeks further south, however, the Macedonians were backwoodsmen. Their archenemy the Athenian orator

Demosthenes exaggerated, of course, when he spoke of Philip of Macedon (see below) as coming "from that Macedonian riffraff which could not even offer a good slave for sale in days gone by" but he must have echoed common Greek prejudices. The Macedonian kings made their own efforts to acquire Greek culture or be accepted as Greeks. King Alexander I (c. 498–454), successfully persuaded the scrutineers of the Olympic Games that his family originally came from Argos with the result that he, if not his people, could compete in the Games. The kings claimed kinship with Heracles (whose roots were in the Peloponnese) and through him with Zeus. There was an important cult center to Zeus on Mount Olympus which was on the southern edge of Macedonian territory.

Political instability was the norm in Macedonia. There was no established rule of succession within the Argeads, and at the death of each king rivals fought over the throne. Succession was by the acclamation of an elite of warriors drawn from the local aristocracies. Their main concern was to ensure the protection of their lands against tribes from the north and incursions from the coast. Grouped around the king they fought alongside him almost as equals but their allegiances were fickle and they could easily defect to a contender. Between 399 and 393 there were no less than five kings of Macedonia, each from a different branch of the royal family. It was hardly surprising that few kings could hope to exploit the full potential of the kingdom.

In 360, Macedonia appeared on the verge of disintegration. After an invasion of Illyrians had killed the King Perdiccas, the Athenians had infiltrated Lower Macedonia in support of a contender to this throne, Argaeus. Macedonia's other neighbors were gathering for the spoils. At this inauspicious moment the throne was taken by Perdiccas' brother, Philip, who was then about twenty-three years old. There was now an astonishing turnaround in Macedonia's fortunes. From the start Philip showed himself to be a politician and soldier of genius, able to use diplomatic guile and military prowess in equal measure. Having spent three years as a hostage in Thebes during its years of dominance, he had learned much from the contact with Epaminondas and gained more understanding of the nature of Greek politics than his predecessors. He got rid of the Athenians by promising to support their demands for Amphipolis, the wealthy trading city they had lost in 424, then bought off the Thracians and another northern tribe, the

Paeonians. In 358 he defeated the Illyrians and assumed control over Upper Macedonia from where he was able to recruit new troops. By 357 he had made a marriage alliance with the Molossians of Epirus. His bride, the formidable Olympias, daughter of the Molossian king, was to provide him with his son Alexander.

With his northern borders all secure (though needing an occasional show of force later in his reign to keep them intact) Philip turned toward the coast. Among his main motives was the search for land with which to reward his aristocratic fellow warriors, the so-called Companions whose loyalties always needed sustaining with booty. Athens, his main rival here, was facing a revolt of her allies (the so-called Social War [from *socius,* ally] 357–5) in the southeastern Aegean and so Philip had the advantage. He finally dashed Athens' hopes of ever recapturing Amphipolis by taking the city himself. Along the coast of the Thermaic Gulf, he seized Pydna, Potidaea, and Methone, where he lost an eye when leading an attack on its walls. Beyond Amphipolis were the gold mines of Mount Pangaeon in Thrace. These were annexed in 356 and their riches, one thousand talents a year, it was said, were diverted to maintaining his army. The powerful city of Olynthos in Chalcidice was taken by treachery in 348. It was razed to the ground and deserted. (The excavated ground plans of its houses have been an invaluable source for Greek domestic architecture.) The success made Philip the master of the Chalcidice peninsula. The land was distributed to his fellow warriors and he could now afford to expand the Companions to draw in suitable men from outside the traditional aristocracy. Attempts by Athens to rally Greek support against these intrusions met with little success and Athens was forced to make peace with Philip in 346.

By 350 Philip had perfected his army. His main innovation was the *sarissa,* a long pike. It meant that his men could engage with hoplites at long range and, safe from the shorter hoplite spears, they did not have to be so heavily armed. This in turn enabled them to march more quickly and maneuver more flexibly. A typical tactic was to use infantry to break through a hoplite line and then send in cavalry, whose horses were the finest in Greece, to break up the phalanx completely. It was not just that his men were well-disciplined and armed, they could be used with impressive versatility. There were contingents of archers and, later, javelin throwers, and the army was equipped with the latest in siege warfare. Much had been learned from Dionysius but Philip is credited with the invention of the torsion catapult. Like all well-organized tyrants Philip had the resources to campaign all the year round and thus make the traditional rituals of warfare obsolete. As Demosthenes put it:

> In the old days the Spartans, like everyone else, would spend the four or five months of the summer 'season' in invading and laying waste the enemy's territory with heavy infantry and levies of citizens, and then would retire again; and they were so old-fashioned, or rather such good citizens, that they never used money to buy an advantage from anyone, but their fighting was of the fair and open kind. But now you must surely see that most disasters are due to traitors, and none are the result of a regular pitched battle. On the other hand you hear of Philip [of Macedon] marching unchecked, not because he leads a phalanx of heavy infantry, but because he is accompanied by skirmishers, cavalry, archers, mercenaries and similar troops . . . I need hardly tell you that he makes no difference between summer and winter and has no season set apart for inaction.
>
> (Translation: J. H. Vince, *Loeb Classical Library Edition*)

Philip's expansion had now achieved a momentum of its own, a momentum based always on the need to reward his men. It was virtually impossible to expand further north over mountain ranges but there was still open country to the south, Thessaly, and to the east, Thrace. Thessaly would be a particularly fine prize. A marriage alliance with the Aleuadae family of Larissa in northern Thessaly gave Philip an entrée and he was able to exploit a continuing conflict between Jason's old home, Pherae, and the rest of Thessaly, which was supported by Thebes. A first attack in 353 on Pherae, which was aided by the Phocians (see below), was a failure. Philip's troops were caught in an ambush and the shock of defeat was so great that his army almost revolted. It showed just how crucial Philip's continuing success was for his survival. The campaign of 352 was more successful. Philip won an important battle at the coastal city of Pagasae (often called the Battle of the Crocus Field) and in recognition of his military prowess the Thessalians elected him *tagos*, the first foreigner ever to hold the post. Another marriage, Philip's sixth, with a local noblewoman cemented the deal.

Now came a chance to intervene still farther south. The Amphictiony, the league of states which controlled Delphi, condemned one of their members, Phocis, for sacrilege. (The real motive of the condemnation seems to have been a desire by Thebes and its allies to humiliate Phocis.) The Phocians in revenge seized Delphi itself (in the spring of 356) and proceeded to use the vast wealth of the sanctuary to raise a mercenary army. They were to hang on for some ten years, gaining some support from Athens and Sparta, both of whom had no love of Thebes. Eventually the Thebans called on Philip for support. Philip used the invitation to march south, bypass the Thebans, and defeat the Phocians who had already troubled him in Thessaly. The members of the Amphictiony had little option but to give Philip a place on their council and it was he who presided over the next games at Delphi.

It is hard to know how much conquest of the remaining Greek states, Thebes and Athens in particular, meant to Philip. Alone, neither was a match for him. The Athenians could harass his coastline with their ships but not confront him on the land. (An expedition to aid Olynthos had failed miserably.) The Thebans still had some military strength, even after 362, but no effective navy. Only by operating in close partnership could they offer a threat. Philip's policy was to keep them separated. It has been argued, by J. R. Ellis, that his main concern was to find a much bigger prize overseas where there would be sufficient booty and prestige for him to sustain the allegiance of his troops. Asia Minor offered the best option and this explains why Philip put such energy into making peace with Athens in 346, deliberately holding up his attack on Phocis, Athens' ally, until the peace (of Philocrates, after an Athenian politician of that name) had been signed. However, it was just this double-dealing that aroused the suspicions of the Athenians. Even though a majority of the Assembly accepted the peace settlement, one Athenian, in particular, came to oppose it. This was Demosthenes, arguably the greatest orator that Athens ever produced.

Demosthenes (384–322 B.C.) had learned his trade the hard way. His father had died when he was seven and when he grew up he found that the family resources had been frittered away by his unscrupulous guardians. He mastered rhetoric in order to retrieve what little remained. Supplementing his income by acting as a speech writer he eventually became a prosecutor (active from 355). Ever more confident in the cut-throat world of Athenian public speaking, he was gradually drawn into politics. By 351 he had sensed the threat Philip offered to Athens' long-term interests and although he accepted the Peace of Philocrates he denounced it as soon as Philip moved against the Phocians. (The wrangling between Demosthenes and Aeschines reported earlier was rooted in their different attitudes to the peace and Demosthenes' speeches have always to be placed in the context of internal Athenian power struggles.) His Philippics, his majestic and relentless speeches against the ambitions of Philip, echo Pericles' funeral speeches in the way they glorify Athens as the defender of democracy.

> Philip knows that even with complete control of all the rest he can have no security while democracy remains in Athens, that in the event of a single setback every element under the sway of force will come to Athens for refuge. You who are her people are not a people naturally given to the selfish pursuit of power, but strong to prevent it in others or wrest it from them, a thorn in the flesh of despotism, and willing champions for the liberation of mankind.
>
> (Translation: A.N.W. Saunders)

Demosthenes thus became a Churchillian voice warning of the dangers of appeasement. By 340 his vision dominated Athenian policy making. Yet it was always a blurred vision. Philip seems to have had no strong ambition to humble Athens and would probably have been happy to keep her as a dependent ally while he concentrated on expansion in the east. This was a possibility that Demosthenes could not admit or accept. Demosthenes also exaggerated the will for resistance among the Greek cities. He assumed that an ancient spirit of freedom still lived and that any city that accepted Philip's hegemony must have been corrupted by his bribes. In fact many welcomed Philip as a protector against more powerful neighbors. (It is also probably true that oligarchies used Philip's support to keep themselves in power.) When Demosthenes called for a crusade against Philip in the northern Aegean he found few ready to risk Philip's hostility in a war that was really only in Athens' self interest. Nothing in this detracts from the essentially heroic nature of Demosthenes' vision.

It is possible to argue that it was Demosthenes' aggressive policy rather than Philip's that conditioned the next moves. Philip appears to have gradually lost hope that Athens would ever maintain the peace of

346 and began to protect himself against the city. While a campaign in Thrace between 342 and 340 was aimed at strengthening Macedonia in the east, it brought Philip close to the Hellespont, the channel through which Athens' vital corn supplies came. In 342 Philip sent mercenaries to Euboea, and Athens had to send a force to remove them. Then, in 340, Athens made an alliance with Byzantium further north at the mouth of the Boshorus. The city, later Constantinople, now Istanbul, occupied a vital strategic position and had formidable defenses. Philip had little option but to try and seize it while writing to Athens to complain that ever since 342 Athens had been acting as if at war with him. In the summer Philip seized a large Athenian grain convoy on the grounds that the corn was being used to supply his enemies. Athens managed to raise the siege of Byzantium (Philip's navy was weak in comparison to hers) and the search was now on for allies among the old subjects of her empire. The biggest catch, however, was Thebes. Demosthenes had been trying to engineer an alliance with the city since 346 and finally this was secured.

This alliance of the two cities, achievable only in the most extreme situations, was what Philip feared most and he knew he would have to deal with it. A dispute within the Amphictiony gave him an excuse to return to central Greece. Once there he hesitated, perhaps hoping for more forces to join him from allies farther south. Finally in August 338 he fell on the Thebans and Athenians on the plain of Chaeronaea in Boeotia. The two armies were matched in numbers but not in the skill of their commanders. The battle began with a traditional phalanx charge but the Macedonians had been trained to fall back in good order. The Athenians believed they were victorious and rushed forward, fatally exposing their ranks. The Macedonian infantry turned to exploit the openings and they were supported by a devastating charge of their cavalry under the leadership of Philip's eighteen-year-old son, Alexander. One thousand Athenians lay dead, another two thousand were made prisoners. The Theban army was destroyed, its elite core fighting on until the last man was killed.

Chaeronaea marked a decisive moment in Greek history. Philip was now fully master of Greece and he set up a new league, the League of Corinth, joined by every state of mainland Greece except Sparta (whose opposition could now be safely ignored). The league guaranteed the autonomy of every city, much as the King's Peace of 386 had done, but this time it was a Macedonian not a Persian who presided over its affairs. This was the first time in Greek history that a stable hegemony had been established over Greece by an outsider. It meant, of course, that the era of the independent city-state was over. Traditionally historians have decried the fact but more recently it has been emphasized how much city life gained from the new stability. Athens, for instance, free to trade without interference, entered one of the most prosperous periods in her history. Her finances were reorganized by the statesman Lycurgus, her main theater was rebuilt, navy revived, and docks and harbors renewed.

Meanwhile the ever restless Philip was now free to turn to a new adventure, an invasion of Persia. A campaign of Greeks to the east had long been urged by the Athenian orator Isocrates as a means of solving the besetting problems of fourth-century Greece. Isocrates argued that such a campaign under Athens and Sparta might unite the Greeks and win land on which they could settle their poor. After Chaeronaea, Isocrates, now in his nineties, urged Philip to take the leadership of the crusade. Philip already had his own motives for taking up the challenge, the persistent need to find resources for his men in an area, Asia Minor, where Persian control over the mass of Greeks and native peoples had always been weak.

A small expedition had already crossed the Hellespont when Philip died at the hand of an assassin at Pella in 336. There was talk that the roots of the assassination lay in a homosexual intrigue and even that Olympias, fearful that Philip would provide an heir to displace her son Alexander, ordered the killing. The truth, however, is lost. His body was returned to the ancient capital of his kingdom, Aegae, the modern Vergina, and here it was cremated, the remains being buried in a purple cloth under a golden oak wreath within a gold casket embossed with the star of the Macedonian royal family. The tomb, with a mass of treasure showing unmistakable Greek influences, was rediscovered in 1976. The damaged right eye socket on the skull found in the casket helped confirm that this was indeed Philip and a reconstruction of his face has been possible.

Philip's had been an extraordinary reign, which has only recently been given the prominence it deserves. German historians have been more sympathetic to Philip than Anglo-Saxon ones, seeing in Philip a forerunner of Bismarck, who used the same mix of diplomacy and military force in unifying Germany in the nineteenth century. English historians have been reluctant to give an accolade to a man who appears to have destroyed the independence of the city-state. There is now more general agreement that Philip lay the foundations, in amassing a territory that had good resources and in building a fine army, that were essential elements of his son Alexander's achievement.

16

Alexander

In A.D. 116 the Roman emperor Trajan, one of the finest soldiers Rome ever produced, reached the mouth of the Euphrates river having overrun Armenia and Mesopotamia, both of which he had incorporated into the Roman empire. Here he was forced to turn back. His new conquests were restless and there were rebellions in the west. Before he left, this stern soldier is reputed to have broken down in tears. He had yearned to emulate his hero Alexander and move, as Alexander had done, even farther into the east.

Trajan was not the first, nor the last, military commander to idealize Alexander, the conqueror of the vast Persian empire, as the greatest soldier of all time, the model by which others judged their own exploits. The Ottoman sultan Mehmed II, conqueror of Constantinople in 1453 had Arrian's *Life of Alexander* (a panegyric to Alexander, and a major source for his life, even though written some four hundred years after Alexander's death) read to him every day and exulted in the fact that while Alexander had conquered Asia from west to east, he had completed the conquest from east to west. Even the rudest soldier in Shakespeare's *Henry V* had been brought up on tales of Alexander's conquests.

Alexander succeeded to the throne on the death of his father Philip in October 336. He had already shown himself to be a tempestuous figure, perhaps not surprising for one who claimed among his ancestors the hero Achilles (through his mother) and Heracles (through his father). Steeped in Homer, perhaps even as a child he lived in a semi-fantasy word of the Greek heroes. But he had prodigious energy and extraordinary qualities of leadership. By the age of eighteen he had held his first command, of the cavalry at Chaeronaea, his father's shattering victory over the Greeks. His relationship with his father was not easy, however. When Philip embarked on yet another marriage, this time to the daughter of a Macedonian noble, Cleopatra, Alexander felt deeply threatened by the chance that he would have a half brother with purer Macedonian blood than his own. There was a terrible row and Alexander even went into exile. He was back by the time of his father's death but only to find that Cleopatra was pregnant.

It was essential for Alexander that he confirm his position with the army and the Macedonian nobility as soon as possible. He was presented with an immediate chance to do so when his neighbors, the Illyrians and Thracians, reasserted their independence and there were similar rumblings of revolt from Athens and Thebes. His presence in Greece was alone enough to overawe the Athenians and Thebans and he assumed the post of *tagos* in Thessaly and leadership of the Corinthian league before returning north. While he was securing the Macedonian borders, however, Thebes chose to revolt. Alexander rushed south and was within reach of Thebes before the city had a chance to find allies. In vain the Thebans called for supporters to join in "destroying this tyrant of Hellas" but the city was stormed. Six thousand Thebans were killed and Alexander used Thebes' surrounding enemies to support him in ordering thirty thousand survivors to be enslaved and the destruction of the city. Meanwhile Alexander's mother, Olympias, had engineered the murder of Cleopatra and her baby, a daughter.

While in Greece Alexander had engineered a pronouncement from the oracle at Delphi that he was invincible. He now turned to the east. His father had sent some ten thousand troops there but they were under increasing pressure from the new Persian king, Darius, who not only confined them to the Hellespont but was building a large Aegean fleet to strengthen himself in the west. Alexander could not abandon these troops but he must have realized too, as his father did, that it was only in Asia Minor that there was a significant chance of victories and the associated plunder that was needed to support his status as king and provide the resources with which to sustain his rule.

Alexander was well served by the army he had inherited from his father. The core of the army was the "Companions," some eighteen hundred drawn from the noble families of Macedonia. The Companions saw themselves as just that, associates of their king rather than subjects. They were supported by a further three thousand cavalry, mainly from Thessaly, and then there was the highly trained Macedonian infantry with its *sarissae.* By now these had had long years of training and could be maneuvred with much greater flexibility than the traditional Greek hoplite. With archers and javelin throwers and even a large contingent of hoplites from Greece this was an efficient fighting force (of some forty thousand men in total before the troops already in Asia were added) and it was also well equipped, with siege equipment, engineers, and surveyors. Alexander was to bring coherent leadership to this force, a leadership reinforced by his own high-risk but galvanizing strategy of fighting at the forefront of any battle. In comparison, the Persian armies were to prove cumbersome. They were made up of a mixture of levies from the empire and mercenaries from Greece. The Greek commanders were continually at odds with the aristocrats who led the Persian troops and, in any case, as hoplites, they were largely obsolete. In the event, neither they nor their counterparts in Alexander's army were used in battle. Alexander himself was to depend heavily on the shock effect of a cavalry charge followed by an advance by the Macedonian infantry.

The Persian empire appeared to be a formidable opponent but its size was its greatest weakness. Its borders stretched from Asia Minor, through Syria, and to the south of Egypt, and then, beyond its heartlands in Mesopotamia, Persia, and Media, as far east as modern Afghanistan. Many of its subject peoples, the Babylonians, Lydians, Phoenicians, Egyptians, for example, had impressive heritages of their own and the strength of their allegiance to the Persian empire was uncertain. The best strategy for an invader was to crush its king, Darius, in battle. So long as the invader then posed as a liberator and proved sensitive to local cultures, the disintegration of the empire could be expected to follow.

Alexander marched in 334. He trumpeted his expedition to the Greeks as revenge for the Persian invasions of 490 and 480 and even followed, in reverse, Xerxes' route of 480 through northern Greece. After crossing the Hellespont he made for the legendary site of Troy and began his campaign with a sacrifice at the supposed tombs of Achilles and Ajax. The sacrifices had their effect. The first encounter with the Persian forces at the River Granicus nearby was a triumph. The Persians had hoped to shelter behind the steep banks of the Granicus but Alexander maneuvred the Companions over the river and they were able to hold off the Persians while the infantry followed. The Persian forces were then virtually wiped out. The surviving Greek mercenaries surrendered but there was to be no mercy for them. (They had, after all, defied the leader of the Corinthian League to which all Greeks were supposed to show allegiance.) Most were massacred. Two thousand who were still alive were sent off as forced labor to Macedon.

The victory was so decisive that it destroyed Persian control over the Greek cities of Asia Minor, among them Ephesus, Priene, and Miletus, and the old Lydian capital of Sardis. They all fell to or welcomed Alexander, and Sardis provided him with his first plunder. The Greeks were promised democracies and patronage and this was enough to secure their support. (An inscription recording Alexander's contributions to the building of a temple to Athena at Priene survives in the British Museum.) Some of the plunder was sent to Athens in reparation, Alexander said, for the destruction Xerxes had inflicted on the city in 480. Farther south, however, the city of Halicarnassus, still garrisoned by Persians, held out. It could be supplied by the sea and so offered a base for the Persian fleet. Alexander was unable to capture it (he had no naval forces equal to those the Persians could raise from the Phoenicians) and so he had to move on, leaving the Aegean and Macedonia itself acutely vulnerable to counterattack. If the Persians' efficient naval commander, Memnon of Rhodes, had not died the following year and Darius had not recalled troops and ships from the west, they would probably have caused serious havoc in Alexander's rear.

For the next few months Alexander made his way through Asia Minor, along the southern coast to Aspendus and Side, then northward into Phrygia and finally, high on the central plateau of Anatolia, to the ancient Phrygian capital Gordium (where the legendary King Midas, whose touch turned objects to gold, had ruled). Here he came across an ancient cart whose yoke was bound by bark. Whoever unraveled it, the legend went, would be lord of all Asia. Alexander had

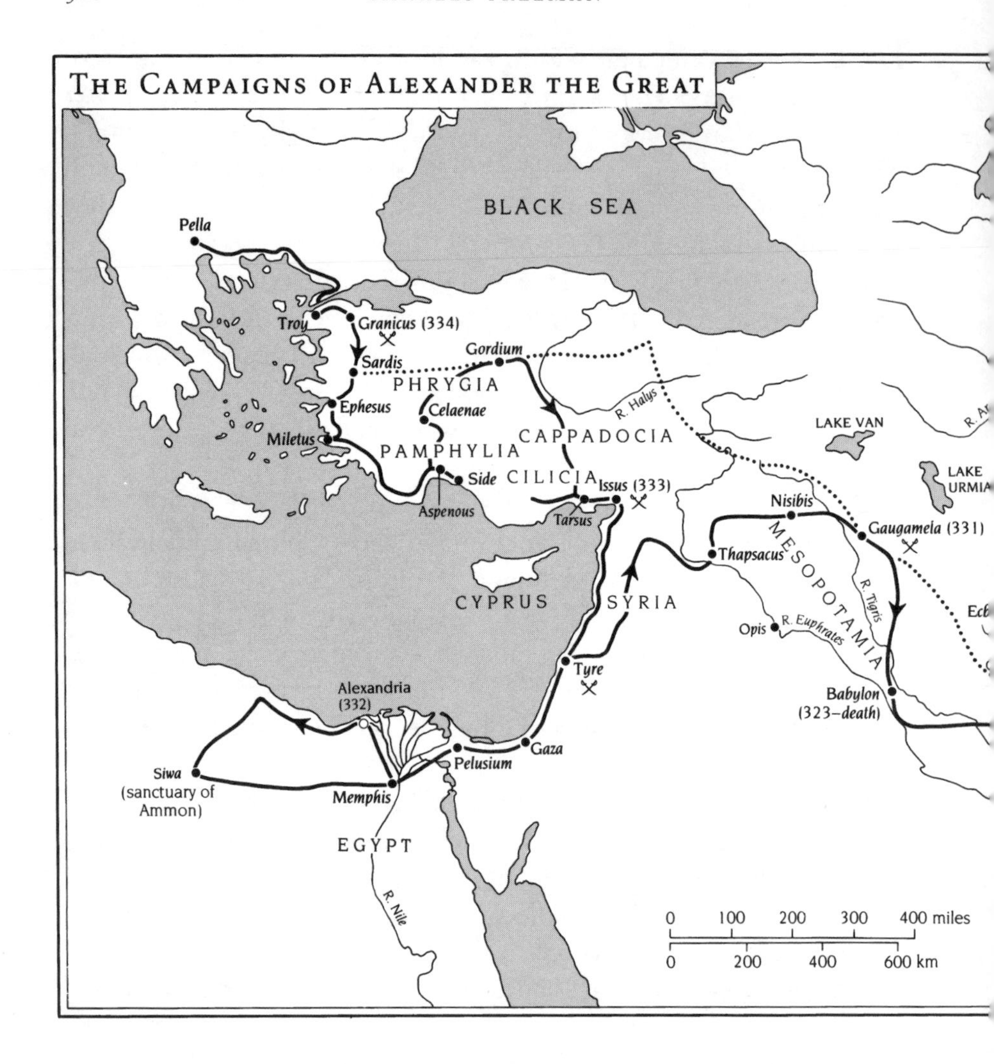

THE CAMPAIGNS OF ALEXANDER THE GREAT

little option but to take up the challenge. Most accounts suggest he simply cut through the knot. An opportune thunderstorm took place as if to confirm the approval of Zeus.

It was now the spring of 333. Resources in the uplands were running low and Alexander had to move southward in search of more fertile land. He moved so swiftly down through the rocky landscape of Cappadoccia to Cilicia that he was able to take the Cilician capital, Tarsus, without a fight and gain more plunder. Here he nearly died after catching a fever while swimming. The whole expedition must have appeared very vulnerable especially now that Darius was gathering his troops. Darius was an experienced commander and he decided to risk

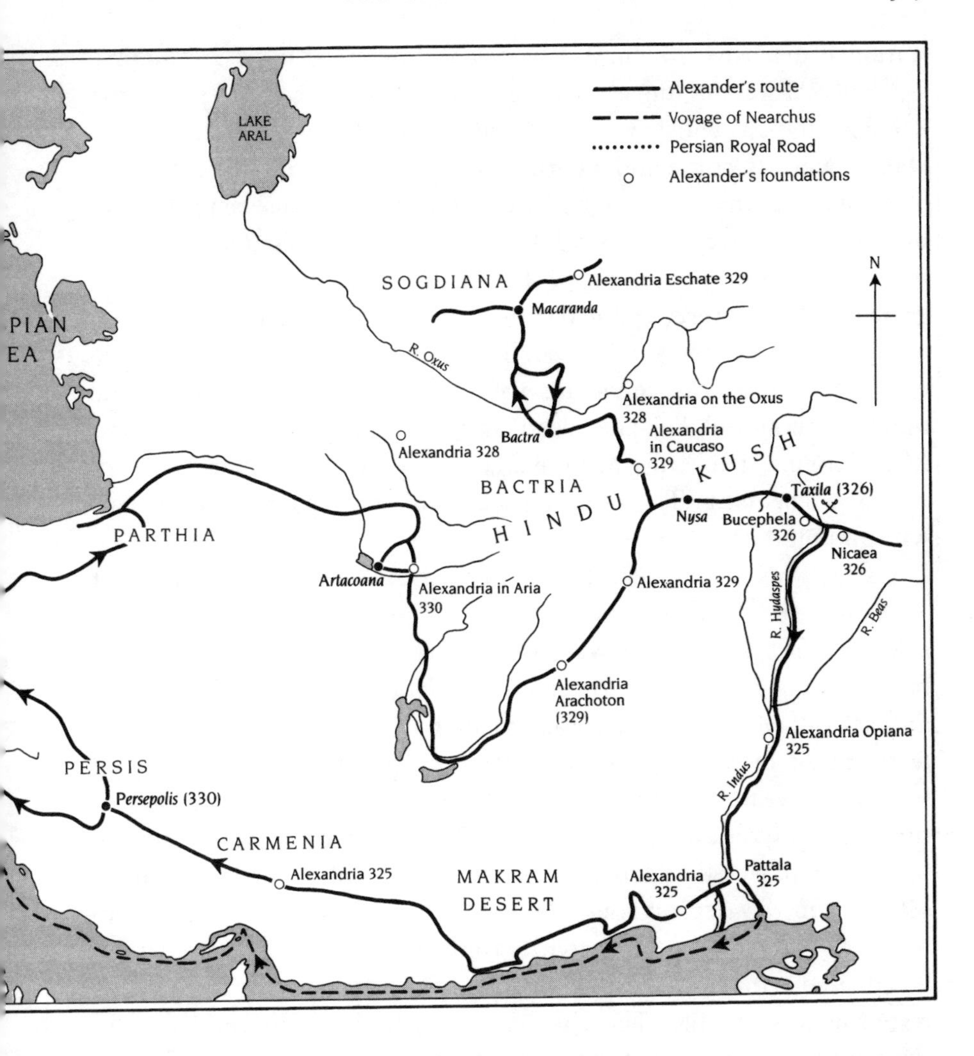

everything on a fixed battle. The bulk of his large army was made up of Persians and Medes but, as with most Persian armies, there was a major contingent of Greek mercenaries, perhaps some thirty thousand. Their resolve must have been strengthened by what had happened to their compatriots after Granicus. Darius was so confident of success that he brought the royal treasure and his wife, mother, and royal princesses with him.

The armies met in September 333 at the eastern end of the Cilician plain above the Gulf of Issus. Darius had taken Alexander by surprise by marching between him and his communication line to Cilicia but the terrain the Persian armies now occupied was not ideal. They were stationed defensively behind a stream and hemmed in by mountains. Typically Alexander himself led the Companions forward to smash the Persian infantry which was on Darius' left. He then turned toward Darius who as commanding from the center. The rest of his army, however, was in trouble. The Thessalian cavalry was being pushed back by the Persian cavalry while his infantry was disrupted as it attempted to cross the stream. In the event, Darius' bodyguard disintegrated under the force of the charge. He fled and, as the news spread, the morale of his army collapsed. The slaughter that followed was so extensive that the Macedonians were to proclaim they had left one hundred thousand Persians dead at the cost of only five hundred Macedonians. This must be an exaggeration but certainly the victory was overwhelming. The royal baggage, full of treasure, and Darius' wife and mother fell into Alexander's hands.

Darius was now prepared to treat Alexander as an equal but Alexander proclaimed himself as Lord of Asia, casting Darius in the role of a usurper. There was no compromise possible and Darius began raising a new army to defend Mesopotamia. Alexander did not, at first, follow him east. His main concern now may have been to protect himself in the west where large areas of the empire, including some of its wealthiest territories, were open to him. He headed back to the coast of Syria. Most of the ancient Phoenician cities welcomed him (and their navies defected so that any chance of a Persian counter-offensive in the Aegean was now lost) but at the city of Tyre, he demanded leadership of the festivities to the local god, Melquart, whom he equated with his ancestor Heracles. The city refused. Alexander's response was terrible. The city was sacked, eight thousand died in the attack itself and two thousand who surrendered were, the Roman sources suggest, crucified. This hysterical reaction was an early sign of a lack of balance in Alexander. Any form of resistance always infuriated him and his response was invariably brutal. He preferred acquiescence and a recognition of his status, now as Lord of Asia. In Egypt, which he reached in 332, he was given the welcome he expected. Proclaimed as a liberator from Persian rule, he was accorded the ancient titles of the pharaohs, son of the sun god Ra, beloved of the great god Amun. (In reliefs at Luxor, Alexander is shown in the iconography of a pharaoh being welcomed by Amun.)

Alexander's stay in Egypt was short. Once he was accepted as pharaoh he had no interest in consolidating his position. However, there were two events of importance during his stay. The first was the foundation on the site of an insignificant village on the Egyptian coast, Rhakotis, of a new city, appropriately enough called Alexandria. It was to become one of the great cities, at times the greatest, of the Mediterranean and some have seen it as Alexander's most important legacy. The second was Alexander's visit to the ancient oracle of the god Ammon, who was equated with Zeus, at the oasis of Siwa in the Libyan desert. It was a difficult journey, some 160 miles (260 kilometers) across open desert, but when he arrived, Alexander, as "pharaoh," received special treatment and seems to have believed he was welcomed by the priests as "the son of Zeus." It tied in with the legends already beginning to form around him, one of which was that Olympias had been impregnated not by Philip but, appropriately, for a "son of Zeus," by a thunderbolt. Alexander might not yet have believed that he was a god himself but the sons of gods enjoyed at the very least the status of hero and Alexander now began to distance himself from the ordinary mortals around him. When news came that Darius would now offer him the whole of his empire to the west of the Euphrates he refused.

A sober assessment of Alexander's reign, apparently shared by his Macedonian commanders at the time, would have suggested that this might be a time to stop and consolidate. Alexander now controlled an enormous empire that, in addition to Greece, included Egypt, Libya, Syria, and Asia Minor. It was wealthy and, especially if the fertility of the Nile valley was effectively exploited, would be self-sustaining. There was every chance that it could be successfully consolidated and defended by its energetic "emperor." However, Alexander never allowed himself to be limited by such sober calculations. His ambitions were limitless and, in any case, Darius, his offers to negotiate spurned, was ready for a new confrontation. He had drawn heavily on the center and east of his empire for new troops and had assembled a huge force of cavalry. He stationed it in a space adequate for its deployment, the plain of Gaugamela in Assyria, on the foothills of the Zagros mountains, and it was here that Alexander, also determined to bring matters to a decisive end, arrived in October 331.

Gaugamela was to prove the most impressive if the closest of Alexander's victories. The Persian forces outnumbered his by probably five to one and on the eve of the battle Alexander is reported to have shown fear for the only time in his life. He soon recovered his composure. He drew up his army with the Companions in their traditional place on the right, the Thessalian cavalry on the left, and the Macedonian infantry in the center. His forces were outflanked by the larger Persian army and so he began advancing at an angle toward the right in the hope of taking the Companions beyond a level ground prepared by the Persians for a charge of scythed chariots and bringing them around the flank of the Persians. His left, forward of the right, was soon engaged with the enemy, while the mass of heavy Persian cavalry was forced to move to their left to confront the Companions before the line was enveloped. As the Persians moved across, however, a gap opened between them and their troops in the center and it was through this that Alexander remorselessly drove the Companions, the Macedonian infantry coming up behind in his support. As the center of the Persian army disintegrated Darius fled again. His army went on fighting well against the Thessalian cavalry (Alexander's left wing) but the news that their king had deserted them with many of his troops left them disheartened and they were destroyed in a Thessalian counterattack. It was another decisive victory for Alexander.

Now the Macedonians were in the heartland of Darius' empire and it was time for booty. In Babylon, Alexander was welcomed as a liberator from Persian rule and his army was able to relax in what was one of the richest and most sophisticated cities of the East. There was vast wealth here as there was in Susa where a treasury of some 50,000 talents in gold and silver bullion and coins was surrendered and farther across the snowcapped Zagros mountains, in Persepolis, the spiritual center of the Achaemenid empire. In Darius' bed chamber at Persepolis alone there was gold worth some 8000 talents. (There were no more than 44 talents of gold on Pheidias' opulent statue of Athena in the Parthenon, an indication of just how modest the wealth of Greece was in comparison with that of the East.) One hundred twenty thousand talents were collected from Persepolis and the city was stripped of its wealth so effectively that no remaining gold there has been found by excavators. In May 330, egged on by an Athenian courtesan by the name of Thais, who had been drinking with the Macedonian commanders, the great palace of Xerxes was set to fire in revenge, it was said, for the sacking of Athens in 480.

The argument that Alexander should have halted and consolidated his rule now becomes even stronger but Alexander had become obsessed by the desire to eliminate Darius and move even farther to the east to the borders of the empire and beyond. The final demise of Darius came at the hands of others. Discredited by his defeats and moving into regions where there was little loyalty to him Darius was captured by one of his cavalry commanders, Bessus, the satrap of Bactria. As Alexander closed in, Darius was stabbed and left to die. Bessus proclaimed himself the new king of Persia but it was a title that was now Alexander's and Bessus was declared a usurper. He was eventually captured, and the traditional punishment of the usurper, the mutilation of his nose and ears, inflicted on him before he was executed.

Alexander drove on into the east but the following years (330–327 B.C.) were harsh and unrewarding ones. He had reached the provinces of Bactria and Sogdiana, now Afghanistan and Pakistan. It was an inherently unstable area (as a later set of invaders, the Russians, found in the 1980s) and Alexander was now fighting a variety of local leaders in a terrain only too suitable for guerrilla resistance. The only way the area could be subdued was through wholesale massacres and enslavements and a major occupation force of some ten thousand infantry, and thirty-five hundred cavalry had to be put in place. Bactria retained a core of Greek cities for centuries. As the area was calmed, Alexander extracted some thirty thousand of its young men for special training as "Macedonian" infantry. He also selected a wife, Roxane, the daughter of a Bactrian noble who had collaborated with him.

These were, inevitably, highly stressful years and they were exacerbated by splits between Alexander and his commanders. Alexander was becoming increasingly isolated, resentful of any attempt to check him and unpredictable in his responses. In 330 he accused his brilliant cavalry commander Philotas of conspiring his death and bullied the army into executing him. Philotas' father, a steady commander from the days of Philip who had criticized Alexander's impetuousness, was also murdered. Then, in 328, came a sobering incident at Macaranda (modern Samarkand) when, after a bout of heavy drinking, Alexander was taunted by Cleitus, a commander who had actually saved Alexander's life when it was threatened at Granicus. Alexander grabbed a weapon and killed Cleitus himself.

In short, Alexander's behavior was becoming increasingly domineering and disturbed. Now that he was king of the Persian empire he had the opportunity to adopt a model of kingship that was only too attractive to his new mood. The Persian kings stood aloof even from the most mighty of their subjects and the distance between ruler and ruled was symbolized by the act of *proskynesis*, a traditional humbling of a subject, however senior, before the king (The supplicant had to bow or lie on the ground before the king and blow him a kiss.) For nearly two hundred years Greek propaganda had ridiculed the despotic demands of the Persian monarchy but now Alexander insisted on *proskynesis* to himself. The Macedonians were horrified and although Alexander later dropped his demands, lasting damage had been done.

Everything was made worse by Alexander's refusals to turn back. In 327 he crossed the passes of the Hindu Kush. As it came down into the Cophen valley his isolated army massacred the inhabitants of any city that resisted it. By 326 Alexander had moved beyond the remote borders of the empire into India itself where at the Battle of Hydaspes he achieved one of the most crushing of his victories against an Indian prince, Porus. On he went but now the monsoons were threatening and when the army experienced some seventy days of continuous rainfall it became deeply demoralized. When he reached the river Beas, it was close to mutiny. Alexander was forced to turn back, concealing his fury at the betrayal by claiming that it was the gods' will shown through the response to a sacrifice that had prompted the decision.

The return from India was down the River Indus in a flotilla, again with the wholesale sacking of the cities which resisted along the way. Garrisons were left to keep order but they appear all to have been wiped out by the native peoples. Alexander himself nearly lost his life when an Indian arrow struck him while he was isolated high on the wall of a city. By July 325 the army was at the mouth of the Indus. A daunting march now lay ahead westward through the Makram desert. It was the kind of challenge Alexander reveled in, partly because, it was said, he knew Cyrus himself, the founder of the empire, had lost a whole army in the desert. The accounts suggest that the following sixty days were exceptionally grueling ones, although it is not clear how many men actually died in the ordeal. Certainly those who returned by sea, through the Arabian Sea and then the Persian Gulf, fared much better. Under a skilled commander, Nearchus, the fleet reached the Tigris without the loss of a single ship. Its success roused Alexander to new ambitions—a circumnavigation of Africa, perhaps even the conquest of the western Mediterranean.

Alexander was now thirty-one but, despite an extraordinarily strong constitution, he was already weakening. Heavy drinking, the effect of wounds and fevers and the continuous stress had taken their toll. However, he now had to consolidate his conquests. During the conquest any Persian satrap who had pleaded loyalty had been left in place with a Macedonian deputy appointed to take care of military affairs and the collection of taxes. However, although the basic structure of the empire remained intact there had been no effective supervision of its officials. The flow of plunder had meant that Alexander had not needed to plan a financial strategy. Many officials had simply assumed that he would never return from the east and corruption and oppression had become widespread. Alexander's response was swift and often brutal. Allegations that his Macedonian administrators had committed atrocities was met with their executions. Most of the Persian satraps were dismissed and replaced with trusted Macedonians. Order was restored but it was one based on fear. There was little attempt to build an effective new structure of government. "As usual," writes A. B. Bosworth, a leading authority on Alexander, "Alexander worked on the short term. It is hard to see any wider policy beyond the basic requirements that the satrapies should remain peaceful with the minimum of expense and that his kingship should be universally and unconditionally recognised."

The major problem was how to integrate Macedonians and Persians. Alexander's sympathies were shown in the way he appropriated Persian royal symbols such as a white-striped purple tunic and the trappings of the Persian court but he also attempted to tie the Macedonians to the court by encouraging them to marry into the Persian aristocracy. In the spring of 324, in a great ceremony at the royal capital at Susa, some ninety Macedonians were married to selected Persian brides. Alexander himself took two royal princesses as his wives, one of them a daughter of Darius. The strategy was ill judged and few of the marriages lasted. The Macedonians themselves had little interest in becoming Persian and there was now increasing dissatisfaction with Alexander's appropriation of an alien culture. Resentment grew when the thirty thousand recruits from Bactria arrived in Susa. They were well trained and seemed destined to replace the Macedonian infantry.

In the summer of 324, the tension exploded. Alexander had taken part of his army up the Tigris to the city of Opis. (He was making the river navigable so that a fleet could use it.) Here he announced that all those Macedonian troops unfit for service would be returned home and replaced by fresh soldiers from Macedon. Though a sound move in principle, the men saw it as a rejection. They jeered that Alexander should send them all home and go it alone with his "father" Zeus. Outraged, Alexander ordered the execution of the ringleaders and started to appoint Persian commanders in their places. At this the mutiny collapsed and there was a highly emotional reconciliation. Eventually some ten thousand Macedonians, loaded with booty, left for home.

Alexander's administrative strategies continued to be based on short-term opportunism. Without any discussion and with little negotiation he announced, at the Olympic Games of 324, that exiles from throughout the Greek world could return to their home cities. For the exiles, many of whom had lost land and livelihood in the political disruptions of the century, it was a wildly popular decision. Twenty thousand of them turned up at the Games to hear the decree read out. For the home cities it was a disaster. Many were overwhelmed by groups of returning refugees claiming land they had lost in power struggles. Ruling groups whom Philip had supported in power found their authority undermined as old opponents came back. In essence, the very stability that Philip had tried to foster in mainland Greece was destroyed by his son. The Greeks who might have hoped to be given some status in Alexander's empire were shown that they mattered as little to him as his other subjects. An anti-Macedonian uprising broke out in Greece as soon as Alexander died (see below).

In his last year Alexander began to plan a major invasion of Arabia. A great harbor was dug out at Babylon and a mixed army of Macedonian and Persian troops was put in training. There were reports too that he might move into the Mediterranean and embassies from as far west as Spain reached Babylon to offer allegiance. However, these months were marked by continuous feasting and drinking. In March of 324 one of Alexander's favorite companions, Hephaistion, died of a fever after a bout of drinking. Alexander's mourning bordered on the hysterical. Comparisons were made with the grief of Achilles after the death of Patroclus. A cult was ordered in Hephaistion's memory and a vast brick funeral monument planned at about 230 feet (seventy meters) high was to be built at Babylon.

These months also saw Alexander elaborating the belief that he was the son of Zeus. It is impossible to know whether Alexander himself believed he had crossed the border between human and divine existence. The sons of gods were not necessarily gods themselves, though it was believed that they could become so after great exploits. (Alexander's ancestor Heracles, a hero by birth, had been accorded divine status as a result of his Labors.) There are indications, however, that Alexander did believe he had become divine. On coins minted at Babylon, he is depicted with a thunderbolt. At banquets he wore the purple robes and ram's head of Zeus Ammon and there is some evidence that the Greek cities were ordered to acknowledge his divinity.

The end was perhaps predictable. One evening in May 323 Alexander was drinking with his companions in celebration of the news that the oracle at Siwa had approved the cult worship of Hephaistion. He is said to have consumed the contents of a great bowl and then fallen ill. The accounts differ. Some say he died immediately, others that he lingered a few days, his troops filing past him when it was clear he was beyond hope of recovery. There were inevitably rumors that he had been poisoned but there is no firm evidence to support them. Whatever the truth, by June 323 Alexander was dead. He was thirty-two.

Alexander may be said to have initiated the ideal of the romantic hero. He was the first Greek to project himself through portraits, in marble or bronze and on coins. He asked to be shown beardless, a sign of youth and vigor, and his chosen pose, realized by his favorite sculptor Lysippus, was to look slightly upward, his gaze distant. In full-size statues, none of which have survived, Lysippus appears to have merged the ideal body of a warrior hero with the real one of Alexander who was actually quite small. Alexander was shown carrying a spear held outward in his hand. The impression was of a dynamic and superhuman character who had achieved his personal supremacy through conquest. Alexander's exploits were further idealized by his main biographers, Arrian and Plutarch, both writing several hundred years after his death. As a result Alexander became one of those figures whose exploits were so deeply ingrained in the European imagination that it is now difficult to assess him objectively. His strengths, his youth, incisive brilliance as a commander, his fearlessness, and boundless curiosity, are compelling ones. One of his better modern biographers (Robin Lane Fox) reminds his readers of Alexander's wider interests, "his hunting, reading, his patronage of music and drama and his lifelong friendships with Greek artists, actors, and architects, . . ." his courtesy to Persian nobles, and his relatively civilized treatment of women. There is certainly some truth in this but overall Alexander has surely been overromanticized. There has been too little questioning of his destruction of the Persian empire—it has been too easily assumed that he was somehow bringing "civilization" to "barbarians" where in fact many of the cultures he conquered were very much older than his own. His curiosity about what lay ahead of him, particularly in the grueling marches to the east, was complemented by his greed for plunder. He had no hesitation about meeting any resistance with repression and massacre. There was nothing noble in his conquest of the east and it is hard to argue that the imposition of Greek culture (through the cities Alexander founded there) brought any long-term benefit to the local inhabitants.

Alexander was essentially an opportunist. He had no aptitude for or skills in long-term administration. Such mundane things bored him. However much he liked to portray himself as a civilized Greek, his treatment of other Greeks, the Thebans, the mercenaries at Granicus, the stable city governments left by his father, was brutal and counterproductive. His major "achievements" were to destroy a loosely structured empire and in the short period in which he ruled over its ruins to create a model of kingship, the monarch as removed, heroic in battle, and the beloved of the gods, which was to prove immensely influential in the Hellenistic and Roman periods, and hence in later European history.

That this would be Alexander's legacy was not at all clear at first. His death left confusion in his vast conquests. There was no obvious heir. His half-brother Arrhidaeus was retarded, his Bactrian wife Roxane was pregnant but even if she gave birth to a son, as she did, there would be a lengthy regency. So matters lay in the hands of his generals. Overall command rested first in the hands of Alexander's senior cavalry officer, Perdiccas, who assumed control as regent for Arrhidaeus and, once he was born, the baby Alexander IV. He handed out subsidiary commands. An able member of Alexander's bodyguard, Lysimachus, was to be responsible for Thrace. In Macedonia, Philip's viceroy there, Antipater (who, in fact, had been so hostile to Alexander that he was rumored to be his poisoner), was left in place. Antipater took it upon himself to subdue the Greek states that revolted under Athenian leadership on the news of Alexander's death (in the so-called Lamian War). This was the moment when Athenian democracy was finally destroyed (voting now depended on a property qualification). A moderate "middle-class" government was prepared to acquiesce in Macedonian control and its accession marked the end of Athens as a force in Greek politics.

The most shrewd of the minor generals was one Ptolemy. He asked Perdiccas for Egypt, was granted it and then achieved a remarkable coup. Alexander's body had been kept in Babylon for two years while an extravagant funerary car was constructed in which to take it back to Macedonia. When the cortege eventually reached the Syrian coast, the body was hijacked by Ptolemy and taken first to the Egyptian capital Memphis and then to Alexandria. Supported by this talisman, Ptolemy consolidated his rule. He knew how difficult it would be for him to be dislodged, and he soon extended his control westward along the African coast. Perdiccas realized he was being out maneuvred and invaded Egypt. As his troops crossed the Nile many were drowned. The rest mutinied and Perdiccas was killed (321).

Antipater was now the senior figure in the disintegrating empire. He moved Arrhidaeus and Roxane's son, officially Alexander IV, to Macedonia but he was now in his seventies and in no state to make a bid of his own for the empire. He needed a strong man to take command of the Asian armies and he chose a formidable figure, a Macedonian general, Antigonus the One-Eyed ("a towering, corpulent figure, with a harsh parade ground voice and a shatteringly heavy laugh" [Peter Green]). Antigonus had his own ambitions and the death of Antipater in 319 gave him his chance to bid for power in Asia. A man of immense energy, he temporarily gained control of Asia from Asia Minor to Persia but his ambitions to take even the rest of the empire were thwarted by Antipater's son Cassander who clung to Macedonia and Ptolemy, still firmly entrenched in Egypt. Antigonus had to come to terms. In 311, in the Peace of the Dynasts, there was a recognition by Antigonus of Cassander, Lysimachus (still in Thrace), and Ptolemy's positions. It was not a settlement which was likely to last, especially as another powerful player emerged, Seleucus. Seleucus had fought as one of Alexander's generals throughout his Persian campaign and had been made satrap of Babylon in 320. He had then been ousted by Antigonus but returned with the help of Ptolemy in 311. He never signed the peace of 311. He was a shrewd and ambitious ruler who sensed the urgency of stabilizing his territories so that he could concentrate on the elimination of his rivals in the west. He settled the far eastern boundary after a negotiation with the king of the emerging Mauryan empire (which came to control the whole Indian subcontinent). One of the terms was the transfer to Seleucus of a fighting force of five hundred elephants. Seleucus then defeated Antigonus at a great battle in 309 or 308, which effectively confined Antigonus to Asia Minor and Greece. For some time, Antigonus, with the help of his son Demetrius, attempted to become leader of the Greek world, promising to support the freedom of the Greek cities. He enjoyed some success in reviving a coalition of Greek cities on the model of the Corinthian League but a failed invasion of Egypt and siege of Rhodes saw his influence on the wane. Seleucus (with his five hundred elephants) and Lysimachus in Thrace finally gave him his match. Antigonus was defeated and killed at the battle of Ipsus, in Phrygia, in 301.

By now any pretense that these warring generals were representatives of Alexander's heirs had vanished. As far back as 317 the ruthless Olympias had had Arrhidaeus murdered to preserve the inheritance for her grandson Alexander IV. Alexander, however, had only survived another seven years until Cassander executed him. The void had to be filled somehow and it was inevitable that the rival generals would eventually take the step of declaring that they were, in fact, kings. Antigonus was the first to do so. In 306, he assumed the title of king and began wearing a diadem, a headdress associated with Macedonian kingship (a particularly fine silver-gilt one was found in the royal tombs at Vergina). Seleucus, Lysimachus, and Ptolemy all followed suit. After their victory at Ipsus, they now ruled unashamedly in their own names and flamboyantly set about establishing dynasties. This was the true moment of transition, when Alexander's legacy, a model of semidivine kingship based ultimately on military force, finally, twenty years after his death, became a living one.

17

The Hellenistic World

"The life has departed from his subject and with sadness and humiliation the historian brings his narrative to a close" lamented George Grote as he concluded his great history of Greece (1846–1856) with the reign of Alexander. In the nineteenth century, the Hellenistic period which follows conventionally from Alexander to the absorption of the Ptolemaic kingdom of Egypt into the Roman empire (30 B.C.), was dismissed by historians as "corrupt" or "imitative" in comparison to the supposed glories of the classical era. This is deeply unfair. Certainly the city-state, the traditional context in which Greek culture had flourished, was no longer the center of political life but this was an age of continuing Greek achievement. There were major breakthroughs in mathematics and science, in particular astronomy and medicine (the subject of the next chapter). There were important new philosophical movements, two, Epicureanism and Stoicism, with a lasting significance. The period sees the birth of pastoral poetry and genres of art such as portraiture, sculpture, and landscape painting. One can hardly dismiss it as second-rate.

The word *Hellenistic* is derived from a German word, "Hellenismus," coined by the nineteenth-century historian J. G. Droysen. He used it to refer to the process of fusion between Greek and non-Greek. The Hellenistic Age, in short, saw the spread of Greek culture from the Mediterranean into Asia, as far east as modern Afghanistan, and to

Egypt, and its fusion with the local cultures. The spread was fostered by Greco-Macedonian rulers and supported by a mass of Greek migrants who came to seek their fortunes in the new kingdoms. Traditionally historians have seen this as a positive process (not least for Christian writers because it was in this expanded Greek world that Christianity was able to spread). More recently they have stressed the continuing resilience of native cultures and the degree to which the Hellenistic world was sustained by the labor and surplus wealth of non-Greeks, especially in Egypt and Mesopotamia. The survival of local cultures was helped by the fact that many Greek cities existed as segregated communities, saw themselves superior to local communities, and did not bother to mix with them. In short, in many areas the impact of the Greeks was comparatively limited.

Four kingdoms had emerged out of the ruins of Alexander's empire. One of them survived for only twenty years. Lysimachus, a former bodyguard of Alexander's, had been given Asia Minor as a reward for his role at Ipsus and he exploited its wealth ruthlessly so that he was able to expand even farther, northward from his original base Thrace, across the Danube and even into Macedonia. His support among the local nobility was never strong, however, and in 281 the ever resourceful Seleucus invaded Asia Minor, defeated and killed Lysimachus and assumed most of Asia Minor for his own.

Although Seleucus himself was assassinated the same year, when he tried to fulfill his own ambitions of securing Macedonia for his kingdom, he died having created the largest of the successor kingdoms. The old heartland of the Persian empire, including Mesopotamia (Babylon), was his and so was the Far East, as far as the border with the Mauryan empire in India, as well as much of Asia Minor. (In the north of Asia Minor, kingdoms such as Bithynia were able to sustain their independence and a Celtic people, the Galatians, migrated to central Asia Minor in the 270s B.C. In the south, Caria and Lycia came under Ptolemaic control.) Traditionally historians have concentrated on the western part of the Seleucid empire, Asia Minor and Syria, but more recent interpretations have stressed how important the breadbasket of the ancient Near East, Mesopotamia, was in underwriting its needs. The capital established by Seleucus, Seleucia-on-Tigris, thrived and was far larger than any Seleucid city in the west. While Seleucia's administrative class was Macedonian, local influences in architecture, for instance, were strong and suggest that the Seleucids had made some form of stable accommodation with the native peoples. The Persian empire's structure of satrapies, provinces under the rule of one man who was directly appointed by the king, was continued (although the Greek word *strategos*, general, was used instead of satrap).

The achievement of Seleucus in creating some sort of order on the Asian mainland was impossible to sustain. In the east the trend was towards disintegration. Bactria, which had been heavily garrisoned by Alexander, broke away in the mid-third century. The northeastern part of the remaining empire was eaten into by the emerging Parthian empire (whose traditional date of foundation is 247), which by the end of the second century B.C. was to rule from the Euphrates to the Indus. Several of the satrapies in the southeast, including Gedrosia and Carmania, probably seceded. In an attempt to regain control of the east, one Seleucid king, Antiochus III "the Great," in a march (209–205 B.C.) reminiscent of that of Alexander himself, reached as far as India but Seleucid control was only effectively restored as far east as Media (and then later lost to the Parthians). There were further losses in Asia Minor when a minor prince, Attalus, defeated the Galatians in 230 B.C., declared himself a king, and began to carve out a kingdom around the commanding site of Pergamum.

The most unsettled area of the Seleucid empire was Syria. Here Seleucus and his successors battled with the Ptolemies who were hoping to extend their kingdom northward from Egypt. There were no less than five wars between the two dynasties in the third century and it was not until 200 that Antiochus III gained control of the whole coast of Syria and Phoenicia, including Palestine, having ousted the Ptolemies. By 190 the empire, having lost its eastern provinces and parts of Asia Minor, consisted of its Babylonian heartland, Cilicia (in southeastern Asia Minor), and the newly acquired Syria. This was still a substantial empire but in the second and first centuries B.C. it was to prove vulnerable to the expanding ambitions of both the Parthians (who had conquered Mesopotamia by the 120s) and the Romans. The last of the Seleucids tried desperately to present themselves in their statues in the pose of Alexander but with little credibility. The annexation of Syria by the Roman general Pompey in 64 B.C. formally marked the end of the empire.

Of the major Hellenistic kingdoms, Ptolemy's was to prove to be the

ILLYRIA
ROMAN REP.
MACEDONIA
Pella
Thessalonica
Pydna
168
Cynoscephalae
197
AETOLIAN LEAGUE
Thermopylae 191
Corinth
ACHEAN LEAGUE
Athens
Black Sea
Byzantium
BITHYNIA
PAPHLAGONIA
Pergamum
Magnesia 190
Ephesus
Priene
Cnidus
RHODES
Tarsus
Antioch
Mediterranean Sea
Palmyra
Alexandria
Jerusalem
EGYPT
Red Sea
0
500
1000 km
0
300
600 miles

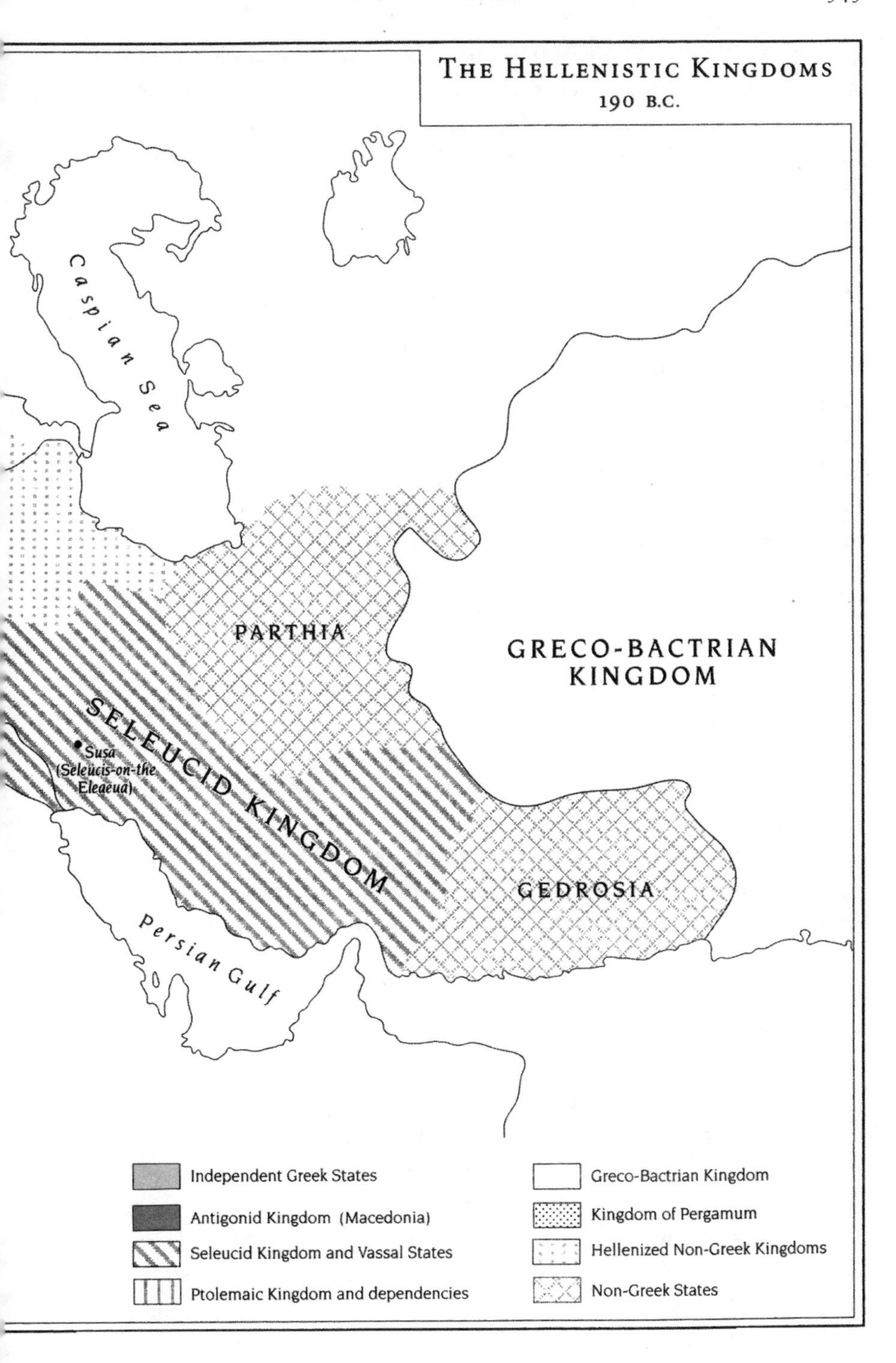
THE HELLENISTIC KINGDOMS
190 B.C.
Caspian Sea
PARTHIA
GRECO-BACTRIAN KINGDOM
SELEUCID KINGDOM
Susa
(Seleucis-on-the Eleaeua)
GEDROSIA
Persian Gulf
Independent Greek States
Antigonid Kingdom (Macedonia)
Seleucid Kingdom and Vassal States
Ptolemaic Kingdom and dependencies
Greco-Bactrian Kingdom
Kingdom of Pergamum
Hellenized Non-Greek Kingdoms
Non-Greek States

wealthiest, the most influential culturally and the last to succumb to Roman rule (in 30 B.C. when the last of the Ptolemies, Cleopatra, finally lost the intricate power game she had been playing with her Roman lovers). Its wealth depended on an economic system, now thousands of years old, by which the large surpluses of grain from the Nile Valley were channeled upward to the king. However, unlike many of their predecessors, the Ptolemies were not isolated within the Nile Valley. They were determined to play on a wider Mediterranean stage and not lose touch with their Greek and Macedonian roots. The Ptolemies clung onto southern Syria until finally dislodged from there by the Seleucids, controlled Cyprus, southern regions of Asia Minor, and many Aegean islands. Rhodes, one of the few Greek city-states to maintain its independence during this period, had an alliance with Egypt that was underpinned by extensive trading links. The determination with which the Ptolemies maintained their overseas possessions suggests that they wanted a buffer zone with which to protect Egypt and also access to raw materials, such as timber, which were in short supply there, and mercenaries. They may well have feared Macedonian expansion into the Aegean and substantial gifts of grain to Athens were used to keep that city's support.

The Ptolemies imposed a Greek-speaking administration on Egypt and none of them, with the exception of Cleopatra at the very end of the dynasty, managed to master Egyptian. Their capital, Alexandria, was never properly integrated into the country (its official title was Alexandria-by-Egypt) and for much of the time they lived isolated from their own peoples. Although they sponsored building programs in the tradition of the pharaohs (among the largest surviving "Ptolemaic" temples are those to the god Horus at Edfu and to Isis on the island of Philae), their hold over their people was bound to be weak. They were forced to arm native Egyptians to help them defend their possessions in Syria but this proved counterproductive: The arms were turned against them. By the end of the third century B.C. Upper Egypt was in fact independent, ruled once again by a native pharaoh. The Aegean islands and Asia Minor were also lost so that by 185 B.C. Cyprus was the only territory outside Egypt under Ptolemaic control. The dynasty itself hastened its fate by tearing itself apart through internal power struggles. The Romans, now beginning to dominate in the eastern Mediterranean, at first sustained the dynasty but then overthrew it in 30 B.C.

Although the impact of the Ptolemies on Egyptian culture was relatively limited, ancient Egypt is still perceived today through Greek eyes. Many important Egyptian myths are recorded only in Greek (and possibly adapted to make sense to Greeks). The word *Egypt* itself comes from the Greek *Aigyptos*. The first compilation of Egyptian dynasties, by the priest Manetho in the third century B.C., one which is still used by Egyptologists as the basis for Egyptian chronology, was sponsored by the Ptolemies. Thebes (the great cult center of the Upper Nile) is the Greek name for the city the Egyptians knew as Waset. The word *pyramid* comes from the Greek *pyramis,* a wheaten cake (which had the same shape as the pyramid). The most important contribution to the later study of Egypt proved to be the custom of issuing decrees in three versions, Greek; demotic Egyptian (the "everyday" native script); and hieroglyphic, the formal script. (The word *hieroglyph* comes from the Greek for "sacred writing.") The Rosetta Stone (named after the village where it was found in 1799 A.D.), now in the British Museum, was inscribed with such a decree. It referred to the cult of a boy king Ptolemy V and dated from 196 B.C. By comparing the texts on the Rosetta Stone, the French scholar Jean-François Champollion was able to decipher hieroglyphics in the 1820s and so open up the lost world of Egyptian sacred texts and literature.

The most "Greek" of the successor kingdoms was, of course, Macedonia and it was the only one in which the rulers and its people shared a common culture. As the birthplace and original kingdom of Alexander it was the most sought after of the thrones but it also was the one whose stability took longest to achieve. Cassander held Macedonia until his death in 297 B.C., then the kingdom collapsed into anarchy and became vulnerable to Celtic war raids (in 279 the Celts even reached as far south as Delphi) and the ambitions of Lysimachus and Seleucus. It was not until 276 that Antigonus Gonatus, the grandson of the Macedonian Antigonus the One-Eyed, was able to bring some stability and establish a dynasty. The old tradition that the rule of the king depended on the support of the Macedonian nobility remained and on the death of Antigonus' son and successor, Demetrius, in 229 the nobility chose a cousin, another Antigonus, as king rather than Demetrius' son who was still a child. In comparison with the other Hellenistic kingdoms Macedonia was never wealthy even though it retained control of Thessaly with its fertile pastures and the gold and silver mines of Mount Pangaeus. When the Romans, shrewd judges of what could be extracted from opponents, imposed an indemnity on Macedonia in 196, they fixed it at only 1000 talents. The Seleucids got stung for 18,000.

How did these kingdoms manipulate their survival? They had to employ a variety of strategies if they were to defend the borders of their kingdoms while keeping the allegiances of their Greek citizens and the acquiescence of their non-Greek populations. The Ptolemies took what they assumed to be a pharaonic model. They adopted appropriate titles, such as Soter, "savior," by Ptolemy I, and married their sisters, believing, incorrectly, that this was a pharaonic tradition. The dynasty also consolidated itself by insisting on cult worship both of living rulers and their predecessors. The Egyptian pharaohs had always been regarded as semidivine and Alexander had suggested that even Greek rulers might be. The Ptolemies drew on these traditions. For the first time rulers used images of themselves as rough warriors or sophisticated aesthetes on coins and in sculptured portraits. They linked themselves to chosen gods. A new god, Serapis, was created by the Ptolemies for the purpose. Serapis was an amalgamation of the ancient Egyptian god Osiris with Apis, a sacred bull worshipped at Memphis, the ancient Egyptian capital. Attributes of Zeus and Dionysus were added to make an all-encompassing god with major cult centers in Alexandria, Memphis, and a new Greek foundation at Ptolemais on the Upper Nile. The cult of Serapis spread into Greece and through the Aegean as a result of Ptolemy's officials taking the cult with them. (There was an important center on Delos.) Queen Arsinoe II the wife (and sister) of Ptolemy II adopted the Egyptian goddess Isis for her support and the worship of Isis also spread to Greece. Both Isis and Serapis were to become major deities in the Greco-Roman world.

The new rulers had learned their lesson from the chaos that had followed Alexander's death. It was essential to secure a stable succession and ideally this meant having a son in place to take over when the king died. A speech of Seleucus I survives which shows how he cleverly secured the support of his army for slotting in his son, Antiochus, as a provincial governor. Antiochus' position was further consolidated by passing on to him Seleucus' second wife, Stratonice. The speech also shows how the Seleucids stressed the personal nature of their rule:

> Then he assembled his army and told them of his exploits and of the extent of his empire, showing that it passed that of

> any of the other successors of Alexander, and saying that as he was now growing old it was hard to govern it on account of its size. "I wish," he said, "to divide it, in the interests of your future safety, and to give a part of it now to those who are dearest to me. It is fitting that all of you, who have advanced to such greatness of domination and power under me since the time of Alexander should cooperate with me in everything. The dearest to me and well worthy to reign are my grown-up son and my wife. As they are young, O pray they soon may have children to aid in guarding the empire. I join them in marriage in your presence and send them to be sovereigns of the upper provinces now. The law which I shall impose on you is not the customs of the Persians and other nations, but the law which is common to all, that which the king ordains is always right." When he had thus spoken the army shouted that he was the greatest king of all the successors of Alexander and the best father.
>
> (Translation from S. Sherwin-White and A. Kuhrt, *From Samarkhand to Sardis*)

All the successor kingdoms based their origins and legitimacy on the idea of spear-won territory and continuing military strength. There was a persistent undercurrent of war throughout the period as frontiers were defended or native uprisings subdued—only two Seleucid kings, in fact, survived to die in their beds. Their kings competed for the battle-worn veterans of Alexander's armies or bought mercenaries from throughout the Greek world. With armies of up to eighty thousand men, as large as any until modern times, and impressive siege equipment, no city-state could challenge them.

The new kingdoms also brought with them the concept of a court, centered on a royal capital. There were Egyptian and Persian precedents to follow although the courtiers themselves were invariably Macedonian or Greek and usually drawn from the city elites. One scholar, Gabriel Herman, has suggested that the traditional friendship links between aristocratic families, which can be traced back to Homeric times, still held fast and provided a pool of candidates for recruitment. The courtiers themselves, known as Royal Friends, included administrators, generals, ambassadors as well as scholars, scientists, philosophers, and poets. The historian Polybius (see below) complained that courtiers intrigued and played one off against each other in their efforts to maintain the ear of the king. Hellenistic courts, it seems, were typical of courts throughout history.

Mercenaries and courts cost money, so the Hellenistic kingdoms needed effective control of their resources. Here the native peoples were expected to play their part. The Ptolemies had a ready-made economic structure in Egypt and the Seleucids, too, adopted, but then developed, the Persian taxation system. The Achaemenid kings had owned vast areas of crown lands including forests and mines and these were taken over by the Seleucids who seem to have taken an active role in increasing their produce. There were also a host of taxes on land, commerce, and salt. Such taxes were used not only to gather revenue but as a means of securing support. A city whose allegiance was shaky could be seduced by granting it temporary immunity from taxation. Under the Seleucids, Greek cities were in theory expected to pay tax equally with others, in practice they were often let off so that a "special relationship" between the king and his cultural kinsmen could be sustained.

Central to Hellenistic rule, in fact, was patronage and show. There is a reminder of the tyrants of the seventh and sixth centuries B.C. in the way that rulers used their wealth for flamboyant display. Games were a popular choice. The traditional Greek games, those of Olympia, the Isthmus, and Delphi, remained, but the ambition of rulers was to create a games which could be seen as *isolympios,* equal in prestige to those of Olympia. A notable example was the Ptolemaia, introduced in Alexandria in memory of Ptolemy I. Then there was a mass of other festivities. Those at Alexandria stand out for their extravagance. A festival to Dionysus organized by Ptolemy II in 275 seemed encased in gold (much of it from the vast quantities released by Alexander's conquests). In a great procession there were 120 boys carrying saffron on gold dishes, a gold mixing bowl that held 150 gallons, a gigantic gold phallus decked out in ribbons and bows, and a display of exotic animals, elephants, camels, peacocks, and even a rhinoceros. A great pavilion housed rows of gold couches for the most distinguished of the guests and there were gold jugs and cups for them to feast from.

Of even greater significance were the building programs of the kings. A precedent had been set by King Mausolus, the satrap of Caria in southwestern Asia Minor (ruled 377–353 B.C.). Although officially subject to the Persian king, he seems to have acted as a free agent in what was a comparatively remote part of the Persian empire and refounded the city of Halicarnassus, birthplace of Herodotus, as his "capital." Before long he began building a hero shrine to himself as city founder. This "Mausoleum" was vast, one of the Seven Wonders of the Ancient World. (The list of these Wonders was first compiled in the second century B.C.) There was a podium some 100 by 120 feet (thirty by thirty-six meters) on which stood an Ionic colonnade and above this was placed a pyramid. The top sculptors of the Greek world, including Praxiteles, were called in to work on its sculptures, the most important of which was a frieze showing dramatic confrontations between Greeks and Amazons. The frenzy, even ferocity, of some of the scenes is in marked contrast to the more restrained styles of classical sculpture although there are precedents from the fifth century in the remote temple to Apollo at Bassae in the Peloponnese. The sculptures at Bassae show similar brutal struggles between men and Amazons (but also between women and centaurs). The region around Bassae was one where mercenaries were recruited and this probably explains why the subject matter of the frieze was so warlike. However, the theme of the frieze is also one in which civilization and good order (represented by the Greeks) are upheld against the forces of disorder. By adopting the same theme, Mausolus was presumably trying to appropriate the mantle of Greek civilization for himself. After his death the Mausoleum became his burial place. It is now vanished although stones from its walls can be seen in the local Crusader castle and some of its sculptures are in the British Museum (as are those from the temple of Bassae).

The Hellenistic rulers followed this model, predominantly through the construction of great cities. The greatest of all was Alexander's foundation, Alexandria. For 650 years it was the showpiece of the eastern Mediterranean, with perhaps half a million inhabitants by the first century B.C. Alexandria was a distinctly Greek city from which most Egyptians were excluded. (One later decree expelled all Egyptians from the city "with the exception of pig-dealers and river boatmen and men who bring down reeds for heating the baths.") It was sustained by the wealth of Egypt (ferried to it along canals which linked it with the Nile) but was also able to exploit its fine position as a double harbor on the coast to become the commercial hub of the Ptolemies' Mediterranean empire. In the first century A.D. a philosopher and rhetorician, Dio, flattered an Alexandrian audience:

> Not only have you a monopoly of the shipping of the entire Mediterranean because of the beauty of your harbours, the magnitude of your fleet, and the abundance and marketing of the products of every land, but also the outside waters that lie beyond are in your grasp, both the Red Sea and the Indian Ocean . . . The result is that the trade, not merely of islands, ports, a few straits and isthmuses, but of practically the whole world is yours. For Alexandria is situated, as it were, at the crossroads of the whole world, of even its most remote nations, as if it were a market serving a single city. . . .
>
> (Translation from A. Bowman, *Egypt after the Pharaohs*)

The most distinctive feature of Alexandria's double harbor was the great lighthouse built on the island of Pharos at the mouth of the harbor to guide sailors along what was a treacherous coast. Four hundred feet (120 meters) high, it was constructed in three stories, the first square, the second octagonal, and the third cylindrical. On its top stood a gigantic statue of Zeus. Its fire was reflected across the sea through mirrors. It was included in some lists of the Seven Wonders of the Ancient World and stood until toppled by an earthquake in A.D. 1375.

Alexandria itself was centered on its rows of palaces, with each ruler outdoing his predecessors in constructing a new one alongside the harbor area so that eventually a quarter of the area of the city was covered in palaces. (The remains of Cleopatra's which collapsed into the harbor after an earthquake have recently been found by divers.) There were two central streets each almost one hundred feet (thirty meters) wide crossing at right angles (the city was laid out in a gridiron pattern by a celebrated architect, Dinocrates of Rhodes) and a mass of *Gymnasia,* theaters, and hippodromes. A great temple complex was constructed in honor of Serapis and embellished in later centuries with colonnades and a library. This library was, however, only a pale imitation of the great royal library of the city, founded by Ptolemy I. Once it was established, collections for its shelves were amassed without any scruple. The official versions of the plays of Aeschylus, Sophocles, and

Euripides were borrowed from Athens and never returned. Rivals were seen off by the simple expedient of forbidding the export of papyrus from Egypt (rolls of papyrus has been used for written texts in the Greek world since at least 500 B.C.). Altogether some five hundred thousand rolls of papyrus may have been accumulated. However, in the first century B.C. large numbers of rolls were lost when fires spread through storehouses when Julius Caesar was fighting in the city. The losses were partially made up when Mark Antony presented his lover Cleopatra with the contents of the royal library at Pergamum, hitherto the second greatest in the Hellenistic world. The library may have been destroyed in a great fire in the palaces in the early 270s.

Next to the library was the museum (literally "shrine of the Muses"). This was essentially a meeting place for scholars who were maintained at public expense and who ran it in common. It enabled the Ptolemies to attract intellectual talent from across the Greek world and it can be assumed, although no official lists survive, that most of the scientists, mathematicians, and medical men who worked in Alexandria were members. Inevitably those who failed to be admitted ridiculed it for the obscurantist interests and petty quarrels of its members (and even for their alcoholism) but it helped make Alexandria the cultural and intellectual capital of the Mediterranean world.

The second capital of the Seleucid empire, after Seleucia, was Antioch (Antiochus was the name of Seleucus' father and of his son). It was founded in 300 by Seleucus I on the left bank of the Orontes in northern Syria. The site overlooked a fertile valley rich in olives and vines. The Orontes valley was an ancient trade route; communications with the rest of the empire and the Mediterranean were good (the first Christian community outside Jerusalem is recorded here) and the city soon flourished. However, little evidence of its greatness survives today within the modern city. Very different is the capital of the Attalids, Pergamum, whose ruins survive largely because the last of the Attalids, Attalus III, bequeathed the city and its surrounding territory intact to the Romans in 133 B.C. Pergamum is a remarkable city, high on an impregnable acropolis overlooking the Caicos Valley in northwestern Asia Minor. The very impregnability of the site had led to its being chosen a holding place for part of the treasure amassed by Alexander and it was this treasure which was used first to surround the site with walls and then to embellish it as a city. Its first successful ruler, Eumenes I (died 261), defeated the Seleucid Antiochus I in 262, and extended its territory but the city's true days of glory began under Attalus I (241–197) who used the city as propaganda for his defeat of the Galatians in the 230s. The Celtic Galatians were recast in the city's sculpture as opposites to the Greeks (in much the same way that Amazons and centaurs were) and as threatening as any other barbarians. One of the most famous survivals of this period, if only in a Roman marble copy of the bronze original, is the *Dying Gaul*, now in the Capitoline Museum in Rome. (*Gaul* is the Roman for *Celt.*) By the reign of Eumenes II (197–160 B.C.) the city had acquired a theater; its celebrated library, second only to that in Alexandria; and gymnasium, all in grandiose style. (The library even had double walls so that damp could not penetrate the books. There is a tradition, disputed by some scholars, that after the Ptolemies banned the export of papyrus from Egypt, the librarians at Pergamum used parchment instead. As the most effective way of storing parchment sheets was to place them one on top of the other as "pages" in a *codex,* Pergamum, arguably, saw the birth of the book.) Each of the rulers also built his own palace and their ruins now run along the eastern edge of the site with, appropriately enough for the city of a Hellenistic ruler, a barracks alongside. The most imposing building, however, was the Great Altar of Zeus, now in Berlin where it was taken by its German excavators in the 1880s. Its frieze was the most ambitious sculptural project in the Greek world since that of the Parthenon 250 years before and shows the Olympian gods battling with the Titans. The Olympians clearly stand for the Attalids, the Titans for the Galatians, who had been finally crushed in 166. This then is a great glorification of military victory, the outcome presented on the frieze as inevitable. The vibrancy and intensity of the struggle reaches such a pitch that the sculptures even spill out onto the steps of the altar.

Pergamum could only be sustained as a city if it had an effective water supply. Remarkably this was brought 29 miles (45 kilometers) from a reservoir that originated more than 1,200 feet (376 meters) above sea level, only 82 feet (25 meters) above the citadel of Pergamum itself. In one of the finest engineering achievements of the ancient world it was brought down through 240,000 linked lead pipes with the pressure maintained so that it was powerful enough to lift the water back up into the city. Here it was stored in a tower and then distributed to the fountains and palaces and even to a sewage system in the city.

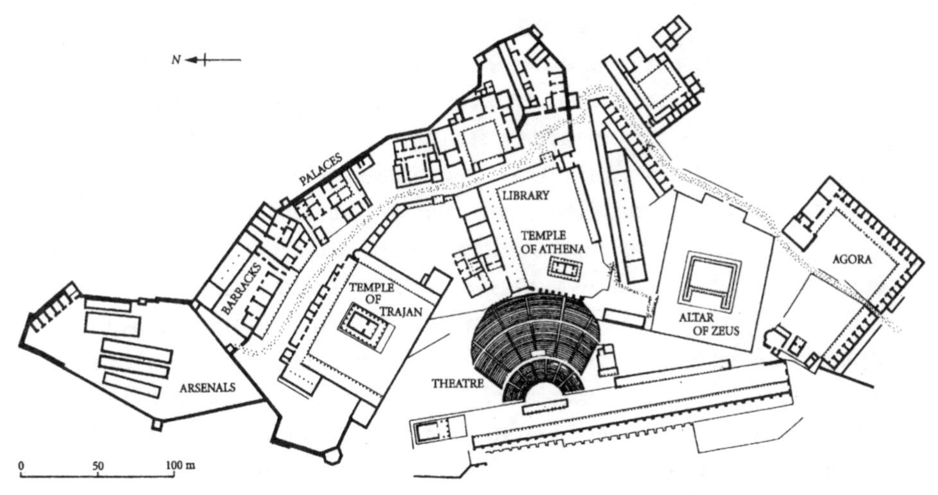

THE ACROPOLIS AT PERGAMUM. In addition to its temples the Acropolis shows the typical concerns of a Hellenistic monarch, for defense (arsenals and barracks) and for culture (a library and theater). Unlike an earlier Greek acropolis, it also holds a royal palace.

These were the showcase cities on a scale and opulence never before equaled in the Greek world. They survived partly on trade and the fertility of their lands, partly on the patronage and accumulated treasures of their rulers. There was a mass of other new Greek cities. Alexander had left a scatter of cities in Bactria. One of them, Alexandria-in-Caucaso in the Hindu Kush was home to three thousand Greco-Macedonian settlers, made up of volunteers or discarded soldiers. They were supported by seven thousand native laborers. Seleucus I and his son Antiochus I were particularly energetic in planting new foundations in their empire, from Bactria in the east to Asia Minor in the west. The modern town of Ai Khanoum, on what is now the Afghanistan border, was the site of a Greek city established in the early third century. Inscriptions from Delphi and fragments of philosophy have been found in the ruins of a Greek-type sanctuary and there was a gymnasium, a library, and even a theater. Its survival, like that of all these remote cities, must have been precarious and it was eventually destroyed by invading tribes in the mid-first century B.C. Some of these cities were fortress towns (it was a a common practice to settle mercenaries as colonists in strategically important areas, a practice also followed by the Romans), others were placed astride important strategic routes, others, along the Persian Gulf, for instance, were designed for trade. In Macedonia a city of enduring importance was Thessalonika, founded by Cassander and named after his wife. Placed on the trade routes between east and west it became the main port of Macedonia, and remains a major city today. Its population was more Greek than Macedonian (although the two were increasingly indistinguishable). At the other end of the Greek world in the city of Ptolemais in Upper Egypt, founded by the first Ptolemy, there was a citizen assembly, a council, magistrates, and *gymnasia,* as in any other Greek city.

The most attractive example of a smaller Hellenistic city is probably Priene in Asia Minor. The original settlement had been destroyed by the Persians after the Ionian revolt (490s) and a new city was founded on the mouth of the river Meander in the fourth century, with the help of patronage by Alexander the Great. It was of good size, with some five thousand inhabitants, but unlike many other cities of Asia Minor, it failed to attract Roman patronage and its contact with the outside world was lost as the River Meander, which it overlooked, silted up. By the time of Augustus (late first century B.C.) it was already isolated, and it was later deserted altogether as malaria spread to the surrounding swamps. The result is that the original plan is left unchanged. Like most Hellenistic cities it was built on a grid plan but any monotony is broken by the hillside on which the city is built. There is a fine theater at the top of the site and below this a gymnasium and then an Agora. This was as much a ceremonial as a commercial center and was marked off by stoas, long colonnades where citizens could meet out of the heat of the sun. The residential streets run crosswise along the contours of the hillside. There is another larger gymnasium at the edge of the site and an impressive temple to Athena (it was this that was built with the help of Alexander). The modern visitor to Priene easily comes to appreciate the scale and atmosphere of a smaller Greek city.

The city-states of mainland Greece were technically independent but they found themselves under continuing Macedonian influence. The Macedonians could never risk losing Greece to rival kings, and Corinth, strategically vital for control of the Peloponnese, was garrisoned for much of the early part of the period. In the 260s Athens led an alliance of Greek city-states, including Sparta, against the Macedonian ruler Antigonus (ruled 277–239 B.C.) but the city was forced into surrender in 261 and the king of Sparta, Areus, killed in the ensuing cleanup operations. Antigonus controlled other cities by imposing pro-Macedonian tyrannies on them. Technical independence was certainly not effective independence.

One response made by cities that found themselves vulnerable in this new world was to form a league. There were two major leagues in Greece, the Aetolian and Achaean. Aetolia was originally an *ethnos* in west central Greece, but in the third century, following a successful defense of Delphi by the Aetolians against the Celts in 279, a federation of states and cities based on Aetolia expanded across central Greece. The league conducted its business through twice yearly assemblies of all men of military age. Between these meetings it was run by a council of several hundred with day-to-day affairs being dealt with by a committee of the council. Besides protecting the shrine of Delphi, the league gave its members some security against Macedonia. Another league, the Achaean, was centred on the northern Peloponnese. Its origins also lay in its distrust of Macedonia but by 225 B.C. its neighbor Sparta seemed a greater threat and the Achaeans reversed their foreign policy and allied themselves with the Macedonians. Both leagues became hopelessly embroiled with the Romans and were eventually crushed by them.

There were a few cities that managed to maintain a true independence, the most prominent being the island of Rhodes. Its important position on the trade routes of the eastern Mediterranean made it an obvious target for Alexander's successors and in 305–4 the city had to fight off a year-long siege by Antigonus' son Demetrius. Triumphant, the city then sold off Demetrius' siege equipment and out of the proceeds constructed a great statue of the local god Helios at the entrance to its harbor. This *Colossus of Rhodes* was another of the Seven Wonders of the Ancient World. By the third century Rhodes' prosperity was assured and it expanded its territory onto the Asian mainland. It survived as an independent Greek state until out-maneuvered by Rome in the 160s B.C.

Those Greek cities within the Hellenistic states had to negotiate their status with their new rulers but this was not difficult so long as the city was prepared to remain loyal. The kings welcomed the support of the more remote cities (and were prepared to buy it, see above) and astute cities themselves adapted to the new situation. They grasped the possibilities of patronage from energetic and wealthy kings who needed their support and who could provide them with effective help.

The sophisticated citizens of Athens knew just how to flatter Demetrius, the son of Antigonus the One-Eyed, presenting him as a divine figure who might actually be able to get things done: "O son of the most mighty god Poseidon and of Aphrodite, hail. For other gods are either far away or have not ears, nor do not exist nor heed us at all but thee we can see in very presence, not in word and not in stone, but in truth, and so we pray to thee" (Translation: F. Walbank). Athens was particularly successful in attracting patronage. The Attalids had adopted Athena as their patron goddess and where better than the city to show themselves off as sophisticated cultural patrons? In the second century B.C. Attalus II of Pergamum donated a resplendent stoa that graced the edge of the Agora. (Such patronage has proved a continuing tradition: the stoa was rebuilt with Rockefeller money in the 1950s A.D.) One of the city-states most successful in gaining outside support was Rhodes. When an earthquake hit the city in 227 the city mounted an effective campaign for disaster relief that left contributors feeling that they were privileged in being allowed to help.

The effects of upheaval from war and unrest and the loss of traditional roles within the city combined with expanded opportunities in the new kingdoms to make this an age of migration. There were, of course, many refugees but Greeks also traveled as traders, mercenaries, pilgrims to shrines and oracles, scholars, and ambassadors. In Egypt migrants from over two hundred cities, some as far north as the Black Sea, were recorded. They were lured by the opportunities of a rich land. "The Egyptians," said one enthusiast, "have anything that exists or is made anywhere in the world, wealth, sports, power, excellent climate, fame, sights, philosophers, gold, young men, a shrine of the sibling gods, an enlightened king, the Museum—everything that one might desire." The continual movements of Greeks across this expanded world saw the breakdown of local dialects so that eventually a common and standard Greek, known as *koine,* became established.

Many people now came into contact with Greeks for the first time. Most experienced them simply as rulers whose culture was exclusive and whose administrations excluded outsiders. (There is some dispute among scholars as to how many native administrators were actually employed in the Hellenistic kingdoms but in most cases administration appears to have been Greek speaking and only open to those who were Greek or who were prepared to learn it. In Egypt there were certainly natives at village level who mastered a smattering of Greek and who were able to carry out basic administrative functions.)

The variety of possible relationships between Greeks and others was wide, from assimilation to complete rejection. In many cases the interaction of Greeks with non-Greeks produced a cautious acceptance of Greek culture. In general, however, the archaeological evidence for assimilation is very difficult to interpret and it is seldom clear whether local cultures adopted Greek culture because it was attractive, because they were told to, or because it provided an avenue for social and political advancement. Different cultures in different contexts would have decided differently. In the Seleucid empire, for instance, at Uruk there is evidence of the local elites possibly intermarrying with local Greeks and adopting Greek names alongside their own. The basic structure of local society remained intact and the adoptions seem to be related to local elites using Greek customs as a means of maintaining their own status. Outside the Greek cities in Egypt, poorer Greeks worked alongside Egyptian peasants and intermarried with them. Children of the marriages were given a mixture of Greek and Egyptian names. However, the overall picture remains of a dominant culture that even if it did not destroy the cultures which they ruled exploited them and was prepared to make relatively few concessions. "I am a barbarian and do not know how to behave like a Greek," moans one camel driver in an Egyptian papyrus.

The best documented example of a culture assimilating itself within the Greek world is that of the Jews. The Jews had been tolerated by the Persians but in the period immediately after Alexander's death the Ptolemies controlled Palestine and their intrusive bureaucracy led to a diaspora of Jews. The largest Jewish community was in Alexandria but the Seleucids were also tolerant and Jewish communities were to be found throughout their western territories. Although the Jews maintained their own communities these gradually became Hellenised and the Torah (the instruction or law of Judaism) and the Hebrew Bible were translated into Greek (the last known in its new version as the Septuagint). One of these Hellenised Jews, who was also, for reasons unknown, a Roman citizen, was a tent maker from Tarsus by the name of Paul. He was to prove one of the most influential figures of the ancient world (see Chapter Twenty).

Some Jews were prepared to go further. In Jerusalem at the time of

Antiochus IV, a group of Jews who claimed that their life had been one of disaster since they had segregated themselves from the Greeks, petitioned the king to be allowed to repudiate their Jewish way of life, build a sports stadium, and intermarry with Greeks. Somehow they removed the marks of their circumcision, presumably so they could take part in games without embarrassment. This was an extreme example of a process of assimilation and it led to a backlash in which traditional Judaism reasserted itself. (See page 371.)

Meanwhile, outsiders to the Greek world could adopt Greek models of art and architecture as Mausolus had done. The kings of the Phoenician city of Sidon, for example, were buried in Greek-style sarcophagi. (The word *sarcophagus*, "flesh eater," comes from the stone of Assos in Asia Minor that was used for coffins. It has a caustic quality that actually destroys the flesh of the dead.) The most celebrated of these, the Alexander sarcophagus of c. 310 B.C., now in the Archaeological Museum in Istanbul, shows in its well-preserved frieze, Alexander at peace, hunting, and at war, at the battle of Issus.

Many traditional institutions of the Greek world survived and continued to be patronized in the Hellenistic world. The Olympian gods remained influential. In Alexandria temples were built to Zeus, Dionysus, and Aphrodite and an enormous temple at Apollo's oracle at Didyma (in Asia Minor, close to Miletus to which it was connected by a ceremonial route) was put in hand. (It was such an ambitious project that six hundred years later, when the Christians moved in to close it down, it was still unfinished.) The round of games went on, old shrines continued to be visited. There were, however, important shifts in perspectives and tastes. The flow of new wealth that entered the Greek world from the East must have threatened traditional economies but also allowed entrepreneurs to grow rich. For the first time in the Greek world there is evidence of a substantial middle class. (Its emergence forced the older families to become more exclusive. In Athens, for instance, the *Gymnasia*, originally simply exercise grounds, became clubs with libraries, lecture halls, and later, baths, attached. Membership was reserved for those from landed families.) The members of this new class live in opulent homes that are decorated with wall paintings, landscapes being a special favorite. The floors are laid with mosaics and the rooms are furnished with a mass of smaller decorative objects.

Women of this class seem to have been better respected. Diadems, tiaras, earrings, necklaces survive as symbols of their new status and marriage contracts of the period allow them to divorce their husbands if these bring other women into the home. There is a new emphasis on sexual relationships that both partners might enjoy. Women are shown being made love to in private bedrooms, no longer simply as the victims of the humiliating public orgies portrayed on so many fifth-century pots. Some women become patrons in their own right, even magistrates, and surviving statues show them dressed much more ornately than before.

The possibility that tenderness can now be shown toward women is reflected in the poetry of the age. Here one Posidippus of Macedonia (born c. 310 B.C.) speaks of the long-dead Doricha. (Doricha was a courtesan whom Sappho's brother Charaxus fell in love with when visiting the Greek trading post of Naucratis on the Nile):

So now the very bones of you are gone
Where they were dust and ashes long ago;
And there was the last ribbon you tied on
To bind your hair, and that is dust also;
And somewhere there is dust that was of old
A soft and scented garment that you wore—
The same that once till dawn did closely fold
You in with fair Charaxus, fair no more.
But Sappho, and the white leaves of her song,
Will make your name a word for all to learn,
And all to love thereafter, even while
It's but a name; and this will be as long
As there are distant ships that will return
Again to Naucratis and to the Nile.

(Translation:
Edwin Arlington Robinson, 1915)

Mingling with traditional beliefs were new ones, as befitted an age of anxiety and social change. The Egyptian gods proved attractive to many (see Chapter Twenty) and ruler cults flourished, but perhaps the most successful goddess was Tyche, Fortune.

Tyche was a daughter of Zeus and is known as early as the eighth century. She stood for both good and bad fortune, although in many sources her "good" side predominates. She now became a symbol of a world where Fate often seemed to rule capriciously. Even cities adopted her as a patroness. (Antioch is a good example.) She was an invisible force (though always personified as a woman draped in voluminous robes) but it was never clear whether she represented some underlying power of providence with power to act for good or ill, or was no more than a symbol of the uncertainty of life. The historian Polybuis, faced with having to explain the rise of Rome, struggled to balance the relative contributions of Tyche and the actions of man.

There were other new ideas thrown up by the times. For Plato and Aristotle, writing earlier in the fourth century, the perfect society was a city and they could not envisage human society happily organized in any other way. The turmoil of the Hellenistic period, with its collapse of traditional city politics, forstered new philosophies which rejected the *polis* as the focus for political and social life. These philosophies had a forerunner in the Cynics who argued that one should turn one's back on the world, the city, the family, and all forms of wealth and social ambition and live in a state of nature. (The word *cynic* meant "doglike" as if a cynic was to live like an animal.) Their originator Diogenes (c. 415 to late 320s B.C.) reduced his possessions to a cloak, a stick, and a purse for holding his money and set out to shock in his behavior. He even defecated in public. When, according to legend, Alexander met him in Greece and asked if he needed anything, Diogenes' request was simply that Alexander should move out of the way of the sun.

Another important movement was skepticism, traditionally thought to have been founded by Pyrrhon of Elis (c. 365–275 B.C.) The Skeptics doubted whether knowledge of any sort was possible. They used Socratic methods to explore the fallacies in any assertion. Although skepticism was ultimately a frustrating philosophical approach it did encourage other schools to define their understanding of what was meant by "knowledge" more clearly. A much more sophisticated attempt at creating a philosophy that offered an alternative to the city was pioneered by Epicurus (341–270 B.C.) Epicurus' own life had been unsettled. The son of a schoolmaster in an Athenian settlement in Samos, his family had been expelled by Macedonians in 322 and he had wandered from city to city along the coast of Asia Minor before arriving in Athens in 306 B.C. He purchased a house with a garden and became the leader of a sect dedicated to propagating his views by living them out in "the Garden."

Epicurus had read widely in earlier philosophy and he followed the Atomists in believing that the world was made up of an infinite number of atoms which were constantly reforming themselves. He developed his own theory that "free" atoms fell toward the ground but occasionally, for no clear reason, swerved, collided with other atoms, and thus formed new matter. The random nature of the collisions ensured that life was never predictable. Fundamental to Epicurus' philosophy was that human life ended at death, the soul dying with the body. It is interesting that he did believe there were gods, made like all other matter, from atoms. Their lives were harmonious and could be taken as models for human behavior but they had no direct influence on the world. One of Epicurus' most passionate beliefs was that no one should live in fear of the gods.

If one simply existed as a set of atoms what was the purpose of life? For Epicurus, who had himself known life as a refugee and who suffered pain from disease, it was *ataraxia,* peacefulness. To achieve this, one should search for pleasure. By pleasure Epicurus did not mean sensual enjoyment, sexual adventuring, or feasting but primarily an absence of pain. To achieve this one should fulfill one's basic needs for food and warmth but without excess and also enjoy any other activity which did not bring mental disturbance. The older Greek values, such as *arete,* virtue, or *dike,* justice, need not be rejected as such but they should not be searched for simply as a matter of duty if the process brought anxiety or guilt. One could never escape the effects of fate but one should cultivate oneself to be so self-sufficient that one could be untroubled by it. Within the fourth century city tensions were so great that, in effect, this meant withdrawing into private life and Epicurus openly advocated the rejection of political activity. Instead, he stressed the importance of friendships and these became almost ritualized in "the Garden" with the celebration of birthdays, the writing of elaborate poems on relationships, and the sharing of endearments. Women and even slaves could participate intellectually in the group although it appears that one of the marks of male friendship was to share one's women partners. In short, personal intimacy and support in fellowship within a withdrawn community replaced the more competitive public life of the city.

Epicureans were, of course, always vulnerable to those who felt they had rejected traditional values; to those who believed they were simply opting out of public responsibilities; and, in later centuries, to Christians who anathematized their religious views. Inevitably, Epicureans tended to be men of private wealth who could afford to withdraw from the world of work and so there was an added charge of elitism. (In this they were forerunners of the Bloomsbury group, who attracted many of the same criticisms.) Nevertheless, Epicureanism appealed to many and spread to other major cities including Rome where the poet Lucretius (first century B.C.) gave one of the fullest accounts of the philosophy in his *On the Nature of Things*. Epicureanism's continuing attraction was seen recently in Italy where a modern translation of Epicurus' works sold a million copies.

Epicureanism needs to be contrasted with Stoicism. Stoicism was founded by Zeno, a Hellenized Phoenician from Cyprus who began life as a trader in the Levant before fulfilling a childhood ambition to come to Athens and be a philosopher. By the year 300 B.C., and now in his early thirties, he had begun to make a name for himself—his philosophy took its name from the Painted Stoa where he taught. Zeno's teachings were written up in a relatively coherent form by a follower, Chrysippes of Soli, but there were always variants and developments from the original ideas and Stoicism developed into a complex philosophical movement that proved attractive to Romans and Christians.

Just as Epicureanism was rooted in a physical conception of the world so was Stoicism. However, the essence of Stoicism was that the *cosmos* was a material unity in which the different elements of which it was made (fire, air, water, and earth) were assimilated with each other in the same way that two liquids could mingle with no distinction between them. Every material part of the universe had its links with and influences on the other. (Astrology, which rests on the assumption that the passage of the stars influence human behavior, was one element of Stoic belief.) Moreover this material was imbued with an active force which totally permeated it. Some called this Zeus; some *pneuma* (breath of a vital spirit); others *logos,* the force of reason, to reflect the Stoic belief that the world did not progress randomly but according to a defined order. In fact Stoics believed that it went through an infinite number of cycles, each one ending in dissolution by fire and then rebirth.

Human beings had their special place within the Stoic *cosmos* as they were the only beings capable of reason and thus of understanding the way the *cosmos* was evolving. In fact, Stoics believed that learning to live within the evolving *cosmos* without stress offered the only chance of virtue, *arete*. In order to work with the *cosmos* rather than against it one needed to show courage, cultivate wisdom, follow a sober lifestyle, and avoid emotional extremes. While it was acceptable to live a life that sought wealth, good health, and a release from pain, these could never be ends in themselves. Equally, if the unfolding of the *cosmos* brought misfortune in its wake the individual had to confront and accept this. There was no intrinsic virtue in opting out of life or retreating, like Epicurus into "a Garden." Zeno actually encouraged his followers to go into the Hellenistic courts. Stoics were found as advisers to the Macedonian kings and in Hellenistic Sparta.

At one level Stoicism is a forbidding creed and one can understand the point made by the Roman statesman and orator Cicero that Stoicism should be taken in sips rather than in gulps. There seems little scope for free will, since the parameters of human behavior are ultimately determined by uncontrollable forces. (How far free will could exist was a major issue in Stoic discussions.) In the last resort Stoics could only advocate endurance and an acquiescence in the order of things and, as such, Stoicism was socially conservative. Although in theory Stoics believed in the common brotherhood of all men, they never challenged the concept of slavery. However, Stoicism served its purpose in providing moral backbone at times of crisis. In Roman times it steadied those confronted by tyrannical emperors or invaders of the empire. The *Meditations* of the emperor Marcus Aurelius (written between A.D. 172 and 180), although drawing on other philosophies than Stoicism, showed the Stoic at its best, as Marcus Aurelius resolutely carried out his duty of defending his empire in the face of appalling odds.

These philosophies reflected the continuing hunger in the Greek mind for exploring life to the depths but they took root, like most ideas do, because they fit the times. They offered a sense of purpose and alternative possibilities of living in an unsettled age. Philosophical writings, however, formed only one part of the mass of literature produced in this fertile age. The vast majority of it has been lost and it is only recently that the scattered fragments, much of it poetry, that have survived have been collected. The loss is all the more serious as Hellenistic literature was an important influence on the Romans. Early

Roman theater, for instance, was dependent on the playwrights of the late fourth century, in particular the Athenian Menander (active 321–289 B.C.). Menander wrote some one hundred plays but only one survives in full (it was found on an Egyptian papyrus) and six in part. This is "New Comedy," to distinguish it from the "Old Comedy" of the fifth century, and its setting, while still in Athens, is domestic. The main theme is frustrated love and the plots of the plays are in Peter Green's words "complicated and improbable, littered with long-lost foundlings, twists of mistaken identity, and supposed courtesans who turn out to be virtuous middle-class virgins, more often than not heiresses into the bargain." Slaves are always more intelligent than their masters; girls raped and made pregnant in the turmoil of festivals find that their rapist is, in fact, the man they wanted to marry all along; foundlings turned out to be heirs. This is a rich mixture, highly successful in the Greek and Roman world and much imitated afterward. The plays of Moliere, Sheridan, the Venetian Carlo Goldoni, Oscar Wilde, and George Bernard Shaw draw on the tradition.

The Hellenistic poets were deeply conscious of the past and were ready to draw on it for inspiration. Apollonius Rhodius, for instance, took Homer for his model in compiling a major epic poem, the *Argonautica*, a reworking of the myth of Jason, his followers the Argonauts, and the quest for the Golden Fleece. It is, like the *Odyssey*, in the tradition of the herioc adventure as a result of which the hero, here Jason, proves himself worthy of his love, Medea, who supports him in overcoming the challenges that confront him. This is, however, a world where the impact of Euripides (himself author of a major play on this myth, *Medea*) is powerful. Women's feelings can now be expressed freely. Here is Medea overcome by adolescent passion:

Like a flame that shaft burned under
Her maiden heart: endless bright sidelong glances
She darted at Jason, her breath fetched quick and laboured
In her heaving breast, all else was forgotten, her spirit
Melted in that sweet ecstasy.

So Love the destroyer
Blazed in a coil round her heart, her mind's keen anguish
Now flushed her soft cheeks, now drained them of all colour.

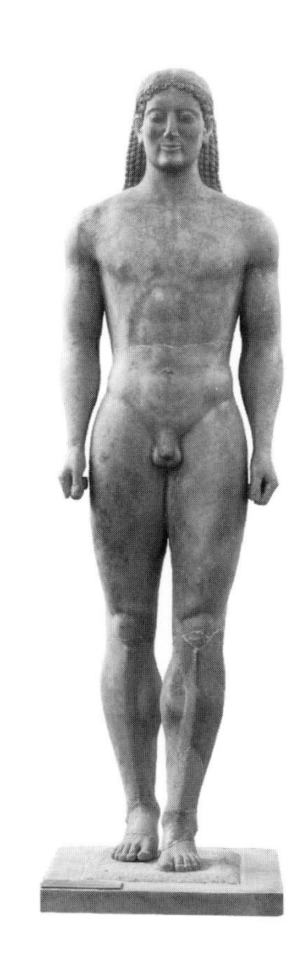

The Egyptian statue with its left foot forward (*far left*) provides an archetype for Greek sculptors, while the influence of the east can be seen in the Lady of Auxerre, probably from Crete, of about 640 BC (*center left*). The *kouros* (this one from Anavissos in Crete) shows the direct influence of Egypt (*left*). The refusal of the Greeks to be constrained by the east can be seen in the Calf Bearer (an Egyptian form developed with real tenderness) from the Athenian Acropolis *c*. 560 (*below left*). By 480 the Greeks have broken through eastern constraints altogether, as in the celebrated Critian boy (*below center*). In 350 the sculptor Praxiteles broke through another convention when he portrayed the goddess Aphrodite in the nude (a Roman copy is shown below, *right*).

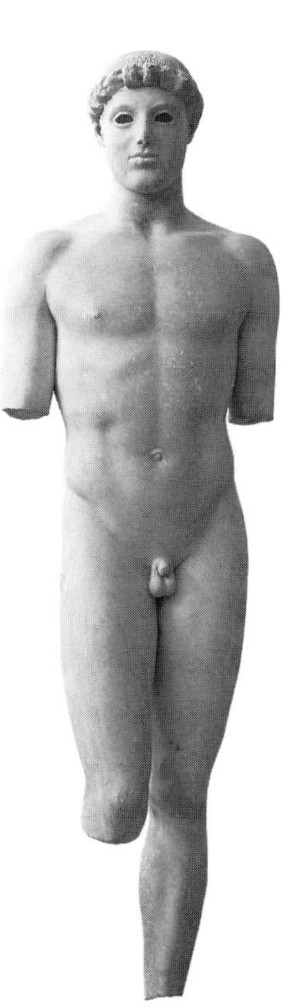

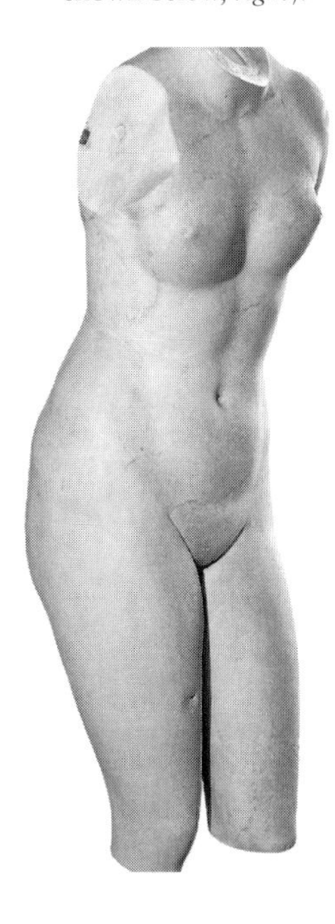

As with pottery, the Greeks found it difficult to portray narrative in sculpture. The limited space of a pediment presents a real challenge. In the temple of Artemis at Corfu (after 600 BC), Medusa is shown alongside her children even though they were born only after her head was cut off by Perseus (*above*). Another approach was to use depth to create a narrative of overlapping figures. A fine example, from about 525 BC, is the north frieze from the Siphnian treasury at Delphi (*below*).

Metopes could also be used to create a series of scenes. At the temple of Zeus at Olympia (*c.* 460 BC) the Labours of Heracles are shown consecutively (*above*). Heracles holds the world with the assistance of his protecting goddess Athena, while Atlas, relieved of the burden, brings back the sacred apples of the Hesperides.

The Parthenon frieze marks the culmination of the use of narrative in temple sculpture as well as being the supreme example of Greek sculpture. Here is the famous scene from the east frieze (*above*) which may show the sacrifice of king Erechtheus' daughters (see the Afterword to Chapter Eleven). Meanwhile a mass of cavalry make their way along the north frieze (*left*).

The girl fixing her sandal from the exquisite temple of Athena Nike on the Acropolis (*c.* 420 BC) is one of the most sensual creations in all Greek art (*left*).

Scenes from daily life

(*left*) A young helmet-maker perfects one of his creations (red-figure cup from *c*. 480 BC).

(*right*) The curves of this vase (of about 450 BC) are used to heighten the emotional effect of this baby being returned to its mother by an attendant.

(*below*) An athlete prepares himself for a javelin throw (red-figure cup of *c*. 470 BC)

(*right center*) A priest and his servant light the sacrificial fire on an altar (red-figure cup, late fifth century BC).

(*left*) A typical Athenian grave *stele* of the late fifth century. It shows Hegeso, wife of Proxenus, ensconced in comfort (note the footstool) and being waited o[n] by a slave.

(*bottom right*) A votive relief from the Piraeus, which shows actors (carrying their masks) making offerings to Dionysus, the god of theater (*c*. 400 BC

Hellenistic sculpture

(*left*) The vigour and inventiveness of Hellenistic sculpture can be seen in this erotic struggle between a satyr and, as the viewer would discover as he walked around the pair, a hermaphrodite.

(*below left*) Scenes from sport were common in Hellenistic art, and few pieces are finer than this portrayal of a jockey astride his galloping horse. The boy, with fragments of the horse, was found in a shipwreck.

(*above right*) The charm of this young girl is enhanced by the relatively large size of the stool, which leaves her dangling above the ground.

(*below right*) By the second century AD individual deities were being given extended powers and interests by worshippers, so that universal goddesses such as Isis or Aphrodite emerge. The panels on Aphrodite's body, in this cult statue from Aphrodisias, show her "interest" in the sun and the moon, animals, sea deities, and the underworld.

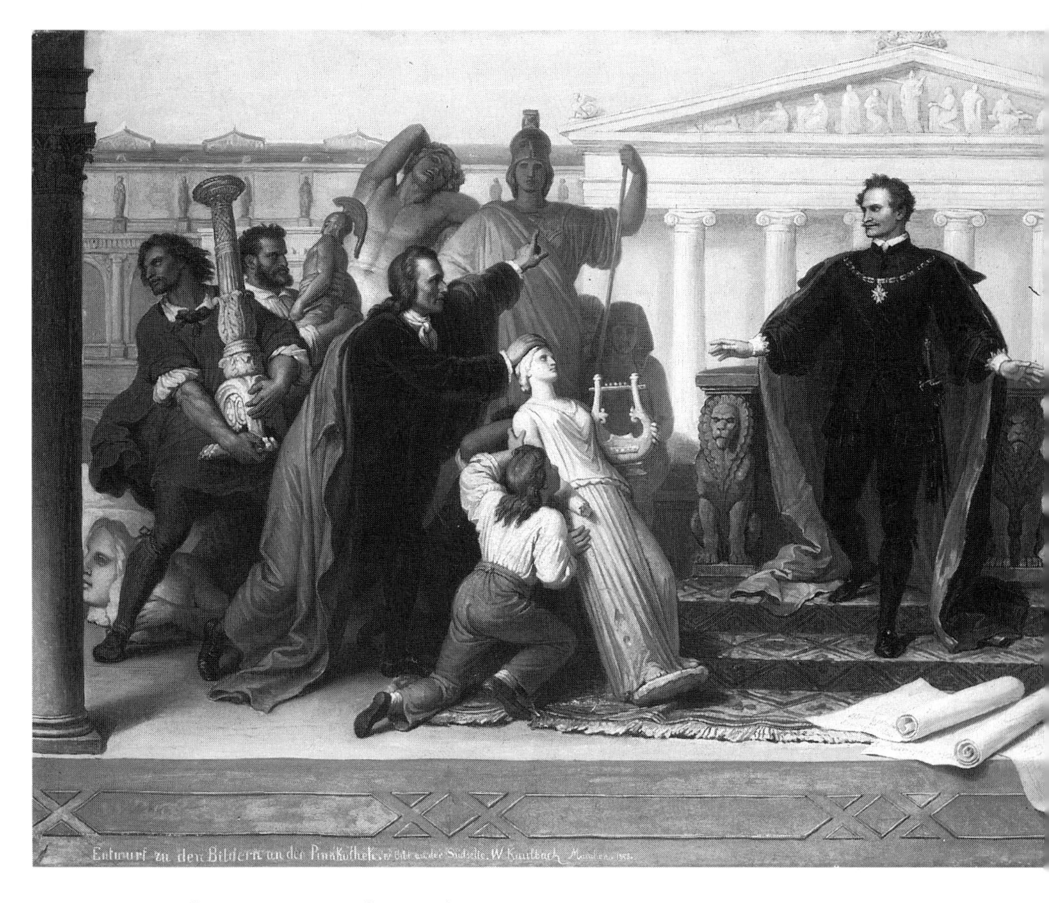

The Appropriation of Greece for Europe

This detail of a fresco of 1848 shows Ludwig I (king of Bavaria 1825–48), one of the major collectors of Greek art, standing in front of the galleries he built, in Greek style, for his art collections. A mass of statuary, torn from its original context, is brought to him. Ludwig's attitude was typical of the nineteenth century, when European rulers, nations and individual collectors believed they had a right to appropriate Greece's heritage for themselves. As a result, many Greek monuments, including the Parthenon and the Great Altar to Zeus at Pergamum, were plundered for their sculpture, which was then rehoused in the museums of northern Europe. These appropriations not only damaged the original buildings but they isolated the sculptures from their original context. The larger finds of more recent excavations are now kept on site so that an appreciation of a city or shrine and its buildings as a whole can be made. The city of Aphrodisias in Turkey is a good example of a site where this will be done.

Quick beat the heart on her breast, as a shaft of sunlight
Will dance on the house wall when flung up from water
New-poured into cauldron or pail: hither and thither
The circling ripples send it darting, a frisson
Of brightness—just so her virgin heart now beat a
Tattoo on her ribs, here eyes shed tears of pity, constant
Anguish ran smouldering through her flesh, hotwired her finespun
Nerve ends, needles in to the skull's base, the deep spinal
Cord where pain pierces sharpest when the unresting
passions inject their agony into the senses.

(Translation: Peter Green)

(As the translator points out, the last lines show that this is an age now familiar with medical symptoms; see Chapter Eighteen.)

Apollonius had been born in Alexandria but his first version of *Argonautica* had been greeted with such ridicule that he left the city for Rhodes where he reworked the epic (hence the addition "Rhodius" to his name). Insofar as one of the themes of the work is the coming of Greek culture to remote areas (the Argonauts explore the Black Sea in their quest) Apollonius may have been indirectly praising the Ptolemies who similarly hoped to spread Greek culture to their territories. If so, his efforts paid off. While he was living in Rhodes he had gained an international reputation as poet and scholar and on his return home in the 260s he was made chief librarian of the Royal Library. His appointment, however, deeply offended another leading member of the library who had been busy compiling the catalogue (in some 120 volumes) and who had hoped for the job himself. This was Callimachus (active from the 280s to 240s B.C.), a native of Cyrene.

Callimachus has been seen as the leading Hellenistic poet. Intellectual, self-absorbed, obsessed with the maintenance of standards, and naturally antogonistic to the more showy, or vulgar, aspects of Hellenistic society and its culture, he has been compared to T. S. Eliot or Ezra Pound. He looked to the lost world of classical Greece and to himself as an exile from it both in time and place. (He even paraded his homosexuality as a badge of his allegiances to an earlier age.) Despite his determination to write a limited collection of restrained, erudite gems of literature, he ended up producing an amazing array of work (800 rolls of papyrus in all, it was said). Almost all is lost but hints of his personality and attitudes come through in what remains. He certainly would have found modern television soap operas hard to take:

I despise neo-epic sagas: I cannot
Welcome trends which drag the populace
This way and that. Peripatetic sex-partners
Turn me off: I do not drink from the mains,
Can't stomach anything public.
(Translation: Peter Jay)

His ideal was the short piece, the epigram, or poetry for a court wedding, full of scholarly allusions. Yet he was not without feeling. Is there any better evocation of personal friendship than Callimachus' lament for his dead friend Heraclitus? It is the nineteenth-century translation by William Cory which has lasted:

They told me, Heraclitus, they told me you were dead,
They brought me bitter news to hear and bitter tears to shed.
I wept as I remembered how often you and I
Had tired the sun with talking and sent him down the sky.

And now that thou are lying, my dear old Carian guest,
A handful of grey ashes, long, long ago at rest,
Still are thy pleasant voices, thy nightingales awake;
For death he taketh all away, but them he cannot take.

Callimachus had a major influence on Roman poets, including Ovid, Catullus, and Propertius, and through them into later European literature. Another major influence on later European literature was the poet Theocritus (active during the first half of the third century B.C.). Theocritus was a native of Sicily although he appears, too, to have lived in southern Italy and then traveled to Alexandria and the island of Cos. Again, only a small proportion of his works survive but among these are the *Idylls*, some of which draw on the shepherd songs of Italy. These inaugurate pastoral poetry, a genre adopted by the Roman poet Virgil in his *Eclogues*, and then passed on into the European tradition. In the first *Idyll* Theocritus tells the story of Daphnis, a herdsman who dies of love for a nymph who has betrayed him. It is a lament which echoes through later European literature (for instance, in Milton's *Lycidas*). In another of the *Idylls*, the poet describes lounging in the countryside with three friends. (Pastoral poets always seem to have an urban background and it is hard to imagine them actually doing any agricultural work.) A nineteenth-century translation enhances its flavor:

there we lay
Half-buried in a couch of fragrant reed
And fresh-cut vine leaves, who so glad as we?
A wealth of elm and poplar shook overhead;
Hard by, a sacred spring flowed gurgling on
From the Nymph's grot, and in the sombre boughs
The sweet cicada chirped laboriously.
Hid in the thick thorn bushes far away
The treefrog's note was heard; the crested lark
Sang with the goldfinch; turtle made their moan,
And o'er the fountain hung the gilded bee.
All of our summer smacked, of autumn all;
Pears at our feet, and apples at our side
Rolled in luxuriance; branches on the ground
Sprawled, overweighed with damsons; while we brushed
From the cask's head the crust of four long years.
(Translation: Charles Stuart Calverley, 1883)

Although it is difficult to make the link between poetry and art, the Hellenistic age was the first in which landscape became a subject for painting. Virtually all the painting of the period has disappeared and one has to travel to Rome to find an example from a surviving house wall on the Esquiline Hill. It is a copy of a Greek original (accompanying words are in Greek) and shows a mythological scene, an episode from Odysseus' journey home to Ithaca. What is particularly interesting is that the landscape dominates the figures. It is an approach that also endures into the European tradition. The French painters Poussin and Lorrain use the same technique, their classical figures half lost in a larger landscape.

The spirit of the age can also be seen in its sculpture. For the first time portraits from life become common. The kings used them for propaganda purposes but benefactors of cities, prominent statesmen (Athens provided a particularly fine statue of Demosthenes in about 280 B.C.), and, above all, philosophers were commemorated with statues that were crowded in among the older buildings of city sanctuaries or in the Agora. So Socrates with his pug nose, and heads of Epicurus, Zeno, and Chrysippes; these last created during their lifetimes or shortly afterward, survive. They served as moral exemplars. A decree on the base of a statue to Zeno praised "his teaching of virtue and temperance to the young . . . for which his life served as a perfectly consistent pattern."

Yet beyond these more formal portraits, there was a new emphasis on luxuriance. It is symbolized, perhaps, by a new decorative column, the Corinthian (the first example of which was actually to be found in the late fifth-century temple at Bassae). The top of the Corinthian column is rich in acanthus leaves that gradually push aside the volutes of the Ionic order from which it develops. Now sculptors felt free enough to mix styles and themes and there is a mass of ornate and even grotesque work. The companions of Dionysus, nymphs and satyrs, had already provided models for less restrained sculpture and now the approach spreads so that a whole range of characters can be portrayed, old women, fishermen, athletes actually performing (rather than standing aloof in glory after the contest). A boy jockey is caught spread-eagled on his horse, a boxer resting his gloves still attached to his hands. There is a preoccupation with the personal, a boy takes a thorn from his foot, an adolescent girl sits on a stool modestly gazing at the ground. Some set pieces, such as the famous Laocoön found in Rome in 1506 and dating from 200 B.C. (Laocoön was a Trojan priest who was destroyed with his two sons by snakes for his impiety) show the almost baroque luxuriance of the period. The agonized and desperate figures are contorted by their struggle with the enveloping snakes. Then there is a fascination with mixed sexuality in the hermaphrodite (literally the result of a union between the messenger god Hermes and Aphrodite). The viewer, coming across what appears to be the statue of a naked woman lying luxuriantly on a cloth, goes around to the other side and finds that "she" has an erect penis. While the art of the Hellenistic period had traditionally been deplored for its vulgarity, there is no doubting its vibrancy, inventiveness, and sheer technical skill.

Within this vibrant world there were two developments which were of essential importance for later history. The first was the survival of traditional (i.e., non-Hellenized) Judaism. As mentioned above, Antiochus IV had supported a group of Jews in Jerusalem who wished to adopt Greek ways. As they paraded their nakedness in local games and undermined Jewish practices the more traditional Jews in the city were outraged. There were revolts which were harshly put down by Antiochus who stationed a garrison in the city and most provocatively of all, imposed a Greek cult on the temple. However, his successor Antiochus V (whose reign began in 164) realized that the policy was counterproductive and demanded that the temple be restored and that the "Jews should regulate their lives according to their ancestral customs." It was too late. A prominent family, the Maccabees, had already taken to the hills around Jerusalem and continued to hold out both against Hellinizing Jews and Seleucid armies. The Maccabees founded their own dynasty and as Seleucid power declined were able to declare full independence in 142 B.C. The legacy of the survival of an intact traditional Judaism based on Jerusalem is an immense one, still coloring world politics in the 1990s.

The second development was the rising power of Rome. The absorption of the Greek world into Roman rule and the impact "*Graecia capta*," Greece in captivity, had on the Romans themselves is the theme of Chapter Nineteen. Before turning to them, however, the most significant of the intellectual achievements of the Hellenistic age, developments in mathematics, science, and medicine, have still to be explored.

18

Mathematics, Science, and Medicine

One of the most remarkable landscapes of the Hellenistic period is the Nile mosaic discovered in the complex of the sanctuary of Fortune Primigenia (in Palestrina, modern Praeneste) in Italy. The original was Alexandrian, probably a commission by the Ptolemies, and it shows a panorama of the Nile in flood. At the top of the picture an expedition of hunters explores the more remote parts of the river and hunts down exotic animals. Then, downriver, there is a representation of pharaonic Egypt, complete with an Egyptian temple. In the foreground, Ptolemaic Egypt has been reached. Greeks, some of them soldiers, are shown in front of the facade of a Greek temple. Doubtless the mosaic had a propaganda purpose—showing off the munificence of the Ptolemies and the fruits of their kingdom—but it illustrates too the curiosity the Hellenistic Greeks had in the natural world. The Nile mosaic shows that an interest in zoology, topography, and botany was an important feature of Greek cultural life.

It was one aspect of the relentless curiosity of an age that also drove men to travel to the farthest reaches of the earth. Alexander had provided the inspiration. Now explorers penetrated as far east as the Ganges and as far south in Africa as modern Somaliland (elephants, an important component of the Ptolemaic armies, were to be found there). A sea captain from Massilia (modern Marseilles), Pytheas, reached Britain and appears to have circumnavigated the island in about 320 B.C. If his measurement of the length of the night is reliable he must have reached a latitude of about sixty-five degrees. One of Aristotle's pupils, Dicaearchus from Messena, is believed to have created a world map about 300 B.C. with a line of latitude marked across from Gibraltar to the Himalayas. An Alexandrian, Eratosthenes, also compiled a map of the world in the late third century, dividing it clearly by lines both of latitude and longitude. His most ambitious project was to measure the circumference of the earth through noting the relative size of a shadow thrown at two points, Alexandria and Syene (near modern Aswan in southern Egypt). He arrived at the figure of 252,000 stades. It depends what quantity is given to a stade (it varied from place to place) but on one measurement (a stade was more than 500 feet [157.5 meters]) he arrived at roughly 200 miles (320 kilometers) from the true figure.

Eratosthenes' calculation, which spanned three disciplines, geometry, geography, and astronomy, was only one among many scientific achievements of the age. The same curiosity can be seen in medicine. From earliest times societies have been preoccupied with finding cures for disease. Like most ancient (and some modern) societies the Greeks searched for help from herbs, incantations, the wearing of charms, and the gods through oracles. In Aristophanes' the *Wasps* a character, Procleon, becomes so obsessed with serving on a jury that he is considered mad. The treatments tried include a ritual purification, a visit to the priests of Dionysus in the hope of working him up into such a frenzy that the madness will be cured, and attendance at the temple of Asclepius on the neighboring island of Aegina. By the fifth century educated Greeks had begun to realize the shortcomings of such approaches. Thucydides records the helplessness of the plague sufferers in Athens in 430 where the doctors could do nothing. Typically, he noted that both those who worshipped the gods and those who did not suffered equally and he speculated as to whether there were natural causes for the disease that might be ascertained. This was the time when Hippocrates of Cos (460–377 B.C.), seen as the father of Western medicine, was beginning his studies.

Virtually nothing is known of Hippocrates, but a jumble of works under his name was assembled as a single corpus in the library at Alexandria about 250 B.C. However, not even one of the works can be attributed to Hippocrates for certain. There are many different styles and approaches and some of them must be far later than Hippocrates as they contain elements of Stoic and Epicurean thought. What unites these works is a belief that, like the *cosmos,* the human body can be understood through a combination of observation and reason. Disease, as one treatise on epilepsy in particular insists, was not the result of the anger of the gods but rather of some specific, possibly ascertainable, cause.

One had to start, therefore, with observation. The Hippocratic doctors prided themselves on careful examinations, noting of symptoms, and building up an understanding of the patient in his environment. This was not a new approach—the Egyptians were known for meticulously examining patients and recording the details of illnesses—but the Greeks went further in trying to understand the reasons for disease so that a rational cure might be applied. "Medicine is not like some branch of enquiry in which everything rests on an unprovable hypothesis," one Hippocratic treatise (*On Ancient Medicine*) put it. "Medicine has discovered a principle and a method through which many great discoveries have been made over a long period and what remains will be discovered too if the inquirer is competent, knows what discoveries have been made and takes them for the starting point of his enquiry."

It followed that the Hippocratic writers saw themselves as superior to everyday practitioners who relied on good-luck charms or the help of the gods, and they sought to distance themselves by insisting on a code of practice for their profession. Hence the origins of the famous Hippocratic oath, still the basis of professional medical practice today. The first task of the doctor, the oath affirms, is to cure the sick and to use his knowledge to this end and not to any evil purpose. He will never take life (abortion is mentioned as well as euthanasia), will always keep secrets imparted to him, and will not abuse his position to have sexual relationships with patients, even if they are slaves.

However, even if there are the makings of a profession here, there was little understanding of anatomy or the functioning of the human body, so what doctors could actually achieve was limited. Originally, dissection was considered an insult to the dignity of the human body, so virtually nothing was known of its main organs. Starved of actual knowledge, the Hippocratic doctors drew heavily on earlier philosophy. In one treatise, *On the Nature of Man,* the healthy body was believed, like the ideal city, to live in equilibrium. Disease came as a result of this equilibrium being upset. The essence of equilibrium lay in the balance between four bodily fluids, the humors, blood, phlegm, black bile, and yellow bile. (The idea of four was a cardinal one in philosophy—four elements, earth, water, fire, and air; four primary qualities, hot, cold, wet, and dry; four seasons, and so on.) The healthy patient was mentally and physically stable but an excess of any one fluid brought disease. An excess of black bile brought melancholy, or blood fever. Close examination, for instance, of a patient's stools or his coughed-up phlegm helped discover what excess there might be. A diagnosis was confirmed by observing the climate and noting the season. The amount of blood in a body was supposed to increase in the spring and this accounted for "spring fevers." Yellow bile was believed to increase in the hot, dry conditions of the summer and account for malarial fevers. (Here cause and effect had got mixed up; the summer is the time when the malaria-bearing mosquitoes flourished and excess bile may be an effect rather than a cause of fever.)

A great deal of emphasis was placed on a careful and thorough examination, partly as a means of building up the confidence of the patient in his doctor. Modern studies have suggested that a feeling of well-being in a patient can be induced by empathetic care of this sort without any further treatment, so there was much good sense here. An attempt to offer a prognosis based on experience of similar cases was also considered a means of building up the necessary confidence between doctor and patient. One important belief was that the body could act to cure itself. Diarrhea was the body's natural way of removing excess bile, coughing of phlegm, menstruation or nosebleeds of blood. (As men were unable to menstruate, it followed that they were more liable to diseases caused by excess blood, among which the Hippocratic doctors numbered gout.) As a result treatment was normally conservative. Drugs were used sparingly. The Hippocratic doctor preferred to stress the importance of good diet and exercise. Sex was recommended, especially for older men. The best of remedies was a balanced life with all things in moderation, a view also recommended by many philosophers. Surgery was reserved only for the most serious cases. The Hippocratic texts forbade it for kidney stones and doubted whether it was of any use for cancer. The likelihood of death from septicemia must have been so high that here again there was good sense in this approach. There was one serious exception to this restrained approach to treatment. Some doctors, although not all, recommended that excess blood should be removed through bloodletting, even to the moment when a patient lost consciousness. The belief in relieving "excess blood" became so deeply embedded in European medical practice that bloodletting was a practice which was to last over two thousand years.

Even if the basis of Hippocratic medicine, the theory of the humors, was flawed, the approach of the Hippocratic doctors must have helped many patients to stay healthy or return to good health. They were right to stress the high proportion of cases in which with careful and supportive attention the body is able to heal itself. If any active cures were to be effected, however, it was essential to move on to a more scientific understanding of the body. This the Greeks attempted to do.

Within his own researches, which included the dissection of animals, Aristotle had made some attempts to explain the function of the heart and brain. Observation of the hearts of chicks as they developed from embryos inside their eggs suggested to him that the heart provided the essential life force of the human body, but he assumed that it was also the seat of the intellect and emotions and that its beat was the result of a boiling of the blood caused by another of the heart's functions, that of a heater for the rest of the body. He believed that the brain and the air inhaled through the lungs provided a means of cooling the blood. It goes without saying that these were major misconceptions (although the heart is still associated with emotional feeling).

Some development of Aristotle's approach was made by Herophilus who worked in Alexandria in the first half of the third century. He was prepared to dissect human corpses as well as animal ones and there is a report (though one first recorded some three hundred years later) that he was given convicts to work on while they were still alive. Hierophilus realized that veins and arteries contained blood (not, as some had argued, air) and distinguished between the veins and the arteries (the blood from arteries is lighter, as, though the Greeks did not know this, it contains more oxygen). He also realized that the pulse originated in the heart though he never grasped the concept of circulation. One of his most important insights was that the pulse rate varied according to the state of health of a patient. He described the liver and the duodenum (its name is from the Latin translation of his word for its length, the breadth of twelve men's fingers) and dissected the eye (the word retina derives from the Greek for *netlike,* his description of one membrane). His most impressive achievement was to isolate nerves and show that they ran back to the brain. For the first time, the central importance of the brain as the seat of sensation had been established.

This work was continued by Erastistratus, also of Alexandria (c. 315–240 B.C.), a master of dissection and careful observation. It was Erastistratus who distinguished between the motor and sensory nerves (those which controlled movement and those which controlled sensation) and began for the first time to map out the brain. He saw the human body as a unity with its different parts related to each other and tried to create a uniform picture of its functioning. He used the analogy of a machine to explain its operations. The alimentary canal pumps the food down into the stomach where it is pounded into smaller pieces and passes into the blood. The blood itself is pumped by the heart, although, like all doctors of the period, Erastistratus did not grasp the idea of circulation. Blood was, he believed, transported in the veins to every part of the body where it was then absorbed into the tissues. Erastistratus made careful examinations of the heart and understood how its valves ran one way only but he maintained one important popular misconception, that the arteries contained air rather than blood. This misconception rested partly on the problems of distinguishing between arteries and other channels of the body, such as the respiratory tract, and partly on observations of dead animals in whom blood naturally withdraws from the arteries (into the veins) on death. (To explain the presence of blood in a human artery, Erastistratus assumed that the blood had been drawn into the vacuum in the arteries after the body had died.)

The dominating figure of Greek scientific medicine comes much later, in the second century A.D. This was Galen, a native of Pergamum who spent his later years, after a training that involved patching up injured gladiators in his home city, in Rome, where he served as physician to the emperors. Galen's dominance rests partly on his own arrogance. "I have done as much for medicine," he boasted, "as Trajan [who ruled from A.D. 98 to 117] did for the Roman empire when he built bridges and roads throughout Italy. It is I and I alone, who have created the true path of medicine." There was, however, good reason for Galen's arrogance. His intellectual appetite was broad and his ambitions for his profession prodigious. Galen had read widely in earlier medical and philosophical works and mastered all that had gone before him. The profession of doctor, he argued, was one which encompassed the whole of human existence. Every doctor, he argued, should be as at home in philosophy and ethics as in medical knowledge. There was no place for narrow specialism.

In many areas Galen adopted the conventional thinking of his predecessors (he was a great admirer of Hippocrates who he believed compiled all his treatises himself) and so placed himself as the heir of a continuing tradition. He adopted the concept of the four humors and the belief that disease was the result of an imbalance in the bodily fluids, for instance. He was an advocate of bloodletting. If Hippocrates was his medical hero, Plato (and to a lesser extent, Aristotle) was his philosophical mentor. Taking Plato's idea that the soul consisted of three parts, the rational part, the spirited, and the appetitive, he tied them to specific locations, the brain, heart, and liver, in his belief that the body should form a harmonious whole.

However, Galen was also able to be critical of earlier work when the results of his dissections showed that it was flawed. He finally put to rest Erastistratus' idea of the arteries containing air by the simple procedure of tying a ligature on an artery and then cutting it below the ligature. Blood was clearly caught in the artery. It was in the practice of dissection that his work was most productive. It was only rarely that he found human corpses to work on, so he used barbary apes instead, as well as pigs, sheep, and goats. His surviving works show that his work was meticulous. He had a macabre party trick in which he cut along the spinal cord of a live pig, showing how each severed nerve destroyed a separate function. He also showed how urine progressed through the ureters into the bladder but could not pass back up them. However, like his predecessors, he failed to understand the way blood circulated through the body and, despite many dissections, he got no further than they had done in understanding the workings of the heart.

Galen wrote extensively and some twenty thousand pages of his works survive. They include textbooks for students (among them *Bones for Beginners*), studies of earlier doctors such as Hippocrates and Erastistratus, and accounts of his own findings. They became authoritative works, especially as Galen argued that the discovery of the human body was a sacred pursuit and that a supreme god had created man for a purpose to which all the functions of his body contributed (there were shades of Aristotle here). Such views meant that Christians could adopt his work and so they remained dominant throughout the Middle Ages, often preventing any further breakthrough. Galen's misconceived version of the working of the heart, which was in line with earlier theories, lasted, for instance, until the seventeenth century when the English physician William Harvey, observing what seems an obvious point, that more blood passed through the heart in an hour than was in the body, finally grasped the idea that it must be circulated.

Medicine was as much a practical as a theoretical activity. A doctor, said Galen, had to be good with his hands and it is clear that Greek physicians did have some success with surgery, particularly in cases of war wounds. (The Romans understood the principle of sterilizing instruments with fire.) In contrast, Greek mathematics dealt almost exclusively in abstractions. By Hellenistic times mathematics had been clearly differentiated as a separate discipline. Aristotle, for instance, had formulated a systematic distinction between *physike* and *mathematike* (the word originates from the Greek word *manthanein,* to learn). *Physike* concerns the study of natural objects while mathematics had developed independently as a branch of thought which dealt predominantly in abstractions. Aristotle distinguished three areas of the subject, arithmetic, plane geometry (the study of two-dimensional figures such as squares and triangles), and solid geometry (the study of volumes such as cubes, cones, pyramids, and cylinders). A major weakness in Greek mathematics was that there was no concept of zero. The idea of nothingness did not seem to make sense to the Greeks. Nor was the concept of algebra grasped in this period. Aristotle's idea that in logic, one could use symbols, A, B, or C, was only adopted for mathematics by one Diophantus of Alexandria working in the mid-third century A.D.

The greatest breakthrough of the Greeks, the principle that mathematics depended on theorems sustained by logical proofs, was already established but there is little surviving evidence of what actually had been proved by 300 B.C. This is why Euclid was so important. Euclid seems to have been active around 300 B.C. in Alexandria but little more is known of him. He apparently ridiculed a student who hoped to make money out of mathematical knowledge and to have told Ptolemy I that there was "no royal road," i.e., short cut, to mastering geometry. There is no evidence that Euclid made any breakthroughs of his own. His genius was as a synthesizer. He collected those theorems that were known and arranged them into a highly systematic set of books, each of which builds on the work of its predecessor. Thus in the *Elements*, as his most enduring work is known, one works through a course in mathematics. It proved to be one of the most influential books in history, the foundation of mathematical training for nearly two thousand years.

Any proof had to start with a set of first principles, assertions which appeared self-evident and on which proofs could be built. Euclid distinguished between "common opinions," which could be used in any area of mathematics and "postulates," which were assumptions which were to be used specifically as a basis for geometrical proofs. Examples might be that all right angles are equal or that lines which are not parallel to each other must meet at a point somewhere. This last postulate (the famous fifth postulate) worried other mathematicians from the start but it was only in the nineteenth century that it, and other postulates, were successfully challenged by Georg Riemann who showed that they were invalid when used on the surfaces of spheres. Essentially, however, Euclid's opinions and postulates hold true within the context (of flat surfaces) in which he set them and he was able to draw a complex set of proofs from them. One of his methods was exhaustion. Suppose one wants to measure the area of a circle. Start by placing inside it a square each of whose corners touch the circumference. Its area can be easily measured. Then in the space between each of the sides of the square and the circumference, draw in an isosceles triangle whose base is the side of the square and whose point reaches the circumference. Go on filling the remaining spaces with triangles until the circle is almost all filled. Add the areas of the squares and triangles together and one has an area which is slightly smaller than that of the circle. Archimedes (see below) took the process one stage further by also placing the circle *within* a square and filling the remaining spaces between the square and the circle with triangles. He thus had two areas within which the true area of the circle must lie. This is what led him to his formulation of π as between $3\frac{10}{70}$ and $3\frac{10}{71}$.

The other method used by Euclid, and also by Archimedes, was that of *reductio ad absurdam,* establishing a proof by showing that its contradiction must be false. The famous example is the proof of whether the number of prime numbers (numbers which can only be divided by themselves or one) are infinite. One starts by assuming the opposite that there *is* a finite number of prime numbers and makes a list of all of them one knows. Then they are multiplied together and one is added to the total. The new total must either be either a prime number or not. If it is not, then there must be, logically, once the "one" has been added, some prime number not yet listed which divides into it. If it is a prime number then there is another to add to the list. Either way there is another prime number to add to the first list. If one then continues by multiplying in the new prime number, adding one again to the total, the same must apply. There must always be further prime numbers and so the number of prime numbers is infinite. The same method, *reductio ad absurdam,* was also used by Euclid to prove the existence of irrational numbers (numbers that cannot be expressed either as whole numbers or as fractions) of which the square root of two is an example. This was a major step forward from Pythagoras' belief that such numbers could not exist because the underlying mathematical coherence of the world depended on all numbers being rational.

The greatest figure of Greek mathematics was Archimedes. Born in Syracuse about 287 B.C. he may have spent part of his early life in Alexandria but he returned home and he lost his life in the sack of Syracuse by the Romans in 211. The most celebrated story about him is that of his famous rush naked through the streets after he had suddenly grasped how his body displaced a volume of water equal to his weight when he got into his bath. It may be a legend but it shows the sheer excitement involved in scientific discovery and is a good story for that reason alone.

It is the range and originality of Archimedes' work which impresses. Much of it was in geometry where he calculated areas and volumes, of circles, cones, and spheres, relating the volume of a sphere, for instance, to the volume of the cylinder which encloses it. He developed a method of relating the areas of objects to each other by dividing them into infinitely thin strips and then "weighing" the strips from each object against similar strips from the other so that the ratios between then in area could be calculated. Archimedes' work, in the determination of the surface area and volume of a sphere, for instance, anticipates the integral calculus. One of his achievements, in his work the *Sand-Reckoner*, was to find a method of notation which could express a really large number. He chose to calculate the number of grains of sand in an entity as big as the universe. Having come to a figure, which we would express as 10^{63}, he tried to find a notation which would encompass it and he produced one which might be expressed as 10^8, itself subject to 10^{16}. This produced a number which was vastly greater even than the one he was trying to notate.

Part of Archimedes' success lay in his ability to use or envisage mechanical ways of dealing with problems and use these as a foundation for finding mathematical proofs of them. He realized, as others before him, the importance of the lever in lifting weights but progressed to work out the principles on which levers worked, showing, for instance, how the further the distance of the operator of the lever from the fulcrum on which the lever rested in comparison with the distance between the load and the fulcrum the less effort was required to lift the load. In this field of statics he went on to explore where the center of gravity in objects of different shapes lay. In all this work Archimedes was never content with simply demonstrating something to be true *mechanically;* he always worried about finding a watertight proof in *geometric* terms. This led to problems. A geometric proof is strictly theoretical and Archimedes was not able to encompass such real-life forces as friction. However, it was the approach that mattered. He was laying the foundation of applied mathematics.

Archimedes' work in hydrostatics, which seems to have been totally original, shows the same progression. Asked by the ruler of Syracuse to find out the true composition of a supposedly gold crown, he suddenly realized (in the famous instance in his bath) that it was a matter of comparing the volume of water it displaced with that displaced by a similar weight of true silver and true gold. He could thus work out whether the crown was wholly gold or an amalgam of metals. He did not stop there but became fascinated with all the problems of hydrostatics. He drew up his observations into principles—an object floating in water displaces a quantity of water equivalent to its own weight, while an object which is too dense to float will display a loss in weight equivalent to the weight of water it displaces. In his second book of hydrostatics, one of his most important works, Archimedes worked out what position in the water differently shaped objects would take if floated in it.

One of the solids which fascinated Archimedes and others was the cone and it was a successor of Archimedes, Apollonius, from Perga in Pamphylia (active c. 220–190 B.C.) who took work in this area to its furthest extreme. Suppose one took a right-angled cone, in other words one whose apex was directly above the center of the circle which formed its base. There were numerous ways of cutting through this solid and a host of questions arising from the cutting. Suppose a cut was made across a cone parallel with its base and the top of the cone removed. Is the area of the circle left on the base equal to that of the base of the cut-off piece? Apollonius went on to make cuts across the cone and named some of the resulting shapes, the ellipse, the parabola, and the hyperbola for the first time. The questions he posed still, apparently, challenge mathematicians today.

Mathematics and science met in the study of the stars. They were always a subject of fascination with the Greeks as they had been for other civilizations including the Babylonians and Egyptians and, as described earlier, Greek philosophy is traditionally seen to begin with Thales' prediction of an eclipse. Parmenides understood that the earth was round and the moon was lit by the light of the sun. By the fourth century the idea that the world was motionless in the center of the universe and that the stars and planets circled around it had become the conventional wisdom. It was espoused by the Cnidian mathematician and astronomer Eudoxus (c. 390 to c. 340 B.C.) who on the basis of crude observations argued that the stars rotated in simple circular movements around the earth. This reflected the assumption that underlay all Greek astronomy that there was an order in the heavens and that a circular, rather than, say, an elliptical, motion was the natural way for this to be expressed. The problem was that even elementary observations of the stars showed that their movements were irregular (the Greek word *planetes* means "the wanderers") but here again the Greeks assumed that even irregularities operated in an orderly way. Eudoxus produced an ingenious explanation for them. He suggested that the earth is encased in a number of concentric spheres which rotate around it. The axes of these spheres are at an angle to each other and they rotate at different speeds. Each of the five planets that Eudoxus distinguished (in addition to the moon and the sun) was, he argued, related to four of these spheres (the sun and moon were related to three each and the rest of the stars to one single sphere, which moved around the earth every twenty-four hours, making twenty-seven in all). A planet was attached to the equator of the innermost sphere and moved round with it but was also subject to the movement of the other three spheres (the outermost two of which were supposed to move in opposite directions to each other). This approach explained many (but not all) of any planet's irregular movements and was accorded great respect by Eudoxus' immediate successors. One of them, Callippus, took things further by adding another seven spheres, including two each for the sun and the moon, to try and deal with the remaining discrepancies. By doing this he was able to calculate the lengths of the seasons and explain the discrepancies in their lengths.

Eudoxus' concept of the universe was primarily mathematical and abstract. Aristotle adopted its underlying concept (of moving spheres) but attempted to conceive of them as a mechanical system. Such an approach posed immediate problems. The spheres had somehow to be fixed to each other and there was no way that each planet's spheres could be kept distinct from those of other planets. Aristotle acknowledged that he was no expert in this area but proposed a further set of spheres to counteract the movements of the others. He eventually needed forty-nine! (A nice idea was that the spheres made music as they moved, a view still prevalent in the sixteenth century. Lorenzo, in Shakespeare's *The Merchant of Venice*, addresses his beloved Jessica. "Look how the floor of heaven is thick inlaid with patens of bright gold. There's not the smallest orb which thou behold'st but in his motion like an angel sings.")

Aristotle made no attempt to challenge the view that the earth rested motionless at the center of the universe. It was, after all, an idea that seemed to receive support from everyday observation. It was noted, for instance, that objects fell toward the earth and rested where they had fallen. This suggested the earth had some power at its center to which all things were attracted and it was assumed from this that the earth was the center of everything in the universe. (But this could only be an assumption. It had to be explained why the stars did not fall in on the earth and so a theory was developed by Aristotle that they were made up of a substance which had no weight.) Then if the earth moved on its axis, how was it that objects floating in the air such as clouds were not left behind as the earth turned? It would be impossible for clouds to move eastward (the direction in which the earth would have to rotate if it did move), for instance, as they could be observed to do. So a geocentric universe became the paradigm around which Greek astronomy developed. However, a hypothesis was put forward by one Aristarchus of Samos (working around 275 B.C.) that the sun and the outer stars remained unmoved and the earth (and, it followed, the planets) rotated around the sun. This hypothesis is only noted in one of Archimedes' works and it is not known whether Aristarchus tried to explain the movements of the planets and stars from it. If he had done so the unnecessarily complicated nature of Eudoxus' approach would soon have been exposed and a much simplier, and, of course, correct explanation for the movements of the planets substituted. As it was, the geocentric approach was to last as the paradigm until the work of Copernicus in the sixteenth century.

If the planets moved around on circles of which the earth was the center, why then did their brightness vary? Two alternative models to explain this appeared at the end of the third century and are associated with Apollonius of Perga, the expert on cones. One model supposed that a planet moved on an epicycle, a circle whose center moved around the circumference of a great circular orbital path (known as the deferent) whose center was the earth. The other supposed that a planet moved around on a circle, one whose center was stationary but not the center of the earth (an eccentric system). Whichever model best fitted the observed movements of the planet could be adopted. (It was assumed that the more simple explanation was likely to be the right one.) The eccentric system, for instance, could be applied to the sun (i.e., the sun moved around the earth but in a circle whose center was not the earth) and so explain the differences in the lengths of the seasons. The epicycle model seemed to explain the wandering movements of the planets. They were simply traveling around the circumference of a small circle whose own center was moving in a circle around the earth. Such a model explained why they might appear to move forward, backward, or appear stationary. If one assumed that the speeds with which planets circled the epicycle and the speed with which the center of the epicycle moved along the deferents might vary, then there was virtually no observation which could not be explained. It was the flexibility of these models that was their chief attraction and they gradually superseded Eudoxus' model of concentric spheres.

At the end of the second century B.C. Hipparchus of Nicaea (in northwest Asia Minor) applied mathematical models to the epicycle/eccentric models in order to predict future movements of the planets and stars. In doing so he founded trigonometry in the shape of a chord table which he devised. (Chords are run from the diameter of a circle to a fixed point on its circumference and the relationship between the angles of different chords can be calculated. It is believed that Indian mathematicians adapted Hipparchus' method to make the first sine table.) Hipparchus was aided by having access to a mass of earlier Babylonian and Greek observations and he also constructed more sophisticated instruments through which he could plot the position of stars. He is said to have compiled a celestial map with some 850 stars on it. His observations were so exact that he was able to spot the slight oscillations in the earth's axis (caused partly by the fact the earth is not an exact sphere) and calculate the shift of two degrees in 160 years, or forty-five seconds a year, when the true figure is fifty seconds. This was the first known recognition of the precession of the equinoxes.

The Greek tradition of scientific astronomy reached it apogée with the work of Ptolemy in the second century. Ptolemy appears to have lived in Alexandria and carried out his observations between A.D. 127 and 141. His *Almagest* ("the greatest," the Arabic name for his astronomical treatise) survives in whole. Like the work of Galen, it is set within earlier conventions. The earth remains motionless at the center of the universe and the movement of stars is essentially circular. Ptolemy adopts the epicycle/eccentric model and is particularly dependent on Hipparchus for much of his data and methods. For instance, he borrows, if only to develop, Hipparchus' Chord Table. However, he also moves on. He devised the armillary astrolabe, a sighting instrument which allowed him to position a star within coordinates of longitude and latitude without the elaborate calculations that earlier instruments required. With this he recognized that the movement of the moon did not fit within the path predicted by the epicycle model. So he developed this model further so that the moon was now assumed to move around an epicycle which itself moved around the circumference of a circle, the center of which in its turn moved around the earth! To further explain the movements of the planets he made an amalgam of the epicycle and eccentric models. The planet moves around an epicycle. This moves around a circle as before, but this deferent circle is an eccentric one in that its center is fixed but is not the center of the earth. Even this elaboration did not work for the observed movements of the planet Mercury and a yet more complicated model had to be devised. It was brilliant work ("an extraordinary achievement, for the rigour of its mathematical arguments, for the range of data encompassed and the comprehensiveness of the results proposed" [Geoffrey Lloyd]), but so long as the earth was considered the center of the universe, totally flawed. Nevertheless, until the astronomical revolutions of the sixteenth century Ptolemy's *Almagest* remained the supreme work of astronomy and was recognized as such by the Arab and early medieval world.

It was a commonplace of Hellenistic belief that the *cosmos* was connected in a "universal sympathy" with one part being able to influence another. The sun was seen to influence the seasons and the moon the state of the tides. It was one step from here to argue that human life might be affected by the stars and the Greek astronomers accepted this as a possibility. Astrology and astronomy were therefore not seen to be in conflict. As the measurement of the stars became more precise, tables of the relative positions of the stars to each other on specific dates could be recorded and so began the idea of creating a personal horoscope based on the day of an individual's birth. Ptolemy considered the nature of astrology in his *Tetrabiblos*. While he accepted the possibility that human behavior might be affected by the stars and that one might even be able to divine the future, he doubted whether one would ever be able to make the link with any precision. Astrology persisted, however. It was supported by the Stoics and was popular among all classes in the Roman empire. It was eventually challenged by Christianity on the grounds that human being were endowed by God with free will and this was incompatible with the influence of outside forces.

Like Galen, Ptolemy had wide interests. He wrote on geography, acoustics, musical theory, and optics. In his work of optics he conducted and repeated experiments like a "true" scientist. For instance, he examined the way that the position in which objects appeared in mirrors varied according to the position taken by an observer and then repeated the examination with convex and concave mirrors to check the angle of reflection. He placed an object in water and measured the angle of refraction when it was viewed through the water from different angles. He then tried to draw up a general theory which encompassed his findings (although it can be seen that he adapted his observations to fit his preferred theory!). Yet for all his down-to-earth research, Ptolemy, again like Galen, never lost his sense of awe at the majesty of the universe:

> *I know that I am mortal, ephemeral; yet when I track the*
> *Clustering spiral orbits of the stars*
> *My feet touch earth no longer: a heavenly nursling,*
> *Ambrosia-filled, I company with God.*
>
> (Translation: Peter Green)

Despite all this speculation and intellectual ingenuity Greek science had virtually no practical applications. The principle of the lever, the pulley, the wedge, and the windlass had all been known before the Hellenistic period and did not necessarily depend on any theoretical background (although once observed, their operation could be described theoretically as Archimedes did for the lever). Archimedes, however, was credited with the invention of a screw which could lift water and a compound pulley with which it was claimed he was able to draw a heavily laden ship towards him single-handedly. When Syracuse was under siege by the Romans, Archimedes was called upon by the king, Hiero, to devise means of defending the city. (Other sources, such as Plutarch, state that Archimedes regarded "every art that ministers to the needs of life as ignoble and vulgar" but this may reflect what Plutarch, writing some 300 years later, believed great mathematicians and scientists ought to think.) It was in war, in fact, that some of the most impressive advances were made, in particular in siege engines where there is some evidence of controlled experiments on the effectiveness of different bores in missile launchers. In other areas, the concept of the screw was exploited to make screw presses (for pressing olives or grapes); cog wheels appeared and there were elementary suction pumps. Water mills are used as a source of milling power. This is a relatively modest list of achievements and there may be two reasons for it. First, there was simply not the mechanical know-how or materials to create machines. Thus, although the power of steam was appreciated, there was no way of creating suitably airtight valves and boilers. Second, and most crucial of all, Greek scientists regarded such applications as beneath their dignity. They were men of knowledge whose purpose was to understand the world as it was, not to change it. Their crucial achievement was to create methods of acquiring and assessing knowledge and here their legacy was immense. What is astonishing is how little recognition of these achievements is made in many introductory books on the ancient Greeks.

19

The Greeks and Rome

By the Hellenistic period, the Greeks had enjoyed a relationship with the Italian peninsula that stretched back over centuries. Perhaps the greatest contribution of the Greeks was to provide a model of city life and, as was seen earlier, the Etruscans had already adopted many aspects of the planned city. Rome itself was not immune from Greek influences in its early history. The city grew up from the eighth century on the plains of central Latium and its position on a major river (the Tiber) gave it access to trade from the Mediterranean world. As with any city foundation, myths were developed and the most popular incorporated easterners. Many centuries earlier, the myth ran, a refugee from the fall of Troy called Aeneas had come to Italy. He had founded a dynasty of kings and the daughter of one of these mated with Mars, the god of war. The offspring were twins, Romulus and Remus. Romulus was to kill Remus and then, like the murderers of mainland Greece, was to go on to found a new city, Rome (traditionally in 753 B.C.). Some later chroniclers even claimed that Rome was a Greek (rather than Trojan) foundation in its own right, although this is likely to have been an invention made to give the city status.

There is no doubt that there was important Greek influence on the development of Rome whether direct through traders or mediated through the Etruscans, many of whom lived in the city. (Legends talk of two Etruscan kings of Rome.) The city did develop monumental public buildings in the late seventh century; it did use an alphabet indirectly derived from Greek models in which to write its language, Latin; and, above all, many of the Roman gods are associated with those of Greece. Like the Greek gods, Roman gods are anthropomorphic. Jupiter shares many of the attributes of the Olympian Zeus. Jupiter's wife Juno is Italian in origin but acquires many of the attributes of the Greek goddess Hera, the wife of Zeus. Minerva, the Roman goddess of handicrafts, has been equated with Athena. A temple to the three was built in Rome on the Capitoline Hill, probably as early as the late seventh century. The only Olympian god to be brought to Rome without meditation through the Etruscans or association with an Italian equivalent was Apollo. He was adopted by the city in 433 B.C. when help was needed to avert a plague. By the end of the fourth century, when Rome had established its power over the Samnites, a number of highly militaristic cults were established in the city to deities such as Victoria and Hercules Invictus, the unconquered Hercules. They are modeled on Hellenistic examples. In the same period there are cases of Romans taking Greek surnames. Later, in 291, the healing god Asclepius, a son of Apollo, was imported, and a temple was erected to him on the Tiber Island. The first history of Rome was written by a Roman, Fabius Pictor, but in Greek as if the city needed to stress its credentials to a wider Greek world. To help prove his point Fabius argued that a Roman festival, the *Ludi Romanes,* showed its Greek origins in the way the procession operated with music, dancers dressed as satyrs, and gods "showing the same likeness as those made by the Greeks."

This early evidence suggests a city still in awe of the much older and opulent Greek cities to the south (or even a wider Greek culture) and using them consciously or unconsciously as a model. Rome, however, was an exposed city and vulnerable to its neighboring tribes. Its overwhelming concern had to be defense. From early days war had been an intrinsic part of Roman society and the avenue to status for its elite. (Among the duties of the senior elected magistrates, the consuls, was command of the armies.) Rome perfected a system by which enemies were treated ruthlessly ("even the dogs were cut up", as the historian Polybius put it) and then converted into allies whose manpower was available for further wars. It was a formidable strategy giving the city major reserves of manpower at little cost. The core of the Roman army, the legions, were highly trained and able to undertake long campaigns. (From around 400 B.C. they were paid and so were freed from having to return to their farms at harvest.) In the late fourth and early third century Rome's status and perceptions of itself as a city were changed by her conquest of the peoples of central Italy, notably the Samnites, a formidable mountain people who held impregnable strongholds in the Apennine range. The major Etruscan cities were also defeated and their cities used as allied strongholds with which to hem in the Celtic peoples of northern Italy. By 295 Rome had become the most powerful city in Italy and the city was then free to look to the Greek south.

By the beginning of the third century most of the cities of Magna Graecia (the Greek settlements of southern Italy) were in decline and on the defensive against the native peoples who were able to raid down from the mountains to the exposed coastal plains where they lay undefended. So they began asking for help from Rome and Rome responded by taking many of them under her protection. The most powerful of the Greek cities, Tarentum on the "instep" of Italy, became suspicious of Rome's intrusions and called on the help of Pyhrrus, king of Epirus in northwest Greece, who brought over a well-trained army to Italy in 280 B.C. This was the first time the Romans had confronted a Hellenistic army and they proved vulnerable to its power and experience. At first Pyrrhus beat the Romans but each time with heavy casualties (hence the term "Pyrrhic victory") and he was finally defeated in 275. Tarentum fell to the Romans in 272 B.C. and Rome's control of the Greek cities was complete. They were bound to the Romans in alliances in which it was tacitly admitted that the Romans sustained the ruling class of each city. There was now no escaping direct contact with the Greek model of city life. In 273 B.C., for instance, a Roman colony (Paestum) was established in the Greek city of Posidonia whose original Doric temples still stood, as they still do. Meanwhile the rest of the Greek world became aware that there was a new player in the politics of the Hellenistic world.

Rome's expansion now took her into direct confrontation with the Carthaginian empire of the western Mediterranean, which included western Sicily, in the so-called Punic Wars. At the end of the First Punic War (242) Sicily was ceded to Rome and in 227 became the first province of what was now an incipient overseas empire. Sicily was home to several major Greek cities. One of them, the wealthy Acragas, had been sacked by the Romans when it hosted a Carthaginian garrison and its twenty-five thousand inhabitants sold into slavery. However, Sicily's largest and wealthiest city, Syracuse, remained independent and became an ally of Rome. During the Second Punic War Syracuse unwisely decided to join Carthage. A siege of the city was led by the Roman Claudius Marcellus, and despite the best efforts of Archimedes to find ways of defending the city, it fell in 211. (Marcellus respected Archimedes' engineering skills and hoped to save his life but the mathematician was killed in the sacking by a common soldier. Marcellus brought Archimedes' astronomical globes back to Rome).

The fall of Syracuse, with its accompanying plunder, was seen by contemporary writers to mark a watershed in the relationship between Rome and the Greeks. Marcellus was blamed with bringing decadent Greek values into the city alongside its art. The Greek historian Plutarch, writing in the late first century A.D., put it as follows:

> Prior to this Rome neither had nor even knew of these exquisite and refined things . . . rather it was full of barbaric weapons and bloody spoils. The Romans blamed Marcellus because he had filled the Roman people, who had hitherto been accustomed to fighting or farming and had no experience with a life of softness and ease, . . . with a taste for leisure and idle talk, affecting urbane opinions about the arts and about artists, even to the point of wasting the better part of a day on such things. But Marcellus, far from sharing this opinion, proclaimed proudly, even before the Greeks, that he had taught the Romans . . . to respect and marvel at the beautiful and wondrous works of Greece.
>
> (Translation: J. J. Pollit, *Oxford History of Classical Art*)

This passage certainly suggests that Rome was deeply unsettled by the influx of Greek art and until recently historians used to divide Roman elite into two camps, those who welcomed Greek culture and those who despised it. It is now accepted that this is much too simplistic. Rome was already a city imbued with Greek influence and Plutarch, who was writing some three hundred years later, is certainly exaggerating when he spoke of the Romans' knowing nothing of these "exquisite and refined things." A far ranging study of the interaction of Rome with the Greeks in the second century by Erich Gruen (*Culture and National Identity in Republican Rome*) argues that the relationship was far less stressful than Plutarch suggests. It was, in fact, essentially a creative one in which the Romans proved strong enough to resist being undermined by the influx of plunder and were able to use Greek culture to forge their own cultural identity. Greek statues brought to Rome, for instance, were often rededicated in Roman temples, not set up in contrast to Roman models. A figure such as Cato the Elder (234–149 B.C.), traditionally seen as the archenemy of all things Greek, was in fact a man who knew Greek culture well and who could use his knowledge of it to define what was important about his own native culture. Hellenism proved to be a creative influence in his work. What was essential, Gruen argues, was for the Romans to keep the perceived extravagances of Greece in check, particularly if they threatened the dignity of individual members of the Roman elite or public order. The historian Polybius details some of the "Greek" activities which were viewed with distaste:

> Some young men squandered their energies on love affairs with boys, others with courtesans, and others again with musical entertainments and bequests and the extravagant expenses that go with them, for in the course of the war with Perseus and the Macedonians they had quickly acquired the luxurious habits in this direction. So far had the taste for dissipation and debauchery spread among young men that many of them were ready to pay a talent for a male prostitute and 300 drachmas for a jar of Pontic pickled fish.
>
> (Translation: Ian Scott-Kilvert)

It has to be stressed that this was the view of a Greek, not of a Roman historian, and one who shared the Roman concern with the potential breakdown of social order that the new wealth might bring. Yet there is no evidence of such breakdown in the second century. The Roman state was stable and well able to maintain control over the more threatening of social and economic changes. A well-known incident is the suppression of Bacchanalian (or Dionysiac; Bacchus was the Roman name for Dionysus) cults and their worship in 186 B.C. By the second century these cults were widespread in Italy. They were suppressed not because they were Greek in origin but because they broke down conventional notions of authority and threatened state control of religious affairs. Those Greek cults that operated within the parameters of state religion remained acceptable. Individual Romans upheld the dignity of their class and state. The contexts in which a Roman could use Greek and those in which he retained Latin were carefully controlled. Even if a Roman could speak fluent Greek, all diplomatic negotiations, even those taking place within Greece and Asia, had to take place in Latin and any embassies coming to Rome had to address the senate in Latin or have their words translated by an interpreter. Thus the Romans could display their dominant status over others. For a Roman to take part naked in Greek games, as a member of the Greek elite would take pride in doing, was seen as degrading of his status. So while temples and other Greek-style buildings (such as basilicas, the all-purpose columned meeting halls that were possibly adapted from the administrative buildings of Hellenistic kings) might be set up in Rome, *gymnasia* were not. Nor were stone theaters. This seems a puzzling restriction as theater was popular in Rome. However, the first theaters were temporary wooden structures erected anew each year. Performances were controlled by the city magistrates. It seems to have been accepted that any permanent stone theater would, in the words of Gruen, "enshrine the drama as an unshakable institution, no longer dependent on the resolve of magistrates."

The complex relationship between Greek and Roman culture in the second century was deepened by the absorption of Greece itself into the Roman empire. The very first direct contact between Romans and mainland Greece came with a raid on pirates on the Illyrian coast in 229 B.C. More was to follow. Rome's main opponent in the Second Punic War, the brilliant Carthaginian general Hannibal, had made an alliance with the king of Macedon, Philip V, and many Romans felt that Philip needed to be punished. When, in 201, Attalus I of Pergamum and the city of Rhodes asked for help against the expansion of Philip, Rome had an excellent excuse for intervening. A gifted commander, Titus Quinctius Flamininus, crossed with an army to Greece in 198 and the following year he destroyed Philip's army at Cynoscephalae in Thessaly.

Rome had no immediate plans to annex Greece and at the Isthmian Games of 196, Flamininus, who presided, announced that Rome intended to leave the cities of Greece, including those of Asia Minor, free and independent. It was a wildly popular move and when the games were over "the Greek spectators almost killed Flamininus with the unrestrained vehemence of their joy and gratitude. Some of them yearned to look him in the face and hail him as their saviour, others pressed forward to touch his hand, and the majority threw garlands and fillets upon him, so that between them they almost tore him to pieces" (Polybius). Cities were soon using Rome as a protector, sending embassies to Rome asking for favors and support in the same way as they did with Hellenistic monarchies. Within a few years, however, Rome began to see Greece as a sphere of interest, an area in which even if she did not rule she could exclude others. This all became clear in 192. The Aetolian League had always seen itself as a buffer against the power of Macedon and it decided to take advantage of the humiliation of Philip by resuming control of some of the cities Philip had surrendered. The Aetolians called on the strong man of the Greek world Antiochus III ("the Great") for support. Antiochus was happy to oblige, especially as he had an agenda of his own, to win back Thrace for the Seleucids. The Romans warned him not to come to Greece but he crossed to the mainland in 192. In 191 at the battle of Thermopylae he was easily defeated. The Romans pursued him back to Asia Minor and thrashed him again near Sardis. With the support of Pergamum they took all his possessions along the coast of Asia Minor and confined him to the east of the Taurus river. His fleet and any influence the Seleucids had had over the Aegean were gone.

Again Rome took no territory for herself. Pergamum and Rhodes shared Antiochus' Asian territory and other cities of the coast were declared independent. Rome's suspicions were aroused again some twenty years later when Philip V of Macedon's son, Perseus, became king. Perseus attempted to revive Macedonian influence in Greece and once again the Romans reacted harshly. At the battle of Pydna in 168 B.C. Perseus' army was shattered by the Roman Aemilius Paullus. It was now that Roman influence in Greece became more direct. Northern Greece was in effect dismembered. The Molossians of Epirus who had aided Perseus were plundered and 150,000, it was said, taken off into slavery. Macedonia itself was split into four republics. Rhodes, originally an ally of Rome but that had done nothing to support Rome in the war, had her trading empire undermined when the Romans created a free port on the island of Delos. Ptolemaic Egypt was increasingly of interest to the Romans, partly because of its wealth and, although they had no immediate wish to annex it, a

Roman envoy there warned off the Seleucid king Antiochus IV when he tried to exploit its weakness by invading.

The final subjection of Greece was not long delayed. A revolt broke out in Macedonia in 150 and after its inevitable crushing Macedonia became a Roman province ruled directly from Rome. The Achaean League now met its own fate. It had always been at odds with Sparta and Rome took Sparta's side and insisted that major cities of the League be allowed their independence. The League resisted what was an attack on its very existence but the Romans crushed the League's forces and, as a terrible example to all Rome's enemies, sacked Corinth so ruthlessly that the site was to remain deserted for a hundred years. (Southern Greece was later to become a separate Roman province, Achaia, and Epirus a province under its own name.) Thirteen years later (133), Attalus III, the last ruler of Pergamum, bequeathed his kingdom to Rome, perhaps to keep it out of the hands of his half brother who was fomenting rebellion against him. The territory was transformed into yet another Roman province, Asia. Of the proud Hellenistic kingdoms, only a diminished Seleucid empire (confined, in effect, to Syria) and Ptolemaic Egypt, whose dynasty was kept in place only through Roman support, now remained.

The story of the coming of Rome to Greece is the subject of the last of the great Greek historians and the only one from the Hellenistic period whose work survives to any extent, Polybius. The son of a rich landowner, Polybius was an Achaean who held the post of cavalry leader for the Achaean League. After the defeat of Pydna, Rome purged the mainland Greek cities of threatening politicians and Polybius was one of a thousand leading Achaeans who was taken as hostage to Rome. He was clearly an attractive and well-educated man and he turned his exile to his own advantage. He was taken on as a mentor by Publius Cornelius Scipio, the adopted son of Aemilius Paullus, the victor of Pydna, who was sympathetic to Greek culture. This gave Polybius access to the heart of the Roman aristocracy and as Scipio's own successful career developed Polybius was able to accompany him to Spain and North Africa. He was present when Scipio sacked Carthage in 146 B.C. By now at home with both the Greek and Roman elite, he played a major role in settling the cities of the Achaean League after their humiliation at the hands of Rome in 146.

Polybius had always been interested in political history and he was fascinated by the process in which in the space of a mere fifty-three

(220–167 B.C.) years, Rome had conquered the Mediterranean world. He later extended his *Histories* to cover another twenty-two years to 145 B.C. Of the original forty books only some five survive complete with fragments only of the rest, but they give a good impression of his style and approach. For Polybius the writing of history has a purpose, to instruct readers in political and military history using contemporary events as a backdrop. Like Thucydides (whom some passages in the *Histories* suggest he had read) Polybius is looking for accuracy and good judgment. He felt this could only be achieved by experience of life itself and he despised the "armchair" historian working only from library material. He liked to be out and about interviewing eye-witnesses and surveying the topography of the areas he was writing about. Like Thucydides he also despised history that was based on legend and emotion, a weakness which he felt was typical of historians of his own day. If they wanted to write in this way, he suggested, they should try writing tragedy.

The story that Polybius had to tell was, in the context of the known world, a universal history. It seems that he found this in itself a satisfying theme, as if the natural end of human affairs was some kind of organic unity. One force underlying this process is, Polybius suggests, *tyche* (fortune). "Fortune," he writes, "has steered almost all the affairs of the world in one direction and forced them to converge upon one and the same goal." Here *tyche* is seen as if it is some kind of providential force guiding history towards some defined end but Polybius also uses *tyche* as an explanation for unexpected events. This confusion is deepened by passages in which Polybius makes it clear that he also believes that the triumph of Roman arms was due to the stability of the Roman constitution and the meticulous way Rome prepared for war. Polybius has earned a small place in the history of political thought for the way in which he relates the Roman constitution as he perceived it, as a mixed one containing elements of monarchy, aristocracy, and democracy in balance with each other, to Rome's success. Modern historians can see that he tried to compress the Roman system of politics into a Greek mold (Aristotle had analyzed systems of government in a similar way) but nevertheless it was a sophisticated attempt to understand the role of political forces in history. Even if he never managed to sort out the relative contributions of human and "divine" elements in the making of history, Polybius deserves his place as an important historian.

With every major victory over Greece a vast triumphal procession of the plunder took place in Rome as the returning general paraded his achievement. Fulvius Nobilior who had subdued the Aetolians brought back 785 bronze statues and 230 marbles ones. After the battle of Pydna it took a whole day for the treasures and loot, including a mass of gold and silver, to be taken through the streets of Rome. Some commanders chose their booty with care and presented it well. Metellus, victor in Macedonia in 148 B.C., selected a celebrated statue group by the sculptor Lysippus of Alexander and his Companions at the battle of the Granicus to bring back, and he then constructed a portico, designed by a Greek architect, to display the 25 statues and other works of art. His buildings included the first marble temple in Rome. Metellus had not only created a grandiose reminder of his military success, he had shown that Greek art could be admired in its own right. So began the age of the connoisseur. The sack of Corinth brought a flood of small decorative bronzes to Rome and these became collectors' pieces. By the mid-first century every wealthy Roman wanted to have a set of Greek statues for his country villa and if there were no originals to be had, Greek sculptors would be employed to make copies.

Drama arrived in Rome first, it is said, when a Tarentine, Livius Andronicus, enslaved by the Romans after the fall of his city, adapted a play from a Greek original. The actors wore Greek dress and the settings remained Greek. The most lively adaptations were those of Plautus (c. 250–184 B.C.) who drew on a wide range of Greek plays. Essentially they were fast-moving musical comedies (in the tradition of Menander) with a mass of stock characters, thwarted lovers, swaggering soldiers, and slaves who had more wit than their masters. Plautus used a theatrical, elevated style and his plays proved highly popular. Everyone from senators (who were given reserved seats), to women and perhaps even slaves attended and the plays were also performed in the countryside outside Rome. The most important dramatist of the midcentury, Terence, a former slave from Africa, made a number of careful adaptations of Menander's plays. He stuck much more closely to Greek originals and although he avoided the theatrical expressions loved by Plautus, preferring to use more everyday language, he appealed to a more discriminating audience. In one of his prologues he complains of how his audience made off when they heard a boxing match or gladiator fight was about to begin. Greek literature came to Rome alongside Greek plays. The most influential poet of the period, Quintus Ennius (239–169 B.C.) was a rarity in that he was a Hellenised Italian (he was probably educated at Tarentum) who was at home equally in Greek and Latin. He is credited with having introduced Hellenistic literature into Rome and to have translated a wide variety of Greek texts into Latin. In his *Annals*, a history of Rome, he wrote the first Latin epic, one that was to become a staple of Roman education.

At first the Romans distrusted Greek philosophy. For traditionalists it was simply too abstract; the arguments were too subtle and spending a day talking seemed to be a waste of time. There seemed to be far better things to do. There is a good story (although it took place in the 90s B.C., it sums up Roman attitudes well) of a Roman proconsul in the east, Gellius Publicola, who assembled all the philosophers in Athens and told them if they could not settle their intellectual differences he would step in and do it for them. Nevertheless from 155 things began to change. In that year an embassy of leading Athenian philosophers arrived in Rome. Sensitive to the Roman stress on public service they did not include an Epicurean. They attracted enthusiastic audiences especially among the young although one of them, the Skeptic Carneades, confirmed the prejudices of conservatives by delivering two speeches on successive days, one arguing that justice was important in politics, the other arguing it was not. It implied (as of course, Plato himself had argued) that words could be used to prove anything, and, what was an equally threatening idea, that the Roman empire might be assessed as unjust.

Nevertheless, the attraction of Greek as a language that could express ideas and provide a means for argument soon became obvious. The scholar Crates of Mallos (who first came to Rome in 159 as an envoy from Pergamum) is credited with introducing *grammatica,* the study of language and literature in both Greek and Latin, and there were some twenty "grammar" schools in Rome by the beginning of the first century B.C. As the chief Roman magistracies were all elected offices, drawn from the nobility and intensely sought after, rhetoric was also a crucial skill and the Greeks clearly the masters of it. The teaching of rhetoric on a Greek model was firmly established in Rome by 90 B.C. Many Romans learned their Greek from slaves who had poured into Rome after the conquest of their countries. Some were much more highly educated than their new masters and it became commonplace for a richer household to have its own Greek doctors and teachers of Greek. The next development was to go to Greece to study philosophy and rhetoric firsthand. Both Cicero and Julius Caesar studied rhetoric in Greece in the first half of the first century B.C.

A new phase in the history of contacts between Rome and Hellenism came in the 80s B.C. Mithradates, king of Pontus in northern Asia Minor, successfully challenged Roman control of Asia and mainland Greece by presenting himself as a descendant of Alexander who had come to liberate Greece. (At one point he instigated an uprising against Italians in which, it was said, some eighty thousand were massacred.) The wars that followed (there were three of them) as the Romans confronted him were highly destructive. The Roman general Sulla punished Athens and other Greek cities for their support of Mithradates and imposed a massive indemnity on the Asian Greek cities. Mithradates was finally defeated by the great Roman commander Pompey and it was in the settlement of Asia that followed that the Seleucid kingdom was destroyed (64–63 B.C.). Syria became a Roman province, and, through a circle of client kingdoms, Roman control of the East was made secure. The wars brought a mass of Greeks to Rome, some of them slaves, many of them refugees, and for the first time Greek intellectuals, both poets and philosophers, became a permanent part of the city's population.

Among the spoils brought to Rome by Aemilius Paullus, the victor of Pydna, had been the royal library of the Macedonian kings. It was ostensibly a gift for his sons but it seems that anyone could consult its contents. One of the Roman commanders in the Mithradatic Wars, Licinius Lucullus, compiled a major Greek library from books he had seized. Sulla brought back the library of Apellicon of Teos from Athens which included the works of Aristotle. Pompey seized the medical books that Mithradates had owned. These libraries were set in fine buildings with colonnades and study rooms. Rome could now boast of having become a center for research into Greek culture that could rival the older cities of Greece. It was in Rome that Andronicus of Rhodes was able to work up a comprehensive edition of Aristotle's books, presenting them in an order that is still used today. (The origin of the word "metaphysics" lies in Andronicus' decision to place the book containing Aristotle's thoughts of the deeper problems of existence after, *meta,* that on physics.)

By the middle of the first century B.C., Romans were able to reflect on the Greek experience and use it to enhance Roman cultural life. The scholar Varro (116–27 B.C.), one of the great polymaths of the age, studied philosophy in Athens and absorbed Greek ways of thinking so extensively that he was able to use Greek models of analysis to carry out the first systematic study of Latin as a language. His study of Rome placed its early history within a Greek context. In his survey of Italian agriculture (*De Re Rustica*) Varro surveyed the changing patterns of farming in Italy, dividing each topic into sections and subsections again following the Greek model of analysis of a topic. Varro also used the Greek pattern of a general education as the basis for a suggested Roman curriculum. It included the traditional Greek subjects, *grammatica,* rhetoric, and dialectic (knowledge of the ways to argue well), arithmetic, geometry, astronomy, and music, to which he added medicine and architecture. Although the two last subjects were dropped by later educators (as too practical for an academic education) the model became the basis of medieval education. The only comprehensive study of architecture from antiquity, Vitruvius' (c. 90 to 20 B.C.) *De Architectura*, is another that approaches its subject in the ordered and systematic way of the Greeks. (Vitruvius included Greek models and made a study of the Greek architectural orders.) Vitruvius took city life to be the ideal and designed the layout of a sophisticated city. His work was a major inspiration to the architects of the Renaissance.

A good example of how the Romans used Greek models for their own ends can be seen in the portrait bust. Traditionally a mask was made of a Roman noble when he died, in an attempt to capture his actual likeness. The Hellenistic Greeks also created portraits but these were always within certain conventions, the nude warrior hero, the bearded philosopher, for instance. The Romans refused to accept many of these models (it would have been deeply embarrassing to be portrayed nude for example) but they did marry the two traditions successfully. An impressive example is a surviving bust of Pompey. His face appears to be an actual portrait; it is chubby and full of bonhomie. His style of hair, however, is copied from one typically given by Hellenistic sculptors to Alexander. So this is the "real" Pompey subtly presented as a conqueror.

By the first century the Roman republic was in collapse. The senate, traditionally the ruling body of the city, now found itself outmaneuvered by ambitious Roman commanders who had built up their large, loyal armies during their conquests overseas. Pompey had been the dominant figure of the 60s, although he has always been careful not to use his troops unconstitutionally. In the 50s a challenge to his position was coming from the younger brilliant commander Julius Caesar, who was using the acclaim brought by his conquest of Gaul to build up popular support in Rome. By the late 50s some form of confrontation between the two men was inevitable. The political system was in atrophy. One response was to withdraw from politics altogether and this accounts for the popularity of Epicureanism among Roman aristocrats in the period. Previously the philosophy had been despised as un-Roman; now it attracted a number of adherents and inspired one of the major poems of the period, Lucretius' *De Rerum Natura* (*On the Nature of Things*).

Another figure sidelined by the confrontations was the orator and statesman Cicero. Cicero had played a prominent role in Roman politics in the 60s but he was too indecisive and lacking in military expertise to survive in the troubled 50s and 40s. He had already written a treatise on oratory in which he had examined the Greek tradition in full (praising Demosthenes as the most complete of the Greek orators) and in his *De Republica* he analyzed Rome's own constitution using a Greek theoretical model of a mixed constitution as Polybius had done. In his final years (45–43 B.C.), nursing his despair over the collapse of the Roman political system and his own private grief over the death of his daughter, Tullia, he set about reinterpreting Greek philosophy for the Romans. It had been a task which many had considered too daunting, partly because Latin was simply not developed enough to deal with the subtle semantic distinctions involved and partly because of the unwieldy mass of material now available to the committed scholar. Cicero specialized in making syntheses of philosophical problems although he seems to have hoped that these syntheses would prove more than this and would stand as works of philosophy in their own right, allowing him to be given a place alongside the Greeks. He had great admiration for Plato and Aristotle but for much of his work Cicero drew on more recent Hellenistic texts. In the *Academica* he tackled the problems of knowledge, in *De Finibus* the ultimate aim of life, in *De Natura Deorum* the nature of the gods, in *De Officiis* the problems of moral philosophy. Cicero was eclectic. He liked to examine a wide range of philosophies (including Epicureanism) with intellectual detachment. His own sympathy, however, was for Stoicism with its emphasis on endurance and commitment to the public good. Stoicism was certainly the most attractive philosophy for the traditional Roman statesman and it was to prove highly influential in the century that followed. (Among the most accessible works on Stoicism are the letters of the statesman Seneca, who, under pressure from Nero "stoically" committed suicide.) When later in western Europe, knowledge of Greek was confined to a few scholars, Cicero's works provided the only comprehensive introduction to Greek philosophy and they defined the main concerns of the subject between the Renaissance and the eighteenth-century Enlightenment.

By the 40s the confrontation between Pompey and Caesar had broken out into civil war. The war spread to Greece. At the battle of Pharsalus (in Thessaly) in 48 B.C. Caesar defeated Pompey and he then pursued him to Egypt. Pompey was murdered as he stepped ashore. Caesar fought his way into Alexandria and took the royal palace. Here a bulky carpet was brought to him. It was unrolled and out of it appeared no less than the Queen of Egypt, the last of the Ptolemies, Cleopatra.

"How would you like to be the wickedest woman in history?" the actress Claudette Colbert was reputedly asked by Cecil B. de Mille when he asked her to play the lead in his version of *Cleopatra* (1934). Cleopatra has haunted the European imagination through the centuries, her image manipulated to cater to every kind of fantasy. "The most complete women ever to have existed, the most womanly woman and the most queenly queen, a person to be wondered at, to whom the poets have been able to add nothing, and whom dreamers always find at the end of their dreams," enthused the nineteenth-century French writer Theophile Gautier. Her image was distorted by painters and dramatists with little regard for historical accuracy. Cleopatra was Greek but she was often portrayed as Egyptian to give her an exotic Eastern allure and, although the accounts suggest that she was bitten by a serpent on her arms and died in her royal robes, an alternative myth was developed that she was bitten on the breasts. Nineteenth-century artists, who needed some kind of cultural or historical excuse to portray nudity, could thus show her naked on her sumptuous deathbed. The "real" Cleopatra is certainly irrecoverable but something can be said of her story. (One of the most vivid accounts of her life is that by Plutarch. Extracts from it are included in the next chapter.)

Ptolemaic Egypt had survived into the first century B.C. but it was a precarious survival as the dynasty's internal power struggles and rising Egyptian national feeling combined to weaken the dynasty's grip. Rome had been hesitant in absorbing Egypt into its empire but was prepared to offer support to the Ptolemies to prevent intruders (such as the Seleucids) taking over the wealthy kingdom for themselves. As happened so often in Rome's history, the initial interest became something much more substantial. The Roman dictator Sulla had to support Ptolemy XI in succeeding to the throne in 80 B.C. He was soon killed by a mob and the son of an earlier Ptolemy became king as Ptolemy XII. This Ptolemy fled from Egypt in 58 B.C. and had to be restored under the auspices of Pompey. When he died in 51 B.C., Cleopatra his daughter, then eighteen, succeeded to the throne with her younger brother, Ptolemy XIII. She attempted to push him aside but the courtiers were outraged at her maneuvers. They managed to expel her (she fled to Syria) and install Ptolemy as sole ruler. Pompey, as the strongman of Roman politics, was again asked to be guardian of the young king and it was this interest which had led him to Egypt (in the hope of reciprocal support) after his defeat by Caesar. Caesar arrived after Pompey's death, and it was then that Cleopatra reappeared in the famous carpet. She knew Caesar, the victor of the civil war, was the man to please if her kingdom was to survive. She was perhaps not as beautiful as later legend made her out to be but she was certainly shrewd, daring, and opportunistic in the use of her sexuality. The effect on Caesar was devastating. One of Rome's finest and most disciplined soldiers, who should have been preoccupied with completing his civil war, was held by her charms in Egypt for six months. They cruised the Nile together and Cleopatra had a son Caesarion, acknowledged as Caesar's. Once the wars were over and Caesar returned to Rome, Cleopatra also went to live in the city.

After the assassination of Caesar (44 B.C.), Cleopatra left for home but the new Roman supremo in the east, Mark Antony, summoned her to him at Tarsus. She upstaged him by arriving in a sumptuous barge suffused with the perfumes of the East. Mark Antony succumbed. He was crude and materialistic in comparison to Caesar but Cleopatra clearly hoped he would serve her purpose. They eventually married and had three children. The climax of their relationship came in 34 B.C. at a great ceremony in Alexandria where they sat together on golden thrones with Cleopatra robed as the goddess Isis. At the ceremony Mark Antony distributed parts of the Roman empire to their children claiming that he was simply adopting Egypt as a client kingdom of the Roman empire. This was his undoing. In Italy, Caesar's appointed heir and nephew, Octavian, was able to portray Mark Antony as the plaything of an unscrupulous woman. Mark Antony had also tried to to link himself to the East by adopting Dionysus as a supportive god. For Romans, Dionysus still smacked of decadence and Octavian highlighted the contrast by aligning himself with Apollo, a god known to Rome for centuries, and associated with reason and good order. So the ancient dichotomy between Dionysus and Apollo was played out on a vast Mediterranean screen. When Antony took Cleopatra with him to Greece in 32 it was easy for Octavian to sell this as a "foreign" invasion of the Roman empire. The two were defeated by Octavian at the battle of Actium in northwestern Greece in 31 B.C. Octavian then pursued them back to Egypt. Mark Antony committed suicide and died in the arms of Cleopatra. The ever resourceful Cleopatra may have tried her luck with Octavian but he was unmoved by her charms and she, too, committed suicide. Egypt, including, of course, the great city of Alexandria, was in Roman hands. Octavian ordered the great sarcophagus of Alexander to be brought to him and he placed a diadem on the mummified head of the conqueror. It was an acknowledgement that the Hellenistic world which Alexander had created had now been fully absorbed into the Roman empire.

As the confrontation between them intensified in the 50s and 40s Pompey and Caesar had used programs of public building as a means of attracting support in Rome. There were still constraints as to what types of building were acceptable. There were no problems in making a votive offering to the gods in the shape of a temple, and displays of Greek art in their own right were acceptable. Pompey, who knew how to push convention to the limit, went further. So far no stone theater had ever been built in Rome. Pompey built a temple to Venus Victrix,

Venus (the Roman equivalent of Aphrodite) as conqueress, but cunningly placed it at the top of a large semicircle of marble steps. Here, in effect, was a theater and it broke the taboo on the building of them. In 23 B.C. a building that was nothing but a theater, the so-called Theater of Marcellus, was dedicated in the city. (It still stands.) Caesar was at first more conventional. He constructed a massive voting enclosure as well as a new Forum (a forum was a Roman town's market place but in grander cities it was constructed as a massive colonnaded square) but once he was in power he set in plans for a major expansion of Rome so as to make it a rival of the Alexandria which had so dazzled him. This was in the flamboyant tradition of the Hellenistic kings. However, Caesar was assassinated before the work could properly begin. When Octavian returned victorious to Rome in 29 B.C., he also worked within Hellenistic examples. He constructed a giant mausoleum for himself, by far the biggest structure in Rome and, as a burial place, second only to that still standing in Halicarnassus.

Yet as he consolidated his position in Rome, Octavian, given the title Augustus, "the revered one", by the senate in 27 B.C., now set about creating a new, more restrained image for himself. He knew, from Caesar's experience, that anything that smacked of kingship was deeply abhorrent to Romans. His building program was cleverly designed to reflect Rome's greatness rather than his own. One of his major projects, for instance, was to restore eighty-two of the city's temples, often by tearing off the more ornate facades to reveal the older more "Roman" structure behind. There was a vast new Forum. It did contain a major statue of Augustus but it also contained a long line of statues of Rome's great commanders and statesmen. Even though Augustus reaffirmed Roman roots, he did so by adopting a Greek style, but it was that of fifth-century classical Greece, in preference to the more unrestrained Hellenistic models. "It was in the balance, simplicity, and dignity of the art of Pheidias and Polycleitus rather than the sumptuousness and realism of Hellenistic art, that artists of the Augustan period found that could convey Augustus' vision of himself as a new Pericles and of Augustan Rome as a new Athens" (J. J. Pollit). The most famous of his statues, the *Prima Porta* portrait found in the villa of Augustus' wife Livia at Prima Porta, has the same approach. Augustus is shown as supreme, the calm hero, removed from the strife of everyday affairs as he might be in a fifth-century sculpture. "The entire body imitates the Classical forms of

Polycleitan sculpture" (Paul Zanker). However, the body is not nude, rather it is shown in armor. On the cuirass, scenes from a recent victory over the Parthians are shown as if they were the cornerstone of a new world order based on the supremacy of Rome. Another of the great buildings of Augustan Rome, the Ara Pacis, the altar of peace, a gift to Augustus from the senate in 13 B.C., used the form of a classical frieze to frame Augustus and his family in procession as "the first family" of Rome. The frieze was carved by Greek craftsmen imported from Athens for the purpose. Here, Greek styles are being selected and transformed in order to create a Roman imperial style.

It was in Augustus' reign, too, that Roman literature reached its maturity. Its models remained Greek but they were used with impressive confidence by the poets of the age. The greatest of these was Virgil. His *Eclogues* consciously draw on the pastoral poems of Theocritus, his *Georgics* are modeled on the *Works and Days* of Hesiod and his *Aeneid* looks back to the epics of Homer. Yet in each case, the genre is used with complete assurance. The poet Horace was steeped in Greek models. He drew on traditions as old as Archilochus and as recent as the epigrams of Hellenistic poetry, yet again he is his own master, exploring personal concerns and the affairs of state with supreme confidence. (Horace is also remembered for his summing up in one of his *Epistles* of the relationship between Greece and Rome: "*Graecia capta ferum victorem cepit et artis intulit agresti Latium.*" [Greece, the captive, took her savage victor captive, and brought the arts into rustic Latium].) The third major poet of the age, Ovid, transposed a mass of Greek mythology into Latin in his *Metamorphoses*, one of the most influential compositions in European literature, the vehicle through which Greek mythology entered the later European consciousness.

In short, by the Augustan age there was a sense of accommodation with Greece, one in which Rome knew its own strengths but was prepared to recognize those of Greece. In the famous words of Virgil in Book VI of the *Aeneid*:

> *Others [i.e., the Greeks] will cast more tenderly in bronze*
> *Their breathing figures, I can well believe,*
> *And bring more lifelike portraits out of marble;*
> *Argue more eloquently, use the pointer*
> *To trace the paths of heaven accurately*

And accurately foretell the rising stars.
Roman, remember by your strength to rule
Earth's people—for your arts are to be these:
To pacify, to impose the rule of law,
To spare the conquered, battle down the proud.
(Translation: Robert Fitzgerald)

It was a measure of just how far Rome had come in dealing with the sophisticated culture that had fallen under its control. The Greco-Roman culture that was the result was to underlie the European intellectual tradition for centuries.

20

The Greeks in the Roman Empire

In A.D. 66, the Roman emperor Nero paid a visit to Greece. He had always praised Greek culture and believed that he had a mission to further it within Rome. In the year 60 he had introduced Greek-style public games to the city and a year later he built its first *gymnasium*. In 65, he had gone so far as to be a performer in the games himself, singing and contributing his own poetry. To more traditional Romans this was still deeply embarrassing and it was perhaps for this reason that Nero decided to head east in 66. "The Greeks alone are worthy of my efforts," he proclaimed. "They really listen to music." In the account given by the biographer Suetonius much of the trip was farcical. Nero ordered all the games to be rescheduled so that he could perform as a singer and reciter of poetry and he added a musical contest to the events at Olympia. While he was performing no one could leave the auditorium (Suetonius tells of women giving birth there and men pretending to be dead so that they could be carried out) and the overawed judges were compelled to give him first prize. He even attempted a chariot race and was declared the winner despite falling out of his chariot. When he returned to Italy he insisted on being treated like Olympic winners of old, with the walls of cities he was traveling through pulled down so he could pass through them. Suetonius loved gossip and was bound to exaggerate what he, as a Roman, saw as humiliating behavior, but the Greeks appear to have seen it differently.

They were flattered by the attention and were understandably pleased when Nero abolished all imperial taxes in Greece. (They were soon reimposed by his successor.) The visit of Nero may have been the moment when the Greeks first felt that they were recognized as a valued part of the empire.

This would not have been possible if the Romans had not achieved peace and stability. Greece itself had suffered appallingly in the first century B.C., both from Roman incursions during the Mithradatic wars and during the civil war. Two of the war's major battles, Pharsalus and Actium, were fought on Greek soil, cities were asked for men and supplies, and the countryside was ravaged by opposing armies. Alongside these disruptions, Greece's wealth had been freely plundered by greedy governors as central control of the empire atrophied in the last years of the republic. Augustus brought order to the empire. He took a personal interest in the appointment of provincial governors, keeping appointments in more sensitive provinces for himself and recognizing that a relatively generous but efficient taxation system was likely to be more successful in keeping peace and increasing revenue than unrestrained exploitation. The secret of success lay in winning over the city elites through the promise that Rome would uphold their power and status and would boost their position through patronage. Inevitably this meant that city democracy atrophied and power was increasingly held by councillors, the *curiales,* who took on the financial responsibility for running their cities, but it brought stability. Mainland Greece itself benefited from its cocooned position within the empire. There was no invasion of the area between the reign of Augustus (30–B.C. to A.D. 14) and barbarian raids in A.D. 267.

The power of Rome in the east was symbolized by the imperial cult that each city was expected to institute. Augustus allowed recognition of himself alongside the city of Rome, personified as a goddess, usually through an imposing temple building. The cult spread quickly. Even in the 20s B.C. many eastern cities had it in place and it gave an essential focus to city life. It was cemented by imperial patronage. "The whole of humanity turns to the *Sebastos* (i.e., Augustus) filled with reverence," as one Nicolaus of Damascus put it. "Cities and provincial councils honor him with temples and sacrifices for this is his due. In this way do they give him thanks everywhere for his benevolence." The most effective of the emperors so far as patronage was concerned was the Greek-loving Hadrian (emperor A.D. 117–138). He had a particular love of Athens and contributed an aqueduct, a library, and a stoa to the city as well as finally completing the temple to Olympian Zeus started by the Pisistratids six hundreds years before. By now Romans could accept Greek conventions in portraiture without embarrassment. In a great marble statue found at the Asclepium, the center of healing, at Pergamum, Hadrian allowed himself to be shown nude, in effect as a *Greek* hero.

By the early second century the Greeks had come to terms with Roman rule, recognizing that it provided the best way to preserve Greek culture and city life. The best known expression of this is the famous hymn of praise of the orator Aelius Aristides addressed to Rome in about A.D. 150. Aelius dwells on the peaceful conditions under which opulent city life can flourish:

> Instead of quarrelling over empire and primacy, through which all wars formerly broke out, some of your subjects . . . relax in utmost delight, content to be released from troubles and miseries, and aware that they are formerly engaged in aimless shadow-boxing. Others do not know or remember what territory they once ruled. . . . Under you, all the Greek cities emerge. All the monuments, works of art and adornments in them mean glory for you . . . seashore and interior are filled with cities, some founded and enlarged under you and by you. Ionia, the great prize, is rid of garrisons and satraps, and stands out as a model of elegance of the world . . . all other competition between cities has ceased, but a single rivalry obsesses every one of them to appear as beautiful and attractive as possible. Every place is full of *gymnasia,* fountains, gateways, temples, shops, and schools. . . . Gifts never stop flowing from you to the cities. . . . Festivity, like a holy, unquenchable fire, never fails, but goes around from one place to another.
>
> (Translation: N. Lewis and M. Reinhold)

The degree to which Greeks could now live comfortably alongside Romans can be seen in the works of Plutarch, a philosopher and biographer (A.D. 46 to A.D. 120) whose home town was Chaeronaea in Boeotia (the scene of Philip of Macedon's victory over the Greeks). Plutarch had traveled widely, from Athens to Egypt and Rome, although much of his later life was spent in Delphi, where he helped

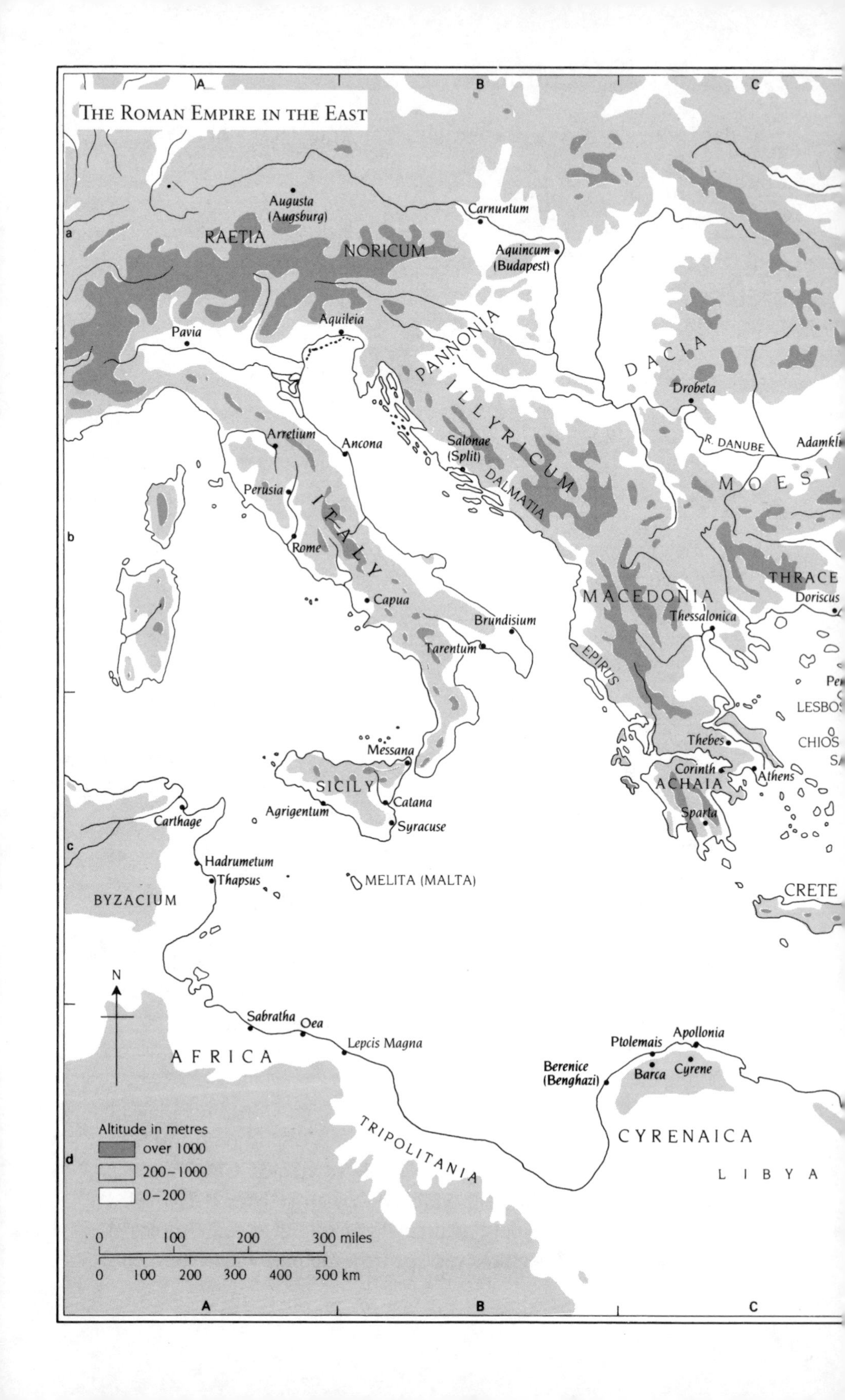
THE ROMAN EMPIRE IN THE EAST
A
B
C
a
b
c
d
Augusta
(Augsburg)
RAETIA
NORICUM
Carnuntum
Aquincum
(Budapest)
Pavia
Aquileia
PANNONIA
ILLYRICUM
DACIA
Drobeta
R. DANUBE
MOESI
Arretium
Ancona
Salonae
(Split)
DALMATIA
Perusia
ITALY
Rome
Capua
Brundisium
Tarentum
MACEDONIA
THRACE
Doriscus
Thessalonica
EPIRUS
LESBOS
CHIOS
Thebes
Corinth
Athens
ACHAIA
Sparta
CRETE
Messana
SICILY
Catana
Agrigentum
Syracuse
Carthage
Hadrumetum
Thapsus
MELITA (MALTA)
BYZACIUM
N
Sabratha
Oea
Lepcis Magna
AFRICA
TRIPOLITANIA
Ptolemais
Apollonia
Berenice
(Benghazi)
Barca
Cyrene
CYRENAICA
LIBYA
Altitude in metres
over 1000
200–1000
0–200
0
100
200
300 miles
0
100
200
300
400
500 km

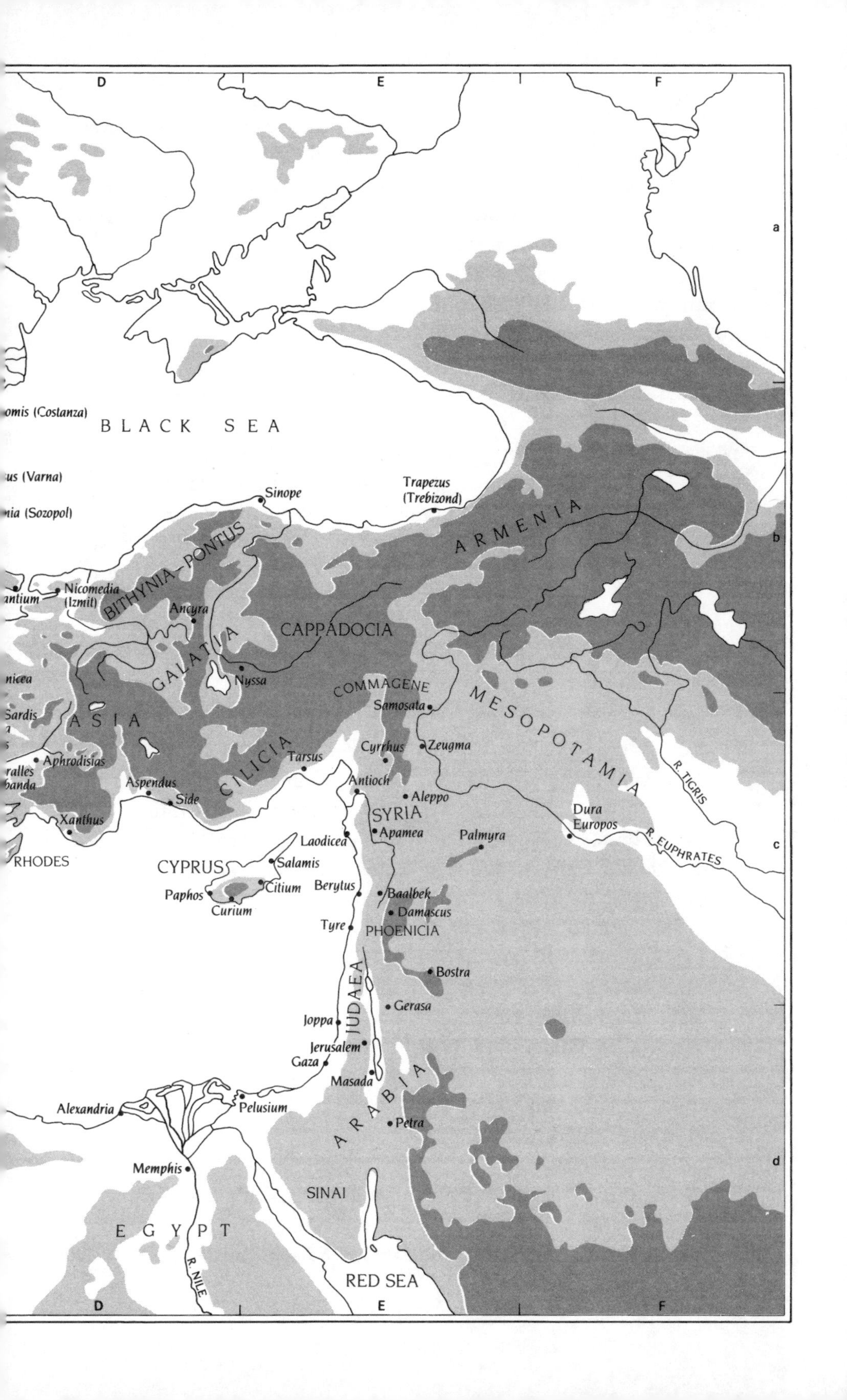
D
E
F
a
b
c
d
omis (Costanza)
BLACK SEA
us (Varna)
nia (Sozopol)
Sinope
Trapezus
(Trebizond)
ARMENIA
BITHYNIA-PONTUS
antium
Nicomedia
(Izmit)
Ancyra
GALATIA
CAPPADOCIA
nicea
Nyssa
COMMAGENE
MESOPOTAMIA
Samosata
Sardis
ASIA
Zeugma
Cyrrhus
Aphrodisias
CILICIA
Tarsus
R. TIGRIS
ralles
banda
Aspendus
Side
Antioch
Aleppo
Xanthus
SYRIA
Dura
Europos
Apamea
Laodicea
Palmyra
R. EUPHRATES
RHODES
CYPRUS
Salamis
Paphos
Citium
Berytus
Baalbek
Curium
Damascus
Tyre
PHOENICIA
JUDAEA
Bostra
Gerasa
Joppa
Jerusalem
Gaza
Masada
ARABIA
Alexandria
Pelusium
Petra
Memphis
SINAI
EGYPT
R. NILE
RED SEA

revive the shrine. He was at ease with the dominance of Rome over Greece while insisting that Greece remained the more sophisticated of the two cultures, In his *Political Precepts* he advises his fellow Greeks how to cultivate the Romans as patrons without arousing their contempt through self-abasement.

In his most enduring work, his *Lives*, Plutarch compares famous Romans with selected Greek equivalents. Cicero, for instance, is paired with Demosthenes and Nicias, the ill-fated commander of the Athenian expedition to Syracuse, with the Roman commander Crassus, who suffered a similar disaster in Persia. Plutarch is fascinated by the characters and moral virtues, or lack of them, in his subjects and in this he makes no discrimination between Greek and Roman. He has the knack of creating atmosphere, particularly around the death beds of his subjects. Among his most famous set pieces is his description of Cleopatra's arriving to meet Mark Antony, a description that Shakespeare was to adapt to describe the scene in his *Antony and Cleopatra*:

> She received several letters, both from Antony and from his friends, to summon her, but she took no account of these orders; and, at last, as if in mockery of them, she came sailing up the river Cydnus, in a barge with gilded stern and outspread sails of purple, while oars of silver beat time to the music of flutes and fifes and harps. She herself lay under a canopy of cloth of gold, dressed as Venus in a picture, and beautiful young boys, like painted Cupids, stood on each side to fan her. Her maids were dressed like sea nymphs and graces, some steering at the rudder, some working at the ropes. The perfumes diffused themselves from the vessel to the shore, which was covered with multitudes, part following the galley up the river on either bank, part running out of the city to see the sight. The market place was left quite emptied, and Antony at last was left alone sitting upon the tribunal . . .

Antony was induced to visit Cleopatra and she dined with him the next evening. He soon succumbed.

> Her actual beauty was not in itself so remarkable that none could be compared with her, or that no one could see her without being struck by it, but the contact of her presence, if you

> lived with her was irresistible; the attraction of her person, joining with the charm of her conversation, and the character that attended all that she said and did, was something bewitching . . . it was a pleasure merely to hear the sound of her voice, with which, like an instrument of many strings, she could pass from one language to another . . .

The fated lovers are finally defeated by Octavian and in Alexandria Antony stabs himself. His dying body is brought to Cleopatra:

> Cleopatra would not open the door but, looking from a sort of window, she let down ropes and cords, to which Antony was fastened; and she and her two women, the only persons she had allowed to enter the monument, drew him up. Those that were present say that nothing was ever more sad than this spectacle, to see Antony, covered all over with blood and just expiring, thus drawn up, still holding up his hands to her and lifting up his body with the little force he had left. As, indeed, it was no easy task for the women; and Cleopatra with all her force, clinging to the rope, and straining with her head to the ground, with difficulty pulled him up, while those below encouraged her with their cries, and joined in all her efforts and anxiety. When she had got him up, she laid him on the bed, tearing all her clothes, which she had spread upon him; and beating her breasts with her hands, lacerating herself and disfiguring her own face with the blood from his wounds, she called him her lord, her husband, her emperor . . .
>
> (Translations: John Dryden, 1683–86)

Plutarch was a leading member of the so-called Second Sophistic (i.e., the second period of the Sophists), a term used to describe an important cultural movement between A.D. 60 and 230. The Second Sophistic centered on major cities such as Athens, Pergamum, Ephesus, and Smyrna (the modern Izmir) and represents a renewal of confidence among the Greeks in their own cultural traditions. There were two major features of the Sophistic: First, there was a revived interest in declamation. Public speakers (*rhetors*) began to enjoy considerable public esteem. Many of them were drawn from wealthy families and their success gave them a new role and status within their cities. They were often sent on missions, to Rome, for instance, in search of patronage. When Smyrna was devastated by an earthquake, Aelius Aristides appealed to the emperors Marcus Aurelius and Commodius for help, which was then granted. The Athenian rhetor Herodes Atticus actually became one of the consuls (143) and tutor to two emperors, Marcus Aurelius and Lucius Verus. He was a major benefactor in his own right, building a stadium and odeon in Athens, a stadium at Delphi, and a nymphaeum at Olympia (a nymphaeum was a shrine to the nymphs, guardian spirits of fresh water, normally in the form of a fountain decorated with sculpture).

The second feature of the Sophistic was a revival of interest in the classical past. This is exemplified by the work of Pausanias from the city of Magnesia in Lydia in his *Description of Greece*, of about A.D. 150. The *Description* focuses on the Roman province of Achaia, i.e., southern Greece. Pausanias has an enthusiasm for Archaic and classical Greece, and, outside the benefactions of Hadrian, hardly notes any building later than 150 B.C. His description of the Athenian Acropolis, for instance, leaves out a temple of Rome and Augustus that was known to have stood in front of the entrance to the Parthenon. He was particularly drawn to the great sites of classical Greece, Athens, Sparta, Delphi, and Olympia—in fact, his *Description* goes from site to site with little mention of the countryside between. Buildings, including their sculptures and now-vanished paintings, are recorded with care, as archaeological excavation has confirmed.

Many of the Sophists' speeches were on classical themes and in their art there was a vogue for copying the work of great sculptors such as Praxiteles (the Cnidian Aphrodite) and Polycleitus (the Spear-Bearer). In many cases copies from this period provide the only indications of what the most famous originals of classical Greece looked like. (These were the examples Winckelmann used for his own studies of "Greek" art.) Hadrian's celebrated villa at Tivoli outside Rome was a showcase of choice pieces, even encompassing a reconstruction of the temple of Aphrodite at Cnidus. A mass of sculpture was copied for it, including the Caryatids on the Erectheum on the Athenian Acropolis, and the statue of the Tyrannicides, Harmodius, and Aristogeiton, again from Athens. There was a deliberate attempt to elevate appreciation of the art by incorporating mythical themes that only the more sophisticated connoisseurs would recognize but, inevitably, the effect was to make such themes the mark of fashionable art throughout the empire. So even in remote corners of the empire one finds gold or silver embossed with the figures of what is now a fully integrated Greco-Roman mythology. (Witness the great dining plate of Mildenhall treasure, an opulent silver banqueting service found in Suffolk in eastern England.) Hellenism has triumphed and has become woven into the western heritage even as Greece itself and Greek culture became cut off from western Europe.

Mainland Greece was not an influential part of the empire. The provinces that most prospered under Rome were those which had good agricultural land or those that were in the front line of the empire's defense. (The legions stationed in these provinces had a major economic impact on their local economies.) Greece was neither of these. As with most parts of the empire there was a trend toward larger landholdings but for many Romans, Greece was to be seen primarily as a tourist destination. Athens was visited for its major attractions while Sparta provided tests of hardiness, including the beating of adolescents, for spectators to watch. Others enjoyed the countryside and romanticized it. The harsh, mountainous environment of the central Peloponnese, Arcadia, the home of the goat-god Pan, was transformed by Roman poets into an imagined landscape of love, poetry, shepherds, and music.

It was in Asia that Greek culture flourished and enjoyed a prosperity not found on the mainland. It had always been true that the Greek cities of Asia Minor had been more opulent than those of mainland Greece but now under the stability of Roman rule they reached new heights. These cities had no independence and relatively little political life and, as a result, their energies were channeled into public building. The ruins of a major city such as Ephesus or Aphrodisias in inland Caria, still in the process of excavation, overwhelm the visitor with the sheer energy of the Greco-Roman world. (These two are chosen because their surviving ruins are so extensive.) There are huge theaters, that at Ephesus could seat twenty-four thousand spectators. (It was here that Paul preached and was thrown out in the rioting that ensued when the silversmiths realized Christianity would bring an end to their lucrative trade in images of Artemis.) The marble seated stadium at Aphrodisias, one of the best preserved in Asia Minor, could take some thirty thousand spectators. These great cities owed their success either to their position or to luck. The city of Aphrodisias had an important shrine to Aphrodite and also access to fine marble so it became a center of sculpture working whose products were exported as far as Rome. (A dazzling array of sculpture has been found in recent excavations on the site.) What cemented its success was its decision during the Mithradatic wars to actively support the cause of Rome. Successive emperors offered patronage and one of its finest buildings was its Sebastion, two parallel porticos, 250 feet long, that led to a temple to Aphrodite. Along the portico, the early emperors of Rome were commemorated in reliefs. The city's main temple to the goddess stood nearby and was enclosed in a massive portico in the reign of Hadrian. The city had a grandiose double Agora, one section nearly 700 feet long and 400 wide, the other 700 by 230. Both again were enclosed by porticos, one in Ionic and the other in Doric style. The so-called portico to Tiberius (emperor A.D. 14–37) surrounded a vast pool, 570 feet long and 90 feet wide and some 3 feet deep. It is a stunning example of how lavishly water could be used for aesthetic effect, though doubtless it was also used for bathing.

Ephesus' origins lay in its fine position on the mouth of the river Cayster at the end of an ancient trade route into Asia Minor. Long associated with the worship of Cybele, the mother goddess of Anatolia, Greek colonists assimilated Cybele with their own Artemis and the temple of Artemis they built in the sixth century, some 360 feet long, was the largest temple ever built by the Greeks. It was destroyed by fire in the fourth century but rebuilt and recognized as one of the Seven Wonders of the Ancient World. Pilgrims to the temple were a major source of revenue. The city was bequeathed to Rome as part of the territory of Pergamum in 133 B.C. but lost its status as a free city when it supported Mithradates and organized the massacre of local Italians. Ephesus was saved as a result of its position. It was an excellent center for trade and administration and it grew rich under the patronage of the emperors. One of its finest buildings, a massive altar to the emperor Lucius Verus (emperor A.D. 161–169), was set up in the second century A.D. This was a work of imperial propaganda. The continuing protection given by Rome is underlined by presenting three generations of the imperial family together facing the onlooker straight on. Modeled, it seems, on the great altar at Pergamum, the altar's reliefs (most of which are now in Vienna) show the triumph of the Romans over the peoples of the east. Ephesus' own citizens contributed to their city's grandeur. The best known of its surviving buildings, the heavily ornate library of Celsus, was dedicated by the family of Celsus, a local man who became consul, in 120. It could hold some twelve thousand books. Ephesus came to eclipse Pergamum as the showcase city of the area.

Ephesus and Aphrodisias were only two of the many important cities of the period. (Antioch in Syria was one of the greatest but little survives of it, and Alexandria remained *the* great city of the east.) There was a mass of smaller but still prosperous towns whose status depended on their public architecture. There was a check list of buildings that any self-respecting city tried to acquire. It included walls, gates, towers, temples, sanctuaries and altars, council houses, theaters, odeons (small theaters suitable for lectures), *Gymnasia,* and libraries. There was a more inventive use of water (brought in by aqueducts) and baths now became prominent. Bath houses, developed in their complete state (of several halls with pools of varying temperatures) by the Romans from southern Italian models, were integrated into the *gymnasia* to provide leisure centers within which one could exercise, bathe, consult books, and pick up prostitutes.

By the third century many cities were so opulently endowed that most of their resources were consumed simply in maintaining existing buildings. This was at a time when the first raids on the empire by "barbarians" were also drawing resources away from the cities. It became increasingly difficult to find local patrons who would willingly finance new building. The main symbol of prestige for a city now became that most ancient Greek institution of all, *agones,* competitive games based on a religious festival. These operated at several different levels. Most cities had games for their own citizens (*Gymnasia* seem to be ubiquitous in the Greek world and Pausanias remarked that a city could not be considered a city unless it had one). At a higher level were the *themides,* where money prizes were competed for, but the most prestigious were the sacred "crown" games in which competition was for no more than a crown or wreath. Many of these were the gift of emperors. Hadrian founded no fewer than three games in Athens and six others in other cities. In Aphrodisias the games were directly modeled on those of Delphi and included not only the full range of athletic events but also competitions in music and drama. The prizes were laurel wreathes.

As the Roman empire stabilized there was a remarkable spread of Greek culture to the East. Greek was the dominant culture, the one by which others appeared to define their own status. Latin, for instance, made almost no inroads in the Greek world or the surrounding provinces to the east. There were, of course, Romans in the Near East, as legionaries, administrators, and traders, but there was only one enclave of Roman culture, at Berytus (modern Beirut), where there was an important school of Roman law. There is virtually no instance of any Greek wishing to write in Latin. (The earliest is the historian Ammianus Marcellinus born in A.D. 330.) Cities farther to the east that wished to improve their status would claim for themselves a Greek foundation myth. In Cilicia (southeast Asia Minor) both Tarsus and its neighbor Aegeae claimed to have been founded by Perseus, the slayer of Medusa. The remote but ambitious city of Aizani in Phrygia boasted that it had been founded by Arcadians but then boosted its "Greek" status by claiming that a cave outside the city was where the infant Zeus had been nursed. A major temple to Zeus was built to celebrate the connection. Many cities adopted the ancient cult of Athena Polias, Athena as protectress of the city. Some cities renamed local landmarks their river, for instance, after Greek examples. So a Greek identity could be constructed.

Greek culture could operate only within a city structure and in rural areas this meant new foundations. The tradition of founding new cities had been one of the policies of Macedonian kings Philip and Alexander and was followed by the Hellenistic monarchs. The tradition was now adopted by Augustus and his successors. In his study of Central Anatolia, for instance, Stephen Mitchell shows how urbanization spread following the imposition of Roman rule. After the Romans had annexed Galatia c. 25 B.C., three cities, one each for one of the main Celtic (Galatian) tribes, including the modern capital of Turkey, Ankara, were founded in about 22 B.C. There were also colonies in Anatolia, settled as homes for the vast numbers of veterans left redundant after Augustus' successful conclusion of the civil wars. Each foundation seemed to spark off more so that by A.D. 70 the whole of central Asia Minor, with the exception of Cappadoccia, was made up of cities and their assigned territories. Their culture was unashamedly Greek, in their style of government, their buildings, and in their adoption of games.

In his important study of the Roman Near East, Fergus Millar examines the spread of Greek culture into Syria, Mesopotamia as far as the Euphrates, and Arabia. Much of this area had been under Seleucid rule but it was in the centuries of Roman rule rather than the Seleucid period that the area became heavily Hellenized. "If there is a single conclusion which emerges from the mass of enigmatic items of evidence from the region," writes Millar, "it is that the Greek language, Greek social structures and Greek frameworks for the construction and worship of deities penetrated to the most remote of rural contexts." Under Roman rule it was "the adoption of the norms of Greek city-culture by both dependent kings and local communities which progressively transformed not only cities, old and new, but a vast network of villages into urban communities using Greek." This extraordinary development, still poorly understood, highlights the impressive resilience, flexibility, and continuing energy of Greek culture. Even after the Arab conquest of much of the Near East in the seventh century, inscriptions continued to be written in Greek in this area for centuries.

With the spread of Greek culture came the spread of Greek cults. The spiritual world of the Greek east in these centuries was one of unbelievable variety. The Olympian gods and their shrines remained, many of them sustained by the prosperity of the day and the largesse of patrons. So it was that the massive temple to Apollo at the oracular site of Didyma was constructed during these centuries (it was never finished); there were new stadia at Apollo's Delphi and fountains at Zeus' Olympia. In Athens, in the first century A.D., the citizens voted overwhelmingly to preserve the traditional sanctuaries from encroachment by new building. An inscription from A.D. 220 restates the procedures for the annual procession from the city to Eleusis, which had now been held annually for some seven hundred years. In Patras near Athens a new temple to Artemis was built and Augustus himself donated the cult statue. At Pergamum a massive sanctuary to the healing god Asclepius was constructed on open ground below the citadel. (Here stood the nude statue to Hadrian mentioned above.) Its major building, the Asclepium, a circular domed building, fronted by a colonnaded entrance, dates from A.D. 150. Many new cities adopted the older cults to give themselves prestige (as Aizani did). Alongside them, the imperial cults were everywhere, acting as talismen of a city's loyalty.

Yet there was also a strong influx of cults from the east. Temples to the gods of Egypt are found in many cities. An Indo-Iranian god, Mithras, spawned a mystery cult that spread through the empire. It centered on small cells of male initiates meeting in caves or underground chambers. A mass of local cults and spiritual activities centered on caves, springs, and minor deities persisted. New religious movements could spring up from nowhere, gain the fervent support of credulous or anxious local populations, and then fade away. When, according to the Acts of the Apostles, Paul and his companion Barnabas visited the city of Lystra they were believed to have cured a lame man. At once they were acclaimed as gods, Paul as Zeus and Barnabas as Hermes. A great sacrifice in their honor was planned until Barnabas persuaded the priests that he was mortal and that his spiritual allegiances lay elsewhere.

None of these cults was mutually exclusive. One could drift in and out of them, combine worship at an altar to Zeus with that to a Roman emperor while fulfilling more deep-rooted spiritual needs in a mystery cult. If there was a trend it was for traditional gods to expand their roles. As seen earlier this had always happened in Greek religion. Gods combined a wide variety of powers and attributes and could always add more, often through absorbing local cults. In the Roman period, however, some gods took on an even more pervasive role. A colossal statue of Aphrodite found at Aphrodisias (and in the museum there) shows the goddess draped in a tunic with five "panels" of scenes outlining the extent of her concerns (which had always centered on love and sexuality). They include the sun and the moon, animals, sea deities (Aphrodite was born in the sea), and the underworld.

The best example of a deity who assumed a universal role is that of the Egyptian goddess Isis. Her worship had gained strength since the fourth century B.C. and she now absorbed powers of every kind. In Apuleius' novel *The Golden Ass* (probably c. A.D. 160), the goddess herself proclaims:

> I am nature, the universal mother, mistress of all the elements, primordial child of time, sovereign of all things spiritual, queen of the dead, queen also of the immortals, the single manifestation of all gods and goddesses that are. My nod governs the shining heights of heaven, the wholesome sea breezes, the lamentable silences of the gods below.

Isis goes on to list the many goddesses whose attributes she has appropriated. She presided over an important mystery cult, initiation into which was an intense mystical experience. "I approached the borders of death," writes Apuleius (whose account is assumed to be autobiographical). "I was borne along through all the elements and then I returned. At midnight I saw the sun blazing with bright light. I came into the presence of the gods who dwell above earth and those who dwell below." (Translations: Robert Graves.)

Even such an intense experience did not threaten conventional beliefs. Apuleius, in fact, records that the chief priest of Isis started the ceremonies with a prayer to the emperor, senate, and people of Rome. However, there were two major religious movements that could not have accepted this precaution. Both believed in a single god, worship of whom precluded any other religious allegiances. They were Judaism and Christianity.

Judaism was, of course, an ancient religion, well rooted in the Greek world. It had spread widely, in the ongoing diaspora, and adapted itself well to Greek culture. Jews may have made up as much as 8 percent of the empire's population. The Hebrew Scriptures were available in Greek: many Jews, in fact, had forgotten Hebrew entirely and abandoned their links to Jerusalem and the Temple there. The extent of the accommodation can be seen in the person of Philo, an Alexandrian Jew (first century A.D.) who was as at home with the works of Plato as with the Greek Bible. In many areas the Jews were tolerated and participated in city life on an equal basis. Inscriptions from many Greek cities, including Aphrodisias, for instance, show Jews as benefactors, often alongside Greeks. However, there were also areas where there were major and deep-rooted tensions between Greek and Jew. Alexandria was the most notorious. There were frequent riots and pogroms and on one occasion the city's Jews were rounded up and forced to eat pork. The emperor Gaius (better known as Caligula, emperor A.D. 37–41) caused further offense when he insisted that a statue of himself be set up in the temple at Jerusalem. In A.D. 66 a major revolt broke out in Judaea which was only suppressed by the Romans in 70, with pockets of resistance holding out longer. The temple was dismantled and its treasures taken off to Rome. After another revolt in the reign of Hadrian, Jerusalem was reconstituted as a Roman colony. This did not prevent the survival of Judaism in the empire as a whole, although the threat to Jewish survival increasingly came from Christianity rather than the Greek or Roman authorities.

The roots of Christianity lay within Judaism. Jesus lived and died within the Jewish world but once his followers absorbed the belief that he had risen from the dead after his crucifixion, he could not be accepted within a tradition which taught that the gulf between God and man was absolute. The spiritual world of the Greeks, where the boundaries between the human and divine were not so rigidly drawn, offered a greater possibility of acceptance. Even so there were difficulties. Jesus had existed as a living person but he was not like other divine figures of the Greek world whose status was dependent on their role as conquerors or kings. Jesus had died as a criminal on the cross. (As one early Christian, Justin Martyr, put it: "The pagans proclaim our madness to consist in this, that we give to a crucified man a place second only to the unchangeable and eternal god, the creator of all.") It was the remarkable achievement of the apostle Paul to create a meaning out of the crucifixion and one that he could proclaim as relevant for all human beings (Jews and non-Jews, slave and free, men and women).

Paul was born probably in the first decade A.D. to a Hellenistic Jewish family of the city of Tarsus in Cilicia, though he was also, unusually for this time, a Roman citizen. His Jewish roots were strong. He had studied in Jerusalem and his letters show virtually no influences from Greek literature. At first antagonistic to Christianity, he was converted after a vision of Christ "on the road to Damascus." It was his determination, energy, and vision of a Christianity that could expand outside its Jewish roots to Gentile; e.g., non-Jewish, communities that fueled his remarkable career. On his missions, reported in the Acts of the Apostles (although there are scholarly disputes over how accurately), he traveled widely, to Jerusalem, through Galatia, Asia, Macedonia, Greece, and even to Rome. In his famous letters, the earliest documents of Christianity, he struggles to set out a coherent vision of Christianity that frees it from the more restrictive elements of Jewish law without breaking its roots with Judaism itself. Although recent research is suggesting that first-century A.D. Judaism was not so monolithic as was once believed and Paul's ideas not quite so original, few if any individuals have succeeded in creating a coherent ideology that has had such an enduring and stimulating effect on later history. Jesus was enshrined at the very core of Christian faith, and it was faith in him as the risen Messiah, rather than rigid adherence to Jewish law which was the key to salvation.

Paul's letters soon became part of a much wider set of sacred texts.

Although some early Christians (notably Marcion, from the Greek city of Sinope on the Black Sea, in the early second century) believed Christianity should break completely with Judaism, Christians retained the Hebrew Scriptures, as their Old Testament. If Jesus was *Christos,* the Messiah, of Jewish tradition, then his coming must be foretold in the Scriptures and these were interpreted accordingly. There were also lives of Jesus, or rather attempts to assess his significance through accounts of his teachings and his trial and crucifixion. According to the gospel of Luke there were many of these (scholars know of some twenty) but by the second century four, those of Matthew, Mark, Luke and John, were given canonical status and the remainder rejected, lost, or suppressed. Like the letters of Paul they were written in Greek.

Unlike any traditional Greek religion, therefore, Christianity rested on sacred texts. This gave it a coherence lacking in other spiritual movements. The tendency of any religious movement in the Greek world was to fragment and Christianity was no exception. Christ as a spiritual leader was adopted within many other cults and beliefs. Gnostics believed that human souls were trapped in their earthly bodies, which could be liberated through the acquisition of knowledge (*gnosis*). They cast Jesus as a mediator between heaven and earth. The Manicheans, who believed that particles of light were trapped in a dark world and needed to be released, equated Jesus with the particles. Some took an intellectual approach to Christianity, interpreting it within a Greek philosophical framework (see below); others, the Montanists of Asia Minor, for instance, relied on direct ecstatic communications from God.

Although the range and diversity of the Old and New Testament texts made any agreed formulation of Christian belief difficult, they provided an authority eventually accepted by all, against which belief could be discussed, and so acted as a focus for the early Christian communities. There was a shared belief in a single god, a risen Christ, and the power of a "Holy Spirit." There was more than this. Paul had preached the importance of faith over adherence to Jewish law but Christians also inherited much of the Jewish ethical tradition. Jews valued chastity and the stability of family life. They visited the sick and supported the poor. This was echoed by the early Christian communities. "We Christians hold everything in common except our wives," said the second-century Tertullian. Three thousand destitute people were being supported by the church in Antioch in A.D. 300.

Shared ritual, including that of baptism, prayers, and fasting, a feeling of belonging to a community, and a belief that one was seen by God as an individual with the possibility of personal salvation all helped sustain the small Christian communities. Women appear to have made up a large part of the membership in early days. A tradition of asceticism made it easier for widows and virgins to be accepted than they were in traditional Greek and Roman communities.

Each community appointed its own bishop. The word *episcipos* ("bishop") had originally been used to describe an administrative official and at first the bishops regulated the community's affairs and conducted relations with neighboring churches. The administrative side of affairs was considered so important, especially after wealthy Christians started giving gifts to the church, that even non-Christians might be appointed bishops if they had the required administrative skills, although they were expected then to convert and master Christian theology. A major role for bishops, developed from the fourth century, was to meet in common council to make doctrine. This was an urgent requirement, especially as Christians were vulnerable to taunts from polytheistic Greeks that they were uneducated and credulous in worshipping a convicted criminal. To acquire credibility Christians needed to explain their faith within the intellectual framework of Greek philosophy.

"And the Word was made Flesh." These famous words from John's gospel mark the earliest integration of Greek philosophy into Christian theology. *Logos*, here translated as "the word," could mean, in fact, many things—"speech," "proclamation," "story," "reason," "rational principle," "logic" are among the possible translations. It has been argued that here the translation of "rational principle" might be more appropriate than "Word" as John seems to be expressing the Stoic belief that there was an underlying principle that governed the unfolding of the *cosmos*. It is this power he is equating with Jesus. (It goes without saying that this phrase, and the issues surrounding it, has been the subject of much scholarly debate.) The point to be made is that, as a phenomenon of the Greek world, Christianity naturally drew on Greek intellectual beliefs as it attempted to formulate its theology. Platonism was the most important influence. The central themes of Platonism, that there was a world beyond the world of the senses that could be grasped through reason and which was the sole repository of "value," survived and were developed by the so-called Middle and Neo-Platonists in the early centuries A.D. The most influential figure was Plotinus, born in Egypt in A.D. 205. Although his is a Roman name (and he taught in Rome for many years), Plotinus wrote in Greek and was certainly imbued with the Greek philosophical tradition.

Recent evaluations of Plotinus' work have seen him as the most important Greek philosopher of the middle Roman empire. Plotinus drew heavily not only on Plato but also Aristotle and the Stoics to produce his own relatively coherent philosophy. He developed Plato's idea of a Supreme Form, the Good, to make it a living force, "the One," which is the ultimate cause of all things, beyond all knowledge. Reality, however, permeates from "the One" but at a number of different levels, at the highest in a divine intellect (similar to Aristotle's unmoved mover), then through a "world soul" in which the soul of each individual participates, and finally, at the lowest level, to the enormously diverse world of matter. The individual who rejects the influence of his body and concentrates on his soul (Plotinus made important contributions to the concept of the soul) can reach back to the higher levels, the world soul, the divine intellect, even to "the One" itself. Then the seeker experiences an ecstatic and mystical moment "when the soul would exchange its present state for nothing in the world, though it was offered the kingdom of all the heavens: for this is 'the One' and there is nothing better."

In the second and third centuries Platonism had already permeated Christian thinking. The Christian god could be presented as the supreme Platonic form, eternal and unchanging, while the other forms, perfect manifestations as they were of their subjects, could be seen as the "thoughts of God." (There was a problem in fitting in Christ, as the Platonists had never believed that any individual could represent a "form" but the idea, articulated by John, that he was the *logos,* "the 'Word' made flesh" could be developed.) Plotinus, although never a Christian, brought a new coherence and depth to this approach. God could be equated with "the One" with individual souls' having the possibility of unity with him. Plotinus thus had a major impact and it was through him that Augustine reached God and Christianity. Another important influence on Christian thought and behavior was Stoicism. Stoicism provided the sense of a cosmic world order under an overriding power and valued modest living and endurance. This appealed to many Christians. It was not simply Greek philosophy as such that was important; it was Greek ways of thinking. Only through

Greek could the subtle distinctions needed to sustain theological positions on the complex issues of the nature of Christ be expressed. So long as the first article of the Church of England declares that God is "without body, parts or passions" or the Nicene Creed states that Jesus is "begotten not made, one in substance with the Father" Greek philosophy lives on in the modern world.

Christianity survived and spread because of the underlying attractions of its communities, its shared texts and beliefs, and its administrative framework. By the third century it was an important force in some, still largely eastern, cities. Yet the refusal of Christians to respect the imperial cults made them vulnerable at times of crisis. In the mid-third century the empire was beset with a mass of different invaders. Defeat could be associated with the faltering of respect for traditional gods and the cult of the emperor. Those, of whom the Christians were the most prominent, who refused to join the rituals were thus seen as undermining the empire itself. Persecution follows. It was not always consistent or universal. It depended very largely on the enthusiasms of local governor or city councilors (although empirewide persecutions were carried out by emperors such as Diocletian). Although many Christian communities collapsed under the pressure of persecution, others gained a new sense of commitment, their martyrs acting as exemplars of Christian fortitude. Christianity continued to grow.

An extraordinary change of fortune occurred in 313, only a few years after Diocletian had launched his persecution. A new emperor of the west, Constantine, proclaimed that Christianity would now be tolerated. Although he himself did not convert to Christianity until the end of his reign, Constantine appears to have recognized that Christianity would give the empire the spiritual cohesiveness it needed as pressures on its borders continued. He backed his decree of toleration with massive resources. Some of the great churches of the Christian world, including those in Jerusalem, were built. It is said that such riches had not been available for new building since the final year of Alexander's life. To give further coherence to his chosen faith Constantine summoned all the Christian bishops to the city of Nicaea, in northwest Asia Minor, in 325 for what was the church's first ecumenical council. The major issue for discussion was the relationship of Jesus Christ to God and the famous declaration of Nicaea that he was "consubstantial, of one substance with the father,"; although it did not settle the issue, it marked a further step in the consolidation of a uniform Christian doctrine.

With imperial support (there was only one non-Christian emperor, the short-lived Julian, after Constantine) Christianity gradually achieved a dominant role in the empire's spiritual life. As doctrine was established at successive ecumenical councils, so were heresies, beliefs incompatible with accepted doctrine, elaborated. An important moment came in 388. A Christian community had burned down a Jewish synagogue. The emperor Theodosius had ordered the local bishop to rebuild it, but under pressure from the bishop of Milan, Ambrose, he relented. Gone was the principle, long upheld by emperors, that one religion would not be privileged against another. The *Gymnasia,* centers of intellectual as much as sporting activities, had disappeared by the 390s. "It was the collapse of the *Gymnasia,* the focal point of Hellenism, more than any other event which brought in the Middle Ages," as one scholar has put it. Bath houses also disappear. At Hieropolis in Asia the bath house becomes a church. By the end of the century there was a concerted onslaught on traditional polytheistic beliefs. The oracle at Delphi was closed down by Theodosius in about 385. In 391 sacrifices were forbidden. Fervent believers from the new monastic communities of Egypt pioneered the destruction of temples. The Serapeum in Alexandria, one of the great temple complexes of the ancient world, was dismantled in 392. The building of the great temple to Apollo at the oracle at Didyma ceases ("templates" for the shapes of column bases are still to be seen on the temple walls). At Aphrodisias the great temple to Aphrodite is given an apse as it is transformed into a Christian church. (As this author was photographing the temple and its apse, the call to prayer rang across the site from a neighboring mosque, a reminder of the sweep of successive spiritual beliefs in the area.) In 415 a prominent female philosopher, Hypatia, was set upon in Alexandria by Christians, stripped naked, and dragged through the streets until she was dead. As shrines lost their aura, they were raided for their treasures with impunity. The statues of Zeus at Olympia and the Aphrodite of Cnidus were taken off to the new eastern "capital" Constantinople. Some institutions held out for longer than others. It was not until the sixth century that the emperor Justinian finally managed to close down Plato's Academy. The old world was in eclipse. When Christians tried successfully to remove a statue of Victory from the Roman senate house a leading senator uttered the swan song of the Greek intellectual tradition. "What does it matter by which wisdom each of us arrives at the truth? It is not possible that only one road leads to so sublime a mystery."

Society could not, of course, be changed overnight. Christianity operated in a society whose conventions and ways of living were centuries old. Many aspects of Greek life, the traditional marriage laws, the institution of slavery, passed on into Christian society. The basilica, the all-purpose meeting halls, which had been ubiquitous in Greco-Roman cities were adopted as the form of new churches. In art images from Greek mythology coexist with Christian ones for some decades. In the marriage casket from the Esquiline treasure (c. 380) a Christian inscription surrounds artwork that is still rooted in classical mythology with a nude Aphrodite/Venus occupying a prominent position in the center of the casket. In some representations Christ is shown being awarded a laurel leaf or portrayed as Apollo.

The erudite travel writer William Dalrymple captures the sweep of the change from Greek to Christian in his visit to the Greco-Roman Museum in Alexandria:

> In gallery after gallery, there is an easy drift of pagan and Christian motifs, styles, subjects and iconographies. The ankh, the Pharaonic symbol of life, appears on early Christian Alexandrian gravestones transformed into an ambiguous looped cross. The image of Isis nursing Horus is now reused in the Christian era unchanged, but now depicts the Virgin suckling the Christ child. Apollo raises a lamb over his shoulders and becomes the Good Shepherd. Dionysian vine scrolls tangle around scenes of the vintage; the same scrolls, hastily baptised with a cross, tangle on unchanged into the Christian era as a Eucharistic symbol. Nereids and victories swoop down from capitals and turn into angels midflight; again deities—Osiris and Aphrodite, Orpheus and Dionysus, Leda and the Zeus-Swan—survive into an afterlife as demons and godlings, removed from the centre of shrines but lurking still unvanquished at the back of Alexandrian churches . . . amid this fizz of dissolving philosophies, this iconographic metamorphis, there is the thrilling feeling of being present at the birth of medieval art. . . .

Constantine was also responsible for the foundation of one of the last great cities of antiquity, Constantinople, on the site of the earlier Greek city of Byzantium, overlooking the Bosphorus. Building began in 324 and the city was dedicated in 330. Its site was superb. It was accessible from land and sea and from both halves of the empire. Although not totally invulnerable from attack it had a good defensive position particularly after its western side was defended by the great expanse of early fifth-century walls, which still stand. However, overall very little remains of its original buildings. There is still the shape of its famous hippodrome where the great chariot races between the opposing factions of the Blues and Greens took place, and standing within it, the base of a column brought from Delphi. The imperial palace has vanished (although recent excavations have revealed some of it). From the sixth century the great church of Santa Sophia survives and the vast cisterns of the palace. (A visit to these provides one of the more memorable experiences open to those interested in antiquity. Recordings of arias from nineteenth-century operas echo through the vast underground halls.)

Constantinople was not planned as a Christian city, although it soon became one as the old gods were displaced. As the empire in the West collapsed in the fifth century it became the home of the emperors who continued to maintain the empire in the East. They were now the representatives of God on earth, maintaining order in an earthly kingdom while God kept order in the heavens. Something new was emerging, a Christian state centered on a virtually impregnable Greek-speaking city that declared itself the heir of Rome. Scholars disagree as to when they should call this new entity the Byzantine empire. Some prefer a date as early as 330, the year of the city's dedication, others prefer to wait until the Arab invasions of the seventh century, others again take the council of Chalcedon, 451, as the starting date. This last seems an appropriate moment to bring this book to a close.

By this time the flourishing city life of the east was also under threat (although many areas of the Greek world continued to be prosperous into the fifth and sixth centuries). The continuous pressures of invaders meant that resources had to be transferred, through taxation and manpower, from the cities to central government. With the coming of the fourth century the pace of building slowed and it seems to have been increasingly difficult to maintain the mass of buildings from earlier eras. The confidence to maintain them also faltered with the spread of Christianity. As bishops took on responsibility for the needs of the poor, one of the major roles of the city councilors was undermined. Many of the traditional buildings of a proud city, temples, *Gymnasia,* and bath houses were redundant in a Christian city.

There were also natural disasters, earthquakes, and plague. Aphrodisias was flooded after earthquakes in the 350s and 360s. Its buildings were repaired in the fifth century, but after a major earthquake in the seventh century they were left in ruins. In the middle of the sixth century, the first outbreaks of bubonic plague hit the Greek cities. As none of the crowded city populations could have developed any immunity, it can be assumed that the death toll was high. In many cities, as a result of plague or general decay, excavation has shown that public buildings were taken over as homes and the grand central streets were built over by those who had withdrawn to the center. War added its toll. The great city of Antioch was sacked by the Persians in the 540s. Invading Slavs and Avars caused considerable damage to Athens in 582. Sparta, Argos, and Corinth were abandoned in the late sixth century, the inhabitants of Corinth taking refuge in Acrocorinth, the citadel above the city. In the seventh century the Arabs overran Egypt and much of the Near East, bringing a new and enduring phase to that region's history. Greek culture did not disappear overnight and the Arabs themselves absorbed the works of many prominent Greeks, primarily Aristotle, but also Plato, Hippocrates, Galen, and the astronomer Ptolemy. In Constantinople, Greek scholarship and a mass of ancient texts survived and these served to fuel a revival of Greek studies in the west (where Greek had been forgotten) from the thirteenth century onward.

By the fifth century Christianity had permeated most parts of the empire and had transformed the spiritual landscape. Much has been said of the enormous diversity of religious belief in the Greek world and the ease with which spiritual experiences could be sought through a variety of coexisting cults. There was no system of authority through which one form of belief was given superiority over any other and this must partly explain why such impressive progress could be made in intellectual and political affairs. The Christian God was something different. While the Greek gods had their own relationships with each other to divert them, and they indulged in every form of "human" activity, including sexual, this God was presented in lonely and unchanging splendor. It was assumed that the behavior of individual human beings was his main concern and by the fourth century aberrant sexual activity (according to some, any enjoyment of the sexual act) was highlighted as a particular area of his interest. While public participation in cults was all that was required in traditional Greek religion, God's knowledge penetrated deep into the human mind. "All things were known to God." He could reward souls after death with admittance to heaven or damn them to hell. (A belief in some form of eternal punishment for wrongdoers in hell dates from early Christianity. One of the joys of heaven, said the second-century theologian Tertullian, would be the ability of saints to watch the torments of those suffering there.) This marks a massive shift in the collective and individual mentality of Greek society and ushers in the Middle Ages. It seems an appropriate place to close this book.

21

Conclusion: The Greek Achievement

The Greeks provided the chromosomes of Western civilization. One does not have to idealize the Greeks to sustain that point. Greek ways of exploring the *cosmos*, defining the problems of knowledge (and what is meant by knowledge itself), creating the language in which such problems are explored, representing the physical world and human society in the arts, defining the nature of value, describing the past, still underlie the Western cultural tradition. In some areas, the creation of mathematics, for instance, the legacy has become a universal one. All mathematicians everywhere work within a framework whose foundations are Greek.

Yet in the late-twentieth century the Greeks can still be something of an embarrassment to the Western world. The male citizens who ran the Greek city-states did so in their own interests. Their women were segregated and marginalized in virtually every area of city life. They were heavily dependent on slaves who, in the more prosperous cities, may have made up 30 to 40 percent of the population. It was clear that the very identity of male citizenship, shown off above all in sculpture, the male represented nude at the height of his physical power, was sustained by having women, slaves, and children classified as something other. (To requote Aristotle, "The slave does not possess the faculty of deliberation at all, the female possesses it but in an indecisive form and the child possesses it but in an imperfect form.") Some Greeks, Plato, for instance, even divided the citizen body itself into the elite who had the capacity to rule others and those whose instincts for pleasure made them unworthy of such a role.

The Greek male also defined himself against outsiders, "the barbarians." As Edward Said has pointed out in his *Orientalism: Western Conceptions of the Orient*, the enduring image of the East, where there are despotic tyrants living in luxury and the mass of people living in subjection, has its roots in the Greek articulation of "barbarism" after the Persian Wars. The Greeks not only created the idea of "barbarism," by doing so they created the notion that some cultures are intrinsically superior to others and this fed into European imperialism. It still lingers in studies of Greece itself. It is usually assumed, as if no discussion of the point was necessary, that Alexander benefited central Asia by his conquest of it.

The nature of Greek society sits uneasily alongside the intellectual and cultural achievements of the Greeks. Here lies the central paradox of the Greek legacy. There has been an understandable tendency to avoid facing up to it in this form, to defuse the issue altogether. One approach has been to suggest that the Greek cultural achievement, dependent as it was on slavery and the suppression of women, must be intrinsically flawed. The status of Homer as "a great poet," for instance, must be something artificially created, sustained by the Greeks themselves and later by the architects of an elitist Western cultural tradition. If this tradition were to be discarded, it is implied, Homer's epics would be seen as poems of no special distinction. In fact, individuals are free to explore the Greek cultural heritage, such of it that survives, on their own terms (though it would be naive to expect one could escape cultural conditioning entirely). Homer, for instance, seems quite capable of looking after himself as a renewed interest in the epics, sustained by several high quality translations of them, has shown in recent years.

Another approach has been to argue that the Greeks were not as objectionable as they were painted. H.D.F. Kitto's *The Greeks* (first published in 1951 but with many reprints and revisions since then) is typical. For Kitto "The Athenian had his faults, but preeminent among his better qualities were lively intelligence, sociability, humanity, and curiosity." Having made this somewhat sweeping generalization, Kitto goes on to defend the Athenian treatment of women against those who have criticized it and concludes, "To say that he [the Athenian] habitually treated one half of his own race [sic] with indifference even contempt, does not, to my mind, make sense." By starting with his assumption that the Athenian is naturally sociable with fellow human beings, the conclusion must surely follow. Kitto then goes on to discuss slavery. Here again things were not that bad. "We know, from vase-painting and other sources, that real friendship between the slave and his owner was not uncommon: it all depended on the individuals concerned. Enslavement, after all, was a haphazard thing. Many a slave was a very decent and intelligent man, and the Athenians were sensible enough to distinguish between the status and the man." Kitto seems to have missed the essence of slavery, that the identity of the Athenian as a free citizen depended on the maintenance of the slave as such. The slave was property and treated accordingly. His evidence could not be believed in an Athenian court unless he had been tortured first and if he was disabled his owner could expect compensation for the damage. It is unlikely that a Greek sat down in the evenings and shared friendship with "the very decent and intelligent men" he had cooped up in the slave quarters (many of whom would have been unable to speak Greek with any competence). As for the women the evidence suggests they were helpless in the face of his sexual demands. And what, one might ask, happened to those slaves who were not gifted with "intelligence or decency"? (In Roman society slaves could be treated equally brutally but many were highly educated Greeks, and friendships, which could be followed by the grant of freedom, were possible.)

No study of the Greeks can hope to recreate the Greeks as they really were. The evidence for that simply does not exist and every work of history operates within the cultural and ideological preconceptions of its writer and his or her times. (History, as has often been said, is a continuous interplay between past and present. Kitto's study of women in classical Athens has as much to say about conservative male attitudes to women in the 1950s as about those of the Greeks.) So what can be said about Greek society and its legacy from the perspective of the early-twenty-first century and a middle-class, middle-aged Western male?

One might start with the assumption that Greek society in the days of the independent *polis* was dominated by male citizens, that citizenship gave privileges and political power to an elite, and that within this elite there was intense competition for individual status. This competition spilled over into a wider Greek world and was displayed both in war and in the Panhellenic games. Fundamental to Greek society was a belief in heroic values, values which were underwritten by a mass of mythological heroes, among them those of the Homeric epics, who acted as exemplars. The crucial point was that there was no unbridgeable gulf between the achievements of the heroes and those of ordinary beings at the peak of their physical strength. The heroes always use their (human) arms, legs, and intelligence. Their weapons are the same as those of ordinary mortals and they never resort to magic to escape from impossible situations. (In fact they can be overcome by them and die.) Ever if the weights lifted, the numbers of enemies killed, the wild animals subdued often need the hero to use superhuman strength, it is only a matter of scale. A mortal, it is implied, could achieve the same if he was just that bit stronger. The lack of any psychological restraint on (Greek, male) achievement seems to have been an important element of Greek culture, and achievement itself was deeply satisfying. The poet Pindar captures the feeling when he tells of victors in the games as coming close to the gods and the heroes of old.

There was also intense competition between males within the city and it had its own important effects. For the city to survive as a stable and defensible community, means had to be found of resolving conflicts through argument. Many arenas developed in which such argument could take place, ruling councils, assemblies, and the law courts. What is clear is that impassioned discussion fostered not only a highly sophisticated language of debate but the rules of argument themselves. As a result the Greeks were able to speak (and write) with impressive lucidity and power. The English historian Macaulay was, of course, writing in the tradition of the nineteenth-century adulation of Greece when he wrote of the Greek language that, "We cannot refuse our imagination to that perfect machine of human thought, to the flexibility, the harmony, the gigantic power, the exquisite delicacy, the infinite wealth of words" but it is true that Greek developed as a superb vehicle for all kinds of oral and written expression. It had the range to deal with topics of every kind and the subtlety with which to explore the nuances of argument. The contrast can be made with republican Rome. Here as late as the first century B.C. Latin was an undeveloped language and one unsuited to argument. The introduction of grammar, rhetoric, and philosophy from Greece and the assimilation of Greek rules of thought into Latin transformed it and proved, in the words of the late Elizabeth Rawson, an authority on the intellectual life of the Roman republic, "a step of primary importance to the history of the west."

However, the Greeks went much further than merely to provide a language. They could stand back and assess their language as a means of expressing ideas and of sustaining power and influence. Thucydides understood only too well how catchphrases were manipulated by those in power (an essential insight in itself, brilliantly explored in the twentieth century by George Orwell). As Simon Goldhill has shown in his *Greek Tragedy* (Chapter One) tragedians continually reflected on the way that language could be used in drama to create a range of effects. This, in fact, was the major worry of Plato who recognized that an argument or belief can be enhanced by its presentation by a skilled speaker and through musical accompaniment. This is how assemblies were swung over by unscrupulous speakers. Instead, argued Plato, the real purpose of language was to be used as a means of reasoning to find the truth behind the false images created by the public speaker. What is important here is not so much the views of the theorists as the sophisticated nature of the discussion about language as a medium for communicating ideas and emotions.

The analysis of language was part of an intellectual experience whose range is astonishing. It includes the foundations of political thought, ethics, metaphysics, drama, mathematics, scientific enquiry, including medicine, ways of presenting art, the presentation of the past. These areas were not only mapped out but the fundamental questions which form the core of these subject disciplines were isolated. What is the meaning of existence? What is it to live a good life? Are numbers a purely abstract phenomenon or do they relate to some form of other reality? Is there a world beyond this one that can be grasped through reason? Are there some underlying physical laws that might explain the nature of matter? Is human nature intrinsically good or does it have to be molded by appropriate laws? Are moral values relative to the situation or absolute? These were not just presented as questions with arguments attached. In drama the dilemmas of life were presented with the appropriate emotional intensity. In Greek tragedy one is confronted with the complex interplay of the forces of reason and unreason in human relationships. The Greeks never shrank from dealing with the mysteries of human existence.

The influence of this on Western society, much of it mediated through the Roman experience, has been immense. Some of the influence has been purely consequential. The Greeks devised a method of housing a cult statue of a god or goddess in a particular kind of building that was surrounded by columns and whose facade was surmounted by a pediment. The Romans adopted (in a modified form) the same concept of a monumental temple and the symmetrical, columned classical facade with pediment was reinvented by Renaissance architects and still holds its power. It is possible that it represents some kind of ideal, in the sense of a Platonic form, and this is why it appeals, but it seems more realistic to say that this is just one way that a building can be constructed and it has proved influential mainly because Greece and Rome have themselves been influential.

The same might be said about drama. The Greeks initiated a particular form of public performance in which individuals impersonate characters in front of an audience and follow through a story about them. The method has proved an excellent way of dealing with dilemmas in a distanced form, of making comments about the ways individuals and societies react, of providing entertainment. Again, partly through the mediation of Rome, drama reentered European culture in the Renaissance and has remained a major art form in itself. In any major city one can find both the original Greek tragedies and a wide range of dramatic offshoots, genetic mutations of the originals, as it were, being performed at the same time. Yet drama is an attribute of Western civilization, if a particularly satisfying one, rather than an intrinsic element of it.

Similarly with the Greek contribution to art. The desire to represent the physical world through representational art and to experience it through music seems to be intrinsic to human existence and the Greeks were no exception to this. Greek music, which was a pervasive element of life and the core of Greek education, has vanished. So has most of Greek art (virtually all Greek painting has vanished and only an estimated one in every thousand bronze statues survives) but enough remains to understand its main concerns. The Greeks grappled with the problems of representation, as artists have had to ever since, and by the fifth century they had managed to provide superb representations of the human body in marble and in bronze. In temple sculpture they had mastered the art of presenting narrative and of using relief work to show perspective. On pottery, the only form of painting which survives in quantity, they used space and the technique of foreshortening to widen the range of what could be represented. These were major achievements in themselves but they also encapsulated particular forms of representation, the male, and later, after Praxiteles, the female nude, the portrait bust, and landscape (both from the Hellenistic period). The Greeks defined ways of seeing things that have not dominated or constrained European art but that have been an important element of it. The same could be said of particular forms of literature which the Greeks made their own, epics (although here the tradition is more universal), lyrics, elegies, pastoral poetry.

The loss of temple pediments, drama, sculptures of nudes, forms of literary expression would not have meant the collapse of Western civilization, although it might have been the poorer for it in ways which are impossible to assess. Is it possible to define aspects of the Greek achievements that have proved fundamental to the way the Western world operates?

Aristotle himself began his works with a survey of what had been achieved in the subject he was tackling. He would sum up what had been said, who had said it, and the problems still left to be solved. In doing so he introduced the idea that the acquiring of knowledge was a cumulative process. One could always hope to make progress from what had been established before although it has to be accepted that, in a world where the capacity of the senses is limited, complete knowledge is never possible. Such an approach was threatened by the Platonic view that all knowledge of reality was, in theory, attainable through the use of reason and it was the Platonic rather than Aristotelian approach that, absorbed within Christian theology, held sway until the sixteenth and seventeenth centuries. Since then Aristotle's view of the possibilities of endless intellectual progress, particularly in the sciences, has again predominated and it is central to the Western experience. It has been underpinned, in a way that was not possible in ancient Greece, by successful practical applications of science to almost every aspect of everyday life. Scientists still operate within the assumption that they are making progress toward full understanding of the physical world.

One cannot make significant intellectual progress, however, without being able to make arguments and develop ways of assessing their validity. The Greeks not only argued, passionately and with immense creativity, they explored the means for argument. They mapped out the areas in which reason might be of use and the extent to which it could sustain absolute knowledge. Aristotle defined a system of logic that was influential until the nineteenth century. The Greeks founded mathematics in the sense that, unlike the Egyptians and Babylonians, they were able to conceive of numbers and shapes as abstractions and then develop theorems that could be sustained by rational proofs. As suggested above, mathematicians operate within the same framework today. It was Plato who postulated that reason was the only way of achieving complete knowledge of a world whose reality was more profound than anything experienced by the other senses. There were immense dangers here and Plato is now respected more for his way of doing philosophy than his ideas. (As Karl Popper has argued in his *The Open Society and its Enemies*, and the experience of the twentieth century has confirmed, it is all too easy for a self-selected thinker to claim to have reached reality and to impose his vision on the society around him). Nevertheless Christian theology remains rooted in Platonism.

However much Plato tried to downgrade the natural world, human senses "know" that it exists in some form, the nature of which needs to be explored. One could simply assume that the natural state of the world is chaos, that inaccessible gods determine the fate of humans, and nothing is predictable (as Archilochus was suggesting in 650 B.C.). From the sixth century B.C. Greek philosophers took the view that there was an underlying order to the *cosmos* which could be discovered through observation and speculation on that observation (the empirical approach) or through reason (Parmenides and Plato). This as Lewis Wolpert has argued in his *The Unnatural Nature of Science* was a major breakthrough. "A scientific mode of thought," he argues, in a chapter entitled "Thales's Leap" originated in Greece. No other society seems to have developed it and "all later developments in science can be traced back to the Greeks." The Greeks not only originated a new way of thinking about the physical world, they deployed considerable ingenuity in developing it. Most of their solutions, as is now clear, were misguided, but one has to be impressed by the attempts, for instance, to find order in the stars. The greatest success seems to have been in mathematics where Archimedes and others provided foundations without which later mathematicians would not have been able to progress.

A society has to find a way of dealing with its past if it is to fully understand itself and the parameters within which it operates. This involves defining the forces which drive human societies. If the motivating force is a god (as in the Jewish historical tradition where God works as a protector of the nation Israel) then this will constrain the way history is written. A victory or defeat in battle is the result of God's favor or anger with his chosen people and is interpreted as such. If a God, or "the gods," are not accorded such a dominating role, then one is forced to see history as created by human beings themselves. The Greek historians took this approach. Herodotus saw the success of the Greeks in the Persian Wars partially in terms of their relationship with their environment. Thucydides was far more cynical about human nature and saw little of nobility in the struggles of the Greeks in the Peloponnesian War. It was, however, because history was in the hands of human beings that it was so brutal. Polybius *was* prepared to accept that an outside force, *tyche,* fortune, might influence history but the nature of his own work suggests that the activities of humans are crucial in shaping the way societies develop. The Greeks also set out ways of collecting and assessing evidence from the past so that some kind of historical truth might be found. "Just as a living creature, if it is deprived of its eyesight, is rendered completely helpless, so if history is deprived of the truth, we are left with nothing but an idle, unprofitable tale," said Polybius. Western historians still work within this tradition.

Greek culture was born within the cockpit of the city and city life was idealized at least until the crises of the fourth century B.C. and the coming of Alexander. Plato and Aristotle could not imagine a harmonious society that was not centered on the city and they were as much founding fathers of political thought as they were of philosophy. This intense concentration on the ideal city spawned much more than the birth of political thought. The perfect city government could not be defined without first establishing some concept of the purpose of human existence, the nature of human happiness and of justice, even the right way to create harmonious individuals. When city life began to collapse it was natural for the Greeks to explore other means of living, outside the protection of the city. The Epicureans related themselves to their mannered friendships safe from the turmoil of public life; the Stoics found a sense of purpose in their membership of the wider human race. Overall, there is an astonishing richness in the variety and sophistication of Greek thought about the nature of life and the art of living.

The flaw of the Greek political system was that it never developed a theory of human rights. Rights and duties were assigned not on a universal basis but on the grounds of status and sex. It is in the Christian tradition with its emphasis that each soul is of equal interest to God that the possibilities of such rights lay, even if they were not fully articulated, as "natural rights," before the eighteenth century. So the religion that destroyed the Greek way of thinking also provided the means of resolving its greatest flaw. Such are the paradoxes of history. They cannot easily be explained away and it is perhaps in their understanding, shown in its greatest maturity in Greek tragedy, that any progress in life destroys old possibilities as much as it creates new ones that the Greeks made one of their most significant contributions to understanding the mysteries of human existence.

There is another major point to be made about the Greeks that is only slowly rising to the forefront of the subject, the resilience of their culture. If one accepts a starting point of the eighth century B.C. (as seen in Chapter Two, one can track elements of Greek culture back further still) and concludes with the fourth century A.D. with the coming of Christianity, then one is talking of a twelve-hundred-year span. The works of Homer, the Olympic Games, the oracle at Delphi remained central to Greek culture for all these centuries. The intense intellectual creativity of earlier centuries may have been lost by the early centuries A.D. but the vitality of Greek city life in the east remained. It is just in these centuries, under the protection of Roman hegemony, that Greek culture was able to expand eastward into Syria, Anatolia, and beyond to the Euphrates. This was no dead or decadent culture as it has been so often portrayed.

This book sees the coming of Christianity as a turning point but Christianity in the East was still essentially a Greek phenomenon. Theological discussion may have been constrained by the elaboration of heresies but there is no mistaking the essentially Greek approach to theology, fervent discussion, subtle analysis, a determination to get to the core of an issue. (As the theologian Gregory of Nyssa put it when in Constantinople in the 380s, "If you ask someone to give you change, he philosophizes about the Begotten and the Unbegotten. . . . If you say to the attendant 'Is my bath ready?,' he tells you that the Son was made out of nothing.") As the empire in the West collapsed, the Greeks continued. The Byzantines might call themselves *Romaioi,* Romans, but by the end of the sixth century Latin had virtually disappeared in the East. In 629 the emperor Heraclius dropped the traditional title *imperator* and adopted the Greek one of *basileus,* which had its origins in the aristocratic households of Homer's epics some fifteen hundred years before. His leading military man was a *strategos,* a general, the term used for Athens' elected military men in the late sixth century B.C. One can then take the story on, as Edward Gibbon does in his *Decline and Fall of the Roman Empire*, to 1453, the capture of Constantinople by the Ottoman Turks.

"The Greek Achievement," then, is remarkable and one can applaud it without having to hide away the elements of Greek society that are unacceptable to the Western world of the year 2000. One can perhaps celebrate not only that achievement but also the fact that we may have reached the point, after the ideological extremes adopted by earlier enthusiasts and detractors, that we are able to assess the Greeks objectively and maturely and to understand the extent to which they have laid the foundations of the Western world.

Date List

Bronze Age Greece

5000–2000. Emergence of the Greek language from Indo-European roots among the mixed population of mainland Greece. Debate continues over more exact dates for the process.
Before 2000 Domestication of vines from wild varieties (which themselves were first known in Greece about 5000 B.C.).
2000. The "palace civilizations" of Crete first become established.
2000–1600. The so-called Old Palace Period of Minoan civilization.
1650. The first use of the shaft graves, Grave Circle B from 1650, Grave Circle A from 1600, at Mycenae on mainland Greece. (The graves were rediscovered by Heinrich Schliemann in 1876.) The graves are used and reused until c. 1500.
1628–1627. Massive volcanic eruption on the Aegean island of Thera (modern Santorini). The trading town of Acrotiri is preserved under the ash.
c. 1600. The Cretan palaces are destroyed (in the aftermath of the Thera eruption?) but are soon rebuilt on a more magnificent scale.
1600–1425. The height of Minoan civilization, the so-called New Palace Period. Crete's trading empire extends to Egypt, the Near East, and the Aegean.
1600–1400. Mycenaean chieftains consolidate their position on the Greek mainland. Their power is sustained by raids overseas and the building of a network of trading activities.
1450–1425. New wave of destruction of Cretan palaces, possibly as a result of earthquakes, internal conflict, or a direct Mycenaean conquest.

The Mycenaeans settle on Crete. They adapt the Minoan Linear A script for their own language, which is an early form of Greek (deciphered by Michael Ventris in 1952). The new script is known as Linear B. By now Mycenaean presence is recorded throughout the Mediterranean from Italy to the coast of Asia and Egypt.
c.1350. The *Kas* shipwreck. The excavation of this trading vessel by George Bass has given a vivid picture of eastern Mediterranean trade in Mycencan times.
1200–1100. Collapse of Mycenaean civilization through internal conflict, earthquakes, or the disruption of trading routes and the settlements themselves by raiders.

1100–800: The "Dark Ages"

1100–950. Migrations of Greeks to the Aegean and coast of Asia Minor following the collapse of Mycenaean civilization.
1050–1000. First use of iron on mainland Greece, at first for weapons and then, by 1000, for agricultural implements.
1100–825. The settlement at Lefkandi provides evidence of the continuation of Greek culture in the Dark Ages. (The "hero's" tomb at Lefkandi is dated to 1000–975 B.C.) Trading links established between Lefkandi and Cyprus and the East.
1050–900. Signs of the revival and independence of Athens demonstrated through its own style of pottery, the so-called protogeometric style.
c. 900. Foundation of Sparta.
850. Greeks from Euboea become drawn into the Mediterranean trading networks of Phoenicians and other peoples of the Near East.
1000–750. The Phoenicians enjoy widespread prosperity as traders throughout the Mediterranean.
(**814.** Traditional date of the foundation of Carthage by the Phoenicians.)
900–725. The age of geometric pottery in Athens. (770–725. "The Dipylon master" provides figures of warriors and mourners on pots.)
825. Greeks are found among other traders at al-Mina at the mouth of the Orontes river.
800. Earliest dedications at the oracle site of Delphi.
776. Traditional date of the founding of the Olympic Games, although the site may well have been used for festivities before that.
c. 775–750. First settlement of Pithecusae (on the island of Ischia off the Italian coast) by Euboean Greeks (and others from the Near East).
(**753.** Traditional date of the founding of Rome.)
750. The Greeks borrow and adapt the Phoenician alphabet for their own use adding vowels. Most Greek communities adopt an alphabet.
750–700. Emergence of first "cities" on mainland Greece, as settlements

define their boundaries, walls, and cemeteries. Appearance of first Greek "temples"; e.g., to Hera on Samos and to Artemis at Ephesus. The earliest surviving hoplite (citizen soldier) helmet dates from 725 B.C. (Argos).
750–700. The *Iliad* and *Odyssey*, traditionally attributed to Homer, reach their final form.
735. The Greeks begin the colonization of Sicily.
(**733.** Foundation of Syracuse by the Corinthians.)
725. Greeks set up a settlement at Cumae on the Italian coast enabling them to trade directly with the Etruscans (as well as to feed themselves).
720. Greek colonization of southern Italy and the Chalcidice peninsula in the northern Aegean now well in hand.

730–620: The So-called Orientalizing Period

A wide range of eastern influences permeate Greek culture.
730–710. Spartan conquest of Messenia and subjugation of its native (Greek) inhabitants, now termed the helots.
c. 700. Hesiod's *Theogeny* and *Works* and *Days.*
The Lelantine War between Chalcis and Eretria marks the end of the old aristocratic Greece. Corinth emerges as the most powerful of the Greek cities. Its so-called proto-Corinthian pottery (725 onward, the Chigi vase, 650 B.C.) becomes the most commercially successful pottery of the period.
First penetration of the Black Sea by the Greeks. (Byzantium founded c. **660,** although permanent Greek settlements were probably not established on the sea until c. **650.**)
The Etruscans adopt the Greek alphabet.
675–640. The poet Archilochus of Paros reaches Thasos about **650** B.C.
669. Defeat of Sparta by Argos at the Battle of Hysiae. The defeat, and a subsequent rebellion of the helots in Messenia, probably initiates the militarization of Spartan society.
660s onward. First Greek traders penetrate Egypt. By **600,** Egyptian influences on Greek sculpture are apparent (in the marble *kouroi,* for instance).
657. Cypselus becomes tyrant in Corinth, overthrowing the aristocratic clan of the Bacchidae. Tyrannies become the most common form of government in the Greek states in the hundred years that follow.
c. 650. Marble is used for sculpture for the first time in Greece.
c. 640. The poetry of the Spartan Tyrtaeus reflects the new importance given to loyalty of citizens to the *polis* (rather than to aristocratic clans).
c. 635. Limestone temple to Apollo at Thermon in northwest Greece, one of the earliest Doric-style temples. The style has reached maturity by **600** (in, for example, the temple to Artemis on Corfu).
630. Cyrene (north Africa) settled by Greek colonists from Thera.

621. Draco's "Draconian" law code in Athens fails to relieve social tensions.

620–480: The Archaic Age

An age in which greater order and formality is brought to Greek culture.

c. 600. Emergence of Ionic order on temples in Ionian cities of Asia Minor.

Foundation of Gravisca, Greek trading post on the coast of Italy, for trade with the Etruscans, makes an intensification of the Greek-Etruscan relationship.

Invention of trireme in Corinth (according to Herodotus).

Foundation of Massilia (the modern Marseilles) by the Phocaeans.

The world's first coinage emerges in Lydia. It spreads to the trading island of Aegina by **595** and Athens by **550.**

Emergence of the Etruscan temple form that shows Greek influences. It is adopted by the Romans.

594. Solon is appointed archon in Athens with full power to reform the state. He initiates an important program of social and political reforms.

585. The starting point of Greek philosophy traditionally marked by the prediction by Thales of Miletus of an eclipse of the sun. The search begins for the underlying structure of the *cosmos*. Thales' fellow Miletians Anaximander and Anaximenes develop their own ideas in the decades that follow.

582–573. The foundation of new Panhellenic games (the Pythian Games at Delphi, **582,** the Isthmian Games, **581,** the Nemean Games, **573**).

c. 580. As the best sites in the western Mediterranean are filled Phoenicians and Greeks clash over Sicily and gradually consolidate their own spheres of influence.

575–560. The temple to Hera at Samos, one of the first monumental Greek temples, shows the influence of monumental Egyptian buildings.

c. 570. Death of the lyric poet Sappho.

c. 570. The so-called François vase, made in Athens, marks the reemergence of Athens as a major pottery-making center.

560. The Spartans are defeated by the Tegeans at the Battle of Fetters and adopt a more conciliatory approach to their neighbors.

560–530. Reign of Cyrus I, the founding king of the Achaemenid empire.

560–546. Pisistratus struggles, with eventual success, to achieve control as tyrant of Athens.

c. 550. The declining status of the Greek aristocracy lamented by the poet Theognis of Megara.

Athenian pottery begins to dominate the Etruscan market.

546. Conquest of Lydia by Cyrus. Subjugation of the Ionian Greek cities of Asia Minor to the new Persian empire.
c. 540. The lost wax methods of casting bronze is first used, on the island of Samos. Large bronze statues from **525** B.C. onward. Bronze now becomes the preferred medium for free-standing statues, although only a tiny proportion survive.
540. The Etruscans and Phoenicians combine to drive out the Phocaeans from their new colony at Alalia (Corsica).
530. The height of black pottery manufacture seen especially in the works of the Athenian painter Exekias.
546–510. The Pisistratids oversee a major building program on the Acropolis and the foundation of new religious festivals such as the Great Panathenaea.
530. Following his exile from Samos the philosopher/mathematician Pythagoras founds a community at Croton in southern Italy.
525. Red figure ware replaces black figure as the main product of the Athenian potters.
c. 520–c. 490. Reign of King Cleomenes of Sparta. His active overseas policy weakens his position at home and leads to his eventual assassination.
522. Darius becomes king of Persia after mounting a coup against Cambyses.
514. Carius crosses the Hellespont into Thrace, where he conducts inconclusive campaigns against the Scythians but maintains a Persian presence in Europe.

Attempted coup in Athens against the Pisistratid tyranny led by Harmodius and Aristogeiton.

510. Pisistratus' son Hippias is overthrown in Athens with the support of Sparta.

Revolution in the use of perspective on pottery by "the Pioneers."

(**509.** Foundation of Roman republic.)

508–507. Reforms of Cleisthenes in Athens lay the foundations for Athenian democracy through the setting up of local deme government.
c. 507. Annexation of the border town of Eleutherae into Athenian territory. The import of its festival to Dionysus to Athens may mark the birth of drama.
c. 504. Formation of Peloponnesian League under Spartan leadership.
501. First election in Athens of the ten generals (*strategoi*) who are to become the most prestigious of the officers of the state in the fifth century.
c. 500. Heraclitus of Ephesus and Parmenides of Elea develop their philosophical ideas.
499–494. Revolt of Ionian Greeks against the Persians. Athens and Eretria provide support. The revolt is eventually defeated at the Battle of Lade.

499. Earliest record of a play by Aeschylus.
498. First surviving poem of Pindar. First *Olympian Ode*, **476**, first *Pythian Ode*, **470**. Pindar remains active, praising victors from throughout the Greek world, until at least **446**.
493. Themistocles becomes an archon at Athens. He initiates the building of the harbor at Piraeus, the first effective harbor Athens has known.
490. Persian invasion of Greece. The Persians land at Marathon north of Athens but are defeated at the Battle of Marathon by the Athenians and Plataeans.
487. First record of the performance of comedies at the Dionysia in Athens.
Ostracism recorded in Athens for the first time.
484. The tragedian Aeschylus achieves his first victory at the Dionysia festival.
482. Themistocles diverts the fruits of a new seam of silver from the Laurion mines to build an Athenian fleet.

480–336: The Classical Age

This era is traditionally seen as the culminating years of the Greek achievement.
c. 480. The so-called Critian boy from Athens traditionally marks the transition from Archaic to classical art.
480–479. A major expedition of the Persian king Xerxes to conquer Greece begins with success but ends in the defeat of the Persian forces at Salamis (**480**) and Plataea (**479**). The Carthaginians (Phoenicians who have settled permanently in the western Mediterranean) attack Sicily and are also defeated.
477. Athens forms the Delian League from among the Aegean cities. Continuing warfare against Persia under the Athenian aristocratic leader Cimon leads to the elimination of the Persian threat but sees the consolidation of Athenian power in the Aegean. Sparta acquiesces in Athenian expansion.
475–450. The relief sculptures on the temple to Zeus at Olympia, the major surviving example of the "Severe Style" in classical art.
472. Aeschylus' *The Persians*, a rare example of a tragedy dealing with a contemporary issue, helps consolidate a contrast between Greeks and "barbarians."
471. Themistocles is ostracized by aristocratic factions in Athens.
470. An attempted secession of Naxos from the Delian League is thwarted by Athens.
470. Birth of Socrates.

468. The tragedian Aeschylus is defeated by Sophocles for the first time in the Dionysia festival.
c. 468. Battle of Eurymedon River (Pamphylia). Cimon destroys a large Persian fleet and, in effect, blunts any chance of an effective Persian counterattack on Greece.
465. The island of Thasos revolts against the League and is subdued by Athenian forces.
464. An earthquake in Sparta is followed by a revolt of the helots. Cimon takes a hoplite army to help suppress the revolt but the Athenian help is rejected.
463. Aeschylus' play *The Suppliants* suggests that democratic ideals are increasingly acceptable in Athens.
461. Democratic revolution in Athens shifts power to the Athenian Assembly. Cimon is ostracized and relations with Sparta are broken off.
461–429. Pericles, one of the leaders of the revolution, maintains his personal supremacy in Athens throughout these years, using the post of *strategos* as the source of his power.
461–445. The first Peloponnesian War between Athens and Sparta. Athens builds the Long Walls (**458**). The first battle between Spartan and Athenian troops is at Tanagra (**457**), and is followed by an Athenian conquest of Boeotia.
458. The *Oresteia* of Aeschylus.
456. Death of Aeschylus.
455. Euripides produces his first play.
454. The Persians defeat a large Athenian fleet that is supporting an Egyptian revolt against Persia in Egypt. The Athenians move the treasury of the League from the exposed island of Delos to Athens.
451. Pericles' citizenship law limits citizenship to those both of whose parents are citizens.
450. The celebrated paradoxes of Zeno of Elea (southern Italy).
449. Assumed date of peace treaty between Athens and Persia. It is followed by the consolidation of Athenian power over the members of the Delian League so that what is in effect an Athenian empire emerges.
447–438. The Parthenon rebuilt in its present form on earlier foundations. Financed by tribute from Athens' empire. The sculptor Pheidias (**490–432**) seems to have been largely responsible for the design and decoration of the temple.
447. The Athenians are defeated at the Battle of Coronea and lose control of Boeotia.
446–445. Thirty-year peace signed between Sparta and Athens.
c. 445. The Athenian Coinage Decree requires members of the League/empire to use only Athenian weights and measures.

443. Athens found a colony at Thurii in southern Italy, an indication of new commercial interests in the West.
441. Sophocles' *Antigone*, one of his most enduring plays.
440s. Herodotus writes his *History of the Persian Wars*.
440–430. Leucippus and Democritus, the "atomists," suggest that all matter is made up of atoms. The sculptor Polycleitus of Argos creates the "ideal" human body based on mathematical proportions.
440. A major revolt against Athens' power is launched by Samos. The revolt is suppressed.
437. The city of Amphipolis is founded by Athens to improve her access to the timber and gold of Thrace.
433. Rome adopts the cult of Apollo when plague threatens the city.
433–431. A drift toward war between Athens and Sparta as Athens supports a revolt by Corcyra against Sparta's ally Corinth and the Spartans realize that an Athenian preoccupation with a revolt in Potidaea weakens her at home.
431. Outbreak of the Second Peloponnesian War. Thucydides begins his history of the war. Euripides' *Medea*. Hippocrates of Cos, Socrates and Protagoras of Abdera are all active in this period.
431–430. The famous funeral oration of Pericles (as reported by Thucydides) proclaims the glory and achievements of Athens.
430. A significant proportion of the population of Athens is killed by plague.
Pheidias completes his gigantic statue of Zeus at Olympia.
430 or shortly afterward. The first production of Sophocles' most famous play, *Oedipus Tyrannus*.
429. Death of Pericles from the plague or a related disease.
428. Plato is born. First production of *Hippolytus* of Euripides.
427. The visit of the orator Gorgias of Leontini (Sicily) to Athens fosters the birth of rhetoric.
The revolt of Mytilene sparks off the debate on its future in the Athenian Assembly.
425–388. The comedies of Aristophanes (*Acharnians*, **425**, *The Clouds*, **423**, *The Birds*, **414**, *The Frogs*, **405**).
425. The stalemate of the Peloponnesian War is broken by the capture of the Spartans at Sphacteria but Athenian hopes of controlling Boeotia end with her defeat by the Thebans at Delium (**424**).
424. The Spartan general Brasidas captures Amphipolis and other Athenian cities in the northern Aegean.
423. Aristophanes' *The Clouds* ridicules Socrates and Sophistic ideas.
421. Peace of Nicias between Sparta and Athens. It is undermined by continued Athenian intrusion in the Peloponnese.
420–400. Building of the Temple of Apollo at Bassae.

418. Battle of Mantineia. Sparta reasserts her control over the Peloponnese by defeating Argos and her ally Athens.
416. The defeat and enslavement of the island of Melos by Athens.
415. Euripides' *The Trojan Women* explores the brutality of war.
The Athenian expedition leaves for Sicily.
413. Disastrous end to the Athenian expedition at Syracuse. The Spartans exploit Athens' weakness by setting up a permanent base at Decelea in Attica to attract runaway slaves.
411. The Spartans seek Persian help to rebuild their navy.
The Council of Four Hundred takes over in Athens. Democracy is restored in **410.** A bitter struggle between Athens and Sparta for control of the Hellespont (through which Athens' corn supplies come).
406. The Athenian naval victory at Arginusae leads to the Assembly's debate on the fate of the generals who left sailors to drown. The generals are condemned to death by a volatile Assembly.
Deaths of Euripides and Sophocles.
405. The *Bacchae* of Euripides is produced for the first time, after his death.
Dionysius I becomes dictator in Syracuse. He maintains himself in power until his death in **367,** presenting a new model of government for the Greek world.
The Battle of Aigospotamae sees the destruction of the Athenian fleet at the hands of the Persian commander Lysander.
404. Surrender of Athens. The government of the Thirty Tyrants is imposed on the city by Sparta. Democracy is restored in a countercoup of **404–403.**
405–395. Lysander is dominant in the Aegean although he loses much credibility after the defeat of the Persian prince Cyrus, whom he has backed as pretender to the Persian throne (**402**). The historian Xenophon (**c. 428–c. 354**) extricates the Greek troops from Persia and recounts the expedition in his *The March of the Ten Thousand.*
399. Death of Socrates after being found guilty of a charge of corrupting the young.
396–347. The philosopher Plato is active throughout these years. He founds the Academy in **387.**
396–394. The Spartan king Agesilaus campaigns to free the Ionian Greeks from Persian control. In retaliation the Persians support Thebes, Athens, and Corinth against Sparta in the Corinthian War (**395–386**). The Athenians use Persian money to rebuild the Long Walls.
395. Thucydides' *History of the Peloponnesian War* is published.
386. In the so-called King's Peace, the Corinthian War is brought to a close. Persia regains control of the Ionian Greeks and maintains her influence in the Greek world.

382. The Spartans seize Thebes.
379. Thebes is liberated and in **378** Athens forms the Second Athenian League to counter Spartan power.
377–353. Rule of Mausulus of Caria, builder of the mausuleum of Halicarnassus.
375–370. The rule of Jason in Thessaly confirms that one-man rule is a serious alternative to city democracy or oligarchy.
371. At the Battle of Leuctra, Thebes comprehensively defeats Sparta and Sparta never recovers. From **371** to **362** Thebes is the most powerful state in Greece.
367. Aristotle joins the Academy.
362. With the death of the Theban leader Epaminondas, Theban power collapses. No Greek city-state is able to take her place.
359. Philip II becomes king of Macedon. He soon consolidates his control of Macedonia and the surrounding area.
358–330. Building of the theater at Epidaurus at the shrine of Aesclepius, one of the finest surviving Greek theaters. The sculptor Praxiteles of Athens (born **c. 390**) and known for his celebrated nude statue of Aphrodite is also active at this time.
357–355. Collapse of Second Athenian League.
356–352. Philip achieves hegemony in central Greece. His growing power is criticized by the Athenian orator Demosthenes (**384–322**) in some of the finest examples of Greek oratory.
356. Birth of Philip's son Alexander, later to become Alexander the Great.
348. Philip of Macedon sacks the north Aegean city of Olynthus. The excavated remains of the city provide a major source of information on Greek houses.
347. Death of Plato. Aristotle leaves Athens but returns in **337** to found his own school, the Lyceum.
340. Athens declares war on Philip. She is joined by Thebes.
338. At the Battle of Chaeronea (in Boeotia) Philip destroys the armies of Athens and Thebes. The age of the independent city-state is over. The triumph of Philip is welcomed by the Greek orator Isocrates (**436–338**), who has long advocated the unification of the Greek world under a single leader.

336–330: The Hellenistic Age

This is a period when the Greeks spread into the Persian empire following its conquest by Alexander. Several monarchs emerge as his successors but overall a more unified Greek culture emerges. The period ends with the incorporation of the Greek world into the Roman empire.
336. Philip launches an attack on Persia but dies in the same year.

Alexander succeeds and rapidly establishes his own control of Macedonia and the Greek states. Sacking of Thebes when the city defies Alexander.
335. The Cynic Diogenes (c. 400–325) reputedly meets Alexander in Corinth and impresses on him the importance of renouncing possessions.
Darius III becomes king of Persia.
334. Alexander launches his invasion of Persia. His victory at Granicus leads to the liberation of the Greek cities of Asia Minor.
333. Alexander defeats the forces of Darius at the battle of Issus.
332–331. Having checked Darius, Alexander travels through Syria (siege of Tyre, 332) to Egypt where he is acclaimed as pharaoh in place of Darius. A visit to the oracles of Ammon at Siwah (Libya) confirms Alexander's belief that he has divine ancestry.
331. Foundation of Alexandria, later to become the most prosperous city of the Mediterranean. (Its famous lighthouse is built at the beginning of the third century B.C.)
Alexander's victory over Darius at Gaugamela allows him to take Babylon, Susa, and Persepolis. The great royal palace at Persepolis is burned to the ground in the following year. Darius is murdered by one of his satraps. The Achaemenid empire is at an end.
330–327. Brutal guerrilla campaigns as Alexander moves through Bactria and Sogdiana.
327. Alexander moves over the passes of the Hindu Kush toward India.
326. Alexander reaches India and achieves his last great victory at the Battle of Hydaspes.
325. Following the refusal of his troops to go farther east Alexander makes the journey back to central Persia via the river Indus and the Makram desert.
324–323. Alexander makes haphazard efforts to bring order to his conquests but his behavior is increasingly unstable. His reaction to the death of his companion Hephaistion gives further evidence of his instability. The announcement that refugees can return to their native cities brings havoc to the Greek mainland.
323. Death of Alexander in Babylon.
322. Death of Aristotle in Euboea.
323–276. A power struggle breaks out among the descendants and officers of Alexander. Alexander's senior cavalry officer, Perdiccas, and Antigonus the One-Eyed fail to control the empire as a single unit as Ptolemy emerges as ruler of Egypt and Seleucis of Babylon.
306. Antigonus assumes the diadem of kingship and other contenders for the empire follow suit. Antigonus is killed at the Battle of Ipsus (301). Three major states eventually emerge from Alexander's empire: Egypt, under the Ptolemies; Macedonia, under descendants of Antigonus; and the Seleucid empire in the east.

321–289. Career of Menander (the New Comedy).
320. Pytheas, from Massilia, makes a circumnavigation of Britain.
307. The philosopher Epicurus founds his school in Athens based on a "Garden" where initiates can seek refuge from the outside world.
305–304. Rhodes fights off a siege by Demetrius, the son of Antigonus the One-Eyed. The Colossus of Rhodes is built out of the proceeds of victory.
300. Stoicism is founded by Zeno in Athens (its name comes from its meeting place in a *stoa,* in Athens).

The most successful textbook in history, Euclid's *The Elements*, is written.

The museum and library are founded by Ptolemy I at Alexandria.

The first world map, showing latitude, is produced by Dicaearchus of Messenia.

Antioch, one of the great cities of the East, founded by Seleucus I.

290. The Aetolian League occupies Delphi and in the next seventy years emerges as the main political entity in central Greece.
c. 287. Archimedes, the greatest mathematician of antiquity, is born at Syracuse.
281. Foundation of the Achaean League, a federation of the city-states of the northern Peloponnese.
280. Pyrrhus of Epirus ships an army to Italy in support of the city of Tarentum and provides the Romans with their first direct contact with the Hellenistic world.
279. Celtic raiders sack Delphi.
276. Antigonus Gonatus, grandson of Antigonus the One-Eyed, restores order to Macedonia and founds the Antagonid dynasty.
c. 275. Aristarchus of Samos puts forward the hypothesis that the earth may go around the sun.

Apollonius Rhodius composes his epic *Argonautica* on Rhodes.

274–271. War between Ptolemy II of Egypt and Antiochus I over Syria. There are subsequent Syrian wars between the two powers in **260–253, 246–241,** and **219–217.**
272. The fall of Tarentum marks the achievement of hegemony of Rome over the Greek cities of southern Italy.
270. The poets Callimachus and Theocritus (founder of "pastoral poetry") are active in Alexandria.
263–241. The emergence of Pergamum as a separate kingdom under Eumenes.
260s. Medical experiments of Hierophilus of Chalcedon and Erasistatus of Ceos lead to important findings on nerves, the pulse, arteries, and veins.
250. The so-called Hippocratic writings, medical treatises, are assembled in the library at Alexandria.

247. Foundation of Parthian empire. The Parthians expand gradually into the Seleucid kingdom.
242. Sicily, and its Greek cities, ceded to Rome by the Carthaginians. (Syracuse remains independent as an ally of Rome.)
238. His defeat of the Galatian Celts inspires Attalus I to rebuild Pergamum as one of the great cities of the Hellenistic world.
229–219. The Hellenistic world receives its first experience of Roman intrusion as the Romans campaign against the pirates of the Illyrian coast.
223–187. Reign of the Seleucid king Antiochus III. Seleucid prestige in Asia is partially restored by Antiochus' major campaign in the east but Antiochus loses his position in the eastern Mediterranean after humiliating defeats by the Romans, **192–188.**
221. Philip V becomes ruler of Macedon.
215. Philip allies with Carthage against Rome.
214–205. Rome declares war on Philip. The first Macedonian War (**214–205**) in which the Romans fight in alliance with the Aetolian League.
211. Death of Archimedes in Syracuse after the city is sacked by the Romans. Large quantities of Greek art enter Rome.
209 (but possibly much earlier). Livius Andronicus introduces Greek drama and epic to Rome.
206–185. Upper Egypt breaks free of Ptolemaic rule.
204. First performance in Rome of a play by Plautus (active **204–184**). Plautus freely adapts original Greek plays.
202. First history of Rome (in Greek) by Fabius Pictor.
200. The mathematician Apollonius of Perge speculates on cones and devises models to explain the movements of the planets.
200–197. The Second Macedonian War between Philip and Rome. Philip is defeated at Cynoscephalae (**197**).
196. The Roman commander at Cynoscephalae, Flamininus, declares that the cities of Greece are free. The Romans leave Greece in **194.**

A record of the thanksgiving of the priests of Memphis to Ptolemy V is inscribed in three languages, including Greek and hieroglyphic Egyptian. Rediscovered at Rosetta on the Nile Delta in **1799** (hence the name Rosetta Stone), it provides the means by which Egyptian hieroglyphics are deciphered.
191. Defeat of Antiochus III by the Romans at Thermopylae.
189. Following the further defeat of Antiochus at Magnesia (**190**) the cities of the Aetolian League are forced to become subject allies of Rome.
186. Suppression of Bacchalanian (imported Dionysiac) cults by Rome. First Greek-style games held in Rome.
c. 180. The bilingual poet Quintus Ennus introduces Hellenistic poetry to Rome and writes the first Latin epic (the *Annals*).

179. Perseus becomes king of Macedonia after the death of his father, Philip.
171–138. Reign of Mithridates I, the first Parthian ruler to achieve full independence from the Seleucids.
168. Defeat of Perseus by the Romans at Pydna is followed by the break-up of Macedonia into four republics.
Humiliation of Antiochus IV by the Romans when he attempts an invasion of Egypt. Ptolemaic Egypt, though independent, falls within the Roman sphere of interest.
167. After the intrusions of the Seleucids and their support of Greek culture in Jerusalem guerrilla warfare breaks out in Judaea under the leadership of Judah Maccabee.
The Greek historian Polybius, a hostage from Greece, arrives in Rome and uses his aristocratic contacts there for material for his *Universal History* (on the rise of Rome).
c. 160s. Building of the Great Altar of Zeus at Pergamum.
160s. The plays of Terence, adapted from Greek originals, bring drama into Rome.
155. Celebrated visit of Greek philosophers to Rome.
148. The suppression of a revolt in Macedonia is followed by its declaration as a province of the empire. The victorious Roman commander Metellus brings back a mass of Greek art to Rome and sets up the first marble temple.
146. The Achaean League is crushed by the Romans and Corinth is sacked. Southern Greece becomes the province of Achaia.
142. Judaea becomes formally independent under Simon Maccabee.
133. The last of the Attalid kings bequeaths Pergamum to Rome and it becomes the Roman province of Asia (**129**).
c. 120. Hipparchus of Nicaea founds trigonometry to further his meticulous observations of the stars, which include an understanding of the precession of the equinoxes.
88–85. Mithradates of Pontus, claiming descent from Alexander, encourages massacre of Roman citizens in Asia and attempts to liberate the Greeks from the Romans.
86. Sulla captures Athens and sacks it. Mithradates is forced to retreat. Roman rule restored to the east.
74–63. Campaigns of Lucullus and Pompey in the east lead to the final defeat of Mithradates and the end of the Seleucid monarchy (**64**). Judaea also comes under Roman rule.
55. Death of the poet Lucretius. His *De Rerum Natura*, the most complete statement of Epicureanism, is published posthumously.
Cicero produces his first literary work, on oratory, and, in **54**, starts *De Republica*. He uses Greek examples throughout.

Pompey creates the first stone theater in Rome.
51. Cleopatra succeeds to the throne of Egypt with her brother, Ptolemy XIII. Shortly afterward she is deposed and flees to Syria.
48–47. Caesar starts an affair with Cleopatra and restores her to the throne of Egypt.
45–44. Cicero's main philosophical works are written in these years and transfer Greek philosophy into the Roman and hence European tradition.
44. Caesar assassinated.
41. Cleopatra meets Mark Antony and becomes his mistress.
38. Virgil's *Eclogues,* which draw on the poetry of Theocritus, are published.
34. Antony and Cleopatra try to upstage Octavian, Caesar's heir, by a great ceremony in Alexandria.
31. The forces of Antony and Cleopatra are defeated by Octavian at the Battle of Actium on the northwestern coast of Greece.
30. Antony and Cleopatra commit suicide. Egypt is annexed by Rome.
c. 30. Andronicus of Rhodes brings together the works of Aristotle (in Rome).

Greece Under the Roman Empire

29. The victorious Octavian builds a mausoleum, modeled on Mausolus' original, for himself in Rome.
29. Virgil's *Georgics* (modeled on Hesiod's *Works* and *Days*) are completed. Publication of Horace's *Epodes*, which use a variety of Greek models.
27. The "restoration" of the Roman republic by Octavian. He is granted the name Augustus. Gradually (**27–2** B.C.) Augustus accumulates enough power to emerge, unquestionably, as the dominant figure in the constitution, and hence ruler of the Roman world including the east.
23. Completion of Vitruvius' *De Architectura,* which draws on Greek originals and that later becomes the most influential work on Roman architecture.
19. Death of Virgil. The *Aeneid*, the greatest of the Roman epics, is preserved for publication by Augustus.
9. The Ara Pacis, an altar carved in classical Greek styles, is dedicated in Rome.
c. 5. Birth of Jesus in Galilee.

A.D.

2–4. The *Metamorphoses* of Ovid bring Greek mythology into Roman and hence European literature.

c. 29–30. Crucifixion of Jesus in Jerusalem. Foundation of early church.
40. Jesus' brother James becomes leader of the "Jewish church" in Jerusalem but as a result of the missionary work of Paul, Christianity spreads more successfully in Gentile communities of the Greek world.
c. 42–54. The letters of Paul, the earliest surviving Christian writings, written in Greek to various Greek Christian communities.
65–100. Composition of the Gospels and the Acts of the Apostles, in Greek.
66. Nero tours Greece and competes in Greek games, making the Greeks feel welcome members of the empire for the first time.
85. The "Jewish" Christian church in Jerusalem is in decline. The future of Christianity now lies with the Greek-speaking Gentile communities.
Plutarch's *Lives* also date from these years.
117–138. Reign of Hadrian. The emperor travels widely and his love of Greece helps integrate the east further into the empire. Hadrian completes a major new suburb of Athens. Period of opulence and self-confidence for the Greeks and Greek culture spreads eastward.
120. Dedication of the library of Celsus at Ephesus.
127–41. Ptolemy of Alexandria, perhaps the greatest of the Greek astronomers, complies his *Almagest.*
150. Panegyrical speech of the Greek Aelius Aristides praises the beneficence of Roman rule. Aelius Aristides is one of the leaders of the Second Sophistic, a revival in the art of Greek oratory.
The physician Galen, the founding father of physiology and the greatest scientist of his day, teaching in Rome.
Pausanias compiles his *Description of Greece.*
The Asclepium, major healing center, at Pergamum.
c. 160. Apuleius' novel *The Golden Ass.*
172–180. *Meditations* of Marcus Aurelius, written in Greek.
190–200. Clement of Alexandria acknowledges that Greek philosophy may be of value to Christians.
244. The philosopher Plotinus settles in Rome. Does important work in developing Platonism.
267. Athens is sacked by the Heruli.
303–312. Last major persecution of Christians under Diocletian and his successor Galerius.
312. The Battle of Milvian Bridge near Rome establishes Constantine as ruler of the western empire.
313. The Edict of Milan, signed by Constantine and Licinius, emperor in the east, introduces empirewide toleration for Christianity.
324. Constantine defeats Licinius and becomes sole emperor. He begins the building of Constantinople and provides material support for the first great Christian churches.

325. Constantine presides over the Council of Nicaea, the first great ecumenical council. The views of Arius, that Jesus was a separate begotten son of God, is condemned.
330. Dedication of Constantinople.
333–379. Life of Basil of Caesarea. Basil establishes that the ideal of monastic life is service to the poor. His monastery has a hospital and a leper colony.
337. Death of Constantine.
361. Julian becomes emperor. The last of the non-Christian emperors, Julian attempts, unsuccessfully, to restore pagan beliefs.
370s. Gradual elimination of the *gymnasia* at the hands of Christians who regard their activities as immoral.
381. Final condemnation of Arianism by the council of Constantinople.
388–395. Theodosius sole emperor. The last reign in which the empire is ruled as a single unit. Under the influence of Ambrose, bishop of Milan, Theodosius uses his power to uphold orthodox Christianity against heresy and paganism.
390s. John Chrysostom preaching in Antioch. Made bishop of Constantinople in **398.**
391. Banning of "pagan" sacrifices. Olympic Games closed down and the gradual elimination of non-Christian sites. The great temple complex of the Serapeum in Alexandria in dismantled in **392.**
394. Theodosius defeats pagan usurper Eugenius at the Battle of the River Frigidus. Traditionally seen as the moment when Christianity is triumphant.
395. The death of Theodosius. The empire is split between his two sons, Arcadius and Honorius, and so an eastern empire emerges.
408–450. Reign of Theodosius II. Constantinople consolidated as the capital of the eastern empire. Image of the emperor as God's representative on earth.
431. Council of Ephesus proclaims Mary to be Theotokos, "the mother of God," and thus plays down the human nature of Jesus.
451. Council of Chalcedon proclaims that Christ had two natures, human and divine, within the same undivided person, but the controversy over the nature of Christ continues.
524. Boethius' *The Consolation of Philosophy.* Boethius is the last Latin speaker to have a comprehensive mastery of Greek and leaves a translation of many of Aristotle's works.
527–565. Reign of Justinian, Justin's nephew.
532. The Nika riots, which almost overthrow Justinian, are suppressed with ferocity.
532–537. Rebuilding of Santa Sophia, one the great buildings of antiquity, in Constantinople.

540. The Sasanians (Persians) sack Antioch. Major outbreaks of plague in the empire.
c. 547–554. The historian Procopius writes his history of Justinian's wars as well as his *Secret History* and *Buildings*.
553. Council of Constantinople fails to resolve the controversy over the nature of Christ.
565. Death of Justinian. The authoritarian and profoundly Christian empire he has sustained is now normally referred to as the Byzantine empire.
582. Athens severely damaged by invading Slavs and Avars. Sparta, Argos, and Corinth abandoned.
610–641. The reign of Heraclius. The Byzantine fight back against the Sasanian empire, almost extinguishing it, but the empire is faced almost immediately by the onslaught of the Arabs.
632. Mohammed's successor, Abu Bakr, leads the attack on the Sasanian and Byzantine empires.
636. Battle of Yarmuk sees the defeat of the Byzantines. Arab conquest of Syria and Palestine.
642. Alexandria lost to the Arabs.
640s onward. A reduced Byzantine state maintains its independence until the sack of Constantinople by the Ottoman Turks in **1453**.

Further Reading

This is not intended to be an exhaustive book list. It includes a selection of books in the main areas of Greek life and culture for those who wish to develop their interest further as well as those sources which have proved particularly helpful in compiling this book. Books cited in the text with their dates of publication are not always included again here.

General Books on the Main Areas of Greek Life

There are standard translations of major works of Greek literature in the Loeb Classical Library and Penguin Classics. Many of the latter have been used here. Excellent translations of Homer include those by Richmond Lattimore and Robert Fagles of the *Iliad* (the second available now on cassette read by Derek Jacobi) and the *Odyssey* by Walter Shrewring in prose or Robert Fitzgerald and Robert Fagles in verse. The translations of Robert Fagles are used in this book. A selection of translations are to be found in A. Poole and J. Maule, (eds.) *The Oxford Book of Classical Verse in Translation* (Oxford, 1995).

The Cambridge Illustrated History of Greece (ed. Paul Cartledge, Cambridge, 1998) has a wide range of essays, many of them excellent, and is very well illustrated though it hardly ventures outside the classical period. General introductions to the Greeks are provided by Kenneth Dover, *The Greeks* (London, 1980) and Paul Cartledge, *The Greeks: a Portrait of Self and Others* (Oxford, 1993) the latter more of a study of "Greekness" than a standard history. A standard one-volume political history is J. Bury and R. Meiggs, *A History of Greece* fourth edition (London, 1975) but this is now rather dated. C. M. Bowra's *The Greek Experience* (London, 1957) is an enduring classic. For the relationship between archaeology and the study of Greece see A. Snodgrass, *An Archaeology of Greece* (Berkeley, 1987) and Ian Morris (ed.) *Classical Greece: Ancient Histories and Modern Archaeologies* (Cambridge, 1994). A recent general source book is M. Dillon and L. Garland, *Ancient Greece* (London, 1992).

Oxford University Press has provided a fine array of companion books. *The Oxford Classical Dictionary* (ed. S. Hornblower and A. Spawforth, third edition, Oxford, 1996) is comprehensive, authoritative but weighty. Many of the articles have been transferred to the more accessible *Oxford Companion to Classical Studies* (same editors, Oxford, 1998). As a general introduction the history and culture of Greece there is J. Boardman, J. Griffin, and O. Murray (eds.), *The Oxford History of Greece and the Hellenistic World* (Oxford, 1991); M. C. Howatson (ed.) *The Oxford Companion to Classical Literature* (Oxford, 1989); John Boardman (ed.) *The Oxford History of Classical Art* (Oxford, 1993); and E. Fantham and others (eds.) *Women in the Classical World* (New York and Oxford, 1994). M. Grant and R. Kitzinger (eds.), *Civilization of the Ancient Mediterranean: Greece and Rome* (New York, 1988) is a major three-volume survey with essays on most aspects of the subject. J. Bryant, *Moral Codes and Social Structure in Ancient Greece* (New York, 1996) covers the full range of Greek history, often from an original angle. A range of essays on Greek history and culture can be found in A. Powell (ed.) *The Greek World* (London, 1995).

The *Cambridge Ancient History* makes its stately, and expensive, way through its second edition. It is often more readable than its format suggests and beginners should not be put off by its forbidding appearance. Individual essays and volumes are cited where relevant below.

For those who wish to get a feel of Greece a readable travel guide is provided by A. and M. Burn, *The Living Past of Greece* (revised edition, London, 1993). There is a host of general guides of which the *Blue Guides* are normally seen as the most authoritative and cover all the areas of the Mediterranean. That on Turkey (2nd edition, by Bernard McDonagh, London, 1995) covers the Greek sites of Asia Minor well. Perhaps more accessible to the general reader are the Companion Guides and Cadogan Guides. *The Companion Guide to Mainland Greece* (Brian de Jongh, revised by John Gandon, Woodbridge, Suffolk, 1989) and *The Companion Guide to the Greek Islands* (Ernle Bradford, revised by Francis Pagan, Woodbridge, 1993) are both to be thoroughly recommended.

Literature, history, and art are woven throughout the main text and so introductory books are given here while books on philosophy, drama, etc., are given in the relevant chapters below. General surveys of Greek literature include Peter Levi, *The Pelican History of Greek Literature* (Harmondsworth, 1985) and, more recently, A. Dihle, *A History of Greek Literature* (London, 1994). The historians are dealt with clearly by T. J. Luce, *The Greek Historians* (London, 1997). The authoritative survey of art by M. Robertson, *A History of Greek Art* (two volumes, Cambridge, 1975) has been distilled into his *A Shorter History of Greek Art* (Cambridge, 1981). See also the many introductions by John Boardman, *Greek Art; Greek Sculpture, the Archaic Period;* and *Greek Sculpture, the Classical Period* (all London, 1988, 1991, and 1985 respectively). Boardman's treatment is conventional but highly authoritative, based on a lifetime of study. Andrew Stewart's *Greek Sculpture* (New Haven and London, 1990) is a more recent major exploration in two volumes. Recent studies that place Greek art within the wider context of culture and society are Andrew Stewart, *Art, Desire and the Body in Ancient Greece* (Cambridge, 1997), Robin Osborne, *Archaic and Classical Greek Art* (Oxford, 1998), and two studies by Nigel Spivey, *Greek Art* (London, 1997) and *Understanding Greek Sculpture* (London, 1996). There is also a well illustrated survey by J. G. Pedley, *Greek Art and Archaeology* (London, 1992). J. Boardman, *The Diffusion of Classical Art in Antiquity* (London, 1994) looks at the impact of the Greeks on other cultures, notably those of Italy. For those who wish to know more of the Near Eastern background, A. Kuhrt's *The Ancient Near East, 3000–330 B.C.*, two volumes (London, 1995) is fundamental.

Chapter One: Recreating the World of Ancient Greece

An introduction to how the Greeks were seen by later generations is provided by Kenneth Dover (ed.), *Perceptions of the Ancient Greeks* (Oxford, 1992). For the nineteenth century there are two fine studies, Richard Jenkyns, *The Victorians and Ancient Greece* (Oxford, 1980) and Frank Turner, *The Greek Heritage in Victorian Britain* (New Haven and London, 1981). Hugh Honour's *Neo-Classicism* (Harmondsworth, 1968) is good on Winckelmann and the quotation is drawn from there. For classical studies in Germany, Suzanne Marchand, *Down from Olympus: Archaeology and Philhellenism in Germany, 1750–1970* (Princeton, 1996) is particularly good. On the "revival" of the classical acropolis I have used Richard McNeal, "Archaeology and the Destruction of the Later Athenian Acropolis," *Antiquity 65* (1991). The first volume of Martin Bernal's *Black Athena* (London, 1987) deals with his theory of the "fabrication" on the ancient Greeks. Beazley's contribution to the study of vase painting is assessed in Chapter One of T. J. Rasmussen and N. Spivey (eds.), *Look-*

ing at Greek Vases (Cambridge, 1991). A selection of J. Burckhardt's thoughts on Greece have recently been reissued with an introduction by Oswyn Murray as *The Greeks and Greek Civilization* (London, 1998).

Ian Morris' important essay "Archaeologies of Greece" comes in the volume he has edited, *Classical Greece: Ancient Histories and Modern Archaeologies* (Cambridge, 1994). W. Connor's comments come in his essay in P. Culham and L. Edmunds (eds.), *Classics: A Discipline and Profession in Crisis?* (New York and London, 1989), a book that provides a useful perspective from which to view the "decline" of traditional classical studies and their adaptation to the modern world.

Chapter Two: The Formation of the Greek World

For a general introduction to the Bronze Age see P. Warren, *The Aegean Civilizations* (2nd edition, Oxford, 1989). An even more recent overview is O. Dickinson, *The Aegean Bronze Age* (Cambridge, 1994). See also the chapter by K. Wardle, "The Palace Civilizations of Minoan Crete and Mucenaean Greece, 2000–1200 B.C. in *The Oxford Illustrated Prehistory of Europe* (Oxford, 1994) (and in the same volume, Mervyn Popham on "The Collapse of Aegean Civilization at the End of the Late Bronze Age"). On Schliemann there is C. Moorehead, *The Lost Treasures of Troy* (London, 1994). John Chadwick's *The Decipherment of Linear B* (Cambridge, 1967) describes the achievement of Ventris and there is also Chadwick's *The Mycenaean World* (Cambridge, 1976). See also W. McDonald and C. Thomas, *Progress into the Past: The Rediscovery of Mycenaean Civilization,* second edition, (Bloomington, 1990). W. Burkert surveys Mycenaean religion and its links with later Greek religion in Chapter One of his *Greek Religion* (Oxford, 1985). On the Sea Peoples see N. K. Sandars, *The Sea Peoples, Warriors of the Ancient Mediterranean* (London, 1978). V. D. Hanson, *The Other Greeks: The Family Farm and the Agrarian Roots of Western Civilization* (New York, 1995) meditates creatively on the relationship between the Greeks and the land. For the Kas shipwreck see G. F. Bass, "Oldest Known Shipwreck Reveals Splendors of the Bronze Age" in the *National Geographic, 172*, no. 6 (December, 1987). Martin Bernal's *Black Athena* (London, 1987 and 1991) aroused great interest but most of the arguments failed to convince scholars. See their responses in M. Lefkowitz and G. Rogers (eds.), *Black Athena Revisited* (Chapel Hill, 1996). On the problem of the ethnic identity of Greeks see J. M. Hall, *Ethnic Identity in Greek Antiquity* (Cambridge, 1997). It has a good summary of the arguments surrounding the Dorian invasion. For the world of the *basilees* see M. Finley, *The World of Odysseus* (Harmondsworth, 1962). See also A. M. Snodgrass, *The Dark Age of Greece: An Archaeological Survey of the Eleventh to Eighth Centuries* (Edinburgh, 1971); Ian Morris, *Burial and Ancient Society: The Rise of the Greek City-State* (Cambridge, 1987); and the introductory chapters of R. Osborne, *Greece in the Making, 1200–479* B.C. (London, 1996). On Hesiod there is Robert Lamberton, *Hesiod* (New Haven, 1988) and the chapter by Jasper Griffin, "Greek Myth and Hesiod" in the *Oxford History*. The authority on geometric art is J. N. Coldstream. See, as an introduction, his chapter "The Geometric Style: Birth of the Picture," in T. Rasmussen and N. Spivey, (eds.) *Looking at Greek Vases* (Cambridge, 1991).

Chapters Three to Eight: General Introductions

Oswyn Murray's *Early Greece*, second edition (London, 1993) takes the story up to 480 B.C. It is a lively and authoritative introduction with a good bibliography. For the Dark Age onward I particularly enjoyed Jeffrey Hurwitt's *The Art and Culture of Ancient Greece, 1100–480* B.C. (Ithaca, 1985), which makes useful connections between literature and art and is alive to the many outside influences on the formation of Greek culture. Another fine and scholarly survey is Robin Osborne's *Greece in the Making 1200–479* B.C. (London, 1996). There is a range of essays in N. Fisher and H. van Wees (eds.), *Archaic Greece, New Approaches and New Evidence* (London, 1998). For art see the early chapters in the works by Spivey, Osborne, and Andrew Stewart, cited in general books above. Especially good is Sarah Morris' *Daidalos and the Origins of Greek Art* (Princeton, 1992). Between them these books will provide the foundations for any further study of the period.

Chapter Three: Homer's World: Heroes and the Coming of the City-State

For a good introduction to the issues surrounding Homer and his times see the Open University reader, C. Emlyn-Jones, (ed.) *Homer, Readings and Images* (London, 1992). M. Finley's *The World of Odysseus* (Harmondsworth, 1962) provides a stimulating introduction to Homer's world. See also the essay "Homer" by Oliver Taplin in the *Oxford History of Greece and the Hellenistic World* and J. Griffin, *Homer on Life and Death* (Oxford, 1980). H. Fraenkel's *Early Greek Poetry and Philosophy* (Oxford, 1975), is a solid readable introduction. Barry Powell's thesis (that the alphabet was introduced specifically to record Homer's epics) is in *Homer and the Origin of the Greek Alphabet* (Cambridge, 1991). For those who wish to follow up Milman Parry see the essays in his *The Making of Homeric Verse* (Oxford, 1971). Oliver Taplin's ideas of how the epics were actually performed is in his *Homeric Soundings* (Oxford, 1992). J. Carter and S. Morris, *The Ages of Homer* (Austin, Texas,

1995) contains the Gregory Nagy essay cited here and a wide range of essays on surrounding "Homeric" issues.

For the formation of the city community see R. Osborne, *Greece in the Making* and I. Morris, *Burial and Ancient Society* both cited for the last chapter. The dipylon evidence is discussed in I. Morris, "Poetics of Power. The Interpretation of Ritual Action in Archaic Greece" in C. Dougherty and L. Kurke, (eds.) *Cultural Poetics in Archaic Greece* (Cambridge, 1993) and in Nigel Spivey and Robin Osborne's books on Greek art. The theme of outlying sanctuaries was raised by F. de Polignac. See his *Cults, Territories and the Origins of the Greek City-state* (Chicago, 1995) and the subject is also analyzed in S. Alcock and R. Osborne, (eds.) *Placing the Gods: Sanctuaries and Sacred Space in Ancient Greece* (Oxford, 1994). Recent work on the development of the polis is gathered in L. Mitchell and P. J. Rhodes (eds.), *The Development of the Polis in Archaic Greece* (London, 1997). For Carla Antonaccio's ideas see her essay "The Archaeology of Ancestors" in Doughty and Kurke, *Cultural Poetics*, cited above.

Chapter Four: An Expanding World: 800–550 B.C.

On Archilochus see Ann Burnett, *Three Archaic Poets: Archilochus, Alcaeus, Sappho* (London, 1998). John Boardman, *The Greeks Overseas* (latest edition, London, 1980) was a pioneering book, which brought much of the evidence together for the first time, and is still very useful. Vol. 3, part 3 of the *Cambridge Ancient History* (Cambridge, 1982) provides a detailed overview of colonization. See also G. Tsetskhladze and F. de Angelis, *The Archaeology of Greek Colonization* (Oxford, 1994) and for the west David Ridgway, *The First Western Greeks* (Cambridge, 1992). Barry Cunliffe's *Greeks, Romans, and Barbarians: Spheres of Interaction* (London, 1988) looks at wider aspects of the relationship. Oswyn Murray, *Early Greece* (London, 1993) is good on Orientalizing as is Boardman. W. Burkert, *The Orientalizing Revolution: Near Eastern Influence on Greek Culture in the Early Archaic Age* (Harvard, 1992) is important. Corinth's role is dealt with by T. Rasmussen, "Corinth and the Orientalising Phenomenon" in *Looking at Greek Vases* cited in chapter 2 above. For those who want to look at the Eastern influences in literature M. L. West's *The East Face of Helicon: West Asiatic Elements in Greek Poetry and Myth* (Oxford, 1997) is an exhaustive analysis. Jeffrey Hurwitt, *The Art and Culture of Ancient Greece, 1100–480 B.C.* is especially good on the development of architecture.

A good summing up of recent research on the Etruscans is G. Baker and T. Rasmussen, *The Etruscans* (Oxford, 1998). On art see Nigel Spivey, *Etruscan Art* (London, 1998) and his essay "Greek vases in Etruria" in *Looking at Greek Vases* cited above.

Chapter Five: New Identities: The Consolidation of the City-State

There is much good material in R. Osborne, *The Making of Greece*, chapters 6–8. For hoplite warfare see W. K. Pritchett, *The Greek State at War* (Berkeley, 1974) and V. D. Hanson, *Hoplites: The Classical Greek Battle Experience* (London 1991). Pauline Schmitt-Pantel's essay is in O. Murray and S. Price (eds.), *The Greek City from Homer to Alexander* (Oxford, 1990), which has many other useful essays. Richard Seaford's *Reciprocity and Ritual: Homer and Tragedy in the Developing City State* (Oxford, 1994) has a mass of material on the archaic state. For coinage the authority is Colin Kraay in *Archaic and Classical Greek Coins* (London, 1976) and there is the more recent C. Howgego, *Ancient History from Coins* (London, 1995).

An introduction to Spartan history is W. G. Forrest, *A History of Sparta, 950–192 B.C.* (London, 1968) and Oswyn Murray also discusses the evidence for the emergence of the Spartan constitution in *Early Greece* cited above. The sources on the tyrants are very fragmentary but for a recent analysis of tyranny see J. McGlew, *Tyranny and Political Culture in Ancient Greece* (Ithaca, 1993). Solon is covered well in Murray's *Early Greece*. Jeffrey Hurwitt's *The Art and Culture of Ancient Greece, 1100–480 B.C.* is good on Pisistatus and see also A. Andrews in the *Cambridge Ancient History*, vol. 3, part 3, chapters 43 and 44, and vol. 4, chapter 4 (Cambridge, 1988). For new thoughts on the phratries see S. Lambert, *The Phratries of Attica* (Ann Arbor, 1993). Generally on the political development of Athens see P. B. Manville, *The Origins of Citizenship in Ancient Athens* (Princeton, 1990).

R. Jenkyns deals well with Sappho in *Three Classical Poets: Sappho, Catullus, and Juvenal* (London, 1982), but also see the following: Peter Green, *In the Shadow of the Parthenon* (London, 1972), Ann Pippin Burnett, *Three Archaic Poets: Archilochus, Alcaeus, Sappho* (London, 1998). There is also a chapter on lyric and elegiac poetry by Ewen Bowie in the *Oxford History of Greece and the Hellenistic World*. The *kouroi* are dealt with in detail by Andrew Stewart in his *Greek Sculpture*. On Pindar see D. Carne Ross, *Pindar* (New Haven, 1988) and Lesley Kurke, *The Traffic in Praise: Pindar and the Poetics of Social Economy* (Ithaca, 1991), which has been used here.

Chapter Six: Underlying Patterns: Land and Slavery

The relationship of the Greeks to their land is a fast changing subject as field surveys become more sophisticated. R. Osborne, *Classical Landscape with Figures* (London, 1987) is a good overview with studies of the relationship between cities and their territories although it is becoming dated. See Alison Burford, *Land and Labor in the Greek World* (Baltimore, 1993) and S. Isager and J. Skydsgaard, *Ancient Greek Agriculture* (London, 1982). V. D. Hanson, *The Other Greeks: The Family Farm and the Agrarian Roots of Western Civilization* (New York, 1995) relates the coming of peasant farming to political change. T. van Andel and C. Runnels, *Beyond the Acropolis: A Rural Greek Past* (Stanford, 1987) explores the changing landscape and agricultural use of the southern Argolid. In I. Morris (ed.), *Classical Greece: Ancient Histories and Modern Archaeologies* there are a number of essays on the problems raised by field surveys. On slavery, Yvon Garlan's *Slavery in Ancient Greece* (Ithaca, 1988) provides a good introduction.

Chapter Seven: Underlying Patterns: Spiritual Life

On Greek religion W. Burkert, *Greek Religion* (Oxford, 1985) is fundamental but many aspects of Greek religion are well surveyed in P. Easterling and J. Muir (eds.), *Greek Religion and Society* (Cambridge, 1985). The chapter by J. Gould, "On Making Sense of Greek Religion" is particularly good as an introduction. In the same book Simon Price looks at the oracle at Delphi. There is also a chapter, "Greek Religion" by Robert Parker in the *Oxford History of Greece and the Hellenistic World* and see chapters 2 and 3, "The Metaphysical World" and "Human Obligations, Values and Concerns" in *The World of Athens: An Introduction to Classical Athenian Culture* (produced by the Joint Association of Classical Teachers, Cambridge, 1984). On the Olympic Games a clear overview is provided by Judith Swaddling in *The Ancient Olympic Games* (London, 1980). Robert Parker's recent *Athenian Religion, a History* (Oxford, 1996) is particularly valuable at looking at religion in the context of a city-state and has been hailed as major work of scholarship in its own right. See also Richard Buxton, "Religion and Myth" in *The Cambridge Illustrated History of Ancient Greece* (Cambridge, 1998). For women and religion there is S. Blundell and M. Williamson, (eds.) *The Sacred and the Feminine in Ancient Greece* (London and New York 1998). For grave monuments see R. Osborne, "The Claims of the Dead," *Archaic and Classical Greek Art* chapter 10, (Oxford, 1998). On myth, see G. S. Kirk, *The Nature of Greek Myths* (Harmondsworth, 1974). More recent overviews of this highly complex area include Geoffrey Buxton, *Imaginary Greece* (Cambridge, 1994) and Ken Dowden, *The Uses of Greek Mythology* (London, 1992).

Chapter Eight: Revolutions in Wisdom: New Directions in the Archaic Age

See the useful introduction by Martin West in the *Oxford History* and chapter 6 (by Christopher Janaway) in A. Grayling (ed.), *Philosophy: A Guide Through the Subject* (Oxford, 1995). See also, for Greek philosophy in general, Terence Irwin, *Classical Thought* (Oxford, 1989) and the chapter on philosophy by Bernard Williams in *The Legacy of Greece* (Oxford, 1984). On early philosophy a standard introduction is E. Hussey, *The Presocratics* (London, 1972). Translations are to be found in G. Kirk and J. Raven, *The Pre-Socratic Philosophers* (Cambridge, 1983). On scientific aspects there is G. Lloyd, *Early Greek Science: Thales to Aristotle* (London, 1974). For the achievement from a modern perspective, there is the chapter "Thale's Leap" in Lewis Wolpert's *The Unnatural Nature of Science* (London, 1992). For more advanced work there is W.K.C. Guthrie, *A History of Greek Philosophy* (Cambridge, 1962–81).

Rosalind Thomas, *Literacy and Orality in Ancient Greece* (Cambridge, 1992) covers the debates over literacy. The links between democracy and literacy in particular are explored in D. Steiner's *The Tyrant's Writ* (Princeton, 1993). William Harris, *Ancient Literacy* (Cambridge, Mass., 1989) dealt with many misconceptions about the nature of literacy. Geoffrey Lloyd's ideas on the relationship between politics and philosophical argument are to be found in his *Magic, Reason and Experience* (Cambridge, 1979). See also his *Revolutions in Wisdom: Studies in the Claims and Practice of Ancient Greek Science* (Berkeley, 1987). For art see the general surveys cited earlier and in particular D. Williams, "The Invention of the Red-Figure Technique" in Rasmussen and Spivey, *Looking at Greek Vases* and Jeffrey Hurwitt's analysis. There is also the essay by J. J. Pollitt in vol. 5 of the *Cambridge Ancient History.* On Cleisthenes there is Josiah Ober's essay "The Athenian Revolution of 509–8" in C. Dougherty and L. Kurke (eds.), *Cultural Poetics in Archaic Greece.* W. Connor's views on the emergence of drama are in an essay "City Dionysia and Athenian Democracy," in J. R. Sears (ed.), *Aspects of Athenian Democracy* (Copenhagen, 1990).

Chapters Nine to Fifteen: The Classical Period General Books

Most of the books mentioned in the "General Books on the Main Areas of Greek Life" concentrate on this period. *The Cambridge Illustrated History of Greece* is particularly stimulating. Translated texts, illustrations, and authoritative essays are well woven together. A fine introduction is provided by J. K. Davies, *Democracy and Classical Greece,* second edition (London, 1993). There is also Simon Hornblower's penetrating *The*

Greek World, 479–322 B.C. (revised edition, London, 1991). Of these two Davies is perhaps more accessible to the general reader. The *Cambridge Ancient History*, vols. 5 and 6 (Cambridge, 1992 and 1994) are fundamental for more specialist study. *The World of Athens: An Introduction to Classical Athenian Culture* (Cambridge, 1984) is useful as is Anton Powell, *Athens and Sparta: Constructing Greek Political and Social History from 478 B.C.* (London 1988). Specifically on art see J. J. Pollitt, *Art and Experience in Classical Greece* (London, 1994).

Chapter Nine: Creating the Barbarian: The Persian Wars

For Persia, see *Cambridge Ancient History,* vol. 4, chapters 1–3 (Cambridge, 1988) and J. M. Cook, *The Persian Empire* (Dent, 1983). Amelie Kuhrt's *The Ancient Near East* deals with the Achaemenid empire in chapter 13 of vol. 2. The Ionian revolt is well covered by Oswyn Murray, chapter 8 of the *Cambridge Ancient History,* vol. 4 and that volume also has two chapters (9 and 10) on the Persian Wars by N.G.L. Hammond. See also A. Burn, *Persia and the Greeks,* 2nd ed., (London, 1984) and P. Green, *The Greco-Persian Wars*, 2nd ed. (London, 1996). J. Morrison and J. Coates look at the mechanics of naval warfare in *The Athenian Trireme* (Cambridge, 1986). On Herodotus see John Gould, *Herodotus* (London, 1989) and T. J. Luce, *The Greek Historians* (London, 1997). See also the comments made on Herodotus by Paul Cartledge in *The Greeks* (Oxford, 1993) and J. Evans, *Herodotus, Explorer of the Past* (Princeton, 1991). E. Hall, *Inventing the Barbarian* (Oxford, 1989) looks at the impact of the wars on Greece. There is also N. Loraux, *The Invention of Tradition* (Harvard, 1986) and the concluding chapters of Sarah Morris, *Daidalos and the Origins of Greek Art.* The sculptures of the temple to Zeus at Olympia are dealt with in all the standard histories.

Chapter Ten: The Fifth Century: The Politics of Power 479–404 B.C.

P. Garnsey, *Famine and Food Supply in the Graeco-Roman World* (Cambridge, 1988) first put forward the thesis that Athens was not as dependent on grain supplies from overseas in this period as originally thought. Michael Whitby's response to this, which I have adopted, is in H. Parkins and C. Smith, (eds.) *Trade, Traders and the Ancient City* (London, 1998). For this chapter the standard narrative histories mentioned in "The Classical Period: General Books" are good. The Athenian Empire is well covered in chapter 5 of Davies, *Democracy and Classical Greece* (London, 1993). See also P. J. Rhodes, *The Athenian Empire* (Oxford, 1985). Thucydides remains the supreme early source though he is now being approached more critically, for instance, by Simon Hornblower in his *The Greek World, 479–323 B.C.* and *Thucydides* (London, 1987). Thucydides is also covered in T. J. Luce, *The Greek Historians* (London, 1997). A short analysis of the war is provided by Davies, *Democracy and Classical Greece*, chapter 7. The fullest survey is that of D. Kagan in four volumes (Ithaca, 1969–81). Details of fighting techniques are covered in the works by Hanson and Pritchett cited for Chapter Five.

Chapter Eleven: The Athenian Democracy

The subject is covered in the "General Books" (page 461) and "General Books for Chapters Nine to Fifteen (page 469). On the religious background R. Parker, *Athenian Religion* (Oxford, 1996), is now the essential introduction. On the archaeological evidence for commercial (and political) activity in the Agora see J. M. Camp, *The Athenian Agora* (London, 1986). On the evolution of democracy see M. Ostwald, *From Popular Sovereignity to the Sovereignity of Law: Law, Society and Politics in Fifth-Century Athens* (Berkeley,1986), and Joseph Ober, *Mass and Elite in Democratic Athens* (Princeton, 1989). For what is known about Pericles see D. Kagan, *Pericles of Athens and the Birth of Democracy* (London, 1990). For the fourth century see Morgen Hansen *The Athenian Democracy in the Age of Demosthenes* (Oxford, 1991). General essays on Athenian democracy are to be found in *The Good Idea: Democracy in Ancient Greece* (New York, 1995). There is much to stimulate in vol. 1 of Paul Rahe's *Republics Ancient and Modern: The Ancient Regime in Classical Greece* (Chapel Hill and London, 1992) and Orlando Patterson's *Freedom in the Making of Western Culture* (London, 1991). Rhetoric is covered in R. Wearly, *The Birth of Rhetoric* (Oxford, 1996). There is also a lot of relevant material in J. Davidson, *Courtesans and Fishcakes, The Consuming Passions of Classical Athens* (London, 1997). T. Webster, *Athenian Culture and Society* (London, 1973) provides a stimulating overview of cultural life in Athens and is relevant for this and the next two chapters.

Joan Connelly's thesis, "Parthenon and Parthenoi: a Mythological Interpretation of the Parthenon Frieze," in the *American Journal of Archaeology* 100 (1996), 53–80. For a study of the frieze in general see Ian Jenkins, *The Parthenon Frieze* (London, 1994) and for the Acropolis as a whole R. Economakis, *Acropolis Restoration* (London, 1994) has a wealth of information arising out of the recent restoration program.

Chapter Twelve: Homage to Dionysus: The Drama Festivals

An overview of Greek drama is given by Peter Levi in chapter 7 of the *Oxford History of Greece and the Hellenistic World* and the chapter by Bernard Knox in vol. 5 of the *Cambridge Ancient History*. For more extended treatment there is S. Goldhill, *Reading Greek Tragedy* (Cambridge, 1986) and P. Easterling (ed.), *The Cambridge Companion to Greek Tragedy* (Cambridge, 1997). T. G. Rosenmeyer's chapter in *The Legacy of Greece* (Oxford, 1994) is also good. For details of each play see Albin Lesky, *Greek Tragic Poetry* (New Haven, 1983). On individual playwrights, J. Herrington, *Aeschylus* (New Haven, 1986), Bernard Knox, *The Heroic Temper: Studies in Sophoclean Tragedy* (Berkeley, 1966), A. Michelini, *Euripides and the Tragic Tradition* (Wisconsin, 1987) and K. Dover, *Aristophanic Comedy* (London, 1972). Martha Nussbaum's analysis of tragic drama in *The Fragility of Goodness* (Cambridge, 1986) is demanding but extremely rewarding.

Chapter Thirteen: Man Is the Measure: Philosophers and Speculators, 450–330 B.C.

For general introductions to issues of morality and individual responsibility see Martha Nussbaum, *The Fragility of Goodness* cited for chapter 12; H. Lloyd-Jones, *The Justice of Zeus* (Berkeley and London, 1983); and B. Williams, *Shame and Necessity* (Berkeley, 1993) (all of which range over both drama and philosophy). For the Greek education system see H. Marrou, *A History of Education in Antiquity* (New York, 1956) and also his chapter in *The Legacy of Greece* (Oxford, 1984). On the philosophy see as an introduction Julia Annas' chapter in the *Oxford History of Greece and the Hellenistic World* and the chapter on philosophy by Bernard Williams in *The Legacy of Greece,* already cited. Chapter 6, by C. Janaway, in A. Grayling (ed.), *Philosophy: A Guide Through the Subject*, takes the story from the pre-Socratics and Sophists through Socrates to Plato. The first part of Richard Tarnas' *The Passion of the Western Mind* (New York, 1991), "The Greek World View," is a thought-provoking introduction. For Socrates see G. Vlastos, *Socrates, Ironist and Moral Philosopher* (Cambridge, 1991). Robert Parker in his *Athenian Religion, a History*, discusses the context of Socrates' trial and there is I. F. Stone, *The Trial of Socrates* (London, 1988), a radical journalist's assessment of the trial. Excellent introductions to Plato and Aristotle are R. M. Hare, *Plato,* and Jonathan Barnes, *Aristotle* (included with Henry Chadwick on Augustine in *Founders of Thought* [Oxford, 1991]), but also available individually in the Past Masters series (both Oxford, 1982). For more advanced work there is R. Kraut, (ed.) *The Cambridge Com-*

panion to Plato (Cambridge, 1992) and J. Barnes, (ed.), *Aristotle* (Cambridge, 1995). For the specific contribution of Plato and Aristotle to political thought there are the first four chapters of J. S. McClelland, *A History of Western Political Thought* (London, 1996). Karl Popper's *The Open Society and Its Enemies* was first published by Routledge, London, in two volumes in 1945. They have republished it in one volume to celebrate its fiftieth anniversary (London, 1995). E. Dodds, *The Greeks and the Irrational* (Berkeley, 1951) is an enduring classic.

Chapter Fourteen: Relationships

On women see as an introduction E. Fantham and others, (eds.) *Women in the Classical World* which includes essays on women in Archaic Greece and in classical Athens. Sarah Pomeroy's *Goddesses, Whores, Wives and Slaves* (New York, 1975) laid the foundation of serious study of the world of women, and her *Families in Classical and Hellenistic Greece* (Oxford, 1997) contains more recent assessments. (The Segal quote is drawn from here.) An excellent overview is provided by S. Blundell, *Women in Ancient Greece* (London, 1995). On the family there is also S. C. Humpreys, *The Family, Women and Death*, second edition (Ann Arbor, 1993) and relevant chapters in A. Powell, *Athens and Sparta: Constructing Greek Political and Social History from 478 B.C.* (London, 1988). See also R. Garland, *The Greek Way of Life* (London, 1990) and *The Greek Way of Death* (London, 1985). For life in Athens in general J. Davidson, *Courtesans and Fishcakes* (cited above) has a wealth of detail. The complex issue of Greek sexuality is dealt within K. Dover, *Greek Homosexuality* (London, 1978); and there is also J. Winkler, *The Constraints of Desire: The Anthropology of Sex and Gender in Ancient Greece* (London, 1990); and D. Halperin, *The Construction of Erotic Experience in the Ancient Greek World* (Princeton, 1990). A. Stewart, *Art, Desire and the Body in Ancient Greece* (Cambridge, 1997) examines how sexuality is portrayed in art. David Cohen's *Law, Sexuality and Society: The Enforcement of Morals in Classical Athens* (Cambridge, 1991) is particularly good and has been drawn on heavily here.

Chapter Fifteen: Transitions: The Greek World in the Fourth Century B.C.

On the fourth century vol. 6 of the *Cambridge Ancient History* (Cambridge, 1994) is fundamental. Shorter accounts are in Davies and Hornblower, already cited. Again Davies is more immediately accessible. The sections on the fourth century in J. Bryant, *Moral Codes and Social Structure in Ancient Greece* (New York, 1996) are helpful. On the Thirty

Tyrants see M. Ostwald, *From Popular Sovereignity to the Sovereignity of Law: Law, Society and Politics in Fifth Century Athens* (Berkeley, 1986). W. Runciman looks at the eclipse of the city in "Doomed to Extinction: The Polis as an Evolutionary Dead End" in O. Murray and S. Price (eds.), *The Greek City: From Homer to Alexander* (Oxford, 1990). On Dionysius there is B. Caven, *Dionysius I, Warlord of Sicily* (New Haven, 1990).

On the Macedonian background see E. Borza, *In the Shadow of Olympus: The Emergence of Macedon* (Princeton, 1990). N. Hammond, *The Macedonian State: Origins, Institutions and History* (Oxford, 1989) continues through to the destruction of Macedonia by the Romans. On Philip II, N. Hammond, *Philip of Macedon* (London, 1994) and the earlier J. Ellis, *Philip and Macedonian Imperialism* (London, 1976).

Chapter Sixteen: Alexander

Two readable biographies are Peter Green, *Alexander of Macedon* (London, 1974) and Robin Lane Fox, *Alexander the Great* (London, 1973). Alexander is still over-romanticized. A study that looks behind the events of Alexander's life is A. B. Bosworth, *Conquest and Empire: The Reign of Alexander the Great* (Cambridge, 1988) and there is now his *Alexander and the East* (Oxford, 1996) which penetrates the distortions of the source material. Bosworth has also contributed the chapters on Alexander in the *Cambridge Ancient History*, vol. 6, chapters 16 and 17. See also A. Stewart, *Faces of Power: Alexander's Image and Hellenistic Politics* (Berkeley, 1993).

Chapter Seventeen: The Hellenistic World

A good introductory survey is F. Walbank, *The Hellenistic World* (London, 1992). *The Oxford History of Greece and the Hellenistic World* has three chapters on the Hellenistic period all worth reading. The fullest account of the period is Peter Green's mammoth study, *From Alexander to Actium* (London, 1990). It includes every aspect of the period including literature. See also the *Cambridge Ancient History* vol. 7, part 1 (Cambridge, 1984) which deals with the period up to 217. On Egypt see A. Bowman, *Egypt After the Pharaohs, 322* B.C.–A.D. *642* (London, 1986). On the Seleucids, S. Sherwin-White and A. Kuhrt's *From Samarkhand to Sardis: A New Approach to the Seleucid Empire* (London, 1993) stresses the legacy of the Babylonians and the Achaemenid empire. The whole issue of the relationships between the Greeks and other cultures is dealt with in A.D. Momigliano, *Alien Wisdom: The Limits of Hellenization* (Cambridge, 1975). There is a chapter "The Hellenistic Period:

Women in a Cosmopolitan World" in *Women in the Classical World*. Forthcoming in Oxford's excellent new History of Art series is J. Henderson and M. Beard, *Hellenistic and Early Roman Art*; and there is the chapter on Hellenistic art by R.R.R. Smith in the *Oxford History of Classical Art* (Oxford, 1993) and J. Pollitt, *Art in the Hellenistic Age* (Cambridge, 1986). For Stoicism and Epicureanism I have found J. Bryant, *Moral Codes and Social Structure in Ancient Greece* very helpful but see also M. Nussbaum, *The Therapy of Desire: Theory and Practice in Hellenistic Ethics* (Princeton, 1994). My descriptions of the Hellenistic and later Greek sites of Asia Minor are based on a recent visit there.

Chapter Eighteen: Mathematics, Science, and Medicine

The achievements of the Greeks in science and mathematics are conveniently summarized in Geoffrey Lloyd's chapter "Science and Mathematics" in *The Legacy of Greece* (Oxford, 1994) and covered in more detail in his *Greek Science After Aristotle* (London, 1973). More searching accounts are contained in Lloyd's other works. See, for instance, his *The Revolutions of Wisdom: Studies in the Claims and Practice of Ancient Greek Science* (Berkeley, 1987). For medicine Roy Porter's *The Greatest Benefit to Mankind* (London, 1997) is a convenient starting point.

Chapter Nineteen: The Greeks and Rome

For the earlier period T. Cornell's *The Beginnings of Rome* (London, 1995) deals with the evidence of early contact with Greece and the Greeks. See also the chapter by J. J. Pollitt "Rome: the Republic and Early Empire" in *The Oxford History of Classical Art* (Oxford, 1993). It will be supplemented by Henderson and Beard's volume *Hellenistic and Early Roman Art* when it appears in the Oxford History of Art series. For the second century A.D. onward E. Gruen, *Culture and National Identity in Republican Rome* is essential (Ithaca, 1992). Elizabeth's Rawson's *Intellectual Life in the Late Republic* (Baltimore, 1985) has a mass of relevant information although Cicero is covered separately in her *Cicero: A Portrait* (London 1995). Elizabeth Rawson also contributed the chapter "The Romans" to Dover (ed.), *Perceptions of the Ancient Greeks* (Oxford, 1992). See also the chapters by Miriam Griffin and Elizabeth Rawson in the *Cambridge Ancient History*, vol. 3 (Cambridge, 1989) and vol. 9 (Cambridge, 1994). For the coming of Rome to Greece there is E. Gruen, *The Hellenistic World and the Coming of Rome* (Berkeley, 1984) and W. Harris, *War and Imperialism in Republican Rome* (Oxford, 1979). On Augustus and his image see the outstanding analysis of Paul Zanker, *The Power of Images in the Age of Augustus* (Ann Arbor, 1988). Polybius is covered by F. Walbank, *Polybius* (Berkeley, 1972). For the changing perspectives of Cleopatra see Lucy Hughes-Hallett, *Cleopatra, History, Dreams and Distortions* (London, 1990).

Chapter Twenty: The Greeks in the Roman Empire

On Greece under Roman rule, see S. Alcock, *Graecia Capta* (Cambridge, 1993). For the imperial cult see S. Price, *Rituals and Power: The Roman Imperial Cult in Asia Minor* (Cambridge, 1984) and the chapter on imperial cults in S. Mitchell, *Anatolia: Land, Men and Gods in Asia Minor* (Oxford, 1993). The last is also good on the spread of city life to a hitherto rural area. Fundamental to the art is J. Elsner, *Imperial Rome and Christian Triumph* (Oxford, 1998), which covers the cultural aspects of the Second Sophistic well. A recent study of the literature of the period is S. Swain, *Hellenism and Empire: Language, Classicism and Power in the Greek World, A.D. 50–250* (Oxford, 1996). On Plutarch see C. Jones, *Plutarch and Rome* (Oxford, 1971). On cultural change in the Near East F. Millar, *The Roman Near East, 31 B.C. to A.D. 337* (Cambridge, Mass. and London, 1993) is important. On the diversity of spiritual life in the Greco-Roman empire and the coming of Christianity see R. Lane Fox, *Pagans and Christians* (London and New York, 1986). On Isis the standard study is R. Witt, *Isis in the Greco-Roman World* (London, 1971). An introduction to Christianity and Greek philosophy is to be found in A. Armstrong's essay in *The Legacy of Greece* (Oxford, 1984). William Dalrymple's *From the Holy Mountain* (London, 1997). The process of Christianization is well described in R. Markus' essay in J. McManners (ed.), *The Oxford Illustrated History of Christianity* (Oxford, 1990). On the same issue see Averil Cameron's *Christianity and the Rhetoric of Empire* (Berkeley, 1991). Averil Cameron's *The Mediterranean World in Late Antiquity* (London, 1993) covers changes in city life. Anything by Peter Brown is worth reading on late antiquity. See his *The World of Late Antiquity* (London, 1971) and *The Making of Late Antiquity* (Cambridge, Mass., 1978).

Chapter Twenty-one: Conclusion: The Greek Achievement

H. Kitto's *The Greeks* (Harmondsworth, 1951) has held its own as a popular introduction for many years but is now dated as the extracts quoted suggest. M. Finley, *The Legacy of Greece* (Oxford, 1984) covers the main aspects of the legacy. L. Wolpert, *The Unnatural Nature of Science* (London, 1992).

Index